Look Smarter Than You Are with Oracle Planning & Budgeting Cloud

interRel Consulting

2nd Edition

interRel Press, Arlington, Texas

Look Smarter Than You Are with Oracle Planning & Budgeting Cloud

interRel Consulting

Published by:
    interRel Press
    A Division of interRel Consulting Partners
    1000 Ballpark Way, Suite 304
    Arlington, TX 76011

All rights reserved. No portion of this book may be reproduced or transmitted in any form or by any means, electronic or mechanical, including photocopying, recording or by any information storage retrieval system without the express written consent of the author or interRel Press except for the inclusion of brief quotations in a review.

Copyright © 2016-Present by interRel Consulting
2nd edition
Printed in the United States of America

Library of Congress Cataloging-in-Publication Data
interRel Consulting
Look Smarter Than You Are with Oracle Planning & Budgeting Cloud

interRel Consulting 1st ed.
    p. 622 cm.
    Includes index.
978-1-365-73345-1

Trademarks
Various trademarked names appear throughout this book. Rather than list all the names and the companies/individuals that own those trademarks or try to insert a trademark symbol every time a trademarked name is mentioned, the author and publisher state that they are using the names only for editorial purposes and to the benefit of the trademark owner with no intention of trademark infringement.

This book is dedicated to astronaut Mark Watney.

Your story was an inspiration to us all.

Thanks to you, we will never give up hope

even when we're in serious trouble.

ABOUT THE AUTHORS

This book is an interRel collaboration of many, many people. Primary authors are:

Opal Alapat (interRel Oracle EPM Cloud Specialist, Oracle ACE Associate, ODTUG Board of Directors)

Opal refuses to date herself, so all she'll say is that she's been wandering around in the EPM and BI space for over 15 years…and something about how side ponytails need to be back in style again. Since joining interRel, Opal has been immersed in all things Oracle EPM/BI Cloud. She's been writing, speaking, and training on Cloud technologies, as well as working with Oracle product development on future releases. When not evangelizing Cloud, Opal enjoys working on her second (volunteer) job, ODTUG, as well as being a complete goofball at home, and eating her way through Dallas' new and exciting cuisines. Visit Opal's blog at http://womaninepm.com/ or follow her on Twitter at @opal_EPM.

Tracy McMullen (interRel Director of Product Strategy, Oracle ACE Director, OAUG Planning Domain Lead)

Tracy, a.k.a. Goddess of all things Oracle EPM and now Oracle EPM Cloud, has been leading the development of EPM and Data Warehousing applications for over 15 years. She helped co-write the Oracle Essentials certification exams with Oracle for Hyperion Planning, Hyperion Financial Management, Essbase, and Data Relationship Management. As if those achievements weren't enough, she's also a certified Project Management Professional (PMP). She's a regular speaker, instructor, mentor, proponent of women in technology, and visionary leader. She currently holds the title for most Hyperion books authored by a single person. Her strong technical background is complemented by comprehensive practical experience, a skill important not only on the job but at home as well where she manages her kids on a daily basis (ok, she attempts to, but with moderate success). Tracy calls interRel "home" and has been there for 10+ years. She is currently the

Director of Strategic Projects. Follow Tracy on Twitter at @TracyAMcMullen1.

Edward Roske (interRel CEO, Oracle ACE Director)

Edward, the leader of the vast interRel empire, was hit by the Hyperion cupid waaaaaay back in 1995. When he saw his first demo of Arbor Essbase (as it was known at the time), he quit his job to become a full-time Essbase consultant. He then went on to become one of the world's first Essbase certified consultants. He was also one of the first people in the world to become certified in Hyperion Planning. In May of 1997, Edward co-founded interRel Consulting. He has been the CEO of interRel ever since, growing the company to a multi-million dollar firm that spans coast to coast. Edward still keeps his technical skills sharp and you can find him evangelizing Oracle EPM and BI (and now Oracle EPM and BI Cloud), as well as billing on customer projects. Edward continues to be a regular speaker at conferences and he's known for his humorous slant on boring technical information. In the last ~20 years, Edward has spoken to over 10,000 people in 15+ countries across 5 continents. Visit Edward's blog at http://looksmarter.blogspot.com/ or follow him on Twitter at @ERoske.

ABOUT INTERREL CONSULTING

Founded in 1997, interRel Consulting is the longest-standing Hyperion partner dedicated solely to implementing EPM/BI solutions for Fortune 500 and mid-size companies, and is the only four-time winner of Oracle's specialized Partner of the Year for BI and EPM. interRel is the 2016 Global EPM & BI Cloud Partner of the Year.

The company is an eight-time Inc. 5000 honoree committed to education with a platform that includes 10+ books in its best-selling technical reference series, "Look Smarter Than You Are with Hyperion;" free, twice-weekly webcasts; the free-access video education platform, Play it Forward, on YouTube; and multi-track EPM/BI Solutions Conferences across the U.S. and Canada. Home to three Oracle ACE Directors and three Oracle ACE Associates, interRel frequently participates in Oracle Technology Network international tours in developing markets. To learn more about interRel Consulting, please visit www.interRel.com.

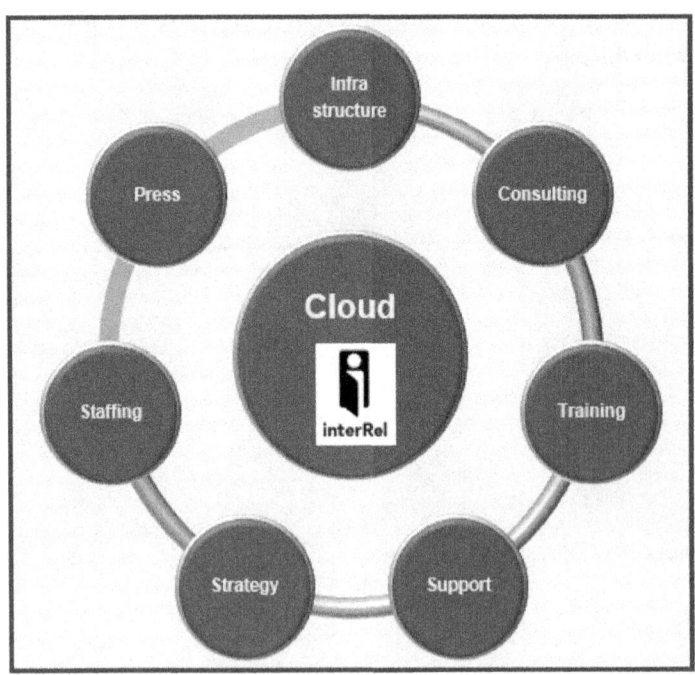

ACKNOWLEDGEMENTS

If we were to thank all of those who assisted us in the creation of this book, we would have to not only personally mention hundreds of people but also several companies and one or two federal agencies (though we will give a special shout-out to those wacky guys over at the Internal Revenue Service: keep it real, yo!). Suffice to say, if this book stands tall, it is only by balancing on the heads of giants.

Thank you to the following individuals who provided significant contributions to this book (content, proofing, and more): Kurt Mayer, Pete Puskar, Summer Watson, Dyana Karcher, Syed Raziuddin, Tanya Shringapure, Ceca Bridges, Kenneth Staudt, and Matt Walker.

A special acknowledgement to Cathy Son, who was a huge contributor to this book and part of the Cloud team that made the first edition of this book possible.

We also want to thank some folks from Oracle whose help was invaluable in writing this book: Al Marciante, Gabby Rubin, Shankar Viswanathan, Matt Bradley, Marc Seewald, Mark Rinaldi, Muthu Ranganathan, Prasad Kulkarni, Sreekumar Menon, Liz Kasabian, Tom Lefebvre, Toufic Wakim, and Karen Imber.

We give our sincerest gratitude to all the people above, and we hope that they feel that this book is partly theirs as well (just without the fame, glory, and most importantly, the royalties).

DISCLAIMER

This book is designed to provide supporting information about the related subject matter. It is being sold to you and/or your company with the understanding that the author and the publisher are not engaged by you to provide legal, accounting, or any other professional services of any kind. If assistance is required (legal, expert, or otherwise), seek out the services of a competent professional such as a consultant.

It is not the purpose of this book to reprint all of the information that is already available on the subject at hand. The purpose of this book is to complement and supplement other texts already available to you. For more information, please see the Oracle documentation.

Great effort has been made to make this book as complete and accurate as possible. That said, there may be errors, both typographic and in content. In addition, due to the accelerated software updates provided by Oracle for EPM Cloud, you might see slight differences in the screen shots and navigation steps compared to your version of Cloud. Therefore, use this book only as a general guide and not as the ultimate source for specific information on the software product. Further, this book contains information on the software that was generally available as of the publishing date. Please note that Oracle Cloud products are ever-changing and some differences are likely to be found between this book and the current versions of the Cloud products.

The purpose of this book is to entertain while educating. The authors and interRel Press shall have neither liability nor responsibility to any person, living or dead, or entity, currently or previously in existence, with respect to any loss or damage caused or alleged to be caused directly, indirectly, or otherwise by the information contained in this book.

We've included a parody storyline to go along with the educational Cloud content - a parody on a recent book and movie. No real clients were harmed in the making of this book

If you do not wish to abide by all parts of the above disclaimer, please stop reading now and return this book to the publisher for a full refund.

FOREWORD

I have been involved in the world of Hyperion Planning for two decades now. While the product has changed immensely, the world of budgeting, forecasting, and planning has changed even more. This presents a challenge not only for us as a software vendor to roll out new features whilst maintaining backward compatibility, but it's even more difficult for our customers to absorb the software changes and to take advantages of the new capabilities. Oracle figured out that the secret to making a planning solution evolve at the rate that the planning world is evolving is to create a Cloud solution... and thus, in 2014, Planning & Budgeting Cloud Service (PBCS) was born.

It quickly became one of the fastest selling services not just in the Oracle EPM suite of products, but in the entire set of Oracle Software-as-a-Services portfolio. It now has both a prebuilt set of frameworks to get companies accelerated into the world of enterprise planning and the ability for companies needing to custom-build their own unique solutions. Now, Oracle Enterprise Planning & Budgeting Cloud is evolving faster than the outside world: Oracle is advancing the world of planning and FP&A groups are rushing to embrace the new planning practices Oracle is helping to pioneer.

While the product has been advancing rapidly, there wasn't any way to learn the entire product in a matter of hours until my friends at interRel wrote the book you're now holding. This is not only the first book on Oracle Enterprise Planning & Budgeting Cloud, as of the end of 2016, it's the only book. I guess that makes it the best book on Oracle EPM Cloud, too, so kudos to them for that.

I'm sure you'll enjoy reading this book as much as I did. It's got content not only on how to use the service but great advice on planning in general. I think that this book will prove a great guide on your planning journey whether you're implementing a traditional budgeting system, a rolling forecast, beyond budgeting, range-based forecasting, graphical planning, or something specific to your industry.

When I started budgeting (way too many years ago to admit), the world was much simpler: ask your cost center managers to enter some estimated dollars for next year, add them up, and then override the numbers you didn't like. Well, the world is much more complex now.

The good news is that you have not only the product but a great book to help you along the way. So good job buying it, and if it doesn't help you, I didn't write it...

Matt Bradley
Sr. Vice President, Development at Oracle
November 30, 2016

TABLE OF CONTENTS

PROLOGUE: THE EPM MARTIAN 1

CHAPTER 1: INTRO TO THE EPM CLOUD 3

   THE DARK DAYS OF SERVERS 3
   THE CLOUD 5
   ORACLE ENTERPRISE PLANNING CLOUD 7
   BUSINESS INTELLIGENCE CLOUD/DATA VISUALIZATION CLOUD 10
   ENTERPRISE PERFORMANCE REPORTING CLOUD 12
   ACCOUNT RECONCILIATION CLOUD 13
   FINANCIAL CONSOLIDATION & CLOSE CLOUD 14
   PROFITABILITY AND COST MANAGEMENT CLOUD 15
   TAX REPORTING CLOUD 16
   ORACLE ANALYTICS CLOUD 17
   DIMENSION MANAGEMENT CLOUD 17
   HYBRID IMPLEMENTATION APPROACH 17

CHAPTER 2: LAUNCH INTO THE CLOUD 19

   CLOUD.ORACLE.COM 19
   CLOUD ROLES, PRIVILEGES, & RESPONSIBILITIES 21
   ORDER MANAGEMENT – MY ACCOUNT 23
   CLOUD ACCOUNT – MY SERVICES 23
   CLOUD ACTIVATION PROCESS 25
   USERS IN THE CLOUD 29
   MANAGE & MONITOR YOUR CLOUD INSTANCE 35
   LOGGING A CLOUD SUPPORT CASE 39

CHAPTER 3: INTRO TO ORACLE PBCS 40

   INTRO TO ORACLE PBCS 40
   USER INTERFACES 40
   NAVIGATE THE SIMPLIFIED UI 41
   MEMBER SELECTION 53
   APPLICATIONS & CUBES DEFINED 56
   VISION APPLICATION DESIGN 58

CHAPTER 4: BUILD AN APPLICATION 61

CREATE AN APPLICATION 61
DIMENSIONS EXPLAINED 67
BUILD SCENARIO DIMENSION 75
REFRESH THE DATABASE 79
BUILD VERSION DIMENSION 84
ACCOUNT DIMENSION EXPLAINED 87
CREATE SMART LIST 92
BUILD ACCOUNT DIMENSION 95
VIEW & ADD YEARS TO YEARS DIMENSION 100
VIEW PERIOD DIMENSION & ENABLE DTS 101
VIEW HSP_VIEW DIMENSION 103
CREATE CUSTOM PRODUCT DIMENSION 104
IMPORT & EXPORT DIMENSIONS 105
USE EXCEL TO UPDATE DIMENSIONS 113
ATTRIBUTE DIMENSIONS 119
SET CUBE DEFINITIONS 126
ASO CUBES 129
VARIABLES 133

CHAPTER 5: INTEGRATE DATA 139

INTEGRATION OPTIONS OVERVIEW 139
IMPORT DATA WITH THE SIMPLIFIED UI 141
EXPORT DATA WITH THE SIMPLIFIED UI 148
INTRO TO DATA MANAGEMENT 150
LOAD DATA FILE USING DATA MANAGEMENT 154
SYNC DATA WITH DATA MANAGEMENT 216
EXPORT DATA USING DATA MANAGEMENT 222
OTHER DATA MANAGEMENT CONCEPTS 235
SYNC DATA WITH DATA MAPS 236
AUTOMATE DATA INTEGRATION 242
REST API 242

CHAPTER 6: CALCULATE DATA 245

INTRO TO CALCULATION MANAGER 245
CREATE BUSINESS RULE IN GRAPHICAL MODE 249
CREATE GRAPHICAL RULE WITH A SCRIPT COMPONENT 255
CREATE BUSINESS RULE IN SCRIPT MODE 260
DEPLOY BUSINESS RULE 266

LAUNCH BUSINESS RULE 267
VIEW BUSINESS RULE STATUS AND SCHEDULE 268
ASSIGN BUSINESS RULE TO FORM 270
EXPORT DATA USING A BUSINESS RULE 271
ASO CUBE BUSINESS RULES 274

CHAPTER 7: CREATE USER INTERFACES 277

DATA FORMS 277
SMART FORMS 325
VALID INTERSECTIONS 328
ACTION MENUS 335
ADD MEMBERS ON THE FLY 338
TASKS 348
DASHBOARDS 352
FINANCIAL REPORTS 360
AD HOC GRIDS & DYNAMIC REPORTS 381
NAVIGATION FLOWS 392

CHAPTER 8: ASSIGN SECURITY 408

NATIVE GROUPS 409
PROVISION APPLICATION-SPECIFIC ROLES 411
SET PBCS APPLICATION SECURITY 414
ASSIGN MEMBER ACCESS 415
ASSIGN FORM ACCESS 418
ASSIGN BUSINESS RULE ACCESS 419
ASSIGN TASK LIST ACCESS 420

CHAPTER 9: AUTOMATE & MIGRATE 422

JOB SCHEDULER 422
EPM AUTOMATE 432
MIGRATION 457

CHAPTER 10: END USER ACTIVITIES 471

NAVIGATE SIMPLIFIED UI 471
REVIEW DASHBOARDS 472
FOLLOW TASKS 472
DATA ENTRY 474
EVERYTHING'S UNDER A MENU 478

SELECT SMART LIST VALUES 481
ENTER TEXT & DATES 481
REFRESH A DATA FORM 482
SAVE A DATA FORM 482
SHORTCUT KEYS 483
AUTOSAVE & UNDO 483
ADJUSTMENTS & DATA SPREADING 484
ATTACHMENTS, COMMENTARY, & DETAIL 488
FORMATTING 494
VIEW MEMBER FORMULAS 496
ANALYZE 496
USE SMART FORMS 500
RUNNING BUSINESS RULES 501
APPROVALS 503
RUN REPORTS 503
SETTINGS 505
ADD MEMBERS ON THE FLY 509
PREDICTIVE ANALYTICS 511
PLAN IN EXCEL USING SMART VIEW 511
RETAIN EXCEL FORMATTING / CUSTOM STYLES 519
MOBILE SUPPORT 521

CHAPTER 11: SANDBOXING 523

ENABLE SANDBOXES 523
ENABLE VERSION FOR SANDBOXING 524
SANDBOXING MEMBERS 525
CREATE A SANDBOX 530
PUBLISH A SANDBOX 532
OTHER RULES ABOUT SANDBOXING 532
MANAGE SANDBOXES 533

CHAPTER 12: MAINTAIN & SUPPORT 535

APPLICATION MAINTENANCE 535
CREATE AND EDIT CUBES 535
CLEAR CUBES 536
DIMENSION MAINTENANCE 538
VIEW AND SET UNDERLYING CUBE PROPERTIES 539
FORCE RESTRUCTURE 544

DELETE APPLICATION 545
VIEW CLOUD VERSION 546
DAILY BACKUPS 547
SET APPEARANCE 547
ANNOUNCEMENTS 548
ARTIFACT LABELS 548
DAILY MAINTENANCE 549
RESTARTING THE PBCS APPLICATION 549
APPLICATION AND SYSTEM SETTINGS 550
CLEAR CELL DETAILS 553
COPY DATA 553
COPY VERSIONS 554
VIEW ACCESS LOGS 555
VIEW ACTIVITY REPORTS 556
APPLICATION DIAGNOSTICS / APPLICATION MONITOR 557
SYSTEM REPORTS 558
CHANGE HISTORY / AUDITING 558
SET ENVIRONMENT NOTIFICATIONS 560
ACADEMY & LEARNING MORE 561

EPILOGUE: THE EPM MARTIAN 563

APPENDIX: *LSTYA WITH ESSBASE* HIGHLIGHTS 564

INTRO TO ESSBASE 564
BLOCK STORAGE DATABASE 572
AGGREGATE STORAGE DATABASE 579
HYBRID AGGREGATION 580
COMPARING ESSBASE DATABASE OPTIONS 581
DIMENSION ORDER FOR BSO CUBE 583

APPENDIX: GLIMPSE INTO EPBCS 585

FINANCIALS FRAMEWORK 585
WORKFORCE FRAMEWORK 588
CAPITAL FRAMEWORK 590
PROJECTS FRAMEWORK 591
ENABLE AND CONFIGURE EPBCS 593
EPBCS VS. CUSTOM PBCS 594

INDEX 596

Prologue:
The EPM Martian

LOG ENTRY: SOL 10, Entry 1

I'm pretty much screwed. That's my considered opinion. Screwed, and not in a good way.
Nine sols into what should be the best EPM implementation of my life, and it's turned into a complete nightmare.
For the record... the EPM implementation didn't die on Sol 9. Certainly the rest of my team thought it did, and I can't blame them. And they'll be right eventually.
So, where do I begin?
Oracle EPM Cloud. Oracle reaching out to send customers to the Cloud and expand the horizons of companies beyond traditional servers…blah, blah, blah. First Hyperion introduced System 9, creating a common workspace for all of the EPM products. They got accolades, fame, and a lovely Solutions conference in their honor. Oracle then bought Hyperion and improved the EPM solution to its current "Business Analytics" state. They got a press release and a boxed lunch at OpenWorld.
Implementing a best practice EPM solution for the Vision Company, a subsidiary of the global dominating Juggling Wolverines Enterprises. Well, that is my mission. Okay, not mine per se. Project Commander McMullen was in charge. I was just one of her crew along with Strategic Architect Joe Aultman, Consolidations Specialist Terrance Walker, Infrastructure Architect Jason Novikoff, and Reporting Analyst Sandy Nozaki-Gonzalez. Actually, I was the lowliest member of her crew, Edward Roske. I would only be "in command" of the mission if I were the only remaining person.
What do you know? I'm in command.
It was a ridiculous sequence of events that led to me and the project almost dying. My client, Vision, needed an EPM solution. They were on board

and ready to move forward before the IT roadblocks started. The hardware was too expensive. It would be costly to upgrade in the future. IT resources at Vision were scarce. So the project was not approved and the Vision finance and ops teams were left without an EPM solution.

On top of that, I was somehow catapulted into the vast expanse which is the Cloud. Now I'm stranded. Why couldn't I be stranded on Mars where they don't have any clouds? Hence, the "I'm screwed" complaint. Really it was Vision that was screwed.

So that's the situation. I have no way to communicate with i.n.t.e.r.R.e.l or Earth. Everyone thinks the project is dead.

But it isn't… Somehow I have to make this work in the Cloud for the Vision Company. If the budgeting and forecasting portion fails, they can't make decisions and the company will fail. If the reporting portion fails, Vision won't be able to find the critical information to pinpoint the source of the problem and the company will fail. If I can't consolidate and close the books, the company will fail.

So yeah. I'm screwed. Oh well. Maybe someday a good-looking, A-list actor like Matt Damon will play me in the movie version of my story…

Chapter 1: Intro to the EPM Cloud

THE DARK DAYS OF SERVERS

This is hard to believe, but in the not too distant past when companies wanted to implement enterprise software they had to call up a computer manufacturer, describe the exact specifications of the computer they wanted, and then wait a few weeks for the machine to be assembled and shipped to the company. Now manufacturers – in an attempt to make computers built from off-the-shelf commodity parts sound more impressive – call these computers "servers."

When I started doing Hyperion back in the '90s, all we had was Essbase and it really didn't require much of a server. The servers back then often had a single CPU and, frankly, were less powerful than the average modern-day smartphone. The good news about this is that a so-called server could be bought by a CFO and placed under her desk without IT ever realizing it. One of these under-the-desk servers was powerful enough to host an entire finance department's implementation of Essbase.

Essbase grew up really quickly and servers did, too. By the turn of the century when Essbase 7 came out, most companies had data centers at their corporate headquarters. These "data centers" were basically a lot of raised, air conditioned floors housing all of the company's servers. Even though it was just a room of chilled computers off in the basement, IT realized that calling them data centers would make them sound more impressive. (Notice the tendency people have of "making things sound more impressive than they really are.")

Around 2004, Hyperion released System 9. It was an enterprise-class suite of EPM (Enterprise Performance Management) and BI (Business Intelligence) tools and it took a trained professional to install System 9 on one or more servers. By this time, most enterprise-class products couldn't be installed by mere mortals.

At about the same time, IT departments realized that having a data center in the company's headquarters wasn't the best use of corporate office space, so they started to move their data centers off-site.

Users would still access the servers as before, but they were now only connected to the corporate servers by – for lack of a better way to put it – really long cables. This is also about the time users stopped knowing where the servers were actually physically located. IT wasn't pleased when they realized that no one actually cared where the servers were physically located.

In mid-2007, Oracle bought Hyperion (now rebranded to "Oracle EPM") and helped turn it into a truly enterprise-class product (Hyperion only thought they had one, but looking back, System 9 was really pitiful compared to what exists now).

With the onslaught of the Great Recession shortly after, IT departments were being forced to cut costs. One of the ways to lower spending was to move their data centers even farther away – preferably near a waterfall (hydroelectric power is cheap) and somewhere cold (to lower the air conditioning needs).

Since most companies couldn't afford to go buy their own building in Norway (in my mind all modern data centers are in Norway, surrounded by little villages straight out of *Frozen*), they started having other companies manage their data centers. So now we had data centers attached to our users by virtual cables and it turned out that no one really cared how their computers talked to the servers as long as it worked.

Now jump ahead several years. In the days after the Great Recession, smartphones became a standard extension of people's hands. The web became the default place to go for information. Applications installed on computers started to become a thing of the past. And flying cars finally became available.

(That last sentence actually isn't true. Despite being promised flying cars since I was a kid, there still aren't flying cars. To be honest, it really annoys me that we'll have self-driving cars before flying cars…but I digress.)

In other words, we became comfortable with storing our information remotely because we could then access it any time from any device. We no longer have any idea where our servers are, who owns them, or how the magic happens that lets us talk to the servers. For all we know, there aren't even physical servers out there and it turns out that no one really cares.

So to make it sound more impressive, we decided to call these far away servers owned by no one in particular that house data and run applications...

> LOG ENTRY: SOL 11, Entry 1
>
> Okay. I've had a good night's sleep and things don't seem as hopeless as they did yesterday. Thinking about this Cloud revolution helped me to feel a little hopeful about my situation. First, I guess I should explain how the Cloud works.

THE CLOUD

Yes, that's right. The "Cloud" is just a cool way of saying servers that are really far away that we don't own. Or to put it a different way, the Cloud is software and services that run on the internet.

Pause for a moment and look down at your smartphone. (It's probably in your hand, in your pocket, or at worst, within arm's reach.) Notice the applications you use most: email, messages, weather, browser, etc. Each one of these is a Cloud application. Your email isn't really stored on your phone: it's on a far flung server somewhere. Your messages are bouncing all around people's servers that you couldn't locate even if you wanted to. The weather app is accessing data stored someplace else. The browser is pulling up information stored around the world. And so on. *Your smartphone is a Cloud-access device.*

As consumers, we're completely comfortable with the Cloud. We don't think we understand the Cloud, but that's just because people have been trying to make us think the Cloud is some complicated thing that can only be understood by rocket surgeons. (I blame the movie *Sex Tape* for this, but I tend to blame that movie for a lot of what's wrong in the world.)

The Cloud has a lot of benefits. Companies no longer have to buy servers. No one has to install (and then patch forever) software on the servers. There's no need to manage the server because *it's now someone else's problem.*

At the time I'm writing this, some IT departments who should know better are afraid of the Cloud (which is weird because those same people in IT are comfortable with their whole personal life being on the Cloud). Is our data secure in the Cloud? What if the Cloud crashes? Is the software in the Cloud any good? Will it slow things down to put them in the Cloud?

A lot of this is fear of the unknown, and, speaking from the standpoint of someone who may not make it through this alive, I have a lot of that fear myself. I know I shouldn't be scared: Cloud companies should be a whole lot better at security than I am. They are better at making sure things shouldn't crash than I am, and they are probably running their Cloud products on far faster servers than I could ever hope to buy... but nonetheless, I'm filled with uncertainty and doubt. Plus the idea that I'm no longer owning my software but rather renting it by the month is a little unnerving (though I do lease my car and rent my apartment).

To recap the key definitions,

- Cloud – software and services that run on the Internet; Physical infrastructure (servers) in massive data centers all over the world
- SaaS (Software as a Service) – software licensing and delivery model
- Software is licensed on a subscription basis – "pay as you grow"
- Centrally hosted, limiting additional hardware
- Accessed via thin client or web browser

Cloud Benefits

The Cloud provides a number of benefits to companies including facilitating the expansion to new geographies, products, or departments. Lower software fees could be found with a SaaS model. IT costs are absolutely reduced with less personnel and equipment required. Relative to EPM, the EPM Cloud can accelerate EPM adoption within your organization. An intuitive user interface means a reduction in training costs. The Cloud allows companies to focus on analytics versus software support. A final bonus is that upgrades and patches are automatically applied (no more waiting for the latest and greatest version).

Oracle Cloud offerings are available via a monthly subscription with self-service sign up, instant provisioning, self-service management, and self-service monitoring.

Cloud Challenges & Considerations

The Cloud is not without some challenges including security management, target and source integration, defining new strategies between IT and the business, what to do with existing software investments, and compliance and reliability concerns.

LOG ENTRY: SOL 11, Entry 2

Is the Cloud "ready" for me? Is it ready for i.n.t.e.r.R.e.1 to implement or Vision Company to use? I think that it's not a matter of *if* I'll be using the Cloud, but rather *when*. It seems like it's coming faster than anyone expected, so maybe it won't kill me after all.

With that comforting knowledge, I took stock of what's in the Cloud for Oracle EPM and BI and here's my situation.

ORACLE ENTERPRISE PLANNING CLOUD

In 2014, Oracle rolled out its first EPM Cloud product and they called it Planning and Budgeting Cloud Service (PBCS). In the early days of the Cloud, companies took their on-premises (also known as "on-premise" by contrarian grammarians or "on-prem" by people in too much of a hurry to utter an extra syllable) products and released limited versions of those products on the Cloud. In Oracle's case, they took Hyperion Planning (which had been around since 2001 and had thousands of companies using it), installed it on some Oracle Exalytics servers, changed the front-end a little, and called it PBCS.

PBCS is a Cloud solution to support planning, forecasting, reporting, and analysis requirements for an organization. Key features include:

- Structured user interfaces to collect and display plans and actuals data
- Customizable tasks and navigation flows to guide users through defined processes
- Secured, central repository for dimensions, data, and calculations
- Powerful business rules and calculations
- Fast reporting and analysis with Financial Reporting and in Excel with the Oracle Smart View Add-in
- Approvals and process management
- Data integration capabilities using Data Management

Highlights of the benefits of PBCS include shortened planning cycles, improved plan & forecast accuracy, flexible modeling and "what-if" analysis, and fast and easy to deployments.

The customer designs and implements the PBCS application to support their specific requirements. This means they create and import their dimensions, build calculation rules, build end user data forms and reports. PBCS contains about of the box features and functions but does not provide out of the box business process frameworks.

Oracle wasn't sure if companies were ready for a Cloud-based EPM solution, but in less than 2 years after the launch of PBCS, over 750 companies had bought it, making it the #1 Cloud-based budgeting product in the world.

Next, Oracle introduced the Oracle Enterprise Planning Cloud option (referred to as EPBCS). EPBCS is a world-class Cloud solution that balances built-in best practice, configurable frameworks with high flexibility. At its core, it leverages the robust Planning and Budgeting Cloud technology, which provides familiar features for powerful analytics, dashboarding, reporting, predicting, and planning. A number of pre-configured, best-in-breed frameworks are delivered with the Enterprise Planning solution and can save customers time when implementing solutions for:

- Financials planning, including income statement, balance sheet, and cash flow (with driver-based or direct input for revenue and

Look Smarter Than You Are with PBCS

expense planning); soon to include Strategic Modeling (a throwback to the Hyperion Strategic Finance technology)
- Workforce planning
- Capital assets planning
- Project financial planning

Customers can upgrade their Enterprise Planning Cloud framework to suit their needs as their business grows. If a customer buys PBCS, there are options directly within the tool to upgrade to EPBCS. Enterprise Planning Cloud is easy to use and easy to maintain through its wizards and intuitive interfaces. It allows customers to spend more time running the business and less time maintaining planning processes. It fits both finance and operational needs by offering scalability to evolve with the business, in addition to transparency and control. The federated architecture allows for operational independence and an aligned planning solution.

In summary, the two pricing scenarios offered today are:

- Original PBCS solution called Oracle Planning and Budgeting Cloud – contains no prebuilt frameworks:

- Enterprise Planning Cloud (also called EPBCS) - contains prebuilt frameworks to support the entire enterprise-wide planning function:

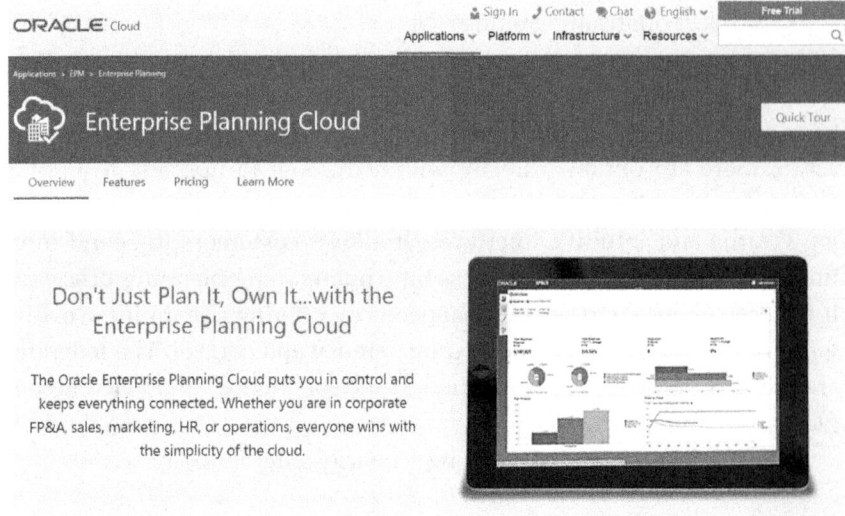

See the appendix in this book for more information on EPBCS.

Oracle sells these Cloud services through the SaaS model: Software as a Service. As I mentioned earlier, you pay by the month to use the software instead of paying a huge amount up front to own the software (and then still having to pay a monthly amount to Oracle to support the software).

BUSINESS INTELLIGENCE CLOUD/DATA VISUALIZATION CLOUD

In September 2014, Oracle released the next Cloud product in the Oracle Business Analytics space: BICS (Business Intelligence Cloud Service). Technically, it's an Oracle BI product (not EPM) but it's in the same family at Oracle and delivers analytics and reporting over the web. It's similar to PBCS in that it took an existing on-premises product, OBIEE (Oracle Business Intelligence Enterprise Edition) and ported it to the Cloud.

It is a different animal than Enterprise Planning Cloud, though, because while Enterprise Planning Cloud delivers application-ready functionality, BICS is more of a platform waiting for you to build your own solutions on top of it. As such, it is not considered to be a SaaS solution, but rather PaaS (Platform as a Service). PaaS is sometimes priced per user and for a set amount of storage. In the case of BICS, Oracle does both. They charge you a monthly fee per user and then they also charge you a flat monthly fee for the underlying Oracle Database Schema Service (sometimes called DBaaS or DataBase as a Schema).

Like Enterprise Planning Cloud before it, BICS quickly started adding functionality that its on-premises version (OBIEE) did not have. Later, one of these awesome features, Visual Analyzer, became available on its own outside of BICS. In November 2015, Oracle started selling DVCS (Data Visualization Cloud Service), which was cheaper than BICS (since it was a subset of BICS) and didn't require a separate fee for the underlying database. Data Visualization Cloud Service focuses on the Visual Analyzer (VA) feature from BICS. DVCS allows users to upload and blend data files and then visualize the data in a multitude of graphical presentations. Users can then share insights and "tell a story" using the story teller mode. Just think... no more death by PowerPoint! Keep discussions interactive and present! DVCS is fully mobile supported and requires 50% fewer clicks to create dashboards (when compared to competitor's tools and BICS Answers and Dashboards).

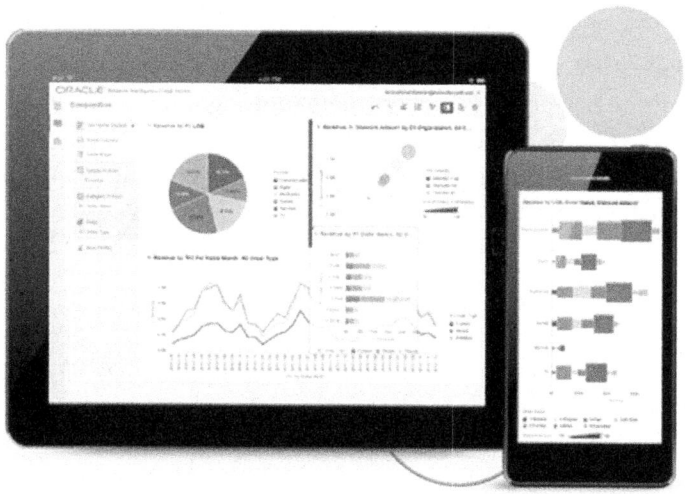

In 2017 Oracle decided to merge Essbase, BICS, and Data Visualizer into one and called it Oracle Analytics Cloud. I'll discuss this in just a moment since I'm taking a chronological approach to introducing Oracle's EPM and BI Cloud products.

> LOG ENTRY: SOL 11, Entry 3
>
> Some BI purists will wonder why we are talking about "BI" in an "EPM" book. The divide of BI versus EPM has always irked Project Commander McMullen. Each involves solutions to help users make better decisions and they will always go hand in hand.

ENTERPRISE PERFORMANCE REPORTING CLOUD

Users have been asked to explain their numbers since, roughly, the beginning of time. When the first tax collector came to the first pharaoh to show him that the expected tax revenue fell short of projections, pharaoh had him beheaded before he could explain that tax revenue was down due to a series of plagues befalling the country. Sadly, the idea that narration should accompany the numbers died with him (and all subsequent tax collectors who simply showed pharaoh the numbers and never got a chance to explain them).

Yes, my knowledge of ancient times apparently is limited to the existence of pharaohs, tax collectors, beheadings, and plagues... and I'm not totally sure there were beheadings. But my point is still valid: the world needs narration. Numbers alone don't tell the whole story and in July 2015, Oracle released Enterprise Performance Reporting Cloud (EPRCS) to solve that problem (and hopefully end future metaphorical corporate beheadings).

Look Smarter Than You Are with PBCS 13

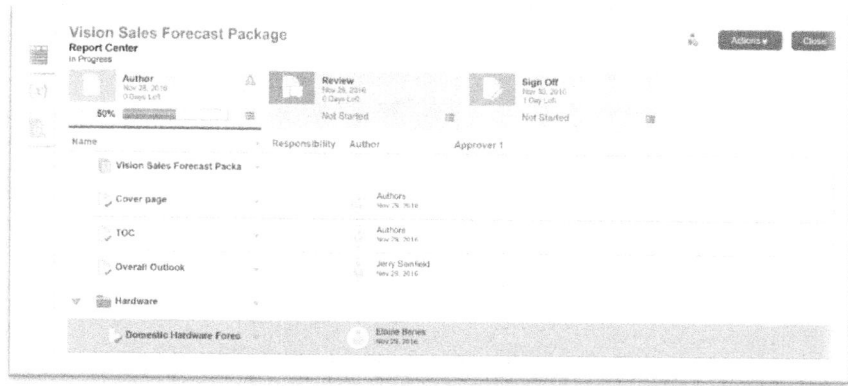

Enterprise Performance Reporting Cloud is not only Oracle's solution for narrative reporting, it's also their first Oracle EPM product to only exist in the Cloud. Created from day one to be a Cloud solution (and not a port of an on-premises product), EPRCS lets users author report packages, review them, and collect commentary on the packages no matter where the data (or the user, for that matter) resides. Like PBCS, EPRCS is sold using a SaaS model.

ACCOUNT RECONCILIATION CLOUD

Oracle Account Reconciliation Cloud is a purpose-built Cloud-based solution that manages, supports, and improves the global account reconciliation process. Leveraging the capabilities of the current release of on-premises Account Reconciliation Manager (ARM), it reduces risk and increases efficiency by leveraging prebuilt reconciliation formats and automating certain reconciliation tasks. Customers can also choose to create their own custom solutions. Built upon best practices for global reconciliation, this solution provides an intuitive interface, interactive and real-time dashboards, and instant visibility into the reconciliation process. Collaboration is driven by role-based tasks and work areas, signoffs, and approvals. Oracle Account Reconciliation Cloud provides flexible balance mapping rules; rule-based thresholds; workflow and audit capabilities; and reporting, monitoring, and analysis. It can integrate data from ERP and EPM systems and supplemental data

14   Chapter 1: Introduction to the EPM Cloud

sources like spreadsheets and databases. Oracle Account Reconciliation Cloud follows the Software as a Service (SaaS) licensing model.

FINANCIAL CONSOLIDATION & CLOSE CLOUD

Oracle Financial Consolidation and Close Cloud (FCCS) is a new, enterprise-wide Cloud solution that provides a consolidation solution to optimize the close cycle. Just to be clear, this is NOT "HFM on the Cloud." FCCS is a newly architected, alternative end-to-end consolidation solution built upon Essbase and delivered on the Cloud. It can be implemented quickly and with less stress and maintenance by providing out of the box functionality. It gives customers visibility into the entire close, consolidation, data collection and management, workflow, audit, monitoring, reporting, and lights out processes. In addition, it can connect to core source systems and comes prebuilt with cash flow, balance sheet, and income statement reporting. It supports IFRS, GAAP, and Multi-GAAP so that customers can feel confident and secure with their regulatory-compliant solution. Some of the common business processes included include full currency support, intercompany eliminations, equity eliminations, adjustments, and detailed data tracking. It can also integrate with Microsoft Office and Enterprise Performance Reporting Cloud (EPRCS). Oracle Financial Consolidation and Close Cloud follows the Software as a Service (SaaS) licensing model.

Look Smarter Than You Are with PBCS   15

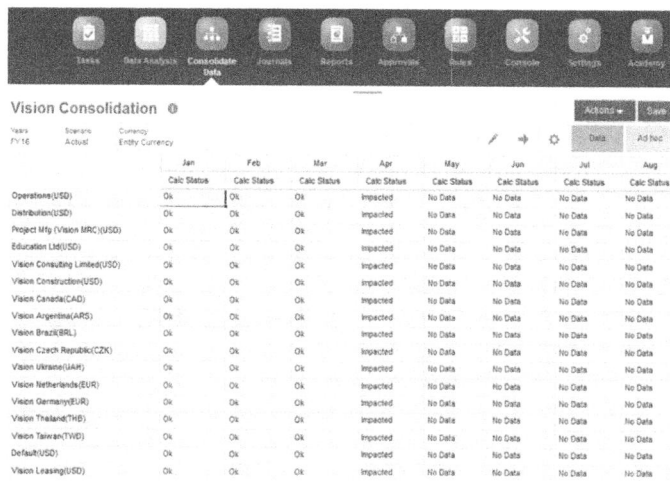

And Oracle didn't stop there. At OpenWorld 2015, they announced that they would be the first company in the world to have a complete EPM suite in the Cloud. Starting early in 2016, they began to roll out Cloud products faster than any company before or since.

PROFITABILITY AND COST MANAGEMENT CLOUD

Oracle Profitability and Cost Management Cloud (PCMCS) is a nearly fully ported version of the successful Management Ledger module of its sister on-premises product, Hyperion Profitability and Cost Management (HPCM) solution. PCMCS answers the most important questions for your organization:

- Am I as profitable as I could be?
- What percentage of my customers, products, channels, etc. are driving most of my profitability? Which ones are unprofitable?
- What proportion of resources to my customers, products, channels, etc. consume?
- What are my true costs to provide services or complete a business process?

PCMCS is a user-driven profitability and cost management solution. Business users create, update and maintain cost allocation logic and profitability models (no scripting required!). It supports dashboarding, profit curves, KPIs, and ad hoc analysis in Excel via Smart View. PCMCS provides full transparency of allocation logic and rules; there are no black boxes in this solution.

This product is architected on an Essbase platform and allows customers to measure their costs and profitability with complex rulesets. Built with a fierce allocation engine, this technology can scale well across an enterprise while still providing flexibility and security. PCMCS is sold using a Software as a Service (SaaS) licensing model.

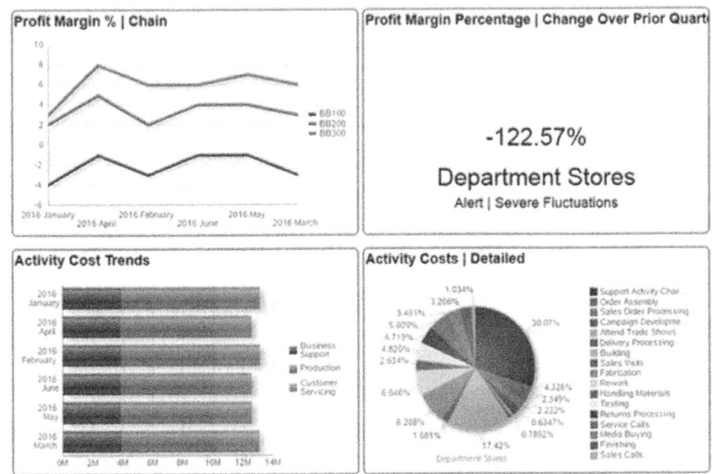

TAX REPORTING CLOUD

Tax Reporting Cloud (TRCS) manages the collection, calculation, and distribution of tax information. This Cloud solution utilizes best practices in tax reporting, allows for tax process improvements, and provides collaboration and transparency between Finance and Tax. TRCS supports state/provincial, federal, and international tax requirements. TRCS integrates with both on-premises HFM and its sister Cloud consolidation service, FCCS.

ORACLE ANALYTICS CLOUD

Essbase is finally in the Cloud! In March 2017 Oracle introduced Oracle Analytics Cloud. This Cloud offering will combine Essbase Cloud, Data Visualization Cloud, and Business Intelligence Cloud together. Within Oracle Analytics Cloud, users can take advantage of the powerful multi-dimensional database, Essbase. Administrators can utilize simplified user interfaces and tools (like Excel spreadsheets) to create and manage Essbase databases. Essbase Cloud will also introduce new features to its on-premises sister, like sandboxing, scenario management, cell status visibility, and enhanced financial intelligence and aggregation. Users will be able to analyze data sets from DVCS, BICS, or Excel via Smart View.

DIMENSION MANAGEMENT CLOUD

Dimension Management Cloud (DMCS) is the tentative name for the upcoming Cloud solution to manage hierarchies, metadata, and attributes across the organization, mirroring the on-premise solution, Data Relationship Management (DRM).

In just over three years of launching their first EPM Cloud product, Oracle will have a complete suite of EPM Cloud solutions.

HYBRID IMPLEMENTATION APPROACH

I was skeptical. What if a company had an on-premises solution and wasn't ready to move their entire EPM suite? Would they be able to go entirely to the Cloud overnight? Luckily, Oracle EPM Cloud was designed to work with the Oracle on-premises solutions. So let's say a company wanted to put part of their EPM / BI strategy into the Cloud and leave part of it in their data center. This is called a "hybrid" solution and there are a number of ways it can play out:

- If your company has existing on-premises EPM tools, they can keep using those and deploy new products into the Cloud. For instance, maybe they've been using HFM for years for financial consolidation. They can still implement PBCS for forecasting and

share the data with HFM using tools like FDMEE (Financial Data Quality Management Enterprise Edition).
- If your company likes the Oracle EPM Cloud products, but is more comfortable with the on-premises products, they can pay for servers and software up-front for the on-premises solutions and pay-as-they-go for the Cloud products.
- If your company wants the production data to stay on-premises, they can still use the Cloud for developing applications. As long as you're on a fairly recent version of the equivalent on-premises product, the Cloud and on-premises applications can be migrated back and forth.
- If your corporation has divisions or departments around the world, you don't have to put all of them onto one platform. Your corporate headquarters might use on-premises Essbase while your remote offices use EssCS (Essbase on the Cloud).

The most likely scenario is that a company with on-premises products will migrate them over time to the Cloud. As IT departments get tired of being hacked, get annoyed at users begging for newer versions, and get pressured to stop spending so much money up-front, the Cloud adoption at your company will take off like a Martian rocket.

```
LOG ENTRY: SOL 11, Entry 4

Knowing all of this about the Cloud... I think
this could maybe work. My project and I just might
make it through alive. I'll just have to EPM the bits
out of this thing.
```

Chapter 2: Launch Into the Cloud

> LOG ENTRY: SOL 11, Entry 5
>
> A launch of the N.A.S.A. space shuttle is complicated, involving hundreds of people, rocket boosters, propulsion systems, abort systems and more.
>
> Would launching Vision's Cloud instance prove to be as involved? As intense? Could I fail before I even started?
>
> Thankfully I have my "Launching into the Cloud" Manual, created by i.n.t.e.r.R.e.l Cloud Specialist Opal Alapat, which documents how to get started, roles and responsibilities, and more. With this resource and all of the documentation at https://cloud.oracle.com, what could go wrong?
>
> 10, 9, 8, 7, 6, 5, 4, 3, 2, 1…

CLOUD.ORACLE.COM

The main place that you need to go to first get started with the Cloud is https://cloud.oracle.com. This site is a one stop shop for all Oracle Cloud customer service subscription needs:

First I'll share some helpful terminology to understand how the Oracle Cloud environment is setup.

Term	What	Where To Manage
Account	Unique customer account May have a single identity domain with many Oracle Cloud services or many identity domains with many Oracle Cloud services May have many Oracle Cloud services Manage account in My Account where you create identity domains, monitor account status and designate other account administrators	Email to activate; My Account
Identity domain	Controls the authentication and authorization of the users who can sign into an Oracle Cloud service May have one or many Oracle Cloud Services Cannot be changed after activation	My Account
Service	Software offering in Oracle Cloud A service will belong to a single identity domain Multiple services may belong to the same identity domain (called a Service Association)	My Services
Service Instance	An instance of a Cloud Service Account could have one or more service instance (for example, you may have 3 different service instances of Enterprise Planning Cloud for different lines of business in your organization)	My Services
Service Name	Service name is the name assigned to the Service that must be unique within the identity domain Cannot be changed after activation	My Services

Now I have understand some of the terminology, I'm ready to take a look at this bad boy.

Look Smarter Than You Are with PBCS 21

To navigate to the Oracle Cloud,
1. Navigate to cloud.oracle.com.
2. Click *Sign in*.

You see a dashboard of options that is role-based. You see options to manage *Cloud Account* (linked to My Services) and *Order Management* (linked to My Account):

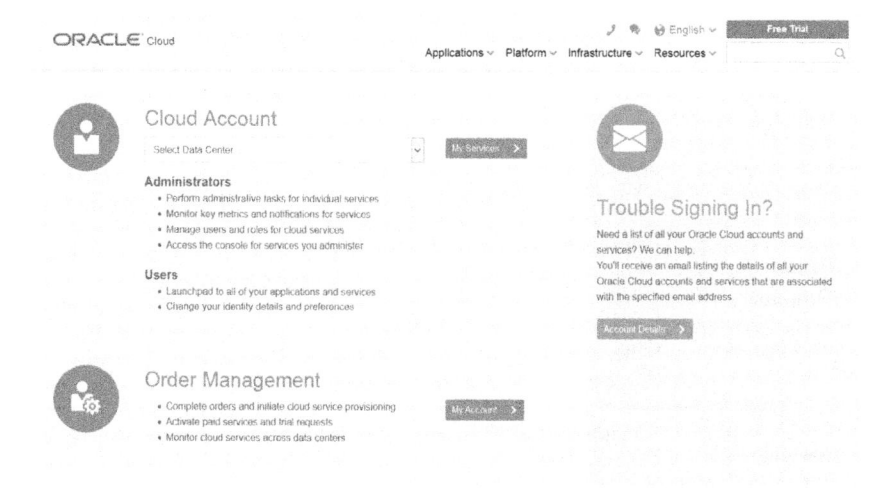

Before we jump into each of these options, let's define the Cloud user roles, privileges and responsibilities.

CLOUD ROLES, PRIVILEGES, & RESPONSIBILITIES

The Cloud supports the following user roles:

Role	Description
Buyer	Makes the initial purchase Designates the account administrator Upsizes, updates, and terminates the paid subscription Note: If you are purchasing more than one Cloud subscription, you may want to consider having the same buyer for all subscriptions
Account Administrator	Uses the My Account section of cloud.oracle.com to activate the Oracle Cloud Services Monitors the status of services Reviews utilization
Identity Domain Administrator	Manages the administrative functions within an identity domain, just like a Service Administrator Uses the My Services section of cloud.oracle.com Adds, removes, and manages users who have access to the services (this is the main difference between this role and the Service Administrator)
Service Administrator	Manages the administrative functions within an identity domain Uses the My Services section of cloud.oracle.com
User	Works within one or more Cloud Services Their service and application role is assigned to them within an identity domain Uses the My Home and Identity Self Service link You can have different types of users: Application Administrators, power users, and end users

Depending on your organization, your Account Administrator, Service Administrator, and Identity Domain Administrator may be the same person. Think through these roles and assignments before activating and setting up your Cloud environment.

ORDER MANAGEMENT – MY ACCOUNT

The Order Management section of cloud.oracle.com allows customers to monitor services for their entire account, across data centers and identity domains. Here, Account Administrators can view information about all of your active, expired, and pending services. This is where you also activate new services, view a dashboard with the status of each of the environments that you have access to, and manage certain Administrator accounts.

My Account URL:

https://myaccount.cloud.oracle.com/mycloud/faces/dashboard.jspx

<u>Username</u>: Use your Oracle account user name
<u>Password</u>: Use your Oracle account password

The My Account ID and password is tied to the Oracle.com ID and password. Your My Services ID and password is NOT tied to the Oracle.com ID and password. So your My Account password and My Services password *could be different*. Try to keep these in sync.

The Account Administrator has access to the dashboard in My Account, which enables them to view metrics and uptime information of the Cloud services. Besides activating the service, the Account Administrator can add Identity Domain Administrators and additional Account Administrators after the service is provisioned.

CLOUD ACCOUNT – MY SERVICES

The Cloud Account (My Services) section of cloud.oracle.com allows Service Administrators and Identity Domain Administrators to manage and monitor all services within a single identity domain. This is where you perform the majority of Cloud management after the services have been activated.

24   Chapter 2: Launch Into the Cloud

Identity Domain & Identity Domain Administrator

The Cloud service must belong to an identity domain. Identity domains control authentication and authorization, i.e. who can log in and the services they can access once they log in. Identity Domain Administrators can create new users and define which Cloud services they can access.

If you have different domains for each Cloud instance, you might not choose the option to "SAVE" the Cloud domain when prompted by your Internet browser:

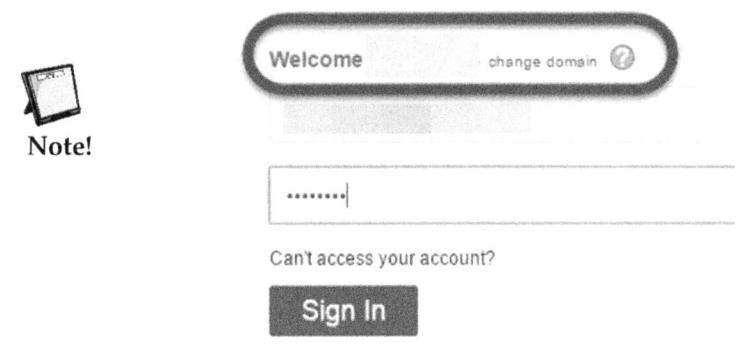

Note!

Once you define the Identity Domain ID, you cannot change it. You can change the *Identity Domain Name* under *My Account* >> *Identity Domain Administration* when you select a specific Cloud instance:

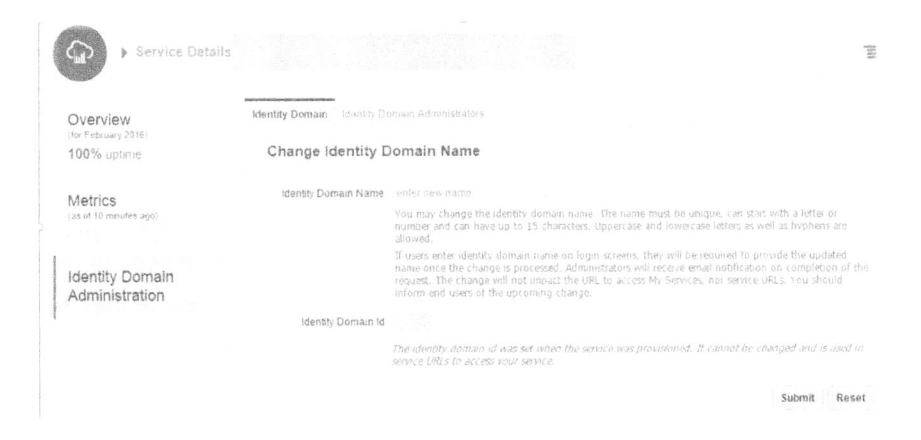

[Screenshot showing Service Details page with Overview, Metrics, Identity Domain Administration sections, and a Change Identity Domain Name form with fields for Identity Domain Name and Identity Domain Id, with Submit and Reset buttons.]

Service Administrator

The Service Administrator has the rights to monitor and manage the service. After activating the service, the Identity Domain Administrator can designate and assign other Service Administrators.

You use My Services to add and manage user access to the service, monitor your service status, and view current and historical usage data.

My Services URL (available after the Cloud service is activated):

https://myservices.usx.oraclecloud.com/mycloud/yourdomain/faces/dashboard.jspx

Username: Use your My Services account username
Password: Use your My Services account password

CLOUD ACTIVATION PROCESS

The general process from initial order to being able to actively use the system is as follows:

1) The buyer places an order for PBCS with the Oracle sales team. Make sure to communicate who is to be the Account Administrator and the email to be used for the Cloud administrative account.

2) In a few days, Oracle activates the account and sends the Account Administrator a welcome email to the new Cloud instance. In earlier Cloud versions, the customer would activate the Cloud instance but now that step is completed by Oracle. A domain ID and service name are automatically assigned by Oracle and you cannot change this ID.
3) In *Order Management* >> *My Account*, the Account Administrator logs in with their Oracle.com ID and password. She then creates a user ID for the Identity Domain Administrator (if that person is different than the Account Administrator).
4) In Cloud Account >> My Services, the Identity Domain Administrator creates other users and assigns their roles including Service Administrators.
5) Service Administrators manages and monitors the service instance from Cloud Account >> My Services.
6) Service Administrators create a new application and manage the application from the service instance.
7) Users access the service instance to work within the application.

After the order is received by Oracle and the instance is activated, Oracle sends an email to log into the Cloud account (note, these emails can change as updates are made to the process):

> Thank you for subscribing to Oracle Enterprise Performance Management. You're the primary administrator for your organization's Oracle Enterprise Performance Management. This includes My Account Administration and My Services Administration.
>
> Your access details, including your user name, temporary password and identity domain name, are included below. As a service administrator you can manage administrative functions related to your Cloud Services, including configuring and managing service instances and performing monitoring and management tasks related to individual services.
>
> **Getting Started:**
>
> - To learn more about Cloud Service roles, review Oracle Cloud User Roles and Privileges.
> - Your Oracle Customer Success Manager (CSM) is your guide in the cloud and will partner with you to help you get the best innovation and value from Oracle's Cloud Services. Visit Oracle Customer Success Managers for additional information. Your CSM will contact you to schedule your onboarding session.
>
> **Access Details**
>
> **My Account Administration**
>
> Use My Account to manage services from all identity domains and data centers, activate services, monitor service status, view historical usage data, and add account administrators.

Once the service is activated, the Dashboard displays the uptime and status of each instance (Pre-Production and Production). This dashboard is accessible at https://myaccount.cloud.oracle.com.

Note! With your Cloud subscription, you get two environments: a Pre-Production and Production instance. In PBCS, each instance may have a single application.

Both the Account Administrator and Identity Domain Administrator (if different people) receive a "Welcome to Oracle Cloud" email. Additional details are included within this email including the URLs for the subscription and the Customer Support ID (CSI) number (you'll need this to log a case with Oracle Cloud Support).

Subscription ID versus Customer Support ID

Note! The Subscription ID is necessary if you need to make changes to your subscription. Your Customer Support ID is necessary if you need to log a support case for the Cloud.

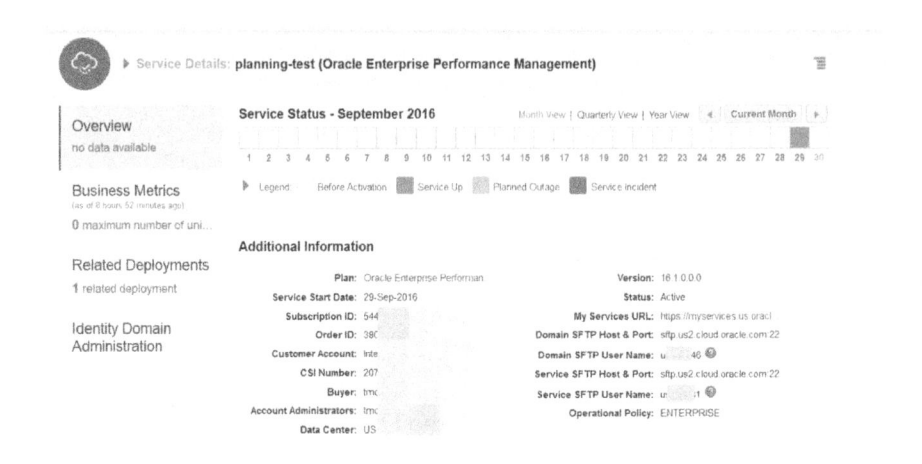

Next, you log into the My Services site with your email and your Oracle password (or possibly a temporary password provided by Oracle via email) and see a similar dashboard view of the service. If using a temporary password, you'll change your password and enter the security question responses when prompted.

A sample My Services URL is as follows:

https://myservices.usx.oraclecloud.com/mycloud/faces/dashboard.jspx

From the Dashboard get the URL of the PBCS service. A sample URL is below:

https://servicename-domainid.pbcs.usx.oraclecloud.com/HyperionPlanning

Now let's walk through the steps to add users!

Users in the Cloud

Create Users in the Cloud

Users can only be created and provisioned by the Identity Domain Administrator through Oracle Cloud My Services. Each Cloud service has its own set of roles in addition to Identity Domain Administrator and Service Administrator.

> **Note!** The processes below are described for PBCS, but they are similar across all Oracle EPM Cloud tools. One obvious difference is that the pre-defined roles differ between technologies.

Before I do anything in the Cloud, I need to set up the users in the Cloud who will be creating and testing the application. I can come back later and add end users at any point. I set up the users in My Services. Note, other Cloud services have different roles but the basic role assignment process for users are the same steps taken here.

> **Note!** For PBCS, users cannot be created within the Simplified Interface. For those familiar with Shared Services and on-premises Hyperion Planning, creating users is different in the Cloud.

PBCS Specific Roles

Within PBCS there are five overarching roles. Within a tool called Access Control (described later in the book), there are more detailed, application-specific roles. However, at the Oracle Identity Management level, only the five exist.

The table below briefly describes the roles available in Oracle Identity Management:

Chapter 2: Launch Into the Cloud

Role	Description
Identity Domain Administrator	Creates users and assigns roles in Oracle Cloud My Services (as mentioned before)
Service Administrator	Functional administrator for an application
Power User	Grants some functional administrator rights such as creating and maintaining forms, Smart View worksheets, business rules, task lists and FRS reports; control approvals process; this is like the Interactive User role in on-premise Hyperion Planning
Planner	Enters data through forms and Smart View, performs ad hoc analysis and drills through to source system
Viewer	Grants view-only access through forms and Smart View

To create users in My Services,
1. If you aren't already there, go to *https://cloud.oracle.com/sign-in*.
2. In the My Services section, select the appropriate Data Center / Region:
3. Click *Sign in to My Services*.
4. Click on *Users*:

|｜| Dashboard   Users   Notifications

5. Click *Add* to create new users.

Note! If the Add, Import, and Export buttons are not available, the user who is logged in has not been granted access to perform those actions.

6. Complete the necessary fields, adding First Name, Last Name, Email, optionally define a user name if you do not want to use email, and Manager Email.
7. In the Simple Role Selection section, select the appropriate service and check *Service Administrator*:

Add User

* First Name: train1
* Last Name: user
* Email: p...@interrel.com
Use email as user name: ☐
* User Name: train1

Manager Email: username@example.com

Roles

Select the roles you would like to assign to the user. You can either use the simple role selection or the advanced selection. Remember to click > or >> icon to complete selection of your roles.

◢ Simple Role Selection

Identity Domain Administrator ☐

Service

Selected Roles — clear
☑ planning-test Service Administrator

▶ Advanced Role Selection

Add   Cancel

Other Roles include Power User, User, and Viewer. I can also choose options if required to define the user as another Identity Domain Administrator or Service Administrator.

Alternatively, the Identity Domain Administrator can go to *Advanced Role Selection* and select users that way.

32   Chapter 2: Launch Into the Cloud

8. Click *Add*.

After the user has been created, a confirmation email is sent to the user's email address.

The Identity Domain Administrator can sort users by roles or by name:

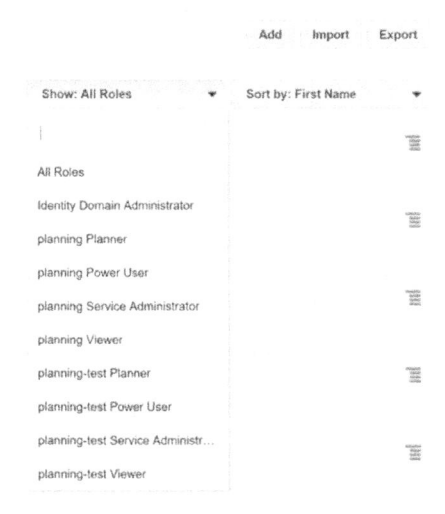

	Add	Import	Export
Show: All Roles ▼	Sort by: First Name ▼		
All Roles			
Identity Domain Administrator			
planning Planner			
planning Power User			
planning Service Administrator			
planning Viewer			
planning-test Planner			
planning-test Power User			
planning-test Service Administr…			
planning-test Viewer			

Identity Domain Administrators can also modify users, reset passwords, manage roles, and remove users in My Services:

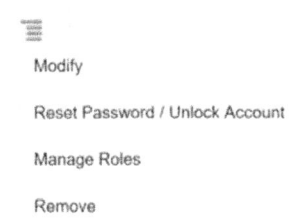

- Modify
- Reset Password / Unlock Account
- Manage Roles
- Remove

Import Users

Oracle PBCS provides a way to import users using a flat file in My Services. In my example below, I'm going to import users into PBCS.

First, I'm going to export the users to get the format of the file.
1. In My Services, click *Users* then *Export*.
2. Save the file and click *OK*.

I now have the template for creating an import file for users. I can use the exported file template and insert in my new users for import. You define the user name, title, and role.

3. Add the following users to the file:

First Name	Last Name	Title	Role
Jerry	Seinfield	VP of Sales	Viewer
Cosmo	Kramer	International Sales Manager – Hardware	Planner
Elaine	Benes	Domestic Sales Manager – Hardware	Planner
George	Costanza	International Sales Manager – Services & Other	Planner
Larry	David	Domestic Sales Manager – Services & Other	Planner
Susan	Ross	Director of Sales – Hardware	Viewer
Frank	Costanza	Director of Sales – Services & Other	Viewer

4. Save as a CSV file.
5. Under users in My Services, click *Import* then *Browse* to select the file.
6. Click *Import*. A notification appears at the top of the page:

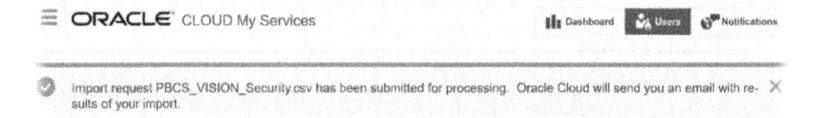

≡ ORACLE CLOUD My Services   Dashboard Users Notifications

Import request PBCS_VISION_Security.csv has been submitted for processing. Oracle Cloud will send you an email with results of your import.

A confirmation email is sent to the email provided with connection information.

7. Once the users have been imported, assign roles by clicking the *Action* icon next to the user, then click *Manage Roles*:

Modify

Reset Password / Unlock Account

Manage Roles

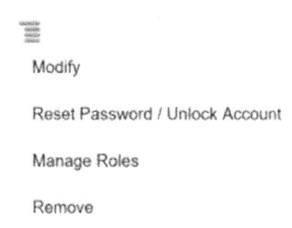

Remove

8. Select the desired role and move it to the right panel for Selected Roles.
9. Click *Save*.

MANAGE & MONITOR YOUR CLOUD INSTANCE

Monitor Service Status

To monitor the status of your Cloud Service,
1. Sign in to My Services and the dashboard displays:

2. Click the service name to open the details page for the service.

The Overview page contains the Overview tile displaying the current month and year, the percentage of time the service was up during the month, and the number of service outages that occurred:

36   Chapter 2: Launch Into the Cloud

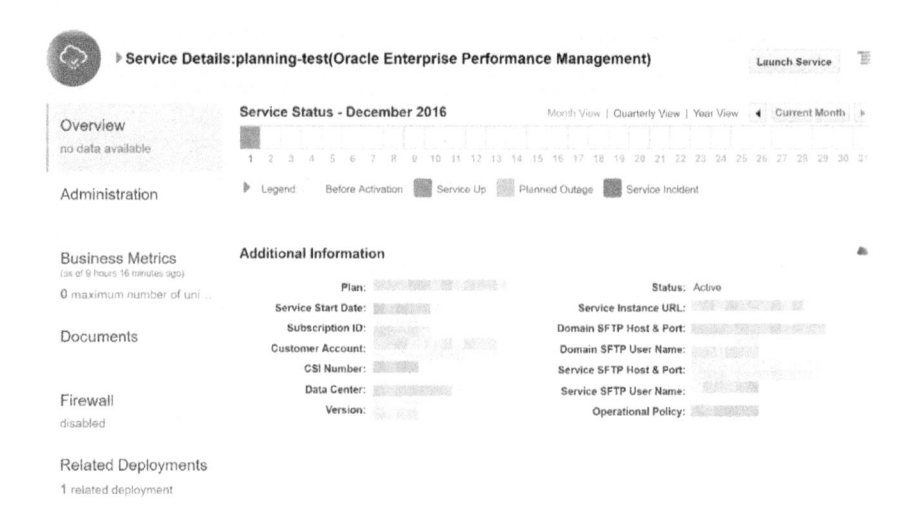

Under Administration, you can define settings for application archiving and lock settings for the entire service:

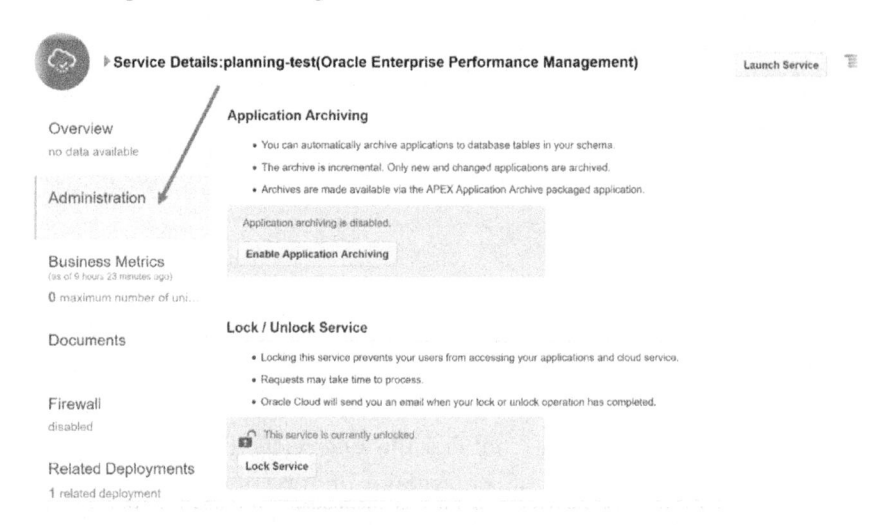

Monitor Usage Metrics

To monitor the usage metrics and see who has logged into the Cloud, click on the *Business Metrics* tile.

Look Smarter Than You Are with PBCS   37

The Business Metrics page contains Historical Usage metrics which display the usage data in the form of a graph that is collected per day for the current service for the past seven days (by default). The Latest Usage metric (at the bottom) shows a snapshot of the last set of metrics collected and when those metrics were collected:

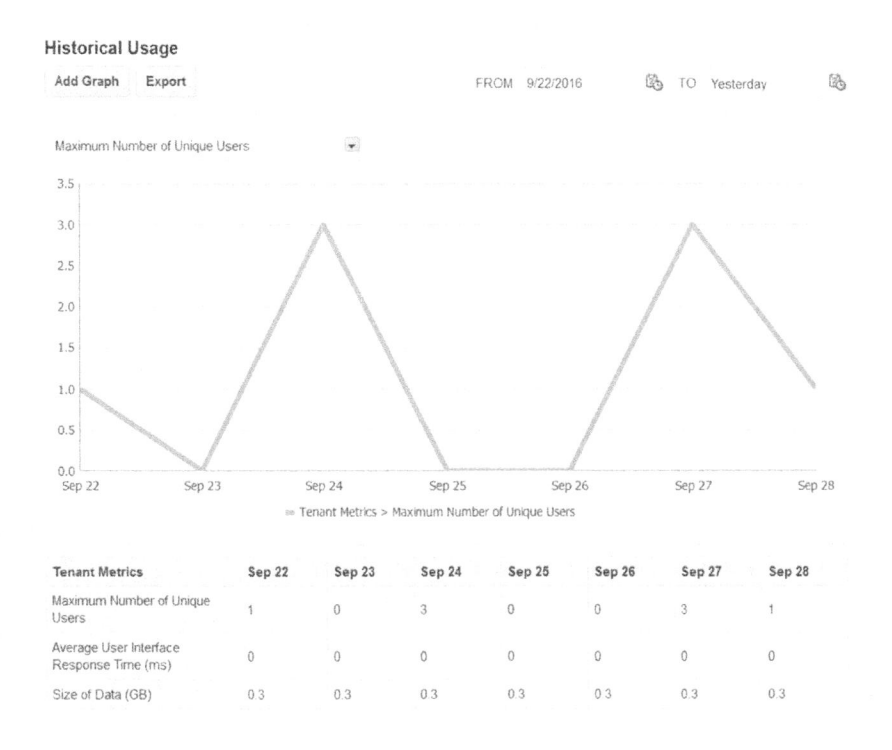

Historical Usage

Add Graph Export   FROM 9/22/2016   TO Yesterday

Maximum Number of Unique Users

— Tenant Metrics > Maximum Number of Unique Users

Tenant Metrics	Sep 22	Sep 23	Sep 24	Sep 25	Sep 26	Sep 27	Sep 28
Maximum Number of Unique Users	1	0	3	0	0	3	1
Average User Interface Response Time (ms)	0	0	0	0	0	0	0
Size of Data (GB)	0.3	0.3	0.3	0.3	0.3	0.3	0.3

Monitor Notifications

To monitor the notifications from Oracle about your Cloud services,

1. Sign into My Services. You are logging directly into your specific Cloud tool.
2. Click *Notifications*:

The My Services Notifications page lists all of the notifications related to the services and displays the following information:

- Name of the Oracle data center where the services are located
- Name of the identity domain to which the services belong
- Four page tabs:
    o **All** – displays all notifications for the services
    o **Applications** – displays only the notifications for the Oracle Software as a Service (SaaS) applications
    o **Platform Services** – displays only the notifications for the Oracle Platform as a Service (PaaS) services
    o **Notification Preferences** – displays the notification preferences (you can receive notifications via email or SMS)

Perform Operations on Services

You can access the My Services application and then drill down to the service details page to perform the following operations:

- Launch service
- Create firewall rules
- View and access related deployments

The *Manage Associations* option in the service details page allows Administrators to manage associations between certain types of services.

Service Association allows different Cloud services to communicate with each other (e.g., Business Intelligence Cloud Service also comes with Oracle Database Cloud Service; these two services are associated together and can share information across services).

LOGGING A CLOUD SUPPORT CASE

To log a case for your Cloud instance, go to http://support.oracle.com/. Choose the *Cloud Support* portal. You can also log a case from My Services.

To use My Oracle Support (MOS),
1. Register your Company with your Customer Service ID (CSI). This was provided in the "Welcome to Oracle Cloud" email that your Account Administrator received after you activated the order.
2. Enter names and emails of all people who need access to MOS, including partners and consultants who may log cases on your behalf.

You should be ready to log a Cloud support case. For more information, you can watch this Cloud Support Webcast: *Essentials Webcast: Oracle Cloud Support (Doc ID 1555872.1)*, which can be found at the following URL:

https://support.oracle.com/epmos/faces/DocumentDisplay?id=1555872.1&displayIndex=1

```
LOG ENTRY: SOL 11, Entry 6

     Success! Launching into Oracle Cloud was WAY
easier than launching a space shuttle. The Vision
Oracle PBCS instance is now in the Cloud and ready
for development!
     ...
     Now what?
```

Chapter 3: Intro to Oracle PBCS

> **LOG ENTRY: SOL 11, Entry 7**
>
> My first mission in the Cloud is to implement Oracle PBCS. I'll worry later about the reporting, dashboarding, and consolidating. That will be whole different set of log entries.
> For now I have a purpose: Vision needs to implement a sales forecasting solution in just sols. So that is what I'm going to do.

INTRO TO ORACLE PBCS

Oracle Planning and Budgeting Cloud Service (PBCS) is a centralized, Cloud-based planning, budgeting, and forecasting solution. Never fear Excel gurus, Microsoft Office integration is also possible with PBCS. Features include: easy to use user interface, powerful calculation capabilities, a central and secured repository, approvals and process management, flexible modeling, Predictive Analytics, powerful reporting and analysis, task lists, and more. You can do both top-down (Target) and bottom-up planning, as well as have multiple versions for iterative planning cycles.

USER INTERFACES

When PBCS was first released, it utilized two user interfaces: the Workspace UI, which is similar to the on-premises Hyperion Planning user interface, and the Simplified UI (new with the first release of PBCS). The Simplified UI or "SUI" is the go forward interface for PBCS. Starting December 2017, Oracle will be retiring the Workspace UI (also known as the "standard interface") for all customers who activated their Planning Cloud subscriptions before July 31, 2016.

The Simplified UI was first developed for tablets, and therefore, has a minimalist look and feel and intuitive navigation:

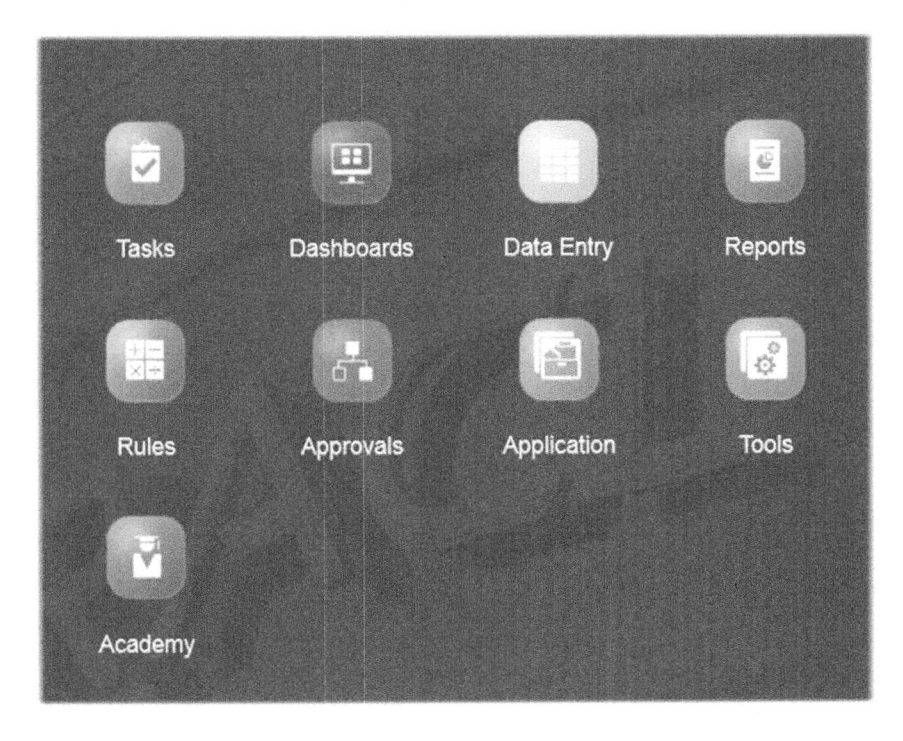

Tasks	Dashboards	Data Entry	Reports
Rules	Approvals	Application	Tools
Academy			

To access the Simplified UI, enter the PBCS URL ending in *oraclecloud.com/HyperionPlanning* sent to your administrator into your web browser.

> **Note!** Check out the latest documentation for supported browsers. We have found Firefox to be the most stable browser for PBCS when using Windows-based machines. In this book, we are using the latest version of Firefox (v45+) for all functionality tests and screen shots.

NAVIGATE THE SIMPLIFIED UI

The Home screen of the Simplified UI for PBCS displays upon login:

42   Chapter 3: Intro to Oracle PBCS

[Screenshot of PBCS home screen showing "February 26, 2017 Welcome Tracy", Activity/Recent/Favorites tabs with "2 Tasks Due Today", and icons for Tasks, Dashboards, Data Entry, Reports, Rules, Approvals, Application, Tools, and Academy.]

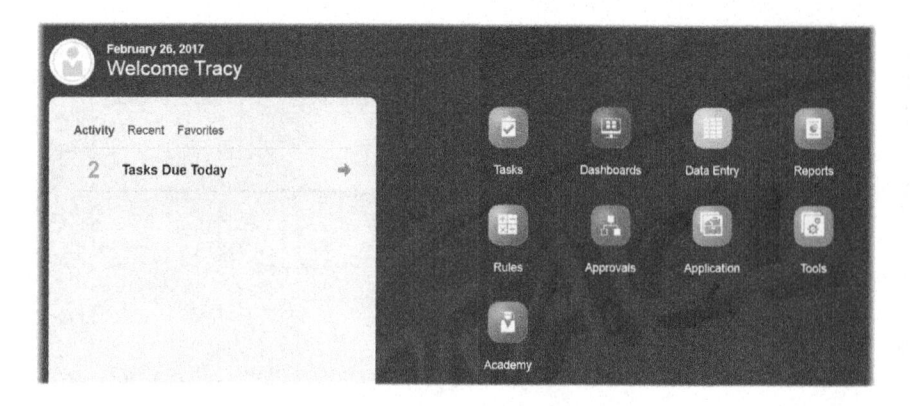

From the home screen of PBCS, users can quickly access announcements via the flip board through *Activity*, recently used places via *Recent*, and *Favorites*.

Note! If you are logging in for the very first time, no applications have been created yet. You will see an initial screen prompting you to create an application.

In addition, you can access a number of icons that will take you to various areas of PBCS:

- **Tasks** – task lists created to guide users through a process; includes dashboards and plans (or data forms)
- **Dashboards** – a listing of editable dashboards created for users and, if provisioned, the ability to create new dashboards
- **Data Entry** – a listing of simple data forms, composite forms, ad hoc grids, and Smart Forms (in earlier Cloud versions you saw this option as "Data" or "Plans")
- **Reports** – run reports in either HTML, PDF, or Excel format
- **Rules** – rules to launch (to create business rules, you go to Calculation Manager via *Navigator >> Create and Manage >> Rules* in the Simplified UI)
- **Approvals** – review and approve plans
- **Application** – administration area focused on the application settings and details

Look Smarter Than You Are with PBCS 43

- **Tools** – administration area focused on important PBCS features and settings to assist with application maintenance and ease of use
- **Academy** – learn more about PBCS through Oracle's documentation and video libraries

If you select one of these icons, a list of cards appears across the top of the UI for easy navigation to each section:

![Navigation bar showing: Tasks, Dashboards, Data Entry, Reports, Rules, Approvals, Academy]

There are two icons that do not display across the top. They are *Application* and *Tools*. These are areas that Administrators may visit frequently for maintenance and troubleshooting.

Application Cluster

In the *Application* cluster, Administrators and users can access a variety of application-focused settings and features. Only administrators can view quick metrics on the overall application by selecting the *Overview* card:

44   Chapter 3: Intro to Oracle PBCS

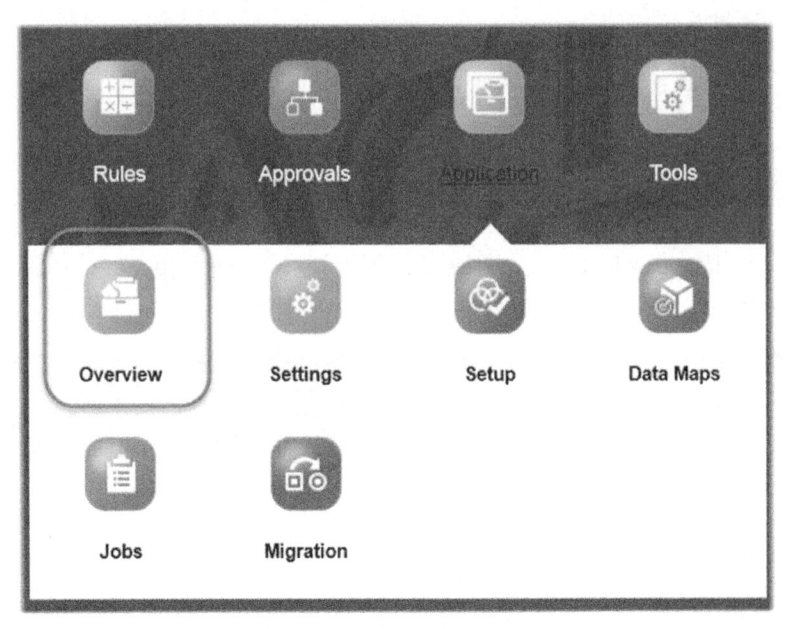

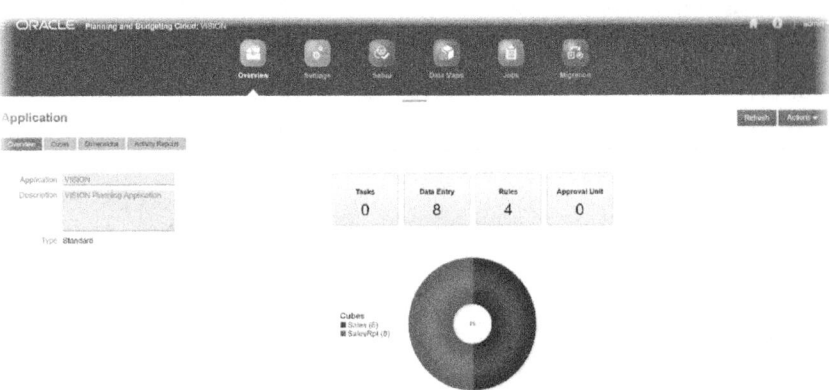

In the *Actions* menu here, Administrators can *Import Data* and *Export Data* (this is data, not dimensions), *Convert to Enterprise* application type (if the EPBCS license is engaged), *Refresh Database* for any changes, *Clear Cube* (both BSO and ASO) of different cross sections of data or all data, *Remove Application* (delete the application), access the *Inbox / Outbox Explorer* (a handy place for getting files to and from the Cloud), and *Manage Sandboxes*:

Look Smarter Than You Are with PBCS 45

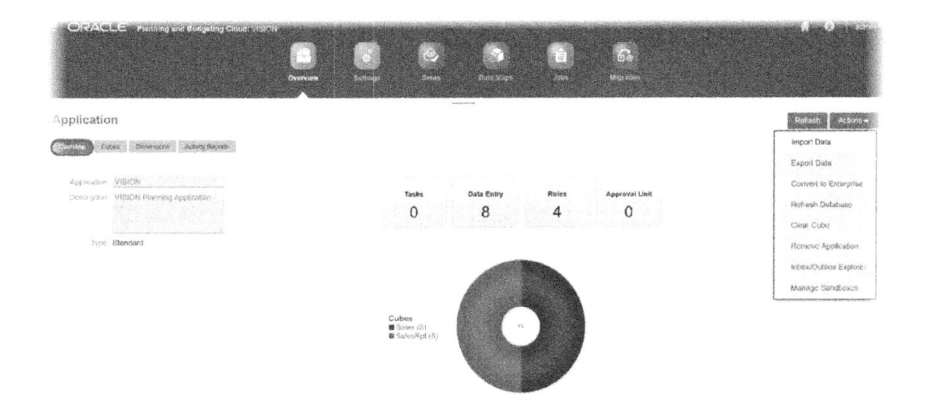

The *Cubes* tab allows Administrators to view and create cubes:

The *Dimensions* tab allows Administrators to view and create dimensions, set the dimension order and dense / sparse settings, and import / export dimensions:

To view dimension properties, click on the dimension (although this only shows you the top level dimension member). To access and view all of the members in the Dimension Editor, you go to *Navigator >> Dimensions* to jump to the dimension editor:

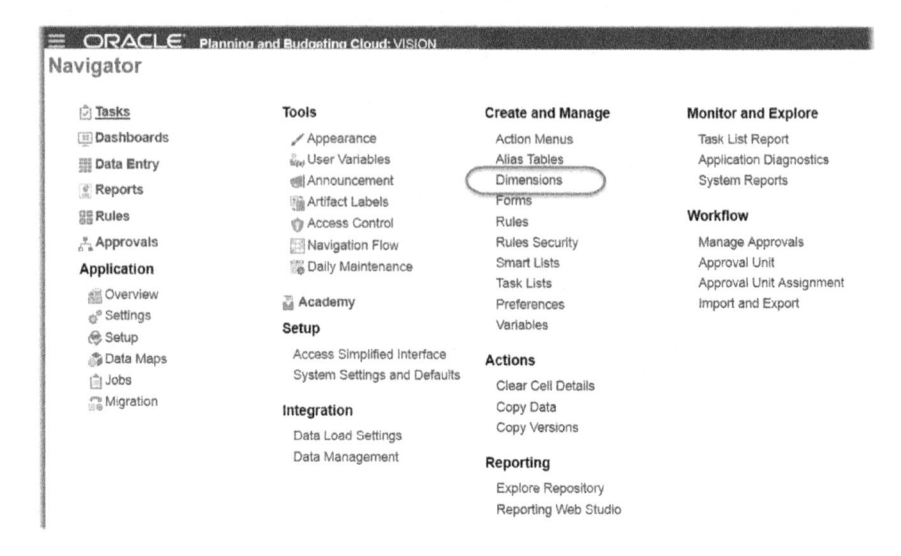

Note! As Oracle adds more features, this Navigator section will change (items could be removed from Navigator and added elsewhere in the Simplified UI).

The *Activity Reports* tab displays the activity reports by day and allows you to download the access logs:

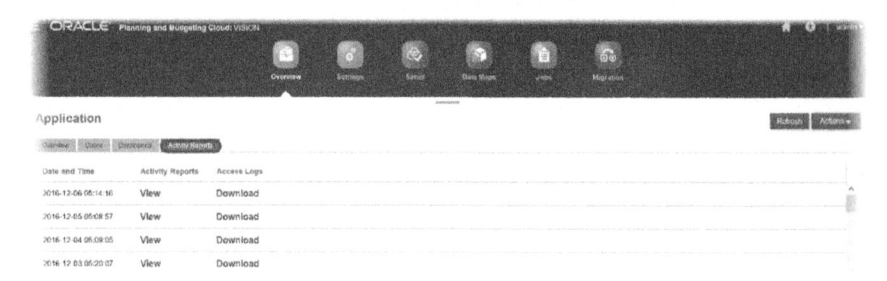

Look Smarter Than You Are with PBCS   47

Once you click *View* next to one of the dates, you'll see a number of useful metrics, like the number of users by day, 30 worst performing user interface actions over 10 seconds, browser version usage, top 10 most active users by usage duration, etc.:

Top 7 User Interface Requests by Duration

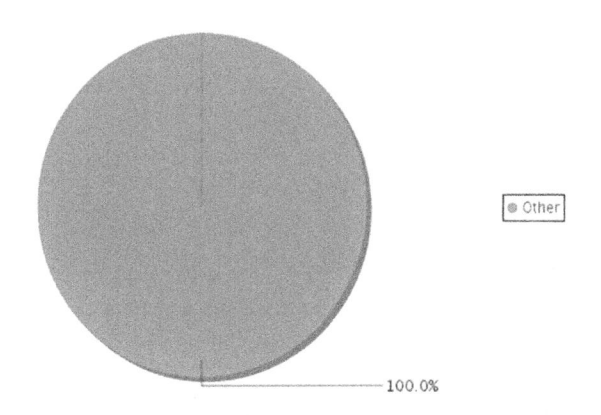

[Pie chart showing 100.0% Other]

UI Request	Duration (Min:Sec)	Executions	Average Duration (Min:Sec)	Min Duration (Min:Sec)	Max Duration (Min:Sec)
Other	00:41	27	00:02	00:00	00:18
Load taskflow	00:00	1	00:00	00:00	00:00

If you click *Download* next to one of the dates, you'll see access information for that date by webpage, IP address, user, action, etc.:

	A	B	C	D	E	F	G	H	I	J
1	Date	Time	URI	Duration (Sec)	Bytes	IP	User	Screen	Action	Object
2	12/5/2016	18:05:18	/HyperionPlanning/	0.397	8297	100.125.1	admin	Other	Other	Other
3	12/5/2016	18:05:22	/HyperionPlanning/faces/LogOn?_afrLoop=5831070599030575&	2.372	16013	100.125.1	admin	Other	Other	Other
4	12/5/2016	18:05:42	/HyperionPlanning/faces/LogOn?_adf.ctrl-state=kdq5qso2g_4	18.096	46010	100.125.1	admin	Other	Other	Other
5	12/5/2016	18:05:43	/interop/feedbackSubmit	0.007	191	100.125.1	admin	Other	Other	Other
6	12/5/2016	18:05:46	/HyperionPlanning/faces/StructureHomeTF/StructureHome?_ad	0.211	918	100.125.1	admin	Other	Other	Other
7	12/5/2016	18:15:44	/HyperionPlanning/faces/StructureHomeTF/StructureHome?_ad	0.136	872	100.125.1	admin	Other	Other	Other
8	12/5/2016	18:15:44	/interop/feedbackSubmit	0.01	116	100.125.1	admin	Other	Other	Other
9	12/5/2016	18:15:44	/HyperionPlanning/faces/StructureHomeTF/StructureHome?_ad	0.109	872	100.125.1	admin	Other	Other	Other
10	12/5/2016	19:00:10	/HyperionPlanning/faces/LogOn	0.263	8147	100.125.1	admin	Other	Other	Other
11	12/5/2016	19:00:11	/HyperionPlanning/faces/LogOn?_afrLoop=5834361890874899&	0.024	16013	100.125.1	admin	Other	Other	Other
12	12/5/2016	19:00:13	/HyperionPlanning/faces/LogOn?_adf.ctrl-state=fvbp726i5_4	0.466	46010	100.125.1	admin	Other	Other	Other
13	12/5/2016	19:00:13	/interop/feedbackSubmit	0.007	191	100.125.1	admin	Other	Other	Other
14	12/5/2016	19:00:14	/HyperionPlanning/faces/StructureHomeTF/StructureHome?_ad	0.107	918	100.125.1	admin	Other	Other	Other
15	12/5/2016	19:01:11	/HyperionPlanning/faces/StructureHomeTF/StructureHome?_ad	0.299	42969	100.125.1	admin	Other	Other	Other
16	12/5/2016	19:01:13	/HyperionPlanning/faces/StructureHomeTF/StructureHome?_ad	0.175	272	100.125.1	admin	EPM Struct	Load taskfl	/WEB-I
17	12/5/2016	19:01:21	/HyperionPlanning/faces/StructureHomeTF/EfsNonFuseNavigato	6.926	88966	100.125.1	admin	Other	Other	Other
18	12/5/2016	19:01:21	/interop/feedbackSubmit	0.005	191	100.125.1	admin	Other	Other	Other
19	12/5/2016	19:01:25	/HyperionPlanning/faces/StructureHomeTF/EfsNonFuseNavigato	0.328	11932	100.125.1	admin	Other	Other	Other
20	12/5/2016	19:01:28	/HyperionPlanning/faces/StructureHomeTF/EfsNonFuseNavigato	0.239	11932	100.125.1	admin	Other	Other	Other

The *Settings* card allows both users and administrators to set preferences and administrators to define application defaults and refresh options:

![Settings card screenshot showing Application Settings with Number Formatting, Approvals, Notifications, and Date Time Display sections]

The *Setup* card allows both users and administrators to view, create, maintain valid intersections for the application (more on this later), and view valid intersection reports:

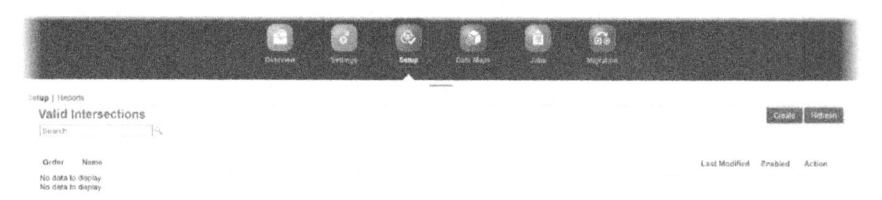

![Setup card screenshot showing Valid Intersections section]

Administrators can navigate to the *Data Maps* card to define, update, and run mappings that push data from one cube to another cube within the PBCS application:

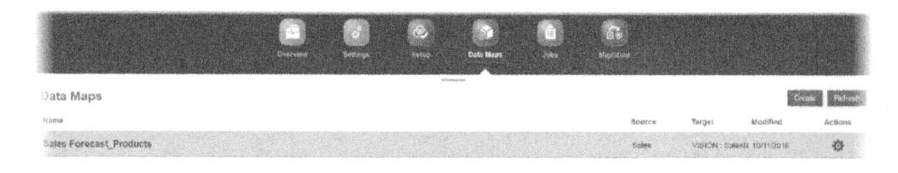

![Data Maps card screenshot showing Sales Forecast_Products mapping]

Both users and administrators can access the *Jobs* card within the *Application* cluster to view recently run jobs, upcoming jobs, and schedule new jobs (to run rules, import data and metadata, export data

Look Smarter Than You Are with PBCS 49

and metadata, refresh the database, clear data from the database, run invalid intersection reports, and push data from one cube to another):

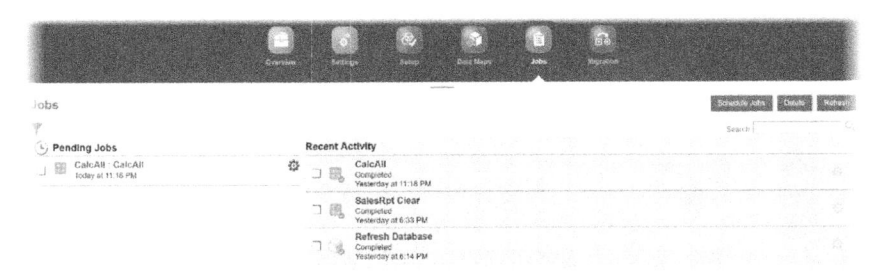

The *Migration* card within the *Application* cluster allows Administrators to export a backup in piecemeal or application entirety, manage daily backup and past snapshots, and view artifact update and migration status reports:

Tools Cluster

In the *Tools* cluster, Administrators and users can use various PBCS features to assist them with application ease of usage and maintenance:

50   Chapter 3: Intro to Oracle PBCS

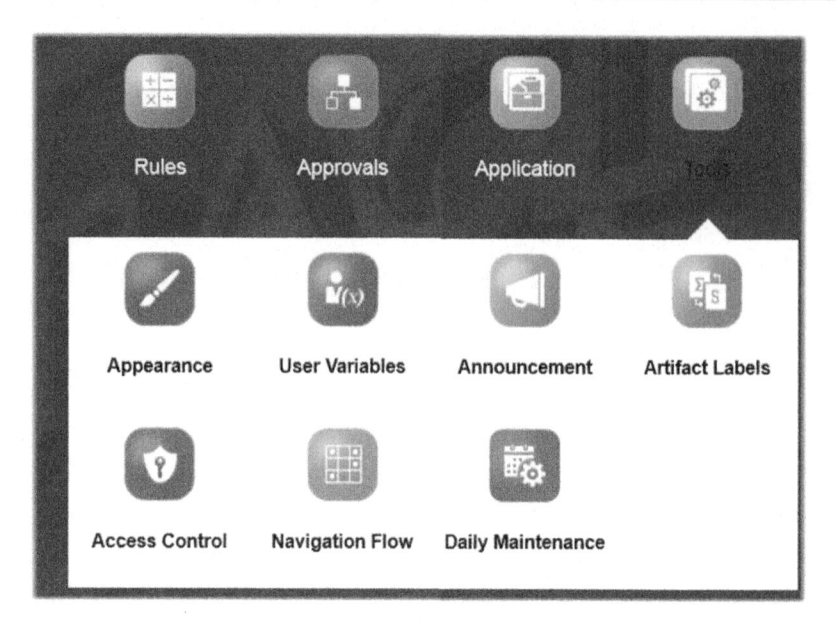

Administrators can setup appearance settings in the *Appearance* card, by designating a logo or background image via URL:

Both Administrators and users can set their user variables in the *User Variables* card:

Look Smarter Than You Are with PBCS   51

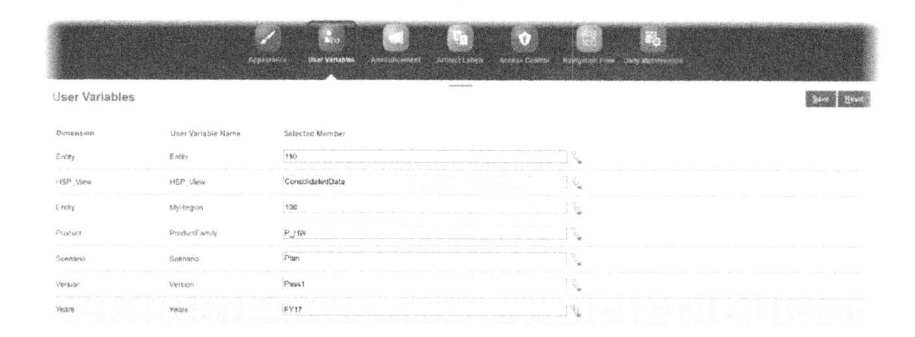

Administrators can set up centralized announcements that all users can view in the *Announcement* card:

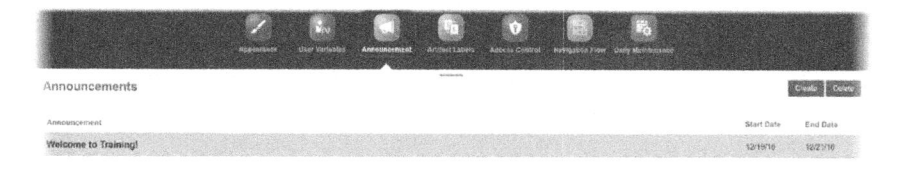

Administrators can set different labels by locale for application artifacts in the *Artifact Labels* card. They can also change the default names for existing objects centrally:

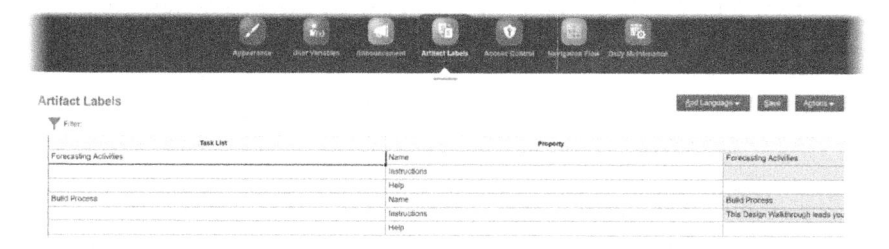

Administrators can manage groups, roles, and run security reports in the *Access Control* card:

52   Chapter 3: Intro to Oracle PBCS

Administrators can manage and create navigation flows (navigation objects that affect the cards and clusters that different user groups see – more on this later) in the *Navigation Flow* card:

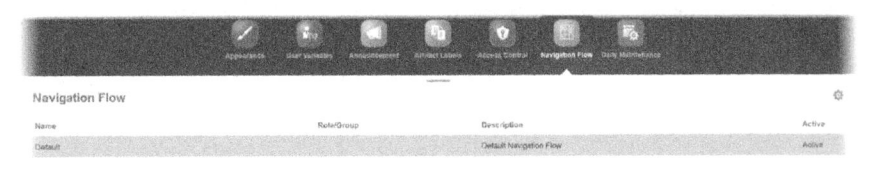

Finally, Administrators can set up the daily maintenance time zone and time in the *Daily Maintenance* card:

Navigator

The *Navigator* icon ☰ is the main navigation method to access all of the PBCS user and administrative functions in one view. Administrators use this option frequently to create and manage the PBCS application:

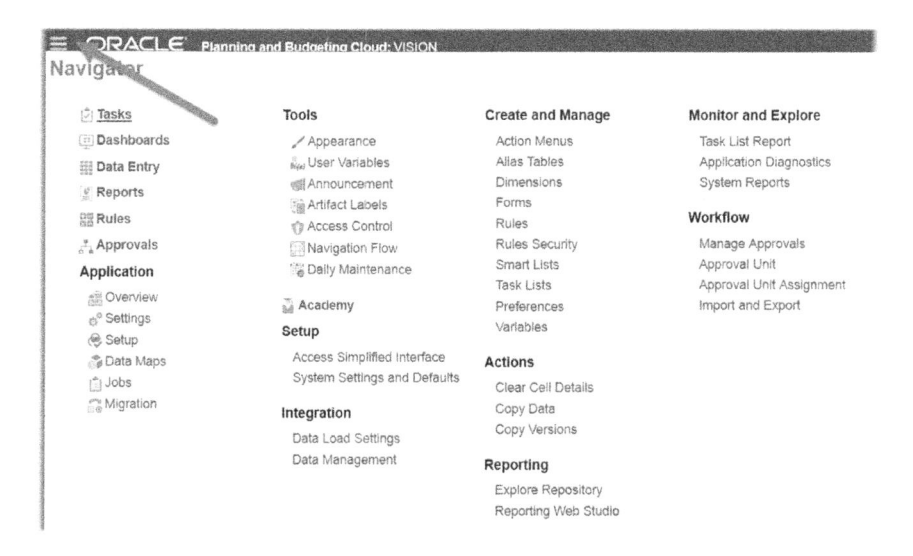

Navigator	Tools	Create and Manage	Monitor and Explore
Tasks	Appearance	Action Menus	Task List Report
Dashboards	User Variables	Alias Tables	Application Diagnostics
Data Entry	Announcement	Dimensions	System Reports
Reports	Artifact Labels	Forms	
Rules	Access Control	Rules	**Workflow**
Approvals	Navigation Flow	Rules Security	Manage Approvals
Application	Daily Maintenance	Smart Lists	Approval Unit
Overview		Task Lists	Approval Unit Assignment
Settings	Academy	Preferences	Import and Export
Setup	**Setup**	Variables	
Data Maps	Access Simplified Interface	**Actions**	
Jobs	System Settings and Defaults	Clear Cell Details	
Migration	**Integration**	Copy Data	
	Data Load Settings	Copy Versions	
	Data Management	**Reporting**	
		Explore Repository	
		Reporting Web Studio	

Throughout this mission, we use Navigator to access different PBCS components but you can also use the out of the box clusters and cards.

MEMBER SELECTION

The Simplified UI has a member selector that you will use throughout PBCS both as an Administrator and user. Members are the metadata elements that describe a number (e.g., "Jan" or "Sales"). More on members in the next chapter. The member selector UI that you use has a common look and feel across the various PBCS components. Once your application is built and you have dimensions and members, users and administrators use the member selection window to select desired member or members. PBCS has revamped this feature to be compatible with the web browser interface.

The member selector allows users to select dimension members as necessary for the planning process. For instance, you can select members for data forms, user variable definitions, rule prompts, rule definitions, Financial Reports, and more. Only valid members are selectable to the user, based on a combination of security and valid intersection rules.

The member selector has three basic sections:

1) Search box
2) Hierarchy navigation columns
3) Settings menu

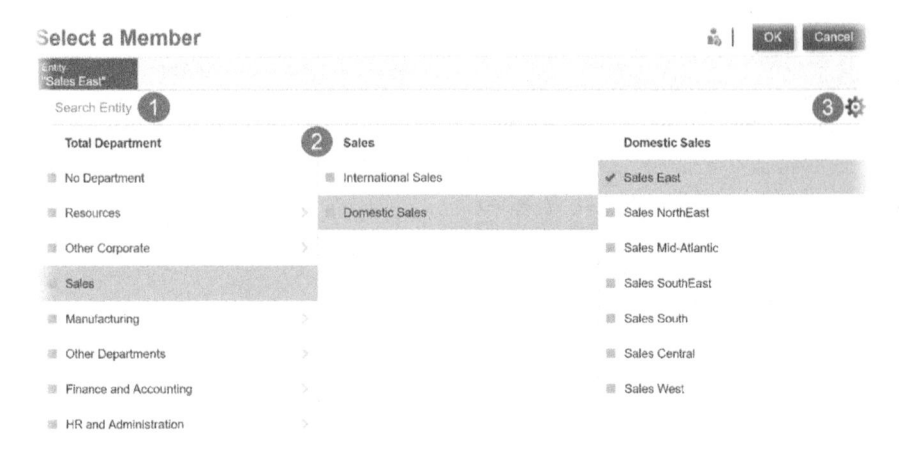

Select a Member			
Entity "Sales East"			
Search Entity (1)			(3) ⚙
Total Department	(2) Sales		Domestic Sales
☐ No Department	☐ International Sales		✓ Sales East
☐ Resources >	Domestic Sales		☐ Sales NorthEast
☐ Other Corporate >			☐ Sales Mid-Atlantic
Sales			☐ Sales SouthEast
☐ Manufacturing >			☐ Sales South
☐ Other Departments >			☐ Sales Central
☐ Finance and Accounting >			☐ Sales West
☐ HR and Administration >			

The search box allows planners to search for a specific member within the dimension. All or part of the member or alias can be used. Also, one or more words can be used. In addition, advanced wildcard searches are allowed. Wildcard searches can include the following types of characters:

- ? – to match any single character
- * – to match zero or multiple characters
- # – to match any single number (0-9)
- [list] – match any single character within a list of characters; a dash can be used to represent a range
- [-list] – match any single character not found within a list of characters; a dash can be used to represent a range

The hierarchy navigation columns are the drill downs into the dimension. This is read left to right, top to bottom. In the previous screen shot, the "Sales" member is highlighted. This then opens the children of Sales into another column. Since the "Domestic Sales" child is also highlighted, the children of Domestic Sales are shown in the third column. Clicking on a member name indicates drill down on the member. Selecting the checkbox to the left of the member name actually selects the member. "Sales East" is checked, therefore, it is the member selected. You can confirm this by looking at the dimension name in the top left of the member selector window – "Sales East" is the member shown there, which indicates selection.

The *Settings* menu allows you to filter, sort, and display member properties within the hierarchy navigation columns. Settings that can be used in conjunction with other settings have checkmarks next to them:

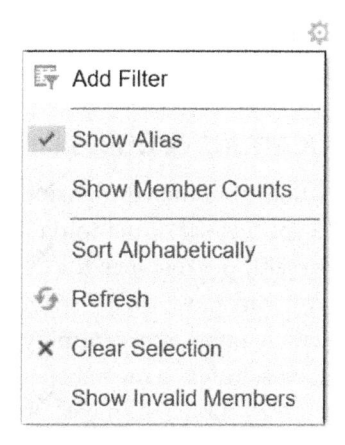

- Add Filter
- ✓ Show Alias
- Show Member Counts
- Sort Alphabetically
- Refresh
- ✗ Clear Selection
- Show Invalid Members

Filtering options include the following. This allows users to filter all members for a given dimension based on relationship functions, specified attributes, member level, or member generation:

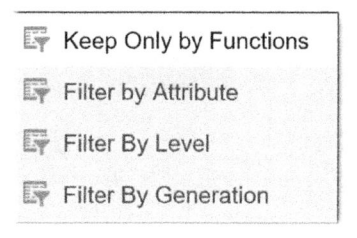

- Keep Only by Functions
- Filter by Attribute
- Filter By Level
- Filter By Generation

Display options include displaying the alias and/or member counts for each parent member. Members that are considered invalid due to valid intersection rules are suppressed.

Sort options include sorting alphabetically. This applies to both member names and aliases.

The *Refresh* option clears all drill downs into the dimension on the member selection screen and takes you back to the top level members.

The *Clear Selection* option clears the current members that are checked. It also clears the current member selected for the dimension.

Finally, the *Show Invalid Members* option displays all members that are suppressed due to valid intersection rules. This option is helpful to understand why certain members are not available for selection.

Once the necessary members are selected by checking the boxes next to them, planners must click the *OK* button in the upper right-hand corner to confirm selection.

APPLICATIONS & CUBES DEFINED

A PBCS application contains dimensions, data, business rules, and interfaces to meet a specific set of planning needs. You can have one application, per environment, per instance for PBCS.

Within PBCS, you can have up to seven cubes (also known as plan types or databases). A cube is a grouping of related dimensions, data, interfaces, and business rules to meet a specific planning need.

You can design the cubes to meet planning and forecasting needs. You might create a summary cube that consolidates data from a custom revenue cube, custom workforce cube, and custom capital expense cube. You might have a separate revenue details cube with actuals details:

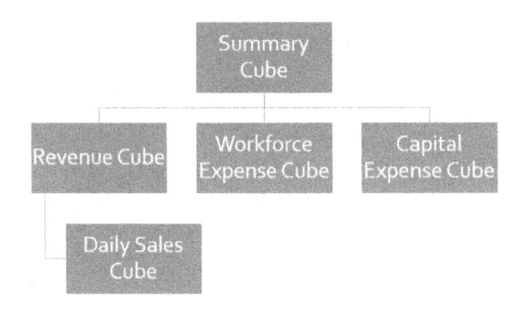

```
                    Summary
                     Cube
        ┌──────────────┼──────────────┐
   Revenue Cube    Workforce      Capital
                  Expense Cube   Expense Cube
        │
   Daily Sales
     Cube
```

The PBCS licensing option does *NOT* include the out of the box on-premises Workforce, Capex, PFP, or Public Sector modules. You can build your own cubes with similar custom logic and interfaces.

Note! Another pricing offering for Oracle PBCS, called Enterprise Planning and Budgeting Cloud (referred to as EPBCS), DOES include prebuilt Financials, Workforce, Projects, and Capex frameworks. They are similar to the on-premises modules.

PBCS utilizes a multi-dimensional database called Essbase to store the numerical data. Each cube has one Essbase database. The Essbase database could be block storage (BSO) databases, aggregate storage (ASO) databases, or in the future, a hybrid aggregation mode database. More on this later and if you are new to Essbase, please review the Appendix on Essbase at the end of the book.

The Planning and Budgeting pricing option allows one application per environment. Each application may have up to three block storage option (BSO) cubes. You may also have the same number of ASO cubes as you have BSO cubes plus one (so this means potentially up to seven cubes within an application). In future versions, BSO cubes can be designed to utilize hybrid aggregation mode. This is important to know when you are designing your application.

The Enterprise Planning licensing option provides prebuilt frameworks for financials, workforce, capex, and projects. Each one of those frameworks is its own set of cubes. You also have the standard three BSO and 4 ASO cubes in addition to the prebuilt frameworks. That is over 11 cubes in one PBCS application!

The PBCS application and cube names are limited to a maximum of eight characters.

Each application and cube have a number of components:

- **Dimensions** – hierarchies of related master data or metadata
- **User Interfaces** – data forms for entering plan data over the Web or in Excel with Smart View, task lists, dashboards and more
- **Business Rules** – objects that are executed to perform pre-defined calculation logic or other operations on data; common business rules include those to roll up data from base data to totals, perform allocations from upper level data to lower levels, perform driver-based calculation logic, copy data and clear data

Some PBCS components may be used across cubes:

- **Task Lists** – guided steps to complete a process
- **Composite Data Forms** – combination view of one or more simple data forms

VISION APPLICATION DESIGN

To meet the sales forecasting needs for Vision I'm going to create an application with two cubes: Sales (BSO) and SalesRpt (ASO):

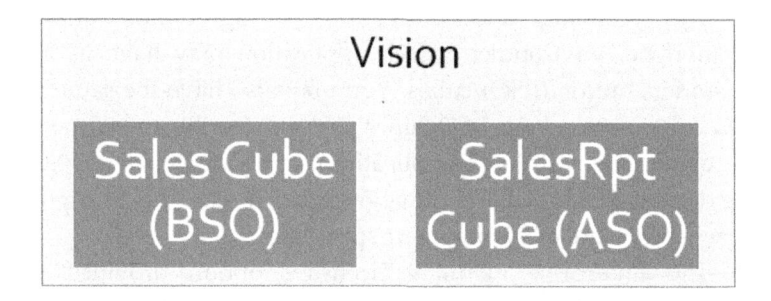

Vision

Sales Cube (BSO)   **SalesRpt Cube (ASO)**

The Sales cube will capture forecast from end users by product and entity. Because I'm so excited about the hybrid capabilities, I'm going to design one of the cubes as a *hybrid cube* (BSO with all upper level sparse members dynamic) even though hybrid is not actually supported yet (as of March 2017). Don't try this at home folks, because I'll repeat, hybrid is not supported (yet). Still, I want to show you the steps to making a BSO cube into a hybrid cube so you'll know. Once hybrid is supported and I've set up the cube properly, I don't have to have any additional aggregation business rules; all upper level members automatically roll up.

Pausing for a moment for a mini-technical deep dive into why I might choose hybrid cube over BSO and ASO cubes in the future (for more details check out the appendix in this book or *Look Smarter Than You Are with Essbase*).

The issue with BSO:

- Limited in the number of dimensions you can realistically build within a plan type
- Large sparse dimensions can't be dynamically calculated
- Stored sparse dimensions increase aggregation time and database size

The issue with ASO:

- Designed for large sparse dimensions but missing powerful BSO calculation engine

The case for Hybrid (future supported feature):

- Combines BSO functionality with ASO performance
- Continues to leverage BSO calculation engine while enabling the use of more (and larger) sparse dimensions
- Reduces the database footprint
- Improves performance
- Not supported for the Cloud (yet)

End users will forecast Units and List Price. I will create a member formula that will calculate revenue for the accounts based on units multiplied by rates. Data will be loaded using Data Management and then product manager Smart List assignments will also be loaded using the Simplified UI. To finish it off, a business rule will be created that will seed forecast data based on loaded actuals data.

The SalesRpt cube will provide more detailed actuals reporting by product, entity, and customer. I'll push the forecast data from the

Sales cube to the SalesRpt cube. No calculations are required for the SalesRpt data and this is a more detailed cube with extra dimensions, so I'm going to create this as an ASO cube.

```
LOG ENTRY: SOL 11, Entry 8

    Not a bad application design, I don't mind
saying. This design uses some best practices and will
illustrate almost all of the PBCS features and
functions.
```

Chapter 4: Build an Application

> **LOG ENTRY: SOL 11, Entry 9**
>
> Now that I have my design for the Vision application, I'm ready to build the application. Fist bump myself for starting this exciting journey! And I was so worried just a few hours ago…

Note! The steps in this book and screen shots are based on PBCS version 16.12, 17.01, 17.02, and 17.03 (December 2016 through March 2017).

CREATE AN APPLICATION

PBCS guides you through the process to create an application. Use the application creation wizard to create the planning and budgeting application.

Note! To follow along the build process, please email info@interrel.com for sample metadata and data files. You can also request an export of this application to import into your environment for testing and learning.

To create an application,
1. Enter the URL for the Simplified UI.
2. Select *Start* in the *Planning and Budgeting* section.

Depending on your Cloud subscription, you might see the option for Financial Consolidation and Close and Tax Reporting, but those are different Cloud solutions. Only choose those options if you are licensed for that product and have intentions on building applications for those specific needs.

The Simplified UI provides three application type options at the beginning of application creation: Lite, Standard, and Enterprise. Below is a summary of these three options:

- **Lite** – this is self-explanatory: a "keep it simple" application type that offers all-in-one planning and reporting models which can be expanded over time
- **Standard** – this application type enables more elaborate and flexible models for more complex business processes
- **Enterprise** – this application type includes built-in planning and budgeting models for Financials, Workforce, Capital, and Project business processes

Note! A Simple Planning application can later be converted into a Standard or Enterprise Planning application, but they cannot be converted backward.

If there are no existing applications in the PBCS instance, the following options appear for creating a new one:

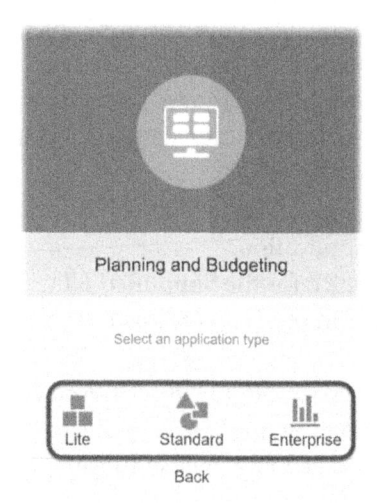

Planning and Budgeting

Select an application type

Lite   Standard   Enterprise

Back

3. Click *Standard* and then *New*.

Look Smarter Than You Are with PBCS 63

Planning and Budgeting

Standard Application
Learn the ropes with a sample demo application, or jump right in and create a new one

Sample   New

Back

4. Enter a name and description for the application. I will call the application "VISION".

Create Application: General

Back | Cancel   General Details Customize Review   Next

* Name: VISION
* Description: Required description

5. Click *Next*.
6. Now fill in the application details:
    a. Select the appropriate calendar options according to application requirements. In my Vision mission, I am choosing years 2010 to 2020; *First Fiscal Month* as "January", and *Even Distribution*.

b. Select the appropriate currency options according to application requirements. I'm choosing a single currency of USD.
c. You can check *Enable rolling forecast for this application* if you would like to automatically create a rolling forecast and specify the period duration. For these steps, I am NOT going to enable it mainly so I can show you how to add this later during application build (in case you want to add this to an existing application).
d. Check *Enable Sandboxes* to allow users to create their own sandboxes as they work on their plans. I'll check the option to enable sandboxes for this application. Note – you cannot enable or disable sandboxes once the application has been created.
e. Name the BSO and ASO Cubes. As mentioned before, I'll name our BSO database "Sales" and our ASO database "SalesRpt":

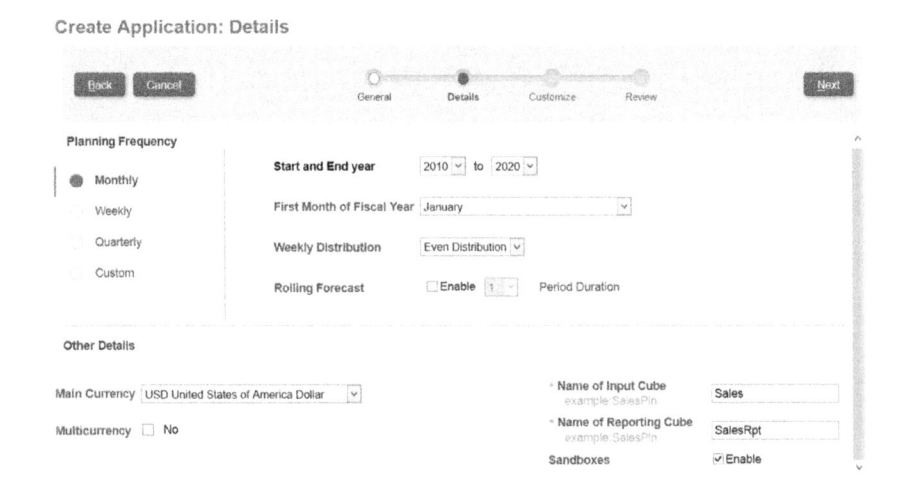

PBCS supports simple currency functionality to meet multi-currency requirements. You can choose this option to use out of the box functionality or create your own custom logic to perform multiple currency calculations and translations.

Notice that I'm creating one BSO cube and one ASO cube for this application. I mentioned earlier that a third option that will be available soon: hybrid aggregation. However, hybrid aggregation is not a formal option in the application creation wizard. The reason why is because a hybrid aggregation cube is really just a BSO cube with the sparse dimensions set to dynamically calculate. So if you want to utilize the hybrid aggregation functionality (in the future), choose BSO. This will make more sense as I go along; the patience will pay off. Also, please review the Appendix on Essbase at the end of the book for more information.

7. Click *Next*.
8. Customizing the application by adding the application metadata and custom dimensions can be done after the application is created and will be discussed in further detail later. If you would like to import metadata during application creation, do the following:
    a. Add any custom dimensions, like Customer and Product.
    b. Attach the appropriate metadata file to the Account, Entity, Customer, and Product dimensions by selecting *Browse* and navigating to the metadata file.

Chapter 4: Build an Application

Create Application: Customize

Metadata and Custom Dimensions

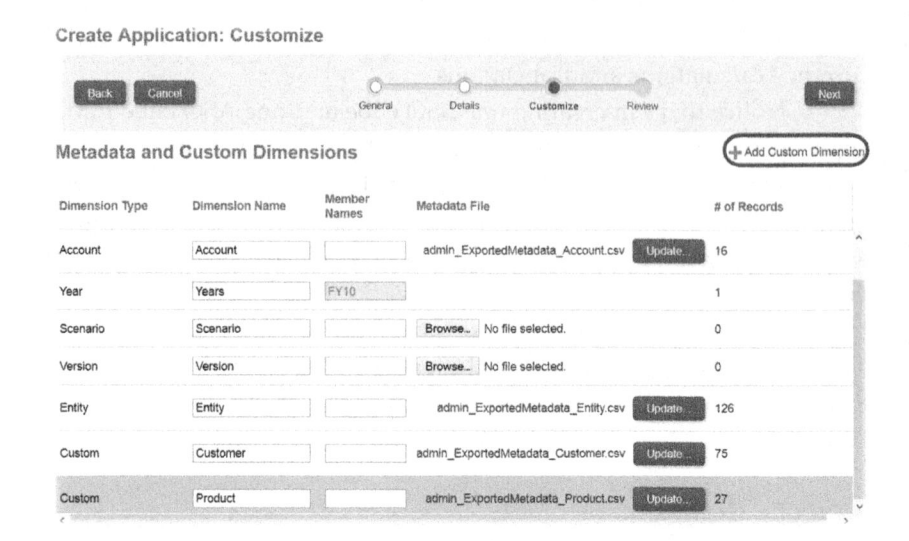

Dimension Type	Dimension Name	Member Names	Metadata File		# of Records
Account	Account		admin_ExportedMetadata_Account.csv	Update	16
Year	Years	FY10			1
Scenario	Scenario		Browse... No file selected.		0
Version	Version		Browse... No file selected.		0
Entity	Entity		admin_ExportedMetadata_Entity.csv	Update	126
Custom	Customer		admin_ExportedMetadata_Customer.csv	Update	75
Custom	Product		admin_ExportedMetadata_Product.csv	Update	27

9. Click *Next*. Review and confirm the application details.

Create Application: Review

VISION - Standard
Required descri...

Planning Frequency : Monthly

Start and End Period	2010-2020 (11 Years)
First Month of Fiscal Year	January
Weekly Distribution	Even Distribution

Other Details

Currency	USD
Multicurrency	No

Cubes
- Input Cube : Sales (7)
- Reporting Cube : SalesRpt (3)

10. Then click *Create*.
11. Wait for the application to create successfully. Click *OK*:

Application Creation Status
Application created successfully.

OK

> LOG ENTRY: SOL 13, Entry 1
>
> Well, that's done. I would celebrate, but recognizing that I only have a short time to complete this application, I had better move onto the next phases.
> I went through the crew's things. Hey – when you are stranded in the Cloud, everything is up for dibs. Surely Project Commander McMullen's iPad had some good movies to entertain myself while stranded in the Cloud.
> Full seasons of Glee and Smash? Seriously? Why couldn't it be Breaking Bad or The Sopranos? I only have musical comedies to watch?
> Well, I guess I won't complain; it's something. Finn and Rachel it is.

DIMENSIONS EXPLAINED

Data is organized within an Essbase database (or cube) into dimensions, or groupings of related data elements in a hierarchical format. To oversimplify, a dimension is something that can be put into the rows or columns of your report or data form like "Periods", "Accounts", "Entities", or "Products". Different databases have different dimensions. In PBCS, dimensions and dimension properties can be edited manually in the dimension editor or imported via a flat file. I will build the dimensions using both methods.

Note! Standard dimensions will already exist in the application (Period, Years, Account, Entity, Scenario, and Version). The HSP_View dimension is created when sandboxes are enabled. To create a new custom dimension, click ✚, but remember that they cannot be deleted once created.

Dimension Types & Member Properties

A dimension can be assigned a dimension type which enables specific functionality and member properties for time and financial intelligence within PBCS. Valid dimension types for PBCS applications include:

- Accounts
- Time
- Country
- Attribute

PBCS assigns the Accounts, Time, and Country dimension types by default. The Country dimension type is used for the multi-currency modules, if that option is chosen during the application creation.

Dimensions also have their own properties in addition to dimension types. In most cases, these properties are applicable for all members, as well as top-level dimension nodes. These properties govern how the member displays to the end user, calculated (if applicable), reported, and more. These are described in the following sections.

Alias

The Alias property provides an alternate name or description for the member. This property is viewed by end users and is assigned by an alias table. You can use multiple alias tables to store different member names for end users to use in planning and reporting. For instance, you might want to have an alias table for "English" and another for "Spanish" so your users can practice their Español when looking at members in forms and reports. PBCS supports duplicate aliases but I recommend trying to keep aliases unique across members and dimensions.

Data Type

Members in PBCS may have a specific data type assigned: Unspecified, Currency, Non Currency, Percentage, Smart List, Date, and Text. I'll further define these data types when discussing the Accounts dimension:

Data Storage

The Data Storage property tells Essbase how the member should be stored back in Essbase. Valid data storage options include:

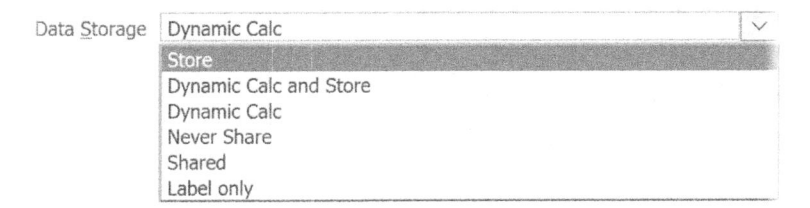

Data Storage	Dynamic Calc
	Store
	Dynamic Calc and Store
	Dynamic Calc
	Never Share
	Shared
	Label only

- **Store** – stores the data value with the member
- **Dynamic Calc and Store** – does not calculate the data value until a user requests it, but stores the data value immediately after the retrieval; this type was designed to be used for infrequently calculated formulas
- **Dynamic Calc** – does not calculate the data value until a user requests it, and then discards the data value
- **Never Share** – does not allow members to be shared implicitly; PBCS creates a lot of "Never Share" members by default so that you can easily send information into summary members for "Target" versions
- **Shared** – shares data between two or more members
- **Label only** – creates members for navigation and grouping and doesn't calculate data at this level; these members (e.g., "Statistical Accounts") usually won't make sense from a logical consolidation standpoint

When should you set a member to *Store* in PBCS? Use the *Store* data storage tab when you need to load data or input data to that member. Set a member to store if that member has a large number of children. Most of the time, your large sparse dimensions are set to Store. (What is a sparse dimension? I'll address this later because it's a somewhat advanced topic.) You may also set dense members with member formulas to store so that a calculation occurs at a level 0 member and then aggregates for all dimensions. I'll do this for my Vision application in just a bit.

In most cases, use the *Dynamic Calc* property for your variances, ratios, averages, and other formulas. You can also set upper level members of a hierarchy to *Dynamic Calc* when those members have just a few children. Oftentimes you set upper levels of the Accounts and Time dimensions (and other dense dimensions) to *Dynamic Calc* to help reduce your database size.

I recommend sticking to *Dynamic Calc* over *Dynamic Calc and Store* unless you have few used sparse members with very complicated formulas.

You should assign *Never Share* to a member that is the only child of its parent (or could potentially be the only child of its parent). Essbase has a built-in feature called "Implicit Sharing", a mischievous gremlin of a function that can cause confusion in your Essbase databases. Essbase tries to be smart for us in this case. When a parent only has one child, the data values for both the parent and the child will always be the same, right? So Essbase decides to only store one value, the child value, which reduces your database size. But this causes issues in loading or inputting data to the parent, who dynamically pulls the data value from the child.

When should you use *Label Only*? Use *Label Only* for members like Scenario, Ratio, or Drivers, whose sole purpose in life is to organize the dimension and hierarchy; members for which it never makes sense to add their children together. A member marked as *Label Only* automatically pulls the value of its first child when referenced. Because of this, when you make a member Label Only you often give its first child a plus (+) consolidation operator and the other children a tilde (~) to designate that only the first child is rolling to the member (more on consolidation properties in the next section). This is entirely to help indicate what's going on in Essbase to a user who might not know that a Label Only member pulls the value from its first child. For example, it makes no sense to add Actual and Budget members together, so you flag the Scenario dimension as *Label Only*.

Valid for Cube

As discussed, a single PBCS application may have multiple cubes or databases. Depending on the dimension, a dimension (or member) may or may not be required for all cubes. The administrator has some flexibility in defining the dimensions and members that are valid and available in the cubes. You can specify how the member should roll up within the hierarchy using the Consolidation property once a member is assigned to one or more cubes.

For the Years and Period dimensions, all members are assigned to all cubes. The administrator cannot change this assignment (the option isn't available), but other dimensions can be changed.

You can, however, assign the consolidation property. What's the consolidation property?

Consolidation Operators

Consolidation properties, also known as consolidation operators, tell Essbase how to roll up the members in the outline. Valid consolidation operators for PBCS include:

- Addition (+)
- Subtraction (-)
- Multiplication (*)
- Division (/)
- Percent (%)
- Ignore (~)
- Never (^)

Note! Never (^) does not aggregate a member up across any dimension in the Essbase database (e.g., prices, index) while Ignore (~) does not aggregate a member up the dimension in which it resides. However, Ignore aggregates for all other dimensions (e.g., Product, Customer).

Two Pass

The two pass member property tells Essbase to "come back and calculate this member at the end." Why is this important? Let's look at an example.

The Accounts dimension is calculated first (I'll explain shortly), which means that Average Price is calculated based on the input members Hardware Revenue and Units. Once I roll up the Time dimension, the monthly Average Price is added together and placed in Q1, as shown below:

	A	B	C	D	E
6		FY16	FY16	FY16	FY16
7		Jan	Feb	Mar	Q1
8	Hardware Revenue	1000	1000	1500	3500
9	Units	100	150	125	375
10	Average Price	10.00	6.67	12.00	28.67

Hmmm... something's not right there. I want Average Price to recalculate after the quarter and year totals for Hardware Revenue and Units have been calculated.

Tag the Average Price member with the two pass calculation property and *Save* it:

Dimensions
Edit Member : Average Price

Member Properties UDA Member Formula

Name	Average Price
Description	
Alias Table	Default
Alias	
Account Type	Saved Assumption
Variance Reporting	Non-Expense
Time Balance	Flow
Skip	None
Exchange Rate Type	No Rate
Source Cube	Sales
Data Storage	Dynamic Calc
Two Pass Calculation	✓

Now Essbase knows to circle back to calculate the correct value after it's finished calculating everything else:

	A	B	C	D	E
6		FY16	FY16	FY16	FY16
7		Jan	Feb	Mar	Q1
8	Hardware Revenue	1000	1000	1500	3500
9	Units	100	150	125	375
10	Average Price	10.00	6.67	12.00	9.33

UDAs

You can create user defined attributes (UDAs) for members on the UDA tab. UDAs provide a way to tag multiple members for analysis, calculations, or data loading. For example, say you want to perform a 10% bonus calculation for all managers managing "Large" markets and a 5% bonus calculation for all managers managing "Small" market accounts. While UDAs can be used to pinpoint those managers for calculating these bonuses, what they can't do is easily give a subtotal for "Large" and "Small" markets – alternate hierarchies or attributes would be a better solution to meet this requirement.

Member Formulas

Because PBCS sits on top of Essbase, I have an amazingly powerful calculation engine at my electronic fingertips. One way to build in calculations for PBCS is through member formulas. These are calculated back in Essbase.

Conditional operators allow for tests based on criteria. An Essbase member formula to calculate "Commission" might use these conditional checks:

```
IF (Sales > 1000)
     Sales * .02;
ELSE
     10;
ENDIF
```

In English-speak, if Sales are greater than 1000, then Commission is equal to Sales times two percent; otherwise, Commission is equal to 10. I'm capitalizing "Sales" and "Commissions" to highlight the fact that these are members in the Account dimension.

Mathematical functions define and return values based on selected member expressions. These functions include most standard statistical functions. An example of a mathematical function would be the standard formula for a Variance calculation for Actual and Budget data:

```
(Actual-Budget)/Actual;
```

Mathematical functions can be used in Essbase member formulas. The member formula for the "Market Share" member uses an index function:

```
Sales % @PARENTVAL (Markets, Sales);
```

In other words, Market Share is equal to the Sales for the current member as a percent of the current member's parent data value for the Markets dimension.

The member formula for the member "Mar YTD" uses a financial function:

```
@PTD(Jan:Mar);
```

The member formula for "Payroll" shows you an example of how to use conditional or Boolean criteria:

```
IF (@ISIDESC (East) OR @ISIDESC (West))
     Sales * .15;
ELSEIF (@ISIDESC(Central))
     Sales * .11;
ELSE
     Sales * .10;
ENDIF
```

To put it in English, for all of the members under and including East and West, Payroll is equal to Sales times 15 percent. For all members under and including Central, Payroll is equal to Sales times 11 percent. For all other members Payroll is equal to Sales times 10 percent.

Note! Essbase member formulas must end with semicolons. If the member name has spaces in it, you must enclose the member name in double quotes.

Now that you are fully fluent in basic PBCS dimension types and member properties, let's turn our attention to building out the all of the dimensions, beginning with Scenario.

BUILD SCENARIO DIMENSION

The Scenario dimension in a PBCS application is used to apply and track different planning methods, as well as create new forecasts. Scenarios can be associated with different time periods and exchange rates. Start period, start year, end period, and end year are Scenario properties that control data form entry. You can also build calculated members into the Scenario dimension to perform variance analysis.

76   Chapter 4: Build an Application

The Scenario dimension is built manually using the dimension editor.

To build the Scenario dimension,
1. Select *Navigator* >> *Create and Manage* >> *Dimensions*:

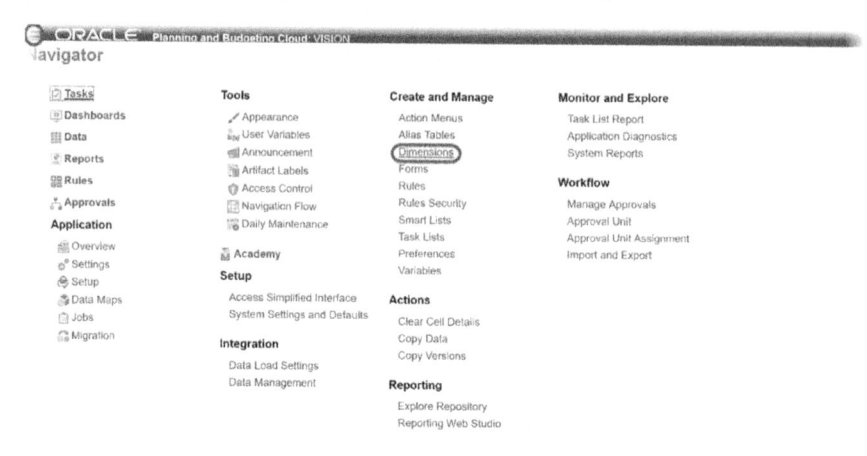

2. Select *Scenario* from the drop-down menu:

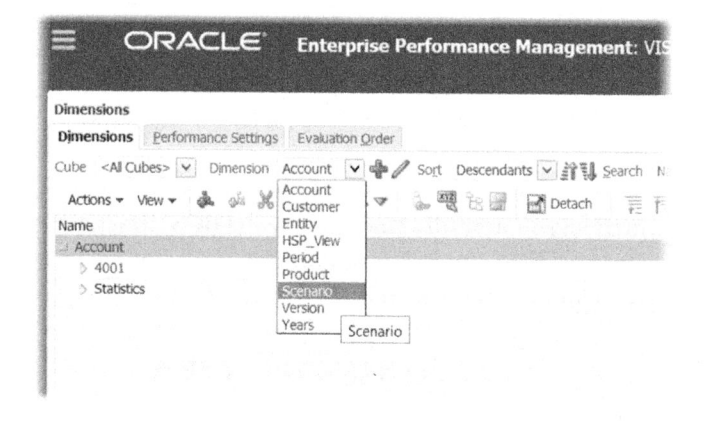

3. Under Actions, use (Add Child) to add new Scenario members.
4. Members can be edited by first selecting the member to edit and then clicking the icon found directly above the

dimension name in the hierarchy tree, or clicking *Edit* under Actions.

Note! There is another Edit icon that is next to the dimension drop-down. This edits the entire dimension and not a specific dimension member. Be careful not to confuse the two edit buttons.

5. Add (or edit) the following members and properties to the Scenario dimension:

Member Name	Start Yr.	Start Period	End Yr.	End Period	Data Storage	Process Management	Data Type
Plan	FY15	Jan	FY16	Dec	Never Share	Y	Unspecified
Actual	FY10	Jan	FY20	Dec	Never Share	N	Unspecified
Forecast	FY15	Jan	FY16	Dec	Never Share	Y	Unspecified
Plan Comments	FY10	Jan	FY20	Dec	Never Share	N	Text
Variance	FY10	Jan	FY20	Dec	Dynamic Calc	N	Unspecified

* If the property is not noted above, accept the default value.

Chapter 4: Build an Application

Note! You'll notice that Scenario members have been created in the application by default, including Plan, Actual, Forecast Variance, and Variance Comments. Edit the properties of those members to match the table above.

Edit Member : Plan

Member Properties | UDA | Member Formula

Name	Plan
Description	
Alias Table	Default
Alias	
Start Yr.	FY15
Start Period	Jan
End Yr.	FY16
End Period	Dec
Include BegBal as Time Period	☑
Enabled for Process Management	☑
Exchange Rate Table	<None>
Hierarchy Type	Not Set
Data Storage	Never Share
Two Pass Calculation	
Plan Type	Sales ☑ Addition
	SalesRpt ☑ Addition
Data Type	Unspecified
Smart Lists	<None>
Enable for Dynamic Children	☐
Number of Possible Dynamic Children	10
Access Granted to Member Creator	Inherit

You can copy an existing scenario member and its properties to a new scenario member using the 📋 (Copy Scenario) icon:

Note!

Dimensions
Dimensions | Performance Settings | Evaluation Order

Scenario
- Plan
- Actual
- Forecast
- Plan Comments
- Variance
- Variance %

If you need users to input data into the BegBalance member, make sure to check the option *Include BegBal as Time Period* for the Scenario member:

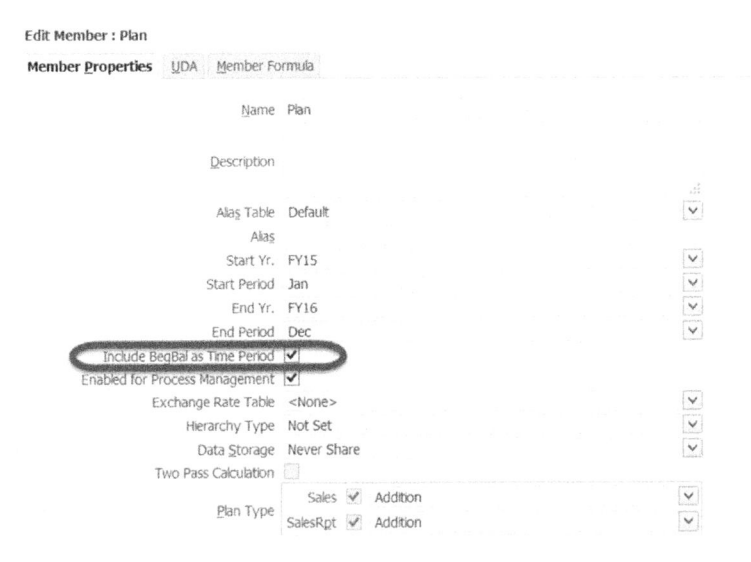

6. Now delete existing Scenario members that are not needed by selecting the member and clicking ✖.

REFRESH THE DATABASE

Any time you make a change to a dimension or member within a dimension, you need to "refresh the database" (a term you will hear and say often as an administrator). This means pushing changes that you make in the PBCS user interface to the underlying Essbase database.

To refresh the database,
1. Select *Navigator* ≡ >> *Application* >> *Overview*.
2. Select *Actions* >> *Refresh Database*:

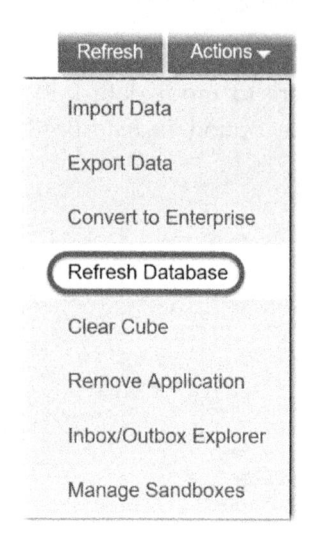

3. Click *Create*, select options, and then click *Refresh Database*:

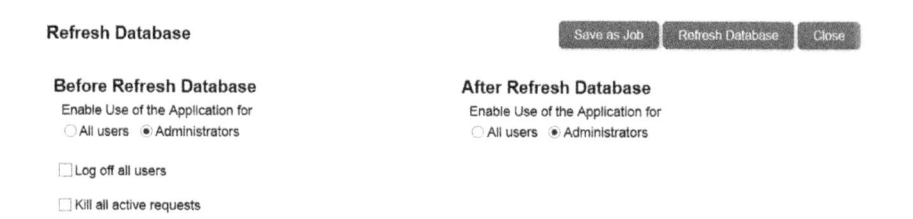

You can optionally save this Refresh Database as a job that can be scripted during a nightly process. You can define options to log off users and/or Administrators while the refresh is occurring (this is a recommended practice).

4. At the warning message, click *Refresh Database* and wait for the following message:

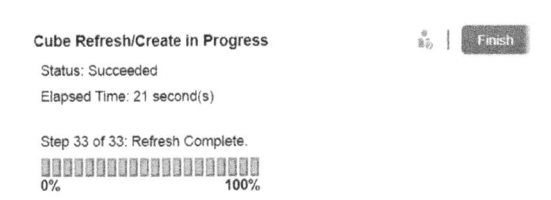

```
Cube Refresh/Create in Progress                    Finish
Status: Succeeded
Elapsed Time: 21 second(s)

Step 33 of 33: Refresh Complete.
▌▌▌▌▌▌▌▌▌▌▌▌▌▌▌▌▌▌▌▌▌▌▌
0%                    100%
```

5. Click *Finish* and then *Close* twice. The refresh is complete.

Note! Refresh the database when there are any metadata or security changes that need to be pushed to Essbase.

Vision Company needs variance calculations for Actual and Plan. To take advantage of the Essbase calculation engine, I'm going to build calculations into the database via a member formula. A member formula is a calculation formula that is assigned to a member in a dimension.

To edit the Variance member in the Scenario dimension,

1. Go back into the dimension editor by clicking the *Navigator* icon, and then under *Create and Manage*, click *Dimensions*, and select the *Scenario* dimension from the drop-down
2. Edit the *Variance* member to match the following properties (be sure that the Data Storage is set to *Dynamic Calc*):

Chapter 4: Build an Application

Dimensions
Edit Member : Variance

Member Properties | UDA | Member Formula

Name	Variance
Description	
Alias Table	Default
Alias	
Start Yr.	FY10
Start Period	Jan
End Yr.	FY20
End Period	Dec
Include BegBal as Time Period	☐
Enabled for Process Management	☐
Exchange Rate Table	<None>
Hierarchy Type	Not Set
Data Storage	Dynamic Calc
Two Pass Calculation	☐
Plan Type	Sales ☑ Addition
	SalesRpt ☑ Addition
Data Type	Unspecified
Smart Lists	<None>
Enable for Dynamic Children	☐
Number of Possible Dynamic Children	10
Access Granted to Member Creator	Inherit

Although listed as options, properties like *Start Year* and *End Period* are not applicable for this member because it is dynamically calculated. Users do not submit data for the "Variance" member.

    3. Click the *Member Formula* tab and enter the following formula:

```
@VAR(Actual, Plan);
```

Dimensions
Edit Member : Variance
Member Properties | UDA | **Member Formula**

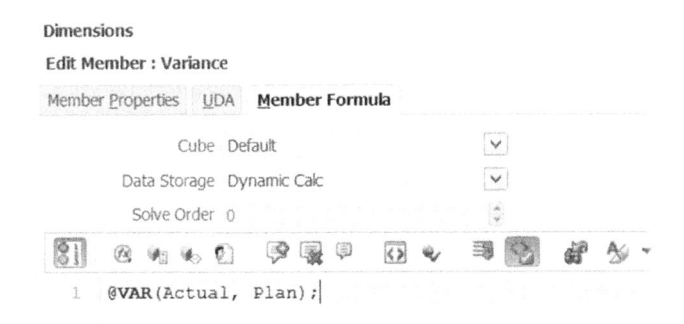

Cube: Default
Data Storage: Dynamic Calc
Solve Order: 0

```
1  @VAR(Actual, Plan);
```

4. *Validate* the formula to ensure that the syntax clears, then click *Save*.
5. Now add a "Variance %" member using the same member properties as the Variance member and enter the following formula:

```
@VARPER(Actual, Plan);
```

6. Go back to the *Navigator* icon, then below *Application* select *Overview >> Actions >> Refresh Database* to refresh the database.

The @VAR and @VARPER are just two of the many Essbase functions. See the Essbase Technical Reference for all of the Essbase calculation functions and examples.

Here's what I am left with for the Scenario dimension (ignore the Security column for now):

Name	Alias (Default)	Description	Security	Start Period	Start Yr.	End Period	End Yr.	Exch. Table
Scenario								
> Plan				Jan	FY15	Dec	FY16	
> Actual				Jan	FY10	Dec	FY20	
> Forecast				Jan	FY15	Dec	FY16	
> Plan Comments				Jan	FY10	Dec	FY20	
> Variance				Jan	FY10	Dec	FY20	
> Variance %				Jan	FY10	Dec	FY20	

BUILD VERSION DIMENSION

The Version dimension is used to differentiate between different drafts of Budget and Plan data. You can model possible outcomes based on more optimistic or less optimistic assumptions like Best Case and Worst Case, or use Version to manage the dissemination of Plan data like Internal and External.

The Version dimension and its members are independent of Scenario members, and Version members are available to all Scenario members. This is because Version and Scenario are two distinct dimensions in the application.

Versions are either defined as Target or Bottom Up. Target versions allow data entry at any level in the hierarchy of dimensions. If data is entered at higher levels, business rules can be created to allocate data down to lower levels. The PBCS administrator has access to create these business rules. In addition, you can copy one Target version to another, which copies data for all levels and members.

Note! Approval tasks are not allowed for Target versions.

Bottom Up budgets only allow data entry at the bottom members of every dimension (level-0 members). Summary members are display-only and aggregate from bottom level members. You can copy data from one Bottom Up version to another.

If *Enable Sandbox* was checked during the application creation wizard, one "Sandboxes" member is created automatically in the Version dimension. When a sandbox is created by a user, a new member is added under the Sandboxes member (e.g., "Sandbox1"). The data in Sandbox1 is stored at the intersection of Sandbox1 and the HSP_View member "SandboxData" (more on the HSP_View dimension later).

To build the Version dimension,
1. Navigate to the dimension editor and select *Version* from the drop-down menu.

2. You will notice that some members are created for you during the application creation process. If that does not match your requirements, please move or delete as necessary.
3. Add (or edit) the following members and properties for the Version dimension (rename BU Version_1 to Pass1 and add Pass2). If the "Final" member has any children members (often created by the app by default), please delete them:

Member Name	Storage	Version Type	Consolidation
Pass1	Never Share	Standard Bottom Up	Ignore
Pass2	Never Share	Standard Bottom Up	Ignore
Final	Never Share	Standard Bottom Up	Ignore

Note! The concept of a "Final" version member does not exist in EPBCS. This should be a consideration for PBCS customers who are interested in upgrading to an Enterprise-type app later.

The resulting Version dimension should look as follows:

Name	Alias (Default)	Description	Security	Type
⊿ Version				
Final				Standard Bottom Up
Pass1				Standard Bottom Up
Pass2				Standard Bottom Up
⊿ Sandboxes				Standard Bottom Up
Sandboxes_Final				Standard Bottom Up
Sandboxes_Pass2				Standard Bottom Up
Sandboxes_Pass1				Standard Bottom Up

Note! There are two additional checkbox options in the member edit window. *Enabled for Process Management* allows the version to be subject to approvals. *Enable Sandboxes* allows users to create their own sandboxes in the application for the selected version (more on sandboxing at the end of the mission).

4. Edit "Final" and check the option to *Enable sandboxes*:

Dimensions

Edit Member : Final

Member Properties | UDA | Member Formula

Name	Final
Description	
Alias Table	Default
Alias	
Type	Standard Bottom Up
Enabled for Process Management	✓
Enable Sandboxes	✓
Hierarchy Type	Not Set
Data Storage	Never Share
Two Pass Calculation	
Plan Type	Sales ✓ Ignore
	SalesRpt ✓ Ignore
Data Type	Unspecified
Smart Lists	<None>
Enable for Dynamic Children	
Number of Possible Dynamic Children	10
Access Granted to Member Creator	Inherit

5. Refresh the database to push the changes to Essbase.

Account Dimension Explained

The Account dimension houses the metrics for the database. While almost every application has an Account dimension, what the dimension contains varies greatly:

- A **financial planning** application has accounts for income statement, balance sheet, and sometimes cash flow
- An **inventory planning** application has measures for beginning inventory, ending inventory, additions, returns, adjustments, and so forth
- A **sales planning** application has measures for sales dollars, units sold, and average sales price
- A **human capital or workforce planning** application has metrics for payroll, unemployment, payroll taxes, sick days, vacation days, years of employment, and so on

The Account dimension is the most important dimension in any application since it lets you define what metrics you're going to plan and analyze. You can safely expect the Account dimension to be unique for each cube.

Before I build the Account dimension, I'll review a few of the Account specific properties.

Source Cube

As the administrator, you can define which accounts are valid for which cubes. If an account is valid for more than one cube, a source cube must be specified. This is where the data is stored. The other cubes reference that data value using the @XREF function. The cubes valid for a member are determined by the cubes assigned to the parent.

Variance Reporting

The Variance Reporting property (also known as Expense Reporting in Essbase circles) is a simple flag that tells downstream calculations and reports whether a positive variance is good or bad. If you're over your target on revenue, everyone is happy. Of course, the opposite is true when you spend too much on office supplies. Well, not everyone will be upset, but you don't want to be making enemies in the Finance Department when it comes time for them to cut you the bonus check for those positive-variance revenues, right?

Let's walk you through an example. If you budget $1,000,000 in revenue and you make $1,100,000, that's a favorable variance of $100,000. Expenses are quite the opposite: if you budget $1,000,000 in marketing expenses and you spend $1,100,000, that's an unfavorable variance of $100,000. In general, you want expense data to have lower actuals than budget.

To allow for this, Planning (and Essbase) uses a property called Variance Reporting. Tag all of your expense accounts with "Expense" and Essbase calculates the variance correctly when using the @VAR or @VARPER functions. Essbase shows a positive variance when Actual data is higher than Budget for revenue or metric accounts. Essbase shows a negative variance for those expense accounts tagged with the Variance Reporting property of "Expense":

	Jan	FY2007	
	Actual	Budget	Variance
Net_Rev	100	75	25
Op_Expense	100	75	-25
Op_Income	#Missing	#Missing	#Missing

The Variance Reporting property should be set to Expense for all measures where budget should be higher than actual.

There is also a "Non-Expense" property. This tags the Account as not an Expense. Essbase calculates the variance by subtracting the budgeted amount from the actual amount to determine the variance.

If you choose an Account Type of *Saved Assumption* (more on this later), you can specify the Variance Reporting property. If you choose any of the other account types, the Variance Reporting property is automatically assigned (though it can be changed). Note, I will discuss account type in just a moment.

Time Balance Property

The Time Balance property is only available in the Account dimension, and is used to tell Planning / Essbase how a given member should be aggregated up the Time dimension.

For example, should Headcount for January, February, and March be added together for Q1 (Quarter 1)? This definitely wouldn't make sense:

	Actual	FY2007			
	Jan	Feb	Mar	Q1	Q2
Headcount	100	125	122	347	#Mis

In most cases, you want Q1 to equal the March headcount (though some might want the average across the periods), or in other words, the last headcount in the period. To get Planning to do this, you tag Headcount with the *Balance* option (in Essbase circles this is known as "Time Balance Last" or "TB Last") so that it takes the last member's value when aggregating time.

Depending on your requirements, you could also assign *First* or *Average*. Here is Q1's headcount, now nicely equaling its last child, Mar (short for March):

	Actual	FY2007			
	Jan	Feb	Mar	Q1	Q2
Headcount	100	125	122	122	#M

What if I have just closed January? Showing the March headcount wouldn't be accurate because March is blank. A second property associated with Time Balance, called "Skip", allows us to define how I handle missing and zero values. In this example, I would want to ignore any blanks (or #Missing). So I set the Headcount account's Time Balance option to *Balance* and then set the Skip option to *Missing*.

Now Q1 correctly shows the January value:

	Actual	FY2007			
	Jan	Feb	Mar	Q1	Q2
Headcount	100	#Missing	#Missing	100	#M

Another example of Time Balance utilization is for inventory analysis members:

- Inventory (~) (Label Only)
  - Opening Inventory (+) (TB First) (Expense Reporting)
  - Additions (~) (Expense Reporting)
  - Ending Inventory (~) (TB Last) (Expense Reporting)

"Fill" is another Time Balance option that automatically "fills" or distributes the parent value to all of its descendants. The "Weighted Average" Time Balance option provides a weighted daily average accounting, with or without Leap Year.

Account Type

The Account Type property dictates how an account flows over time and how the account's sign calculates when performing variance calculations. Each account member is assigned an account type:

- **Expense** – Flow and Expense
- **Revenue** – Flow and Non-Expense
- **Asset** – Balance and Non-Expense
- **Liability** – Balance and Non-Expense
- **Equity** – Balance and Non-Expense
- **Saved Assumption** – user Defined Time Balance and user Defined Variance Reporting

The "Saved Assumption" account type is often used to store drivers like headcount, square feet, or units sold. Once Saved Assumption is selected, you define variance reporting and time balance properties for the member.

Data Type

The Data Type property determines how values are stored in account members and, if multi-currency is used, the exchange rates used to calculate values. Valid data type options include Unspecified, Currency, Non Currency, Percentage, Smart List, Text, and Date.

An account member with a data type of "Text" allows users to enter free-form text comments or information for the account at the intersection of other dimension members. For example, if your Capital Expense application has an account called "Asset Model Number", users can input a specific model number by item.

Hierarchy Type

I'll discuss the Hierarchy Type member property shortly when we get to the ASO cube section. This property does not apply for block storage cubes.

Exchange Rate Type

The Exchange Rate Type is only enabled if the Data Type is set to *Currency* and the application is multi-currency. It includes the following options:

- **Average** – uses account's average exchange rate
- **Ending** – uses account's ending exchange rate
- **Historical** – uses account's exchange rate that was in effect when the earnings for a "Retained Earnings" account were earned or the assets for a "Fixed Assets" account were purchased (for example)

Smart Lists

Simply put, Smart Lists are customized drop-down menus that users can access within data forms. Smart Lists allow Administrators to control a list of values for users to select. Users may not type in the cell of a member that is of a Smart List type. You can create a data element as a Smart List in a PBCS application, in place of a regular dimension (which helps with performance and database size). Once you've created a Smart List, you can use its values in member formulas:

I'm going to go ahead and create the Smart List first so it will be available when I create dimensions later.

CREATE SMART LIST

To create a Smart List,

1. Select the *Navigator* icon.
2. Under *Create and Manage*, click *Smart Lists*.
3. Under Actions, click *Create* to add a new Smart List:

4. Name the Smart List. It can't have any spaces or special characters. Also type in the Label, the text to be displayed to users once the Smart List is selected. Labels can have spaces and special characters. I will create a Smart List for the Product Managers in Vision Company.
5. Select the *Display Order*, *#Missing Drop Down Label*, and *#Missing Form Label*:

```
Smart Lists
Create Smart List
Properties  Entries  Preview
              * Smart List  Product_Manager
                   * Label  Product Manager
              Display Order  ID    v
  #Missing Drop Down Label
      #Missing Form Label  Form Setting    v
   Automatically generate ID ☐
      Create From Members ☐
          Member Selection
```

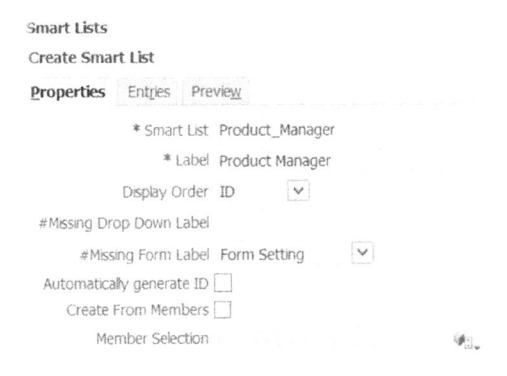

You can define the following parameters for Smart Lists:

- **Smart List** – unique name of the Smart List; can only contain alpha-numeric and underscore characters, no special characters or spaces
- **Label** – display text when the Smart List is selected
- **Display Order** – determining factor for how the Smart List entries are ordered: by ID, name, or label
- **#Missing Drop Down Label** – text to be displayed when the value for a Smart List entry is #Missing
- **#Missing Form Label** – determines whether or not the Smart List #Missing setting or the form #Missing setting governs what displays for #Missing values
- **Automatically generate ID** – have the system generate the unique numbers that control the order of the Smart List entries; if this is checked, the sort order cannot be customizable
- **Create From Members** – if checked, the Member Selection option becomes available and the system creates the Smart List based on the dimension hierarchy chosen in Member Selection; user security for the dimension is honored and any changes made to the dimension hierarchy selected are dynamically updated in the Smart List
- **Member Selection** – determines what hierarchy the Smart List used to populate the Smart List values

6. Check *Automatically generate ID* to have the system generate the numeric ID for each entry in the Smart List. Leaving this unchecked allows ID values to be customized.
7. Click the *Entries* tab.
8. Click ✚ to add entries to the Smart List.
9. Type in the required *Name* and *Label* fields.

As I mentioned above, the *Label* is the text displayed to users and it auto-populates with the value entered into the *Name* field. If the option to *Automatically generate ID* was selected, then the *ID* field also auto-populates.

10. Create the following entries for the Product_Manager Smart List.
11. Once finished, click the *Preview* tab.
12. If all looks good, click *Save*:

Smart Lists

Edit Smart Lists : Product_Manager

Properties | Entries | **Preview**

Drop Down View

Rachel ▾

Table View

Label	ID
Rachel	1
Ross	2
Chandler	3
Monica	4
Pheobe	5
Joey	6
Jerry	7
Elaine	8
George	9
Kramer	10
Larry	11
David	12
Susan	13
Putty	14

Our Smart List can now be assigned to a member in a dimension. Back to the Account dimension; it's time to build!

BUILD ACCOUNT DIMENSION

To build the Account dimension,

1. Navigate to *Dimensions* under *Navigator* ≡ >> *Create and Manage*.
2. Select *Account* from the dimension drop-down menu.
3. Edit the "Statistics" member and ensure that the properties match the following:

Name	Statistics
Description	
Alias Table	Default
Alias	
Account Type	Saved Assumption
Variance Reporting	Non-Expense
Time Balance	Flow
Skip	None
Exchange Rate Type	No Rate
Source Cube	Sales
Hierarchy Type	Dynamic
Data Storage	Label only
Two Pass Calculation	☐
Plan Type	Sales ☑ Ignore
	SalesRpt ☑ Ignore
Data Type	Unspecified
Smart Lists	<None>
Enable for Dynamic Children	☐
Number of Possible Dynamic Children	10
Access Granted to Member Creator	Inherit

4. Under "Statistics", change the properties for the following "children" members (members placed under the Statistics member) to match the following:

Member Name	Account Type	Source Plan Type	Data Storage	Consolidation	Data Type
Units	Saved Assumption	Sales	Store	Ignore	Unspecified
List Price	Saved Assumption	Sales	Store	Ignore	Currency
Average Price	Saved Assumption	Sales	Dynamic Calc	Ignore	Currency

If the property is not noted in the table, accept the default value.

Now that the "Statistics" hierarchy is complete, let's add a "Total Revenue" hierarchy to the Account dimension.

5. Select the *Account* dimension name and click (Add Child).
6. Type "4001" as the member name and "Total Revenue" as the alias. Set the properties according to the following:

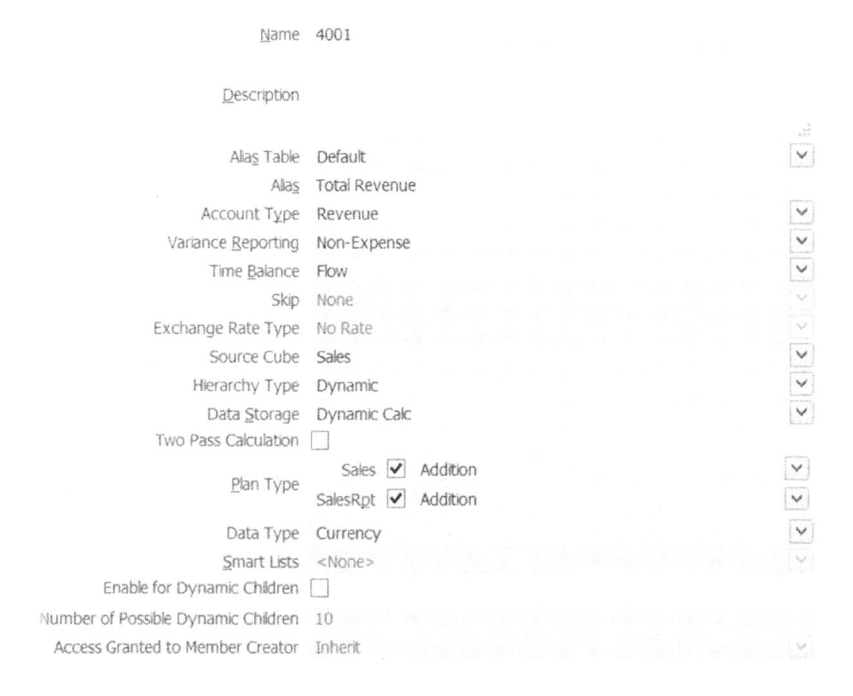

Name	4001
Description	
Alias Table	Default
Alias	Total Revenue
Account Type	Revenue
Variance Reporting	Non-Expense
Time Balance	Flow
Skip	None
Exchange Rate Type	No Rate
Source Cube	Sales
Hierarchy Type	Dynamic
Data Storage	Dynamic Calc
Two Pass Calculation	☐
Plan Type	Sales ☑ Addition
	SalesRpt ☑ Addition
Data Type	Currency
Smart Lists	<None>
Enable for Dynamic Children	☐
Number of Possible Dynamic Children	10
Access Granted to Member Creator	Inherit

7. Ensure that the following "children" members have been added to 4001 (Total Revenue) and have the following properties set:

Member Name	Alias	Account Type	Source Plan Type	Data Storage	Consolidation	Data Type
4110	Hardware Revenue	Revenue	Sales	Store	Addition	Currency
4120	Support Revenue	Revenue	Sales	Store	Addition	Currency
4130	Consulting Revenue	Revenue	Sales	Store	Addition	Currency
4140	Training Revenue	Revenue	Sales	Store	Addition	Currency
4150	Miscellaneous Revenue	Revenue	Sales	Store	Addition	Currency
4160	Payment Discount	Revenue	Sales	Store	Addition	Currency

8. Refresh the database.

I will load in Actual data by account. For Forecast, however, I will calculate revenue based on inputs from users. Now that I've added all the Account members, I'm going to go back and add some member formulas. These members will have Data Storage set to *Store* and I'll use the <Calculate Data Form> option in data forms so this will automatically calculate for users. I'm using *Store* instead of *Dynamic Calc* because I want this member formula to execute at level 0 members only and then aggregate for upper level dimensions.

9. Ensure that the *Average Price* member has the following member formula:

```
"4110"/"Units";
```

10. Edit the *4110* member and ensure that it has the following member formula:

```
IF (@ISMBR("Forecast"))
  "Units"*"List Price";
ENDIF
```

11. Edit the *4120* member and ensure that it has the following member formula:

```
IF (@ISMBR("Forecast"))
  "4110"*.18;
ENDIF
```

Note! If a member formula is pasted in, sometimes it may not validate due to a different quotation format (or other character issue). Try manually typing in the quotes or the entire formula instead.

Now I am ready to add the Account member for the Product Manager Smart List.

12. Add an Account member named "Product Manager" with the following properties. Note the *Smart List* Data Type and the *Product_Manager* selection for the Smart Lists property:

Chapter 4: Build an Application

Name	Product Manager
Description	
Alias Table	Default
Alias	
Account Type	Revenue
Variance Reporting	Non-Expense
Time Balance	Flow
Skip	None
Exchange Rate Type	No Rate
Source Cube	Sales
Hierarchy Type	Not Set
Data Storage	Never Share
Two Pass Calculation	☐
Plan Type	Sales ☑ Ignore
	SalesRpt ☑ Ignore
Data Type	SmartList
Smart Lists	Product_Manager
Enable for Dynamic Children	☐
Number of Possible Dynamic Children	10
Access Granted to Member Creator	Inherit

13. Click *Save*.
14. Refresh the database.

The "Product Manager" Account member and Smart List will make its appearance when I build data forms later in my mission.

VIEW & ADD YEARS TO YEARS DIMENSION

"Years" is one of two Time dimensions. The "Years" dimension contains the calendar years which were determined when the application was created.

I'm going to add an "All Years" member and go over how to add more years to the application. The "All Years" parent member allows users to view the accumulated data across multiple years – for example, an asset's total depreciation through its end date. You can also define this member in the application creation process.

To view the Years dimension,

1. Navigate to *Dimensions* under *Navigator* ≡ >> *Create and Manage*.
2. Select *Years* from the drop-down menu.
3. Review the Years members. Notice that there is no summary year member.
4. To add an "All Years" member, simply go to *Action* >> *Add "All Years"* or click (Add "All Years"):

```
Dimensions
Dimensions   Performance Settings   Evaluation Order
Cube  Sales         Dimension  Years
Action ▼  View ▼  ✚ ✖ ⚙ ✏ ⚙
   Add Years        Ctrl+W    ault)    Description
   Remove Years     Ctrl+Del
   Add "All Years"  Ctrl+6
   Edit Year        Ctrl+E
   Options          Ctrl+P
   Show Usage       Ctrl+U
FY17
FY18
FY19
FY20
```

To add additional years to the PBCS application (because time does not stand still),

5. Select the *Years* dimension in the dimension editor.
6. Select *Action* >> *Add Years*.
7. Enter the number of years to add and click *OK*.
8. Refresh the database.

VIEW PERIOD DIMENSION & ENABLE DTS

It is standard for a PBCS application to have two Time dimensions. The second time dimension is Period, which includes periods like months, weeks, and quarters. The calendar for the Period dimension was created during the application creation wizard.

Chapter 4: Build an Application

To view the Period dimension,
1. Navigate to *Dimensions* under *Navigator* >> *Create and Manage*.
2. Select *Period* from the drop-down menu.
3. Explore the members and add the full month name as an alias, if desired (*Actions* >> *Edit* or ✎ icon, type in Alias and *Save*).

If users need to enter data into the BegBalance member (e.g., for statistical, Smart List, or free form text accounts that aren't stored by period), make sure to check *Include BegBalance as Time Period* under Scenario members properties:

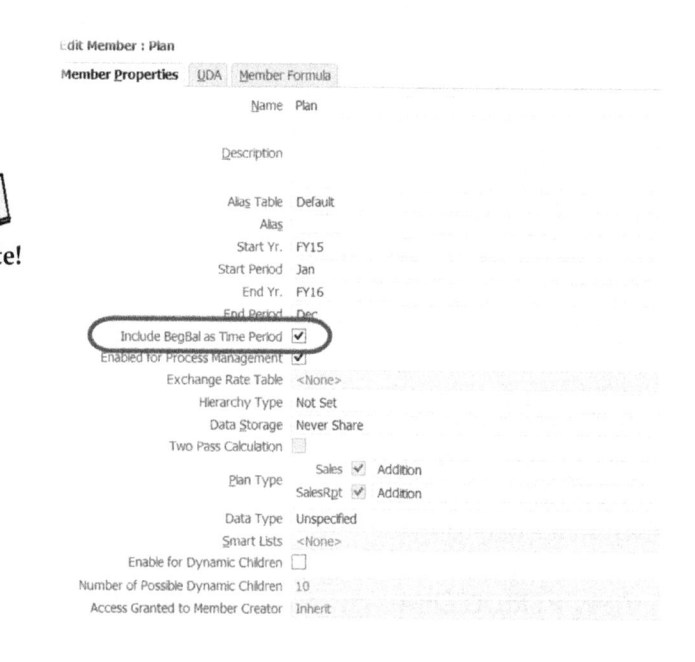

Note!

Edit Member : Plan

Member Properties | UDA | Member Formula

Name	Plan
Description	
Alias Table	Default
Alias	
Start Yr.	FY15
Start Period	Jan
End Yr.	FY16
End Period	Dec
Include BegBal as Time Period	✓
Enabled for Process Management	✓
Exchange Rate Table	<None>
Hierarchy Type	Not Set
Data Storage	Never Share
Two Pass Calculation	☐
Plan Type	Sales ✓ Addition
	SalesRpt ✓ Addition
Data Type	Unspecified
Smart Lists	<None>
Enable for Dynamic Children	☐
Number of Possible Dynamic Children	10
Access Granted to Member Creator	Inherit

Dynamic-time-series (DTS) allows users to retrieve dynamic 'to-date' totals from the PBCS database.

To enable DTS,

1. In the Period dimension, select *Action* >> *DTS* or click (DTS).
2. Check the options for *YTD* and *QTD*, and assign the correct generations as follows:

Period : Dynamic Time Series

Series	Enabled	Generation	Alias Names
Y-T-D	✔	1	
H-T-D	☐	Unassigned	
S-T-D	☐	Unassigned	
Q-T-D	✔	2	
P-T-D	☐	Unassigned	
M-T-D	☐	Unassigned	
W-T-D	☐	Unassigned	
D-T-D	☐	Unassigned	

3. Click *Edit Alias Names* to add an alias, if desired.
4. Click *Save*.
5. Refresh the database.

VIEW HSP_VIEW DIMENSION

The HSP_View dimension is created when sandboxes are enabled and members are automatically created. Neither the dimension nor its members can be altered, and the members should not be reordered within the dimension.

The members in the HSP_View dimension include:

- **ConsolidatedData** – dynamically calculated member that retrieves data from the SandboxData member when it is available; otherwise, it retrieves the data from the BaseData member
- **BaseData** – where data is stored when users are working in a non-sandbox view in a form
- **SandboxData** – where data is stored when users work in a sandbox

To view the HSP_View dimension,
1. Navigate to *Dimensions* under *Navigator* ≡ >> *Create and Manage*.
2. Select *HSP_View* from the drop-down menu.
3. Explore the members and their properties.

Note! For aggregations to work in the Sandbox view, sparse dimension parent members (such as Entity or custom dimensions) must be set to *Dynamic Calc*. This is also true for Hybrid Aggregation Mode once it is supported.

Because who doesn't love to play in a sandbox, I have a whole chapter dedicated to Sandboxing at the end of the book.

CREATE CUSTOM PRODUCT DIMENSION

PBCS allows many custom dimensions for a cube; however, it is best to limit the number of dimensions for any application. Some examples of custom dimensions include Customers, Employees, Products, and Projects. Custom dimensions can be assigned to specific cubes (meaning each cube can have unique dimensions that don't have to belong or exist in another cube). Once created, a dimension cannot be deleted without going through some serious gyrations.

To create a custom dimension,
1. Select *Navigator* ≡ >> *Application* >> *Overview*.
2. Select the *Dimensions* tab:

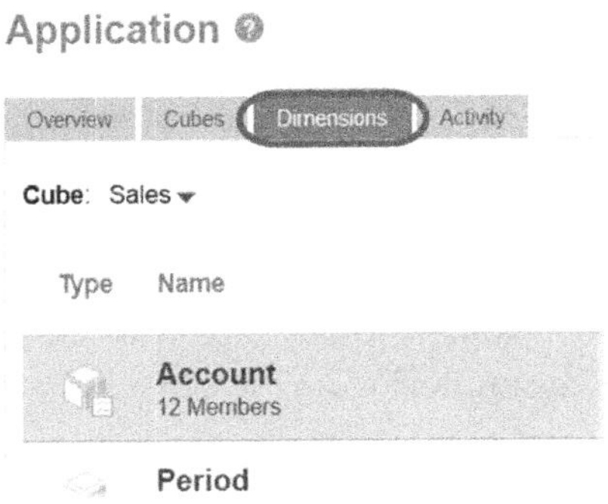
Application
Overview
Cubes
Dimensions
Activity
Cube: Sales
Type
Name
Account
12 Members
Period

3. To the right, you see buttons for Create, Import, and Export. Click *Create*.
4. Type in "Product" for the dimension name and check *Enabled* for both Sales and SalesRpt cubes. Leave the other options as default:

Create Dimension
Product
Default
Cube
Enabled
Sales
SalesRpt

5. Click *Done*.
6. Refresh the database.

Now that the Product dimension has been created, it's time to prepare the import file.

Import & Export Dimensions

Up until now I have defined all the dimensions manually through the dimension editor. Dimensions can be imported using the "Import Metadata" or "Export Metadata" function in the Simplified UI.

So when I say "metadata", most of the time in PBCS, I mean "dimensions." Flat files are the only available source in PBCS. Data Management does not support the import or export of dimensions (yet).

Export a Dimension

You can easily create a template to help get the import file ready by exporting a dimension. You may also want to export dimensions for other purposes (for example, loading to other systems). The dimension is exported in a "parent-child" format; generational or level exports of dimensions are not supported.

To export a dimension,
1. *Navigator* >> *Application* >> *Overview* >> and choose the *Dimensions* tab.
2. Click the *Export* button, then *Create*.
3. Check the box next to Product and click the option for *Comma delimited* (default):

```
Product
0 Members          ● Comma delimited  ○ Tab delimited  ○ Other           No details are available.
```

4. Click *Export*. Save the file (which normally defaults to your Downloads folder) and open (search for the most recent *ExportedMetadataFile* zip file). You should see the following in Excel (well, as many columns as we could show in a single screen shot):

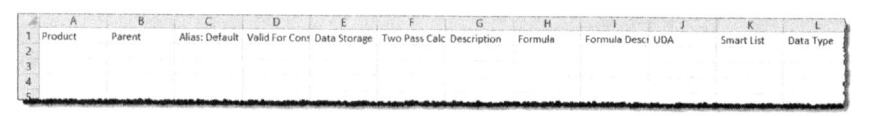

```
   A        B       C             D            E           F            G          H       I              J      K          L
1 Product  Parent  Alias: Default Valid For Cons Data Storage Two Pass Calc Description Formula Formula Desc UDA Smart List Data Type
2
3
4
```

I can now use this file to build my Product dimension file for importing. I like to use Notepad++ or other text editors when creating these files. If I use Excel, I need to be careful with members with only numbers as the member name (e.g., "4110" as an Account member name) since those are viewed as numeric values. Using a text editor like Notepad++ avoids that and other common CSV headaches.

Import Members for Product Dimension

Now to import members for the Product dimension,
1. Create the Product dimension by completing the template (or email info@interrel.com for a copy of the file). Save the template as a CSV file.

Once the template has been completed, it should look something like the following (not all properties are shown):

Product	Parent	Alias: Default	Valid For Consolidations	Data Storage	Two Pass Calculation	Description	Formula	UDA
P_TP		Product Total Product	FALSE	dynamic calc	FALSE		<none>	
P_000	P_TP	No Product	FALSE	store	FALSE		<none>	
P_HW	P_TP	Hardware Products	FALSE	dynamic calc	FALSE		<none>	
P_TP1	P_HW	Computer Equipment	FALSE	dynamic calc	FALSE		<none>	
P_100	P_TP1	Product X	FALSE	store	FALSE		<none>	
P_110	P_TP1	Sentinal Standard Notebook	FALSE	store	FALSE		<none>	
P_120	P_TP1	Sentinal Custom Notebook	FALSE	store	FALSE		<none>	
P_130	P_TP1	Envoy Standard Netbook	FALSE	store	FALSE		<none>	
P_140	P_TP1	Envoy Custom Netbook	FALSE	store	FALSE		<none>	
P_150	P_TP1	Other Computer	FALSE	store	FALSE		<none>	
P_160	P_TP1	Tablet Computer	FALSE	store	FALSE		<none>	
P_TP2	P_HW	Computer Accessories	FALSE	dynamic calc	FALSE		<none>	
P_200	P_TP2	Accessories	FALSE	store	FALSE		<none>	
P_210	P_TP2	Keyboard	FALSE	store	FALSE		<none>	
P_220	P_TP2	Software Suite	FALSE	store	FALSE		<none>	
P_230	P_TP2	Monitor	FALSE	store	FALSE		<none>	
P_240	P_TP2	Modem	FALSE	store	FALSE		<none>	
P_250	P_TP2	Network Card	FALSE	store	FALSE		<none>	
P_260	P_TP2	Game	FALSE	store	FALSE		<none>	

Parent members have been set to *Dynamic Calc* so I can leverage hybrid aggregation mode in our cube (remember, when hybrid aggregation mode is supported in the future, I must tag upper level members tagged as "Dynamic Calc" to utilize the hybrid engine). In most production applications, you will likely set upper level sparse members to *Store* until hybrid aggregation is supported.

2. Select *Navigator* >> *Application* >> *Overview* and choose the Dimensions tab.
3. Click *Import*, then *Create*.
4. Navigate to the *Product* dimension and click *Browse…*
5. Select the Product CSV file. Click *Open*.
6. Click *Import* (at the top of the screen).
7. Do not check the option to *Refresh Database if Import Metadata is successful:*

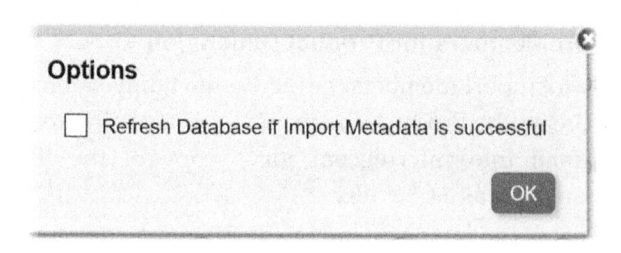

Chapter 4: Build an Application

> **Options**
>
> ☐ Refresh Database if Import Metadata is successful
>
> [OK]

The *Refresh Database if Import Metadata is successful* option forces PBCS to refresh the metadata to Essbase if there are no issues with the metadata import. This is a necessary step when you change the application structure – otherwise, the changes won't be reflected to the users until the refresh has occurred. However, refreshing the database is a maintenance task and has an impact to any users that are currently connected. Therefore, I will defer the refresh of the database to later.

8. Click *OK*, then *OK* again.
9. Click *Refresh* at the top of the page and you should see your Product dimension now has members and the last import information:

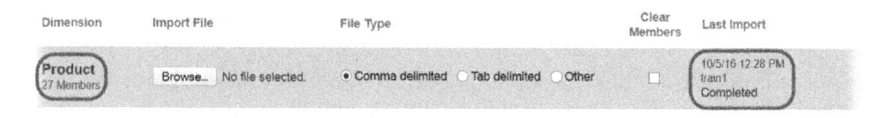

Dimension	Import File	File Type	Clear Members	Last Import
Product 27 Members	Browse... No file selected.	● Comma delimited ○ Tab delimited ○ Other	☐	10/5/16 12:28 PM Iran1 Completed

10. Click the *Completed* link. If there are errors during the import process, they are displayed in the next screen.
11. Check out the Product dimension in the dimension editor:

Look Smarter Than You Are with PBCS   109

Name	Alias (Default)	Data Storage	Custom Attributes
Product		Store	
P_TP	Total Product	Dynamic Calc	
P_000	No Product	Store	
P_HW	Hardware Products	Dynamic Calc	
P_TP1	Computer Equipment	Dynamic Calc	
P_100	Product X	Store	
P_110	Sentinal Standard Notebook	Store	
P_120	Sentinal Custom Notebook	Store	
P_130	Envoy Standard Netbook	Store	
P_140	Envoy Custom Netbook	Store	
P_150	Other Computer	Store	
P_160	Tablet Computer	Store	
P_TP2	Computer Accessories	Dynamic Calc	
P_200	Accessories	Store	
P_210	Keyboard	Store	
P_220	Software Suite	Store	
P_230	Monitor	Store	
P_240	Modem	Store	
P_250	Network Card	Store	
P_260	Game	Store	
P_270	Camera	Store	
P_280	Television	Store	
P_SVC	Services	Dynamic Calc	
P_TP3	Computer Services	Dynamic Calc	
P_291	Training_P_291	Store	
P_292	Miscellaneous_P_292	Store	
P_293	Maintenance_P_293	Store	
P_294	Consulting_P_294	Store	

12. Refresh the database to push changes to Essbase.

Using the same process as the Product dimension, let's build the Entity dimension. To follow along the build process for the Product and Entity dimension, please email info@interrel.com for sample flat files.

Note! You can import and export dimensions over the web (*Administration >> Import and Export* menu). The Outline Load Utility is used behind the scenes for this feature.

Import Members for Entity Dimension

The Entity dimension differentiates between organizational entities. This dimension can be called Organizations, Cost Centers, Departments, Locations, etc. Process management (or approvals; how plans are promoted up the hierarchy) primarily follows the Entity hierarchy structure.

To build the Entity dimension with a flat file,
1. Create an Entity CSV file using the same process as the Product dimension (or email info@interrel.com for a copy of the file):

Entity	Parent	Alias: Default	Valid For Cons	Data Storage	Two Pass C
Total Entity	Entity		FALSE	dynamic calc	FALSE
TD	Total Entity	Total Department	FALSE	dynamic calc	FALSE
0	TD	No Department	FALSE	store	FALSE
100	TD	Resources	FALSE	dynamic calc	FALSE
110	100	Facilities Resources	FALSE	store	FALSE
111	100	West Region Resources	FALSE	store	FALSE
112	100	East Region Resources	FALSE	store	FALSE
120	100	Machine Resources	FALSE	store	FALSE
130	100	Computer Resources	FALSE	store	FALSE
140	100	Communications Resources	FALSE	store	FALSE
200	TD	Other Corporate	FALSE	dynamic calc	FALSE
210	200	US Organization	FALSE	store	FALSE
220	200	CAD Organization	FALSE	store	FALSE

Note! Column headers are case-sensitive and must match the template exactly. Our recommendation is to do an export of the dimension metadata for the exact file format.

2. Save as a CSV file.
3. Select *Navigator* >> *Application* >> *Overview* and choose the Dimensions tab.
4. Click *Import*, then *Create*.
5. Navigate to the Entity dimension and click *Browse…*
6. Select the Entity CSV file and click *Open*.
7. Click *Import*, *OK* and *OK* again.
8. Click *Refresh* until the import is complete, then check for any errors.
9. Refresh the database.
10. Check out the Entity dimension in the dimension editor:

Name	Alias (Default)	Data Storage
⊿ Entity		Never Share
⊿ Total Entity		Dynamic Calc
⊿ TD	Total Department	Dynamic Calc
0	No Department	Store
⊿ 100	Resources	Dynamic Calc
110	Facilities Resources	Store
111	West Region Resources	Store
112	East Region Resources	Store
120	Machine Resources	Store
130	Computer Resources	Store
140	Communications Resources	Store
> 200	Other Corporate	Dynamic Calc
> 403	Sales	Dynamic Calc
> 500	Manufacturing	Dynamic Calc
> 601	Other Departments	Dynamic Calc
> 700	Finance and Accounting	Dynamic Calc
> 800	HR and Administration	Dynamic Calc
Enterprise Global		Store
Unspecified Entity		Store
No Entity		Store
> Management Rollup		Dynamic Calc

OK, the dimensions are all built for the Sales cube. Now to explore some metadata administration options.

Export Multiple Dimensions

I already completed these steps to export a single dimension to get a file template that I can use for importing. You can choose to export more than one dimension at a time if required.

To export multiple dimensions (use the same steps discussed earlier),

1. Select *Navigator* ≡ >> *Application* >> *Overview* and choose the Dimensions tab.
2. Click the *Export* button, then *Create*.
3. Check the box next to *Account*, *Entity*, and *Product*.
4. Click the radio button for *Comma delimited* (or *Tab delimited* if preferred):

Chapter 4: Build an Application

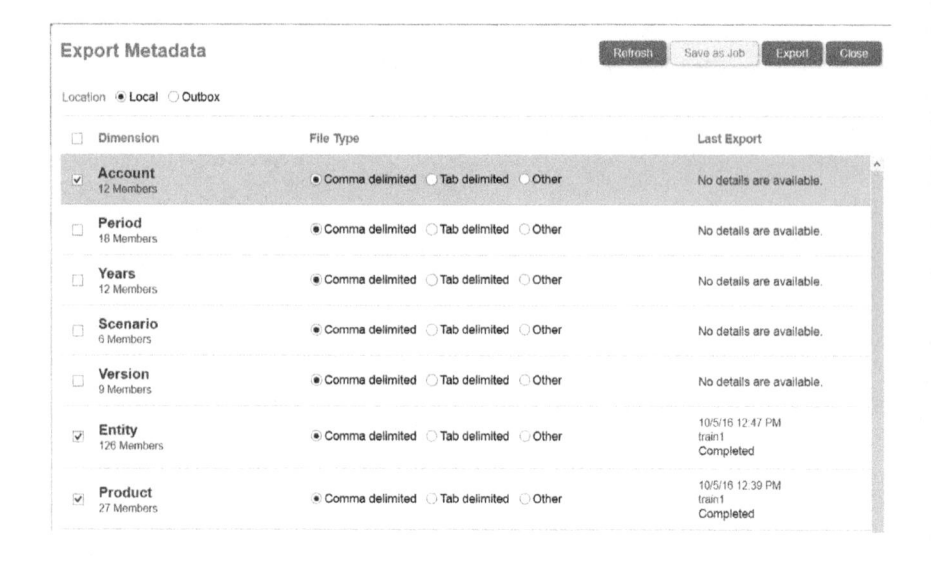

5. Click *Export*.
6. Click *OK* to save files:

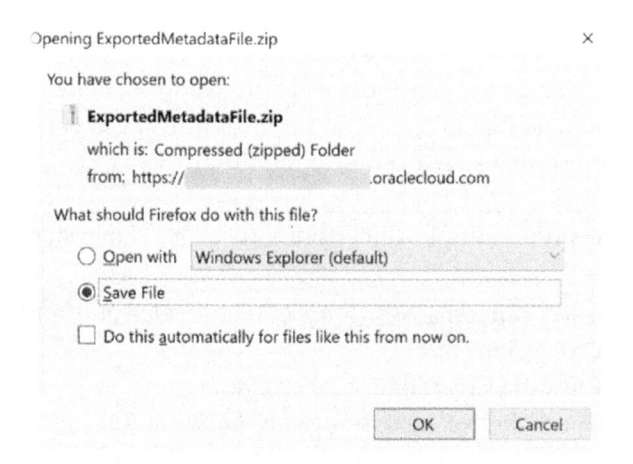

7. Open the compressed folder and open a file to view:

- train1_ExportedMetadata_Account
- train1_ExportedMetadata_Entity
- train1_ExportedMetadata_Product

The resulting file is as shown below:

Account	Parent	Alias: Default	Valid For Con:	Data Storage	Two Pass	Descript Formula
4001	Account	Total Revenue	FALSE	dynamic calc	FALSE	<none>
4110	4001	Hardware Revenue	FALSE	store	FALSE	IF (@ISMBR("Forecast"
4120	4001	Support Revenue	FALSE	store	FALSE	If (@ISMBR("Forecast"
4130	4001	Consulting Revenue	FALSE	store	FALSE	<none>
4140	4001	Training Revenue	FALSE	store	FALSE	<none>
4150	4001	Miscellaneous Revenue	FALSE	store	FALSE	<none>
4160	4001	Payment Discount	FALSE	store	FALSE	<none>
Statistics	Account		FALSE	label only	FALSE	<none>
Units	Statistics		FALSE	store	FALSE	<none>
List Price	Statistics		FALSE	store	FALSE	<none>
Average Price	Statistics		FALSE	store	FALSE	"4110"/"Units";
Product Manager	Account		FALSE	never share	FALSE	<none>

Note! Remember, parent-child format is the only supported export option for PBCS today. This sort of stinks because Cloud products like Business Intelligence Cloud Service (BICS) and Data Visualization Cloud Service (DVCS) only support generational dimension formats.

USE EXCEL TO UPDATE DIMENSIONS

I've now updated dimensions over the web and I've imported dimensions from a flat file. I can also use Microsoft Excel! With PBCS, administrators can update metadata in Excel with the Smart View add in.

To use Excel to update dimensions and members,
1. Click the caret next to your username in the top right corner of the page and select *Downloads*:

114   Chapter 4: Build an Application

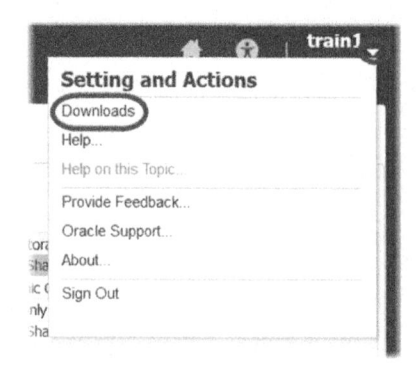

2. Scroll down and select *Download* for the *Planning Admin Extension*.
3. Install the utility using the default options.
4. Open Excel and go to the Smart View ribbon.

If you have an older version of Smart View installed, you might have to uninstall and reinstall the version available in PBCS. To install Smart View, click the caret next to your username in the top right corner of the page and select *Downloads*. Scroll down to Smart View and click *Download from Oracle Technology Network* and follow the prompts to install.

5. Configure Smart View to connect with the PBCS instance. Go to *Options* and within the *Advanced* section type in the Shared Connections URL. A sample of the URL is below:

<https://<your PBCS URL through oraclecloud.com>/workspace/SmartViewProviders>

6. Click *OK*.

7. Connect to the instance. Click the *Panel* (very left of the Smart View ribbon), then click *Shared Connections*:

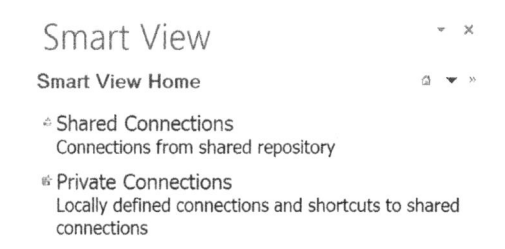

```
Smart View
Smart View Home
 ⁃ Shared Connections
   Connections from shared repository
 ⁃ Private Connections
   Locally defined connections and shortcuts to shared connections
```

8. You should be prompted to log into PBCS. Enter the domain and login credentials.
9. From the Panel drop-down menu, select *EPM Cloud*.
10. Expand the server and application folder. Since I installed the administrator utility, I see a new "Dimensions" folder:

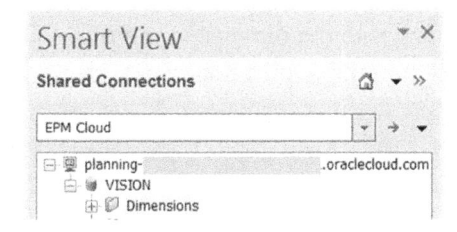

```
Smart View
Shared Connections
[EPM Cloud]
  planning-                   .oraclecloud.com
    VISION
      Dimensions
```

11. Open the *Dimensions* folder.
12. To edit a dimension, right-click it and select *Edit Dimension*. I'll edit the Account dimension.
13. Drill down the Account dimension by selecting the cell with the dimension name.
14. Navigate to the Planning Ad Hoc ribbon and *Zoom In* >> *All Levels*.

I can do *Zoom In* on *All Levels* because I know my dimension is pretty small; for large dimensions, I might want to zoom into specific sections of the dimension hierarchy. I can use other ribbon options like *Keep Only* or *Remove Only* to narrow my focus on the desired members.

The dimension shows in Excel with all the column properties:

	A	B	C	D	E	F	G	H	I
1		Parent Member	Default Data Storage	Data Type	Sales Consol op.	SalesRpt Consol op.	Account Type	Variance Reporting	Time Balance
2	Account		Never Share	Currency	Ignore	Ignore			
3	4001	Account	Dynamic Calc	Currency	Addition	Addition	Revenue	Non-Expense	Flow
4	Statistics	Account	Label only	Unspecified	Ignore	Ignore	Saved Assumption	Non-Expense	Flow
5	Product Manager	Account	Never Share	Smart List	Ignore	Ignore	Revenue	Non-Expense	Flow

From this worksheet, I can add and edit members and member properties. To insert a new member, simply right-click and use plain ol' Excel functionality. Type in the new member name in the blue section and then enter the member properties:

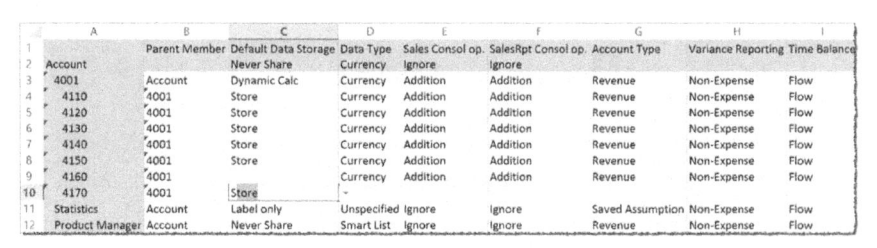

	A	B	C	D	E	F	G	H	I
1		Parent Member	Default Data Storage	Data Type	Sales Consol op.	SalesRpt Consol op.	Account Type	Variance Reporting	Time Balance
2	Account		Never Share	Currency	Ignore	Ignore			
3	4001	Account	Dynamic Calc	Currency	Addition	Addition	Revenue	Non-Expense	Flow
4	4110	4001	Store	Currency	Addition	Addition	Revenue	Non-Expense	Flow
5	4120	4001	Store	Currency	Addition	Addition	Revenue	Non-Expense	Flow
6	4130	4001	Store	Currency	Addition	Addition	Revenue	Non-Expense	Flow
7	4140	4001	Store	Currency	Addition	Addition	Revenue	Non-Expense	Flow
8	4150	4001	Store	Currency	Addition	Addition	Revenue	Non-Expense	Flow
9	4160	4001	Store	Currency	Addition	Addition	Revenue	Non-Expense	Flow
10	4170	4001	Store	-					
11	Statistics	Account	Label only	Unspecified	Ignore	Ignore	Saved Assumption	Non-Expense	Flow
12	Product Manager	Account	Never Share	Smart List	Ignore	Ignore	Revenue	Non-Expense	Flow

To save changes to the dimension in PBCS, click *Submit Data*. The changes are reflected in the application:

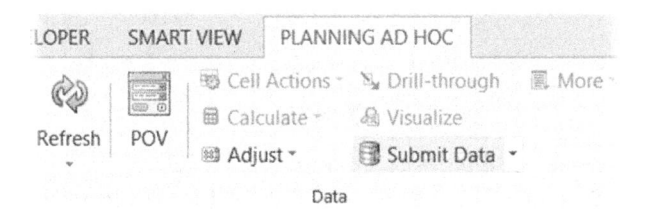

Submit Data has not refreshed the database or pushed changes back to Essbase yet. To refresh the database from Smart View, right-click *Dimensions* in the Smart View Panel and select *Refresh Database* to save changes to Essbase:

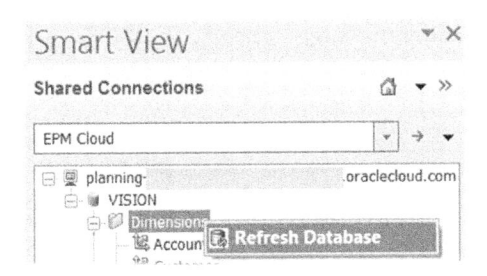

A window appears asking what you'd like to refresh. Click *Database* and then click *Refresh*:

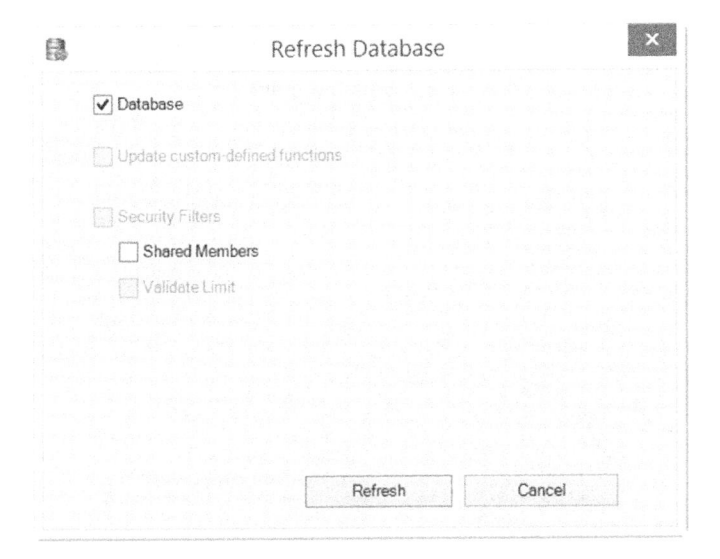

The options here relate to the various refresh options. *Database* and *Security Filters* should be used when dimension hierarchies have changed. When updating security filters, the option to refresh *Shared Members* (members that appear in more than one sub-hierarchy across a single dimension) as well as *Validate Limit* are available. As there are no shared members in this updated dimension and we're not concerned about hitting the security filters limit, these options won't be selected. Not selecting options improves performance. *Update custom-defined functions* updates PBCS custom-defined functions for the application. This option is grayed out, as it does not apply to this application.

15. A warning message appears. Click *OK*:

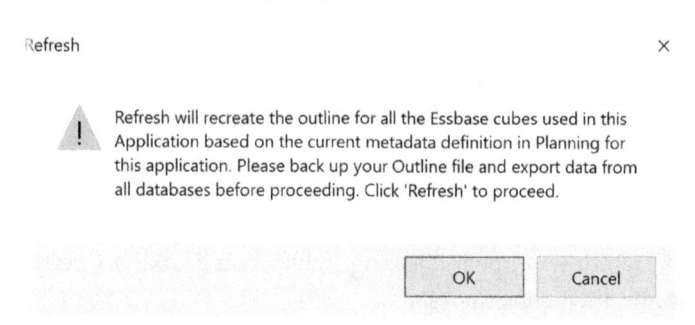

Refresh

> Refresh will recreate the outline for all the Essbase cubes used in this Application based on the current metadata definition in Planning for this application. Please back up your Outline file and export data from all databases before proceeding. Click 'Refresh' to proceed.

OK   Cancel

16. A progress bar appears to show you the refresh progress. When the refresh is complete click *Finish*:

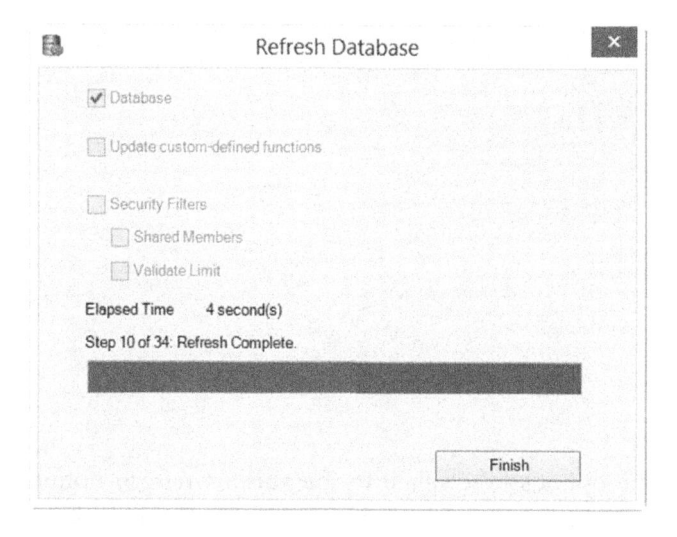

Refresh Database

- ✓ Database
- ☐ Update custom-defined functions
- ☐ Security Filters
-   ☐ Shared Members
-   ☐ Validate Limit

Elapsed Time   4 second(s)
Step 10 of 34: Refresh Complete.

Finish

17. Upon refreshing the Smart View sheet, the new member appears as part of the Account dimension list:

	A	B	C	D	E	F	G	H	I
1		Parent Member	Default Data Storage	Data Type	Sales Consol op.	SalesRpt Consol op.	Account Type	Variance Reporting	Time Balance
2	Account		Never Share	Currency	Ignore	Ignore			
3	4001	Account	Dynamic Calc	Currency	Addition	Addition	Revenue	Non-Expense	Flow
4	4110	4001	Store	Currency	Addition	Addition	Revenue	Non-Expense	Flow
5	4120	4001	Store	Currency	Addition	Addition	Revenue	Non-Expense	Flow
6	4130	4001	Store	Currency	Addition	Addition	Revenue	Non-Expense	Flow
7	4140	4001	Store	Currency	Addition	Addition	Revenue	Non-Expense	Flow
8	4150	4001	Store	Currency	Addition	Addition	Revenue	Non-Expense	Flow
9	4160	4001	Store	Currency	Addition	Addition	Revenue	Non-Expense	Flow
10	4170	4001	Store	Currency	Addition	Addition	Revenue	Non-Expense	Flow
11	Statistics	Account	Label only	Unspecified	Ignore	Ignore	Saved Assumption	Non-Expense	Flow
12	Product Manager	Account	Never Share	Smart List	Ignore	Ignore	Revenue	Non-Expense	Flow

ATTRIBUTE DIMENSIONS

Block storage cubes are limited in the number of dimensions that you can have per database (by practicality, if nothing else). The maximum dimensions in BSO is usually around nine to 10 dimensions, and the fewer, the better. To address this limitation, I can utilize attribute dimensions which are associated with a base stored dimension that provide an additional level of grouping.

For instance, for Vision's product dimension, they might want to also analyze Product Start Date, Product Type, and Target Group. Since all these "dimensions" are really just alternate ways of divvying up the Product dimension (in this example), attribute dimensions might be a good design choice.

Attribute dimensions are dimensions that can be placed in the rows or columns in forms and reports with some special considerations. Just like regular dimensions, they define characteristics about the data that is loaded to PBCS. They have hierarchies and members just like any other dimension.

One of the special qualities of attribute dimensions is that adding them to the outline does not impact the size of the Essbase database. You can add a virtually unlimited number of attribute dimensions.

You can analyze sum totals, minimums, maximums, averages and counts of members in attribute dimensions which certainly isn't possible with UDAs.

Attribute dimensions are supported in block storage and aggregate storage cubes. Attributes are supported for analytic purposes in addition to filtering or calculation purposes. They can be used in valid intersection definitions.

Varying attributes over time are not supported in PBCS. You would use Smart Lists instead of attributes if the attribute can change over time.

But wait, before you get too excited, know there are performance considerations! Attribute dimensions are always dynamically calculated in block storage cubes which could mean slower performance any time an attribute is referenced in data forms and retrievals. I'll also need to watch how hybrid aggregation cubes will support attribute dimensions in the future.

In some cases, the design decisions are clear cut on when to use UDAs versus alternate hierarchies versus attribute dimensions versus Smart Lists. In other scenarios, the answer is less obvious. Let's review some design decision points.

When should you use Attributes?

Use when the attribute does not vary over time; it has a one-to-one relationship with its base member.

Use attributes when you need to identify a group of members for calculation purposes or you want to filter for members in a data form based on an attribute. This use case is available for both BSO and ASO cubes.

Attributes are very helpful when performing comparisons based on certain types of data or when performing calculations based on characteristics. Attributes can be used in cross tabular views in data forms, reports, and dashboards.

When not to use Attributes?

Do not use attributes when you need to define characteristics that vary over time. For example, let's say I have "Employee Status" as an attribute dimension based on the "Employee" dimension. Jack was run over by a bus in October and his employee status was changed from "Active" to "Inactive" to reflect his untimely death. If I run reports for the month of January, it will look like Jack was "inactive/no longer with us" for that month. Jack was alive and kicking for months January through September, but Oracle Enterprise Cloud has no way of knowing this because employee status is solely tied to the Employee dimension.

If you need to track how an attribute changes over time, make the attribute an account tied to a Smart List. Or you could make it a stored dimension (but watch out and don't add too many dimensions).

Do not use attributes when you need to calculate a value by placing a formula on a member (member formulas aren't allowed on attribute members). Watch out for attributes when you need to improve retrieval performance (attributes are dynamically calculated and can be slow at times).

Types of Attributes

There are four types of attribute dimensions: Text, Numeric, Boolean, and Date.

Text attributes are the default type and are used to describe text characteristics.

When AND, OR NOT, <, >, =, >=, <=, <>, !=, IN, and NOT IN operations are performed on text dimensions, Essbase makes logical comparisons for text attribute dimensions. Not always the most logical thing to do, but it's there all the same.

Numeric attribute dimensions contain numeric values at level 0. You can perform AND, OR NOT, <, >, =, >=, <=, <>, !=, IN, and NOT IN operations on numeric attribute dimensions. You can group numeric values into ranges (using the ":" symbol) and include these numeric values in calculations.

Boolean attribute dimensions contain exactly two members (that are defined by the user): True and False, Left and Right, Yes and No, Up and Down, Dog and Cat, or any other two members that you want. Once the two Boolean member names are defined, you must use the same names for all Boolean attribute dimensions in the database. When you perform AND, OR NOT, <, >, =, >=, <=, <>, !=, IN, and NOT IN operations on Boolean attribute dimensions, Essbase translates true to 1 and false to 0.

Date attribute members must contain date members at level-0 that are formatted properly. Valid date formats are mm-dd-yyyy or dd-mm-yyyy. All dates must be after 01-01-1970 and before 01-01-2038.

AND, OR NOT, <, >, =, >=, <=, <>, !=, IN, and NOT IN operations can be performed on Date attribute dimensions. Date values can be also included in calculations.

There are five ways to calculate attribute data: Sum, Count, Average, Minimum, and Maximum. Sum is the default when you don't specify which one to use, but you can use the other calculations as though it was yet another dimension.

There are a few rules when it comes to building attribute dimensions and members:

- Consider the implication of dynamic calculations as reporting on attribute dimensions can be slow
- Define attribute dimensions on sparse dimensions only
- You cannot tag attribute members as a shared members
- You cannot tag attribute members as two-pass calculation
- You cannot assign a UDA to attribute members
- You cannot use consolidation symbols or formulas

Create an Attribute Dimension

I won't create an attribute for my Vision application but I'll show you the basic steps in case you want to add an attribute dimension to your application.

To create an attribute dimension and its members,
1. Select *Navigator* >> *Create and Manage* >> *Dimensions*:
2. Select the desired sparse dimension from the Dimension drop down.
3. Select the dimension member name in the Dimension Editor (if you highlight any other member in the hierarchy, the *Custom Attributes* button is disabled).
4. Select the *Custom Attributes* button:

Dimensions

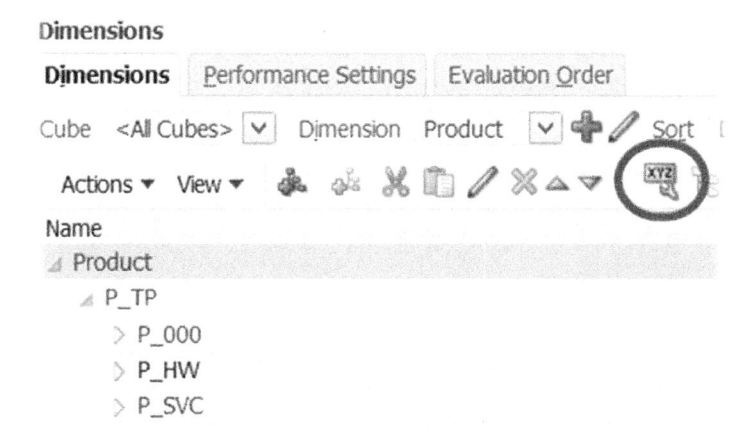

Dimensions | Performance Settings | Evaluation Order

Cube <All Cubes> Dimension Product Sort

Actions ▼ View ▼

Name
- Product
  - P_TP
    - P_000
    - P_HW
    - P_SVC

5. Select the *Add* button in the left panel to create a new attribute dimension.
6. Enter the name of the custom attribute: "Product Type" and select *Text* as the Data Type:

Create Attribute

Name Product Type
Data Type Text
Is Indexed Attribute? ✔

Save   Cancel

7. Click the *Save* button.
8. Add the Attribute members by selecting *Add Child* or *Add Members* icons in the right panel:

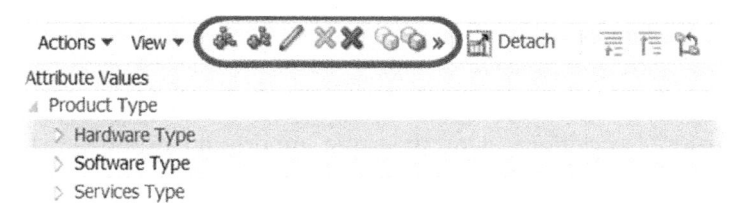

Actions ▼ View ▼   Detach

Attribute Values
- Product Type
  - Hardware Type
  - Software Type
  - Services Type

You can also add aliases by clicking the *Add Alias* icon:

Actions ▼   View ▼   🛠 🛠 ✏ ✖ ✖ 🔍   📋 Detach

Attribute Values
⊿ Product Type
   > Hardware Type
   > Software Type
   > Services Type

You can also move attribute members up and down using the arrow icons.

Associate an Attribute to Base Member

The next step for attributes is to associate the attribute members to the base members of the base dimension. In the example below, I need to assign a product type to the actual product.

9. Select the desired member in the Product dimension and click the *Edit* button. Select the *Attribute Values* tab.
10. Assign the appropriate attribute value ("Hardware Type") by selecting the radio button and using the arrow keys to move the member to the Assigned Attribute value window:

11. Click *Save* and *Close*.
12. Repeat for the other members.
13. Finally refresh the database.

Note you can upload attribute dimensions and attribute dimension associations using the same import and export functionality of the Simplified Planning UI discussed in the previous section.

I walked through an example of creating a text attribute dimension, but remember, you can create numeric, date, and Boolean attributes.

Once the attribute dimension is created and you can select them in forms just like stored dimensions (more on data forms in a bit):

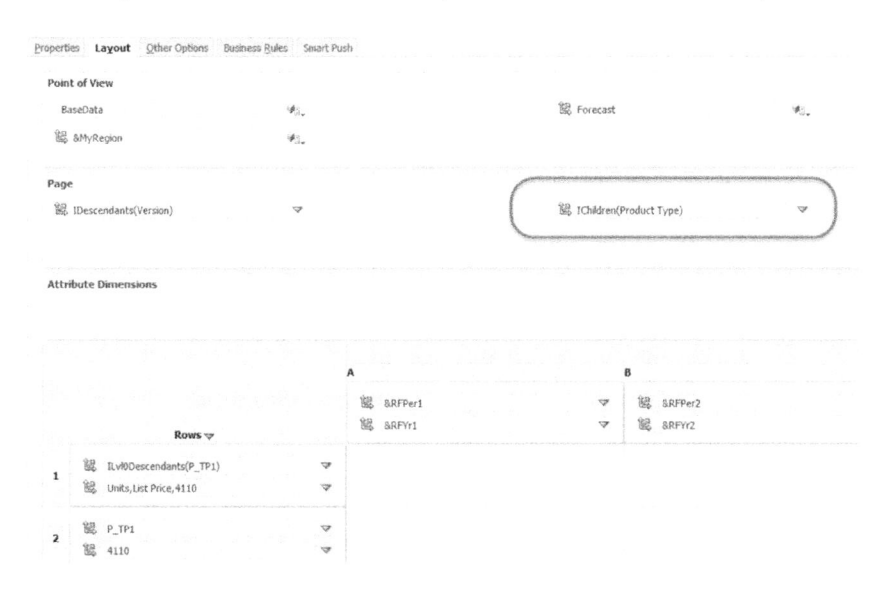

You can also filter members in data forms using attribute dimensions:

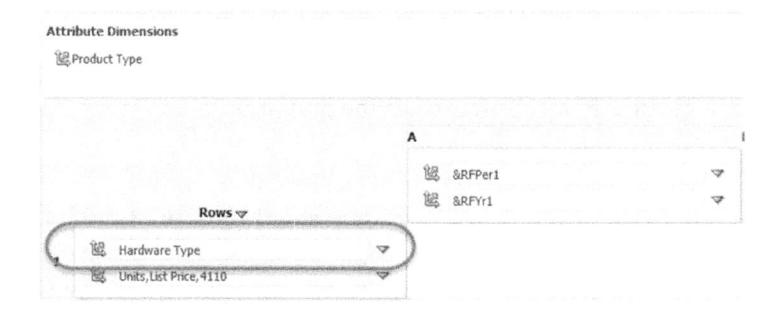

SET CUBE DEFINITIONS

Set Dimensions as Dense or Sparse

For BSO cubes, dimensions are assigned a property of dense or sparse, which impacts how the underlying database is created. This setting affects application performance.

Dense data occurs often or repeatedly across the intersection of all member combinations. You will most likely have data for all periods and most of your accounts for member combinations.

Sparse data occurs periodically or sparsely across member combinations. Dimensions like Entity or Product are usually sparse. Please review the appendix on Essbase at the end of the book for a more comprehensive look at this topic.

To set dimensions as dense or sparse,
1. Select *Navigator* ≣ >> *Application* >> *Overview*.
2. Click the *Dimensions* tab.
3. Check the box for *Dense* for the *Account* and *Period* dimensions to tag them as dense.
4. Leave the other dimensions unchecked to tag them as sparse.
5. Refresh the database.

Dimension Order for BSO Cube

Dimension ordering is critical to Essbase performance in BSO cubes. Can't I just order alphabetically? NO!

First, a few definitions to understand the different types of dimensions (this helps us figure out the best order):

- **Dense dimensions** – dimensions that define the internal structure of the data block; they should reside at the top of the outline definition order
- **Aggregating Sparse dimensions** – dimensions that are sparsely populated across other dimensions and are aggregated from the bottom level to upper levels; these dimensions should reside directly after the last dense dimension in the outline order (placing these dimensions as the first sparse dimensions positions

them to be the first dimensions included in the calculator cache, which gives them an ideal location for optimized calculation performance)
- **Non-Aggregating Sparse dimensions** – dimensions that organize the data into logical slices and don't have a large number of "rollup" members (e.g., Scenario, Version, and Years); not crucial for these dimensions to be included in the calculator cache because their members are typically isolated in FIX statements of calculation scripts for business rules

With these types of dimensions in mind, a common order is to create the "hourglass on a stick." The general starting point would be to have Period first, then Account. The aggregating sparse dimensions would go next in the outline order, followed by the non-aggregating sparse dimensions. If there is a sparse dimension that is frequently in rows, consider moving that dimension to be the first sparse dimension after the dense dimensions.

There is no one right answer. Test iterations of dense and sparse dimensions to figure out the optimal settings for your BSO cubes.

Note! Outline order only matters for BSO cubes.

Now let's actually set the dimension order using the "hourglass on a stick" method.
1. Select *Navigator* >> *Application* >> *Overview* >> then select the *Dimensions* tab in the Simplified UI.
2. Choose the *Sales* cube.

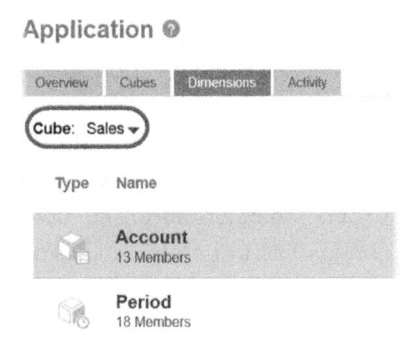

128   Chapter 4: Build an Application

3. Using the arrows in the *Order* column, move the dimensions according to the following:

Note that Period is listed first, then Account. Since there are no other dense dimensions, Entity, the largest sparse dimension, comes next. After that, the other sparse dimensions are listed by member size.

Set Evaluation Order

To make certain objects like Smart Lists or percentages available in data forms, you must set the evaluation order for dimensions. Evaluation order specifies which data type prevails when a data intersection has conflicting data types. Since I have a Smart List member in the Account dimension, I will set the evaluation order for Account as "1".

To set the evaluation order for dimensions,

1. Select *Navigator* >> *Application* >> *Overview* >> then select the *Dimensions* tab:

2. For the Sales cube, set the *Evaluation Order* for Account as 1:

3. Refresh the database.

```
LOG ENTRY: SOL 13, Entry 2
Time to see what the good Project Commander
brought for music.
90's hip hop. Darn it, McMullen.
```

Now that my BSO cube is fully configured, I'm ready to turn my attention to ASO cubes.

ASO CUBES

About ASO Cubes

ASO cubes function like BSO cubes for the most part. They can be used in data forms, you can load data, and you can report and analyze on ASO cubes. The key difference and why you might want to use an ASO cube: this type of Essbase database supports much larger databases (more dimensions and more members). They are ideal for detailed actuals where you only need to aggregate or roll up the dimension hierarchies (and no complicated business rules are required).

The ASO cube will be used in the Vision application for reporting purposes (hence the cube name "SalesRpt"). This cube has an extra dimension, "Customer." In this cube users can report and analyze actuals by customer even though they do not plan at that level. I still want to push Forecast into this cube so Vision users can do variance analysis and then drill to details on customer actuals.

ASO cube dimensions and members have a couple of unique properties that you need to define.

Solve Order

The *Solve Order* member property tells Essbase "here is the order to complete calculations" for ASO databases. Why is this important? You want to calculate the correct numbers in the correct order. Think order of operations for basic math. 4 + 5 * 2 does not equal (4 + 5) * 2. Solve order is the way you control the order of calculations in ASO databases.

Hierarchy Type

In ASO cubes, there are two types of hierarchies: stored and dynamic. Stored hierarchies aggregate according to the structure of the outline. In our example, months roll up to quarters up to a year total in the Period member. This aggregation is really fast (the nature of ASO databases), but stored hierarchies may only have the + consolidation for any member and ~ consolidation tags for members under a "Label Only" parent (other assigned consolidation tags are ignored). Also, stored hierarchies cannot have member formulas and there are a few other restrictions on Label Only assignments.

Dynamic hierarchies are calculated by Essbase (instead of being aggregated like in stored hierarchies), so all consolidation tags and member formulas are processed. The evaluation order for the calculation of members is dictated by the solve order as mentioned above. Dynamic hierarchies, as expected, do not calculate as fast as stored hierarchies.

You can also have multiple hierarchies within a single dimension. The hierarchies within a dimension can be stored, can be all dynamic, or can have one hierarchy stored and the other hierarchy dynamic.

Multiple hierarchies can contain alternate hierarchies with Shared Members or completely different hierarchies.

ASO Cube Considerations

A few other ASO cube considerations include:

- Smart Lists and text measures are supported
- Predictive Analytics (discussed in the end user section) is supported

- PBCS does not generate XREFs on ASO databases (remember XREF is a function that shares data for a member from one BSO cube to another)
- Because PBCS does not require all base dimensions on an ASO database, approvals may not apply to the ASO database if an approvals dimension is missing; if this is the case, normal security would apply
- Dynamic time series members are not supported for ASO cubes
- You can build some calculation rules in Calculation Manager for ASO cubes

Build Custom Customer Dimension with Flat File

I will add a customer dimension, for just the ASO cube, for reporting purposes. Since there are many customers for our application, I will do this using the flat file method. If you are unsure about some of the steps below, look back to the Import & Export Dimensions section of this chapter.

To build a custom, customer dimension with a flat file,
1. Select *Navigator* ▤ >> *Application* >> *Overview*.
2. Click the *Create* button.
3. Type in "Customer" for the dimension name and check *Enabled* for ONLY the SalesRpt cube. Leave other options as default.
4. Click *Done*.

Now that the Customer dimension has been created, it's time to prepare the import file. First I'll export the dimension (even though it is empty) to get the correct file format.

5. Select *Navigator* icon ▤ >>*Application* >> *Overview*.
6. Click the *Export* button, then *Create*.
7. Check the box next to *Customer* and click the option for *Comma delimited* (default).
8. Click *Export*. Save the file and open the template.

Chapter 4: Build an Application

9. Create the Customer dimension by completing the template (or email info@interrel.com for a copy of the file). Save the template as a CSV file.

Once the template has been completed, it should look something like the following (not all properties are shown):

Customer	Parent	Alias: Default	Valid For Cons	Data Storage	Two Pass	Descript	Formula
Total Customer	Customer		FALSE	never share	FALSE		<none>
Large Enterprise	Total Customer		FALSE	never share	FALSE		<none>
A10001	Large Enterprise	WalStores	FALSE	store	FALSE		<none>
A10002	Large Enterprise	Texxon Industries	FALSE	store	FALSE		<none>
A10003	Large Enterprise	Clover	FALSE	store	FALSE		<none>
A10004	Large Enterprise	Specific Motors	FALSE	store	FALSE		<none>
A10005	Large Enterprise	Phillips 66	FALSE	store	FALSE		<none>
A10006	Large Enterprise	Mustang Motors	FALSE	store	FALSE		<none>
A10007	Large Enterprise	SVC Health	FALSE	store	FALSE		<none>
A10008	Large Enterprise	Valerian Energy	FALSE	store	FALSE		<none>
A10009	Large Enterprise	DividedHealthGroup	FALSE	store	FALSE		<none>
A10010	Large Enterprise	Spherizon	FALSE	store	FALSE		<none>
Mid Cap Enterprise	Total Customer		FALSE	never share	FALSE		<none>
B10011	Mid Cap Enterprise	Circle Energy Solutions	FALSE	store	FALSE		<none>
B10012	Mid Cap Enterprise	Hawk Materials	FALSE	store	FALSE		<none>
B10013	Mid Cap Enterprise	ABB Educational Services	FALSE	store	FALSE		<none>
B10014	Mid Cap Enterprise	Landmoon Systems	FALSE	store	FALSE		<none>
B10015	Mid Cap Enterprise	Adminiteam	FALSE	store	FALSE		<none>
B10016	Mid Cap Enterprise	TaylorAng Stores	FALSE	store	FALSE		<none>

Note the valid cube columns should be for the SalesRpt cube:

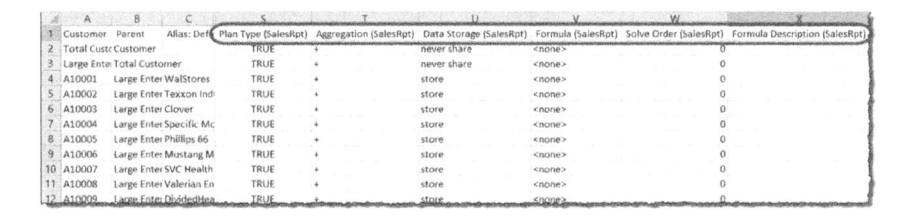

	A	B	C	...	Plan Type (SalesRpt)	Aggregation (SalesRpt)	Data Storage (SalesRpt)	Formula (SalesRpt)	Solve Order (SalesRpt)	Formula Description (SalesRpt)
1	Customer	Parent	Alias: Def		Plan Type (SalesRpt)	Aggregation (SalesRpt)	Data Storage (SalesRpt)	Formula (SalesRpt)	Solve Order (SalesRpt)	Formula Description (SalesRpt)
2	Total Custc	Customer			TRUE	+	never share	<none>	0	
3	Large Ente	Total Customer			TRUE	+	never share	<none>	0	
4	A10001	Large Enter	WalStores		TRUE	+	store	<none>	0	
5	A10002	Large Enter	Texxon Ind		TRUE	+	store	<none>	0	
6	A10003	Large Enter	Clover		TRUE	+	store	<none>	0	
7	A10004	Large Enter	Specific Mc		TRUE	+	store	<none>	0	
8	A10005	Large Enter	Phillips 66		TRUE	+	store	<none>	0	
9	A10006	Large Enter	Mustang M		TRUE	+	store	<none>	0	
10	A10007	Large Enter	SVC Health		TRUE	+	store	<none>	0	
11	A10008	Large Enter	Valerian En		TRUE	+	store	<none>	0	
12	A10009	Large Enter	DividedHea		TRUE	+	store	<none>	0	

10. Select *Navigator* ▦ >> *Application* >> *Overview*.
11. Click *Import*, then *Create*.
12. Navigate to the Customer dimension and click *Browse...*
13. Select the Customer CSV file. Click *Import*, *OK*, and *OK* again.
14. Click *Refresh* at the top of the page until you see a "Completed" notice.

15. Click the *Completed* link. If there are errors during the import process, they are displayed in the next screen.
16. Check out the Customer dimension in the dimension editor (*Navigator* >> *Create and Manage* >> *Dimensions*):

Name	Alias (Default)	Data Storage	Custom Attributes
Customer		Store	
Total Customer		Never Share	
Large Enterprise		Never Share	
A10001	WalStores	Store	
A10002	Texxon Industries	Store	
A10003	Clover	Store	
A10004	Specific Motors	Store	
A10005	Phillips 66	Store	
A10006	Mustang Motors	Store	
A10007	SVC Health	Store	
A10008	Valerian Energy	Store	
A10009	DividedHealthGroup	Store	
A10010	Spherizon	Store	
Mid Cap Enterprise		Never Share	
Small Business		Never Share	
Public Sector		Never Share	
Home and Home Office		Never Share	
No Customer		Never Share	

17. Edit the Customer member and set the hierarchy type to *Store*.
18. Refresh the database.

VARIABLES

Variables have many wonderful functions, one of which is to help reduce manual maintenance on forms, scripts, reports, etc. In addition, variables can help users by providing flexibility with member selection. In this section I'll explain two different types of variables: user variables, which users can control and change; and substitution variables, which can be used system-wide and are controlled and changed by administrators.

Create User Variables

User Variables act as filters in data forms, enabling PBCS to focus on the members they are interested in. Once the User Variables are created by users, they can associate it with a data form so that they can plan in a data form tailored for each individual user. User Variables can be "dynamic," meaning users can change their variable member selection within a data form if enabled by the administrator. User Variables may be defined for both stored dimensions and attribute dimensions.

To create a User Variable,

1. Select *Navigator* ≡ >> *Create and Manage* >> *Variables*.
2. In the User Variables tab, click ✚.
3. Select the dimension that the user variable is associated with, then enter a name. Select "Entity" for the Dimension Name and call it "MyRegion":

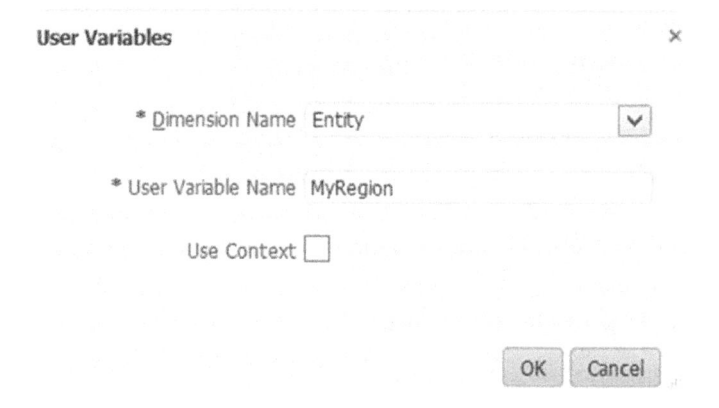

User Variables

* Dimension Name: Entity
* User Variable Name: MyRegion

Use Context ☐

OK   Cancel

4. Click *OK*.
5. Add another user variable for the Product dimension and call it "ProductFamily".
6. Click *OK*.

You should have the following:

Variables

Dimension	User Variable Name
Entity	MyRegion
Product	ProductFamily

The variable definition that we have set so far allows the user to select any member in the dimension for which they have security. You can further define what users can select by defining the User Variable Definition. For example, if I wanted to limit MyRegion to only allow users to select the sales regions, I can define this in the User Variable Definition section, using the member selection to select the members. I use a function so that if new regions are added to the dimension, they are automatically available for users to select:

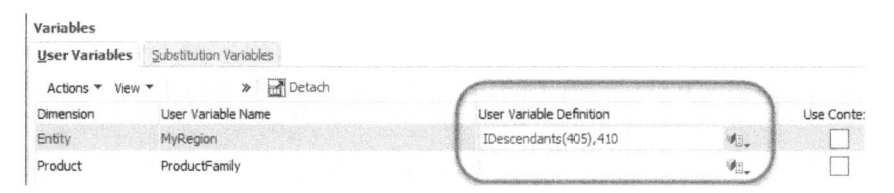

Dimension	User Variable Name	User Variable Definition	Use Conte:
Entity	MyRegion	IDescendants(405),410	
Product	ProductFamily		

Another possible use case: if I created a user variable called "SandboxVersion", I would only want users to be able to choose between the different members for sandbox versions:

Chapter 4: Build an Application

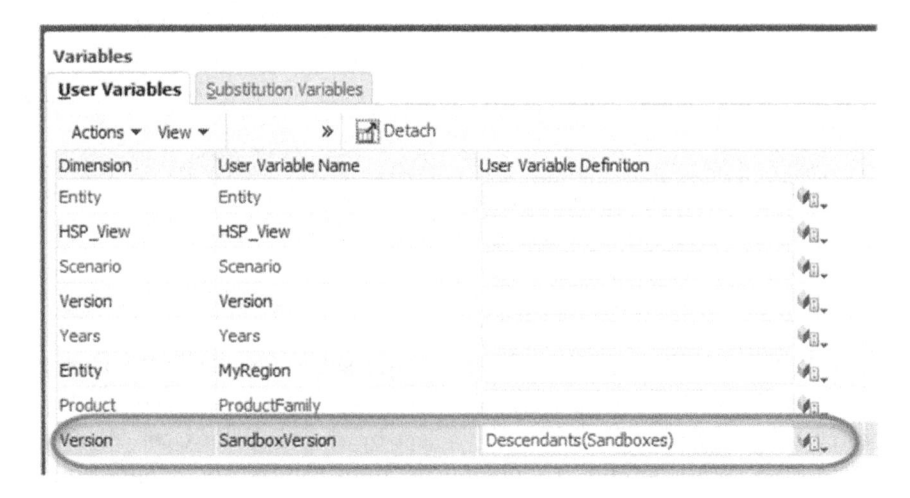

Variables			
User Variables	Substitution Variables		
Actions ▼ View ▼		» Detach	
Dimension	User Variable Name	User Variable Definition	
Entity	Entity		
HSP_View	HSP_View		
Scenario	Scenario		
Version	Version		
Years	Years		
Entity	MyRegion		
Product	ProductFamily		
Version	SandboxVersion	Descendants(Sandboxes)	

I can now select these user variables in data forms (instead of hard coding member selections). More on this when I get to the data forms section.

Select User Variable Members

In order to open forms, each user must select a member for each User Variable that has been set up. This is quite simple to do.

To set your User Variable,

1. Select *Navigator* ▦ >> *Tools* >> *User Variable Options* tab.
2. Use the Member Selector to make selections for each user variable, or type in the member name if the exact spelling is known:

User Variables

Dimension	User Variable Name	Selected Member	
Entity	MyRegion	410 International Sales	
Product	ProductFamily	Computer Services	

3. Click *Save*.

I'll put these user variables to work in the data forms section!

Create Substitution Variables

Substitution Variables are variables that serve as a placeholder for specific members. These variables can be used in data forms, calculation scripts, reporting and analysis tools, and much more. Common Substitution Variables include CurrentMth, CurrentYear, and PriorYear. Instead of modifying 20 different months that were hardcoded into your forms or calculation scripts, you can just change the value of the Substitution Variable every month. The application administrator will need to change the values of the variables monthly or yearly, as they change.

To create a Substitution Variable,
1. Navigate to *Navigator* ☰ >> *Create and Manage* >> *Variables*.
2. In the Substitution Variables tab, click ✚.
3. Type in "CurrentYear" for the *Name* and "FY16" for the *Value*:

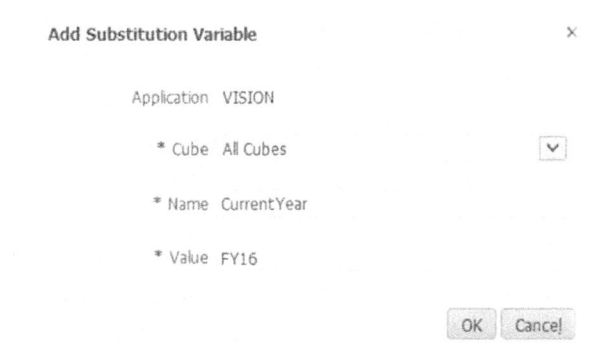

```
Add Substitution Variable                          x

        Application  VISION

        * Cube       All Cubes                  v

        * Name       CurrentYear

        * Value      FY16


                                          OK    Cancel
```

4. Click *OK*. The substitution variable entry appears on the screen.
5. Create another substitution variable for "PriorYear" and assign "FY15" as the value.
6. Create another substitution variable for "ForecastYear" and assign "FY17" as the value.

You can manually update Substitution Variables in the UI or you can automate the update with EPM Automate (more on this later).

```
LOG ENTRY: SOL 13, Entry 3

    With the application built, I'm feeling pretty
good about this PBCS thing. Next on my list is
loading data. How hard could that be?
```

Chapter 5: Integrate Data

Oracle PBCS provides a number of methods for both loading data into and exporting data out of applications. Data can be imported using the Simplified UI with an Essbase data format or PBCS/"Hyperion Planning" data format. A business rule can be used to export data.

PBCS data can be integrated using on-premises Financial Data Quality Management (FDMEE) beginning with release 11.1.2.4.200. FDMEE is a business users "ETL" (Extract-Transform-Load) tool. FDMEE provides a graphical interface to define sources and targets and maps them together to integrate data. FDMEE has long been used with on-premises Hyperion applications and now supports integration to the Cloud. A separate license for FDMEE is required if you want to use this method.

Data can also be integrated using Data Management (which is a "lite" version of FDMEE on the Cloud). Data Management comes with your PBCS subscription and can be used to both import and export data to and from the Cloud, as well as between Cloud pods.

Flat files and other EPM Cloud services are the only available source for Data Management and the PBCS Simplified UI. I will walk through the Data Management and Simplified UI data load methods in this portion of the mission.

While I will not cover the steps to build a data integration for FDMEE, the steps are similar to the steps addressed in the Data Management section; the main difference is that on-premises FDMEE delivers more supported sources and targets, scripting capabilities, and many other features

INTEGRATION OPTIONS OVERVIEW

PBCS data can integrate directly with other Oracle EPM Cloud services like FCCS, PCMCS, and ARCS using Data Management. Other supported sources for direct connectivity include Oracle Fusion Financials Cloud. Both the Data Management tool and Simplified load method support the loading of numerical data and text-based data loads (Smart List intersections, free form text data).

The following list provides a summary of the different ways to load data to and export data from PBCS.

Options to load data into PBCS include:

- **Native Essbase format via Simplified UI** – use when a source file can be provided in the specific / required format; a good use case is when moving data across the same cubes (production to test); flat files are supported
- **Hyperion Planning format via Simplified UI** – use for loading numerical data, free form text, and Smart List data; this format has a very specific format with a "POV" column; flat files are supported
- **Data load rules in Data Management** – use when loading data files of different formats and when mapping and / or drill through is required (use when you don't have an Essbase or Planning data file format); flat files are used for on-premises sources and direct connectivity is available for other EPM Cloud Services
- **Data load rules in on-premises Financial Data Quality Management (FDMEE)** – use when you have purchased full version FDMEE; it a great solution for Hybrid Cloud/on-premises integrations; supported FDMEE sources, on-premises Hyperion sources, and direct connectivity to other EPM Cloud services are available

Options to synchronize data between cubes include:

- **Synchronize Data in Data Management** – use to push data between BSO and ASO cubes within a PBCS application
- **Data Maps via Simplified UI** – use to push data between BSO and ASO within a PBCS application; can be used in data forms for real time syncing

Options to export data from PBCS include:

- **Native Essbase format via Simplified UI** – use to move data across environments (pre-prod to prod) or backup of data; flat files in native Essbase format are supported
- **Hyperion Planning format via Simplified UI** - use to export out numerical data, Smart Lists, and free form text intersections; easy to apply filtering to export specific data sets; flat files in Planning format are supported
- **Delimited data file in Data Management** – use to export data to load to other EPM Cloud applications or flat files to load to other systems; flat files are supported and direct connectivity is available to other EPM Cloud Services
- **Data load rules in FDMEE** – use to export data to load to other systems; great for Hybrid Cloud/on-premises integrations; supported FDMEE targets are available
- **Business Rule with DATAEXPORT function in Calculation Manager** – use export data to load to other systems; easy to apply filtering to export specific data sets; flat file only

Other methods for Cloud integration:

- **REST API** - scripted interface in conjunction with EPM Automate utility; this option uses a scripting/programming interface to integrate data between Cloud and other systems; almost any source is available

IMPORT DATA WITH THE SIMPLIFIED UI

Load Data with Native Essbase Format

You can load data to PBCS using the native Essbase format in the Simplified UI. A good use case for this option is when you want to move entire data sets from one application to another with the exact same dimensionality (e.g., moving data from pre-production to production or on-premises to Cloud).

Free-form data loading is a simple method for loading data to Essbase. The data file can be loaded as is without any explicit description of its contents (i.e. no load rule), but the data MUST be in the natural order for Essbase. So what is the natural order for Essbase? Essbase must encounter a member from every dimension before a data value. Any valid dimension / member / alias name combination is acceptable. Data is read according to the member names Essbase finds.

The steps to load the Essbase data format are mostly the same steps to load data with the Planning format.

Load Data with Planning Format

You can load data to PBCS using the native Planning format in the Simplified UI. Under the covers, the Simplified UI is using the Outline Load Utility functionality from on-premises Hyperion Planning. This is a one way to load Smart List data intersections and free form text members.

This format is pretty specific. The first column is where data is loaded to. The second column is the driver members where data is loaded to (I like to use account members as the driver members). The next column is the POV, which is basically the rest of the dimension members where data should be loaded. This can be tricky to create from other source systems as the POV must be enclosed in double quotes (as shown in the next screen shot). It is pretty easy to create this format if you have a SQL database to generate the file. The final column is the Data Load Cube name.

Here is a sample Planning Simplified UI data file displayed in Notepad++ text editor:

```
Product, Product Manager, Point-of-View, Data Load Cube Name
P_100, Rachel, "0, FY16, Actual, Final, BaseData, Jan", Sales
P_100, Rachel, "0, FY16, Actual, Final, BaseData, Feb", Sales
P_100, Rachel, "0, FY16, Actual, Final, BaseData, Mar", Sales
P_100, Rachel, "0, FY16, Actual, Final, BaseData, Apr", Sales
P_100, Rachel, "0, FY16, Actual, Final, BaseData, May", Sales
P_100, Rachel, "0, FY16, Actual, Final, BaseData, Jun", Sales
P_100, Rachel, "0, FY16, Actual, Final, BaseData, Jul", Sales
P_100, Rachel, "0, FY16, Actual, Final, BaseData, Aug", Sales
P_100, Rachel, "0, FY16, Actual, Final, BaseData, Sep", Sales
P_100, Rachel, "0, FY16, Actual, Final, BaseData, Oct", Sales
P_100, Rachel, "0, FY16, Actual, Final, BaseData, Nov", Sales
P_100, Rachel, "0, FY16, Actual, Final, BaseData, Dec", Sales
```

Be careful when updating this file. Excel can really screw this file up, as it tends to remove commas, add additional quotes, and more:

Product	Product Manager	Point-of-View	Data Load Cube Name					
P_100	Rachel	"0	FY16	Actual	Final	BaseData	Jan"	Sales
P_100	Rachel	"0	FY16	Actual	Final	BaseData	Feb"	Sales
P_100	Rachel	"0	FY16	Actual	Final	BaseData	Mar"	Sales
P_100	Rachel	"0	FY16	Actual	Final	BaseData	Apr"	Sales
P_100	Rachel	"0	FY16	Actual	Final	BaseData	May"	Sales
P_100	Rachel	"0	FY16	Actual	Final	BaseData	Jun"	Sales
P_100	Rachel	"0	FY16	Actual	Final	BaseData	Jul"	Sales
P_100	Rachel	"0	FY16	Actual	Final	BaseData	Aug"	Sales
P_100	Rachel	"0	FY16	Actual	Final	BaseData	Sep"	Sales
P_100	Rachel	"0	FY16	Actual	Final	BaseData	Oct"	Sales
P_100	Rachel	"0	FY16	Actual	Final	BaseData	Nov"	Sales
P_100	Rachel	"0	FY16	Actual	Final	BaseData	Dec"	Sales

To load data using the Simplified UI in Planning format,
1. Select *Navigator* ▦ >> *Application* >> *Overview*.
2. Choose *Actions* >> *Inbox / Outbox Explorer*.
3. Click *Upload*.
4. Click *Browse…* to find and upload the prepared file. Mine is called "ProductManagerLoad.csv".
5. Click *Upload File* and the file is uploaded into the Inbox / Outbox Explorer:

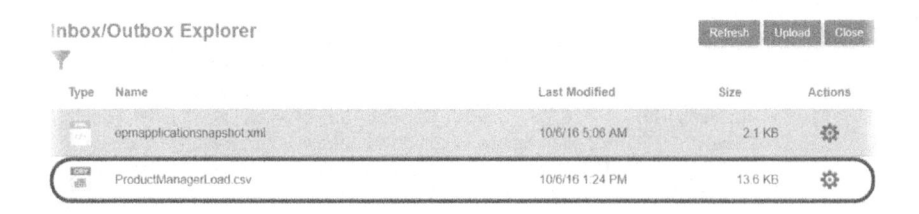

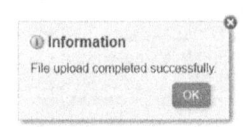

Chapter 5: Integrate Data

[Inbox/Outbox Explorer screenshot showing opmapplicationsnapshot.xml and ProductManagerLoad.csv files]

[Information dialog: "File upload completed successfully." with OK button]

6. Click *OK*, and then *Close*.
7. Choose *Actions >> Import Data*:

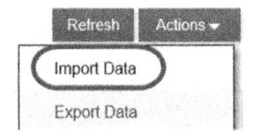

[Actions menu showing Import Data and Export Data options]

8. Click *Create*.
9. Define the import information:

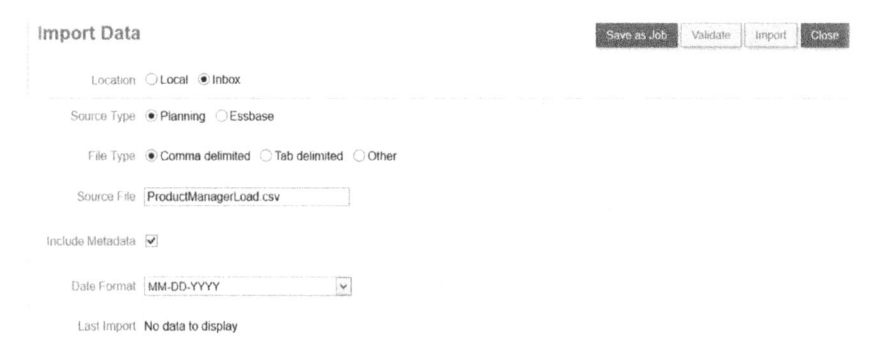

[Import Data dialog showing:
- Location: Local / ●Inbox
- Source Type: ●Planning / Essbase
- File Type: ●Comma delimited / Tab delimited / Other
- Source File: ProductManagerLoad.csv
- Include Metadata: ✓
- Date Format: MM-DD-YYYY
- Last Import: No data to display]

The following options are available for the Planning import type:

- **Location** – location of the file; either locally on the user's computer or on the Cloud server

- **Source Type** – format of the source file; either Planning or Essbase native format
- **File Type** – type of delimiter used in the source file; either comma, tab, or one that the user specifies
- **Source File** – name of the source file
- **Include Metadata** – specify to load metadata along with application data; this checkbox is selected by default; deselecting this option improves performance, but you must already have the required metadata in the application; deselecting this option also prevents members from shifting their position within the outline
- **Date Format** – date format options if date types are used in the source file
- **Last Import** – not selectable; last date and time an import was attempted

The following options are available if the import type is Essbase:

- **Source Type** – format of the source file; either Planning or Essbase native format
- **Cube** – which cube to load data to
- **Source File** – name of the source file
- **Last Import** – not selectable; last date and time an import was attempted

10. Click *Save as Job*.
11. Enter the job name "ImportProductManager", click *Save*, and then *OK*.
12. The job is created. Click *Close*.
13. Schedule the job (or run now on demand).
14. Select *Navigator* ▤ >> *Application* >> *Jobs*.
15. Click *Schedule Jobs*:

146   Chapter 5: Integrate Data

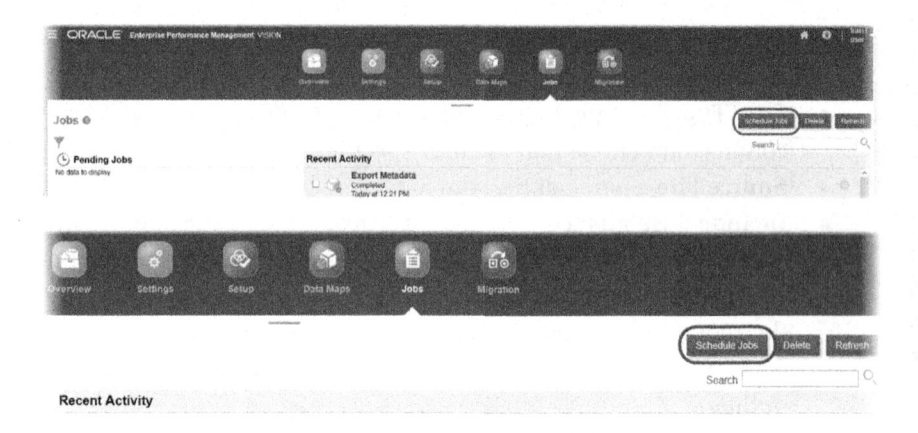

16. Enter the following job information:
    a. What type of job is this: *Import Data*
    b. When do you want to run this job: *Run Now:*

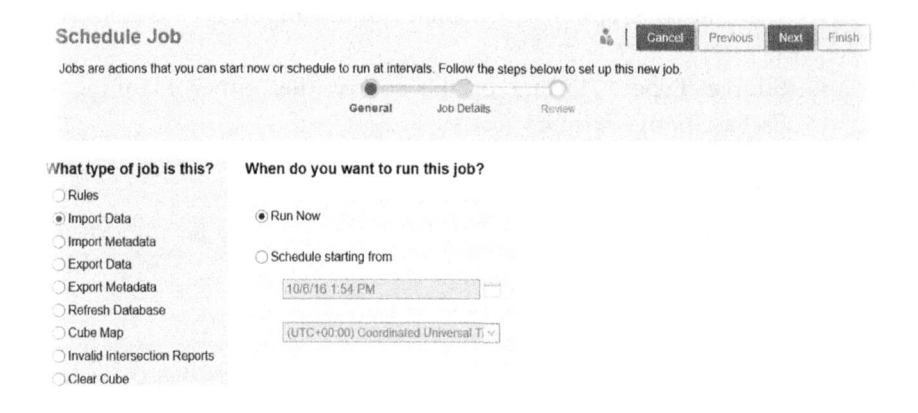

17. Click *Next*.
18. View the Job Details:

Look Smarter Than You Are with PBCS   147

Schedule Job

Jobs are actions that you can start now or schedule to run at intervals. Follow the steps below to set up this new job.

General — Job Details — Review

Import Data
Select an Import Data job

Job Name

ImportProductManager

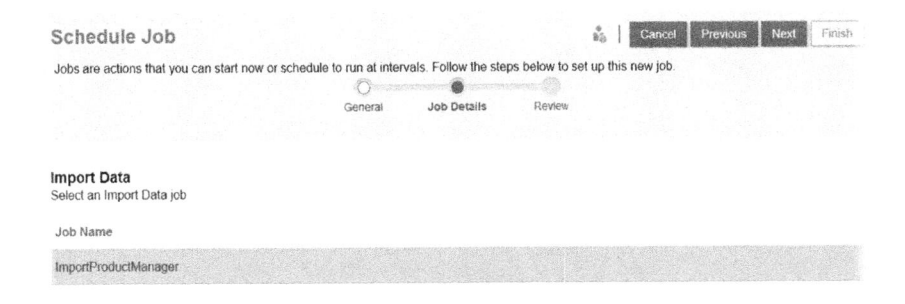

19. Click *Next*.
20. Review the job information and click *Finish*.
21. You can view the job progress in the console:

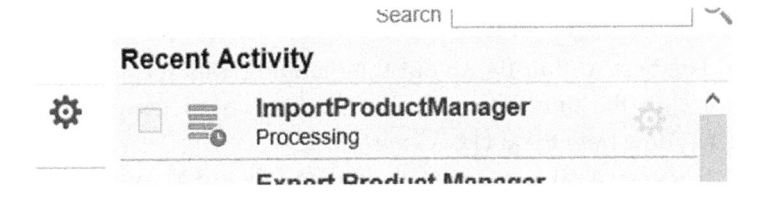

Recent Activity

ImportProductManager
Processing

Export Product Manager

22. When the job is complete, you can select the job to view the process details:

Import and Export Status

Load Id: 21	Start Time: 10/6/16 3:30:49 PM
Type: Data Import	End Time: 10/6/16 3:30:51 PM
Run By: train1	Records Read: 192
Dimension: Product	Records Processed: 192
Job Status: Completed	Records Rejected: 0

Show: Errors ▼
Category   Record Index   Message
No data to display

To check that the data load was successful, you can create a data form to view the data (I'll do this in the next chapter). Once you've created the data form, you can verify the data load with a data form (I called mine "Check Product Manager Load" data form):

EXPORT DATA WITH THE SIMPLIFIED UI

Export Data Using the "Export Data" in Simplified UI

The best way to figure out the Planning data format is to export data through the Simplified UI first to give you a template. It's also handy to know how to quickly export data.

Data can easily be exported using the Export Data function in the Simplified UI if needed.

To export data in the Simplified UI,
1. Select *Navigator* ≡ >> *Application* >> *Overview*.
2. Go to Actions and click *Export Data*.
3. Click *Create*.
4. Keep the default options:

Set *Dynamic Members* to "Exclude" when you know you do not need to export dynamically calculated members (this executes much faster).

Now a slice of data needs to be defined to customize the export. Click the hierarchy icon next to each dimension name to select the members.

When inside the Select Members screen:

- Click on a parent name to show its children
- To add a relationship function, click the function icon *fx* next to the appropriate member
- To select just a single member name (for the Point of View), click the box to the left of the member name

5. Make the following Slice Definition selections.
   a. **Row** – Account: Descendants ("4001")
   b. **Column** – Period: ILvl0Descendants(YearTotal)
   c. **Point of View** – BaseData, FY16, Actual, Final, Descendants(TD), Descendants(P_TP):

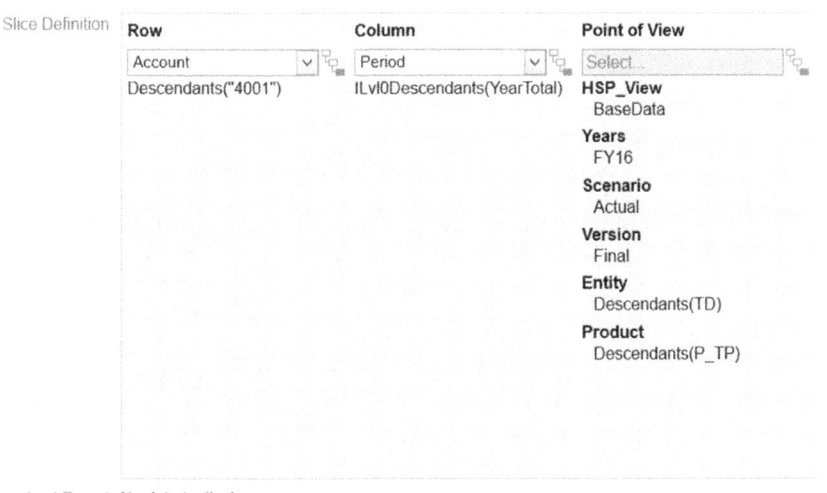

Slice Definition	Row	Column	Point of View
	Account Descendants("4001")	Period ILvl0Descendants(YearTotal)	Select... HSP_View BaseData Years FY16 Scenario Actual Version Final Entity Descendants(TD) Product Descendants(P_TP)

Last Export No data to display

6. Click *Export* and wait for the data export to complete:

Data Export

0%   100%

Data is currently being exported...

OK

7. Save the .zip file. Then open it and note the Planning format (remember Excel can mess up the POV column pretty easily).

Note, you cannot export data from the Simplified UI in an Essbase format. The Essbase format is used in the migration snapshots when you take snapshots of your application (more on this later).

Export Data Using a Business Rule

You can also export data from BSO cubes using business rules and the Data Export function. Check out the Calculate Data chapter for more information.

INTRO TO DATA MANAGEMENT

As I mentioned earlier, Data Management within PBCS is another one of the ways you can load data and export data. Data Management is a "lite" version of Financial Data Quality Management Enterprise Edition (FDMEE) and is the data integration tool for PBCS (along with other EPM Cloud products).

Data Management today can import and export flat files from any source to and from PBCS, integrate data across EPM Cloud Services and other supported Oracle Cloud solutions, perform mapping translations, and sync data across cubes.

Data Management is a more robust integration solution and has a few more steps than the simplified UI. With more steps, I get greater flexibility and functionality. The overall steps to load data using Data Management are as follows. Don't worry – I'll explain each of the steps in more detail as I go through this chapter / portion of the mission.

Data Management Steps to Build an Integration

#	Task / Term	Term Definition	Where to Perform the Task
1	Define System Settings	System settings are default settings (or system level profiles) that you define that will apply to the entire system	*Setup >> Configure >> System Settings*
2	Define Application Settings	Application settings are default settings (or application level profiles) that you define that will apply to target application	*Setup >> Configure >> Application Settings*
3	Define **Source** System	Where you will load data from; for Enterprise Planning Cloud this is a flat file	*Setup >> Register >> Source System*
4	Define app as a **Target** (Optionally set drill flag to *Yes*)	Where you will load data to; for Enterprise Planning Cloud this is the Enterprise Planning Cloud application or an export of the Enterprise Planning Cloud application data	*Setup >> Register >> Target Application*
5	Define **Import Format** (including defining Drill URL to source)	Determines which columns are extracted from the source system, how the data is stored in the Data Management staging table and import mapping information	*Setup >> Integration Setup >> Import Format*
6	Create a **Location**	Associates Import Format with Target Application and combines mapping and data load rules for Target	*Setup >> Integration Setup >> Location*

#	Task / Term	Term Definition	Where to Perform the Task
7	Define **Mappings** (Data Source, Period, Category Mappings)	Map source fields to Target Application (any delimited data file can be mapped to target application; define period mappings and category mappings)	*Setup >> Integration Setup >> Period Mapping*
8	Define Logic groups (optionally)	Define Logic groups, check rule groups, and check entity groups	*Setup >> Data Load Setup >> Logic Group*
9	Create a **Data Load** Rule	Defines what file to run; if file is left blank, user is prompted at run time	*Workflow >> Data Load >> Data Load Rule*
10	**Execute** (which will load data to the Workbench and / or Target application)	Will load data to the Data Management staging tables and / or Target application)	*Workflow >> Data Load >> Data Load Rule* or *Workflow >> Data Load >> Workbench*

That is quite a few steps, so I'm going to create my own acronym to remember the steps: S_T_IF_Lo_Ma_DL_E (*"Stiflomadle"*: Create Source, Create Target, Define Import Format, Define Location, Define Mappings, Define Data Load Rule, and finally Execute).

An important concept in Data Management is Point of View or POV. Sources are loaded by POV. A POV is made up of a POV Location, POV Period (month and year), and POV Category. If you are loading a single Actuals source file, you may just have one location. If you are loading files from multiple sources, you might have more than one location. Data Management is geared to load data for a single period (Period POV), but loading for multiple periods is supported. A POV category is telling Data Management – do I want to load to Actual or Budget?

Note! Today's version of PBCS Data Management does NOT have all of the features and functions available in on-premises FDMEE, such as scripting. This is mostly due to Cloud security precautions. However, the near-term roadmap for on-premises FDMEE includes hybrid Cloud / on-premises support, which will allow it to integrate with PBCS as well as on-premises applications.

PBCS only allows one Data Management application. Because of this requirement, Data Management performs some of the setup steps for you with PBCS:

- **Target Applications** – two application targets are automatically created as [Appname] and [Appname_Export] (so you can load data to the application and export data from the application)
- **Default Import Format** – when you create a PBCS application, a default import format is automatically created with the name [Appname_1]; use this import format to map a source data file to a Planning application
- **Default Location** – default Location is automatically created with the name [Appname_1]

Navigate to Data Management

To navigate to Data Management in the Simplified UI,
1. Select *Navigator* >> *Integration* and click *Data Management*.

A separate window for "Data Management" opens. Data Management has two main sections, Workflow and Setup:

154   Chapter 5: Integrate Data

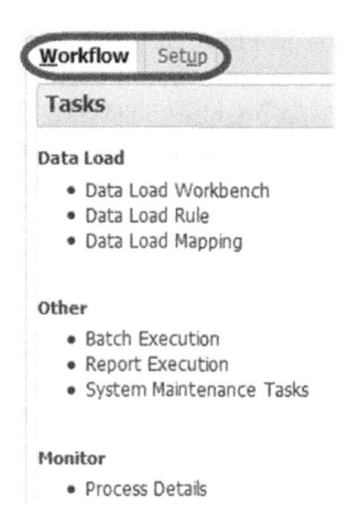

> **Workflow** | Setup
>
> **Tasks**
>
> Data Load
> - Data Load Workbench
> - Data Load Rule
> - Data Load Mapping
>
> Other
> - Batch Execution
> - Report Execution
> - System Maintenance Tasks
>
> Monitor
> - Process Details

Tasks in Data Management are grouped by Workflow and Setup.

LOAD DATA FILE USING DATA MANAGEMENT

Data File Requirements

Data Management file requirements must follow these guidelines:

- Supported delimiters include:
    o   comma (,)
    o   exclamation (!)
    o   semicolon (;)
    o   colon (:)
    o   pipe (|)
    o   tab
- PBCS supports single period or multiple period load (with periods across the columns)
- PBCS also supports multi-column load of numeric data for any dimension (periods and years are supported in the rows of the file)

Define System Settings

To define the System Settings,
1. Click the *Setup* tab.

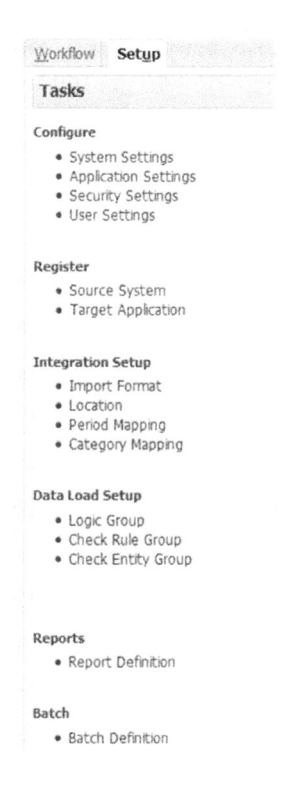

```
Workflow  Setup
Tasks
Configure
   • System Settings
   • Application Settings
   • Security Settings
   • User Settings

Register
   • Source System
   • Target Application

Integration Setup
   • Import Format
   • Location
   • Period Mapping
   • Category Mapping

Data Load Setup
   • Logic Group
   • Check Rule Group
   • Check Entity Group

Reports
   • Report Definition

Batch
   • Batch Definition
```

2. Click the *System Settings* link under Configure.
3. Then change the Profile Type to *All* to see all of the possible System Settings available.

System settings are default settings that apply to the entire system (all target applications in Data Management). Usually, you can leave most of the System Settings blank to accept Data Management defaults. Here are a few you should consider setting:

- **Log Level** – this setting specifies the level of detail included in the Data Management process log. The default value is "4" which

is recommended for production. Set to a value of "5" for the most verbose option that should be used during development.
- **Batch Size** – this setting is used to adjust performance. When data is loaded, this setting determines how many records are stored in the cache before being committed. Set to a higher number for better performance, but avoid setting it too high as the application can become unstable.

Define Application Settings

To define the Application Settings,
1. Still within the *Setup* tab, click the *Application Settings* link under *Configure*.

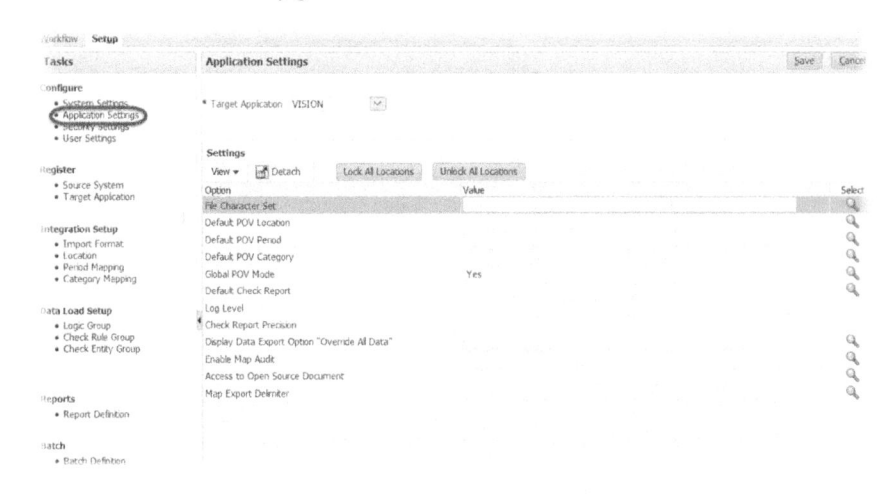

[screenshot of Application Settings page]

The first step in setting up data loads is to define application settings. Application settings are default settings (or application level profiles) that you define which apply to the Target application (and override any System Settings for that particular application). You select a Target application and then define the application settings. Since PBCS only allows one application, two application targets are automatically created as *Appname* and *Appname_Export* (so you can load data to the application and export data from the application).

You can set each of these Application Settings, or leave them blank to accept the Data Management defaults:

- **File Character Set** – specify method for mapping bit combinations to characters for creating, storing, and displaying text (e.g., UTF-8)
- **Default POV Location** – the POV location that should come up by default
- **Default POV Period** – the POV period that should come up by default
- **Default POV Category** – the POV category that should come up by default
- **Global POV Mode** (Yes or No) – when this is set to *Yes*, other POVs are ignored
- **Default Check Report** – define the type of Check Report to use at the application level (either picking a pre-defined Check Report or a custom report that you create)
- **Log Level** – define level of detail to display in the log (1 = least detail and 5 = greatest detail); logs are displayed in *Process Details >> Log*
- **Check Report Precision** – number of decimals for check report
- **Display Data Export Option "Override All Data"** (Yes or No) – option that, when enabled, will display the "override all data" option for data exports which will clear data for the entire application
- **Enable Map Audit** (Yes or No) – creates audit records for the Map Monitor reports
- **Access to Open Source Document** (Administrators or All Users) – determines access level to the Open Source document
- **Map Export Delimiter** (!, , ; or |) – the application default delimiter used for exported mappings; in prior versions exports of mappings could only be done via .csv files

In Application Settings, you can choose to click *Lock All Locations* which prevents data from being loaded for a designated period and category. To unlock locations, choose *Unlock All Locations:*

Chapter 5: Integrate Data

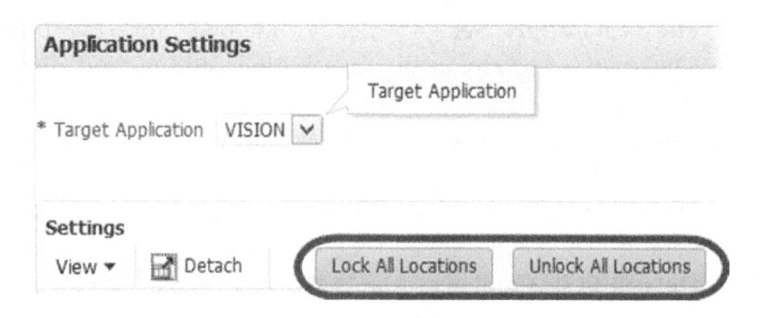

2. For example, if I wanted to prevent users from loading data for Feb-16 actuals, I could select those members and click *OK*:

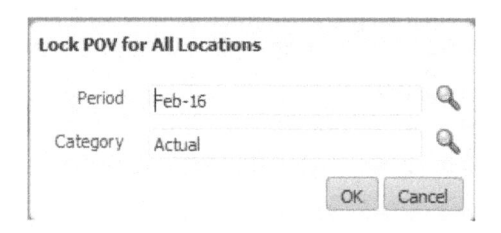

I'll continue on and define the application settings for my Vision data load.

3. Select the application to load data to. In this case, I will select *VISION*.
4. Type "Yes" in the Global POV field:

Application Settings	
* Target Application	VISION

Settings	
View ▼ Detach	Lock All Locations Unlock All Locations
Option	Value
File Character Set	
Default POV Location	
Default POV Period	
Default POV Category	
Global POV Mode	Yes

5. Click *Save*.

Define Source System

To define a source system,
1. Under the Setup tab and Register section, click *Source System*.
2. Review the *File* source system that is created by PBCS by default.

The Source System section is where I define the information about where I am loading data from. The "File" source already exists by default since it is the only source available in PBCS (for now). If you are loading data from an Oracle Fusion ERP data file, there is an additional step to identify the file as a Fusion file.

For file-based source systems, you see the name, type, description, and drill through URL for the source (to learn more about drill through, check out Oracle's tutorial video – https://goo.gl/sxD6IL).

You can add new source systems, edit source system details, and delete sources. The option to *Configure Source Connection* is used for Oracle Fusion file sources (not regular file sources).

The File type already exists by default since it is the only source available in PBCS. I could use this source system but I'm going to create a new one to show you the process from start to finish:

Chapter 5: Integrate Data

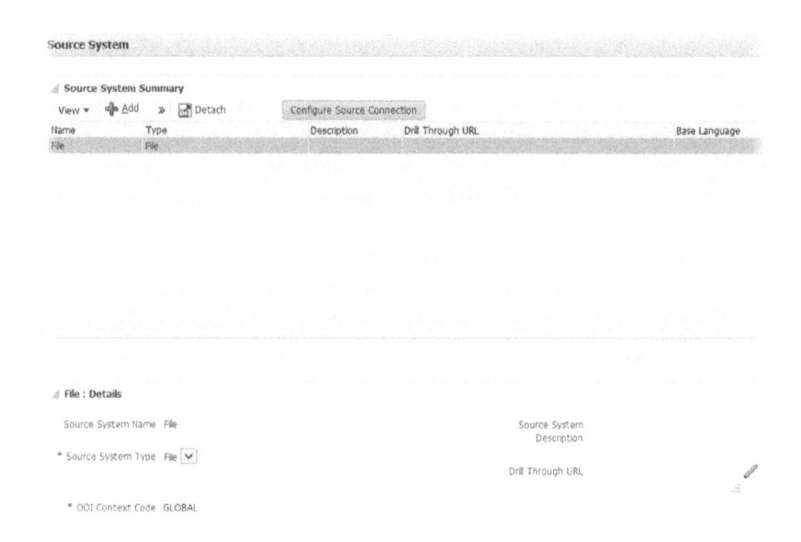

3. Click the *Add* ✚ icon to add a new source system.
4. Enter *Source System Name* as "Vision Data File" with a *Source System Type* of "File", and a *Source System Description* of "Vision Actual Data Load File":

5. Click *Save*.

Define Target Application

Now that Data Management supports Cloud to Cloud integration, when you click *Add* to add a new target, it can be a little confusing. *Local* is used for a target Cloud app on the same pod. *Cloud* is used for a target Cloud app on a different pod:

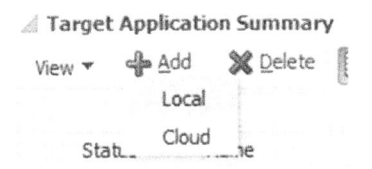

Target Application Summary

View ▾ ＋ Add ✖ Delete

Local
Stat... Cloud ...ne

To review the setup and properties for a target application,
1. Click *Setup* >> *Register* >> *Target Application*.

The BSO application defined in PBCS (in this case, VISION) already exists by default as a target application along with any ASO cubes.

2. Click on the *VISION* target application.

You see the dimensions listed in the Dimension Details tab. Each dimension is assigned a *Target Dimension Class* and a *Data Table Column Name*. You can also check the option to *Create Drill Region*, as well as define the sequence.

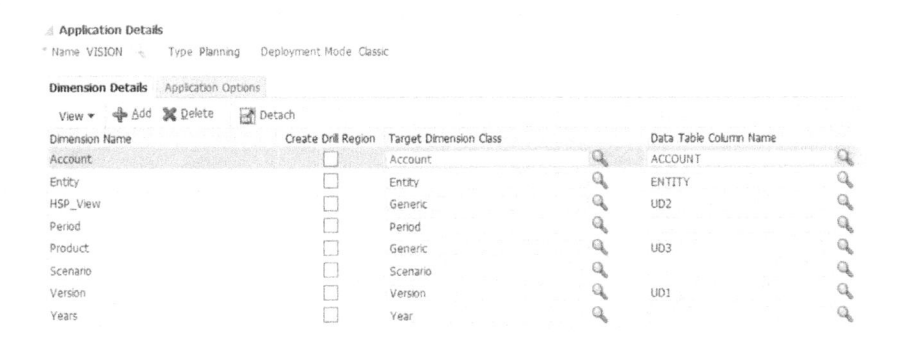

Application Details

* Name VISION Type Planning Deployment Mode Classic

Dimension Details Application Options

View ▾ ＋ Add ✖ Delete Detach

Dimension Name	Create Drill Region	Target Dimension Class	Data Table Column Name
Account	☐	Account	ACCOUNT
Entity	☐	Entity	ENTITY
HSP_View	☐	Generic	UD2
Period	☐	Period	
Product	☐	Generic	UD3
Scenario	☐	Scenario	
Version	☐	Version	UD1
Years	☐	Year	

3. If all dimensions are not listed in Dimension Details, add a new row to include the missing dimension. Data Management reads the dimensions from PBCS and assigns the Target Dimension Class and Data Table Column Name.

4. Define or update the appropriate Target Dimension Class and Data Table Column Name using the magnifying glass icon if it doesn't match the above image.

A *Target Dimension Class* is a property that is defined by the dimension type. For example, dimensions with months rolling to quarters and Year correspond to the Period dimension class. Account dimensions correspond to the Account dimension class, and so forth. Generic classes are used for most Custom dimensions. The dimension classes Employee, Position, Job Code, Budget Item, and Element are all used for Public Sector Budgeting (ignore these for PBCS). You can add or update the assigned Target Dimension Class. Valid Target Dimension classes are shown below:

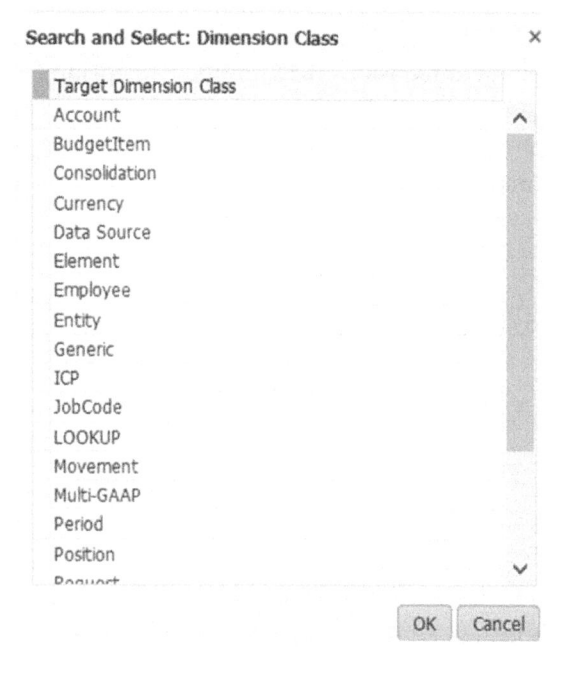

```
Search and Select: Dimension Class            ×

Target Dimension Class
  Account
  BudgetItem
  Consolidation
  Currency
  Data Source
  Element
  Employee
  Entity
  Generic
  ICP
  JobCode
  LOOKUP
  Movement
  Multi-GAAP
  Period
  Position
  Product

                               OK    Cancel
```

5. Make sure Entity is tagged as *Entity* (and not Country).
6. Make sure Years is tagged as *Year*.

The *Data Table Column Name* is the name of the column in the Data Management staging table where the dimension value is stored.

7. Set the Account dimension to *Account* for the Data Column Name, the Entity dimension to *Entity*, and the rest of the dimensions to UD*x*.

ICP (Intercompany Partner) does not apply for PBCS. You can either type in the Data Column Name or click the *Search* icon to select it:

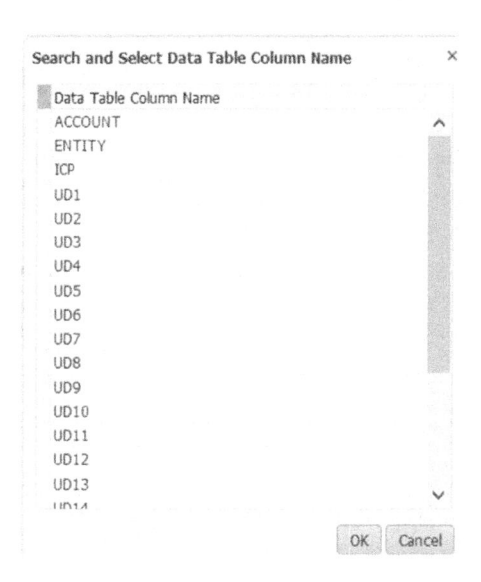

```
Search and Select Data Table Column Name        ×

Data Table Column Name
ACCOUNT
ENTITY
ICP
UD1
UD2
UD3
UD4
UD5
UD6
UD7
UD8
UD9
UD10
UD11
UD12
UD13
UD14

                                    OK    Cancel
```

Do not specify a Data Table Column Name for the Year, Period, or Scenario dimensions. These should be left blank since those members are defined by the POV.

8. Select the *Application Options* tab to review and define parameters for Load Method, Batch Size, Drill Region, and Date Format (leave all as default):

Chapter 5: Integrate Data

Property Name	Value	Select
Load Method	Numeric Data Only	
Batch Size	10000	
Drill Region	No	
Date Format	MM-DD-YYYY	

Load Method is the type of data load that will be completed. There are two methods available: *numeric* and *all data types with security*. The "numeric" load method allows only numeric data to be loaded and ignores Planning data security. The "all data types with security" data load option allows all Planning data types to be loaded: numeric, Smart List, text, and date. If a non-administrator loads data using this method, only up to 500,000 rows can be loaded and Planning security is enforced.

Batch Size is the batch size used to write data to files (the default is 10,000). Batch size is covered above under System Settings. *Drill Region*, if marked "Yes," is used for drill through.

Date Format allows you to specify a specific format for the date data. The following options are available:

- DD-MM-YYYY
- MM-DD-YYYY
- YYYY-MM-DD

Use *Refresh Metadata* to synchronize application metadata from the target application and display any new dimensions (important if you add a new dimension). Use *Refresh Members* to synchronize members from target dimensions (important when you need to update mappings):

Look Smarter Than You Are with PBCS 165

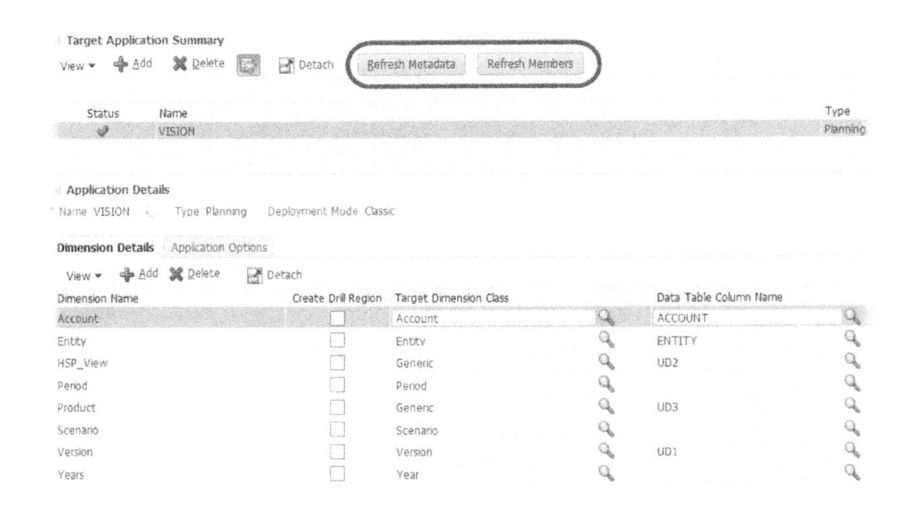

9. Click *Save*.

Since the Vision application has already been defined, let's create a target application for the SalesRpt ASO cube.

Note! Target applications can only be created once per Planning cube or Essbase database. Custom applications can have multiple target applications attached to them. If you ever need to delete a target application, select it and click ✖. All data load rules associated with it are also deleted.

To add the SalesRpt Target application,

1. Click ✚ under Target Application Summary and select *Local*.
2. Select *Essbase* as the Type:

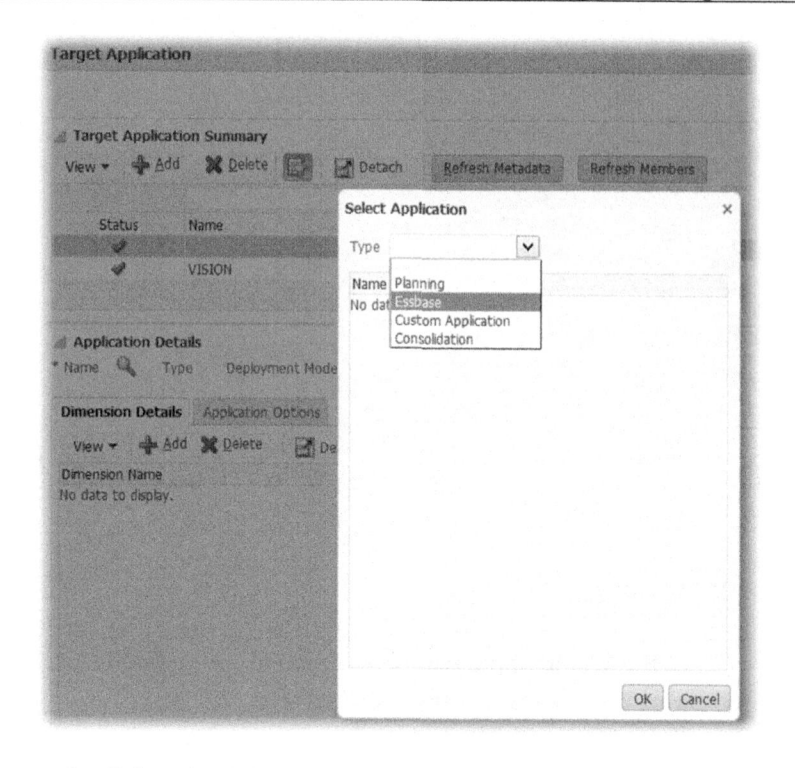

3. Select the ASO application name, *AVISION-SalesRpt*:

4. Click *OK*.

Many of the Dimension Details populate automatically, but they may not be correct.

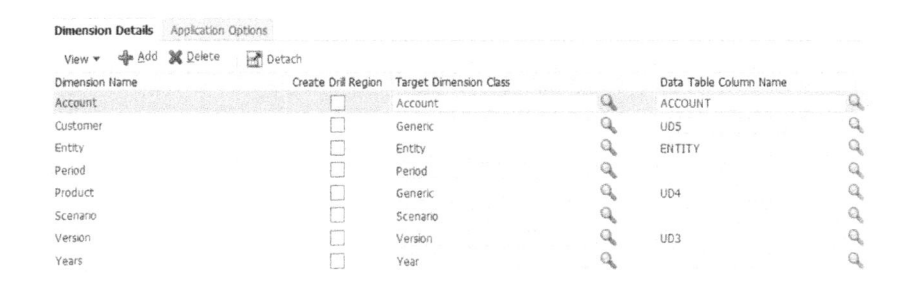

Dimension Name	Create Drill Region	Target Dimension Class	Data Table Column Name
Account	☐	Account	ACCOUNT
Customer	☐	Generic	UD5
Entity	☐	Entity	ENTITY
Period	☐	Period	
Product	☐	Generic	UD4
Scenario	☐	Scenario	
Version	☐	Version	UD3
Years	☐	Year	

5. Set *Entity* Dimension Name to *Entity* Target Dimension Class and *Entity* Data Table Column Name.
6. Set *Version* Dimension Name to *Version* Target Dimension Class and *UDx* Data Table Column Name.
7. Set *Scenario* Dimension Name to *Scenario* Target Dimension Class.
8. Ensure that Years, Period, and Scenario Dimension Names do not specify a Data Table Column Name. These should be left blank since those members are defined by the POV:

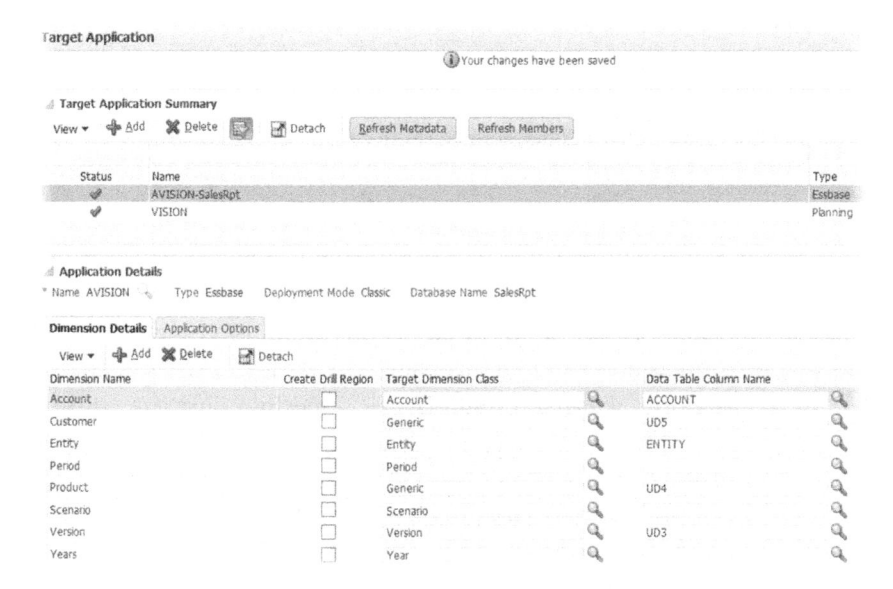

Target Application

Your changes have been saved

Target Application Summary

Status	Name	Type
✓	AVISION-SalesRpt	Essbase
✓	VISION	Planning

Application Details

* Name AVISION   Type Essbase   Deployment Mode Classic   Database Name SalesRpt

Dimension Details

Dimension Name	Create Drill Region	Target Dimension Class	Data Table Column Name
Account	☐	Account	ACCOUNT
Customer	☐	Generic	UD5
Entity	☐	Entity	ENTITY
Period	☐	Period	
Product	☐	Generic	UD4
Scenario	☐	Scenario	
Version	☐	Version	UD3
Years	☐	Year	

9. Click *Save* to save the target application.

168   Chapter 5: Integrate Data

One last note for now – a custom application target is used to export data from PBCS. I'll cover this in the Export section in just a bit.

Define Import Format

The import format defines which columns are extracted from the source system, how the data is stored in the Data Management staging table, and import mapping information.

To define the import format,
1. Under the Integration Setup section within the Setup tab, click *Import Format*.

The Import Format Screen consists of three sections:

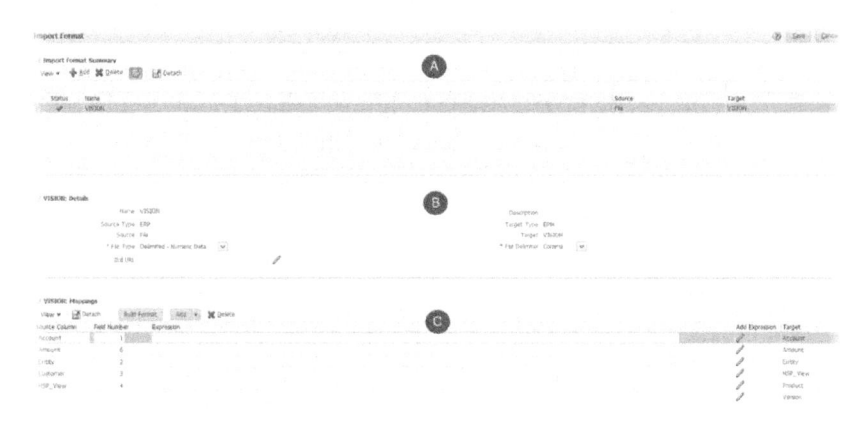

[screenshot of Import Format screen with sections labeled A, B, C]

A. **Import Format Summary** – lists the import formats and details about source and target applications; new import formats are added in this pane
B. **Import Format Details** – specific import format configurations: name, source and target information, file type, drill through, etc.
C. **Import Format Mappings** – maps source file columns to target dimensions, as well as data columns

PBCS creates an import format by default for the BSO cube. Select the *VISION* import format and review the import format details. I could use this import format but I'll create a new import format so you can see the process from start to finish.

2. Click ✚ to add an import format.
3. Under Details, name the import format "Load Vision Actuals".
4. For the Source, select *Vision Data File* from the drop down menu.
5. Specify the File Type as *Multi Column – Numeric Data* to match the load file format:
6. For Target, select *VISION*.

```
Load Vision Actuals: Details
         Name   Load Vision Actuals              Description
       Source   Vision Data File                      Target  VISION
  * File Type   Multi Column - Numeric Data   * File Delimiter  Comma
    Drill URL
```

7. Click *Save*. Note that until you save the new import format, Mappings appear to be blank.

The file that I am going to load has multiple data columns which is why I chose *Multi Column – Numeric Data* for the File Type. Other valid options are:

- *Fixed (Numeric or All Data Type)* – for set column widths for single period loads; uses fixed character lengths
- *Delimited (Numeric or All Data Type)* – for variable column widths for single period loads; uses delimiters like commas
- *Multi Column (Numeric or All Data Type)* – for variable column widths for multiple data columns (like periods); uses delimiters like commas

The Fixed and Delimited options are best used when loading a single period. Multi Column is best used when loading multiple periods or any other type of multiple data column file. The "numeric" option indicates that the data loaded are all numeric. The "all data type" option allows for text, date, and Smart List data to be loaded:

Load Vision Actuals: Details

Name	Load Vision Actuals	Description	
Source	Vision Data File	Target	VISION
*File Type	Multi Column - Numeric Data	*File Delimiter	Comma
Drill URL	Fixed - Numeric Data		
	Delimited - Numeric Data		
	Multi Column - Numeric Data		
	Delimited - All Data Type		
	Fixed - All Data Type		
	Multi Column - All Data Type		

Supported delimiters are:

- comma (,)
- exclamation (!)
- semicolon (;)
- colon (:)
- pipe (|)
- tab

I'm going to use the Import Format Builder to help build my definition. The Import Format Builder supports both Fixed and Delimited files (though it does not support tab-delimited files).

8. Select *Build Format*.

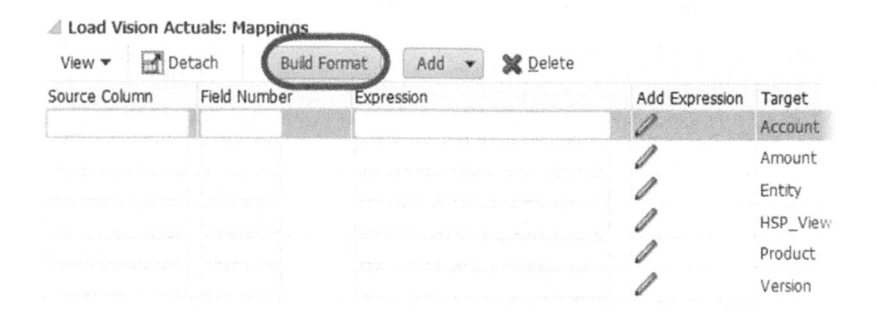

Load Vision Actuals: Mappings

View ▼ | Detach | **Build Format** | Add ▼ | ✖ Delete

Source Column	Field Number	Expression	Add Expression	Target
			✎	Account
			✎	Amount
			✎	Entity
			✎	HSP_View
			✎	Product
			✎	Version

9. Select *Upload* then *Browse…* to find and upload the file.
10. Browse and select the "Vision_Actual_Dollars_FY14.csv" file.
11. Click *OK*:

Look Smarter Than You Are with PBCS 171

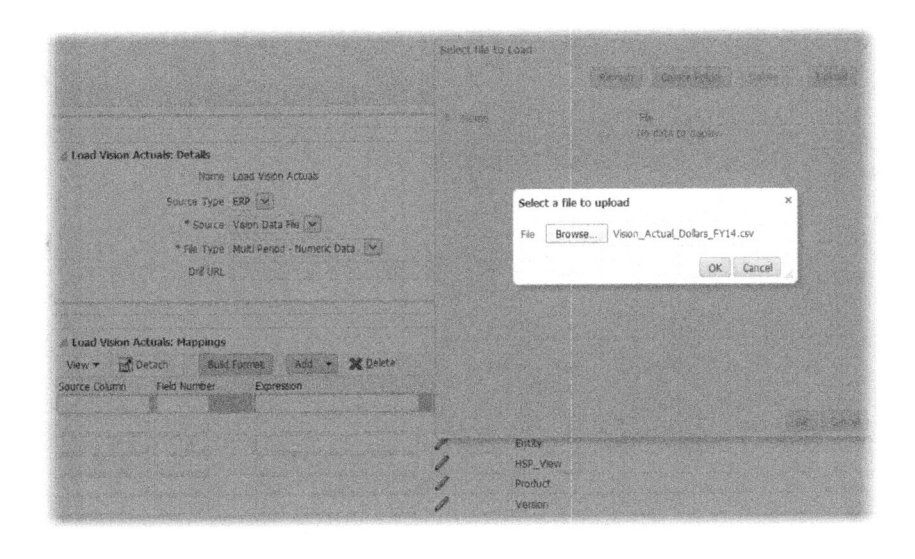

12. Select the file and click *OK*:

13. The Import Format Builder displays:

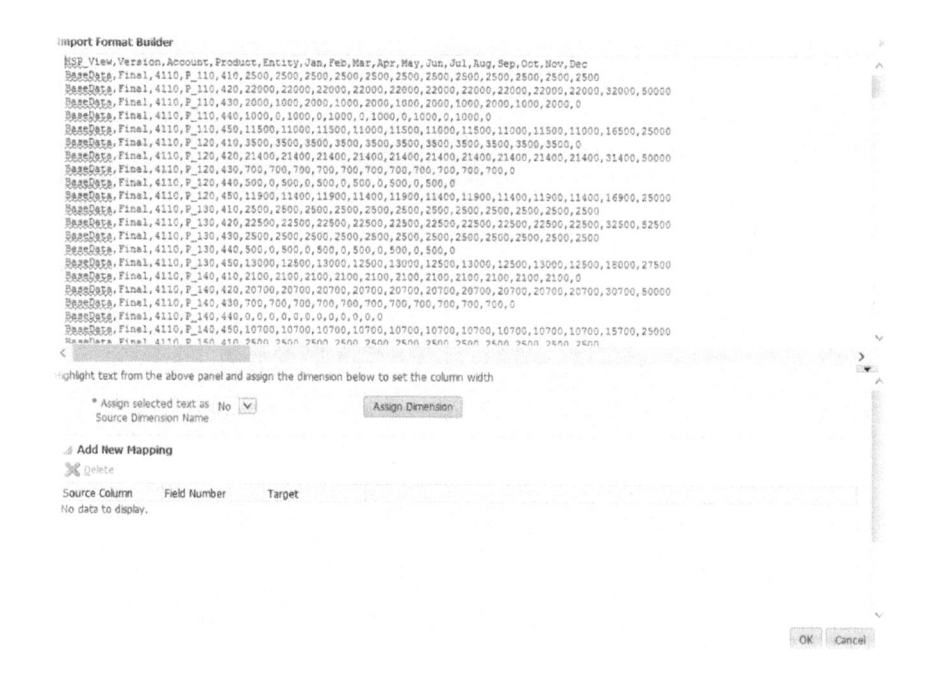

14. Select *HSP_View* text.
15. Set *Assign selected text as Source Dimension Name* to *Yes*.
16. Click *Assign Dimension*:

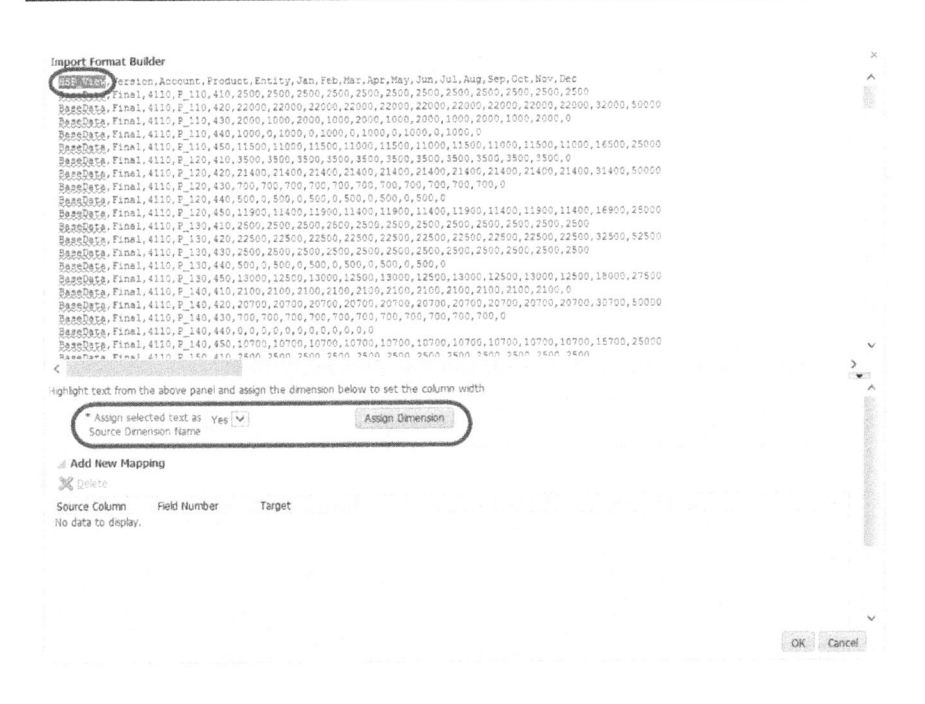

17. Make sure *Source Dimension Name* is set to *HSP_View*.
18. Set the *Target Dimension* to *HSP_View*.
19. Leave *Field Number* as 1.
20. Click *OK*:

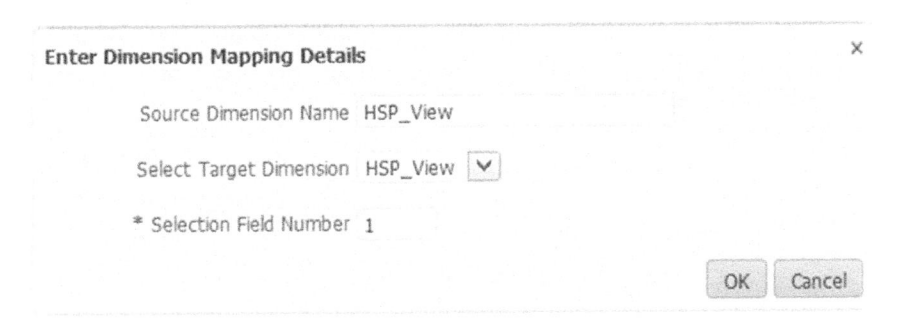

21. The first mapping row is added:

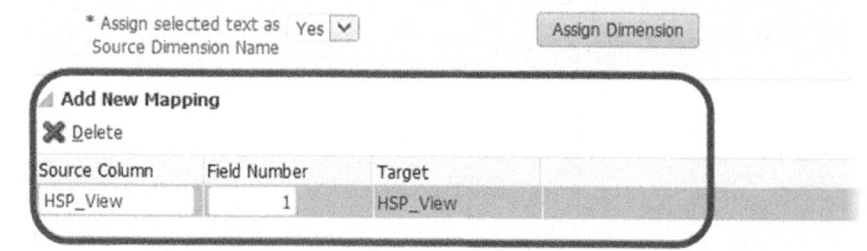

Chapter 5: Integrate Data

Highlight text from the above panel and assign the dimension below to set the column width

* Assign selected text as Source Dimension Name: Yes

[Assign Dimension]

Add New Mapping
✖ Delete

Source Column	Field Number	Target
HSP_View	1	HSP_View

22. Select *Version* text.
23. Set *Assign selected text as Source Dimension Name* to *Yes*.
24. Click *Assign Dimension*:

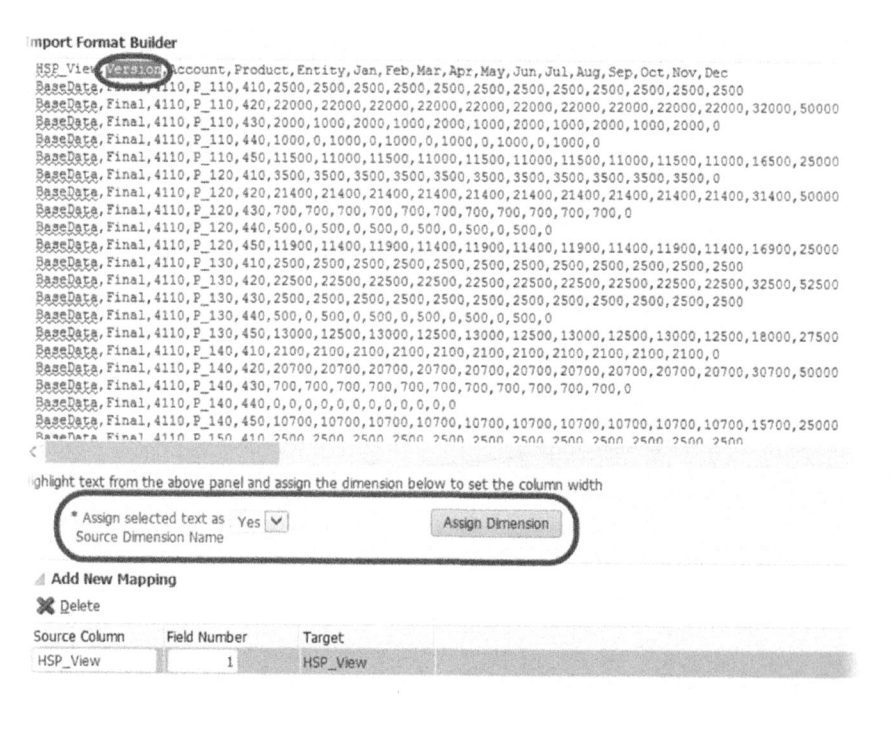

Import Format Builder

```
HSP_View  Version  ccount,Product,Entity,Jan,Feb,Mar,Apr,May,Jun,Jul,Aug,Sep,Oct,Nov,Dec
BaseData, Final, 4110, P_110, 410, 2500, 2500, 2500, 2500, 2500, 2500, 2500, 2500, 2500, 2500, 2500, 2500
BaseData, Final, 4110, P_110, 420, 22000, 22000, 22000, 22000, 22000, 22000, 22000, 22000, 22000, 22000, 32000, 50000
BaseData, Final, 4110, P_110, 430, 2000, 1000, 2000, 1000, 2000, 1000, 2000, 1000, 2000, 1000, 2000, 0
BaseData, Final, 4110, P_110, 440, 1000, 0, 1000, 0, 1000, 0, 1000, 0, 1000, 0, 1000, 0
BaseData, Final, 4110, P_110, 450, 11500, 11000, 11500, 11000, 11500, 11000, 11500, 11000, 11500, 11000, 16500, 25000
BaseData, Final, 4110, P_120, 410, 3500, 3500, 3500, 3500, 3500, 3500, 3500, 3500, 3500, 3500, 3500, 0
BaseData, Final, 4110, P_120, 420, 21400, 21400, 21400, 21400, 21400, 21400, 21400, 21400, 21400, 21400, 31400, 50000
BaseData, Final, 4110, P_120, 430, 700, 700, 700, 700, 700, 700, 700, 700, 700, 700, 700, 0
BaseData, Final, 4110, P_120, 440, 500, 0, 500, 0, 500, 0, 500, 0, 500, 0
BaseData, Final, 4110, P_120, 450, 11900, 11400, 11900, 11400, 11900, 11400, 11900, 11400, 11900, 11400, 16900, 25000
BaseData, Final, 4110, P_130, 410, 2500, 2500, 2500, 2500, 2500, 2500, 2500, 2500, 2500, 2500, 2500
BaseData, Final, 4110, P_130, 420, 22500, 22500, 22500, 22500, 22500, 22500, 22500, 22500, 22500, 22500, 32500, 52500
BaseData, Final, 4110, P_130, 430, 2500, 2500, 2500, 2500, 2500, 2500, 2500, 2500, 2500, 2500, 2500
BaseData, Final, 4110, P_130, 440, 500, 0, 500, 0, 500, 0, 500, 0, 500, 0
BaseData, Final, 4110, P_130, 450, 13000, 12500, 13000, 12500, 13000, 12500, 13000, 12500, 13000, 12500, 18000, 27500
BaseData, Final, 4110, P_140, 410, 2100, 2100, 2100, 2100, 2100, 2100, 2100, 2100, 2100, 2100, 2100, 0
BaseData, Final, 4110, P_140, 420, 20700, 20700, 20700, 20700, 20700, 20700, 20700, 20700, 20700, 20700, 30700, 50000
BaseData, Final, 4110, P_140, 430, 700, 700, 700, 700, 700, 700, 700, 700, 700, 700, 700, 0
BaseData, Final, 4110, P_140, 440, 0, 0, 0, 0, 0, 0, 0, 0, 0, 0
BaseData, Final, 4110, P_140, 450, 10700, 10700, 10700, 10700, 10700, 10700, 10700, 10700, 10700, 10700, 15700, 25000
BaseData, Final, 4110, P_150, 410, 2500, 2500, 2500, 2500, 2500, 2500, 2500, 2500, 2500, 2500, 2500
```

Highlight text from the above panel and assign the dimension below to set the column width

* Assign selected text as Source Dimension Name: Yes

[Assign Dimension]

Add New Mapping
✖ Delete

Source Column	Field Number	Target
HSP_View	1	HSP_View

25. Make sure *Source Dimension Name* is set to *Version*.
26. Set the *Target Dimension* to *Version*.
27. Leave *Field Number* as "2".

28. Click *OK*:

Enter Dimension Mapping Details

Source Dimension Name Version

Select Target Dimension Version

* Selection Field Number 2

OK   Cancel

29. Repeat the same steps to define the remaining mapping rows through Entity, selecting the Target Dimension that matches the Source Dimension Name for each field.

This is what things should look like so far:

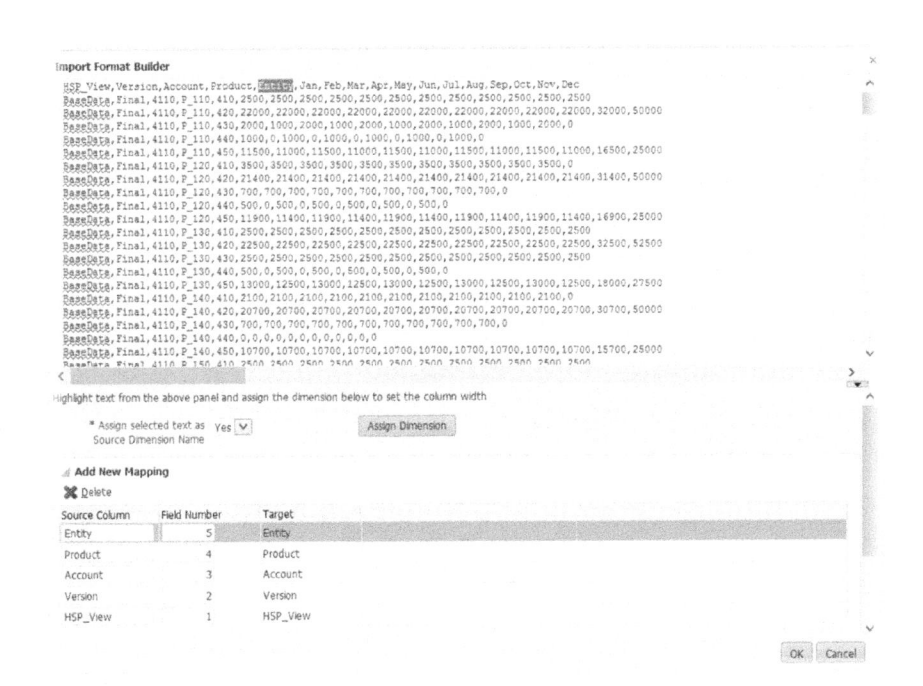

```
Import Format Builder
HSP_View,Version,Account,Product,Entity,Jan,Feb,Mar,Apr,May,Jun,Jul,Aug,Sep,Oct,Nov,Dec
BaseData,Final,4110,P_110,410,2500,2500,2500,2500,2500,2500,2500,2500,2500,2500,2500,2500
BaseData,Final,4110,P_110,420,22000,22000,22000,22000,22000,22000,22000,22000,22000,22000,32000,50000
BaseData,Final,4110,P_110,430,2000,1000,2000,1000,2000,1000,2000,1000,2000,1000,2000,0
BaseData,Final,4110,P_110,440,1000,0,1000,0,1000,0,1000,0,1000,0,1000,0
BaseData,Final,4110,P_110,450,11500,11000,11500,11000,11500,11000,11500,11000,11500,11000,16500,25000
BaseData,Final,4110,P_120,410,3500,3500,3500,3500,3500,3500,3500,3500,3500,3500,3500,0
BaseData,Final,4110,P_120,420,21400,21400,21400,21400,21400,21400,21400,21400,21400,21400,31400,50000
BaseData,Final,4110,P_120,430,700,700,700,700,700,700,700,700,700,700,700,0
BaseData,Final,4110,P_120,440,500,0,500,0,500,0,500,0,500,0,500,0
BaseData,Final,4110,P_120,450,11900,11400,11900,11400,11900,11400,11900,11400,11900,11400,16900,25000
BaseData,Final,4110,P_130,410,2500,2500,2500,2500,2500,2500,2500,2500,2500,2500,2500,2500
BaseData,Final,4110,P_130,420,22500,22500,22500,22500,22500,22500,22500,22500,22500,22500,32500,52500
BaseData,Final,4110,P_130,430,2500,2500,2500,2500,2500,2500,2500,2500,2500,2500,2500,2500
BaseData,Final,4110,P_130,440,500,0,500,0,500,0,500,0,500,0
BaseData,Final,4110,P_130,450,13000,12500,13000,12500,13000,12500,13000,12500,13000,12500,18000,27500
BaseData,Final,4110,P_140,410,2100,2100,2100,2100,2100,2100,2100,2100,2100,2100,2100,0
BaseData,Final,4110,P_140,420,20700,20700,20700,20700,20700,20700,20700,20700,20700,20700,30700,50000
BaseData,Final,4110,P_140,430,700,700,700,700,700,700,700,700,700,700,700,0
BaseData,Final,4110,P_140,440,0,0,0,0,0,0,0,0,0,0,0,0
BaseData,Final,4110,P_140,450,10700,10700,10700,10700,10700,10700,10700,10700,10700,10700,15700,25000
BaseData,Final,4110,P_150,410,2500,2500,2500,2500,2500,2500,2500,2500,2500,2500,2500,2500
```

Highlight text from the above panel and assign the dimension below to set the column width

* Assign selected text as Yes   Assign Dimension
Source Dimension Name

Add New Mapping

✕ Delete

Source Column	Field Number	Target
Entity	5	Entity
Product	4	Product
Account	3	Account
Version	2	Version
HSP_View	1	HSP_View

OK   Cancel

30. When you get to the columns containing the values by month, select all of the months:

Import Format Builder

```
HSP_View,Version,Account,Product,Entity,Jan,Feb,Mar,Apr,May,Jun,Jul,Aug,Sep,Oct,Nov,Dec
BaseData,Final,4110,P_110,410,2500,2500,2500,2500,2500,2500,2500,2500,2500,2500,2500,2500
BaseData,Final,4110,P_110,420,22000,22000,22000,22000,22000,22000,22000,22000,22000,22000,32000,5000
BaseData,Final,4110,P_110,430,2000,1000,2000,1000,2000,1000,2000,1000,2000,1000,2000,0
BaseData,Final,4110,P_110,440,1000,0,1000,0,1000,0,1000,0,1000,0,1000,0
BaseData,Final,4110,P_110,450,11500,11000,11500,11000,11500,11000,11500,11000,11500,11000,16500,2500
BaseData,Final,4110,P_120,410,3500,3500,3500,3500,3500,3500,3500,3500,3500,3500,3500,0
BaseData,Final,4110,P_120,420,21400,21400,21400,21400,21400,21400,21400,21400,21400,21400,31400,5000
BaseData,Final,4110,P_120,430,700,700,700,700,700,700,700,700,700,700,700,0
```

31. Set *Assign selected text as Source Dimension Name* to *No*.
32. Click *Assign Dimension*.
33. Type "Amount" for the *Source Dimension Name*, set the *Target Dimension* to *Amount*, set the *Selection Field Number* to "6".
34. Click *OK*:

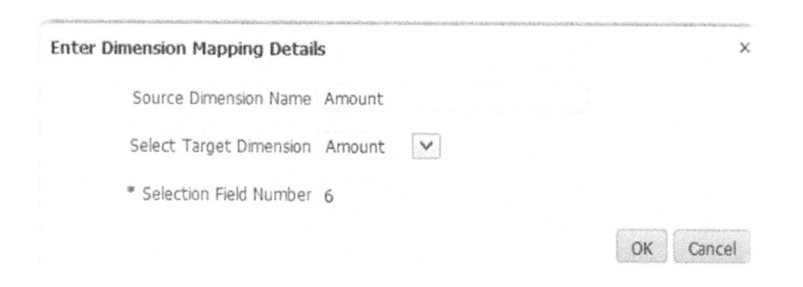

Enter Dimension Mapping Details

Source Dimension Name   Amount

Select Target Dimension   Amount

* Selection Field Number   6

OK   Cancel

The end result should look as follows:

Add New Mapping
Delete

Source Column	Field Number	Target
Amount	6	Amount
Entity	5	Entity
Product	4	Product
Account	3	Account
Version	2	Version
HSP View	1	HSP View

OK   Cancel

35. Click *OK* to add the new mapping.
36. The final step is to use an expression to identify the Amount columns. Type "Column=6,17" to specify Column 6 as the first data number and Column 17 as the last data number:

Load Vision Actuals: Details				
Name	Load Vision Actuals		Description	
Source Type	ERP		Target Type	EPM
*Source	Vision Data File		*Target	VISION
*File Type	Multi Period - Numeric Data		*File Delimiter	Comma
Drill URL				

Load Vision Actuals: Mappings

View ▼ Detach Build Format Add ▼ ✖ Delete

Source Column	Field Number	Expression	Add Expression	Target
Account	3			Account
Amount	6	Column=6,17		Amount
Entity	5			Entity
HSP_View	1			HSP_View
Product	4			Product
Version	2			Version

Make sure there are no spaces in your expressions or you will receive an error message.

37. Click *Save* to save the import format.

Note that I did not define Scenario, Period, or Year. Scenario is defined in the Category mapping. Period and Year are defined in the POV upon data load rule execution.

Import file formats support a number of expressions which are helpful for reading and parsing data files. Supported expressions include:

- Conversion of nonstandard numeric signs
- Conversion from European to US notation
- Padding fields with leading fills
- Padding fields with trailing fills
- Multiplying by whole number and decimal factors
- Disabling zero suppression

For file-based mappings you can add a mapping row to define additional specifications for the import file. You can define:

- **Skip** – to skip rows with no data or zeros or specific accounts

- **Attribute** – load up to 13 additional attributes to the staging table which can be helpful in drill through and for documentation purposes
- **Description** – load up two description columns
- **Currency** – load data in currency other than the default currency
- **Dimension** – allows you to concatenate fields for file-based data; to use this option, select the dimension, start and end positions, and the expression

You can concatenate source system fields as needed to map to a target dimension. While I did not use these features, it is good for you to know they exist. Check out the Oracle *Administering Data Management for Oracle Enterprise Performance Management Cloud* online documentation for more information.

Define Location

Locations associate Import Format with Target Application, and combines mapping and data load rules for Target.

Important information about a location:

- A location has one source system
- A location is assigned one import format
- A location is assigned one or more data load rules
- A location is assigned one data load mapping
- A location is the level at which a data load is executed
- Duplicate locations with the same source system and target application are allowed
- You can create different locations that use the same import format where the target application and dimensionality are the same
- Parent locations are supported. You can define mappings at a parent location and the related or "children" locations use those mappings. Use this feature when you have multiple locations loading data using the same chart of accounts

- A location can be assigned a logic account group (a logic account group contains one or more logic accounts that are generated when a source file is loaded; logic accounts are calculated accounts derived from source data)
- Security can be applied to locations and are enabled under Security Settings. Location security allows a Service Administrator to assign users to specific Data Management Locations through user groups with a view to securing data and mapping rules for a user or a group of users

You can also enable free form text using Data Management scripts in locations.

To set up a location,
1. Under Integration Setup in the Setup tab, click *Location*:

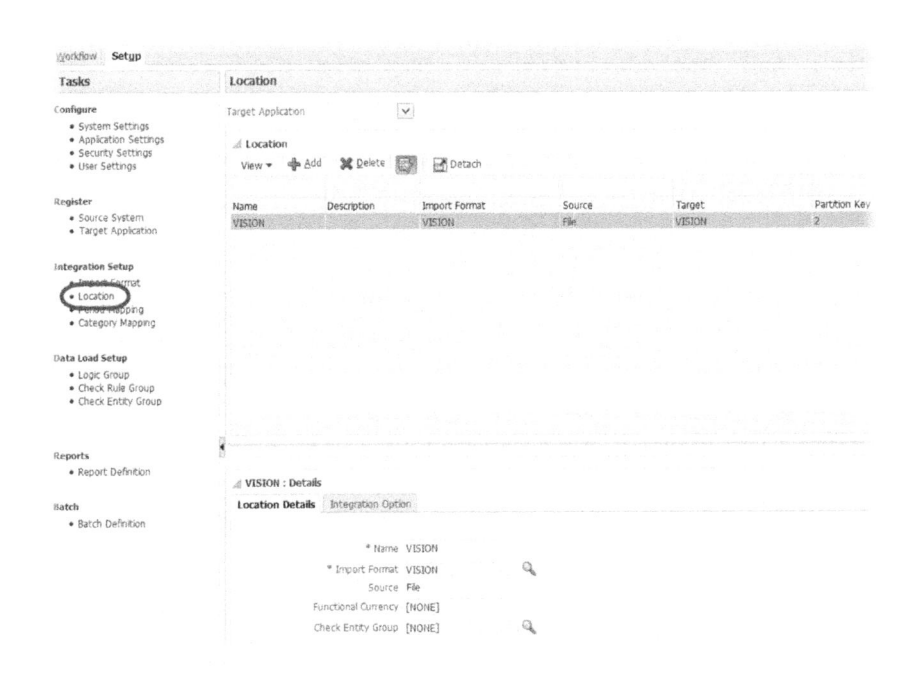

2. Click ✚ to create a new location.

180   Chapter 5: Integrate Data

3. Enter the following Location details, leaving some of these settings to default to [NONE] or blank (e.g., *Accounting Entity* is used for ERP loads from Fusion or E-Business Suite; the default behavior for *Check Entity Group* is to run for each entity):

```
: Details
Location Details   Integration Option

         * Name  VisionSales_Loc                    Description
         * Import Format  Load Vision Actuals       Parent Location
              Source  Vision Data File             Target   VISION
         Functional Currency  [NONE]               Logic Account Group  [NONE]
         Check Entity Group  [NONE]                Check Rule Group  [NONE]
```

4. Click *Save*.

LOG ENTRY: SOL 14, Entry 1

I keep asking myself… why is the Save button all the way at the top in Data Management? Why aren't Finn and Rachel together? Why did Notorious B.I.G. have to leave us so soon?
   I think being isolated in the Cloud with Data Management, Glee, and McMullen's '90s hip hop music is getting to me.

Define Period Mapping

Period mappings define the mapping of ERP calendars and EPM application year and periods. Period mappings may be defined in a global mapping, application mapping, or source mapping. Use *Global Mapping* when your target applications get data from sources with calendar definitions. If you are loading data from multiple sources with varying complex calendar definitions, use *Application Mapping*. *Source Mapping* is used for adapter-based integrations, which are not available for PBCS.

To define a period mapping,
1. Under Integration Setup in the Setup tab, click *Period Mapping*:

In the Global Mapping tab, all entries should be populated with the years specified at application creation (in my case, FY10 to FY20). The Period Key and Prior Period Key fields are not relevant to PBCS applications. I will focus on the Target Period Month and Year Target:

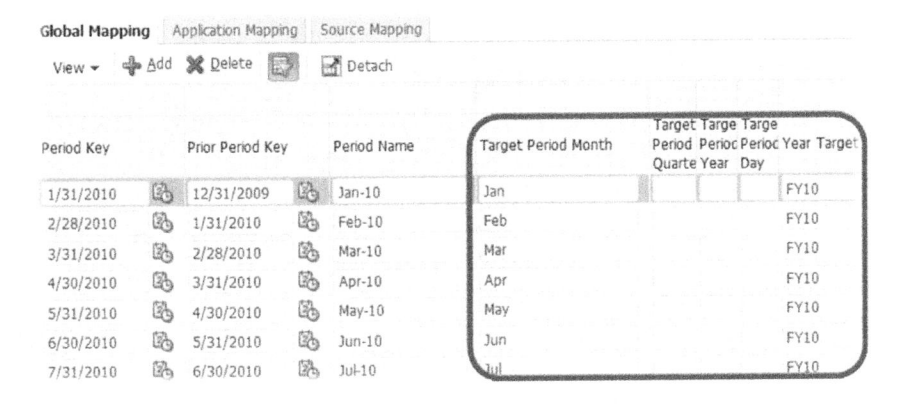

2. Ensure that all target months and years match up to the *Period Name*.
3. Press *Save* when done.

Define Category Mapping

Category mappings map scenarios from source systems to targets. For example, your ERP system might use "Budget" scenario but in PBCS you have a "Plan" member. You would define a category mapping to match these two elements.

Global Mapping defines mappings that cross multiple applications (so you only have to set them once). Most of the time "Actual" from a source maps to "Actual" in a Target. This is a good candidate for a global category mapping.

Application Mapping defines category mappings that are specific for a target application.

I will define my category mappings as global.

To define a category mapping,
1. Under Integration Setup in the Setup tab, click *Category Mapping*.
2. In the Global Mapping tab, click ✛ to enter a new row.
3. Enter *Category* as "Actual", *Frequency* as "Monthly", and *Target Category* as "Actual".
4. Enter *Category* as "Forecast", *Frequency* as "Monthly", and *Target Category* as "Forecast".
5. Enter *Category* as "Plan", *Frequency* as "Monthly", and *Target Category* as "Plan".
6. If you see any other rows (e.g., "Current"), delete them. Your screen should look like the following:

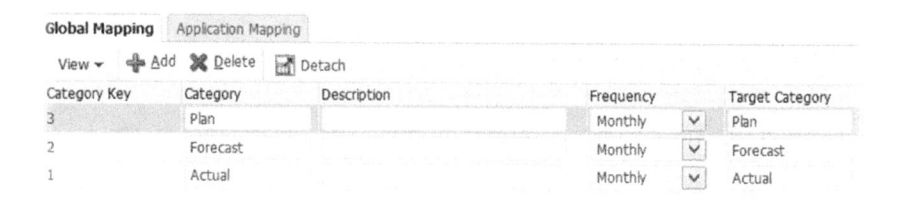

Category Key	Category	Description	Frequency	Target Category
3	Plan		Monthly	Plan
2	Forecast		Monthly	Forecast
1	Actual		Monthly	Actual

7. Click *Save* (at the top of the screen).

> LOG ENTRY: SOL 14, Entry 2
>
> Finally the setup is complete! Can I load data? No. Not yet. Ugh. Now that I think about it, the first time I created a data load in Essbase that also seemed to have a million steps. I'll be patient as I complete this first data load.
> Maybe.

Define Data Load Mapping

I now will switch to the Workflow section, where I will define member maps and data load rules.

Member maps are defined in Data Load Mapping. I must map members for all target dimensions. Member mappings are used during the data load process to load data to the appropriate members in the target dimension. This is where I can map or transform data from the source to the target (e.g., if I have five GL accounts that I would like to map into one summary PBCS account, I define that mapping here).

You will not map Period or Scenario dimensions because you already did that in the Setup section under Period Mapping and Category Mapping.

Valid member mapping types include:

- **Explicit** – source value is matched exactly and replaced with the target member value (e.g., your source file has a column with values "current" and you want to load that to "Final" version member in the Version dimension)
- **Between** – range of source values is replaced with one target member value (e.g., I want to specify accounts 6000-6999 should be loaded to "COGS" member in PBCS)
- **In** – list of source accounts to be mapped to one target member value
- **Multi-Dimension** – define a member mapping based on multiple column values (e.g., you are combining Cost Center column and Department column to map to Entity dimension members in PBCS)

- **Like** – string in the source value is matched and replaced with target member value

Special characters to be used in Like mappings:

Special Character	How to Use	Example / Use Cases
Asterisk (*) Wildcard	Represents source value; you can add a prefix or suffix	Use when source members match target members exactly – use * to *; for example, A* would take source value "6001" and load to member "A6001"
Question Mark (?) Wildcard	Strips a single character from a source value; you will probably use this in an expression	?* would take source value "A6001" and load to member "6001"
<1> returns first concatenated segment, <2> returns second concatenated segment, <3> returns third concatenated segment, and so on… <4>, <5>	Processes rows that have concatenated values separated by an underscore "_" and extracts corresponding value; can use with ? but not *	<2> would take source value "A_6001" and load to member "6001"
<BLANK>	Processes only rows that contain spaces; use to map to "No_XXX" members in the target In on-premise FDMEE, <BLANK> does not recognize an actual blank; it only recognizes a space	<BLANK> as source and "No_Product" would load any rows with blank values to "No_Product" member

Multiple mappings might apply to a specific source value. Within each mapping type (except for Explicit), mapping is evaluated in alphabetical order according to Rule Name.

Format masks are also supported in Data Management mappings (available for all mapping types except Explicit). You might use #FORMAT when replacing segments from the source value, replacing segments with string operations, and replacing segments with string operations using prefixes or suffixes. For example, a source value might look like "ABC-6001" and you want to load to a member, "ABC-Account-6001-Expense". Using the format mask syntax with special characters generates this result.

To ignore a member mapping, select the source value and then in *Target Value*, enter "IGNORE". Data is not loaded for any source values defined with IGNORE mapping.

To create a data load mapping,
1. In the Workflow tab, click *Data Load Mapping*:

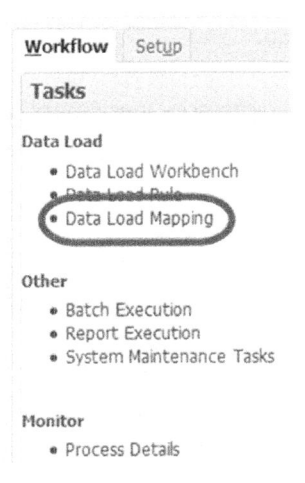

```
Workflow    Setup

Tasks

Data Load
   • Data Load Workbench
   • Data Load Rule
   • Data Load Mapping

Other
   • Batch Execution
   • Report Execution
   • System Maintenance Tasks

Monitor
   • Process Details
```

2. At the bottom of the screen, choose the Location just created, *VisionSales_Loc*. Change the period and category to match the image below:

Chapter 5: Integrate Data

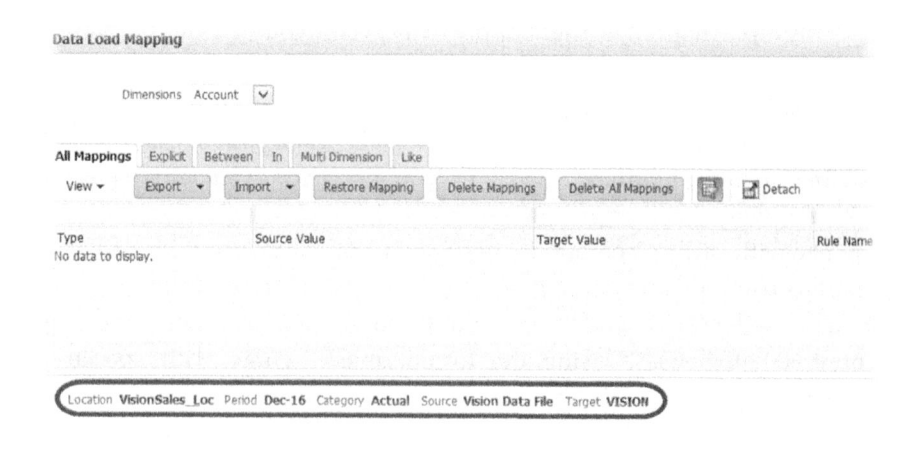

Now I need to complete the appropriate mappings for each target dimension.

3. Choose the *Account* dimension from the drop down list near the top of the Data Load Mapping screen.
4. Select the *Like* tab.

Note! Data Management processes these mappings from left to right: *Explicit* first, then *Between*, *In*, *Multi Dimensional*, and then *Like*.

5. Click ✚ to add a row into the mapping (note that you can add multiple rows in a mapping for Like, if requirements dictate; you can also delete rows).
6. Enter "*" as both the *Source Value* and *Target Value*, call the *Rule Name* "DirectMapAccount", and *Description* "All accounts should load no mapping required":

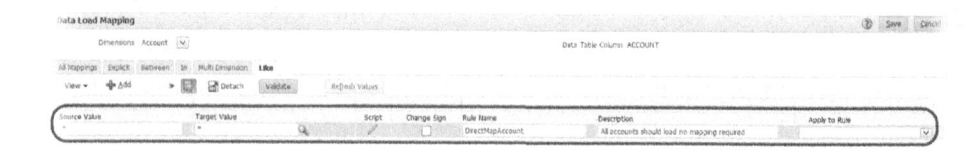

Note! The "Rule Name" name is a misnomer in Data Management. This is actually a name for the mapping created and it is unique across locations. Data Management processes these maps in alphabetical order after left to right based on operation, so the name you choose can be critical in the mapping process. Once a match is found then it maps and moves to the next record. Rule Names can handle numbers as well as text, so numbers can be used to force process order. Numbers, however, are processed as text.

7. Click *Save*.
8. Choose the *Entity* dimension from the drop down list.
9. Select the *Like* tab.
10. Click ✢ to add a row into the mapping.
11. Enter "*" as the *Source Value* and "*" as the *Target Value*, call the *Rule Name* "DirectMapEntity" and *Description* "All entities should load no mapping required":

12. Click *Save*.
13. Choose the *Product* dimension from the drop down list.
14. Select the *Like* tab.
15. Click ✢ to add a row into the mapping.
16. Enter "*" as the *Source Value* and "*" as the *Target Value*, call the *Rule Name* "DirectMapProduct", and *Description* "All products should load no mapping required":

188   Chapter 5: Integrate Data

17. Click *Save*.
18. Choose the *HSP_View* dimension from the drop down list.
19. Select the *Explicit* tab.
20. Click ✚ to add a row into the mapping.
21. Add "BaseData" as the *Source Value* and "BaseData" as the *Target Value* and add a description. I could have used the Like mapping as I did earlier, but I wanted to show you the steps for a different mapping method. I would use this if the source file had "Base Data" and I needed to map to "BaseData" in the target:

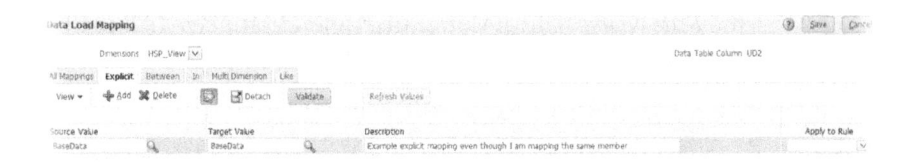

22. Click *Save*.
23. Choose the *Version* dimension from the drop down list.
24. Select the *Explicit* tab.
25. Click ✚ to add a row into the mapping.
26. Add "Final" as the *Source Value* and "Final" as the *Target Value* and add a description. As before, I could have used the *Like* mapping. I would use this if the source file had "Current" and I needed to map to "Final" in the target:

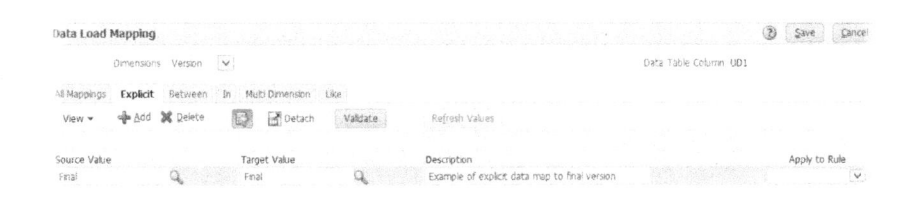

Once you're done, you can check all mappings in the *All Mappings* tab by cycling through each dimension in the drop down. All dimensions except Scenario, Period, and Years need to be mapped in this manner. This view is helpful because it is possible to combine mapping requirements (e.g., using *Explicit*, *Like,* and *Between*) for a single dimension. You can only view the mappings for a single dimension at a time.

Note! If you have mappings that are valid for many locations then it's recommended that you create a parent location and define the mappings there.

27. Click *Save*. Check that all dimensions in the drop down are mapped.

Export & Import Excel Mappings

Mappings may be updated in a more granular fashion via the Data Load Mapping interface in FDMEE, which allows exporting or importing maps for one or more dimensions.

To download an Excel Import Template, select *Import >> Download Excel Template*:

Chapter 5: Integrate Data

```
Data Load Mapping

            Dimensions  Version  [v]

All Mappings  Explicit  Between  In  Multi Dimension  Like
  View ▼     Export ▼    Import ▼    Restore Mapping
                         Current Dimension
  Type                   All Dimensions
  Explicit               Import From Excel
                         Download Excel Template
```

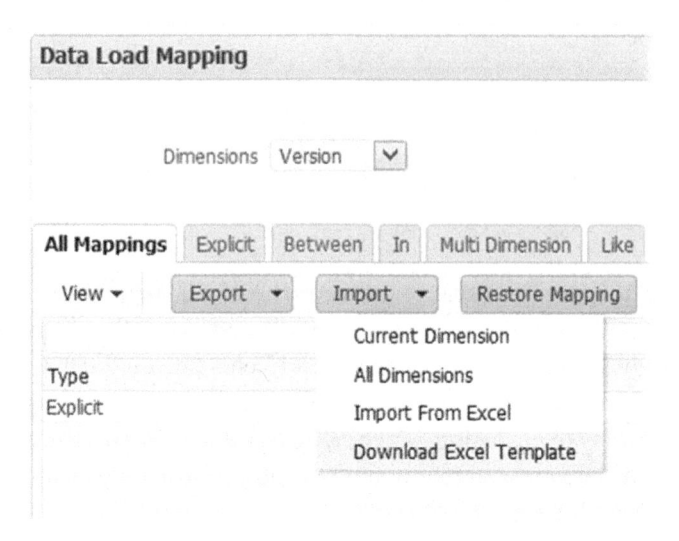

Here are some guidelines for creating the mapping template:

- Mapping templates may not have any blank lines
- Do not insert lines into the mapping template
- You may only have one mapping template per workbook
- Create a separate workbook for each dimension

Follow these additional instructions to complete your Excel mapping template:

Look Smarter Than You Are with PBCS 191

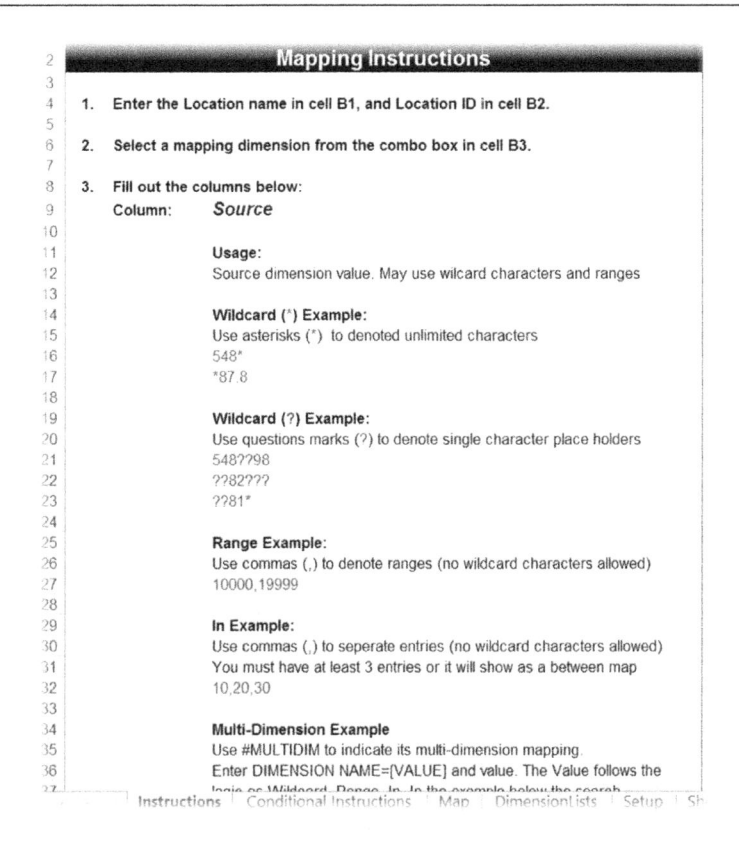

```
Mapping Instructions
1. Enter the Location name in cell B1, and Location ID in cell B2.
2. Select a mapping dimension from the combo box in cell B3.
3. Fill out the columns below:
   Column:   Source

             Usage:
             Source dimension value. May use wilcard characters and ranges

             Wildcard (*) Example:
             Use asterisks (*) to denoted unlimited characters
             548*
             *87.8

             Wildcard (?) Example:
             Use questions marks (?) to denote single character place holders
             548??98
             ??82???
             ??81*

             Range Example:
             Use commas (,) to denote ranges (no wildcard characters allowed)
             10000,19999

             In Example:
             Use commas (,) to seperate entries (no wildcard characters allowed)
             You must have at least 3 entries or it will show as a between map
             10,20,30

             Multi-Dimension Example
             Use #MULTIDIM to indicate its multi-dimension mapping.
             Enter DIMENSION NAME=[VALUE] and value. The Value follows the
```

Once the template is ready, you can import the Excel template with all mappings. Choose the dimension from the drop down list, then click *Import* >> *Import From Excel*:

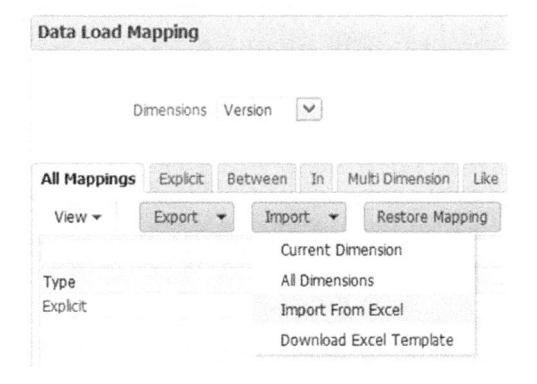

You'll specify the file and then define options to merge or replace mappings. You can also export existing mappings for a single dimension or all dimensions.

Exporting Mapping

To export a mapping, click *Export*:

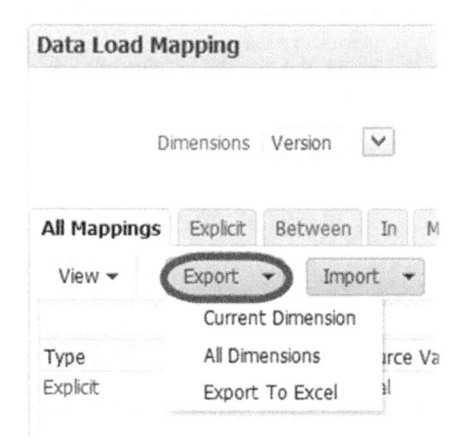

The following *Export* options are available: *Current Dimension* exports the current dimension for the current location (POV) to a comma-delimited flat file in the PBCS Home folder. When prompted, enter a file name (including .txt or .csv extension) and click *OK*. Then select the file from Home and click *Download* to download it locally. Other options from the Specify file location window include *Delete* and *Upload*:

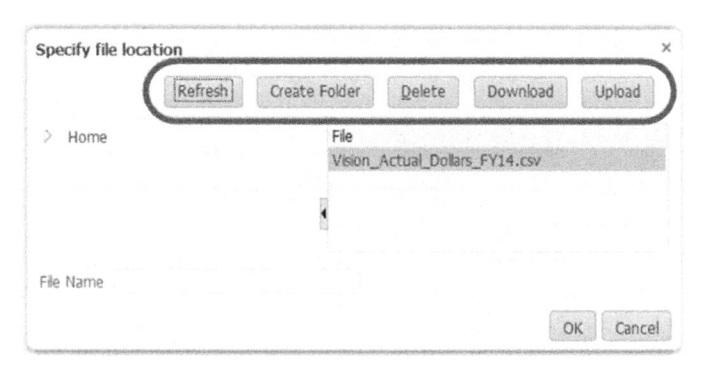

All Dimensions provides the same functionality as Current Dimension above, except all dimensions are exported for the current location (POV). *Export to Excel* exports the mapping as a formatted report that is intended for business users. It prompts to open and save the Excel file locally. This is a report only, but it may be used to coordinate mapping changes but may not be directly imported to FDMEE.

Importing Mapping

To import a mapping, click *Import*:

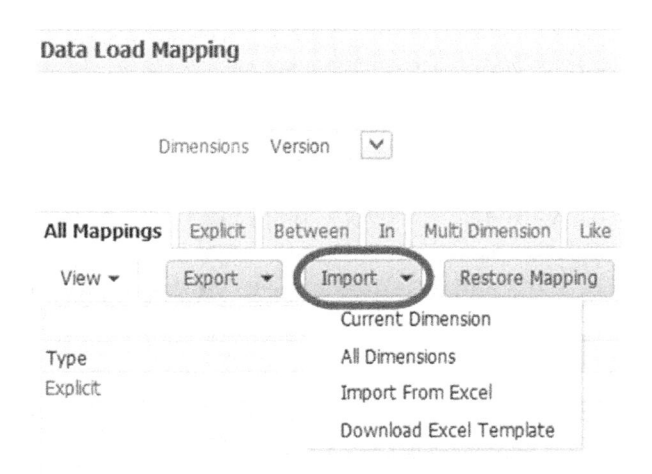

The following *Import* options are available: *Current Dimension* – imports mapping from a comma-delimited flat file for the current dimension and current location (POV). When prompted, click *Upload* to upload a file, or select an existing file from the PBCS Home folder (or subfolder), and click *OK*. *All Dimensions* provides the same functionality as *Current Dimension* above, except all dimensions are imported for the current location (POV). *Import from Excel* imports the mapping from the Excel Template (see below). *Download Excel Template* prompts the user to open and save the Excel Template file locally. Instructions are included in the file. This provides a user-friendly alternative to exporting and importing a mapping via comma-delimited flat file.

After selecting a file to import, a prompt appears with the following import mode and validation options:

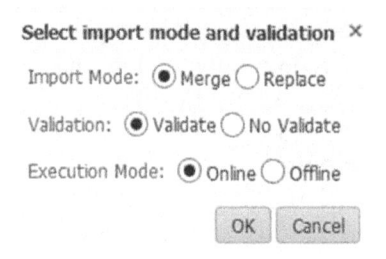

> **Select import mode and validation**
>
> Import Mode: ● Merge ○ Replace
>
> Validation: ● Validate ○ No Validate
>
> Execution Mode: ● Online ○ Offline
>
> OK   Cancel

- **Import Mode**
  - **Merge** – add to / update existing mapping
  - **Replace** – replace all existing mapping
- **Validation**
  - **Validate** – checks mapping for any invalid target members
  - **No Validate** – does not check mapping for invalid target members
- **Execution Mode**
  - **Online** – executes immediately (recommended)
  - **Offline** – executes in the background (check status under Process Details)

Create Data Load Rule

I'll create a data load rule now that I've completed the member mappings. A data rule is defined for a single location. You may have many data load rules that load to your target application, allowing for loads from multiple sources.

To create a data load rule,
1. On the Workflow tab, navigate to *Data Load >> Data Load Rule*.
2. Check that your POV at the bottom of the screen is set to the "VisionSales_Loc" Location and "Actual" Category. (Ignore Period – that is defined in Execution because this is a multi-period file.)
3. Click *Add* ✛.

4. Enter the name "Load Vision Sales Actuals":

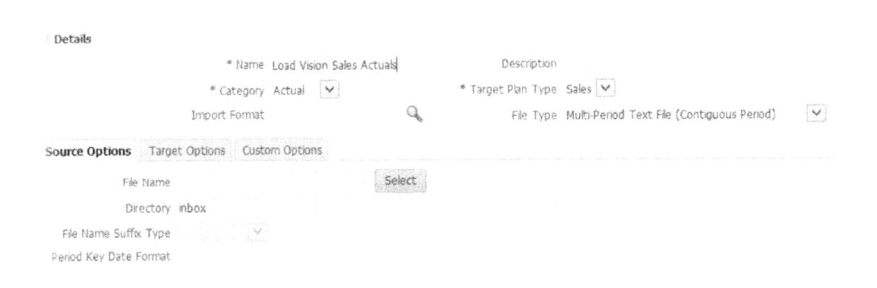

5. Select *Actual* for Category.
6. Select *Sales* for Target Cube.
7. Select *Load Vision Actuals* for Import Format:

Defining the import format here is an optional step. You can choose to overwrite the import format that is defined with the location. If you do not select anything here, the default import format for the location is used (in my case, I picked the same import format so I'm really using the same import format definition).

8. Click *Save*.
9. Under Source Options click *Select*.
10. Click *Upload* and browse to the file *Vision_Actual_Dollars_FY14.csv*, then click *OK*.
11. Select the file *Vision_Actual_Dollars_FY14.csv* and click *OK*.
12. Leave all other options set to the default.
13. Click *Save*.

196   Chapter 5: Integrate Data

The data load rule is now saved and ready for use.

> **LOG ENTRY: SOL 14, Entry 3**
>
>   Finally the data load rule is complete! Can I load data?
>   Yes! Yes, I can.
>   Boy, I never thought I would get here but here I am. Ready to load data into the Cloud with Data Management!

Execute Load Rule to Load Data

Before I run the load process, I want to revisit how Data Management loads data. Data Management imports source data to a staging table and then load to the target. I can do this in two steps or all in one step.

Source ➡ **Staging Table** ➡ **Target**

I can execute the load rule from the *Data Load Rule* section:

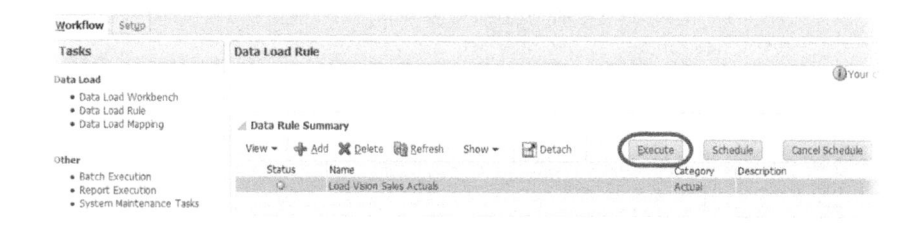

1. Once ready to load, select the desired load rule (in my case *Load Vision Sales Actuals*) and click *Execute*.

You have the option to *Import from Source* which imports into Data Management's staging table. You can stop there if you would like, or you can continue and export the data from the Data Management staging table and load to the target.

2. Check the options to:
    a. *Import from Source*
    b. *Export to Target*
3. Specify the Start Period and End Period (in my case I'm loading data from Jan-14 to Dec-14).
4. Set Import Mode to *Replace*.

Available import modes / load methods for files are *Append* (new rows are appended to rows in the staging table for the POV) or *Replace* (replace all rows in the staging table for the POV). Remember that the POV is the Location, Period, Year, and Scenario. *Append* is useful when a particular location has multiple source files. The first source file may be loaded as *Replace* and subsequent source files may be loaded as *Append*.

5. Set Export Mode to *Replace Data*:

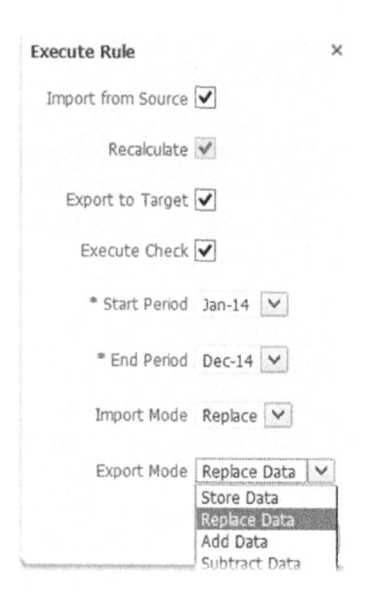

Export Mode defines how data is exported from the staging table and loaded into the target.

Available options for Export Mode include:

- **Store Data** – inserts file from source and replaces any value that currently exists in the target
- **Add Data** – adds the value from the source to the value that exists in the target
- **Subtract Data** – subtracts the value from the source to the value that exists in the target
- **Replace Data** – clears all data in the target for the POV currently being loaded and then loads the source file

Another option, *Override All Data* (clears ALL data in the target), is available but only if it is enabled in *System Settings* or *Application Settings*.

Note!

- **Import Mode** – controls how the data is imported to the Data Management staging table
- **Export Mode** – controls how the data is exported from the Data Management staging table to the target application

The example above loads data to one set of accounts all the way from source to target. If there is a need to load multiple files, one option is to accumulate it all in FDMEE first and then load it to the target at one time. To do this, set the first load's Import Mode to *Replace* and do not select the option to *Export to Target*. This replaces all previously existing FDMEE data records with the first data file set. Then for each subsequent data file load except the last, change the Import Mode to *Append* so that records are appended to the underlying Data Management staging table only. Otherwise, the data loaded for the first set of accounts is cleared in the Data Management staging table when each new data set is loaded. Continue to not select *Export to Target* in these subsequent loads. On the final data file load, keep the Import Mode as *Append*, finally check the option to *Export to Target*, and set the Export Mode to *Replace*. This adds the last data file's records into the staging table and then load all of the accumulated data records from the staging table to the target.

Note!

When loading multiple sets of data or multiple data files, change the Import Mode to *Append* and the Export Mode to *Store Data* or *Add Data* so that records are appended to the underlying Data Management staging table. Otherwise, the data loaded for the first set of accounts is cleared when the second data set is loaded.

6. Click *Run*. You should receive a message indicating that the process is running in the background. Make a mental note of the Process Id:

Chapter 5: Integrate Data

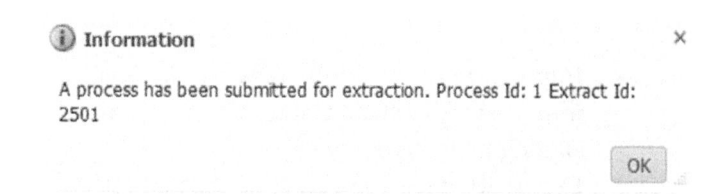

> ⓘ Information   ✕
>
> A process has been submitted for extraction. Process Id: 1 Extract Id: 2501
>
> OK

You can view the load process status in the top of the Data Load Rule window, within the *Data Rule Summary* section.

7. Click the *Refresh* button after at least 10 seconds to see the status:

8. For more details on the process, go to *Monitor >> Process Details*:

Note! Process Details give you a lot of great information in the log file. For instance, the log file can tell you how many records go through a specific mapping.

Look Smarter Than You Are with PBCS 201

9. View logs and search for "Error" to see if any errors have occurred (though the log file can be confusing).

Note! Data cannot be loaded to members that are tagged as Dynamic Calc or are not level-0.

Workbench

The *Data Management Workbench* helps me monitor and view each of the stages of the Data Management load process. The Workbench allows you to interact with each of the stages (Import, Validate, Export, and Check), drill back to source details, and more. The Workbench, however, does not support multi-period loads, so you have to view data for a single period:

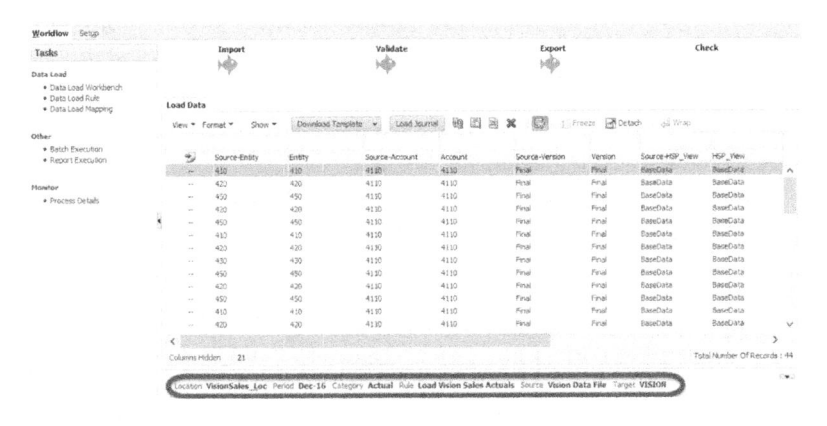

The Workbench consists of four sections:

- Workflow grid
- POV bar
- Status
- Data grid

The workflow grid lets users process data from start to finish. The four main stages are listed as headers here. Fish icons (the illustrious "fishies" that this product is known for) mark the status of each step. If a step is completed successfully, the fish turns orange. ᓫ᷈ If the step is unsuccessful, the fish turns gray. ᓫ᷈ The four stages of processing data are as follows:

- **Import** – loads data from the source
- **Validate** – checks to ensure that all source members are mapped
- **Export** – loads the valid members to the target application
- **Check** – verifies the accuracy of the data with user-defined rules

The POV bar is accessible at the bottom of the workbench screen.

Location **VisionSales_Loc** Period **Dec-16** Category **Actual** Rule **Load Vision Sales Actuals** Source **Vision Data File** Target **VISION**

This governs the Location, Period, Category (Scenario), and Data Load Rule that processes data. The status shows the current status of the data processing. The data grid allows users to import, view, verify, and export data from source systems, as well as drill through to the source data and view mapping details.

> **LOG ENTRY: SOL 14, Entry 4**
>
> Did you see how Data Management uses fish across the top of the screen to illustrate the stage of the data integration process (Import, Validate, Export, Check)? Being a huge fan of Aquaman, I love the fishies!

Once I create my data forms, I'll be able to verify and view that data in PBCS:

Check Actuals Data Load

Scenario	Entity	Version
Actual	International Sales	Jerry1_Version
Jerry1_Version		

		FY14	FY15	FY16
		⊞ YearTotal	⊞ YearTotal	⊞ YearTotal
⊞ Total Product	⊞ 4001:Total Revenue	401720	1498358.75	

Load More Data

I need to load the rest of my data for the Vision application. Do I have to go through all of the "Stiflomadle" steps? No – I can actually reuse the same source, target applications, import formats, locations, and mappings. All I need to do is create a new data load rule that points to the new data file.

To load FY15 data,
1. Navigate to the *Data Load >> Data Load Rule* section.
2. Check that your POV is set to the *VisionSales_Loc* Location and *Actual* Category. (Ignore Period – that is defined in Execution because this is a multi-period file.)
3. Click ✚ to add a new Data Load Rule.
4. Enter the name "Load Vision Sales Actuals-FY15".
5. Select *Load Vision Actuals* for Import Format.
6. Select *Actual* for Category.
7. Select *Multi-Period Text File (Contiguous Period)* for File Type.
8. Select *Sales* for Target Cube.
9. Under Source Options, click *Select*.
10. Click *Upload* and *Browse...* to the file *Vision_Actual_FY15.csv*.
11. Leave all other options set to default.
12. Click *Save*:

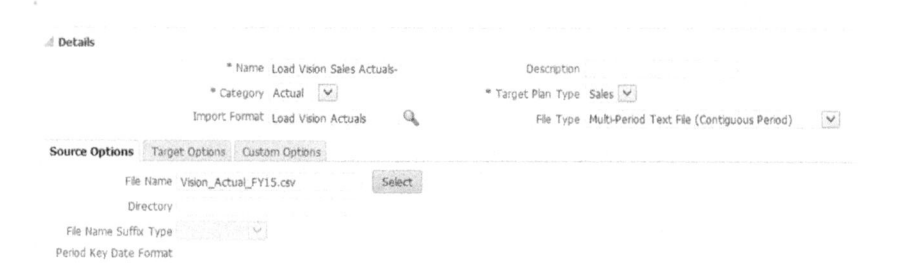

13. Highlight the "Load Vision Sales Actuals-FY15" data load rule and click *Execute*.
14. Check the options to:
    a. *Import from Source*
    b. *Export to Target*
15. Specify the Start Period and End Period (in my case I'm loading data from Jan-15 to Dec-15).
16. Set Import Mode to *Replace*.
17. Set Export Mode to *Replace Data*.

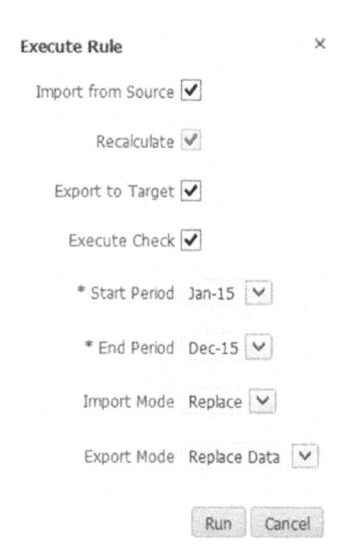

18. Click *Run*. You should receive a message indicating that the process is running in the background.

Look Smarter Than You Are with PBCS   205

19. Navigate to *Process Details* to view data load status (click *Refresh* until the load is complete):

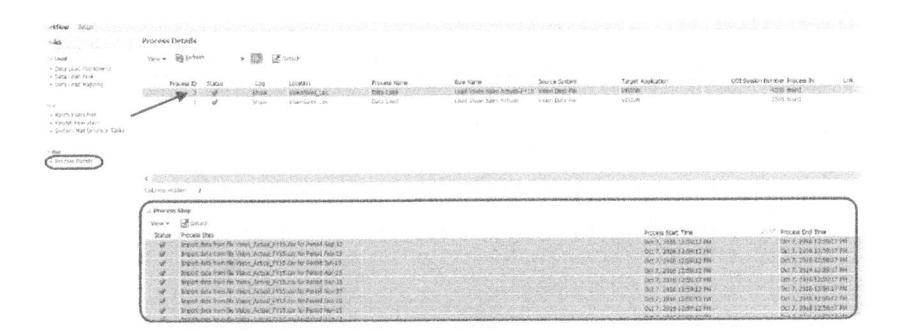

Now I need to load FY16 data. To do this,
1. Navigate to the *Data Load >> Data Load Rule* section.
2. Check that your POV is set to the *VisionSales_Loc* Location and *Actual* Category. (Ignore Period – that is defined in Execution because this is a multi-period file.)
3. Click ✚ to add a new Data Load Rule.
4. Enter the name "Load Vision Sales Actuals-FY16".
5. Select *Actual* for Category.
6. Select *Multi-Period Text File (Contiguous Period)* for File Type.
7. Select *Sales* for Target Cube.
8. Select *Load Vision Actuals* for Import Format.
9. Under Source Options, click *Select*.
10. Click *Upload* and *Browse...* to the file *Vision_Actual_FY16.csv*.
11. Leave all other options set to default.
12. Click *Save*:

13. Highlight the "Load Vision Sales Actuals-FY16" data load rule and click *Execute*.
14. Check the Options to:
    a. *Import from Source*
    b. *Export to Target*
15. Specify the Start Period and End Period (in my case I'm loading data from Jan-16 to Dec-16).
16. Set Import Mode to *Replace*.
17. Set Export Mode to *Replace Data*.
18. Click *Run*. You should receive a message indicating that the process is running in the background.
19. Navigate to *Process Details* to view data load status (click *Refresh* until the load is complete).

Load Data to ASO Cube

Next, I need to load data to the ASO Cube, SalesRpt. Do I have to go through all of the "Stiflomadle" steps? This time, yes because I have a new target application to load data to.

My source called "File" has already been defined so no further steps are required under source application.

To add the SalesRpt Target application (if you did not create previously; if AVISION-SalesRpt target exists, jump to the Import Format step),

1. Click the *Setup* tab >> *Register* >> *Target Application* link.
2. Click ✚ under Target Application Summary.
3. Select *Essbase* as the Type:

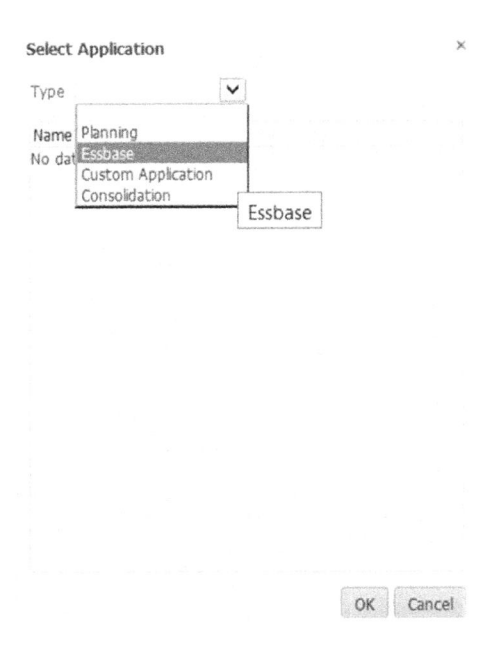

4. Select the ASO application name, *AVISION-SalesRpt*.
5. Click *OK*.

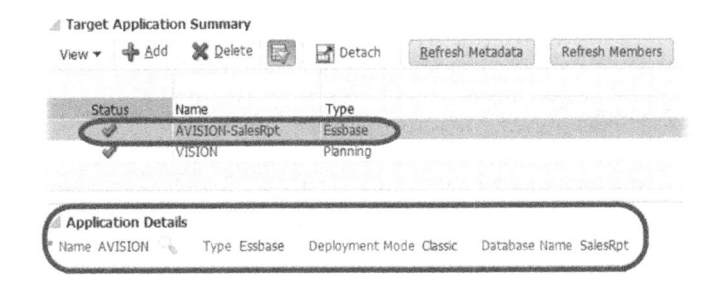

Many of the Dimension Details populate automatically. Make sure you set Entity to *Entity* for Target Dimension Class (sometimes it will default to Country).

6. Review the Dimension Details tab.
7. Set Entity to *Entity* Target Dimension Class.
8. Set Version to *Version* Target Dimension Class.
9. Set Scenario to *Scenario* Target Dimension Class:

Target Application Summary

Status	Name	Type
✓	AVISION-SalesRpt	Essbase
✓	VISION	Planning

Application Details

*Name AVISION   Type Essbase   Deployment Mode Classic   Database Name SalesRpt

Dimension Details | Application Options

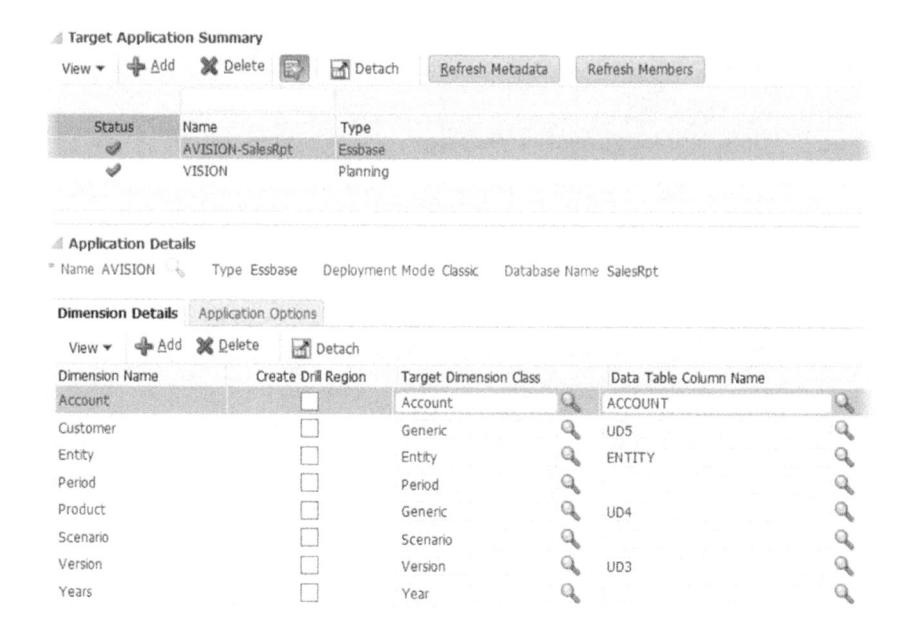

Dimension Name	Create Drill Region	Target Dimension Class	Data Table Column Name
Account	☐	Account	ACCOUNT
Customer	☐	Generic	UD5
Entity	☐	Entity	ENTITY
Period	☐	Period	
Product	☐	Generic	UD4
Scenario	☐	Scenario	
Version	☐	Version	UD3
Years	☐	Year	

10. Click *Save* to save the target application.

Next I need to define the Import Format. To do this,

11. Under *Integration Setup* on the *Setup* tab, click *Import Format*.
12. Click ✚.
13. Under *Details*, enter the following information. Specify the File Type as *Multi Column – Numeric Data* to match the load file format and click *Save* when done:

Load SalesRpt_IF: Details

Name Load SalesRpt_IF   Description
Source Vision Data File   Target AVISION-SalesRpt
*File Type Multi Column - Numeric Data   *File Delimiter Comma
Drill URL

The file that I am going to load has multiple periods, which is why I chose *Multi Column – Numeric Data*. Other valid options are *Fixed* (for set column widths to identify fields) or *Delimited* (individual data values use delimiters like quotation marks). These two options are used when loading a single period.

I'm going to use the Import Format Builder to help build my definition. The Import Format Builder supports both Fixed and Delimited files (though it does not support tab-delimited files). You could alternatively manually build the mapping rows.

In this step, I am mapping the Source columns in the data file to the target application dimensions.

To do the mapping,
14. Select *Build Format*.
15. Select *Upload* to upload the file.
16. *Browse...* and select the *SalesRpt_Load_Data_FY14.csv* file (email info@interrel.com for a copy of this file and the next two files).
17. Click *OK*.
18. Select the file and click *OK*. The Import Format Builder displays.
19. Select *Account* text.
20. Set Assign selected text as Source Dimension Name to *Yes*.
21. Click *Assign Dimension*.
22. Make sure Source Dimension Name is set to *Account*.
23. Set the Target Dimension to *Account*.
24. Leave Field Number as "1":

210   Chapter 5: Integrate Data

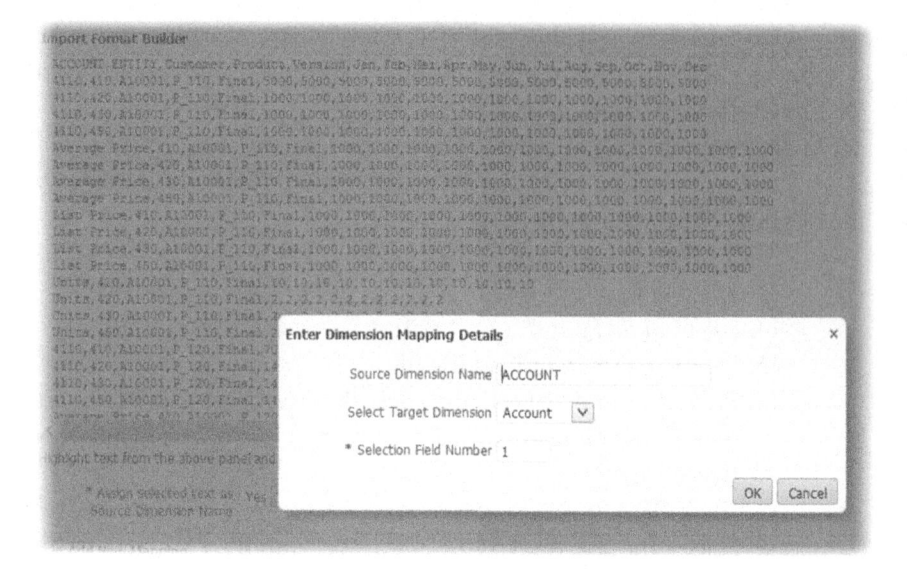

[screenshot of Import Format Builder with "Enter Dimension Mapping Details" dialog showing Source Dimension Name: ACCOUNT, Select Target Dimension: Account, Selection Field Number: 1]

25. Click *OK*. The first mapping row is added.
26. Repeat the above steps, assigning the columns / fields to the matching target dimension.
27. When you get to the columns containing the values by month, select all of the months.
28. Set Assign selected text as Source Dimension Name to *No*.
29. Click *Assign Dimension*.
30. Enter *Amount* as the Source Dimension Name, select *Amount* as the Target Dimension, leave the default Selection Field Number and click *OK* and then *OK* again.
31. The final step is to use an expression to identify the Amount columns. Type "Column=6,17" in the Expression field and set the Field number to "6" (the first column of data numbers). The end result should look as follows:

Load SalesRpt_IF: Details

Name	Load SalesRpt_IF	Description	
Source Type	ERP	Target Type	EPM
* Source	Vision Data File	* Target	AVISION-SalesRpt
* File Type	Multi Period - Numeric Data	* File Delimiter	Comma
Drill URL			

Load SalesRpt_IF: Mappings

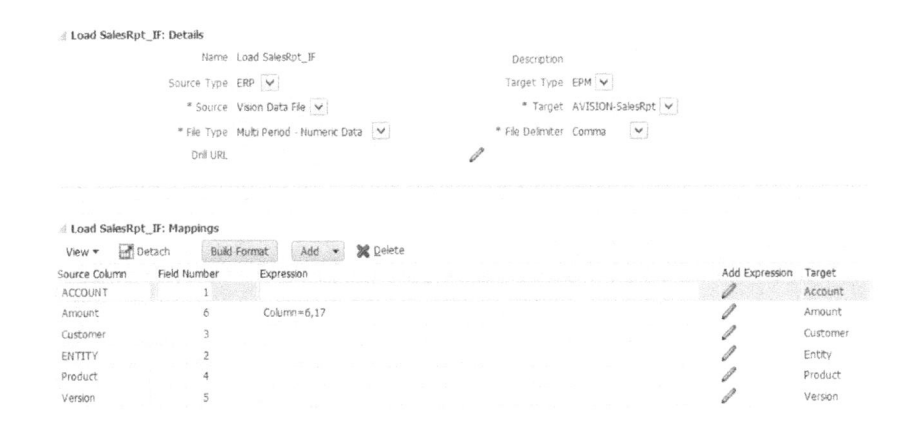

Source Column	Field Number	Expression	Add Expression	Target
ACCOUNT	1			Account
Amount	6	Column=6,17		Amount
Customer	3			Customer
ENTITY	2			Entity
Product	4			Product
Version	5			Version

32. Click *Save* to save the import format.

Note that I did not define Scenario, Period, or Year. Scenario is defined in the Category mapping. Period and Year are defined in the POV upon execution.

Next I need to define the Location to associate the import format with the target application.

33. Under Integration Setup on the Setup tab, click *Location*.
34. Click ✚ to create a new location.
35. Enter the following Location Details and leave the other fields as the default:
    a. *Name*: SalesRpt_Loc
    b. *Import Format*: Load SalesRpt_IF
    c. *Source*: Vision Data File
    d. *Target*: AVISION-SalesRpt:
36. Click *Save*.

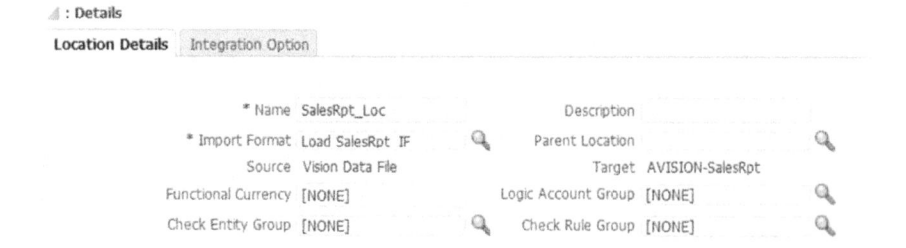

Chapter 5: Integrate Data

* Name	SalesRpt_Loc	Description	
* Import Format	Load SalesRpt IF	Parent Location	
Source	Vision Data File	Target	AVISION-SalesRpt
Functional Currency	[NONE]	Logic Account Group	[NONE]
Check Entity Group	[NONE]	Check Rule Group	[NONE]

To use the global period and category mappings,

37. Under Configure on the Setup tab, click *Application Settings*.
38. Select *AVISION-SalesRpt* and type "Yes" for *Global POV Mode*:

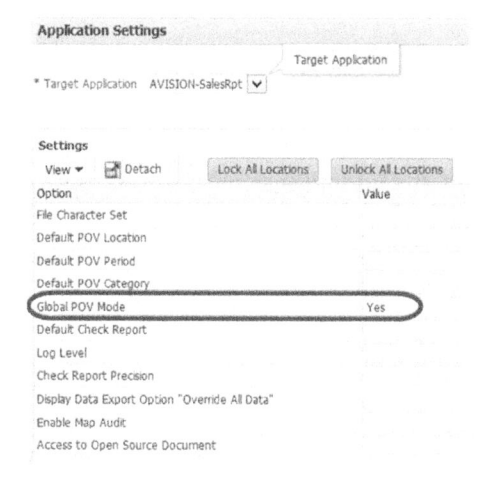

Application Settings

* Target Application AVISION-SalesRpt

Settings

Option	Value
File Character Set	
Default POV Location	
Default POV Period	
Default POV Category	
Global POV Mode	**Yes**
Default Check Report	
Log Level	
Check Report Precision	
Display Data Export Option "Override All Data"	
Enable Map Audit	
Access to Open Source Document	

39. Click *Save*.

I now will switch to the Workflow section where I will define member maps and data load rules.

40. On the Workflow tab, click *Data Load Mapping*:

Look Smarter Than You Are with PBCS 213

Workflow Setup

Tasks

Data Load
- Data Load Workbench
- Data Load Rule
- Data Load Mapping

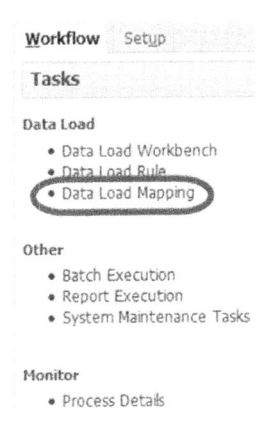

Other
- Batch Execution
- Report Execution
- System Maintenance Tasks

Monitor
- Process Details

41. On the POV bar, choose the newly created location, *SalesRpt_Loc*:

Select Point of View

* Location SalesRpt Loc
Period Dec-16
Category Actual
Set as Default

OK Cancel

Now I need to complete the appropriate mappings for each target dimension.

42. Choose the *Account* dimension from the drop down list.
43. Select the *Like* tab.
44. Click ✚ to add a row into the mapping.
45. Enter "*" as the Source Value and "*" as the Target Value, and call the Rule Name "DirectMapAccount":

46. Click *Save*.
47. Choose the *Entity* dimension from the drop down list.
48. Select the *Like* tab.
49. Click ✚ to add a row into the mapping.
50. Enter "*" as the Source Value and "*" as the Target Value and call the Rule Name "DirectMapEntity".
51. Click *Save*.
52. Choose the *Product* dimension from the drop down list.
53. Select the *Like* tab.
54. Click ✚ add a row into the mapping.
55. Enter "*" as the Source Value and "*" as the Target Value and call the Rule Name "DirectMapProduct".
56. Click *Save*.
57. Repeat these steps for the remaining dimensions so mappings are defined for every dimension.
58. Click *Save*. Check that all dimensions in the drop down are mapped.

I'm finally ready to create my data load rule.

59. Navigate to the *Workflow* tab >> *Data Load* section >> *and select Data Load Rule*.
60. Check that your POV is set to the *SalesRpt_Loc* Location and *Actual* Category. (Ignore Period – that is defined in Execution because this is a multi-period file.)

61. Click ✚ to add a new Data Load Rule.
62. Enter the name "Load Vision SalesRpt Actuals-FY14".
63. Select *Actual* for Category.
64. Select *Multi-Period Text File (Contiguous Period)* for File Type.

ASO cubes will only have one database so you do not select a Target Cube.

65. Select *Load SalesRpt_IF* for Import Format.
66. Under Source Options, click *Select*.
67. Click *Upload* and *Browse...* to the file *SalesRpt_Load_Data_FY14*. Select this file.
68. Leave all other options set to default.
69. Click *Save*:

70. Click *Execute*.
71. Check the Options to:
    a. *Import from Source*
    b. *Export to Target*
72. Specify the Start Period and End Period (in my case I'm loading data from Jan-14 to Dec-14).
73. Set Import Mode to *Replace*.
74. Set Export Mode to *Store Data*:

```
             Execute Rule                    ×

                 Import from Source ✔

                         Recalculate ✔

                      Export to Target ✔

                       Execute Check ✔

                  * Start Period  Jan-14  ∨

                   * End Period  Dec-14  ∨

                    Import Mode  Replace  ∨

                   Export Mode  Store Data  ∨

                             Run     Cancel
```

75. Click *Run*.
76. Navigate to *Process Details* to view data load status (click *Refresh* until the load is complete).
77. Create two more data load rules using the steps above to load data for FY15 and FY16 into the SalesRpt cube using the respective data files.

```
LOG ENTRY: SOL 14, Entry 5

I wonder how the Texas Rangers are doing.
```

SYNC DATA WITH DATA MANAGEMENT

Data Management supports the synchronizing and mapping of data across EPM source and targets. In the case of PBCS, this means sharing data across cubes. Sharing data between two EPM data sources is called "data sync" in PBCS Data Management.

Note! You cannot share data via Data Management directly to on-premises applications. With Data Management, you still must use files to navigate in a hybrid world (on-premises and Cloud). However, with PBCS release 16.04 (April 2016), on-premises FDMEE can now be used to point to Cloud EPM sources and targets.

I'll now create a data synchronization process between my BSO cube to ASO cube (note – I can also do that through Smart Push functionality). I'll use the same Data Management "Stiflomadle" steps to create this integration (Create Source, Create Target, Define Import Format, Define Location, Define Mappings, Define Data Load Rule and finally Execute). One difference with data sync is that I do not need to create source and target applications because they already exist.

Note! Once Data Management objects are created, they must be deleted manually to be fully removed. Objects in Data Management will remain even after deleting the PBCS application.

When Dimensionality Differs in Source and Target

One fun new requirement is needed in this integration. I'm trying to set up data sync between my two cubes (Sales → SalesRpt). The Sales cube has the *HSP_View* dimension which is not in the SalesRpt cube. SalesRpt cube has the *Customer* dimension which is not in the Sales cube. So how to map these two dimensions?

If the source app contains a dimension that does not exist in the target app:

- Specify the dimension in the data load rule source filter and choose a default member to pull from.
- If the dimension does NOT map to any other dimension in the target app, then no other action is required

If the target app contains a dimension that does not exist in the source app, just leave the Source Column pick list empty.

Setting Up a Data Sync Process in Data Management

The artifacts below will push FY14 Actual data from the Sales cube to the SalesRpt cube.

To set up a data sync integration in Data Management,
1. Select *Navigator* >> *Integration* >> *Data Management*.
2. Navigate to the *Setup* tab and then *Import Format*.
3. Create a new import format called "SyncSalesToSalesRpt" and fill in the details as shown.
   a. **Name**: SyncSalesToSalesRpt
   b. **Source**: Vision
   c. **Target**: AVISION-SalesRpt:

Import Format

▸ : Details

* Name: SyncSalesToSalesRpt   Description:
* Source: VISION   * Target: AVISION-SalesRpt
Drill URL:

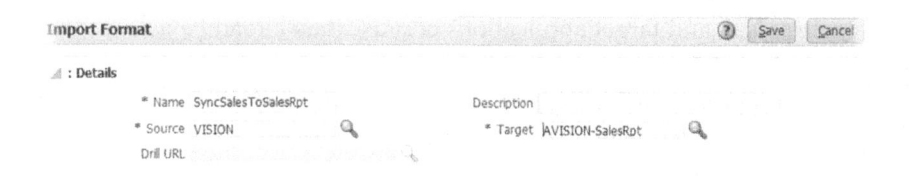

4. Click *Save* to save the import format.
5. Assign the mappings from the source to target as follows, leaving the target Customer dimension blank for the source application, as there is no Customer dimension within the Sales cube:

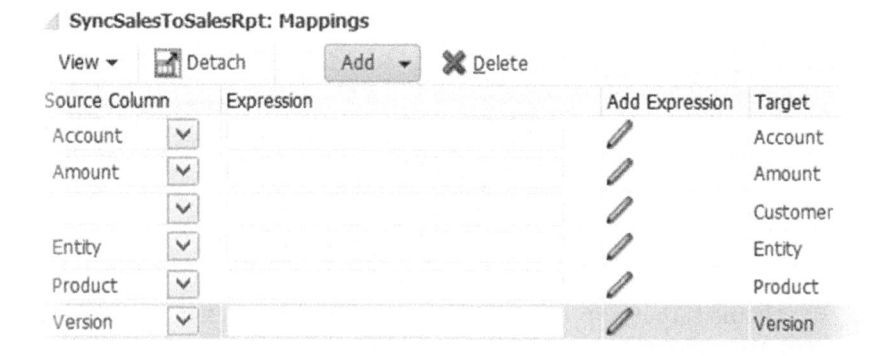

SyncSalesToSalesRpt: Mappings

View ▾   Detach   Add ▾   Delete

Source Column	Expression	Add Expression	Target
Account			Account
Amount			Amount
			Customer
Entity			Entity
Product			Product
Version			Version

6. Click *Save* to save the import format again.
7. Navigate to *Location* and create a new one.
8. Name it "SalesToSalesRpt_Loc" and then fill in the details as shown below.
   a. **Name:** SalesToSalesRpt_Loc
   b. **Import Format:** SyncSalesToSalesRpt:

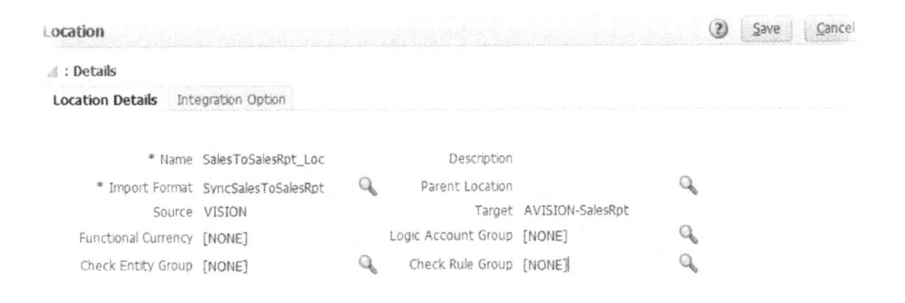

```
Location                                                              Save   Cancel
: Details
Location Details   Integration Option

              * Name   SalesToSalesRpt_Loc        Description
     * Import Format   SyncSalesToSalesRpt        Parent Location
              Source   VISION                     Target              AVISION-SalesRpt
  Functional Currency  [NONE]                     Logic Account Group [NONE]
    Check Entity Group [NONE]                     Check Rule Group    [NONE]
```

9. Click *Save* to save the location.
10. Navigate to the *Workflow* tab and then *Data Load Mapping*.
11. Change the location to the new "SalesToSalesRpt_Loc" location:

```
Location  SalesToSalesRpt_Loc  Period Dec-14  Category Actual  Source VISION  Target AVISION-SalesRpt
```

12. For the Account, Entity, Product, and Version dimensions, do a "Like" mapping with an asterisk in both the Source Value and Target Value fields. Name each Rule Name "DirectMapX" where "X" is the dimension name:

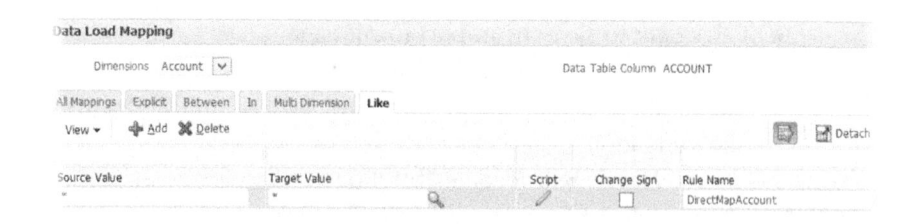

As there is no Customer dimension in the source, it's important to select a default member to map to in the target.

13. In the Customer dimension, add a *Like* mapping.
    a. Enter an *asterisk* in the Source Value field
    b. Enter "No Customer" in the Target Value field
    c. Name the Rule Name "DirectMapCustomer":

14. Click *Save* to save the mapping.
15. Navigate to the *Data Load Rule* area.
16. Create a new data load rule and fill in the details as shown below.
    a. **Name**: SalesToSalesRpt_rule
    b. **Category**: Actual
    c. **Period**: Default
    d. **Source Cube**: Sales

Details

* Name	SalesToSalesRpt_rule	Description	
* Category	Actual	Target Plan Type	
* Period Mapping Type	Default	* Source Plan Type	Sales

As the Sales cube has an HSP_View dimension and the SalesRpt cube does not, it's important to add a source filter to map to a single member. In addition, since only Actual data is being sent over, a source filter should be added to limit to only the appropriate Actual Version member.

To set up the required source filters,
17. Navigate to the *Source Options* tab.
18. Add two source filters, as shown below.
    a. Add a filter condition "BaseData" for the HSP_View dimension
    b. Add a filter condition "Final" for the Version dimension:

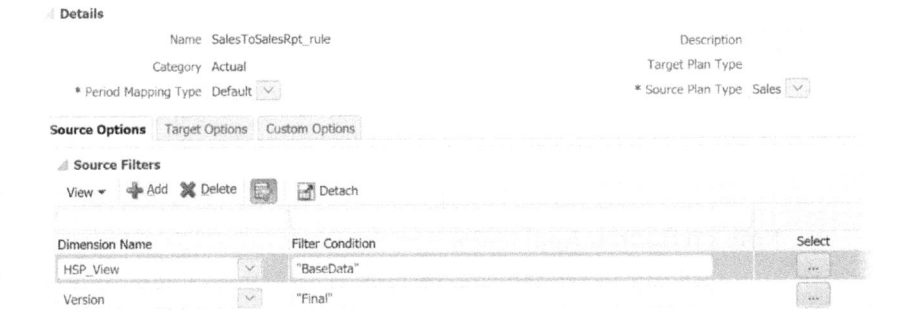

Details

Name	SalesToSalesRpt_rule	Description	
Category	Actual	Target Plan Type	
* Period Mapping Type	Default	* Source Plan Type	Sales

Source Options | Target Options | Custom Options

Source Filters
View ▼ ➕ Add ✖ Delete Detach

Dimension Name	Filter Condition	Select
HSP_View	"BaseData"	...
Version	"Final"	...

19. Click *Save* to save the rule.
20. *Execute* the rule.

It might take several minutes, but this rule should execute successfully. Once it does, verify that the Actual FY14 data matches between Sales and SalesRpt via ad hoc grid or analysis or in a data form that I create in an upcoming chapter.

EXPORT DATA USING DATA MANAGEMENT

Data Management can also export PBCS data to a file (from both BSO and ASO cubes). I'll use the same Data Management "Stiflomadle" steps to create this integration (Create Source, Create Target, Define Import Format, Define Location, Define Mappings, Define Data Load Rule and finally Execute).

Note on Source Application

Within Data Management for PBCS, cubes are available as sources by default.

Create a Custom Target Application

To export data out of PBCS, you first need to create a target application (actually with PBCS applications, one is created by default but I'll walk you through the steps so you understand the process from start to finish). The custom target application is defined with the requirement dimensionality. Instead of writing data to a target, Data Management generates a data file.

A few things to note about custom target applications and exporting data:

- Data is written to the file in this order: Account, Entity, UD1, UD2, UD3...UD20, Amount
- A few options are not valid for custom target applications
- Metadata rule is applicable
- POV category is not validated in Data Load Rules
- Target values are not validated in Data Load Mappings
- Check Rules can be created but they can't be based on target values

When the option to export the data file is enabled, Data Load Execution creates an output file named "*<Target App Name> <Process ID>.dat*". The file is placed in the *<APPL ROOT FOLDER>/outbox* directory. You can access the file from the Process Details page.

If this step hasn't already been done, create a custom target application,

1. Click *Setup >> Register >> Target Application.*

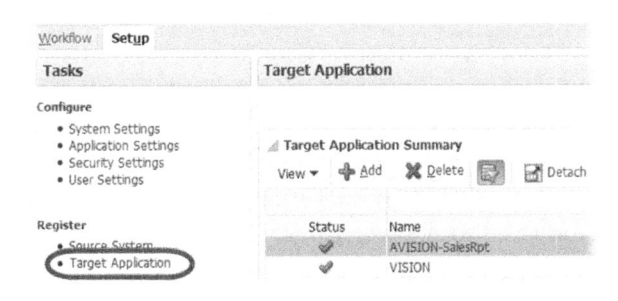

2. Click ✚ to add a target application.
3. Choose *Custom Application*:

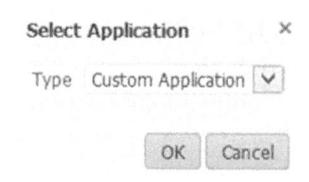

4. Click *OK*.
5. Enter the target application name "SalesRpt_Export":

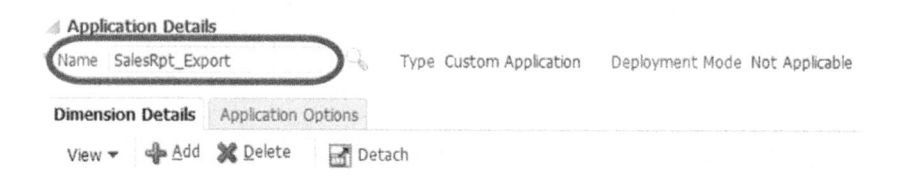

6. Define the following Dimension Details including Dimension Name, Target Dimension Class, Data Table Column Name, and Sequence:

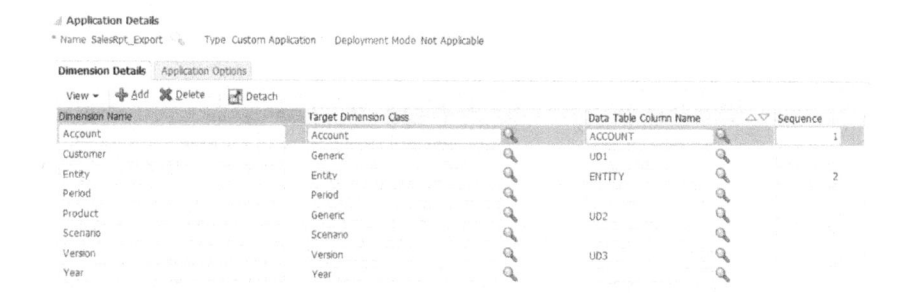

Make sure Entity dimension is set to Target Dimension Class of *Entity*, Account dimension is set to *Account* Target Dimension Class, etc. Incorrect assignments of Target Dimension Classes could cause issues down the line.

7. Click the *Application Options* tab.
8. Set Enable export to file to "Yes".
9. Set Delimiter (available delimiters include comma, pipe, exclamation point, semi-colon and colon).

10. Enter the File Name for Download as "SalesRpt_Export_Data".

This is the name of the file that is copied to the LCM folder. You can use EPM Automate to download the file or you can download it manually through the Simplified UI:

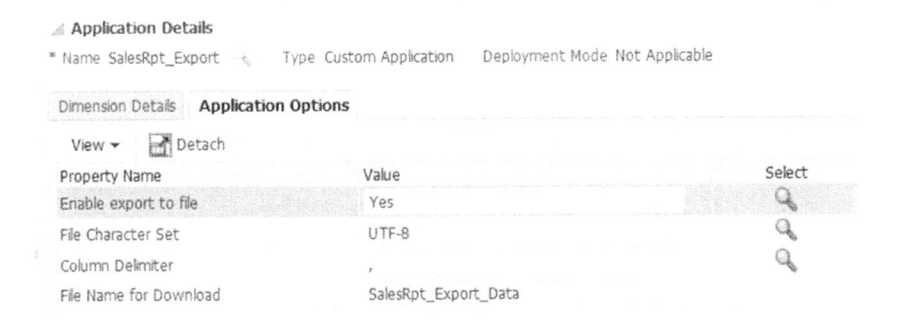

Application Details

* Name SalesRpt_Export   Type Custom Application   Deployment Mode Not Applicable

Dimension Details   **Application Options**

View ▼   Detach

Property Name	Value	Select
Enable export to file	Yes	🔍
File Character Set	UTF-8	🔍
Column Delimiter	,	🔍
File Name for Download	SalesRpt_Export_Data	

11. Click *Save* to save the target application.
12. Go to *Application Settings* and select the SalesRpt_Export target application to set Global POV Mode to "Yes" and Display Data Export Option "Override All Data" to "Yes":

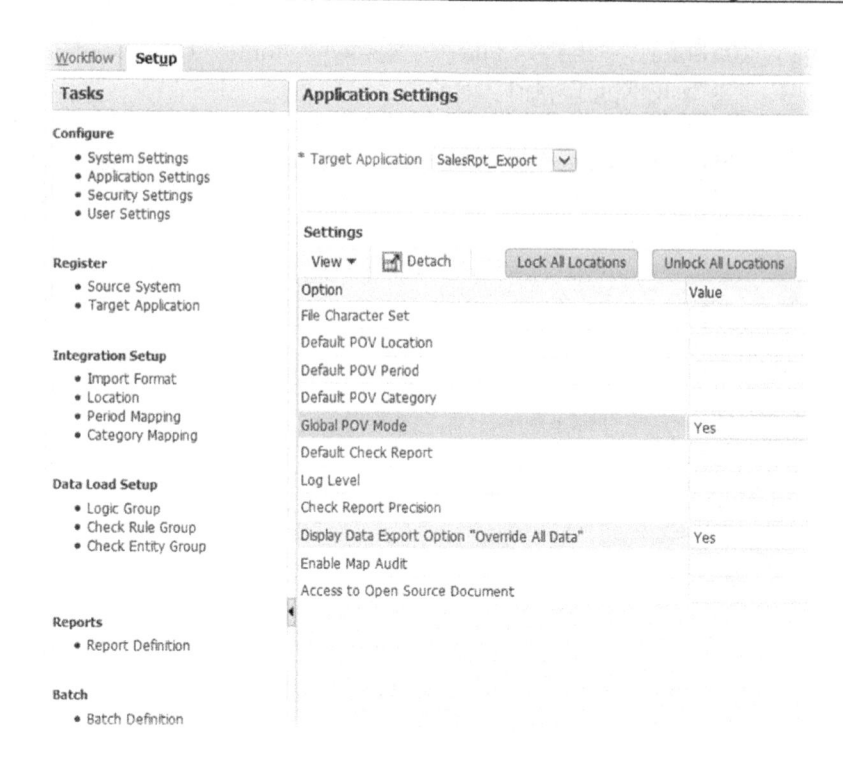

Global POV mode ignores all other POVs. *Display Data Export Option "Override All Data"* displays the Override All Data Option from the Execute screen when I run the data load rule.

13. Click *Save* to save the application settings.

Define the Import Format

1. Select *Setup >> Integration Setup >> Import Format*.
2. Click ➕.
3. Enter the Import Format definition information:
   a. **Name**: "Export_SalesRpt_IF"
   b. **Description**: Optional
   c. **Source Type**: EPM
   d. **Source**: AVISION-SalesRpt
   e. **Target Type**: EPM
   f. **Target**: SalesRpt_Export:

Look Smarter Than You Are with PBCS 227

Import Format

: Details

* Name Export_SalesRpt_IF   Description Export SalesRpt Data
Source Type EPM   Target Type EPM
* Source AVISION-SalesRpt   * Target SalesRpt_Export
Drill URL

4. Click *Save* to make the mappings fields appear.
5. Enter the import format mappings, selecting the source column dimensions and match to the Target application dimensions:

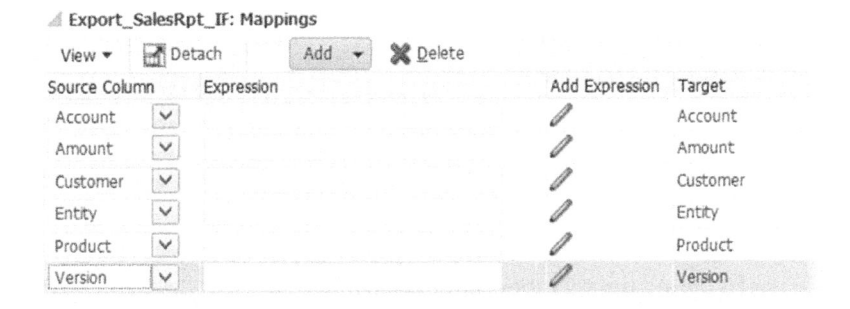

Export_SalesRpt_IF: Mappings

Source Column	Expression	Add Expression	Target
Account			Account
Amount			Amount
Customer			Customer
Entity			Entity
Product			Product
Version			Version

6. Click *Save* to save the import format.

Define Location

1. Select *Setup >> Integration Setup >> Location*.
2. Click ➕.
3. Enter the location information:
   a. Name: "Export_SalesRpt_Loc"
   b. Import Format: *Export_SalesRpt_IF*
4. The Source and Target are automatically populated:

: Details
Location Details | Integration Option

* Name	Export_SalesRpt_Loc	Description	
* Import Format	Export SalesRpt IF	Parent Location	
Source	AVISION-SalesRpt	Target	SalesRpt_Export
Functional Currency	[NONE]	Logic Account Group	[NONE]
Check Entity Group	[NONE]	Check Rule Group	[NONE]

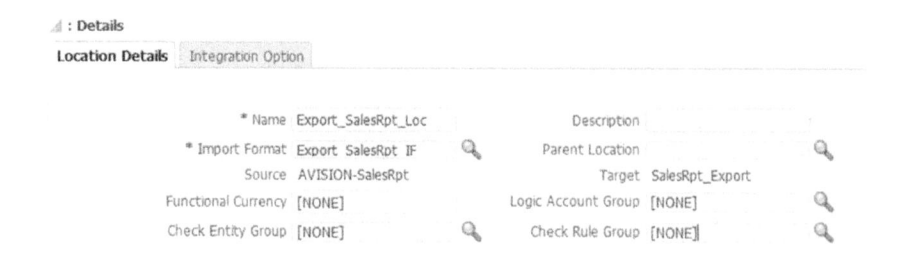

5. Click *Save* to save the location.

Period and Category Mappings

I can use the global mappings for Period and Category, so no need to do any further steps.

Define Data Load Mappings

I do need to define the member mappings from the source to the target.

To define the member mappings,
1. Select *Workflow >> Data Load >> Data Load Mapping*.
2. Choose the Location just created, *Export_SalesRpt_Loc*, for the POV (located at the bottom of the screen):

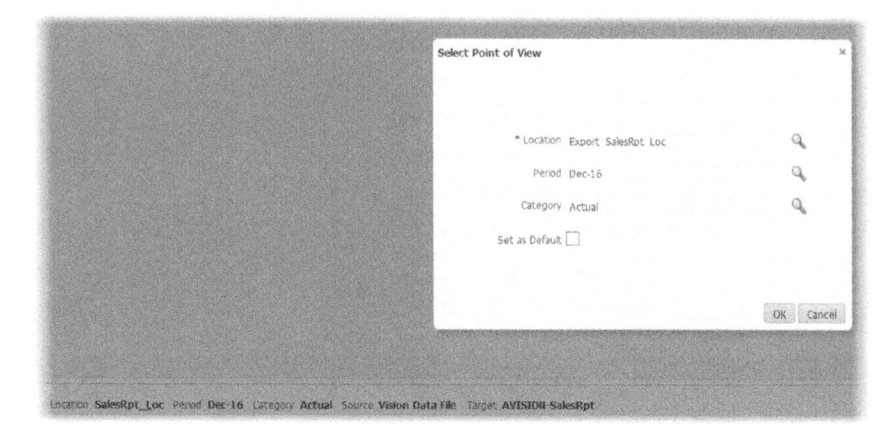

Select Point of View

* Location	Export SalesRpt Loc	
Period	Dec-16	
Category	Actual	
Set as Default ☐		

OK   Cancel

Location SalesRpt_Loc Period Dec-16 Category Actual Source Vision Data File Target AVISION-SalesRpt

Look Smarter Than You Are with PBCS 229

Now I need to complete the appropriate mappings for each target dimension.
3. Choose the *Account* dimension from the drop down list.
4. Select the *Like* tab.
5. Click ✥ to add a mapping row.
6. Enter "*" as the Source Value and "*" as the Target Value and call the Rule Name "DirectMapAccount":

7. Click *Save*.
8. Choose the *Entity* dimension from the drop down list.
9. Select the *Like* tab.
10. Click *Add* to add a mapping row.
11. Enter "*" as the *Source Value* and "*" as the *Target Value* and call the *Rule Name* "DirectMapEntity"
12. Click *Save*.
13. Choose the *Product* dimension from the drop down list.
14. Select the *Like* tab.
15. Click *Add* to add a mapping row.
16. Enter "*" as the *Source Value* and "*" as the *Target Value* and call the *Rule Name* "DirectMapProduct".
17. Click *Save*.
18. Repeat for the rest of the dimensions (Customer and Version).

Define Data Load Rule

Now I need to define the data load rule,
1. Navigate to the *Workflow* >> *Data Load* >> *Data Load Rule* section.

2. Check that your POV is set to the *Export_SalesRpt_Loc* Location and *Actual* Category (ignore Period – that is defined in Execution):

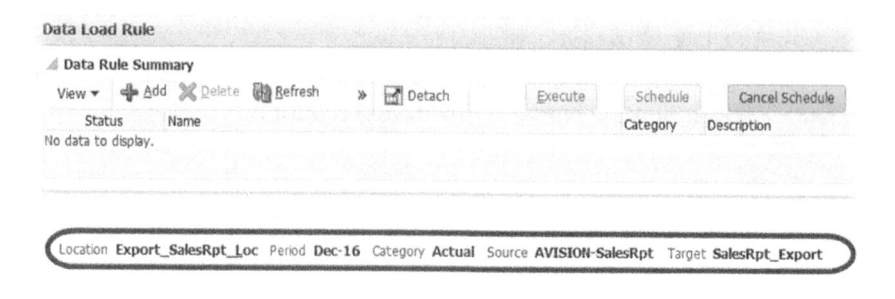

3. Click ➕.
4. Enter the name "Export SalesRpt DLR".
5. Click *Save*.
6. Select the *Source Options* tab. Under Source Filters, you can add filters to the source (e.g., you only want to extract a specific account or set of products).
7. Optionally click ➕ under Source Filters.
8. Select the dimension and then select the ▫ icon to use member selection to select members that you want to extract. For now, I will export everything so I'll leave Source Filters blank.
9. Set Extract Dynamically Calculated Data to *Yes* (to allow dynamically calculated data to be extracted).
10. Optionally enter Data Precision and the Data Number of Decimal:

Look Smarter Than You Are with PBCS 231

[Screenshot of Details pane showing Name: Export SalesRpt DLR, Category: Actual, Period Mapping Type: Default; Source Options tab with Source Filters (no data to display) and Source Parameters listing Extract Dynamic Calculated Data: Yes, Data Precision, Data Number of Decimal; Location: Export_SalesRpt_Loc, Period: Dec-16, Category: Actual, Source: AVISION-SalesRpt, Target: SalesRpt_Export]

- **Extract Dynamic Calculated Data:** "Yes" – include dynamically calculated values or "No" – don't include dynamically calculated values
- **Data Precision** – number of decimal places to be exported (focused on the accuracy of the data); default value is 16
- **Data Number of Decimal** – maximum number of decimal positions to be exported (focused on legibility of the number); valid values are 0 - 16. If this parameter is not specified, the Data Precision number is used

11. Select the *Target Options* tab.
12. Some of these properties should populate by default based on target application settings. Make sure the *File Name for Download* is defined (I'll find the file in our PBCS Inbox / Outbox):

232　　　　　　　　　　　　　　　　　　　Chapter 5: Integrate Data

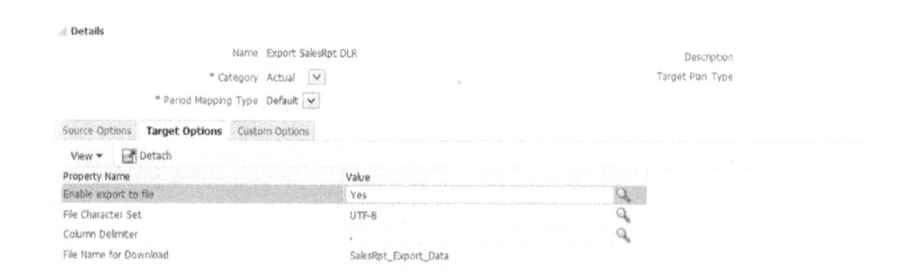

Details		
Name	Export SalesRpt DLR	Description
* Category	Actual	Target Plan Type
* Period Mapping Type	Default	

Source Options | **Target Options** | Custom Options

View ▼ Detach

Property Name	Value	
Enable export to file	Yes	
File Character Set	UTF-8	
Column Delimiter	,	
File Name for Download	SalesRpt_Export_Data	

13. Click *Save*.

Execute Data Load Rule to Export Data to a File

Remember Data Management imports source data to a staging table and then loads to the target. I can do this in two steps or all in one step.

Source ▶ Staging Table ▶ Target

To execute the data load rule and export data,
1. Select the *Export SalesRpt DLR* Data Load Rule and click *Execute*.
2. Set Start Period to *Jan-14*.
3. Set End Period to *Dec-14*.
4. Check Options to *Import from Source* and *Export to Target*.
5. Set Import Mode to *Replace* if it is not already selected by default:

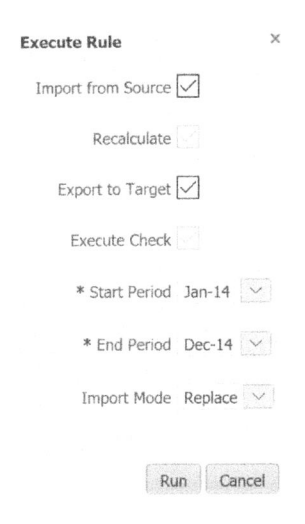

6. Click *Run*.
7. Check the data load process under *Monitor >> Process Details*:

8. Show the log and search for "Error" to see if any errors have occurred (though the log file can be confusing).
9. Scroll to the right of the screen and under the "Output File" column click *Download* to download the file.

Access Exported Data in PBCS

Now that the export is complete, you can access the data file in the PBCS Inbox/Outbox Explorer. To do this,
1. Navigate back to the Simplified UI for PBCS.
2. Select *Navigator* >> *Application* >> *Overview*.
3. Select *Actions* >> *Inbox / Outbox Explorer*:

Chapter 5: Integrate Data

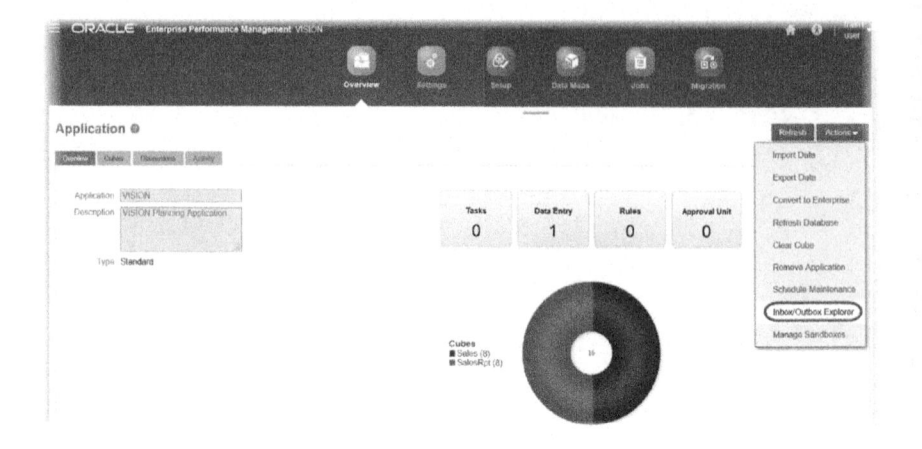

4. You can access the exported data file here (this can also be automated with EPM Automate) to download:

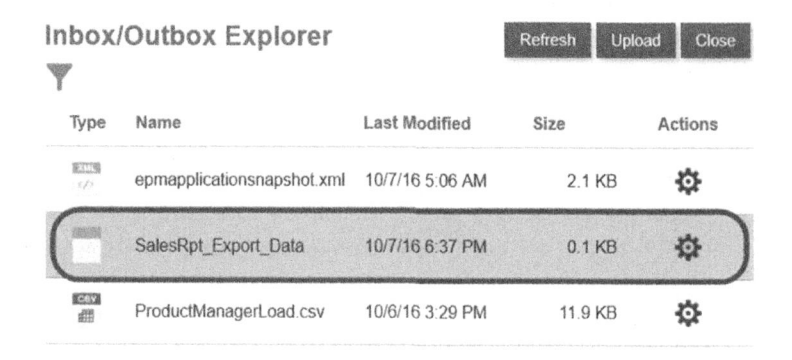

5. To download the file, select the *Actions* icon and choose *Download File*:

Inbox/Outbox Explorer

Type	Name	Last Modified	Size	Actions
XML	epmapplicationsnapshot.xml	10/7/16 5:06 AM	2.1 KB	⚙
	SalesRpt_Export_Data	10/7/16 6:37 PM	0.1 KB	⚙
CSV	ProductManagerLoad.csv	10/6/16 3:29 PM		

✖ Delete
⬇ Download File

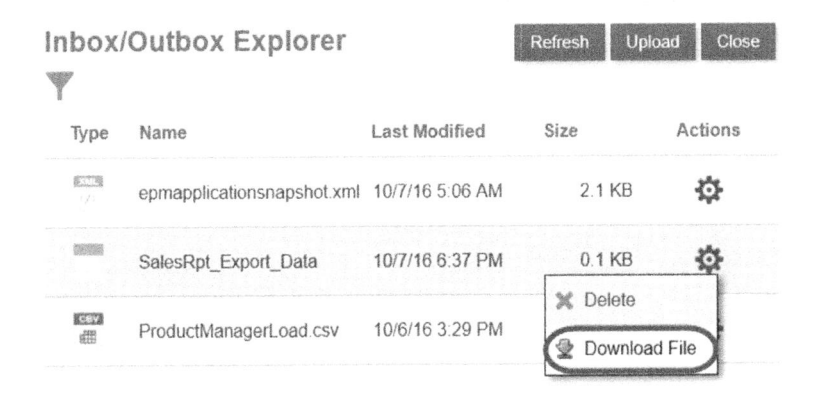

Voila! I have exported data from PBCS (ASO cube). The steps to export data for BSO cubes are the same steps and of course all of this can be automated with EPM Automate (more on this later).

OTHER DATA MANAGEMENT CONCEPTS

Batches

Batches are supported in Data Management and allow you to combine one or more data load rules in a batch and execute them at one time. Batch jobs may run in serial or parallel mode. A number of batch parameters are defined, including POV settings for the batch. Period parameters can be derived based on the POV settings. Finally, batches can be grouped together. To access, go to *Setup >> Batch >> Batch Definition*:

Reports Definition

Data Management has prebuilt reporting functionality to provide information and auditability about your data integrations. To access this, go to *Setup >> Reports >> Report Definition*:

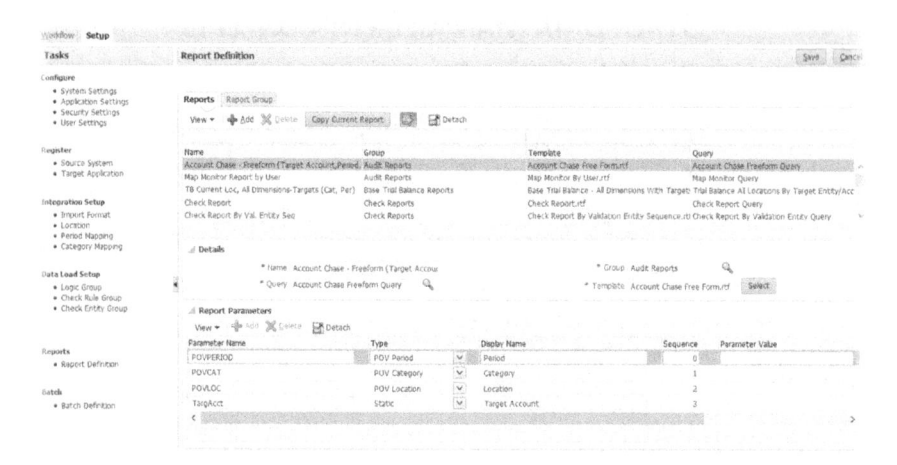

SYNC DATA WITH DATA MAPS

An alternative to syncing data using Data Management is to use the "Map to Reporting" or "Data Maps" feature of PBCS. You can map data across cubes within your PBCS application, dimension to dimension, or Smart List to dimension. These are called "data maps" in the Simplified UI. For Vision, I want to share Forecast data from Sales

(BSO cube) to SalesRpt (ASO cube). Later I will see that these maps can be attached to data forms and run by the end user, if enabled.

If the dimension names are the same between the source and target databases, the mappings automatically match up (they should in PBCS because everything is self-contained within the application). By default, the members selected are level-0 members of the dimension selected. You can further refine the selected members by using the Member Selection – for example, if you just want to map the Forecast Scenario for the Forecast years. You can update the member selection to choose the desired slice of data to push from source cube to the target cube. If you are pushing data to an ASO database, you should only map level zero members in the target database.

Data maps may be defined for sparse and dense dimensions.

The *Smart List to Dimension* mapping feature allows Smart List data to be pushed to a reporting cube where that Smart List exists as a dimension. Users can slice and dice and report subtotals by the Smart List.

Create Data Maps

To create a data map,
1. Select *Navigator* >> *Application* >> *Data Maps*.
2. Click *Create*.
3. Name the data map "Sales Forecast_Products".
4. Select Sales (BSO) as the Source cube and SalesRpt (ASO) as the Target cube:

Sales Forecast_Products
Tap description to edit

Source
VISION
Sales ▼

Target
VISION
SalesRpt ▼

5. In the Source column, use the following table to select members from each dimension to copy to Target:

Chapter 5: Integrate Data

Dimension	Members
Account	ILvl0Descendants(Account)
Entity	ILvl0Descendants (Entity)
Period	ILvl0Descendants (Period)
Product	ILvl0Descendants (Product)
Scenario	Forecast
Version	Final
Years	ILvl0Descendants (Years)
HSP_View (Unmapped)	BaseData

There are different ways to design your data map, depending on how you want to control the data push and whether or not you allow users to "real time" sync from a data form. If you're using a data map independently, then you can define it how you want. The key here is to understand the structures of the hierarchies in both the source and target. In addition, you want to be cognizant of the underlying architectures of the cubes. For instance, when going from a BSO cube to an ASO cube, you need to send only level-0 member data.

Note! When using relationship functions in a data map, be careful on how many you use. Relationship functions can max out the underlying algorithm used behind the scenes, as functions are replaced with hardcoded members.

6. Dimensions that are not in common between the cubes also need mappings. In the Target column, select *No Customer* for the Customer dimension (Unmapped):

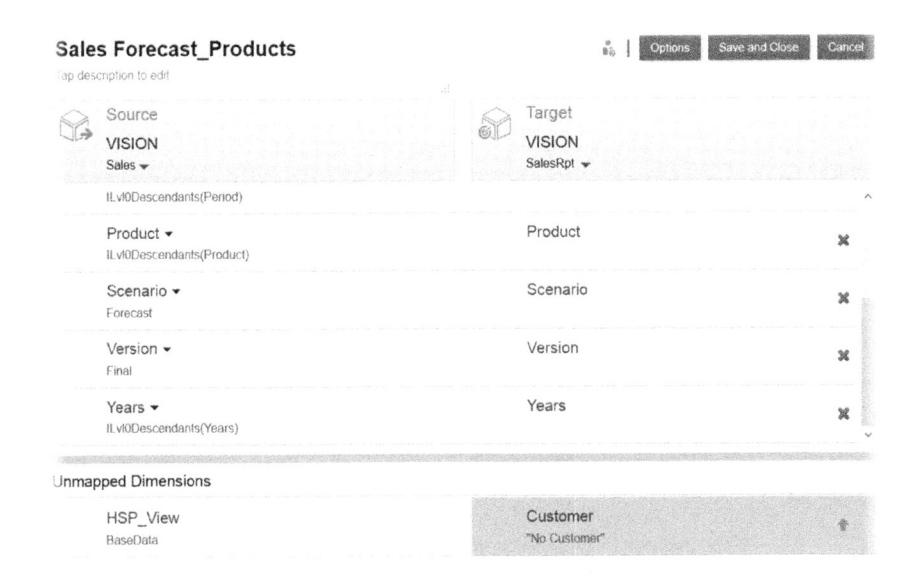

If you select *Options*, you can optionally define whether you want to copy *Comments*, *Attachments*, and / or *Supporting Detail* to a non-reporting cube (meaning ASO reporting cubes are not applicable to this situation). The *Collate* option determines how comments and attachments are copied in the case when there are not one-to-one mappings between the source and target. If *Collate* is checked, then the *Comments and Attachments* are combined and then sent to the target. If *Collate* is unchecked, only the last source cell's *Comments and Attachments* are copied. In the case of *Supporting Detail*, if there is not a one-to-one mapping then supporting details aren't copied:

240   Chapter 5: Integrate Data

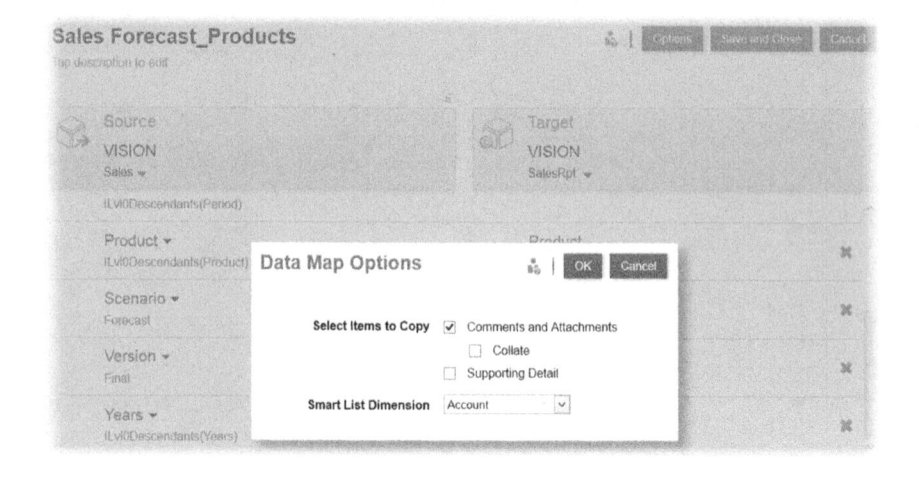

[Screenshot of Sales Forecast_Products data map with Data Map Options dialog showing Select Items to Copy: Comments and Attachments (checked), Collate, Supporting Detail; Smart List Dimension: Account]

7. Review and click *Save and Close*.

Execute a Data Map

Now that the data map is defined, you can push all data from the source cube to the target cube. Click ⚙ and choose *Push Data* or *Clear and Push Data*. *Push Data* uses the data map to push data based on how the data map currently exists, independent of any additional Smart Push configurations in data forms. *Clear and Push Data* first clears the data intersections in the target application based on the definitions in the data map, and then replace them.

Note! *Clear and Push Data* only works with member names, not member aliases.

Look Smarter Than You Are with PBCS 241

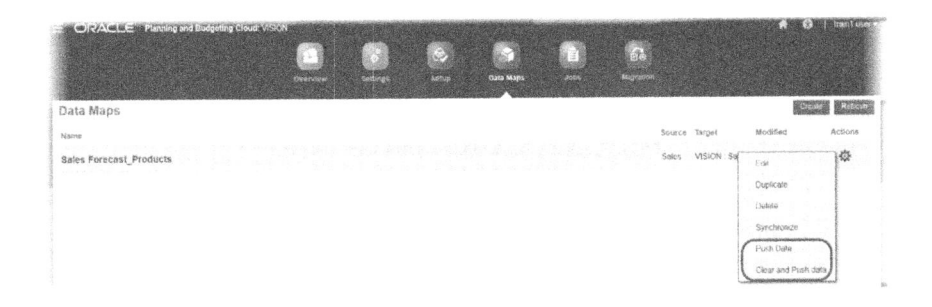

Data maps may also be executed from a data form or dashboard if Smart Push is enabled.

Synchronize Smart Lists in Reporting Applications

It is possible to map Smart Lists to physical dimensions in reporting applications. This type of situation requires that the Smart List entries in the source cube be mapped to physical members within the target cube. To synchronize the two, the *Synchronize* feature should be used. This can be found within the same Actions menu next to the data map:

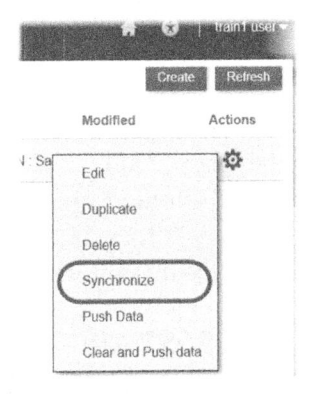

Once clicked, this adds all reporting dimension members to the Smart List. Smart List members are never deleted as a result of this action. You need to run *Synchronize* if you add new members before the maintenance window occurs on that same day; otherwise you could receive an error message about "new members not being found in the target."

AUTOMATE DATA INTEGRATION

You can automate all of these steps with EPM Automate. The EPM Automate Utility may be downloaded from PBCS. This utility allows you to remotely perform tasks in Cloud instances. You can automate a number of data integration tasks including:

- Import and export metadata
- Import and export data
- Run business rules on data
- Copy data from one database to another; typically from a block storage database to an aggregate storage database, or from a block storage database to another block storage database
- Upload files into service instance
- Upload files into the Planning Inbox / Outbox
- Upload files into Data Management folders and initiate import process by running data load rules
- Run a Data Management batch rule and get the output log file
- Download files from the Planning Inbox / Outbox and from Data Management folders
- List the files in the Inbox / Outbox
- Delete files from the Inbox / Outbox
- Update one or more substitution variables

For more information, see the Automation chapter / mission.

REST API

One other way to integrate data with Oracle PBCS is to use the more technical / programming route of REST APIs. First, an Application Program Interface (API) is, by definition, one piece of software that talks to another piece of software based upon certain routines, protocols, tools, and interfaces. The REST API is an API that falls into the category of an architectural style, or a concept that is a simple interface that transmits data using the already established HTTP methods without using any additional messaging layer such as SOAP. It works similar to how the communication happens between a web server hosting a web site and a client over the http protocol.

REST is short for **RE**presentational **S**tate **T**ransfer and can work with many of the EPM Automate Utility commands to integrate data between Oracle PBCS and other systems. A few basics about REST API:

- It relies on a client-server architecture
- It is resource-based versus action-based (as in SOAP). The resources are identified by uniform resource identifiers (URIs).
- All communications are performed via representation in XML or JSON format
- HTTP methods (verbs) are used (e.g., GET, PUT, POST, DELETE)
- In REST, everything is a resource. Every resource is identified by a unique identifier, thus making it easy to focus and request a specific piece of information. The request is in the form of a uniform resource identifier (URI), which identifies the resource – such as a file or folder on which to operate

REST API clients and browser add-ins are freely available on the web. The REST API add-in for Firefox is very easy and simple to use.

REST API works with EPM Automate to integrate data. EPM Automate is essentially a tool that wraps around and makes calls to the REST APIs. Nothing more, really. It's the least technically complex (and thus least powerful) way to make REST API calls. Other ways from Oracle to use writing programs or scripts include Java, cURL, or Groovy.

For more information on using REST API with Oracle PBCS, see the Oracle documentation.

Meanwhile, back on earth...

They decided to announce the tragedy on the regularly scheduled Tuesday webcast. i.n.t.e.r.R.e.1 has been having these webcasts every Tuesday and Thursday for years, delivering tips and tricks information on all of the Hyperion products. They never had to deliver bad news (well, except maybe a few times when Oracle made a strategic change in direction, like no more support for ODI). What could be worse than losing Edward Roske? Oracle announcing they would stop selling Hyperion products?

Danielle White, Marketing and Press Director for i.n.t.e.r.R.e.1, delivered the agreed upon statement: It was a sad day. We lost Edward Roske and the Vision EPM project today...

Immediate weeping could be heard across the Tuesday i.n.t.e.r.R.e.1 webcast (well, that was what Danielle imagined because on GoToWebinar everyone was muted). No more snarky jokes from Roske? It was impossible to imagine.

Chapter 6: Calculate Data

> LOG ENTRY: SOL 15, Entry 1
>
> I need to calculate data and I have an idiotically dangerous plan for this requirement. And boy, do I mean dangerous. But I really don't have much choice. I'm going to build business rules in Calculation Manager.

PBCS, much like its counterpart, on-premises Hyperion Planning, offers a variety of ways to calculate data. The combination of inherent member properties, member formulas, and custom business rules in Calculation Manager allows PBCS to create intelligent calculations primed for consumption by administrators and business users. Common business rules in PBCS include:

- Aggregate and consolidate data
- Allocate data
- Clear data
- Copy data
- Seed forecasts based on actuals
- Perform driver-based calculations
- Perform data validation and checks

This section will cover one of the more powerful ways to calculate data via business rules in Calculation Manager. I'll cover some very basic business rule examples. Note, there is so much more you can do with business rules and Calculation Manager.

INTRO TO CALCULATION MANAGER

Simply put, a business rule calculates PBCS data with a series of commands, functions, and equations. In PBCS, rules can only be created in Calculation Manager since EAS, Essbase Administration Services, is not available (for any legacy Hyperion administrators out there).

Chapter 6: Calculate Data

In Calculation Manager, you can design rules in a graphical environment that supports calculation ranges, conditions, scripts, and loops; display the calculation flow in a graphical way; use pre-defined templates for standard calculations; create your own custom templates definition; and design and use variables and run-time prompts. You can copy or share rules across Planning applications, as well as share components across rules. Objects are organized in the calculation library by objects, or in a tree structure.

> **Note!** Once a rule is created in Calculation Manager, it must be deleted manually to remove it. Objects in Calculation Manager will remain even after deleting the PBCS application.

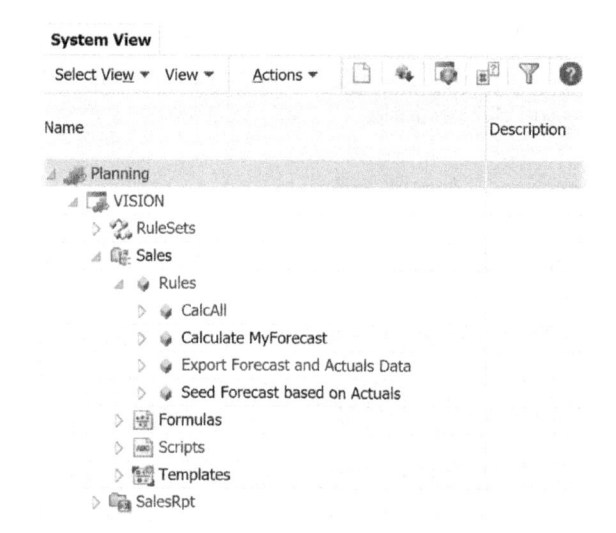

System View

```
Select View ▼   View ▼   Actions ▼

Name                                                Description
▲ 🗂 Planning
   ▲ 🗂 VISION
      ▷ 🗂 RuleSets
      ▲ 🗂 Sales
         ▲ 🗂 Rules
            ▷ ● CalcAll
            ▷ ● Calculate MyForecast
            ▷ ● Export Forecast and Actuals Data
            ▷ ● Seed Forecast based on Actuals
         ▷ 🗂 Formulas
         ▷ 🗂 Scripts
         ▷ 🗂 Templates
      ▷ 🗂 SalesRpt
```

The System View is where you can view and manage your business rules (Open, Debug, Delete, Print, Export, Refresh, Validate, Deploy, Compare Scripts, Copy, Create Shortcut, and Save as Template):

Look Smarter Than You Are with PBCS 247

When you create and edit a business rule, the following layout displays:

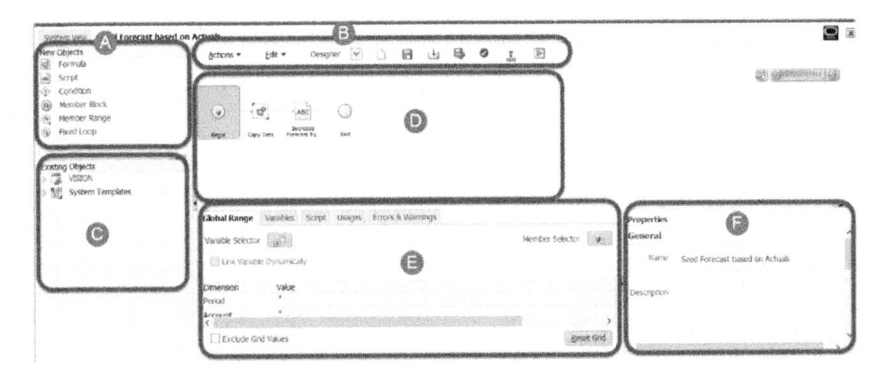

A. **New Objects** – pre-defined objects that you can drag into the main business rule layout; you'll be prompted to enter the parameters for the object

B. **Business Rule menu bar** – all of the available actions for the business rule like Save, Save As, Validate, Debug (helpful when troubleshooting), Analyze (to see if you've written an optimized script or not), Deploy, and more
C. **Existing (System) Objects** – you can save components for reuse in other scripts; access those saved objects in this section along with pre-defined templates from Oracle including:

- System Templates
  - Clear Data
  - Copy Data
  - Amount-Unit-Rate
  - Allocate - Level to Level
  - Allocation
  - Aggregation
  - SET commands
  - Currency Conversion

D. **Main layout** – visual data flow of the business rule; make sure to add captions for each component so the graphical flow is easy to read
E. **Details section** – displays the details for the selected component in the main layout
F. **Properties** – context-sensitive information panel to define properties for the selected component

There are two methods of creating rules: Graphical Mode and Script Mode. Graphical Mode is suited for those less experienced in scripts, due to the templates and script wizards that it provides. Script Mode is for more experienced developers who do not need a visual of the script or any step-by-step guidance.

Once a rule is created and saved in Calculation Manager, you must deploy the rule for launch in PBCS. Business rules and rule sets are run from the PBCS web interface or the Smart View client by users with appropriate access.

CREATE BUSINESS RULE IN GRAPHICAL MODE

For the Vision application, I'm going to create a simple business rule to show you how to use the graphical interface. I'm going to use the pre-defined templates to create a script that aggregates everything because this is a rule most BSO cubes need. I technically don't need this script in my Vision application because I've set all upper levels of dimensions to dynamic because I'm eagerly anticipating hybrid aggregation support in this sales forecasting application. However, until hybrid is supported in PBCS, administrators will want to leverage aggregation rules like this one and tag upper level sparse members to store.

To create a business rule in graphical mode,
1. Select *Navigator* ▣ >> *Create and Manage* >> *Rules*. The Calculation Manager appears.
2. In System View, expand *Planning* >> *VISION*.
3. Expand the *Sales* database and right-click on *Rules*.
4. Click *New* to create a new business rule:

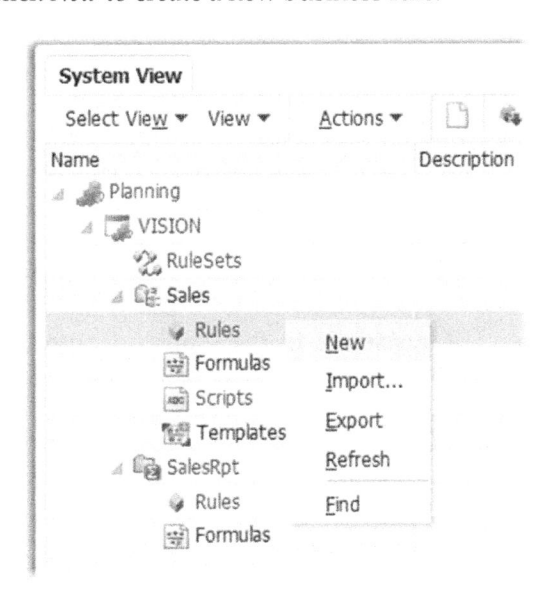

5. Name the rule "CalcAll". Leave other properties at their default values:

New Rule

Name	CalcAll
Application Type	Planning
Application	VISION
Cube	Sales

Help   OK   Cancel

6. Click *OK*.
7. Explore the *System Templates* list within the *Existing Objects* panel:

- System Templates
  - Clear Data
  - Copy Data
  - Amount-Unit-Rate
  - Allocate - Level to Level
  - Allocation
  - Aggregation
  - SET commands
  - Currency Conversion

8. Drag *SET commands* to the graphical representation of the business rule, between "Begin" and "End":

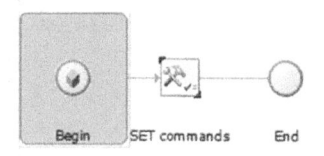

Begin — SET commands — End

Note! If you can't view the graphical interface due to the "a plugin is needed to display this content" error, then download and install Adobe Flash Player version 10 or later.

9. In the Data Volume section, select *Calculates all data blocks* for the UPDATECALC property. This turns off intelligent calculation, which only calculates data that has been changed after the last calculation:

SET commands Wizard
1. Data Volume

1. Data Volume

(UPDATECALC) Specify whether to calculate only dirty blocks, such as updated data blocks and their dependent parents, or all data blocks
Calculates all data blocks

(CLEARUPDATES) Specify when data blocks are marked as clean
Default

(EMPTYMEMBERSETS) Specify whether to stop the calculation within a FIX command if the FIX evaluates to an empty member set
Default

(FRMLBOTTOMUP) Specify whether to optimize the calculation of complex formulas on sparse dimensions in large database outlines
Default

Back   Next   Save   Finish   Exit

10. Click *Save*, then *Exit*.
11. Click the *Script* tab to see the code:

Chapter 6: Calculate Data

```
1  FIX ("BaseData")
2  /* Start Template:SET commands*/
3  SET UPDATECALC OFF;
4  /* End Template:SET commands*/
5  ENDFIX
```

12. Drag the *Aggregation* template icon to the graphical interface for the business rule, between "SET commands" and "End".
13. The Aggregation Wizard appears. Click *Next* until the "Full dense Aggregation" section appears.
14. In the Full dense Aggregation section, select *Account* for Dense dimension 1 and *Yes* for the property following:

Aggregation Wizard
Information > Point of view > Full dense Aggregation

Full dense Aggregation

Select the dense dimensions to aggregate fully

Dense dimension 1
Account

Does dense dimension 1 have stored, non-level 0 members?
Yes

Dense dimension 2

Does dense dimension 2 have stored, non-level 0 members?
No

If you have stored, non-level 0 members, a CALC DIM is generated for that dense dimension.

[Back] [Next] [Save] [Finish] [Exit]

15. Click *Next*.

16. In the Full sparse Aggregation section, select *Entity* for Sparse dimension 1 and select *No* for the property following. Select *Product* for Sparse dimension 2 and select *No* for the property following:

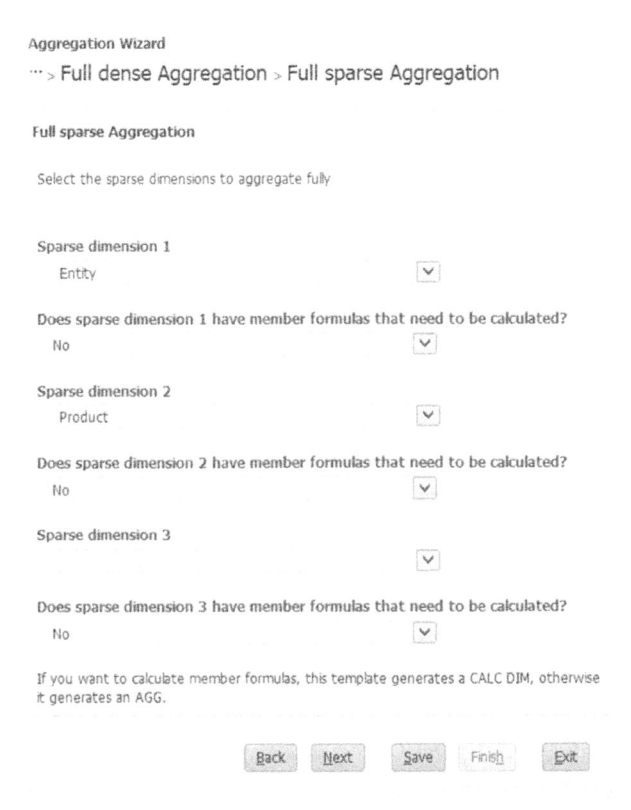

Aggregation Wizard
··· > Full dense Aggregation > Full sparse Aggregation

Full sparse Aggregation

Select the sparse dimensions to aggregate fully

Sparse dimension 1
Entity

Does sparse dimension 1 have member formulas that need to be calculated?
No

Sparse dimension 2
Product

Does sparse dimension 2 have member formulas that need to be calculated?
No

Sparse dimension 3

Does sparse dimension 3 have member formulas that need to be calculated?
No

If you want to calculate member formulas, this template generates a CALC DIM, otherwise it generates an AGG.

[Back] [Next] [Save] [Finish] [Exit]

17. *Save, OK,* then *Exit.*
18. Click the *Script* tab to see the written code:

```
1 /* Start Template:Aggregation*/
2 CALC DIM ("Account");
3 AGG ("Entity");
4 AGG ("Product");
5 /* End Template:Aggregation*/
```

Chapter 6: Calculate Data

Note! Remember that in our Vision application build, I don't really need this calc script to roll up data because upper members in the BSO cube are set to dynamic. In your real life application, until hybrid is supported, this calc would make sense.

19. Click the *End* icon in the graphical representation and click the *Script* tab to view the entire script:

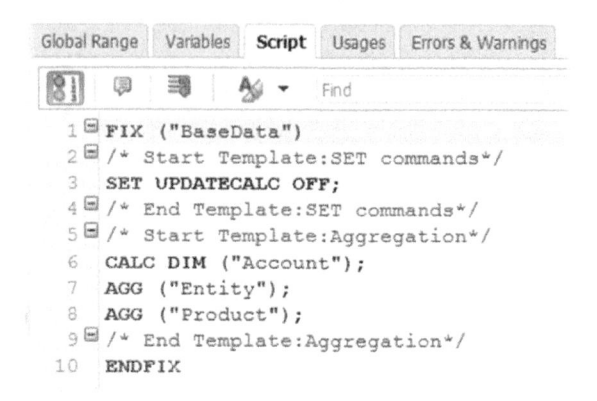

```
1  FIX ("BaseData")
2  /* Start Template:SET commands*/
3  SET UPDATECALC OFF;
4  /* End Template:SET commands*/
5  /* Start Template:Aggregation*/
6  CALC DIM ("Account");
7  AGG ("Entity");
8  AGG ("Product");
9  /* End Template:Aggregation*/
10 ENDFIX
```

Note! Note that if you have sandboxing enabled for the application, Calculation Manager automatically inserts a "FIX" statement at the very beginning of the rule. Most of the times this is good…sometimes it can be tricky if you're trying to write in script mode.

20. Use the menu bar to *Validate* then *Save* the rule:

Save does not automatically perform the *Validate* step – you need to *Validate* as a separate action step. You can use the *Validate and Save* option instead to tackle both actions in one step.

CREATE GRAPHICAL RULE WITH A SCRIPT COMPONENT

Now let's create a graphical rule that I do need in our Vision application. Vision would like to seed its forecast based on actuals data. I can use a business rule to do that. This time I'm still going to create a graphical rule and use a pre-defined Calc Manager template. But I'm also going to insert a script component (where I can write the logic directly); this is sort of a hybrid approach to business rule writing. You can take advantage of many of the Calc Manager features (like the flow diagrams, captions, printing, etc.), but still write your own logic if you prefer.

To create a graphical business rule,
1. Create a new business rule. Call it "Seed Forecast based on Actuals".
2. Drag the *Copy Data* template into the blank rule area.
3. Enter the following POV:
    a. *Period*: @RELATIVE(Period,0)
    b. *Account*: Units, "List Price"
    c. *Entity*: @RELATIVE(Entity,0)
    d. *Product*: @RELATIVE(Product,0)
    e. *Version*: Final
    f. *HSP_View*: BaseData

Chapter 6: Calculate Data

Copy Data Wizard
Information > Point of View

Point of View

Define the Point of View to use for copying data

Select members to restrict the data copy

Use Predefined Selection   Member Select

Dimension	Value
Period	"@RELATIVE("Period", 0)
Account	"Units","List Price"
Entity	"@RELATIVE("Entity", 0)
Product	"@RELATIVE("Product", 0)
Years	
Scenario	
Version	"Final"
HSP_View	"BaseData"

4. Copy data from *FY15, Actual*:

Copy Data Wizard
Information > Point of View > Copy From

Copy From

* Select members from which to copy data

Use Predefined Selection   Member Select

Dimension	Value
Years	"FY15"
Scenario	"Actual"

5. Copy data to *FY16, Forecast*:

Copy Data Wizard
Information > Point of View > Copy From > Copy To

Copy To

* Select members to which to copy the data

Use Predefined Selection   Member Select

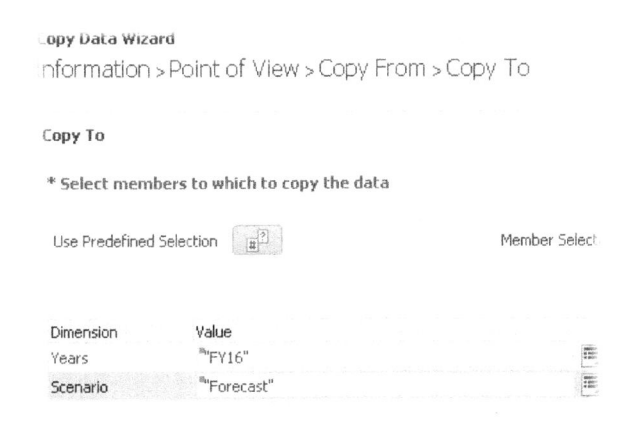

Dimension	Value
Years	"FY16"
Scenario	"Forecast"

6. Leave Options blank – you do not want to alter the data during the copy.

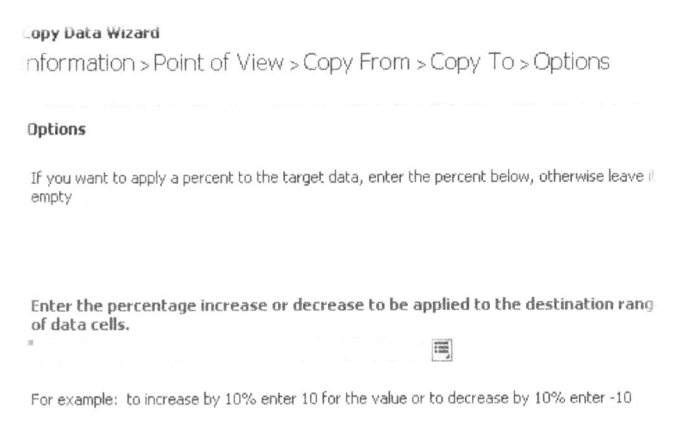

Copy Data Wizard
Information > Point of View > Copy From > Copy To > Options

Options

If you want to apply a percent to the target data, enter the percent below, otherwise leave it empty

Enter the percentage increase or decrease to be applied to the destination range of data cells.

For example: to increase by 10% enter 10 for the value or to decrease by 10% enter -10

7. Note that at any time I can go back and edit the entered parameters for the template:

Chapter 6: Calculate Data

Point of View
Select members to restrict the data copy

- Period @RELATIVE(Period, 0)
- Account "Units", "List Price"
- Entity @RELATIVE(Entity, 0)
- Product @RELATIVE(Product, 0)
- Version Final
- HSP_View "BaseData"

Copy From
Select members from which to copy data

- Years FY15
- Scenario Actual

Copy To
Select members to which to copy the data

- Years FY16
- Scenario Forecast

8. Click *Finish*.
9. Now drag a *Script* component into the rule after the Copy Data component:

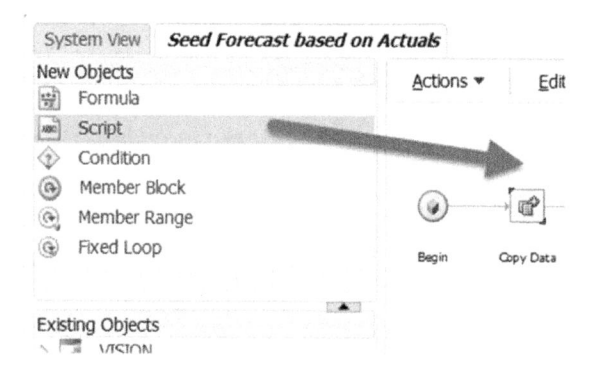

Seed Forecast based on Actuals

New Objects:
- Formula
- Script
- Condition
- Member Block
- Member Range
- Fixed Loop

Existing Objects:
- VISION

10. Type in the following logic into the script area:

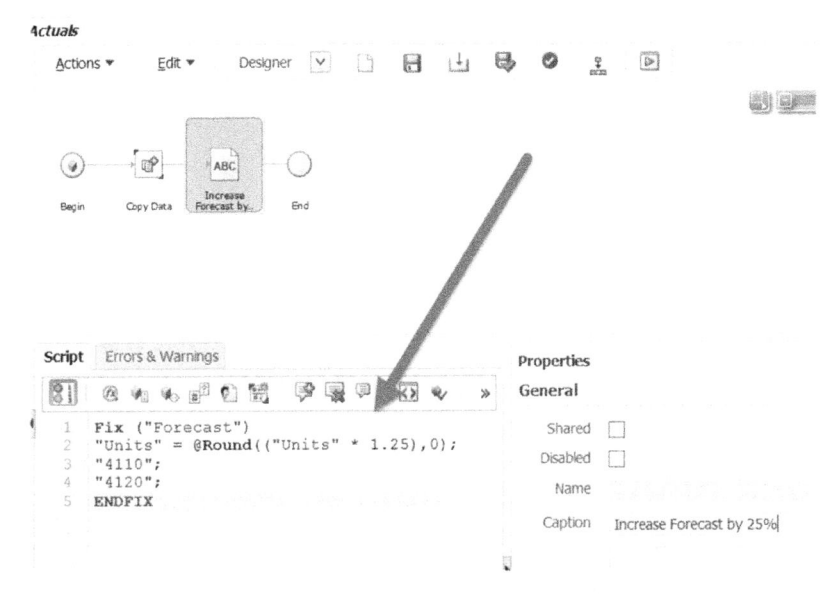

```
Actuals
Actions ▼    Edit ▼    Designer
```

[Business rule flow: Begin → Copy Data → Increase Forecast by... → End]

```
Script  Errors & Warnings

1  Fix ("Forecast")
2  "Units" = @Round(("Units" * 1.25),0);
3  "4110";
4  "4120";
5  ENDFIX
```

Properties
General
Shared   ☐
Disabled ☐
Name
Caption   Increase Forecast by 25%

11. Add a caption "Increase Forecast by 25%".

Notice that the business rule calculates the two account members "4110" and "4120" which have member formulas associated with them. "4110" is based on units and price:

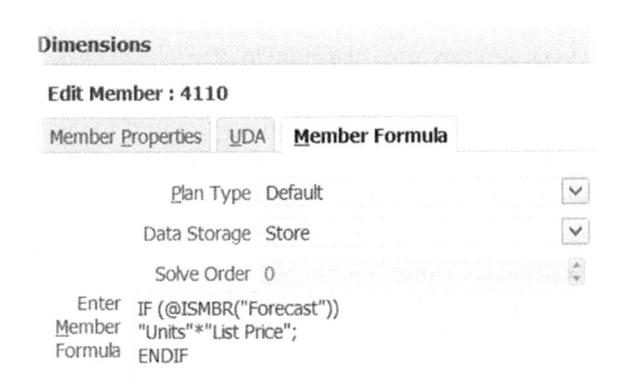

Dimensions

Edit Member : 4110

Member Properties | UDA | **Member Formula**

Plan Type   Default
Data Storage   Store
Solve Order   0
Enter Member Formula   IF (@ISMBR("Forecast"))
                       "Units"*"List Price";
                       ENDIF

12. "4120" is based on the "4110" revenue:

```
Edit Member : 4120

Member Properties   UDA   Member Formula

                Plan Type  Default
             Data Storage  Store
              Solve Order  0
          Enter    If (@ISMBR("Forecast"))
          Member   "4110"* .18;
          Formula  ENDIF
```

13. Use the menu bar to *Validate* then *Save* the rule (or you can also choose *Validate and Save* icon in one step):

CREATE BUSINESS RULE IN SCRIPT MODE

Experienced Hyperion Administrators might prefer to write the business rule scripts and skip the graphical user interface. If you choose to write the business rule in script mode, there are a few simple rules to follow (these same rules apply to script objects like the one I inserted in the previous business rule):

- End every statement with a semicolon
- You can break a statement onto multiple lines, but the end of the statement must have a semicolon
- If a member name contains spaces or starts with a number, surround it with "double quotes." Spaces between member names, commands, and functions do not matter.
- Start comments with /*
- End comments with */
- Calc scripts are not case-sensitive
- Use the Debug mode to troubleshoot your script one section at a time

There are many more rules, but these are the important ones that people tend to forget, causing them to wonder for hours why their business rule scripts aren't working.

You can switch to edit in script mode by switching the drop down box from "Designer" to "Edit Script." Thankfully when writing scripts, Calc Manager has several icons / functions / tools to help you build your logic (mouse over each icon to see the available options):

```
FIX ("Forecast")
  "Units" = @Round(("Units" * 1.25),0);
  "4110";
  "4120";
  AGG("Product", "Entity");
ENDFIX
```

Because I have to finish this in a few hours, I can't spend any more time on all of the Calc Manager features (that could be its own separate mission and book). There are many online resources and your helpful partner, i.n.t.e.r.R.e.l, can provide more information on business rules and Calculation Manager.

Until hybrid aggregation is supported, you will likely want to create a business rule for users that will calculate forecast for just the entity (or product). Why recalculate the whole database? Shouldn't I just calculate that entity and any impacted entities? Yes. You should only calculate what you have to; this has big performance benefits for users during the planning cycle.

I will create a business rule that runs a focused aggregation using run-time prompt variables to prompt users for their department and desired version and a substitution variable to focus the rule for a specific year. I'll create the run-time prompt variables first, and then write the business rule script.

Variables

Before I move forward, let me explain a little more on variables. Variables are like placeholders in a business rule for a specific purpose.

Chapter 6: Calculate Data

They can be defined at the global, application, cube or business rule level. Calculation Manager supports two types of variables: execution and replacement variables. Supported variables include numeric, string, dimension, member or members, cross-dimension, percent, integer, member range, string as a number, date as a number, and array. A common variable is a run-time prompt variable which prompts users to enter a value to put into the variable. In Vision's case, I am going to prompt the users to select a department member and version member.

To create variables for business rules,
1. Select *Navigator* >> *Create and Manage* >> *Rules*. The Calculation Manager appears.
2. Within the System View tab, navigate to *Actions* >> *Variable Designer*:

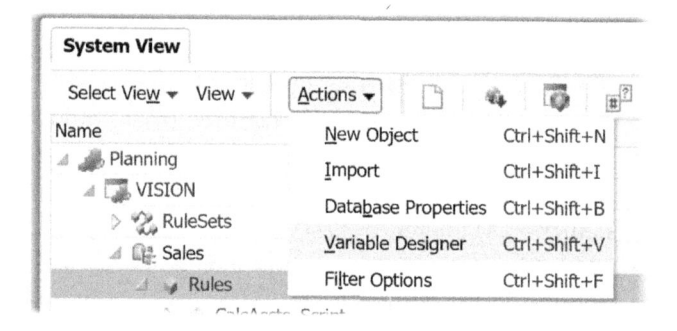

System View		
Select View ▼ View ▼	Actions ▼	
Name	New Object	Ctrl+Shift+N
▲ Planning	Import	Ctrl+Shift+I
▲ VISION	Database Properties	Ctrl+Shift+B
▷ RuleSets	Variable Designer	Ctrl+Shift+V
▲ Sales	Filter Options	Ctrl+Shift+F
▲ Rules		

Note! Variables can also be created through the variable selector screen.

3. Then switch over to the *Variable Designer* tab.
4. In the left panel, navigate down and then right-click on the *VISION* application and click *New*:

```
System View   Variable Designer
Varia_ble Navigator
    Planning
      <Global>
      VISION
         Sale   New
         Sale   Refresh
                Export
                Find
```

5. In the Properties section, name the variable "Department_Var".
6. Select *Member* for Type.
7. Click the radio button for *Dimension Type* and select *Entity* in the drop down menu:

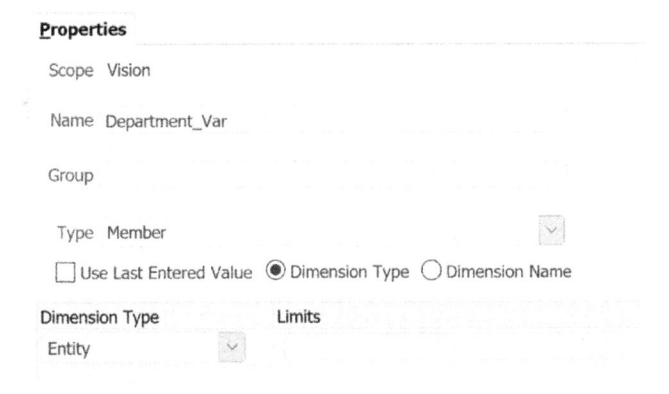

```
Properties

Scope   Vision

Name    Department_Var

Group

Type    Member
        ☐ Use Last Entered Value  ● Dimension Type  ○ Dimension Name

Dimension Type              Limits
Entity
```

8. Check the box for *RTP* (run-time prompt) and type "Select Department" for the RTP Text:

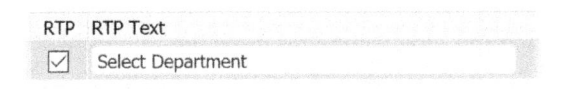

```
RTP   RTP Text
 ☑    Select Department
```

9. Create a "Version_Var" and "Year_Var" using the same principles.

The following variables should be listed in the Variable Designer:

Name	Description	Type	Default Value
Department_Var		Member	
Version_Var		Member	
Year_Var		Members	"FY13"

Note! Notice "FY13" was selected as Year_Var's Default Value. Default values can be chosen to make the user selection of run-time prompts a little easier.

Now that the variables are done, on to writing a business rule using the script mode!

To create a business rule in script mode,
1. In the Calculation Manager, expand the *Sales* database and right-click on *Rules*.
2. Click *New* to create a new business rule.
3. Name the rule "Calculate MyForecast". Leave other properties as default.
4. Click *OK*.
5. Before doing anything else, in the menu bar, change the drop-down value to *Edit Script*:

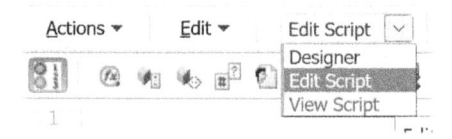

6. When the screen changes, type the following:

```
FIX ("Forecast", &ForecastYear, {Version_Var})
FIX ({Department_Var})
"4110";
"4120";
AGG("Product");
ENDFIX
@IANCESTORS({Department_Var});
ENDFIX
```

Notice the use of the RTP variables I created earlier. The syntax for referencing a Calc Manager variable is to enclose the variable name with "{}". The syntax for referencing a substitution variable is to prefix "&" before the substitution variable name.

The line of code that says @IANCESTORS ({Department_Var}) only calculates the entity passed to it from the data form and any ancestor members, making this a much faster business rule.

7. Click the *Script* tab to review the final code:

```
Calculate MyForecast

1  FIX ("Forecast", &ForecastYear, {Version_Var})
2  FIX ({Department_Var})
3  "4110";
4  "4120";
5  AGG("Product");
6  ENDFIX
7  @IANCESTORS({Department_Var});
8  ENDFIX
```

Variables | Script | Usages | Errors & Warnings

```
1  FIX ("BaseData")
2  FIX ("Forecast", &ForecastYear, Pass1)
3  FIX (403)
4  "4110";
5  "4120";
6  AGG("Product");
7  @IANCESTORS(403);
8  ENDFIX
9  ENDFIX
```

Note! Again, if you have sandboxing enabled for the application, Calculation Manger automatically inserts a FIX statement at the very beginning of the rule. Most of the times this is good... sometimes it can be tricky if you are trying to write in script mode.

Note! The FIX statement containing BaseData should be in every rule or script when user sandboxes are enabled. See the section on HSP_View in the Build Dimensions section for more information.

8. Click the *Variables* tab and enter or select values for *Department_Var* and *Version_Var*.
9. *Validate*, then *Save*.
10. Now update the substitution variables to list the rolling forecast variables since this business rule are attached to the rolling forecast data forms:

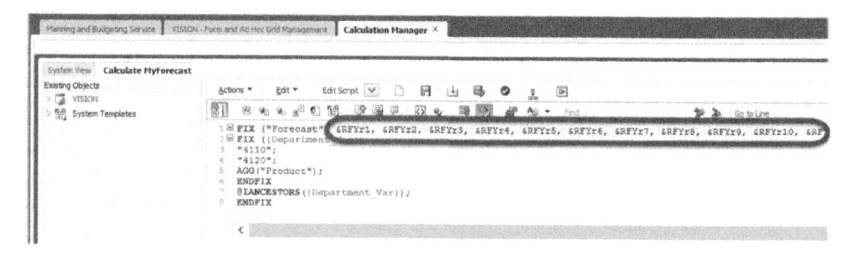

DEPLOY BUSINESS RULE

Once a business rule has been created, it must be deployed to be available in PBCS. I'll deploy the business rules I created.

To deploy the business rule,
1. In Calculation Manager, select the desired rules (control-click to multi-select).
2. Right-click and select *Deploy*:

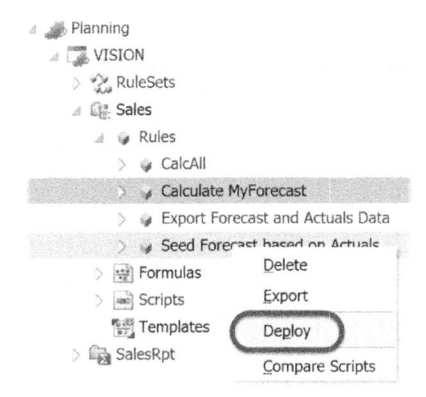

3. When the following message shows, click *OK*:

> **Deployment Status**
> The deployment was successful.

Once deployed, the rule can be assigned to a form and launched in the PBCS application.

LAUNCH BUSINESS RULE

You can launch business rules either from Calculation Manager or PBCS. We'll launch from PBCS, as this is the method that most users use.

To launch the business rule,
1. In the main menu, click the *Rules* icon.
2. The complete listing of business rules for which users have access displays. Administrators see every rule.
3. Click the arrow icon for *Launch* next to the business rule you'd like to execute:

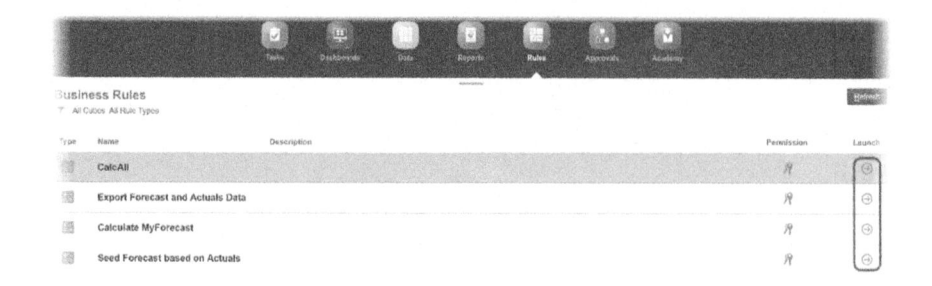

VIEW BUSINESS RULE STATUS AND SCHEDULE

The Job Console provides a way to view the status of business rules that are run for PBCS.

To access the Job Console,

1. Select *Navigator* >> *Application* >> *Jobs*

Here you can view pending and recently completed jobs within PBCS such as business rule launches and database refreshes:

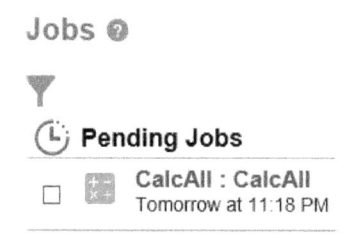

Within PBCS, it is also quite simple to schedule jobs using the Jobs Console. I will schedule the *CalcAll* business rule to run nightly at 12AM.

To schedule a rule,

1. Select *Navigator* >> *Application* >> *Jobs* and click *Schedule Jobs:*

2. Select the type of job, give the job a name, then designate when and how often the job should run:

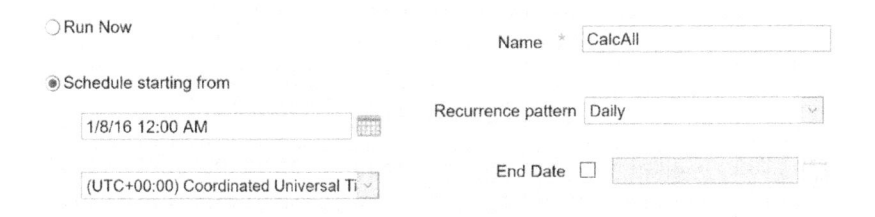

3. Click *Next*.
4. Select the rule by clicking *Select* to the right of the business rule of your choice. Click *Next*.
5. Review the scheduled job and click *Finish*.

The scheduled job appears in the Jobs Console:

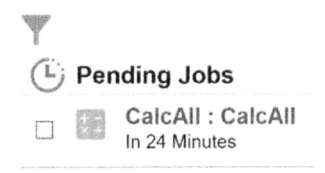

If an error occurs, you can view the error details by clicking the job name:

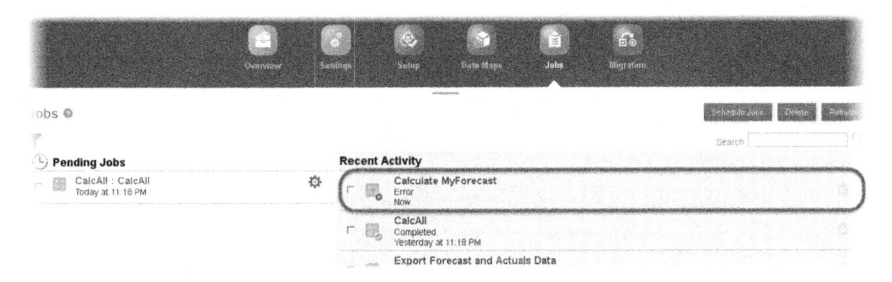

Job Details

Application Name	VISION	Start Time	1/30/16 2:51:20 AM
Plan Type	Sales	End Time	1/30/16 2:51:20 AM
Job Status	Error		
Prompt Text	Cannot calculate dimension member [410] with restricted member [410]		
Select Version			

I'll come back to the Job Scheduler later on other types of automation.

ASSIGN BUSINESS RULE TO FORM

The "Calculate Form" business rule is automatically created for every form. It calculates subtotals for the members on the data form (more on data forms in just a bit). Note, if every member on your data form is stored input or dynamically calculated, you do not have to "Calculate Form."

You can also assign custom business rules to a data form, using the arrows to move over the desired business rule to the "Selected Business Rules" section. For the assigned business rule, you can specify the following:

- **Run Before Load** – runs the business rule when the user opens the data form
- **Run After Save** – runs the business rule when the user clicks the save button on the data form
- The user may be prompted if a run-time prompt is included in the business rule. You can select the option, **Use Members on Data Form**, to pass the members on the data form through to the run-time prompt and then optionally *Hide Prompt* to hide the run-time prompt from the user.

While I haven't created a data form yet, I want to show you the steps to assign business rules in data forms.

To assign a business rule to a data form,
1. Select *Navigator >> Create and Manage >> Forms* and edit the *Sales Forecast – Products* data form.

2. Navigate to the *Business Rules* tab:

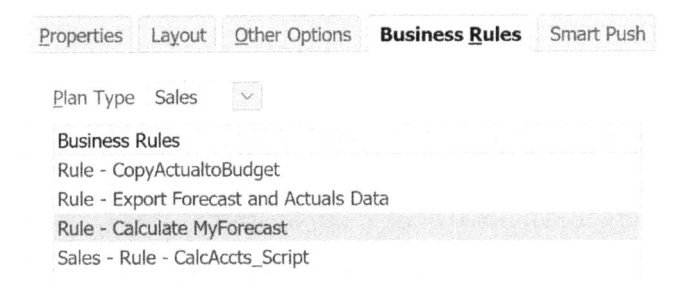

   > Properties | Layout | Other Options | **Business Rules** | Smart Push
   >
   > Plan Type   Sales
   >
   > Business Rules
   > Rule - CopyActualtoBudget
   > Rule - Export Forecast and Actuals Data
   > **Rule - Calculate MyForecast**
   > Sales - Rule - CalcAccts_Script

3. Add the *Calculate MyForecast* business rule to the right panel:

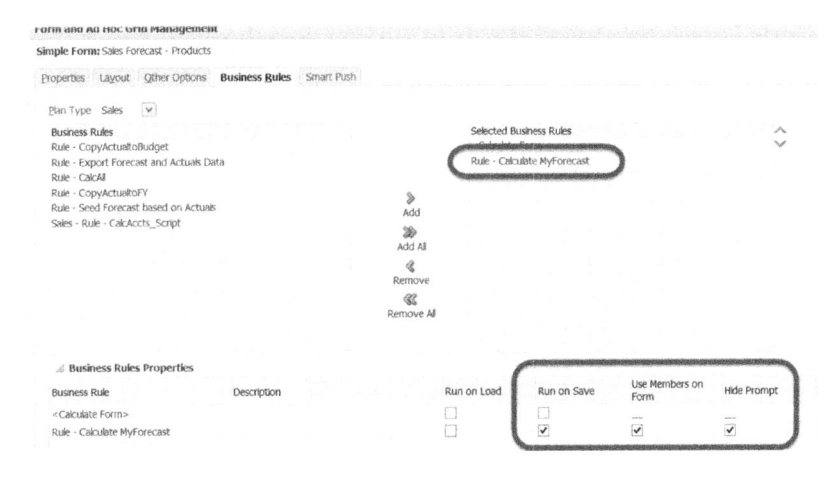

4. In Business Rule Properties, check the *Run on Save*, *Use Members on Form*, and *Hide Prompt* boxes for the rule.
5. Click *Finish*.

EXPORT DATA USING A BUSINESS RULE

While I'm on the topic of exporting data, I'll cover one last way to export data from PBCS. You can create a business rule and use the DATAEXPORT calculation script command. This command allows you to extract data to a text file or relational table. Placing this command within FIX statements and IF statements allows you to isolate the desired data to be pulled. You can then load the extracted data to a source cube.

The full process can be automated with the Job Scheduler and scheduled to run as needed. There are Data Export Options to define behavior for the export:

```
SET DataExportDecimal <n>;
SET DataExportLevel "ALL" or "LEVEL" or "INPUT";
SET DataExportColFormat ON or OFF;
SET DataExportColHeader "<Dimension Name>";
SET DataExportDynamicCalc ON or OFF;
SET DataExportOverwriteFile ON or OFF;
SET DataExportDimHeader ON or OFF;
```

Review the example export business rule script below that exports Forecast and Actual data to a file in the Inbox / Outbox Explorer called "VisionForecastDataExport2.txt".

```
FIX ("BaseData")
SET DataExportOptions
{
            DataExportLevel "ALL";
            DataExportColFormat ON;
            DataExportColHeader "Account";
            DataExportDynamicCalc ON;
            DataExportOverwriteFile ON;
            DataExportDimHeader OFF;
};

FIX("Forecast", "Actual",
@Relative("Years",0),
@Relative("Entity",0),
@Relative("Product",0),
"BegBalance":"Dec",
"Units",
@Relative("4001",0),
"4001",
@Relative("Version",0))

DATAEXPORT "File" ","
"/u03/lcm/VisionForecastDataExport2.txt" "NULL";
ENDFIX
ENDFIX
```

Create the business rule in the PBCS application and call it "Export Forecast and Actuals Data". Use the Job Scheduler to schedule the business rule if desired.

Whenever the business rule is run, it creates a text file that can be viewed and downloaded in the Inbox / Outbox Explorer. To go to the Inbox / Outbox Explorer, navigate to *Navigator >> Application >> Overview >> Actions >> Inbox / Outbox Explorer*:

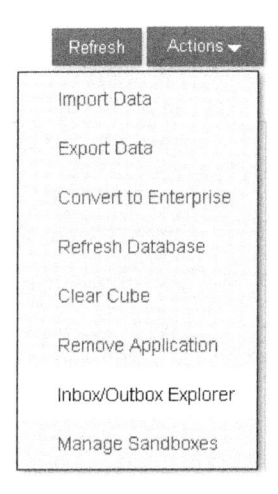

Since the business rule script specifies to overwrite the file, the file is replaced every time the rule is launched:

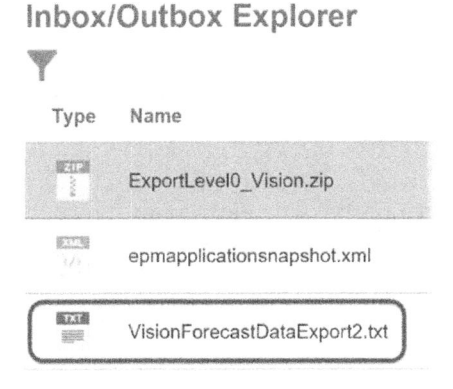

ASO Cube Business Rules

Business rules are supported for ASO cubes with some considerations and limitations. You follow the same steps to create a business rule for an ASO cube in the graphical interface.

The graphical interface is the only supported interface for ASO cubes (scripting is not supported). There are three pre-defined templates that you can use to build business rules for your ASO cube: Point of View, Allocation, and Formula. The Point of View template defines the focus for the business rule. The Allocation template allocates values from a source to a destination based on a driver. This template supports single dimension allocation. The Formula template allows you to build a simple formula calculation:

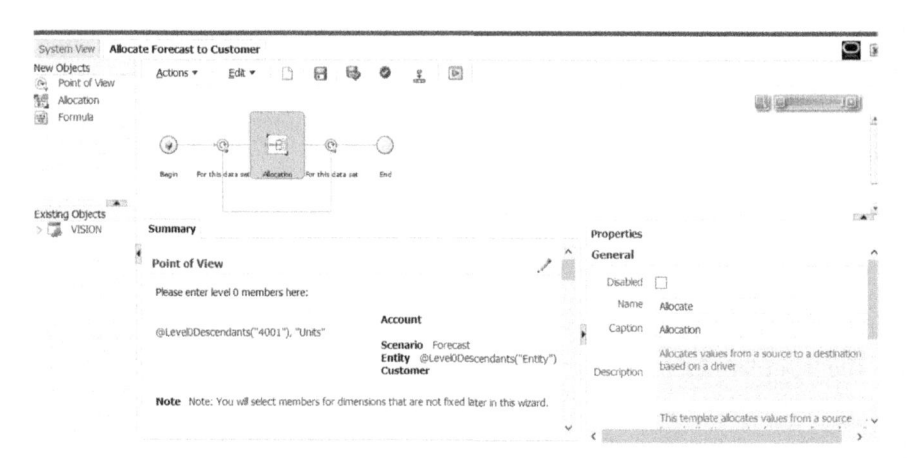

One other handy task that you will need to do for your ASO cubes: partial data clears. At some point, you will want to clear part of the data in an ASO cube but not all of the data.

To perform a partial data clear in an ASO cube,
1. Open Calculation Manager.
2. Click the icon for *Database Properties*.
3. Right-click on the desired cube and select *Clear >> Partial Data*.

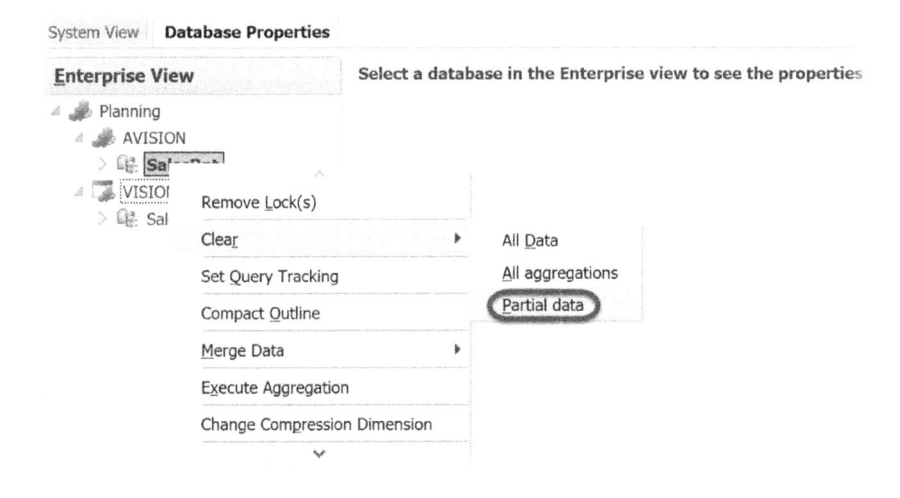

[Screenshot showing Database Properties menu with Clear > Partial data highlighted]

4. Enter the MDX expression defining the data slice that you would like to clear; for example:

```
{([Actual],[Final])}
```

MDX is the syntax that is used with ASO cubes. For more information on MDX and ASO, check out the Oracle documentation.

5. Choose the option: *Physical* or *Logical*.

A *Physical* clear actually clears the data (which may take a little longer) and the *Logical* clear creates an offsetting slice of data (which goes a little faster). If you have time, choose *Physical*. If clearing data during the day (while users are in the system), choose *Logical* and then come back at night and run a physical clear.

6. Click *OK* and the data should clear for the specified slice.

As I mentioned at the beginning of the chapter, I've only skimmed the surface with the foundations of Calculation Manager and business rules. For more information and examples, check out the Oracle documentation and i.n.t.e.r.R.e.l.'s webcasts and Play It Forward videos.

> **LOG ENTRY: SOL 15, Entry 2**
>
> Well, the implementation is still going! Calculation Manager worked and it wasn't dangerous at all! Really easy in fact and it met all of my calculating, aggregating and allocating needs.

Look Smarter Than You Are with PBCS 277

Chapter 7: Create User Interfaces

> LOG ENTRY: SOL 16, Entry 1
>
> Finally! Something users can see and touch and love.
> Wait. That sounded a bit awkward. What I meant to say is… I'm excited to finally create the user interfaces in PBCS.
> It is a little lonely in the Cloud by myself…

DATA FORMS

Data forms are the way for users to enter and review plan data. Data forms can be accessed over the web or in Excel via Smart View:

Manage Form Folders

Data forms may be organized into form folders and security may be applied at the form folder or form level.

To create a form folder,
1. Select *Navigator* >> *Create and Manage* >> *Forms*.
2. Create a Form Folder in the left panel by clicking .
3. Call the Form Folder "Vision users". Click *OK*.

Create

* Enter the name for the new folder Vision Users

OK   Cancel

Data Form Basics

A data form is a structured interface that administrators create for end users. There are two types of data forms: Simple and Composite. A simple form is created against a single cube with members assigned to the rows, columns, pages (drop-down menu), and point of view (POV). A composite form is comprised of two or more simple forms.

When you create a simple data form, the first tab allows you to define and update data form properties:

- Data form name
- Description
- Source cube
- Data form instructions

You can add detailed instructions for the data form and use formatting, URLs, and more to create a helpful guide to end users.

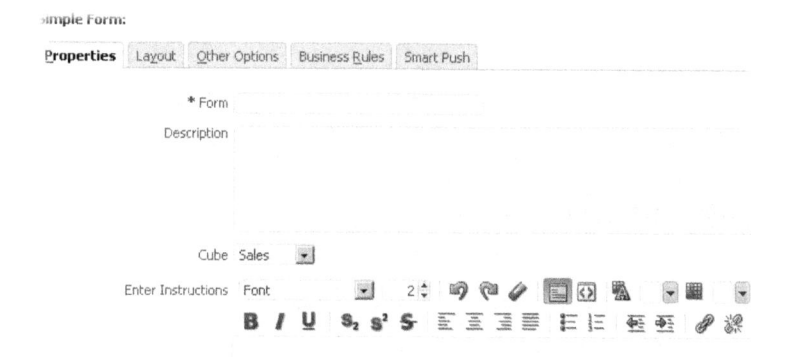

Simple Form:

Properties | Layout | Other Options | Business Rules | Smart Push

* Form

Description

Cube Sales

Enter Instructions Font

On the Layout tab, you must have at least one dimension and member in a row and column. A dimension can exist in one place only – the row, column, page, or point of view. The Point of View section defines one member only from the dimensions assigned to this section. You can use the member selection icons to select members for the point of view or manually type the member name in:

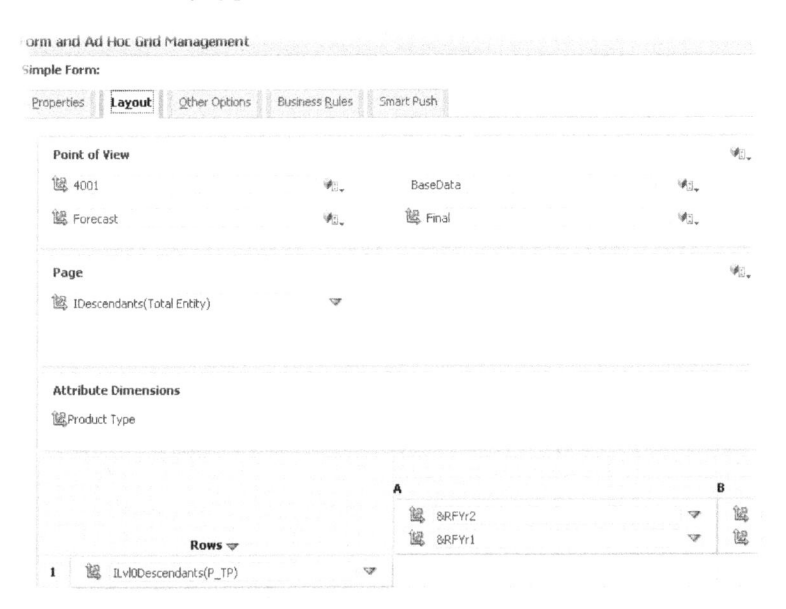

```
orm and Ad Hoc Grid Management
Simple Form:
 Properties  | Layout |  Other Options  | Business Rules | Smart Push

Point of View
  4001                          BaseData                  
  Forecast                      Final                     

Page
  IDescendants(Total Entity)

Attribute Dimensions
  Product Type

                                     A                    B
                                  8RFYr2                  
                        Rows ▽    8RFYr1                  
  1     ILvl0Descendants(P_TP)
```

The Page section may house one or more dimensions. These dimensions display the selected members at the top of data forms in the form of a drop-down menu. The rows and columns of a data form are the "meat" of the form. You can define one or more rows / columns. You may place one or more dimensions in a row section or column section. You can drag and drop to move dimensions around the Layout definition.

You may insert additional columns or rows into a data form (each column / row is also known as a "segment." You can also add a data column / row or a formula column / row:

280   Chapter 7: Create User Interfaces

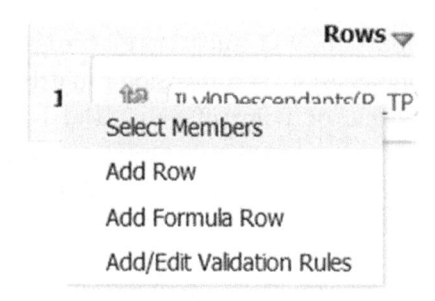

```
                                      Rows
        ]      ⬚   ILvlnDescendants(P   TP
               Select Members
               Add Row
               Add Formula Row
               Add/Edit Validation Rules
```

One of the cool features added in the fall of 2016 is the ability to support Attribute dimensions in forms. Attributes can be configured to filter members for the base dimension or viewed in the page, rows, and columns of a data form.

Member Selection

When you choose to use Member Selection to define members in the Point of View, Page, Row, and Column sections, click ⬚ or ⬚ and then ⬚ Edit. The Member Selection window displays:

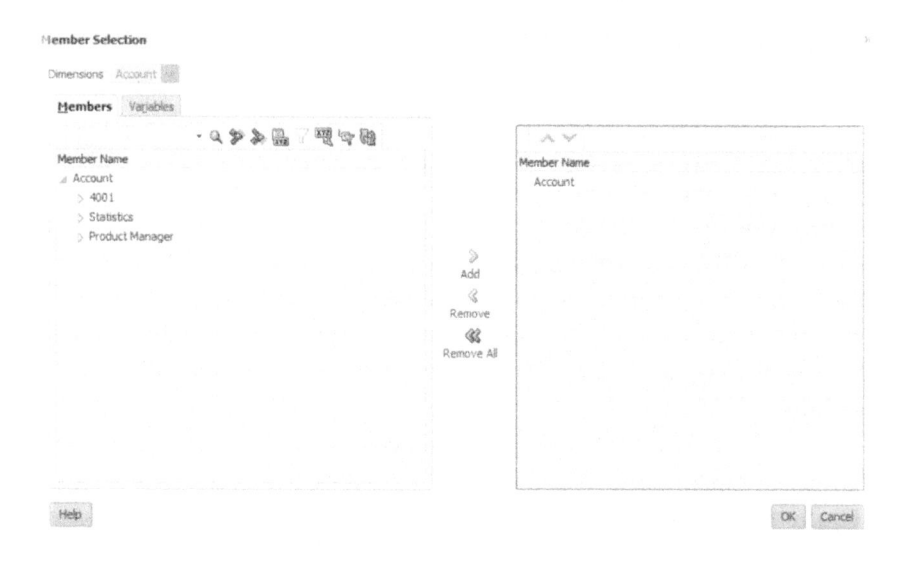

```
Member Selection
Dimensions  Account
Members   Variables
                      · Q 🔍 📋 🗒 🗒 🗒
Member Name                                    Member Name
 ▲ Account                                      Account
   > 4001
   > Statistics
   > Product Manager
                                 ▷
                                Add
                                 ◁
                               Remove
                                 ◁◁
                              Remove All

Help                                              OK    Cancel
```

From this window, you can navigate the dimension to select members. You can choose whether you want to search by member name, alias or different combinations of member name and alias by selecting the *Display* icon:

Type in the search bar and click the magnifying glass icon to search for members:

Other options include "keeping" or retaining member selections by Attributes or Level:

Instead of specific members, you can also insert applicable substitution variables and ranges of substitution variables, user variables, or filter members by associated attributes on the Variables tab in the Member Selection window:

Chapter 7: Create User Interfaces

Member Selection

Dimensions: Account

Members	Variables

> User Variables

Substitution Variables

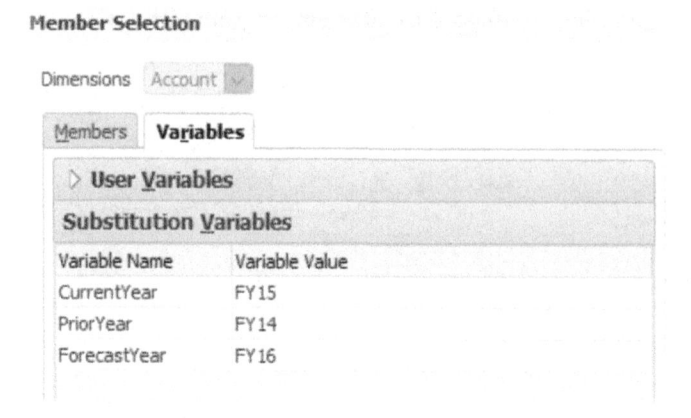

Variable Name	Variable Value
CurrentYear	FY 15
PriorYear	FY 14
ForecastYear	FY 16

Use the arrow keys to move members between the dimension and variables list and Selected Members section:

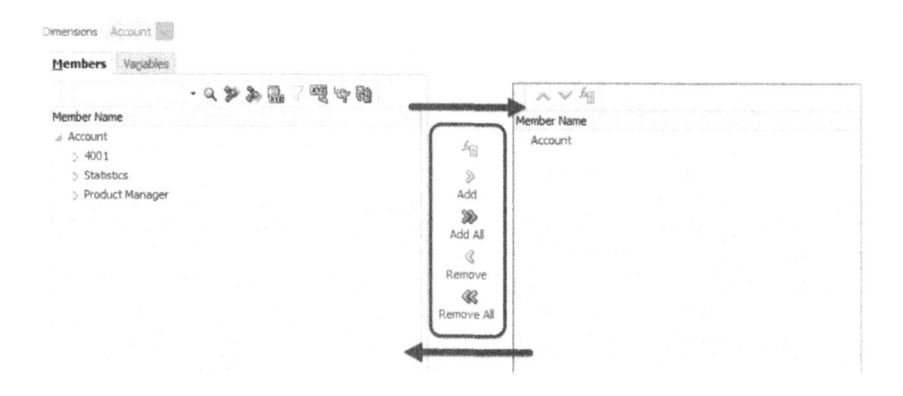

Dimensions: Account

Members | Variables

Member Name
- Account
  - 4001
  - Statistics
  - Product Manager

Member Name
- Account

(Add, Add All, Remove, Remove All)

Before moving the selected member, you can also choose whether to move the member itself, or children of the member, or descendants of the member (or other available functions):

Functions provide two benefits:

- A faster way to pick a list of members
- Making the data form dynamic

As the dimension evolves over time (as members are added or removed), the form automatically displays the correct list.

An example of a function may be pulling in the children of Product (so that you have a dynamic list of the product categories displayed on the form) or level-0 Descendants of Revenue (so that you always have a complete list of level-0 revenue accounts listed in the data form).

You can also choose to add an *Add Exclusion* definition for members selected. For example, I can select descendants of "Total Entity" but I do not want the "Enterprise Global" member. From the data form definition, I select the option to *Add Exclusion:*

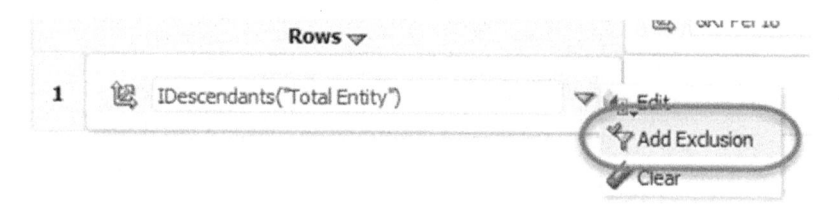

I then select the member(s) to exclude from the member definition:

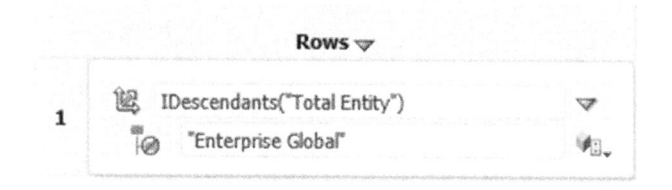

You can *Edit* the member selection, *Edit* the exclusion member selection, *Remove Exclusion* to delete the exclusion, or *Clear* the current member selection as needed:

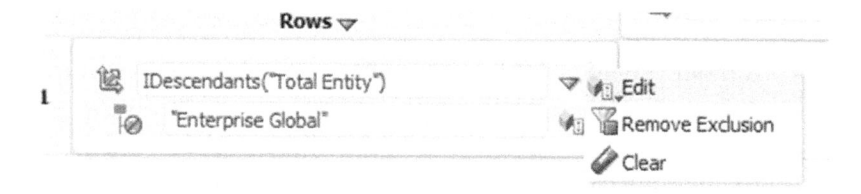

Data Form Options

Most of the data form options are defined on the Layout tab on the collapsible right panel:

Look Smarter Than You Are with PBCS 285

Grid Properties

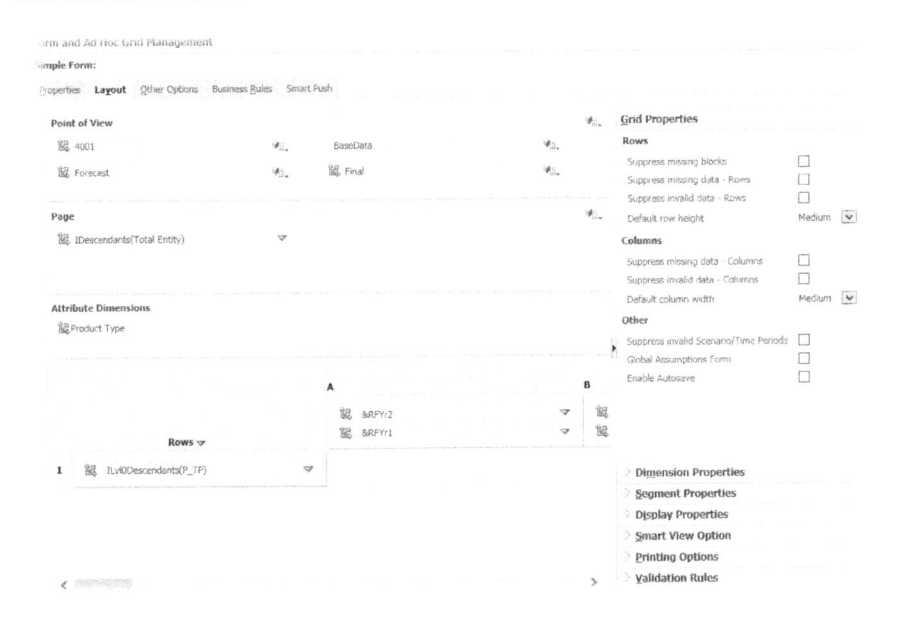

The Grid Properties apply to the entire grid:

- **Suppress missing blocks** – suppresses entire blocks that do not have data. This setting can help with performance when suppressing a large number of rows, such as 90% or more. This option can degrade performance if few or no rows are suppressed.
- **Suppress missing data – Rows** – suppresses any rows that do not have data
- **Suppress invalid data – Rows** – suppresses any rows with invalid data
- **Default row height** – allows you to choose the row height displayed
    - o **Medium** – default option
    - o **Size-to-Fit** – force all text to fit in the displayed space
    - o **Custom** – enter a custom value
- **Suppress missing data – Columns** – suppresses any columns that do not have data

- **Suppress invalid data – Columns** – suppresses any columns with invalid data
- **Default column width** – allows you to choose the column width displayed
    - **Small** – display 7 decimal places on the data form
    - **Medium** – display 10 decimal places on the data form
    - **Large** – display 13 decimal places on the data form
    - **Size-to-Fit** – force all column headings to fit in the displayed space
    - **Custom** – display over 13 decimal places on the data form; can enter a value up to 999
- **Suppress invalid Scenario/Time Periods** – links the form to the start and end time periods set up within the Scenario dimension. Any periods outside of the Scenario range are suppressed.
- **Global assumptions form** – specifies the form as a "Global Assumptions Form"; this type of form contains global assumptions data that can be migrated with its data from Pre-Production to Production via LCM
- **Enable autosave** – when checked, allows users to use Ctrl-Z to undo their actions; also saves the data when users navigate between cells

Dimension Properties

You can also set options for each dimension. Simply select a dimension and the dimension properties display:

- **Apply to all POV dimensions** – for POV dimensions only; applies selected properties to all POV dimensions
- **Apply to all column dimensions** – for column dimensions only; applies selected properties to all column dimensions
- **Apply to all page dimensions** – for page dimensions only; applies selected properties to all page dimensions
- **Apply to all row dimensions** – for row dimensions only; applies selected properties to all row dimensions

- **Member name** and **alias** – choose whether the data form should display the member name or alias (or both if the dimension is in the rows)
- **Member formula** and **description** – allows users to view member formulas and description (or both if both are checked)
- **Hide dimension** – hide the dimension on a data form (helpful to "clear" real estate on the data form)
- **Show consolidation operators** – show consolidation operators
- **Show currency** – for the Entity dimension only; displays the currency attached to that entity
- **Start expanded** – for column or row dimensions only; if you have a hierarchy selected for the dimension (e.g., IDescendants of "YearTotal"), you can decide whether you want the hierarchy to start expanded or collapsed
- **Drill on shared members** – for column or row dimensions only; allows shared parent members to be drillable

Once you have the settings defined you can choose the option to *Apply to all [column, row, page, or POV dimensions*, which applies the settings to all columns / rows / page / POV members (saving you some time in the data form definition process).

Segment Properties

For each dimension, you can create multiple segments (which really means that you can have multiple rows and columns in a data form). For each row or column, you can define the properties.

The following Segment properties are available:

- **Apply to all rows** – applicable to row segments only; applies properties to all rows; uncheck to set different properties by individual rows
- **Apply to all columns** – applicable to column segments only; applies properties to all columns; uncheck to set different properties by individual columns
- **Hide** – hide the segment so it is not displayed on the data form

Chapter 7: Create User Interfaces

- **Read-only** – create a read-only segment in the data form to allow comparing old, read-only data with new, editable data
- **Show separator** – create a bold border before the segment to visually distinguish parts of the data form
- **Suppress hierarchy** – for columns, do not display line breaks
- **Suppress missing data** – suppress missing data for the selected segment only
- **Suppress invalid Scenario/Time Periods** - links the segment to the start and end time periods set up within the Scenario dimension. Any periods outside of the Scenario range are suppressed in the segment.
- **Column width** – applicable to column segments only; change the default column width size
- **Row height** – applicable to row segments only; change the default row height
- **Enable drop-down for dimensions** – one checkbox per dimension in row segment; applicable to row segments only; allows you to create drop-down member selection boxes for each checked dimension

Once you have the segment settings defined you can choose the option to *Apply to all rows / columns* (saving you some time in the data form definition process).

Display Properties

The Display properties control the overall display of the data form. You can choose to:

- **Make form read-only** – the entire form is "grayed out" with no data entry possible by users
- **Hide form** – hides the forms from end user access – helpful for simple forms that are used in composite forms
- **Display missing values as blank** – use this option when you don't want to see #MISSING
- **Enable account annotations** – allows users to enter account annotations (aren't used as frequently now that Planning has

Smart Lists and free-form text measures so you probably won't ever check this option)
- **Allow multiple currencies per entity** – applicable for applications that use the out of the box currency logic
- **Enable mass allocate** – carefully consider this option; do not enable for the end-user masses (behind the scenes, Mass Allocate runs business rules)
- **Enable grid spread** – enables grid spreading (only enable this feature on data forms that are set up for "grid spread")
- **Enable cell-level document** – allows users to view and attach documents
- **Message for forms with no data** – enter a custom message to tell users what they should do if no data displays when the form opens
- **Hide save confirmation message** – hides the confirmation message when users save data on the form

Smart View Option

The Smart View options allow you to set options for when users interact with the form through Smart View. There are options for disabling specific web form features like spreading, formatting, and repeating member labels.

Printing Options

You can define the default printing options for the data form, including whether supporting detail or comments should print. You can also use printing options for defining formatting, precision options, and more.

Validation Rules

You can define validation rules for grids, rows, columns, or cells within a data form. These rules evaluate user input using condition logic. Through validation rules, you can apply criteria to highlight certain data conditions (e.g., if budget versus actual variance is greater than 10 percent, highlight the cell with an orange background) and also prohibit plans from being promoted up through the approvals hierarchy until all validation rules are met. I'll create a validation rule in just a bit.

Other Options

Back in the data form designer, once you've finished the Point of View, Page, Row, and Column member selections, and have defined the data form options, you are ready for the Other Options tab. Click *Next* to move to Other Options or choose the Other Options tab. You can define options for precision, context menus, and dynamic user variables (I'll cover menus and user variables later in the book).

Business Rules

You can assign one or more business rules to a data form. The "Calculate Data Form" business rule is automatically created for every form. It calculates subtotals for the members on the data form. (Note: if every member on your data form is stored or dynamically calculated, you do not have to use "Calculate Data Form".)

You can also assign custom business rules to a data form using the arrows to move over the desired business rule to the Selected Business Rules section. For the assigned business rule, you can specify the following:

- **Run before load** – runs the business rule when the user opens the data form
- **Run after save** – runs the business rule when the user clicks the save button on the data form
- The user may be prompted if a run-time prompt is included in the business rule. You can select the option **Use members on data form** to pass the members on the data form through to the run-time prompt. You can also optionally select **Hide prompt**, which hides the run-time prompt from the user

Now that I have the Data Form basics down, I'm going to build a simple form that allows users to enter forecast data for the Sales entities of Vision Company.

Build a Simple Form

To build a simple form,
1. Click the *Vision Users* folder.
2. Then explore the options in the *Actions* menu:

Form and Ad Hoc Grid Management

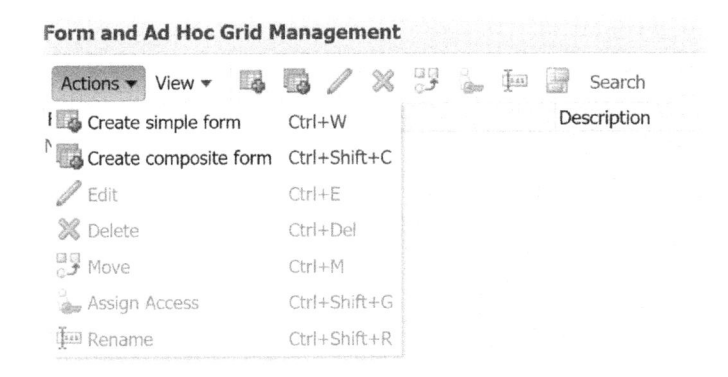

Create simple form	Ctrl+W
Create composite form	Ctrl+Shift+C
Edit	Ctrl+E
Delete	Ctrl+Del
Move	Ctrl+M
Assign Access	Ctrl+Shift+G
Rename	Ctrl+Shift+R

3. Click *Create simple form*.
4. Name the form and add a description if desired. I'm going to call this one "Sales Forecast – Products".
5. Note the Cube and make sure *Sales* is selected.
6. Add instructions for form users if desired:

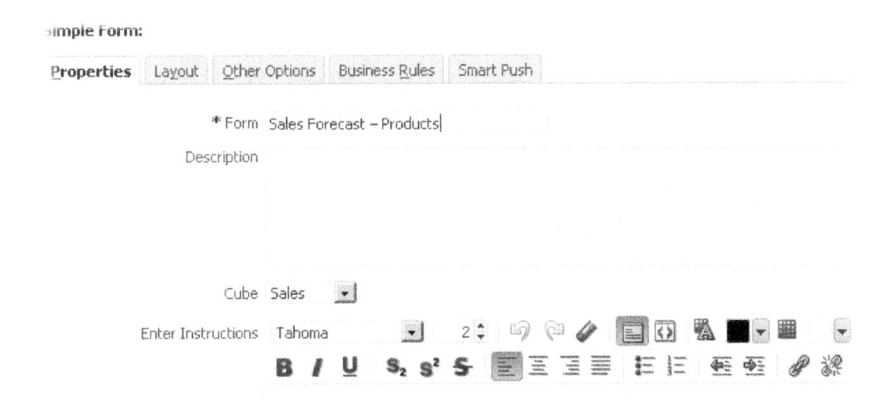

Properties | Layout | Other Options | Business Rules | Smart Push

* Form: Sales Forecast – Products
Description
Cube: Sales
Enter Instructions: Tahoma

Note! All kinds of formatting options are available for form instructions including: font type, font color, indentation, bullets, and alignment. You can also add dynamic URL links.

7. Click *Next* to move on to the Layout tab.

In the Layout tab, I drag dimensions to the Row, Column, or Page from the Point of View. I can select the members I want through the Member Selector and also adjust Dimension and Segment properties in the right panel.

8. Click and drag the icon to the left of the dimension names to move Period and Years to the Columns section of the layout:

Period
Years

Note! Click the column (e.g., "A") or row (e.g., "1") identifier to view the Segment Properties.

9. Drag *Product* and *Account* to the Rows. Click on one of these dimension names to explore the Dimension Properties in the right panel. For the Products and Accounts dimensions, make sure that the properties for *Member Name* and *Alias* are checked.
10. Drag *Version* to the Page section.
11. Leave HSP_View member *BaseData*. Also leave *Entity* and *Scenario* in the Point of View:

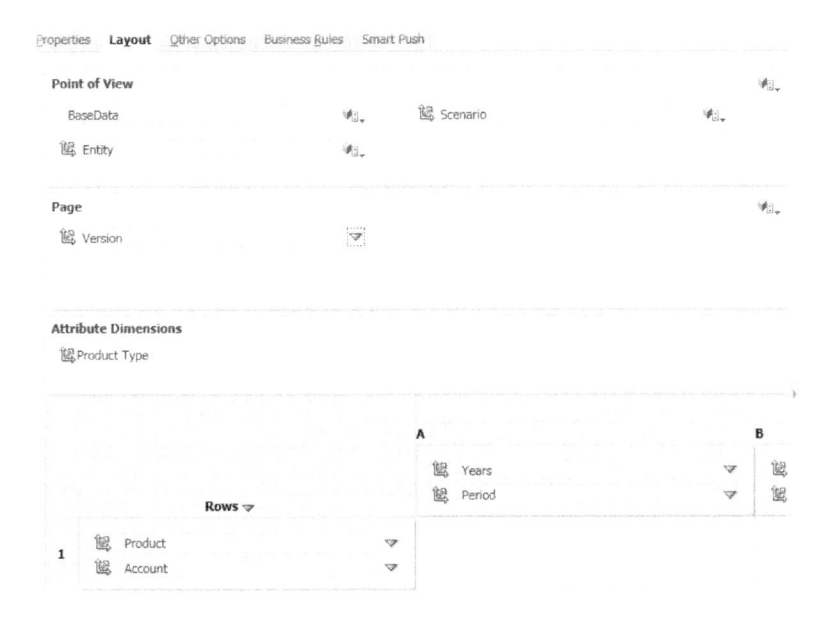

The next step is to select members for each dimension.

Select Members in Data Form

I'll now select the other members for the remaining dimensions in the Sales Forecast – Products data form.

12. Click ▼ next to the *Account* dimension in the Rows section and select Edit. The Member Selector opens:

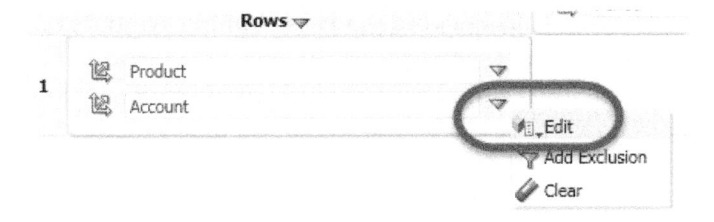

13. Change the display in the Member Selection so you can view aliases by selecting the *Display Properties* icon. Switch to *Alias*:

Chapter 7: Create User Interfaces

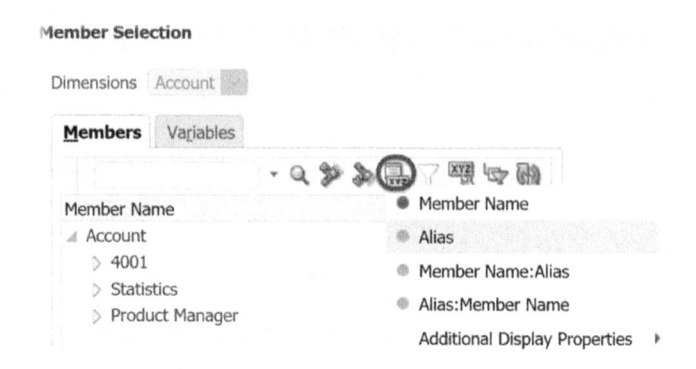

Member Selection

Dimensions Account

Members | Variables

Member Name
- Account
  - 4001
  - Statistics
  - Product Manager

- Member Name
- Alias
- Member Name:Alias
- Alias:Member Name
- Additional Display Properties ▸

On the Members tab icon menu, several options are available to assist form developers with selecting and finding members for forms. The search text box allows developers to search for specific members within the hierarchy:

Members | Variables

A search term can be entered into the search field. Once the magnifying glass is pressed, the term is searched on in the current dimension. The drop-down next to the search field allows for more refined searches within: member names, aliases, descriptions, and / or UDA's. The flashlight icons also search up or down from the current member highlighted within the dimension. Searches include shared members. In addition, they are not case sensitive and searches can be restricted to exact matches, word searches, multiple word searches, and / or wildcard characters.

The next icon is the *Display Properties*, explained previously:

Members | Variables

The *Keep Only by Functions* icon activates once a member is selected within the dimension. This allows a developer to pinpoint on a specific subset of dimension members using the keep only feature with relationship functions:

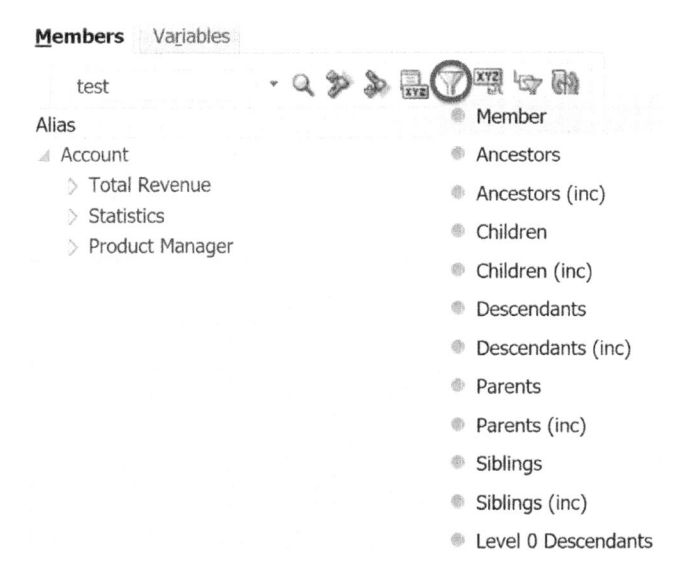

```
Members   Variables

  test

Alias                              Member
  Account                          Ancestors
    Total Revenue                  Ancestors (inc)
    Statistics                     Children
    Product Manager
                                   Children (inc)
                                   Descendants
                                   Descendants (inc)
                                   Parents
                                   Parents (inc)
                                   Siblings
                                   Siblings (inc)
                                   Level 0 Descendants
```

The *Keep Only by Attributes* icon only applies to attributes. If attributes are part of the design, the attribute, an operator, and a value can be used in conjunction to filter to specific members:

```
Members   Variables

  test

Alias                Keep Only by Attr                                    X
  Account                                    Attributes
    Total Revenue    Attributes    Operator              Variable Value
    Statistics
    Product Manager                                       OK    Cancel
```

The *Keep Only by Levels or Generations* icon allows member filtering by either level or generation. Once Level or Generation is selected, a corresponding number is selectable:

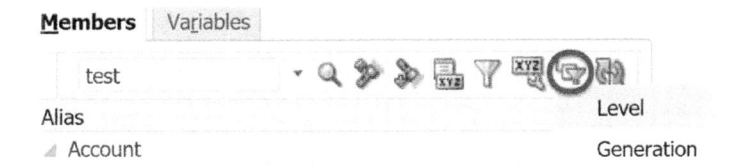

```
Members   Variables

  test

Alias                              Level
  Account                          Generation
```

296　　　　　　　　　　　　　　　　Chapter 7: Create User Interfaces

Finally, the *Refresh* icon removes the filters and then refresh the display:

Now you can see the aliases instead of the member names:

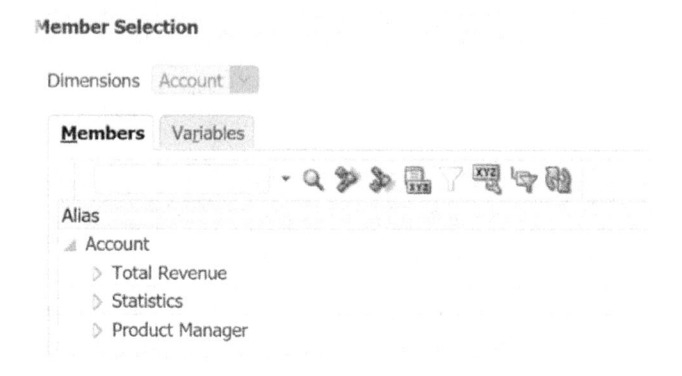

14. Drill down the *Account* hierarchy and select *Units*, *List Price*, and *Hardware Revenue* by clicking on them and moving them to the right. Alternatively, search for the Account names in the search bar.

For the Product dimension, I display all the level-0 members of "Computer Equipment" (member name "P_TP1") to display all the Computer Equipment products.

15. Click ▽ next to the Product dimension, select Edit and click *Computer Equipment* on the left panel.

16. Click :

> Add
>> Add All
< Remove
<< Remove All

17. Select *level-0 Descendants*.

"ILvl0Descendants("Computer Equipment")" appears in the right panel. This function returns all of the lowest level members under "Computer Equipment":

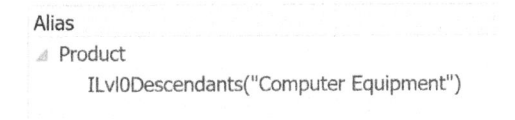

Alias
▲ Product
ILvl0Descendants("Computer Equipment")

18. Click *OK*.

Computer Equipment and its level-0 descendants appears on the data form. Next, I want to create a row that gives me the total Hardware Revenue for all Computer Equipment. I'll have to create another row to do this.

19. Right-click the row number (if there is only one row, click the "1").
20. When the menu appears, select *Add Row*:

Chapter 7: Create User Interfaces

1 — ILvl0Descendants(P_T
Select Members
Add Row

2 — Add Formula Row
Delete Row
Move Row Down
Add/Edit Validation Rules

A new row with the same members as the previous row appears.

21. Click [▼] next to the Account dimension and select Edit. Change the display property to *Member Name*:

Members | Variables

Member Name
▲ Account
  ▷ 4001
  ▷ Statistics
  ▷ Product Manager

● Member Name
● Alias
● Member Name:Alias
● Alias:Member Name
Additional Display Properties ▶

22. Select *4110* as the Account and *Computer Equipment (P_TP1)* as the Product.
23. Add two more rows until there are a total of four rows.
24. Select the members for each row according to the following (first two rows should be defined already):

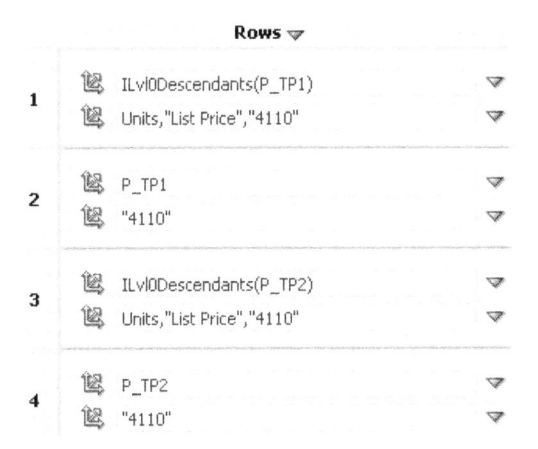

Look Smarter Than You Are with PBCS   299

	Rows ▽	
1	ILvl0Descendants(P_TP1) Units,"List Price","4110"	▽ ▽
2	P_TP1 "4110"	▽ ▽
3	ILvl0Descendants(P_TP2) Units,"List Price","4110"	▽ ▽
4	P_TP2 "4110"	▽ ▽

For the Entity dimension in the POV, I display all the members selected as the MyRegion user variable.

25. Click located in the Point of View section.
26. Choose *Entity* from the Dimensions drop-down list.
27. Click the *Variables* tab:

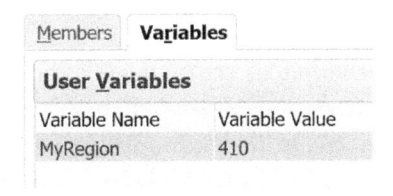

Members	**Variables**
User Variables	
Variable Name	Variable Value
MyRegion	410

28. Add the *MyRegion* variable to the right panel.
29. Choose *Scenario* from the Dimensions drop-down list.
30. Add the *Forecast* member to the right panel.
31. Click *OK*.
32. Finally, click and *Edit* for the Page.
33. Add all the descendants of Version using .
34. The end result should be the following:

300   Chapter 7: Create User Interfaces

```
Properties   Layout   Other Options   Business Rules   Smart Push

Point of View
    BaseData                                      Forecast
    &MyRegion

Page
    IDescendants(Version)
```

35. Click *Save*.

Enable Dynamic User Variables in Data Form

Now that I've defined the user variable MyRegion in the data form, the form automatically filters based on what the user has specified in their preferences. This means that the user would have to go back to Preferences to change their selected member if they don't want what's currently set for MyRegion. To save the user some clicking, you can enable *Dynamic user variables* on a data form and let the user change the value within the form (so they don't have to navigate back to preferences). Once you enable dynamic user variables, users can change the user variable member within the form.

Dynamic user variables create flexible data forms that users can tailor for their desired sections of the database, reducing the number of data form objects to create and administer (versus the administrator creating multiple data forms for multiple data groups).

To enable dynamic user variables,
1. In the Sales Forecast – Products data form, select the *Other Options* tab.
2. Towards the bottom right corner, check *Enable dynamic user variables*.
3. Move the *MyRegion* user variable to the right panel:

Dynamic User Variables	
Available User Variables	Selected User Variables
ProductFamily	MyRegion

Now I'll define the Years and Period dimensions by setting up a rolling forecast.

Create Rolling Forecast

Rolling forecasts are continuous forecasts that continue past the annual fiscal period end. The periods within the rolling forecast period should roll up together even when they cross fiscal or annual years. Companies typically forecast for 12 month, 18 month, or 24 month cycles.

When allowing for rolling forecast forms, the required substitution variables are created on the fly and the values assign to them automatically. These and other substitution variables can be controlled and managed within PBCS.

Note! In the current version of PBCS, once you enable rolling forecast, all new forms automatically place the rolling forecast variables for period and year in the columns. You can update or change the period and year columns if desired, changing members, deleting columns and / or moving to the POV or page.

To set up a rolling forecast in a form,
1. Go back to the *Layout* tab and right-click *Column A* to select *Rolling Forecast Setup*:

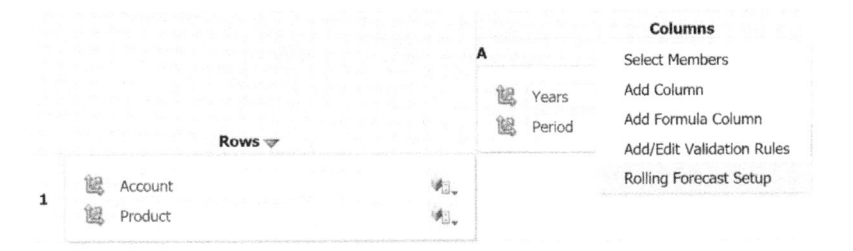

		Columns
	A	Select Members
	Years	Add Column
	Period	Add Formula Column
Rows		Add/Edit Validation Rules
1 Account		Rolling Forecast Setup
Product		

302   Chapter 7: Create User Interfaces

2. Type "RF" as the prefix for the substitution variables that is generated for the rolling forecast.
3. Select Start Year, Start Period, and Number of Periods, which I select as *FY16, Jan,* and *18* respectively:

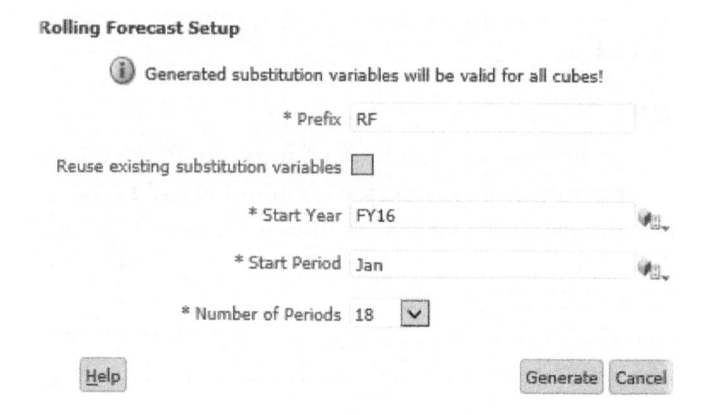

Rolling Forecast Setup

> Generated substitution variables will be valid for all cubes!

* Prefix: RF
Reuse existing substitution variables ☐
* Start Year: FY16
* Start Period: Jan
* Number of Periods: 18

4. Click *Generate*.

Substitution variables &RFPer1 through &RFPer18 and &RFYr1 through &RFYr18 appears in the columns.

5. Click *Preview* to visually see the data form:

Scenario Forecast	Entity 410	MyRegion 410	Version Final			
Final						
				Jan FY16	Feb FY16	Mar FY16
P_100:Product X		Units				
		List Price				
		4110:Hardware Revenue				
P_110:Sentinal Standard Notebook		Units		6	6	6
		List Price		1200	1200	1200
		4110:Hardware Revenue		7200	7200	7200
P_120:Sentinal Custom Notebook		Units		6	6	6

6. Click *Save*, then *Finish* to complete the form.

Shift Rolling Forecast Periods

When shifting rolling forecast periods, the shift is auto-generated for all forms which have been set up for rolling forecast using the same variables.

When you are ready to "shift" the variable values to the next forecast period,
1. Go to *Data* in the main menu and open one of the data forms using the rolling forecast variables. I open the *Sales Forecast – Products* form.
2. Click the first column containing the variable.
3. Go to *Actions* and select *Set Rolling Forecast Variables*:

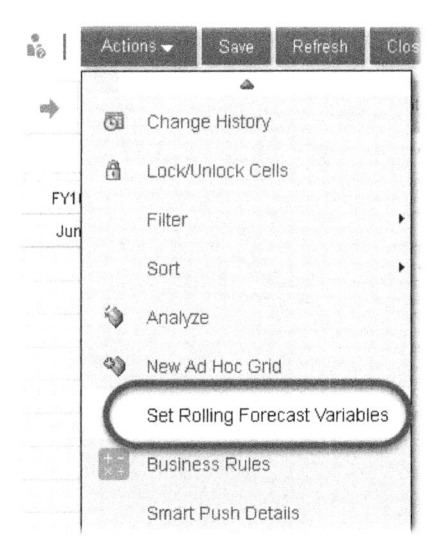

4. Towards the bottom, select "1" where it says *Shift Values By*:

5. Click *Apply*.

Years and Periods shift by one. You can review the substitution variables created during the rolling forecast form design by going to *Navigator* >> *Create and Manage* >> *Variables*. The values of the variables can be edited manually there.

Use Save As to Create Data Form

The *Save As* button can be used to easily create a form similar to an existing form. I'll create two data forms from the first one using Save As.

To create the second data form,
1. Open the *Sales Forecast – Products* data form and click *Save As*.
2. Name the new form "Sales Forecast – Services & Other".
3. Select members according to the following Layout:

Simple Form: Sales Forecast – Services & Other

Properties | **Layout** | **Other Options** | **Business Rules** | **Smart Push**

Point of View
- BaseData
- &MyRegion
- Forecast

Page
- IDescendants(Version)

Attribute Dimensions
- Product Type

	Rows		A
			&RFYr1
			&RFPer1
1	P_291		
	4140		
2	P_292		
	4150		
3	P_294		
	4130		

4. *Preview* the form, *Save*, and then *Finish*.

Sales Forecast – Services & O...

Scenario	Entity	MyRegion	Version
Forecast	410	410	Final

Final

		FY16	FY16	FY16
		Jan	Feb	Mar
P_291:Training_P_291	4140:Training Revenue			
P_292:Miscellaneous_P_292	4150:Miscellaneous Revenue			
P_294:Consulting_P_294	4130:Consulting Revenue			

To create the third data form,

1. Open the *Sales Forecast – Products* data form and click *Save As*.
2. Name the new form "Sales Forecast – Support".
3. Select members according to the following Layout:

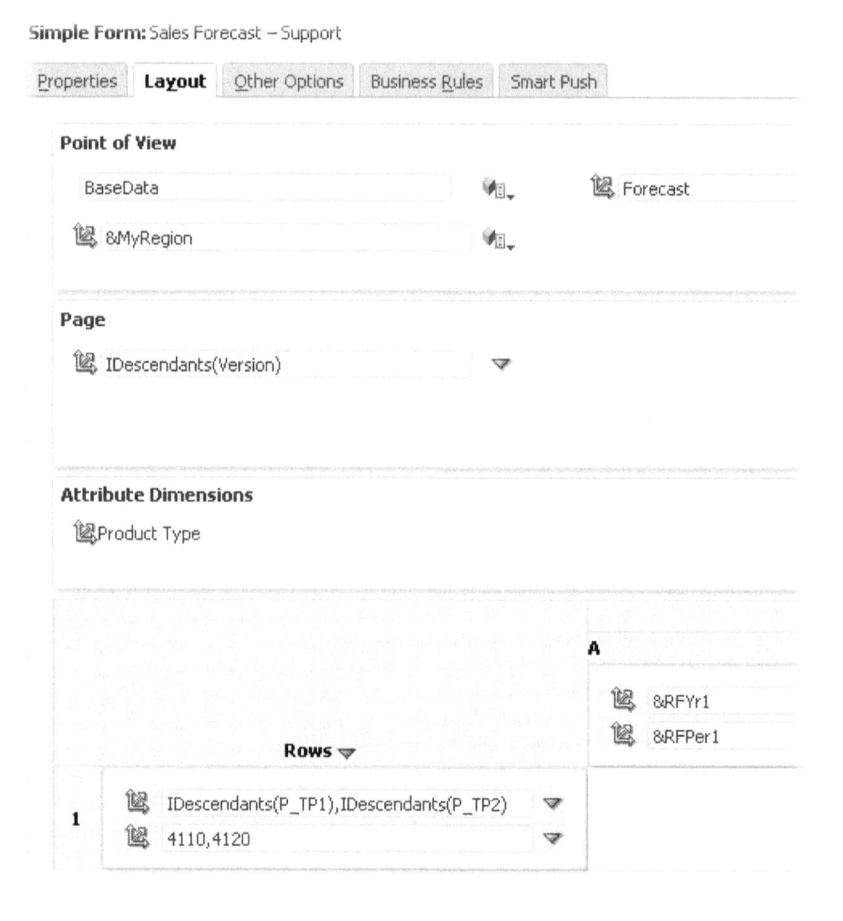

Simple Form: Sales Forecast – Support

Properties | **Layout** | Other Options | Business Rules | Smart Push

Point of View
- BaseData
- Forecast
- &MyRegion

Page
- IDescendants(Version)

Attribute Dimensions
- Product Type

A
- &RFYr1
- &RFPer1

Rows

1 | IDescendants(P_TP1),IDescendants(P_TP2)
  | 4110,4120

4. In addition, for the Product Dimension Properties, check the boxes for *Alias* and *Start expanded*.
5. Check the Account Dimension Property options for *Member Formula* and *Alias*.
6. *Preview* the form, *Save*, and then *Finish*.

Sales Forecast – Support ⓘ

Scenario	Entity	MyRegion	Version
Forecast	410	410	Final
Final			

		FY16 Jan	FY16 Feb	FY16 Mar
Product X	Hardware Revenue *f*			
	Support Revenue *f*			
Sentinal Standard Notebook	Hardware Revenue *f*	7200	7200	7200
	Support Revenue *f*	1296	1296	1296

Note! Any rows with members that include member formulas or are tagged as Dynamic Calc appear gray to indicate *Read Only*. You can tell that the ability to view member formulas has been enabled on this data form because of the function symbols displayed.

Note! In the *Sales Forecast – Support* data form, Computer Equipment and Computer Accessories are expanded by default to display all of their descendants. Simply click the "-" icon to the left of the member name to contract the hierarchy.

Create Summary Form

Next, I'm going to create a summary form to view the aggregation of the Accounts entered in the other Sales Forecast forms.

1. Open one of the previous forms and use *Save As* to create a form with the following layout (call the form *Sales Forecast Summary*):

308   Chapter 7: Create User Interfaces

Simple Form: Sales Forecast Summary

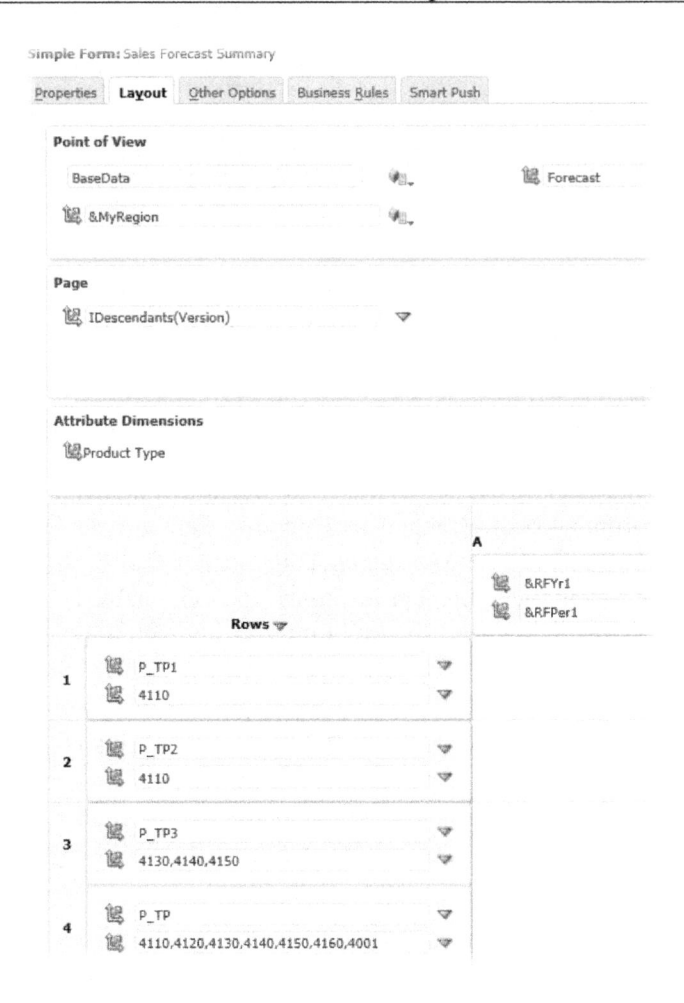

Properties | **Layout** | Other Options | Business Rules | Smart Push

Point of View

| BaseData | | Forecast |
| &MyRegion | | |

Page

IDescendants(Version)

Attribute Dimensions
Product Type

		A
		&RFYr1
	Rows	&RFPer1
1	P_TP1	
	4110	
2	P_TP2	
	4110	
3	P_TP3	
	4130,4140,4150	
4	P_TP	
	4110,4120,4130,4140,4150,4160,4001	

2. Open *Grid Properties* and check *Suppress missing blocks* and *Suppress missing data – Rows*:

Grid Properties

Rows

Suppress missing blocks	☑
Suppress missing data - Rows	☑
Suppress invalid data - Rows	☐
Default row height	Medium

Columns

Suppress missing data - Columns	☐
Suppress invalid data - Columns	☐
Default column width	Medium

Other

Global Assumptions Form	☐
Enable Autosave	☐

3. *Preview* the form, *Save*, and then *Finish*. Open it up:

Sales Forecast Summary

Scenario	Entity	MyRegion	Version
Forecast	410	410	Final

Final

		FY16	FY16	FY16
		Jan	Feb	Mar
P_TP:Total Product	4110:Hardware Revenue	27040	27040	27040
	4120:Support Revenue	4867.2000000000	4867.2000000000	4867.2000000000
	⊟ 4001:Total Revenue	31907.2	31907.2	31907.2

Note! Since the Sales Forecast Summary form does not contain level-0 members, the members are shaded gray to indicate *Read Only*. Users are not able to enter data into these cells.

Use Smart Lists in Data Forms

The last form I will create will be used to assign Product Managers to all the products at Vision Company. Remember the Product Manager Smart List I created earlier? I will use the Product Manager account for this data form.

310   Chapter 7: Create User Interfaces

To create a data form containing a Smart List,
1. Create a new simple form and name it *"Assign Product Manager"*.
2. Drag *Account* and *Period* to the Columns.
3. Drag *Product* to the Rows.
4. Drag *Years* to the Page.
5. Leave *HSP_View*, *Entity*, *Scenario* and *Version* in the POV.
6. Using ![icon], select *Pass1* for Version, *Plan* for Scenario and *0*, or *No Department*, for Entity.
7. For Years, select *FY16* to *FY21*.
8. For Account, select the *Product Manager* member.
9. For Period, select all level-0 members (months).

There are many methods to select level-0 members for any dimension, but the easiest method is to click the desired dimension, then click the *Keep Only by Functions* icon ![icon]. Click the *level-0 Descendants* option:

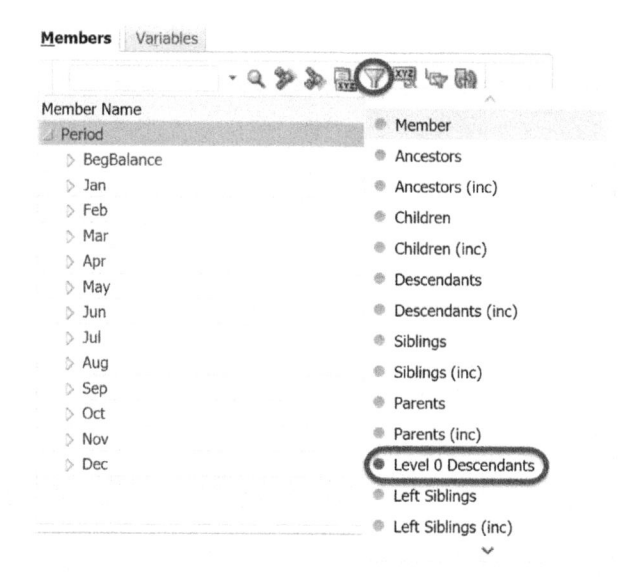

Member Name	
Period	● Member
▷ BegBalance	● Ancestors
▷ Jan	● Ancestors (inc)
▷ Feb	● Children
▷ Mar	● Children (inc)
▷ Apr	
▷ May	● Descendants
▷ Jun	● Descendants (inc)
▷ Jul	● Siblings
▷ Aug	● Siblings (inc)
▷ Sep	● Parents
▷ Oct	● Parents (inc)
▷ Nov	(● Level 0 Descendants)
▷ Dec	● Left Siblings
	● Left Siblings (inc)

Only level-0 members appear on the left panel. Highlight all members except *BegBalance* by clicking the *Jan* and *Dec* member while holding the *Shift* key. Move the members to the right panel.

10. For Product, select all level-0 products.
11. In the Product Dimension Properties, check *Member name* and *Alias*.

The Columns and Rows should resemble the following:

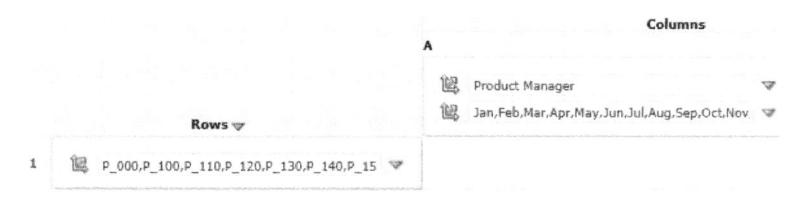

	A	Columns
		Product Manager
		Jan,Feb,Mar,Apr,May,Jun,Jul,Aug,Sep,Oct,Nov
1	P_000,P_100,P_110,P_120,P_130,P_140,P_15	

12. Click *Save*, and then *Finish* (though I could just click *Finish*, which also performs a Save).

Open a Data Form

To view all the forms I have created,
1. Go to the main menu and click *Data*.
2. Expand the *Vision Users* folder to display the forms.

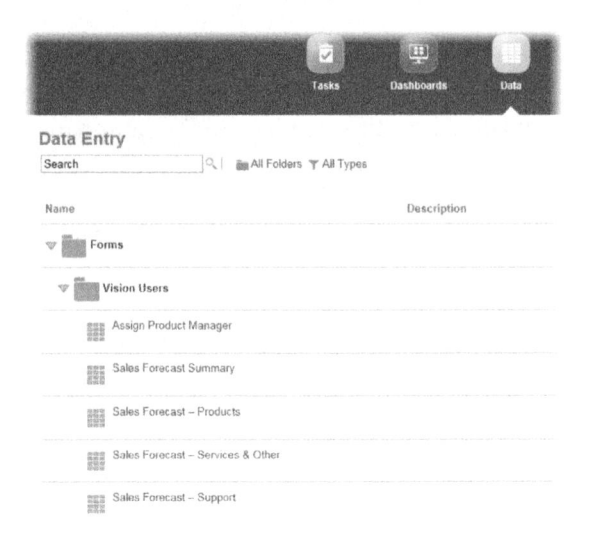

Chapter 7: Create User Interfaces

Data Entry

Name	Description
▼ Forms	
▼ Vision Users	
Assign Product Manager	
Sales Forecast Summary	
Sales Forecast – Products	
Sales Forecast – Services & Other	
Sales Forecast – Support	

3. Select the *Assign Product Manager* data form and the form opens.
4. The result should look similar to the following:

Create Composite Form

Now that all the simple forms have been created, let's use a few of them to create a composite form. A composite form is a data form that combines two or more data forms into a single object. Data forms can be from the same or different cubes. You can choose to combine Page and Point of View member selections so that users select a member from a drop-down once and both data forms within the composite are updated. When combining data forms, you can choose a horizontal, vertical, or tabular orientation.

One important note is that composite forms are not supported in end user navigation flows as of March 2016. You might want to stick with simple data forms for your PBCS application design and use navigation flows with cards, clusters, and tabs for end user navigation in the simplified user interface.

You can also achieve a similar user experience using the PBCS Dashboards feature (though Dashboards are not supported in Smart View yet).

To create a composite form,
1. Select *Navigator* >> *Create and Manage* >> *Forms*.
2. Select the *Vision Users* folder. Then from Actions, select *Create composite form*.
3. Name the form "Sales Forecast – Composite".
4. Navigate to the *Layout* tab. In Section Properties, click ⊕, check all the Sales Forecast forms and click *OK*:

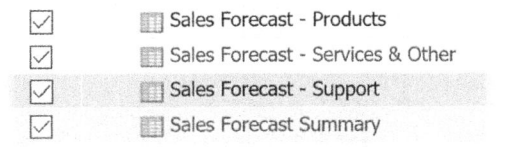

   ☑ Sales Forecast - Products
   ☑ Sales Forecast - Services & Other
   ☑ **Sales Forecast - Support**
   ☑ Sales Forecast Summary

5. Click in Section Properties to display forms as tabs within the composite:

314 Chapter 7: Create User Interfaces

Section Properties

Forms
- [ ] Sales Forecast - Products
- [ ] Sales Forecast - Services & Other
- [ ] Sales Forecast - Support
- [ ] Sales Forecast Summary

Form Name

	Name		
Height	Automatic	⌄	0
Width	Automatic	⌄	0
Forms per Row	Automatic		
Forms per Column	1		

[ ] Set scope for all common dimensions as global

6. Check the option to *Set scope for all common dimensions as global*. This allows any POV and Page settings to persist across the tabs.
7. Select *Preview*, then click *Finish*. The form should look similar to this:

Sales Forecast - Composite

Sales Forecast - Products	Sales Forecast - Services & Other	Sales Forecast - Support	Sales Forecast Summary

Scenario	MyRegion	Version				
Forecast	410	Pass1				

		Oct FY15	Nov FY15	Dec FY15	Jan FY16
P_100:Product X	Units	86	106		
	List Price	30	30		
	4110:Hardware Revenue	2580	3180		
P_110:Sentinal Standard Notebook	Units	151	151		
	List Price	250	250		
	4110:Hardware Revenue	37750	37750		
P_120:Sentinal Custom Notebook	Units	106	106		

Enable Autosave for a Data Form

Administrators have the option to enable *Autosave* when creating data forms. Autosave is cool feature that saves data input into a cell when a user tabs out of the cell. If a user mistakenly saves data by tabbing out of a cell, a Ctrl+Z shortcut undoes the mistake.

If Autosave is enabled, the cells turns green to indicate a saved cell:

		Oct FY15	Nov FY15	Dec FY15
Training_P_291	4140:Training Revenue	500	700	750
Miscellaneous_P_292	4150:Miscellaneous Revenue			
Consulting_P_294	4130:Consulting Revenue			
Total Product	4120:Support Revenue	9895.5	9895.5	6606

Additionally, an option to *Run Form Rules* on Autosave can be enabled by the administrator to update dynamically calculated cells that depend on the autosaved cell values that were input by the user. If rules were run, *Ctrl+Z* undoes any input and rules that were run as a part of the Autosave.

To enable autosave on a data form,
1. Create a new form by clicking *Save As* on the Sales Forecast – Products form and name it "Sales Forecast – Products Autosave":

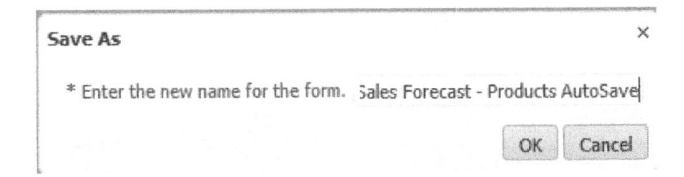

Save As   ×

* Enter the new name for the form.   Sales Forecast - Products AutoSave|

OK   Cancel

2. On the *Layout* tab, under Grid Properties, check the option to *Enable Autosave* and *Run Form Calc on Autosave*:

Chapter 7: Create User Interfaces

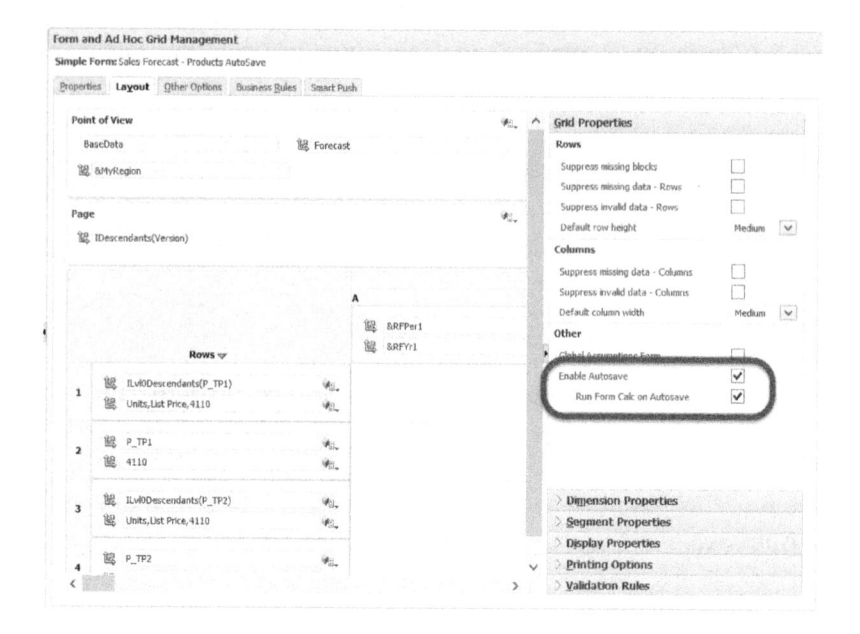

3. In the *Business Rules* tab, make sure the *<Calculate Form>* business rule is selected and checked for *Run on Save*:

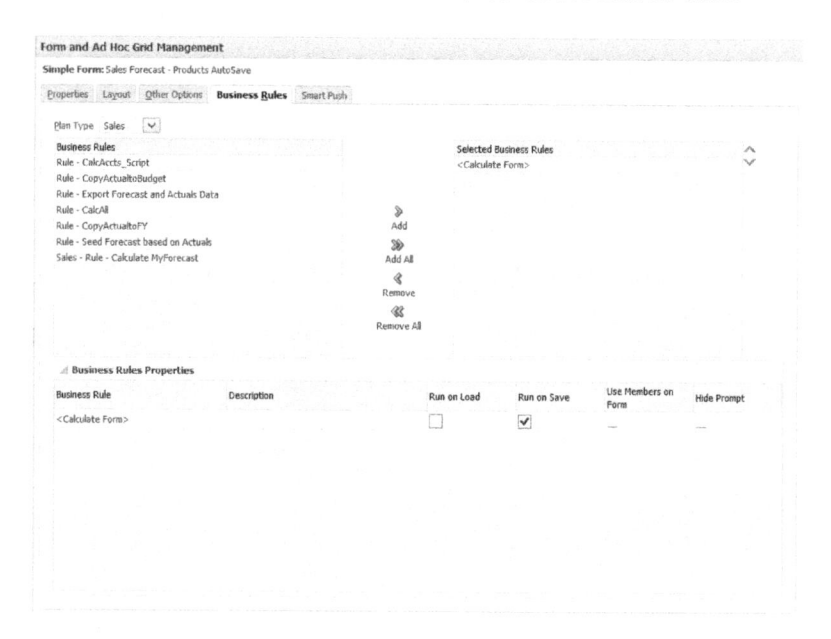

4. Click *Finish* to save and exit the form definition.
5. Navigate back to *Data Entry* in the Home screen.
6. Open the *Sales Forecast – Products Autosave* form and test out my very favorite new feature.
7. Enter values for Units for product P_110.

The cell should turn green for *Units* along with the cell for *4110:Hardware Revenue* (this is a calculated account; remember in the dimension definition, I defined the member formula for this account member):

Sales Forecast - Products Aut...

Scenario	MyRegion	Version
Forecast	410	Final

Final

		Oct FY15	Nov FY15	Dec FY15	Jan FY16
P_100:Product X	Units				
	List Price				
	4110:Hardware Revenue				
P_110:Sentinal Standard Notebook	Units	5	5	5	5
	List Price	1000	1000	1000	1200
	4110:Hardware Revenue	5000	5000	5000	6000
P_120:Sentinal Custom Notebook	Units	13	13		13
	List Price				

Enable Smart Push on a Data Form

Smart Push allows users to push data from a data form, executing the data map I created earlier. It's meant to provide a quick update to reporting cubes based on planning data entry. It can be used on both simple and composite data forms. Smart Push is also supported from dashboards.

There are some guidelines you need to consider when using Smart Push:

- Smart Push has to use at least one data map
- You can use Smart Push to push data from a BSO cube to either a ASO or BSO cube only
- Smart Push honors metadata and approvals security

- At least one of the dense dimensions (Account or Period, generally) needs to be set as a dimension-to-dimension mapping in the data map
- If the target cube dimensionality changes, you need to synchronize the data in the data map

To enable the Smart Push of data from Sales to SalesRpt, I'll need to attach the data map I created previously to a form.

To attach a data map to a form,
1. Select *Navigator* ▤ >> *Create and Manage* >> *Forms*.
2. Edit the *Sales Forecast – Products* form.
3. Navigate to the *Smart Push* tab.
4. Click ✚ and select the *Sales Forecast_Products* data map.
5. Optionally you can check the option to *Run on Save*.

Now it's time to configure the Smart Push settings on the data form. There are three main options that are relevant here. The first two allow you to overwrite the original data mapping dimension selections:

- **Use form context** – push data for all members on the data form
- **Overwrite selection** – overwrite the list of members on the data form as the source of the data with your own dimension definition; this can't be used when the Use Form Context option is checked
- **Run on save** – when checked, this kicks off a data push once the data form is formally saved by the user; if unchecked, then the data push must occur manually by the user through the *Actions* >> *Smart Push Details* menu option for the form; the data map does not appear under Smart Push Details if this option is checked

If you choose to leave the defaults for *Use Form Context*, data from all members on the form are pushed, regardless of what's specified in the data map. Since data from a BSO cube is being pushed to an ASO cube, this is problematic, as ASO cubes are set up to accept level-0 data.

Therefore, *Use Form Context* shouldn't be used for the Products dimension, as the form contains upper level members.

If you choose to overwrite the selection, be careful here – the syntax within the Overwrite section is not validated. Therefore, you can accidentally reference the wrong dimension, which leads to an error.

Note! Oracle recommends Smart Push be used strategically and on summary forms that consolidate data. Automatic push should also be limited, as users may tend to push incomplete data.

6. Change the settings so that they match the following:

Smart Push

Dimension	Use Form Context	Overwrite Selection	Run on Save	Delete
Account	☑			
Entity	☑			
Period	☑			
Product	☐			
Scenario	☐			
Version	☐			
Years	☐			

7. Click *OK*.

You should have the following:

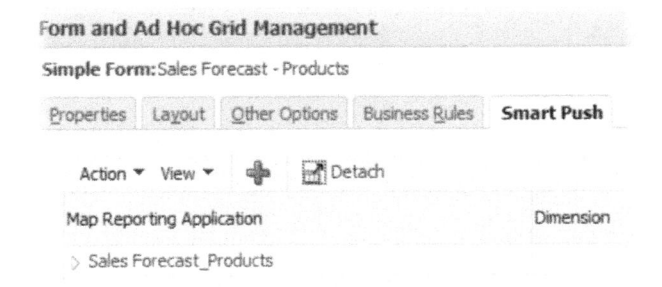

Form and Ad Hoc Grid Management

Simple Form: Sales Forecast - Products

Properties | Layout | Other Options | Business Rules | **Smart Push**

Action ▼   View ▼   ➕   Detach

Map Reporting Application   Dimension

> Sales Forecast_Products

320   Chapter 7: Create User Interfaces

As mentioned above, if you don't want to use the members in the form as the focus for the data push, you can change the *Overwrite Selection* to level-0 products. You need to uncheck the option *Use Form Context* first:

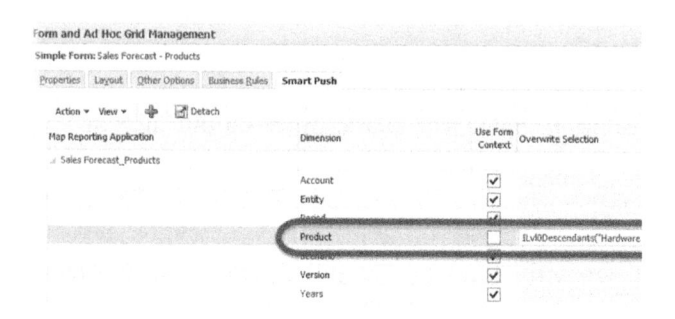

Note!

Finally, it's time to execute copy data from Sales to SalesRpt using Smart Push within a form.

To execute Smart Push,
1. In the Simplified UI, click *Data* from the main menu.
2. Open the *Sales Forecast – Products* form.
3. Go to *Actions >> Smart Push Details*:

4. Click the *Sales Forecast_Products* data map to execute the Smart Push:

Smart Push

📊 Sales Forecast_Products   [Close]

The following image appears if the Smart Push was successful:

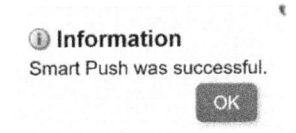

> ⓘ **Information**
> Smart Push was successful.
> [OK]

Check that the data was transferred from the Sales cube to the SalesRpt cube by connecting to the SalesRpt cube and viewing the data in Smart View with ad hoc analysis. The following shows the copied data in Smart View:

	A	B	C	D	E	F	G	H	I	J	K	L
12	Product X	Units	#Missing	#Missing	#Missing	#Missing	#Missing	#Missing	#Missing	#Missing	#Missing	#Miss
13	Product X	List Price	#Missing	#Missing	#Missing	#Missing	#Missing	#Missing	#Missing	#Missing	#Missing	#Miss
14	Product X	Hardware	#Missing	#Missing	#Missing	#Missing	#Missing	#Missing	#Missing	#Missing	#Missing	#Miss
15	Sentinal Standard	Units	10	10	10	10	10	10	10	10	10	
16	Sentinal Standard	List Price	500	500	500	500	500	500	500	500	500	
17	Sentinal Standard	Hardware	5000	5000	5000	5000	5000	5000	5000	5000	5000	5
18	Sentinal Custom	Units	10	10	10	10	10	10	10	10	10	
19	Sentinal Custom	List Price	700	700	700	700	700	700	700	700	700	
20	Sentinal Custom	Hardware	7000	7000	7000	7000	7000	7000	7000	7000	7000	7
21	Envoy Standard	Units	10	10	10	10	10	10	10	10	10	
22	Envoy Standard	List Price	500	500	500	500	500	500	500	500	500	
23	Envoy Standard	Hardware	5000	5000	5000	5000	5000	5000	5000	5000	5000	5
24	Envoy Custom	Units	10	10	10	10	10	10	10	10	10	
25	Envoy Custom	List Price	700	700	700	700	700	700	700	700	700	
26	Envoy Custom	Hardware	7000	7000	7000	7000	7000	7000	7000	7000	7000	7

Or you can create a new data form that would capture the data that was pushed over (in my example below, I created a master detail composite form that has a simple form for Sales cube on top and a simple form for SalesRpt on bottom):

Chapter 7: Create User Interfaces

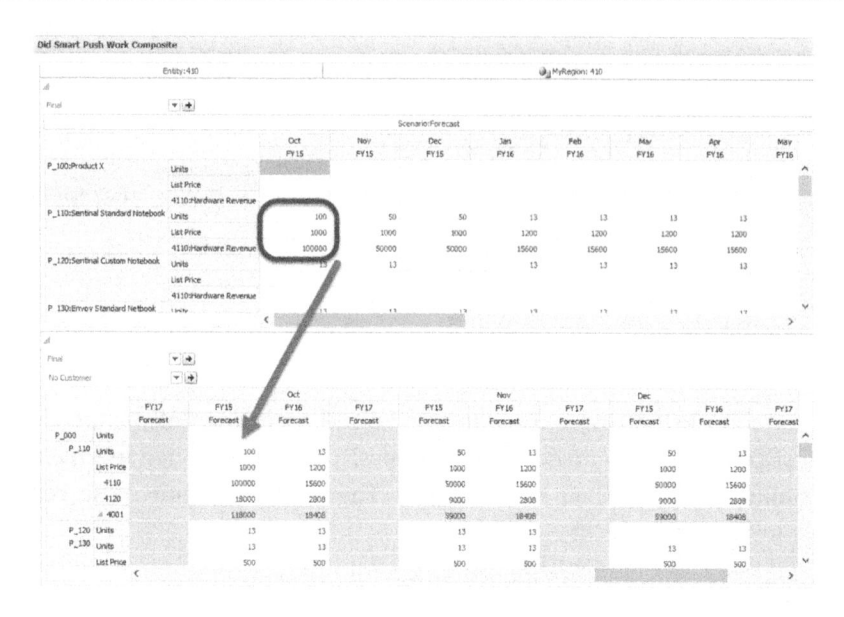

[Screenshot of "Did Smart Push Work Composite" form showing two grids with Entity:410, MyRegion:410, product rows P_100:ProductX, P_110:Sentinal Standard Notebook, P_120:Sentinal Custom Notebook, P_130:Envoy Standard Netbook across months Oct FY15 through May FY16, with a handwritten "7" circling values in the Oct FY15 column; lower grid shows P_000, P_110, P_120, P_130 across FY17 Forecast through FY17 Forecast columns.]

Sometimes this feature can behave a little wonky. It seems to be a little finicky when you use functions in the member selection. Hardcoded definitions, though not ideal, are the most consistent. Make sure to synchronize mappings after metadata changes to dimensions:

[Screenshot showing "Sales Forecast_Products" row with Sales, SalesRpt, 2/1/2016, and a dropdown menu listing: Edit, Duplicate, Delete, Synchronize (circled), Push Data, Clear and Push data.]

Other workaround tips (for now, if you have issues) are to update data forms that need Smart Push to have members match the definitions in the data map (with no references to upper level dynamic members).

Master Composite Forms

Master Composite forms are supported in PBCS. These composite forms allow you to define dimension members in one source or master form and have it apply to the target forms. The target forms need to have the dimensions for which context is being passed in the Page or POV area of the target form. Master detail forms provide two significant advantages:

1) You can visualize the source and target forms within the same content area.

2) You can see the immediate impact on several dependent forms within the same composite form.

To tag a form as the master form, edit the form and go to the *Layout* tab. Right-click the desired form and click *Tag as Master Composite Form*:

Note! The master form dimensions apply to the entire composite form; therefore, there can only be one master form.

Other Form Options

I've just highlighted the possibilities with data forms, but there are many more features I have not fully covered. Other form features include defining validation rules for grids, rows, columns, or cells within a data form:

The options to enable Account Annotations, print Supporting Details, automatically save data entry with Autosave, allocate data using

324   Chapter 7: Create User Interfaces

Mass Allocate, utilize client side spreading with Grid Spread, and attach cell-level documents are also available in data forms:

Display Properties	
Make form read-only	☐
Hide Form	☐
Display missing values as blank	☑
Enable account annotations	☐
Allow multiple currencies per entity	☐
Enable Mass Allocate	☐
Enable Grid Spread	☑
Enable cell-level document	☑
Message for forms with no data	

Additionally, member name / alias display, the ability for users to see member formulas in data forms, and other dimension properties can be enabled:

Dimension Properties	
Account	
Apply to all row dimensions	☐
Member name	☑
Alias	☑
Member Formula	☑
Hide dimension	☐
Show consolidation operators	☐
Start expanded	☑

Manage Data Forms

Select *Navigator* >> *Create and Manage* >> *Forms* to manage data forms. From the *Forms and Ad Hoc Grid Management* section, you can edit, move, rename, assign access, or delete data form folders or data forms by selecting the appropriate task from the *Actions* drop-down menu or icon from the menu bar. You can also Search for a particular form:

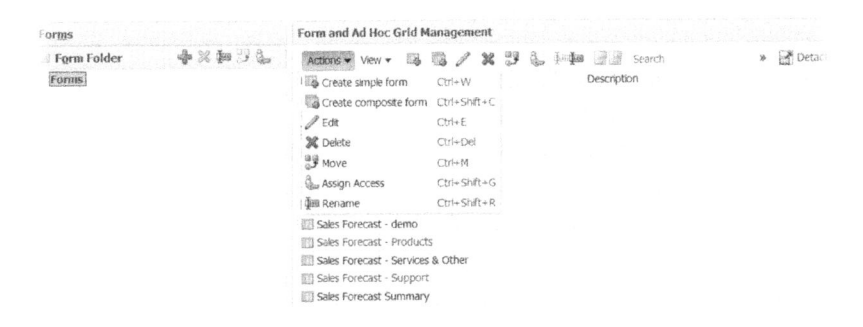

```
Forms                    Form and Ad Hoc Grid Management
  Form Folder            Actions ▼  View ▼                    Search              Detai
    Forms                   Create simple form      Ctrl+W              Description
                            Create composite form   Ctrl+Shift+C
                            Edit                    Ctrl+E
                            Delete                  Ctrl+Del
                            Move                    Ctrl+M
                            Assign Access           Ctrl+Shift+G
                            Rename                  Ctrl+Shift+R
                         Sales Forecast - demo
                         Sales Forecast - Products
                         Sales Forecast - Services & Other
                         Sales Forecast - Support
                         Sales Forecast Summary
```

Some of the options mentioned above are discussed further in the End User Activities section of this chapter. For more information on data forms, view the Oracle *Working with Planning for Oracle Planning and Budgeting Cloud* online documentation or reach out to info@interrel.com for tips, tricks, and design best practices on data forms.

Finally, the data forms are complete.

SMART FORMS

About Smart Forms

Smart Forms are a new feature to the Oracle planning and budgeting world. They are data forms based on ad hoc grids that use Excel formulas and calculate data on the client side rather than in Essbase. Oracle calls these Excel formulas "business calculations." These calculations do not affect metadata within the application and can be executed both in the web and in Smart View.

You assign a grid label (a custom header) to the Excel formula header row or column in the Smart Forms. These required grid labels replace member names in the ad hoc grid.

Smart Form features include the ability to:

- Support Excel formulas with most Excel functions
- Support Excel formatting
- Support Excel cell merging

- Be created in Smart View
- Be used by end users like any old data form in the web or Smart View
- Create a sandbox from a Smart Form

Administrators and power users can create Smart Forms in Smart View. They must provision access to the Smart Forms for users. Users may access Smart Forms either within the Simplified UI or Smart View.

Why would users want to use Smart Forms? If the calculations on a form are done directly on a form, users may experience better performance and a more enjoyable user experience. Formulas use a syntax that everyone is familiar with – Excel!

Create a Smart Form

To define a Smart Form,
1. Connect to the application with Smart View.
2. Select a form in the Panel and click *Ad hoc analysis* at the bottom. Alternatively, open an ad hoc grid.
3. Add grid labels and Excel formulas as desired. The example below is using the SUM Excel formula to add up quarters:

Q1	Q2	Q3	Q4	Q1+Q2	Q3+Q4
474	474	474	352	948	826
27240	27240	27240	27240	54480	54480
259200	259200	259200	219600	518400	478400

4. In the Planning Ad Hoc ribbon, click *Save As Smart Form*:

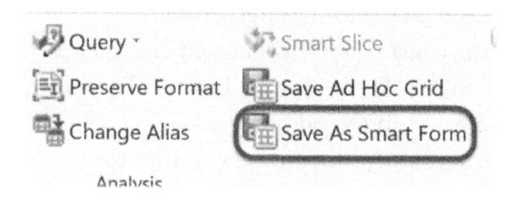

5. Name the grid "FY14_Actual_Smart Form", keep the default Forms root folder, and add a description if desired:

Once the Smart Form has been saved, it can be seen in the Smart View Panel, under the root Forms folder:

This Smart Form can also be seen in the Simplified UI. To access Smart Forms, go to *Data Entry* and click the Smart Forms tab:

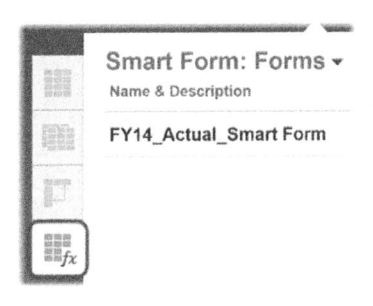

328   Chapter 7: Create User Interfaces

The grid labels and the Excel calculations can be seen in the Smart Form. Hover over the calculated cells to see the formulas:

Q1+Q2	Q3+Q4		
948	826		
54480	54480		
Row Total ProductList Price Column Q1+Q2 54480 This cell is read-only Formula:=SUM(D3:E3)			

You have to follow a few rules when it comes to Smart Forms:

- You must enter grid labels in order to save the business calculations in the Smart Form; expect wonky behavior if empty space is entered instead of a grid label
- Grid labels may be entered at any dimension location for an axis
- Grid label names may not match any member name or alias
- Member functions are not supported in the Smart Form definition

You can view Smart Forms in the Form definition area, but you cannot edit the form.

VALID INTERSECTIONS

Valid intersections allow administrators to define rules, called valid intersection rules, to restrict invalid data entry for users. Cells in data forms containing invalid intersections are shown as read-only. This restriction speeds the planning process and optimizes the information available to users. Valid intersection definitions may be defined based on stored dimensions or attribute dimensions.

For this application, I'm going to create a rule that allows users to enter data for accounts related to Computer Services while preventing users from entering units for Computer Services members in the *Forecast Sales – Products* form, since forecast for this product is entered in dollars. I'm also going to make sure users enter data for the matching product – account combinations.

Create Valid Intersection Rule

To create valid intersections,
1. Select *Navigator* ▤ >> *Application* >> *Setup:*

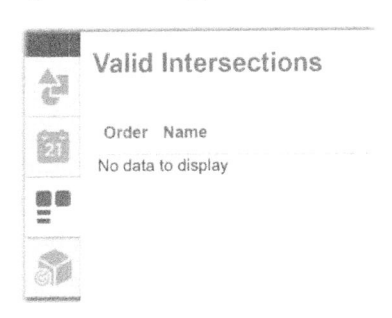

Valid Intersections

Order Name
No data to display

2. Click *Create*.
3. Name the valid intersection rule "Services&Other _Accounts" and add a description:

Services&Other_Accounts

To allow users to enter data into the Support, Consulting, Training and Misc. Revenue accounts for Services & Other products. Data entry into the Units and List Price accounts disabled.

4. Select *Product* as the anchor dimension.
5. Next, click *Add Dimension* and select *Account*.

Note! Depending on which dimension is designated as the anchor dimension, the valid intersections of data will vary. In our case, Product is the anchor dimension and Account is the non-anchor dimension, which means that only the selected accounts are valid for the selected products. All accounts are valid for products that were not selected.

6. Click *Add Rule*.
7. Click the drop-down arrow for Product and select *Edit*:

330　　　　　　　　　　　　　　　　Chapter 7: Create User Interfaces

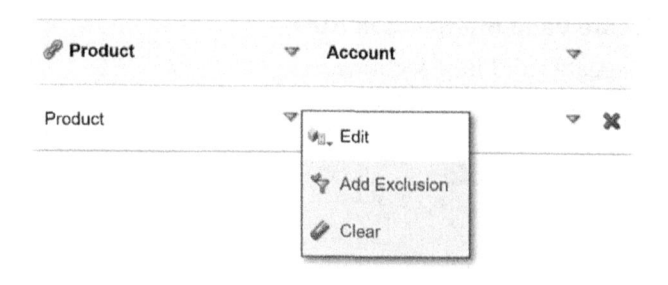

8. Select ⚙ in the upper right-hand corner and choose to *Show Alias*.
9. Navigate to *Computer Services* then select the member "Training_P_291":

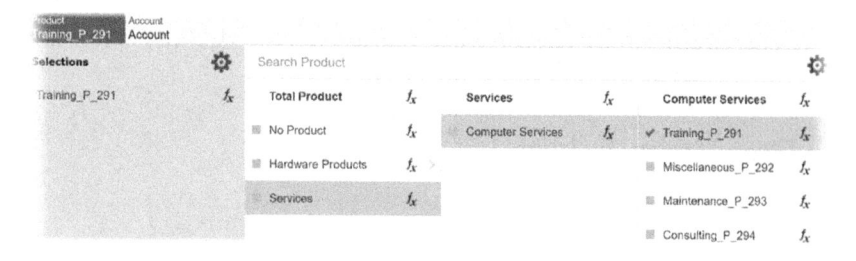

10. Click the *Account* tab.
11. Select *Total Revenue* ("4001") to open its children and select *Training Revenue* ("4140") (or search for "4140"):

12. Click *OK*.

Note!

To remove or uncheck members: highlight the member to remove, click ⚙ in the selections panel and click *Remove*:

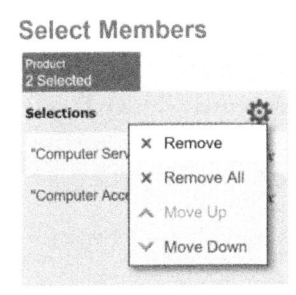

Note!

If you would like to add a filter or show the alias instead of the member name, more setting options are available in settings (⚙ located in the right-most panel of the member selector):

13. Check that you have the following selections for the valid intersection rule:

Services&Other_Accounts

To allow users to enter data into the Support, Consulting, Training and Misc. Revenue accounts for Services & Other products. Data entry into the Units and List Price accounts disabled.

Product	Account
P_291	4140

14. Add additional rules and type in the member names for both Product and Account, as shown below:

Services&Other_Accounts

To allow users to enter data into the Support, Consulting, Training and Misc. Revenue accounts for Services & Other products. Data entry into the Units and List Price accounts disabled.

Product	Account	
P_291	4140	
P_292	4150	
P_293	4120	
P_294	4130	

The purpose of the rule is to ensure that inputs are entered at the correct intersections of Product and Account (e.g., the Training Product member is valid for only the Training Revenue account and the Consulting Product member is only valid for the Consulting Revenue account).

15. Click *Save and Close* at the top right.

To edit, duplicate, delete, or move a valid intersection, click ⚙ in the main Valid Intersections page:

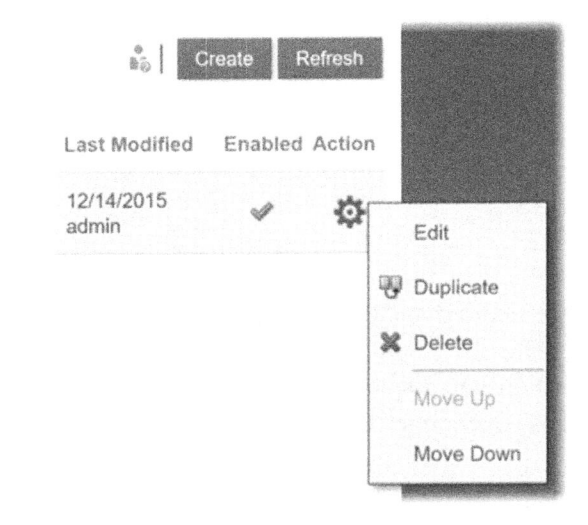

Note!

16. Ensure that the rule is enabled with a ✓ (disabled valid intersections have a grey check mark).
17. Check that the Valid Intersection Rule has been correctly set up using the Analyze capabilities in PBCS Simplified UI or in Smart View (see sections *Analyze* and *Ad Hoc Grids* – located in End User Activities).

Valid Intersections & Data Forms

I created a form to check if the valid combinations worked. It worked! This PBCS stuff is awesome:

Did the Valid Intersections Work

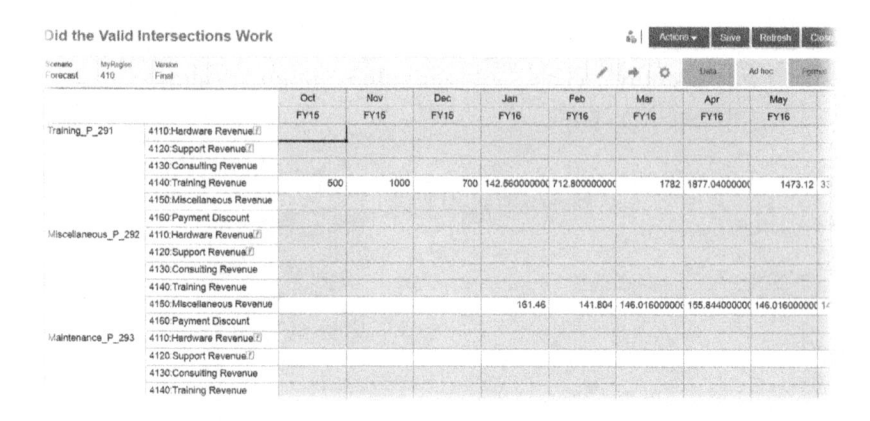

			Oct FY15	Nov FY15	Dec FY15	Jan FY16	Feb FY16	Mar FY16	Apr FY16	May FY16
Training_P_291	4110:Hardware Revenue									
	4120:Support Revenue									
	4130:Consulting Revenue									
	4140:Training Revenue		500	1000	700	142.56000000	712.80000000	1782	1877.04000000	1473.12
	4150:Miscellaneous Revenue									
	4160:Payment Discount									
Miscellaneous_P_292	4110:Hardware Revenue									
	4120:Support Revenue									
	4130:Consulting Revenue									
	4140:Training Revenue									
	4150:Miscellaneous Revenue				161.46	141.804	146.01600000	155.84400000	146.01600000	
	4160:Payment Discount									
Maintenance_P_293	4110:Hardware Revenue									
	4120:Support Revenue									
	4130:Consulting Revenue									
	4140:Training Revenue									

A few notes about data forms and valid intersections:

- Invalid sections are displayed as read only
- If you mouse over an invalid section, a tool tip displays:

> Row Miscellaneous_P_2924110:Hardware Revenue Column Dec FY15 This cell is read-only because it is defined as an invalid intersection.

- If invalid intersections are in the POV and / or page, a warning displays
- Valid intersections apply to run-time prompts launched within PBCS Web or Smart View (but not Smart Forms)
- Attribute dimensions are supported for valid intersections (as of February 2017)
- You can't import valid intersections yet

Invalid Intersection Reports

You can create an invalid intersection report to locate data that does not meet valid intersection requirements. This situation can happen erroneously through a data load or business rule calculation.

To create and run an invalid intersection report,
1. Select *Navigator >> Application >> Setup*.
2. Click the *Invalid Intersection Reports* tab.
3. Click *Create*.

4. Enter a name and description. Type "Account-Product Data Check".
5. Select the cube. Choose *Sales*.
6. Select members for the POV: Entity, Scenario, and Version.
7. Optionally add another dimension to the report.
8. Click *Save and Run Now*.

The report displays and hopefully no invalid data sets are found:

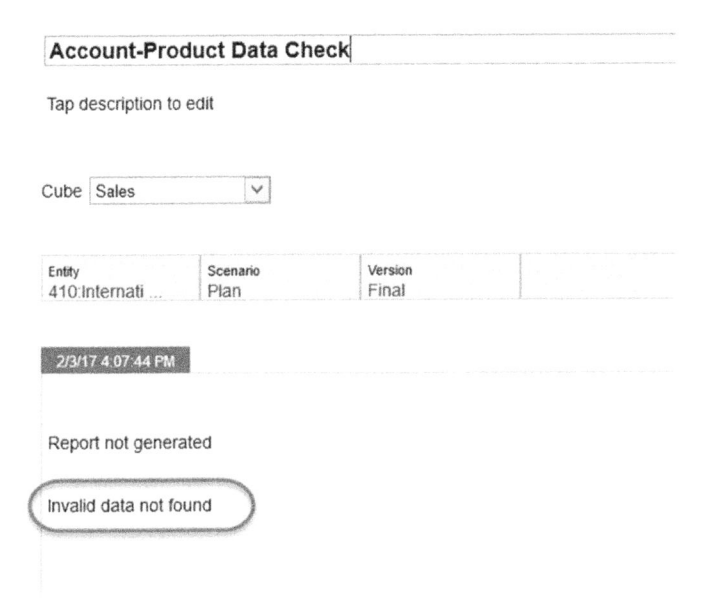

Account-Product Data Check

Tap description to edit

Cube: Sales

Entity	Scenario	Version
410:Internati...	Plan	Final

2/3/17 4:07:44 PM

Report not generated

Invalid data not found

ACTION MENUS

Another handy set of tools that you can add to data forms are menu items for an action menu. These objects provide users a quick way to launch related data forms, business rules and URLs.

Create Action Menu

To create an action menu,

1. Select *Navigator* >> *Create and Manage* >> *Action Menus*.
2. Click to create a new menu.
3. Name the menu. I'm going to call it "Sales Forecast".

4. Once it has been created, edit the menu (✎).
5. Click ♣ (Add Child) while in the Sales Forecast menu. (Adding a "child" really just means creating a menu.)
6. Name the Menu Item and Label "View Forecast Summary".
7. Select *Form* as the Type and click ✚ to select the *Sales Forecast Summary* form:

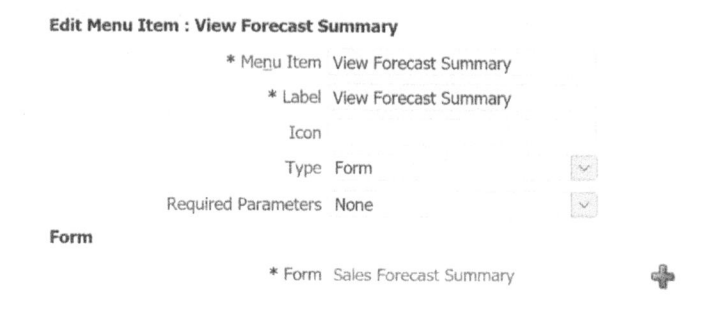

Edit Menu Item : View Forecast Summary

* Menu Item	View Forecast Summary	
* Label	View Forecast Summary	
Icon		
Type	Form	⌄
Required Parameters	None	⌄

Form

* Form	Sales Forecast Summary	✚

8. Click *Save*.
9. Click the *Add Sibling* icon to add another option to the menu:

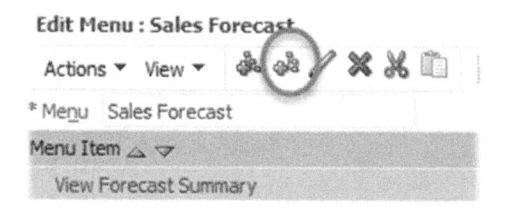

Edit Menu : Sales Forecast

Actions ▼ View ▼ ♣ ♣ ✎ ✖ ✂ 📋

* Menu   Sales Forecast

Menu Item △ ▽

View Forecast Summary

10. Name the Menu Item and Label "Calculate Forecast".
11. Select *Business Rule* as the Type and click ✚ to select the *Calculate MyForecast* business rule.

You can optionally add a custom Window Title, OK Button Label, Cancel Button Label, and Launch Confirmation Message. If left blank, the default PBCS behavior applies. You can choose to launch the rule in a separate window and hide any prompts:

```
Add Sibling : View Forecast Summary
                    * Menu Item  Calculate Forecast
                       * Label  Calculate Forecast
                           Icon
                           Type  Business Rule           [v]
            Required Parameters  None                    [v]
Business Rule
                           Cube  Sales         [v]
               * Business Rules  Calculate MyForecast    [v]
                      View Type  Classic View  [v]
                   Window Title
                OK Button Label
            Cancel Button Label
    Launch Confirmation Message
      Launch in a separate window  [ ]
                    Hide Prompt  [ ]
```

12. Leave the remaining options blank and click *Save*.

Assign Action Menu to Form

To assign the action menu to a form,

1. Select *Navigator* ≡ >> *Create and Manage* >> *Forms*.
2. Edit the Sales Forecast – Products form and go to the *Other Options* tab.
3. In the Context Menus section, move the Sales Forecast menu to the right panel:

Context Menus

Available Menus		Selected Menus
	⟩	Sales Forecast
	⟫	

4. Click *Finish*.
5. Back in the Home screen, go to *Data* and open the *Sales Forecast – Products* form.

6. Click the *Actions* menu. I can see the menu item that I created at the top of the drop-down list:

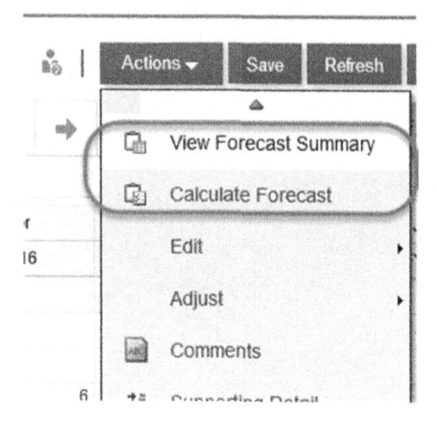

ADD MEMBERS ON THE FLY

A cool feature I might want to enable for users is called "add new members on the fly," which allows users to add members dynamically from within forms. If enabled and configured by the administrator, end users can add new sparse dimension members through data forms and enter data for those new members (without performing a database refresh). This same on-premises functionality is available through PBCS.

The administrator can manage this process by setting boundaries on: how many members can be added, identifying the parent of the new members, and performing the initial configuration for this feature. Placeholder members are created under the covers and not visible to users until they've added their new sparse member. Users can add a single new member at a time on the data form.

To configure this, settings need to be set properly in: the sparse dimension of choice, business rules, and the data forms. I'll start by some initial configuration steps in the desired dimension.

Note! These steps are completed by a PBCS administrator.

To allow for dynamic "members on the fly" within a dimension for a specific parent,
1. In the Simplified UI, select *Navigator >> Create and Manage >> Dimensions*.
2. Select a sparse dimension from the drop-down. I'm going to choose *Product*.
3. Create a new parent for these dynamic members or select an existing one. I'm going to add a new parent to the root called "New Products".

There are a few settings specific to enabling dynamic members.

4. Check *Enable for Dynamic Children*.
5. Select how many maximum children you'll allow users to add to it, as well as the type of access rights. I'm going to allow 25 maximum children members and *Inherit* permissions:

Chapter 7: Create User Interfaces

Add Sibling : Product : P_TP

Member Properties | UDA | Member Formula

Name	New Products
Description	
Alias Table	Default
Alias	
Hierarchy Type	Not Set
Data Storage	Never Share
Two Pass Calculation	
Plan Type	Sales ☑ Addition
	SalesRpt ☐ Ignore
Data Type	Unspecified
Smart Lists	<None>
Enable for Dynamic Children	☑
Number of Possible Dynamic Children	25
Access Granted to Member Creator	Inherit

Inherit
None
Read
Write

Now I'll need to refresh the database to create the placeholders for the dynamic members in the database. To do this,

6. Select *Navigator >> Application >> Overview*.
7. Select *Actions >> Refresh Database* and refresh the database.
8. Once the refresh is complete and successful, click *Finish*.
9. Click *Close* and then *Close* again to get completely out of the Refresh Database screens.

Next, it's time to create the Calculation Manager rule that will prompt users for the member name and optionally other information for the new member.

To create the Calc Manager business rule,
1. Select *Navigator >> Create and Manage >> Rules*.
2. Choose *Actions >> New Object*.
3. Make the selections necessary to create a new business rule within the Sales cube of the Vision app.

Look Smarter Than You Are with PBCS 341

    a. **Application Type**: Planning
    b. **Application**: Vision
    c. **Cube**: Sales
    d. **Object Type**: Rule
    e. **Name**: "AddDynamicProducts":

New Object

Application Type	Planning
Application	VISION
Plan Type	Sales
Object Type	Rule
Name	AddDynamicProducts

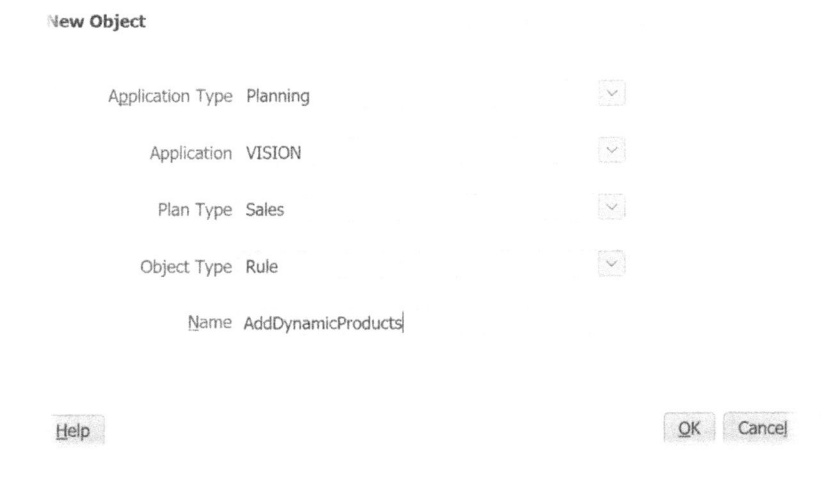

Help   OK   Cancel

4. Click *OK*.

The new business rule editor opens. Now I need to set up the new business rule so that it allows for the creation of dynamic members.

5. The "Begin" step in the graphical interface should be highlighted by default. While highlighted, on the bottom right-hand side find the Properties window and check the option to *Create dynamic members*:

Chapter 7: Create User Interfaces

Properties

Location

Application VISION
Plan Type   Sales

Options

Create dynamic members ☑
Delete dynamic members ☐
Enable Notifications   ☐

Next, a variable needs to be added. This needs to be a run-time prompt that accepts the new product names.

6. Within the *Global Range* tab, select the *Variable Selector* button:

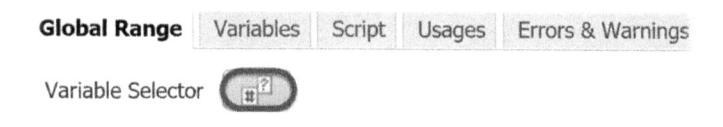

| Global Range | Variables | Script | Usages | Errors & Warnings |

Variable Selector

7. Click *Create* to create a new variable:

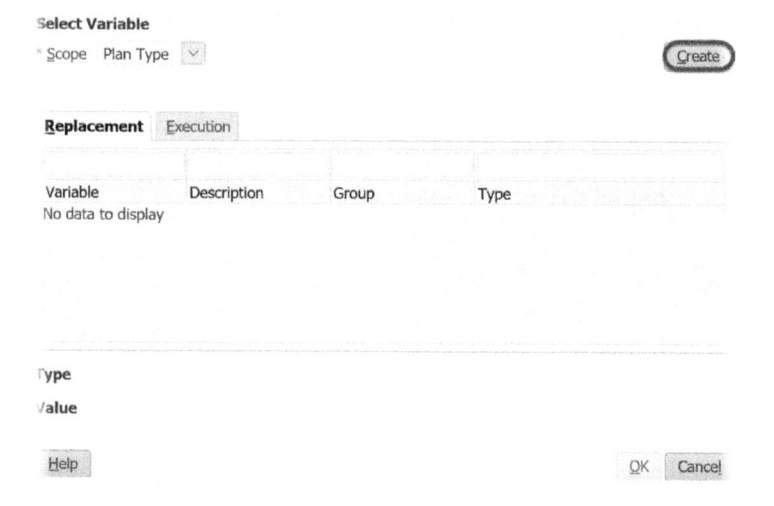

Select Variable

* Scope Plan Type ⌄   Create

Replacement Execution

| Variable | Description | Group | Type |

No data to display

Type
Value

Help   OK   Cancel

8. In the left-hand pane, navigate down the Planning tree until the *Sales* cube is highlighted:

```
System View    AddDyna
Variable Navigator
  ▲ Planning
    > <Global>
    ▲ VISION
       > Sales
       > SalesRpt
```

9. Then within the Variable Designer tab, select *Actions >> New* to create a new variable:

```
Variable Designer
        Replacement   Execution
        Actions ▼
          New      Ctrl+Shift+V
          Save     Ctrl+S
          Refresh  Ctrl+Shift+R
```

10. Enter the properties of the new variable, as shown below.
    a. **Dimension:** Product
    b. **Limits:** @RELATIVE("New Products",0)
    c. **RTP:** Checked
    d. **RTP Text:** Add New Products
    e. **Dynamic Member Parent:** "New Products"

It's critical that the parent of the new dynamic members be specified in the "Dynamic Member Parent" field:

344   Chapter 7: Create User Interfaces

[Properties panel screenshot showing Scope: VISION.Sales, Name: AddProducts, Type: Member, Dimension: Product, Limits: "@RELATIVE("New Products", 0)", Default Value, RTP RTP Text: Add New Products, Dynamic Member Parent: "New Products"]

11. Click the *Save* icon to save the variable.
12. Navigate back to the rule.
13. Within the Global Range window, specific the new variable as the range of the Products dimension:

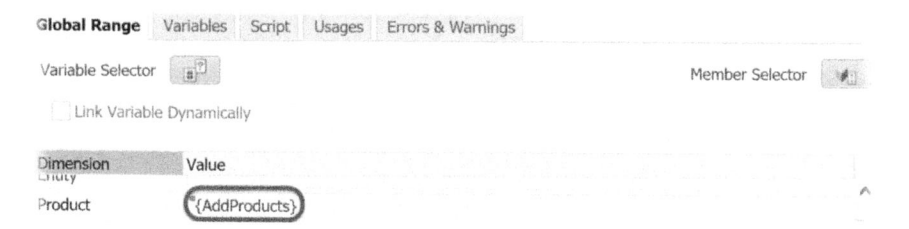

[Global Range screenshot showing Variable Selector, Dimension: Product, Value: {AddProducts}]

14. Save the rule. Click *OK* when you receive the confirmation.
15. Validate and deploy the rule.
16. You should receive a message that the deployment was successfully.

> **Deploy**
> The deployment was successful.

17. Close out of Calculation Manager.

This rule simply adds the new product member. You may also want to add additional prompts to collect information from users in this step, prompting them to enter the forecast units and average price.

Now let's create an action menu that will be assigned on a data form that will run this business rule. This is the construct that allows users to add members dynamically.

1. Select *Navigator* >> *Create and Manage* >> *Action Menus*.

Look Smarter Than You Are with PBCS 345

2. Create a new menu by selecting the green plus symbol or going to *Actions >> Create Menu*.
3. Name the menu "Products Menu":

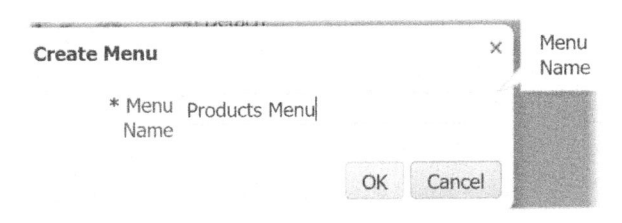

4. Edit the menu.
5. Click the *Add a child* icon to add the first menu item:

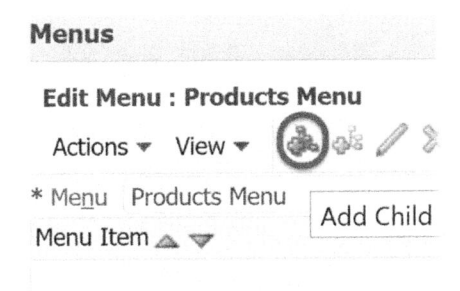

6. Enter the properties of the new menu item.
   a. **Menu Item**: Add New Products
   b. **Label**: Enter new product members
   c. **Type**: Business Rule
   d. **Required Parameters**: None
   e. **Cube**: Sales
   f. **Business Rules**: AddDynamicProducts
   g. **View Type**: Classic View:

Chapter 7: Create User Interfaces

* Menu Item	Add New Products
* Label	Enter new product members
Icon	
Type	Business Rule
Required Parameters	None

Business Rule

Plan Type	Sales
* Business Rules	AddDynamicProducts
View Type	Classic View
Window Title	
OK Button Label	
Cancel Button Label	
Launch Confirmation Message	
Launch in a separate window	☐
Hide Prompt	☐

7. Save the menu item and then close out of the Actions Menu window.

Next, it's time to create a Planning data form with the new menu. This is the vehicle through which users will add members dynamically.

1. Select *Navigator >> Create and Manage >> Forms*.
2. Go to *Actions >> Create simple form* or click 📝.
3. Set the name of the form and add an optional description:

Form and Ad Hoc Grid Management

Simple Form:

| **Properties** | Layout | Other Options | Business Rules | Smart Push |

* Form	Add Product Members
Description	This form allows users to add up to 25 new products

Since the primary goal of this data form is to add new products, I'll create a simple form.

4. Select the Layout tab and define the dimension layout so that it matches the following:
   a. **POV Account**: Units
   b. **POV Scenario**: Forecast
   c. **POV Entity**: No entity
   d. **POV HSP_View**: BaseData
   e. **POV Version**: Final
   f. **POV Month**: &CurMth
   g. **Rows**: IDescendants(New Products)
   h. **Columns**: &ForecastYear:

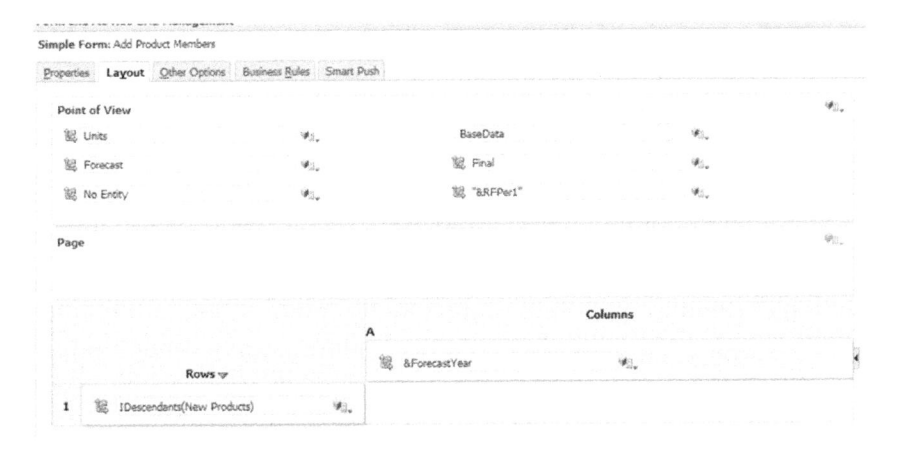

5. Add the menu in the *Other Options* tab:

348   Chapter 7: Create User Interfaces

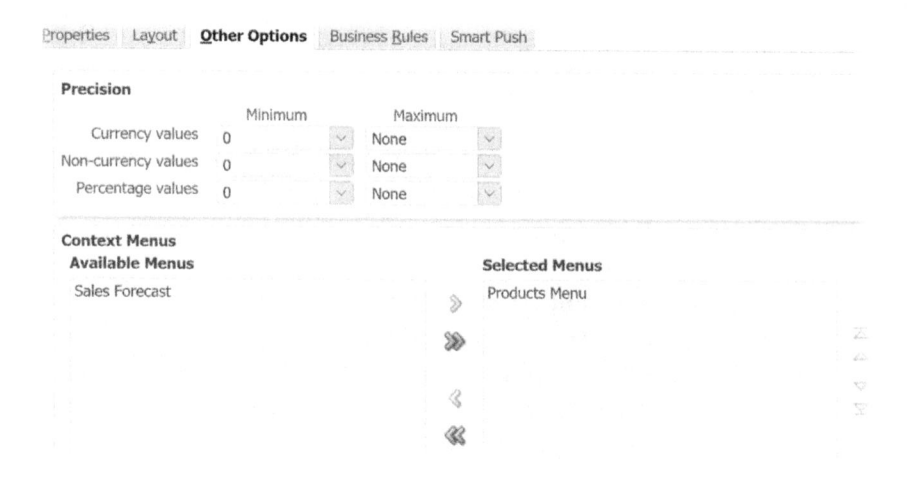

[Screenshot of form editor showing Properties, Layout, Other Options, Business Rules, Smart Push tabs. Precision section with Currency values, Non-currency values, Percentage values all set to Minimum 0 and Maximum None. Context Menus section with Available Menus "Sales Forecast" and Selected Menus "Products Menu".]

6. Save the form and then close it.

Finally, let's test out the final product. Can an end user really add a member on the fly and enter data? Yes! We'll find out in in the End User Activities portion of this mission.

TASKS

Budgeting and forecasting often requires users to perform multiple activities or tasks to complete the process. Tasks are lists of PBCS steps to guide users through the planning process, listing the tasks to be completed with instructions and due dates. Administrators and power users can create and manage tasks and task lists.

A task list can include the following in PBCS Simplified UI:

- URL
- Form
- Business Rule
- Manage Approvals
- Descriptive

Create Task Lists

Like forms, you can create Task List folders to group task lists:

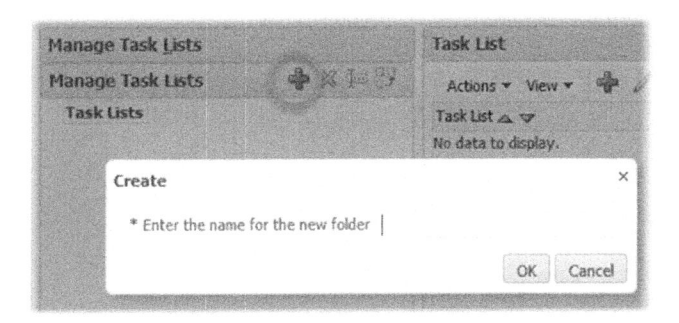

To create a task list to guide users through the forecasting process,
1. Select *Navigator* >> *Create and Manage* >> *Tasks Lists*.
2. Under Actions, click *Create Task List*.
3. Name the task list "Forecasting Activities".
4. Select the pencil icon to *Edit* the Forecasting Activities Task List.
5. Under Actions, click . (Add Child adds a new item to an existing task list.)
6. Enter a name for the task, in our case, "Enter Sales Forecast – Products".
7. Select *Form* as the Type and use to select the radio button to the left of the appropriate form.
8. Optionally set a Start Date, End Date, and Alerts:

Chapter 7: Create User Interfaces

Edit Task List - Forecasting Activities

Task - Enter Sales Forecast – Products

- Task: Enter Sales Forecast – Products
- Type: Form
- Form: Sales Forecast – Products
  - ☐ Set Page Member Defaults
- Duration: 0
- Start Date: ☐
- End date: ☐
  - ☐ Repeat Every 0 Hour(s)
- Alert: ☐
  - ☐ Repeat Every 0 Hour(s)
- Dependency

Alerts display: Green = On Schedule, Yellow = Approaching End Date, Red = Overdue. If End Date is checked, you can send emails when a task is not completed by the due date. Optionally, you can select the Dependency check box if the completion of this task is dependent upon completing the primary task.

9. Add instructions for users to provide more guidance.
10. Click *Save*.
11. Repeat steps 5-10, but for the Sales Forecast – Services & Other form. Add Sibling instead of child for step 5.
12. Repeat steps 5-10 again for the Sales Forecast Summary form. Use *Add Sibling* instead of *Add Child* for step 5.

The completed task list should look as follows:

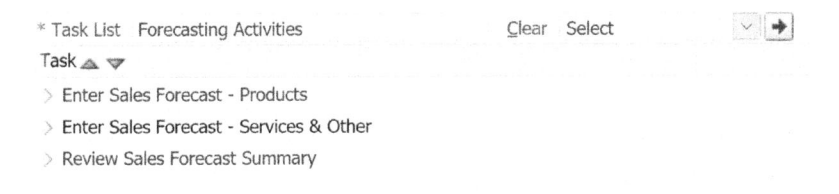

```
* Task List   Forecasting Activities              Clear   Select
Task ▲ ▼
> Enter Sales Forecast - Products
> Enter Sales Forecast - Services & Other
> Review Sales Forecast Summary
```

13. Click *Save*.

To view or go through the task list, click *Tasks* in the PBCS main menu.

Note! To save some time, you can also use *Save As* to duplicate an entire task list.

From the Manage Task Lists section, you can create, rename, edit, move, or delete task lists and task list folders. This is also where you assign user access for specific task lists:

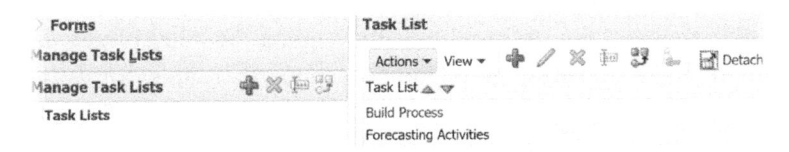

```
> Forms                          Task List
Manage Task Lists                 Actions ▼  View ▼  ✚ ✏ ✖ ▦ ⫶  ⬚ Detach
Manage Task Lists    ✚ ✖ ▦ ⫶     Task List ▲ ▼
   Task Lists                     Build Process
                                  Forecasting Activities
```

To copy a task list, use the "Save As" option from within the desired source task list.

Monitor Tasks

As an administrator you will want to monitor the status of a specific task list, understanding what steps have been completed and what tasks are outstanding. To view task list status, simply click the Tasks icon from the Home screen:

352   Chapter 7: Create User Interfaces

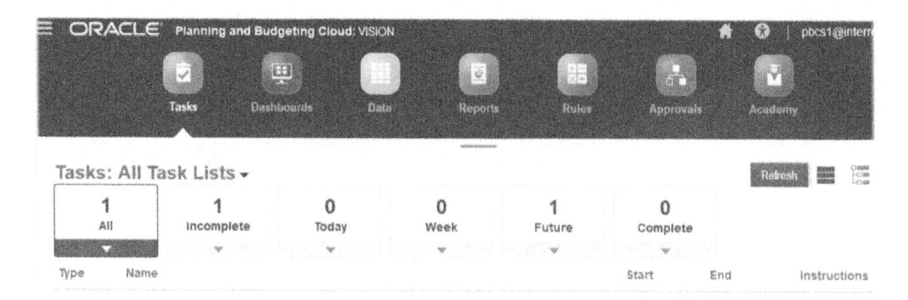

You can filter, sort, and view all of the tasks for which you are provisioned. You can toggle between a list of the task lists and a hierarchical view of the task lists (I prefer to use the hierarchical view):

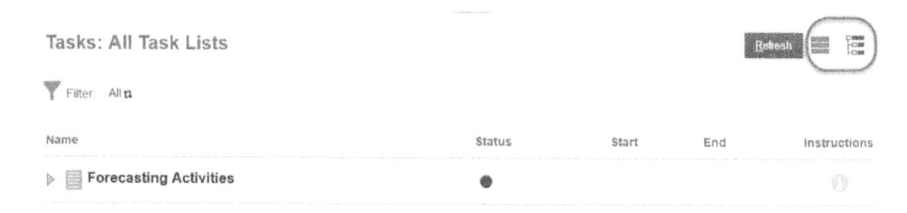

DASHBOARDS

Dashboards are interactive user interfaces that allow users to visually analyze the information they need in one place. Objects included in the dashboards include: dashboard header, forms, charts, webpages, and commentary text. Charts are based on existing forms. You can edit data directly in a dashboard. Sometimes the forms you create are not ideal for displaying in dashboards due to the number of rows / columns included. You might need to create specific data forms to support dashboard requirements.

Dashboards are a great alternative over composite forms because you can combine charts, commentary, external URLs, with editable forms all in one view. The only "catch" is that dashboards are not yet supported in Smart View in Excel.

Keep in mind the following attributes about dashboards in PBCS:

- May have up to six editable forms

- May have up to nine types of charts such as area, bar, bubble, column, doughnut, funnel, gauge, scatter, radar, and tile
  - Tile chart type displays a specific value or metric
  - Gauge chart type functions much like a gas gauge for a car
- Links are supported to external websites
- You can add text sections to a dashboard for explanations and commentary
- Global POVs are supported
- Dashboard sections may be defined vertically or horizontally
- Dashboard sections can be fixed sized or dynamic

Create Dashboard

To create a dashboard in PBCS,
1. In the Home screen, go to *Dashboards*.
2. Click *Create*.
3. Enter a Dashboard Name "Sales Forecast Home".
4. Drag "Sales Forecast Summary" data form into the main layout:

5. Drag "Sales Forecast Summary" data form into the main layout again, placing it just above the first "Sales Forecast Summary." A blue bar highlights when the form is ready to be "dropped":

354   Chapter 7: Create User Interfaces

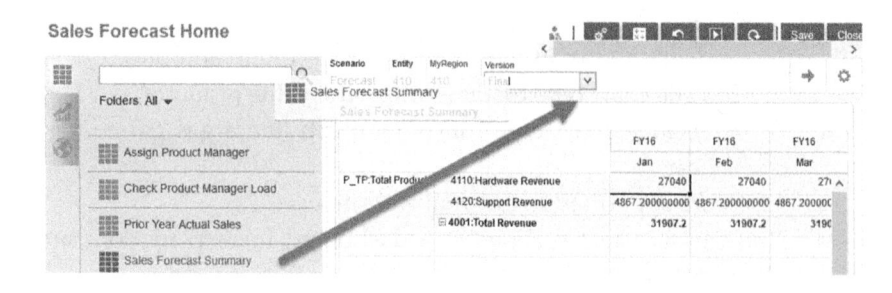

The data form name is automatically assigned as the section header. If you'd like to add a custom header, click on the *Settings* icon:

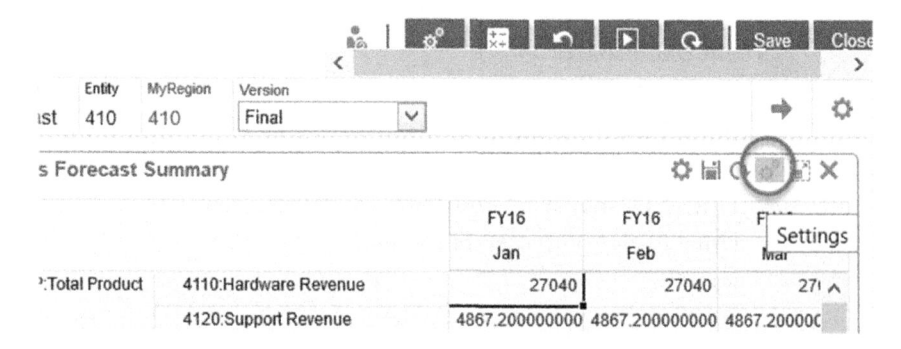

Under *Settings,* you can define custom headers and chart types for the data.

6. Select the *Settings* icon for the top section (first "Sales Forecast Summary" form listed).
7. Leave the default header and default height but change the chart type to *Bar*:

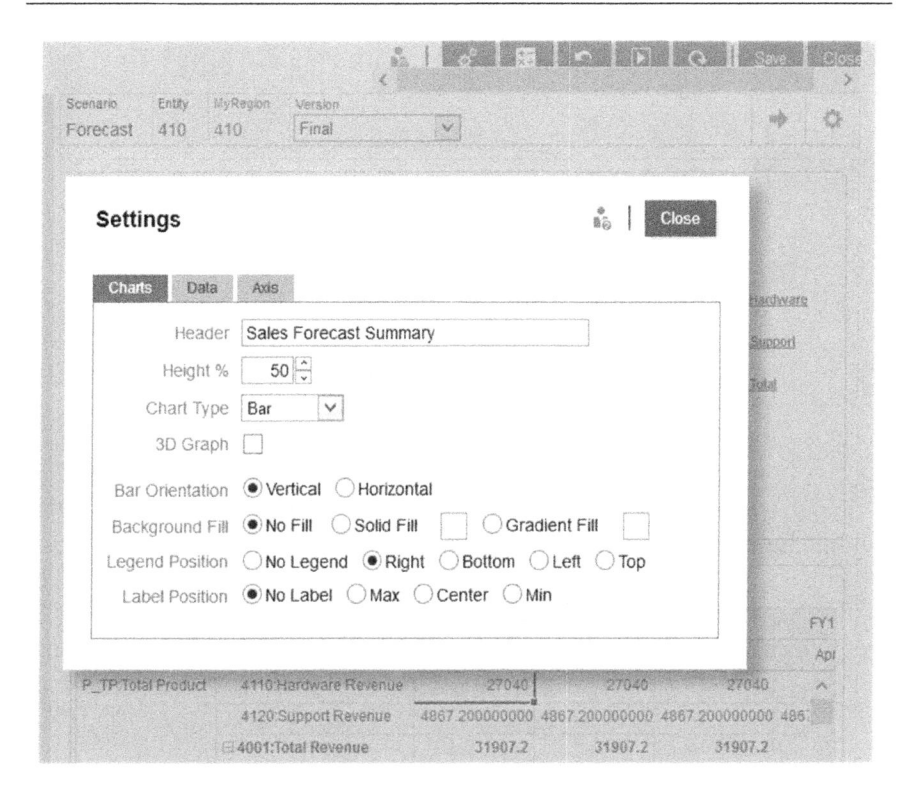

A number of options display depending on the chart type selected like: 3D display, chart orientation, background fill, legend position, and label position.

8. Leave the other options to the default setting.

Notice you can also change the data source for the chart on the *Data* tab:

356   Chapter 7: Create User Interfaces

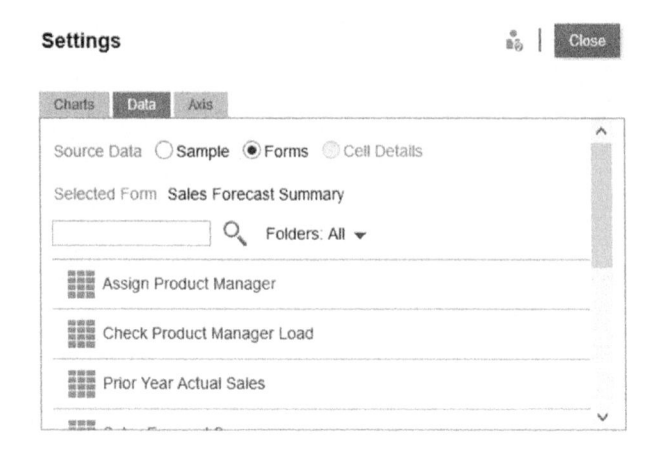

You can define axis settings on the *Axis* tab, accepting automatic limits for X and Y axis or manually setting the limits yourself:

The top

9. Click *OK*. The top section now displays as a bar chart:

Look Smarter Than You Are with PBCS 357

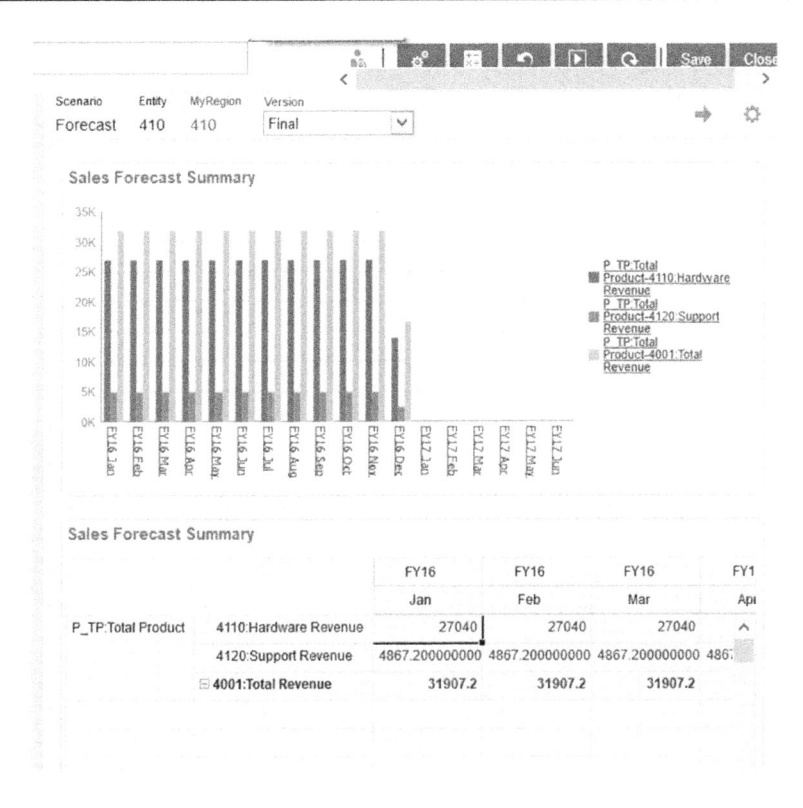

An alternative order to creating a dashboard is to start with the *Chart Types* icon on the left and drag in the type of chart I want to display. I can then select the data form containing the source data:

358   Chapter 7: Create User Interfaces

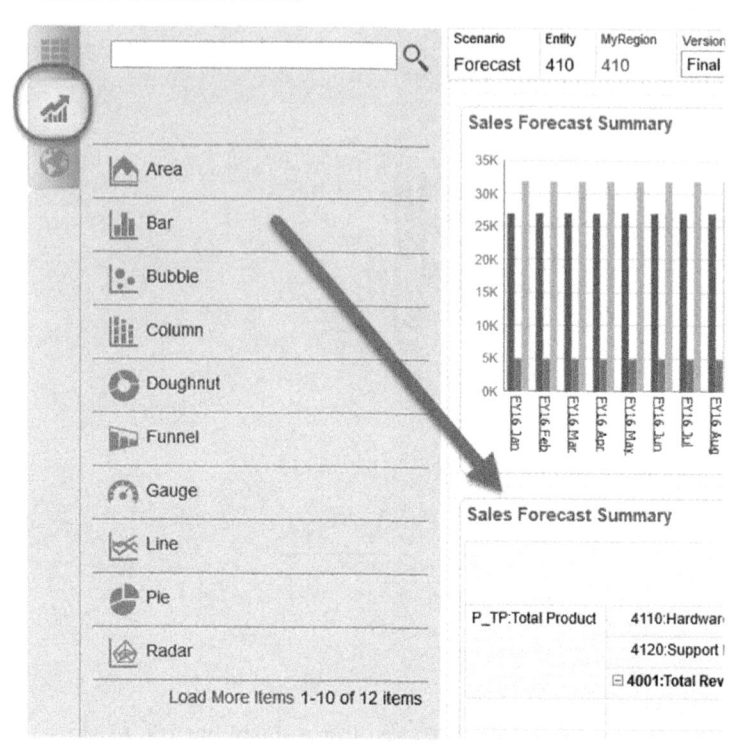

10. Open the *External Artifacts* tab on the left and drag the *Commentary* object to dashboard:

Look Smarter Than You Are with PBCS 359

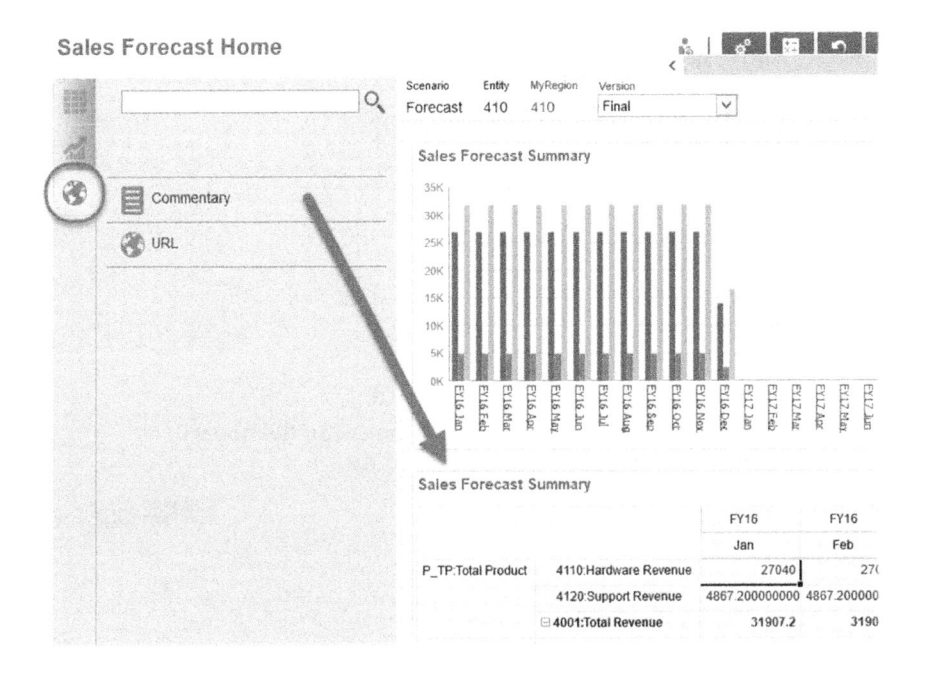

11. Add commentary and format the text:

12. Click *Close*.

Other Dashboard overall settings include:

- *Dashboard Settings* to define name, borders, layout, POV bars, and global POV bars

Chapter 7: Create User Interfaces

- Assigning business rules to a dashboard with *Run Before Load*, *Run After Save*, *Use Members on Form*, and *Hide Prompt* parameters:

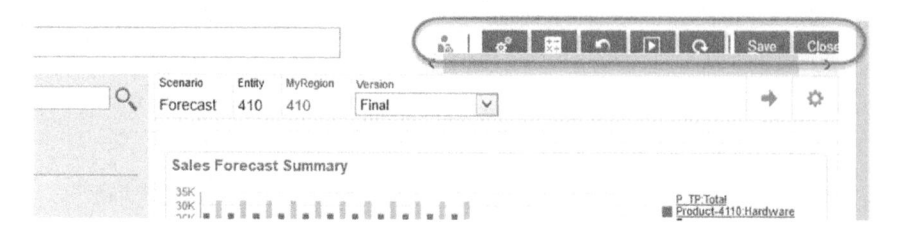

13. Click *Save* to save the dashboard.
14. Click the *Play* icon to review the entire dashboard:

FINANCIAL REPORTS

Financial Reporting (FR) is a reporting solution for Oracle EPM to create nicely formatted, printable reports. Report designers build and define reports. When reports are executed, they retrieve information from the database as it currently exists, including any recent data changes. Therefore, a report could display different values each time it is run if the data changes frequently.

It is often desirable to keep a copy of a report that is run at a specific point in time, similar to a photograph or a Polaroid. This records the data as it existed at that point in time. Financial Reporting accomplishes this by creating "Snapshots." Snapshots are essentially reports with stored data values that can be viewed at any time. Since the data is stored, the report is not rerun against the database and data values remain static. After a snapshot is created, changes to the data in the database will not be reflected in that snapshot. Snapshots are stored in the reporting and analysis repository *(Navigator >> Reporting >> Explore Repository)*.

Books are a collection of reports. A book can include both reports and snapshots, although they typically contain one or the other and offer an easy way to work with multiple reports. Other artifacts from the reporting and analysis repository can be included in the book with the reports and snapshot reports. These can include the file types: text, HTML, PDFs, and Microsoft Office files (Word, Excel, and PowerPoint). Books are created by selecting *File >> New >> Document* from the reporting and analysis repository.

Note! Snapshots and books can only be created in the PBCS reporting and analysis repository.

The Oracle EPM Smart View add-in provides integration with Financial Reporting. You can import report images from Financial Reporting into Word or PowerPoint. You can also import report grids from Financial Reporting into Word, PowerPoint, or Excel. This is sometimes helpful for presentations or documents where you need to pull EPM Cloud information and combine it with external information.

Standardized, formatted reports are created using Financial Reporting Studio (FRS). The original FRS was installed as a desktop client. The desktop version of FRS will be available until May 2017, when it will be completely replaced with the new web version.

A new web studio for Financial Reports was released in March 2016. Most of the same Financial Reporting Studio concepts apply with the new user interface. In fact, you can open existing FR reports with the new Reporting Web Studio. The new Reporting Web Studio is launched from the Simplified UI (*Navigator >> Manage >> Reporting Web Studio*).

I'll first be creating a Sales Revenue by Product report in the FR web studio to explore the neat functionality Financial Reporting has to offer. Finally, I'll show how to create a book combining multiple reports together into a single PDF/HTML deliverable. This is not a comprehensive guide for Financial Reporting. For full documentation, please refer to Oracle's *Financial Reporting Studio User's* guide or the *Designing with Financial Reporting Web Studio for Oracle Planning and Budgeting Cloud* guide.

Create Report in Financial Reporting Studio (Web)

With the PBCS release in March 2016, FR web studio was added to the set of tools available to users on the Cloud interface. The web studio requires no client installation and continues to bridge the gap in functionality with the desktop software. In May 2017, the web studio will be the only way to build reports in FR, as Oracle will stop shipping the desktop software at that point in time.

To create a new report in FR Web Studio (note there are a lot of steps in this task),

1. Select *Navigator* >> *Reporting* >> *Reporting Web Studio*. A new window launches with the FR web studio:

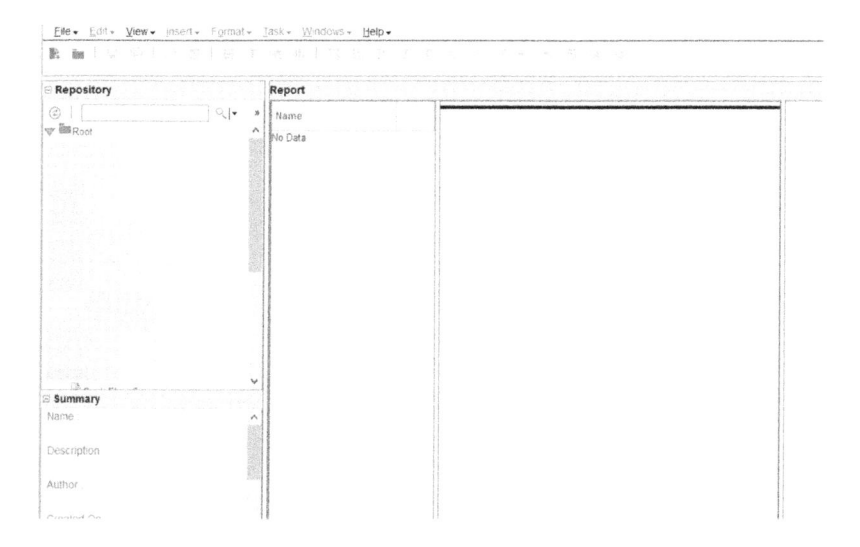

2. Click the first icon, *New Document*, to create a new report:

Four objects that can be inserted into reports include:

- Grids
- Text objects
- Images
- Charts

Create a Grid

3. Click the *Grid* icon and create the shape of the grid with a click, drag, and release on the report.
4. To create a Grid, I need to connect to a database connection. The database connections available to the FR desktop studio are also available here, as they are managed centrally. Point to the same *SalesRpt* connection and then type in the login credentials:

Database Connection Properties

Data Sources

| SalesRpt | ∨ |

[New Connection]

User Name

| admin |

Password

| •••••••• |

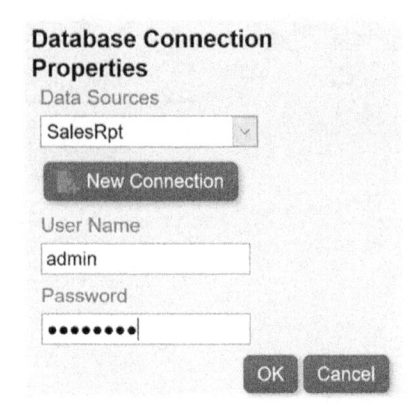

[OK] [Cancel]

5. Click *OK*. The Dimension Layout opens.
6. Click and drag the following dimensions from the POV to the Pages, Columns, or Rows:

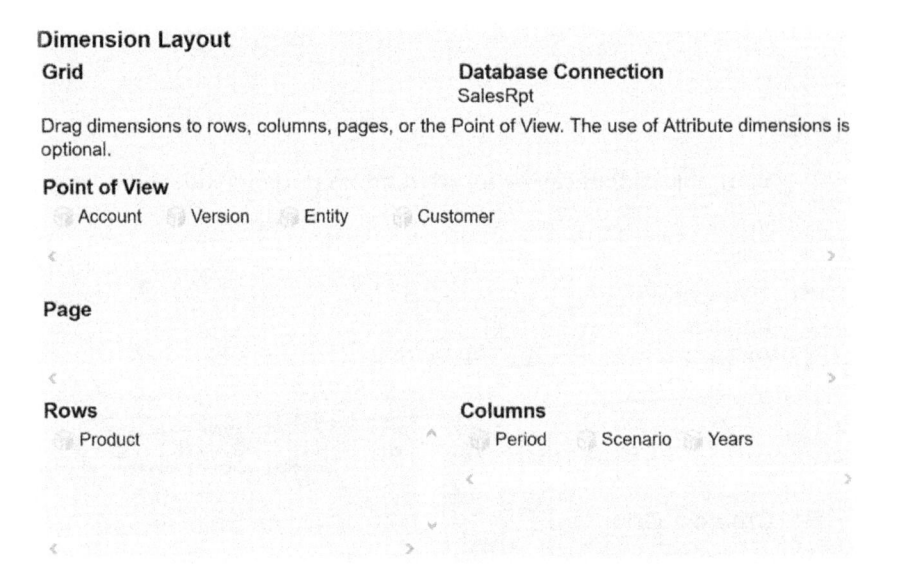

Dimension Layout

Grid **Database Connection**
SalesRpt

Drag dimensions to rows, columns, pages, or the Point of View. The use of Attribute dimensions is optional.

Point of View
  Account   Version   Entity   Customer

Page

Rows **Columns**
  Product   Period   Scenario   Years

7. Click *OK*.
8. Double-click each dimension in the grid to select the desired members. Double-click *Product*. Expand the dimension and then check the box next to the Services member ("P_SVC").

Then click the member function drop-down at the top and select *Descendants (Inclusive)*:

Select Members

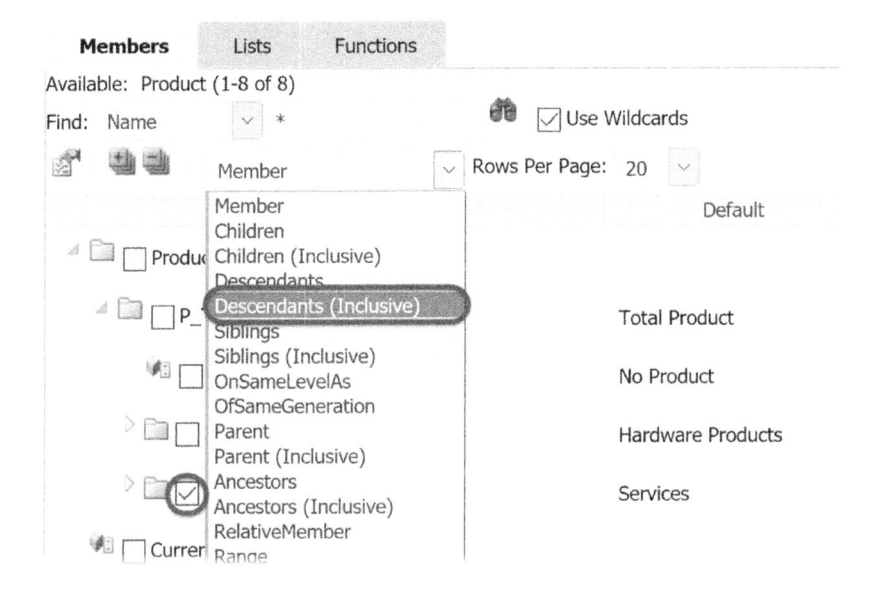

Members	Lists	Functions

Available: Product (1-8 of 8)

Find: Name ∨ *   ☑ Use Wildcards

Member ∨   Rows Per Page: 20 ∨

- Member — Default
- Children
- ☐ Produc Children (Inclusive)
- Descendants
- ☐ P_ **Descendants (Inclusive)** — Total Product
- Siblings
- Siblings (Inclusive) — No Product
- OnSameLevelAs
- OfSameGeneration
- ☐ Parent — Hardware Products
- Parent (Inclusive)
- ☑ Ancestors — Services
- Ancestors (Inclusive)
- RelativeMember
- ☐ Currer Range

9. Move the selection to the right. Then remove the previously default-selected *Product* selection.

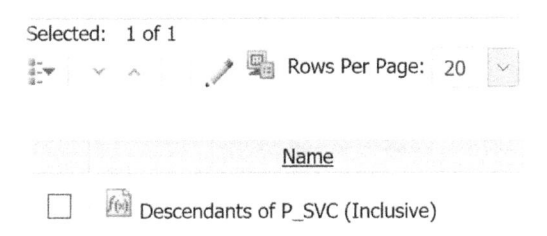

Selected: 1 of 1

Rows Per Page: 20 ∨

Name

☐ Descendants of P_SVC (Inclusive)

10. Click *OK*.
11. I'm going to display Actual data for an entire year. Double-click *Scenario* and select *Actual*.
12. Double-click *Period* in Column A and remove the default *Period* member.
13. Navigate to the *Functions* tab:

Select Members

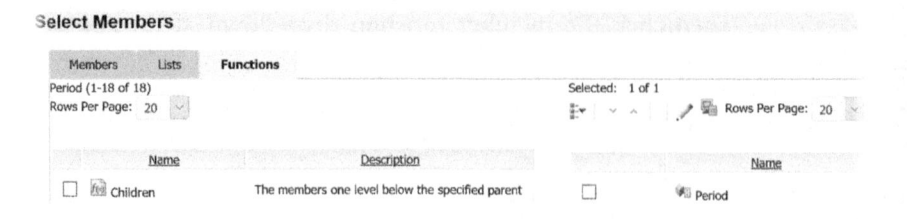

Members	Lists	**Functions**			
Period (1-18 of 18)			Selected: 1 of 1		
Rows Per Page: 20					Rows Per Page: 20

Name	Description		Name
☐ Children	The members one level below the specified parent	☐	Period

14. Check the box next to the *Range* function. Then move it to the right pane.
15. Within Parameters for Range, select *Jan* as the StartMember and *Dec* as the EndMember:

Select Members

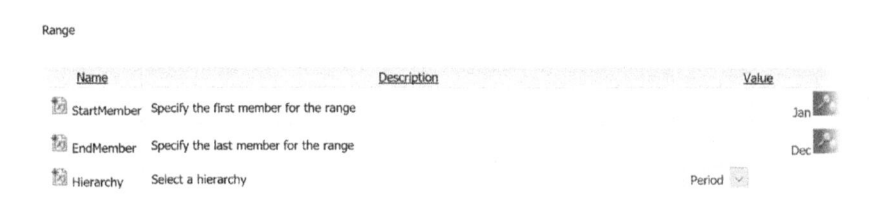

Range

Name	Description	Value
StartMember	Specify the first member for the range	Jan
EndMember	Specify the last member for the range	Dec
Hierarchy	Select a hierarchy	Period

16. Click *OK*.
17. In addition to your Range from Jan to Dec, add the *YearTotal* member.
18. Click *OK*:

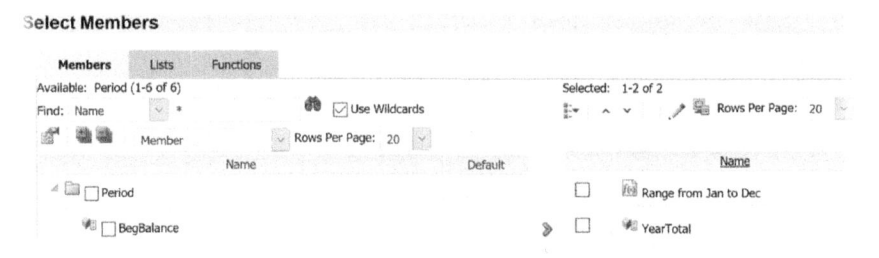

Select Members

Members	Lists	Functions			
Available: Period (1-6 of 6)			Selected: 1-2 of 2		
Find: Name		☑ Use Wildcards			Rows Per Page: 20
Member		Rows Per Page: 20			

Name	Default	Name
▸ ☐ Period	☐	Range from Jan to Dec
☐ BegBalance	☐	YearTotal

19. Double-click *Years* in Column A and remove the default Years member.
20. Select the checkbox next to *Prompt for Years* and move it over:

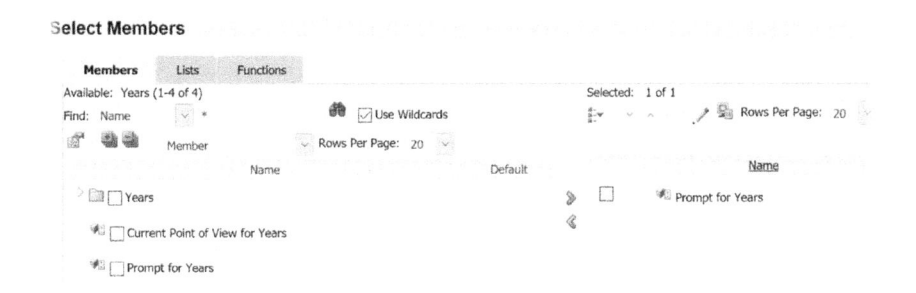

21. Click *OK*. Fill in the details of the prompt and click *OK*:

22. Your report build should now be designed as follows:

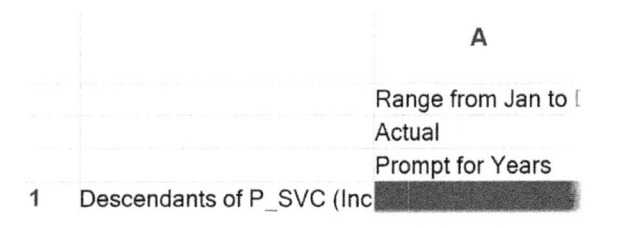

	A
	Range from Jan to [
	Actual
	Prompt for Years
1	Descendants of P_SVC (Inc

The default grid name for the first grid in any report is named "Grid1". To change the grid name, click the top left corner of the grid, and change the name in the *Grid Properties* pane to the right:

Note!

Grid Properties - [SalesRpt_G

SalesRpt_Grid

Database Connection
SalesRpt

Dimension Layout

Now that the grid dimensions have been defined, I still need to define the dimensions in the POV.

23. Near the top, click each dimension in the POV and make the following selections:

Account: 4001   Version: Final   Entity: Total Entity   Customer: Total Customer

Now let's format the grid. To do this,

24. Click the row that contains *Prompt for Years* so that the entire row is highlighted:

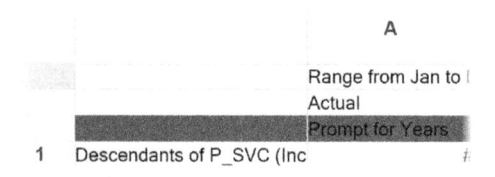

		A
		Range from Jan to
		Actual
		Prompt for Years
1	Descendants of P_SVC (Inc	

25. In Row Properties on the right, check the box for *Hide Always*:

Look Smarter Than You Are with PBCS   369

> **Row Properties**
> Row Height   18
> ☑ Hide Always
>
> ☑ Adjust Row Height to Fit

26. Highlight the cells you would like to format:

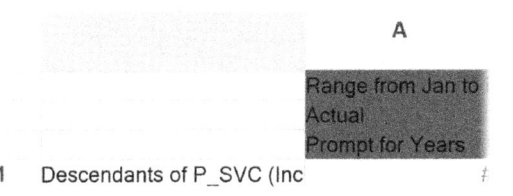

> | | A |
> |---|---|
> | 1 | Range from Jan to Actual Prompt for Years |
> | | Descendants of P_SVC (Inc |

27. Right-click the cells and click *Format*.
28. Explore the formatting tabs and change cells as desired (bold, center, add prefixes to data, create borders, etc.):

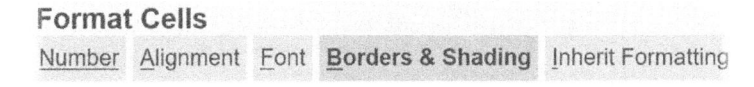

Format Cells
Number Alignment Font **Borders & Shading** Inherit Formatting

Note! You can also insert more rows of data, text, or even formulas in the report grids. Column and Row Properties allow more formatting options as well.

Create a Text Box

Now's a good time to save the report. To do this,

29. Click the *Save* icon, name it, and save it in the *Vision >> Sales* repository folder. It should be saved as *Reports* type:

370　　　　　　　　　　　　　　　　　　Chapter 7: Create User Interfaces

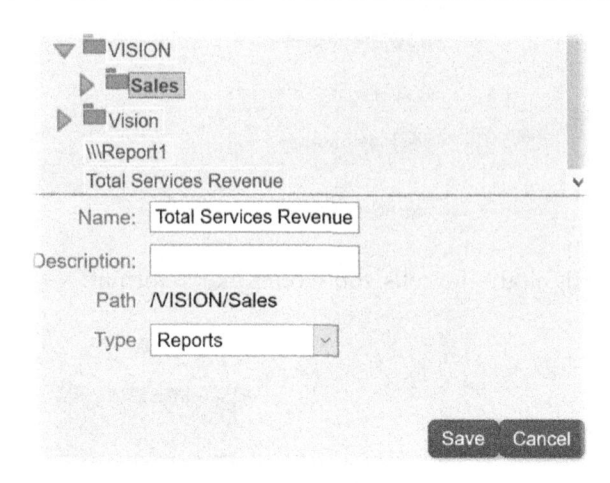

30. Navigate back to the *Report Properties* by clicking on the report name in the left pane:

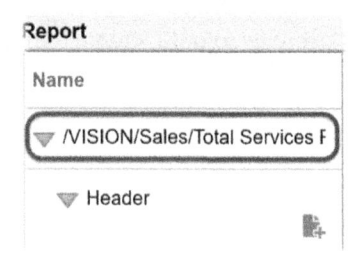

31. Click the *Text* icon at the top:

32. Click, drag, and release in the report header to create the shape of the text box.
33. Type in a title for the report and format the font and alignment.
34. Insert text functions, like *Member Name*, to make text more dynamic.

You should have something like the following:

Total Services Revenue - <<MemberName("SalesRpt_Grid", 1/A/1, Scenario)>> <<MemberName("SalesRpt_Grid", 1/A/1, Years)>>

(Report in Thousands)

Add a Chart

In the March 2016 update for FR, the chart engine was updated to improve rendering performance and functionality. Charts are available to both desktop and web studio clients.

To add a chart to the report,

35. Click the report name to see the report properties.

Now I'll be able to move around objects on the report to make space for a chart. I'm going to keep the header at 0.5 inches. I'm also going to move down the grid, as I want the chart at the top of the report.

36. Click the *Chart* icon on the menu bar and then draw a chart box above the grid:

37. In the chart editor window, change the *Chart Properties*:

372   Chapter 7: Create User Interfaces

Chart Properties - [Chart1]

Name

[SalesRpt_Chart]

Chart Type

[Bar ⌄]

Grid

[SalesRpt_Grid ⌄]

Legend Items from Grid
- ⦿ Rows
- ○ Cols

Data Range

Rows	Cols
☑ 1	☑ A

☐ Include Auto Calculation

[Format Chart]

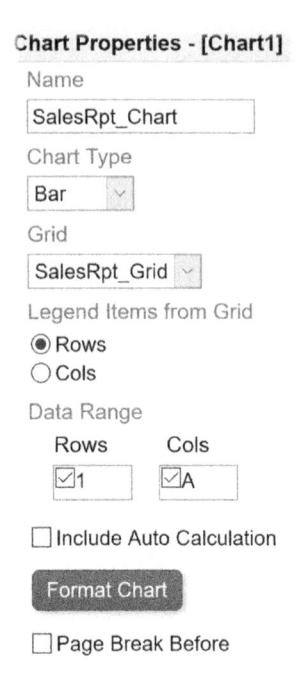

☐ Page Break Before

38. Click *Format Chart* to change specific aspects of the chart. In the *Appearance* tab, add a chart title:

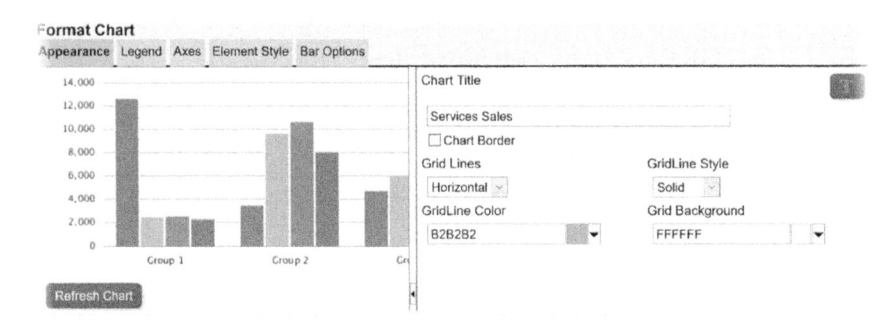

Format Chart

Appearance | Legend | Axes | Element Style | Bar Options

Chart Title: Services Sales

☐ Chart Border

Grid Lines: Horizontal ⌄   GridLine Style: Solid ⌄

GridLine Color: B2B2B2   Grid Background: FFFFFF

[Refresh Chart]

39. Play with whichever other settings make sense for this report.
40. Click *OK*.
41. Back in the main Chart Properties, change the position of the chart so that it's vertically aligned to the top and horizontally centered. To get to the position settings, use the expander next to Position:

Look Smarter Than You Are with PBCS 373

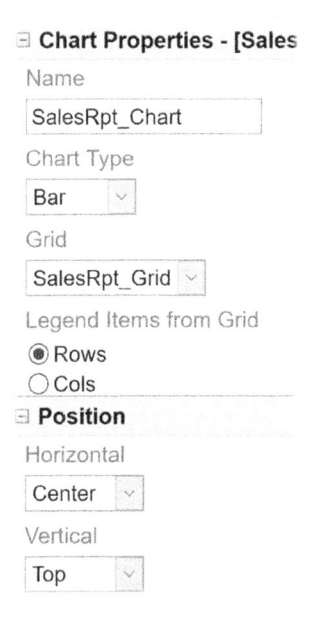

Chart Properties - [Sales
Name
SalesRpt_Chart
Chart Type
Bar
Grid
SalesRpt_Grid
Legend Items from Grid
● Rows
○ Cols
Position
Horizontal
Center
Vertical
Top

42. Do the same for the grid, but change the Vertical alignment to *Relative*.

Save and View the Report

43. *Save* the report.
44. Click the *PDF Preview* icon to run the report and view as a PDF:

45. Specify the Year to view in the report and click *OK*.
46. View the report:

Total Services Revenue - Actual FY14

(Report in Thousands)

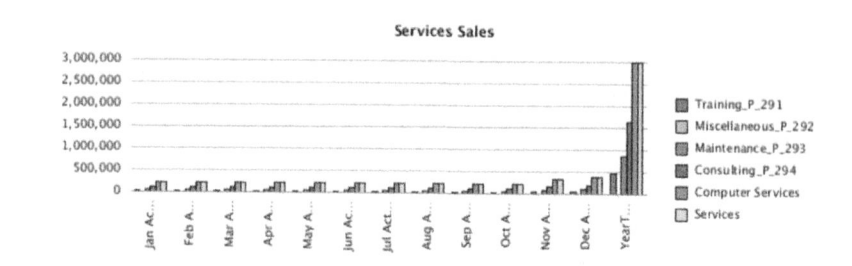

Services Sales

	Jan	Feb	Mar	Apr	May	Jun	Jul	Au
Training_P_291	36,368	35,520	35,968	35,520	36,368	35,520	36,368	3
Miscellaneous_P_292	1,818	1,776	1,798	1,776	1,818	1,776	1,818	
Maintenance_P_293	65,462	63,936	64,742	63,936	65,462	63,936	65,462	6
Consulting_P_294	127,288	124,320	125,888	124,320	127,288	124,320	127,288	12
Computer Services	230,937	225,552	228,397	225,552	230,937	225,552	230,937	22
Services	230,937	225,552	228,397	225,552	230,937	225,552	230,937	22

Other Report Properties

You define paper size, orientation, margins, and how to fit the report objects in the Page Setup dialogue. Select *File>>Page Setup* to define these settings:

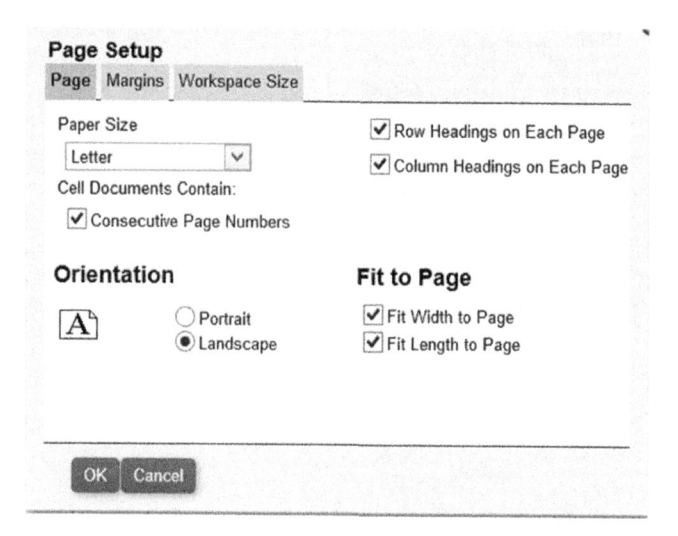

Page Setup

Page | Margins | Workspace Size

Paper Size: Letter
☑ Row Headings on Each Page
☑ Column Headings on Each Page

Cell Documents Contain:
☑ Consecutive Page Numbers

Orientation
○ Portrait
● Landscape

Fit to Page
☑ Fit Width to Page
☑ Fit Length to Page

OK | Cancel

Look Smarter Than You Are with PBCS 375

Positioning report objects involves placing objects in the desired positions in the report workspace. For example, you can position a text box on the top left of the report, and position a grid in the center of the report. How you position objects affects both the online report and the printed page. You position report objects by specifying position property values or using the workspace rulers to position objects.

It's important for the appearance of your report to be able to position objects because report objects can change size depending on the amount of data they contain. You can set the position of a report object relative to other report objects above it and to its left. This means if report objects above the given report object increase or decrease in size, the given report object moves as necessary to maintain the same distance between it and other report objects.

If you don't position a report object, the report object is always printed at its current location regardless of whether report objects above it or to its left increase or decrease in size.

Create a Second Report

1. Using the similar steps above, create a report with the following definition:

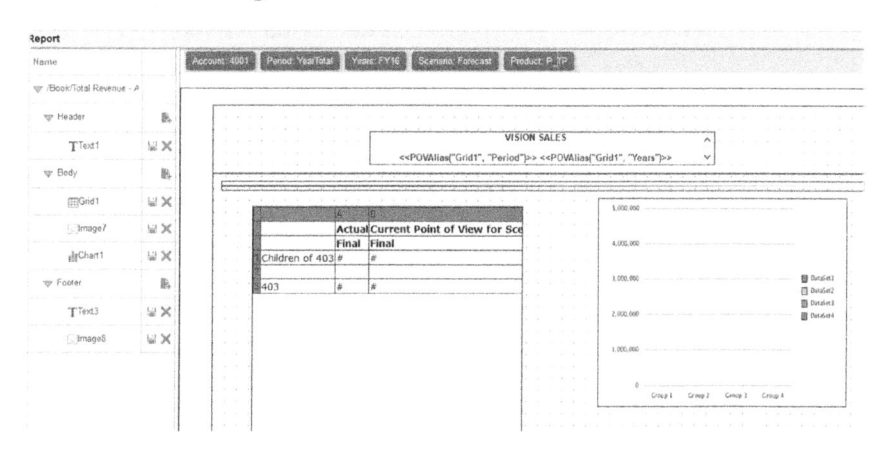

[Report layout screenshot showing Name, Book/Total Revenue, Header with Text1, Body with Grid1, Image7, Chart1, Footer with Text3, Image8, and a preview showing VISION SALES with POVAlias grid and chart data]

2. Set the chart properties to the following:

Chapter 7: Create User Interfaces

Chart Properties - [Chart1]

Name: Chart1

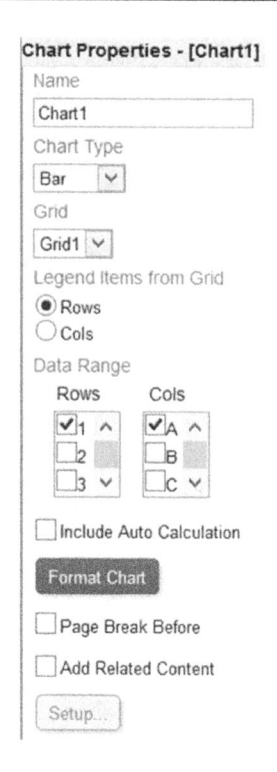

Chart Type: Bar

Grid: Grid1

Legend Items from Grid
- ● Rows
- ○ Cols

Data Range

Rows	Cols
☑ 1	☑ A
☐ 2	☐ B
☐ 3	☐ C

☐ Include Auto Calculation

[Format Chart]

☐ Page Break Before

☐ Add Related Content

[Setup...]

3. Save the report as "Total Revenue-Actual vs. Plan".

Combining Reports into a Book

Financial Reporting supports the creation of books. A book is a single object/report package that contains one or more Financial Reporting documents and may also contain external content like Word documents. In most companies, a set of reports are run each week, month, and quarter. Instead of having to run each of these reports individually, Financial Reporting can group these reports into report books. This is done using the Book Editor. It is in this editor that the reports are identified and POV selections are provided. A table of contents is created for the book. You can collate the reports within the printed table of contents by report or by member selection. I'm going to create a book that contains the two reports we just created.

To create a Financial Reporting book,

Look Smarter Than You Are with PBCS 377

1. If not already open, select *Navigator* ☰ >> *Reporting* >>*Explore Repository*.
2. Go to *File* >> *New* >> *Document*:

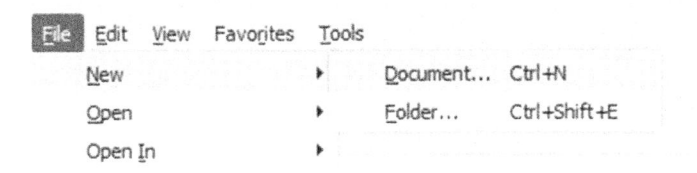

```
File  Edit  View  Favorites  Tools
      New           ▶    Document...  Ctrl+N
      Open          ▶    Folder...    Ctrl+Shift+E
      Open In       ▶
```

3. Keep the default of *Collect Reports into a Book*:

| Planning and Budgeting Service | Explore: / | **New Document 1** ✕ |

1. Select a Task

Select a Task

What would you like to do?

◉ Collect Reports into a Book
○ Batch Reports for Scheduling

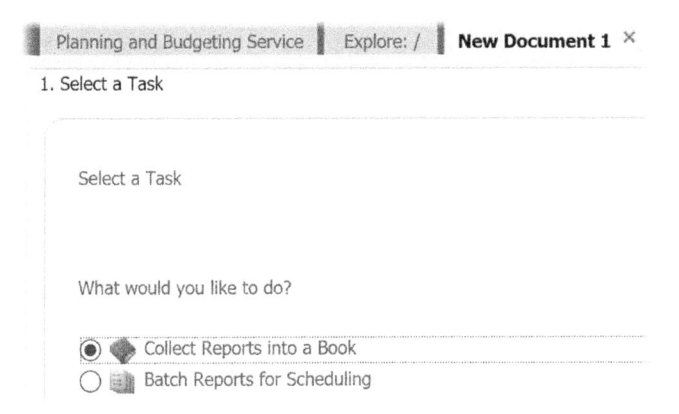

4. Click *Next*.
5. Add the two reports created in the above sections and then click *Finish*:

378   Chapter 7: Create User Interfaces

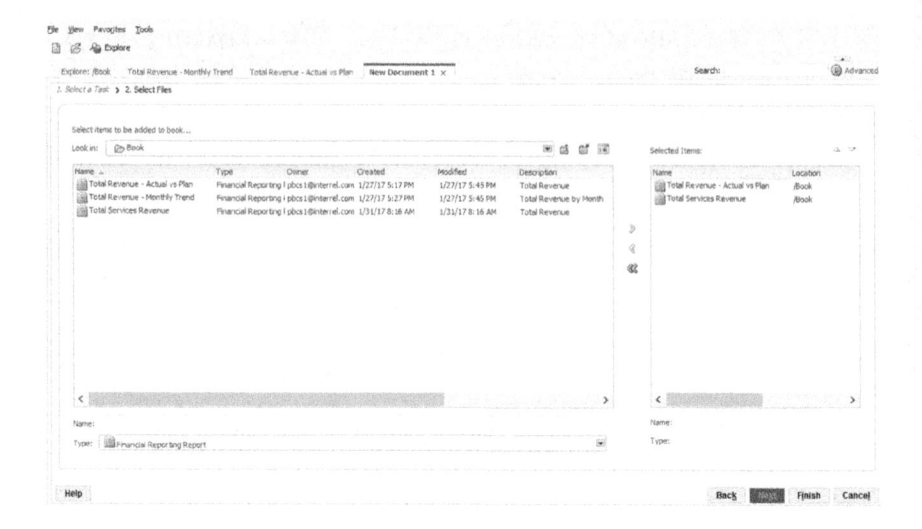

6. Change the drop-down to *Book Setup* and make changes as necessary:

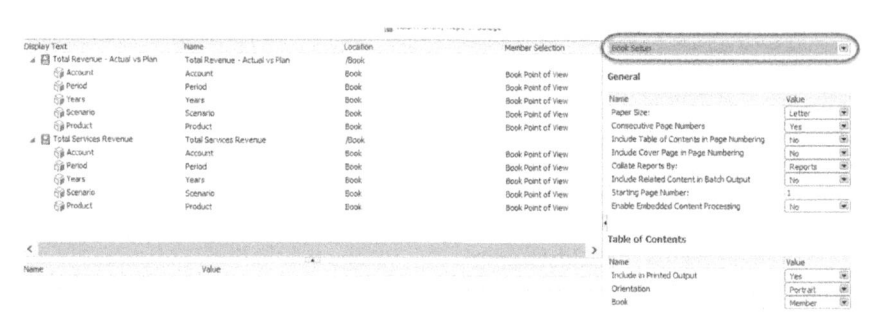

7. Save the object as *Vision Monthly Report Package*:

8. Choose to preview the book to ensure that it's working correctly.

And there you have it! Both reports are now combined into a single Financial Reporting book.

Scheduling Reports and Books in Batches

Batches allow you to schedule reports and books to run simultaneously. To create a batch, select *File >> New >> Document* from the repository and select *Batch Reports for Scheduling*. After all the reports and books are included and the prompts defined, save the batch. You can then run the batch manually or schedule it to run automatically:

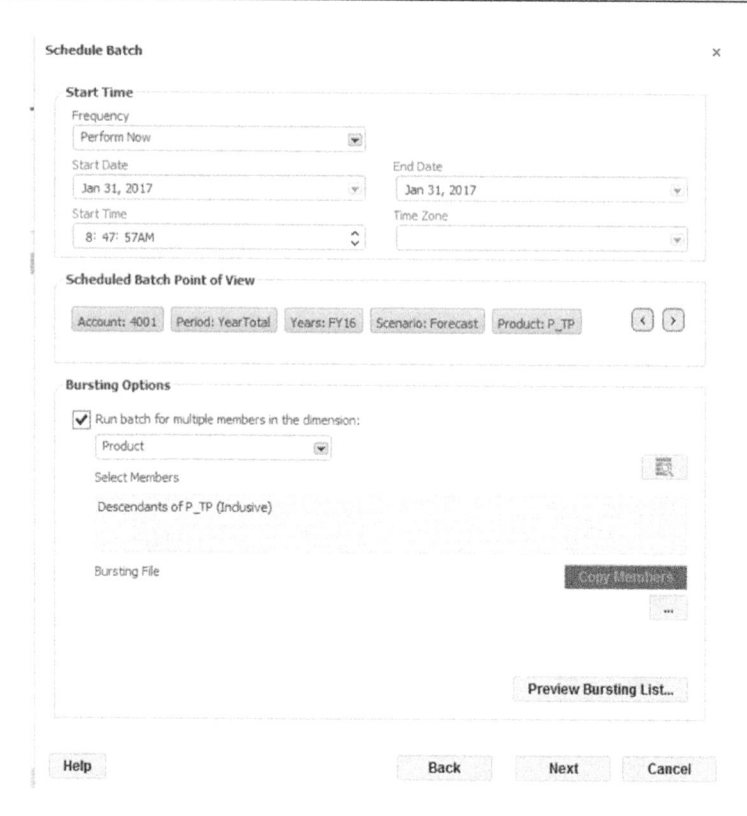

Batches also support batch bursting. This feature provides an easy way to distribute reports (e.g., you want to send a PDF of the P&L report to a non-Cloud user). With batch bursting you can run a batch for more than one dimension member on the Batch POV. You can send the output to the Planning Inbox/Scheduler Output folder, a file system folder, Cloud repository, or email to one or more recipients. When sending the output to emails, you can send different members to different emails (so one person could receive the P&L for the East Region and a different person could receive the P&L for the West region).

I've only skimmed the surface with the functionality in Financial Reporting. Make sure to check out the Oracle documentation and/or attend one of i.n.t.e.r.R.e.l.'s training classes.

AD HOC GRIDS & DYNAMIC REPORTS

Ad Hoc Grids

Ad hoc grids are focused data slices created by users that are saved for reuse within the PBCS application. Users choose the dimensions and members that they want to see in the rows, columns, and page section and are not confined to the data form definition and layout. The user interface is a "grid" versus a "data form." Users can still update data in ad hoc grids and administrators can update the ad hoc grid definitions.

To create an ad hoc grid,
1. Open up a data form. Go to *Actions* >> *New Ad Hoc Grid*:

Or within the ad hoc grids, click *Create*.

2. Choose the cube *Sales* and click *Create*:

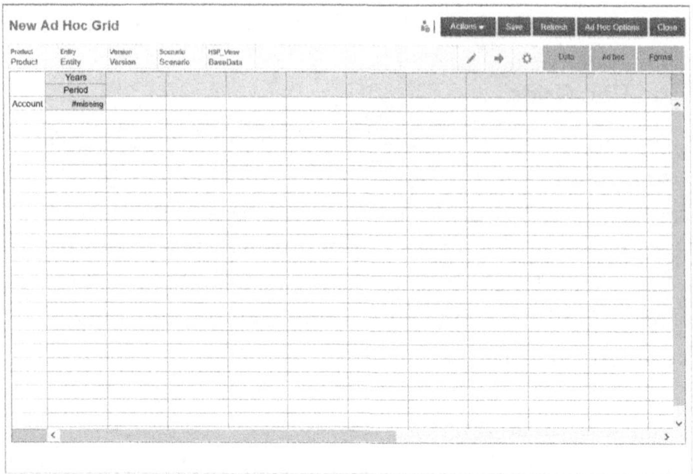
New Ad Hoc Grid
Actions
Save
Refresh
Ad Hoc Options
Close
Product
Entity
Version
Scenario
BaseData
Data
Ad hoc
Format
Years
Period
Account
#missing

Analyze to Build the Ad Hoc Grid Layout

With the blank grid, users can select members for each dimension and use the *Ad Hoc* menu to zoom, move, and pivot dimensions as they wish. However, you might find it helpful to use the UI to build your ad hoc grid.

3. Click the *Ad Hoc* icon to show the Ad hoc panel:

New Ad Hoc Grid
Actions
Save
Refresh
Ad Hoc Options
Close
Product
Entity
Version
Scenario
HSP_View
BaseData
Data
Ad hoc
Format
Years
Period
Account
#missing
Select Members
Zoom
Expand All Levels
Move
Pivot
Remove Selected
Keep Selected
Change Alias

Look Smarter Than You Are with PBCS   383

4. Drag *Product* from the POV to the columns.
5. Select *Years* and click the *Page Pivot* icon. This pivots to the POV.
6. Select *Period* and click the *Page Pivot* icon. This pivots to the POV:

New Ad Hoc Grid						
Years	Entity	Version	Scenario	HSP_View		
Years	Entity	Version	Scenario	BaseData		
	Product					
	Period					
Account	#missing					

7. Drag *Entity* into the Rows.
8. Pivot *Account* into the Page. This pivots to the POV.

The result should look as follows:

New Ad Hoc Grid

Account	Period	Years	Version	Scenario	HSP_View
Account	Period	Years	Version	Scenario	BaseData
	Product				
Entity	#missing				

9. Update the POV member selections by selecting the dimension in the POV and choosing the member through the member selection process, or click ✎ and select each member through the member selection icon there:

384   Chapter 7: Create User Interfaces

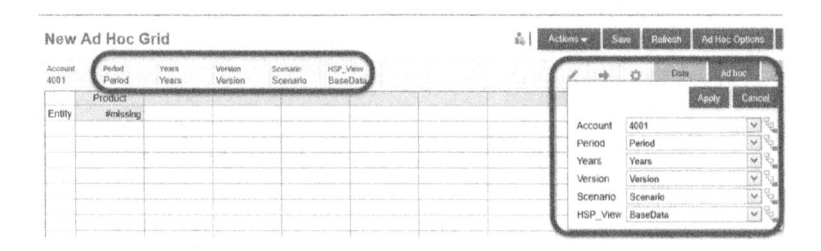

10. Update the POV to:
    a. Account = 4001 (Total Revenue)
    b. Period = YearTotal
    c. Years = FY16
    d. Versions = Final
    e. Scenario = Forecast
    f. HSP_View = BaseData

Period	Years	Account	Version	Scenario	HSP_View
YearTotal	FY16	4001	Final	Forecast	BaseData
Final					

	Product
Entity	17882846.64800

11. Double-click on *Entity* within the grid to zoom down. Zoom until you get to Sales numbers "403" (and then choose the option to *Keep Selected)*:

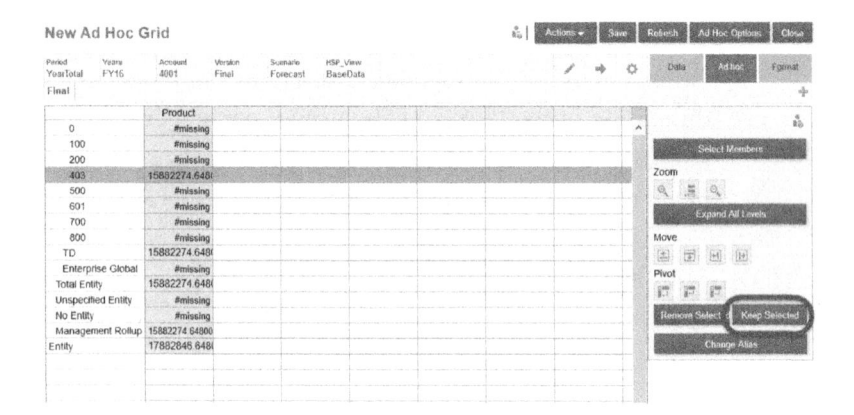

Look Smarter Than You Are with PBCS 385

12. Now zoom in on Product using the *Zoom In* icon in the Ad hoc panel. Click the icon twice.

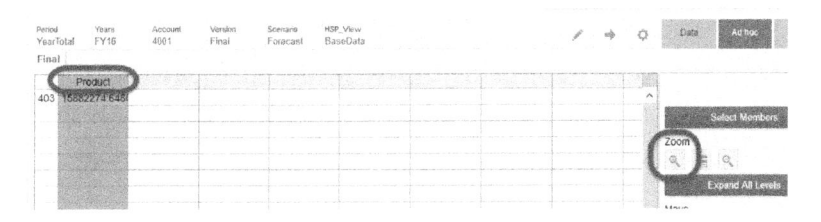

13. Choose *Product* and *Remove Selected*.
14. Click on the *Data* icon:

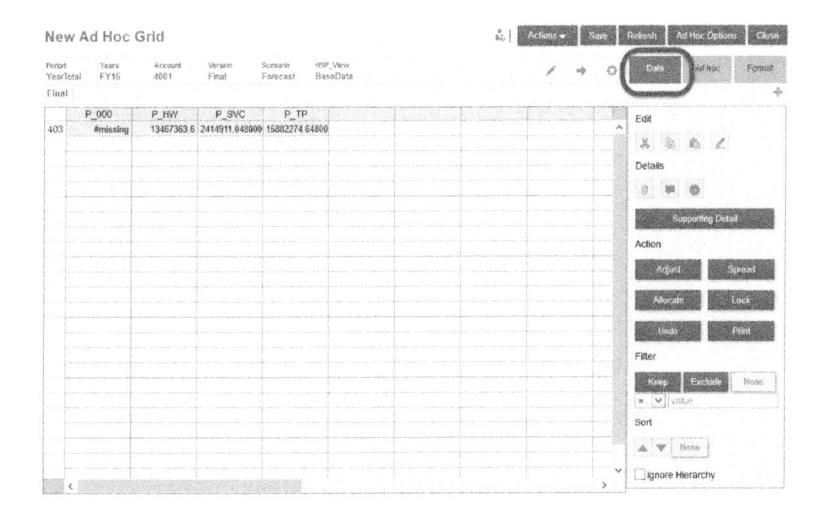

Notice that many of the actions that you perform within data forms are available in ad hoc grids, like: entering and viewing supporting detail, viewing change history, adjusting, spreading, locking, and printing:

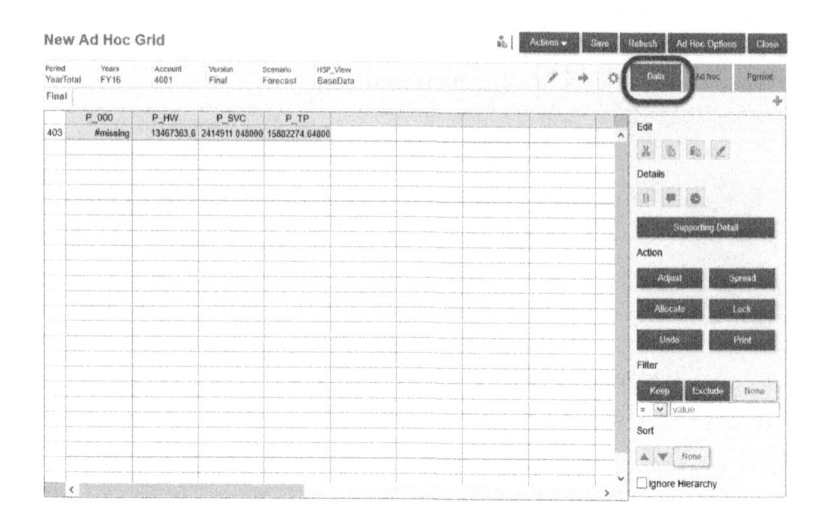

15. Click on the *Format* icon. Drill down on member "403".

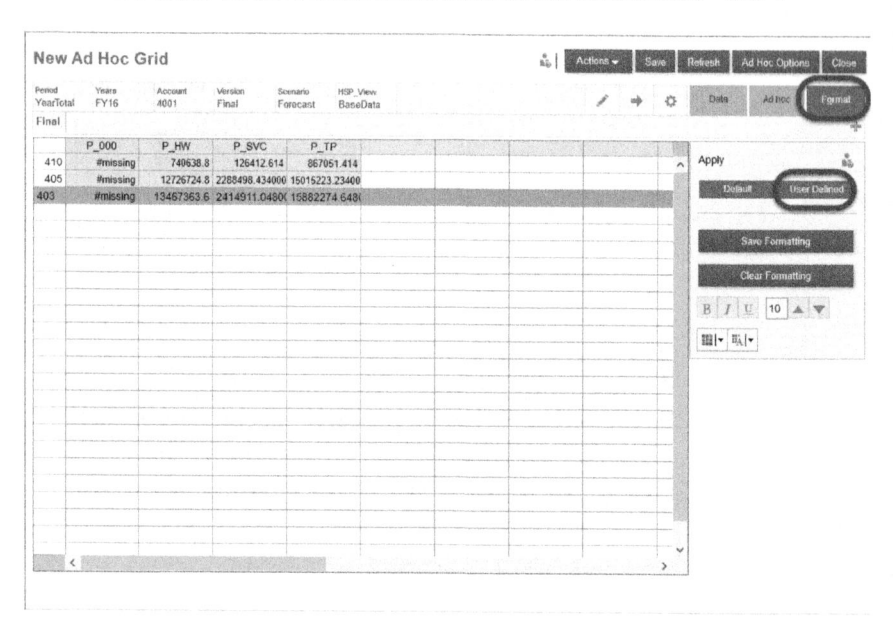

16. Select *User Defined*.
17. Apply formatting to the total rows and columns. Make sure to click *Save Formatting* as you go.
18. Click *Ad Hoc Options*.

19. Change the options to match the following and click *Save*:

Ad Hoc Options

Member inclusion: ☑ Include selection, ☐ Within selected group
Zoom in levels: ● Next level, ○ All levels, ○ Bottom level
Ancestor Position: ○ Top, ● Bottom
Navigate without refreshing data: ○ Yes, ● No

Display: ○ Member name, ● Member name and alias, ○ Alias
Alias Table: Default
Indentation: ○ None, ● Subitem, ○ Totals

Suppress
Zeros: ☐ Row, ☐ Column
Missing Data: ☑ Row, ☑ Column
☐ Repeat Members
☐ Missing Blocks on Rows

Precision
	Minimum	Maximum
Currency values	0	0
Non-currency values	0	0
Percentage values	0	0

Use Currency member precision setting ☐

Replacement
#Missing/#NoData: -
#NoAccess: #noaccess
Submit zeros: ☐

These same Ad Hoc Options are also covered in the Analyze section. You can set the default options for ad hoc actions for member inclusion, display of member name and / or alias, zoom behavior, indentation, ancestor position, navigation with / without data, suppression, precision, and replacement. As with all forms and grids, formatting options are also available.

20. Click *Actions >> Save Ad Hoc Grid*:

388   Chapter 7: Create User Interfaces

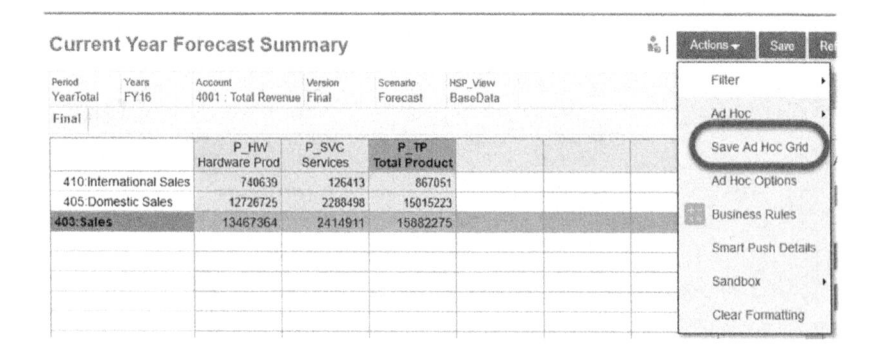

21. Save the grid as "Current Year Forecast Summary". Choose *Ad Hoc Form* and click *Save*:

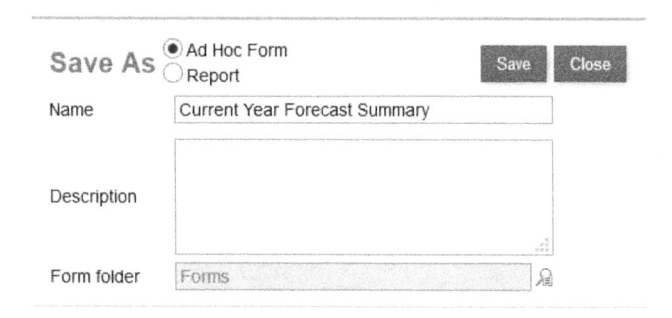

22. Go to *Data Entry* >> *Ad Hoc: Forms* to navigate back to the grid.

Manage Ad Hoc Grids

Select *Navigator* >> *Create and Manage* >> *Forms* to manage ad hoc grids (along with data forms). From the Forms and Ad Hoc Grid section, you can move, rename, assign access, or delete ad hoc grids by selecting the appropriate task from the *Actions* drop-down menu or icon from the menu bar. You can also Search for a particular form.

Note! You cannot edit the ad hoc grid from this section.

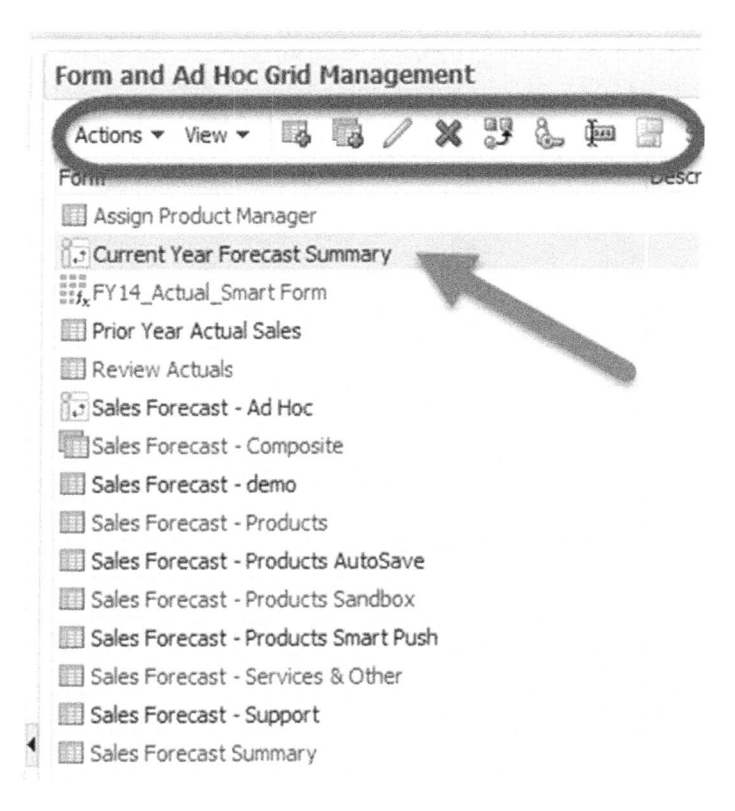

Look Smarter Than You Are with PBCS 389

Form and Ad Hoc Grid Management

- Assign Product Manager
- Current Year Forecast Summary
- FY14_Actual_Smart Form
- Prior Year Actual Sales
- Review Actuals
- Sales Forecast - Ad Hoc
- Sales Forecast - Composite
- Sales Forecast - demo
- Sales Forecast - Products
- Sales Forecast - Products AutoSave
- Sales Forecast - Products Sandbox
- Sales Forecast - Products Smart Push
- Sales Forecast - Services & Other
- Sales Forecast - Support
- Sales Forecast Summary

Dynamic Reports

Essentially, dynamic reports are ad hoc grids saved as a report. These reports are dynamic because the data shown depends on the dimension members selected from the Page menu.

To create a Dynamic Report,
1. Under *Data,* open the *Current Year Forecast Summary* ad hoc grid (if not open).
2. Click *Actions* >> *Save Ad Hoc Grid*:

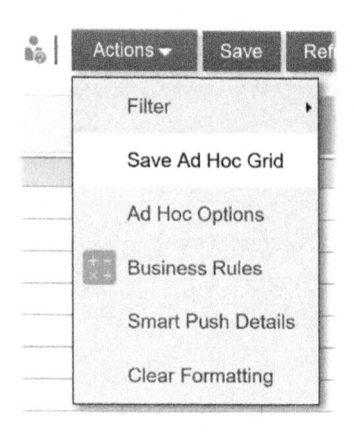

3. The *Save As* window opens. Click the radio button for *Report*, name the report "Current Year Forecast Summary Dynamic Report", and click *Save*:

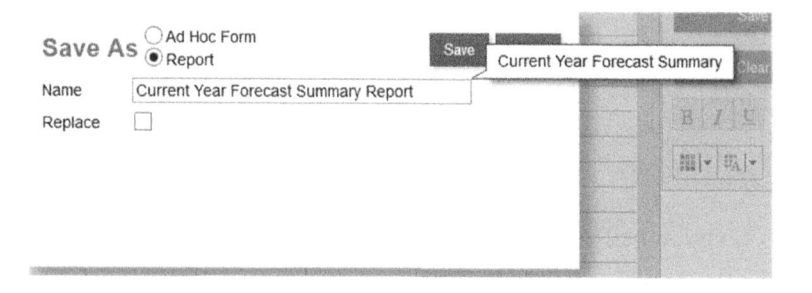

The dynamic report is saved in *Reports* from the main menu.

4. Click the *HTML* view to see dimension options:

Current Year Forecast Summary Dynamic Report

Page: YearTotal, FY16, 4001 Total Revenue, Final, Forecast, BaseData

	P_HW Hardware Products	P_SVC Services	P_TP Total Product
410 International Sales	740,639	126,413	867,051
405 Domestic Sales	12,726,725	2,288,498	15,015,223
403 Sales	13,467,364	2,414,911	15,882,275

Export In Query-Ready Mode

Page 1
Current Year Forecast Summary Dynamic Report   Confidential   Tuesday, February 02, 2016

The data will change depending on the page option selected. Our example had a single page selection because all dimensions were defined in the POV or the rows and columns.

Note! The page options vary depending on how the ad hoc grid was set up.

Ad hoc grids and dynamic reports may be opened in Smart View by switching to the *Reporting Settings* drop-down option within Shared Connections:

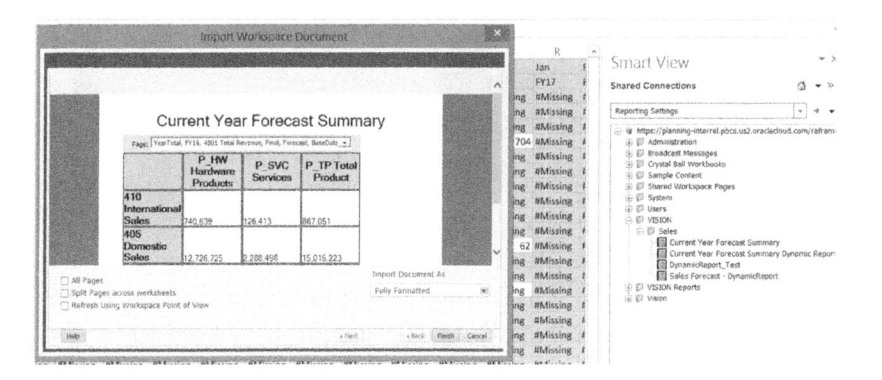

NAVIGATION FLOWS

Countdown please. We are now down to our final user interface for PBCS. Navigation Flows! So what is a Navigation Flow? A navigation flow is a way to customize the tiles (now called "clusters" and "cards") on the Simplified UI home screen. You've been using a navigation flow from the first time you logged into PBCS! This is the default navigation flow for PBCS:

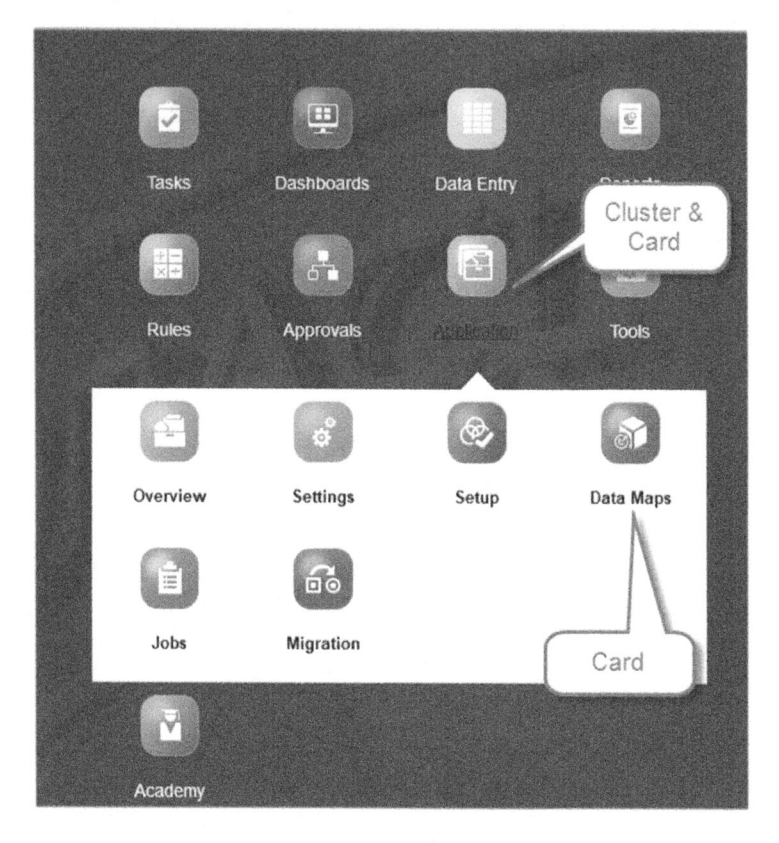

With navigation flows, you can configure which cards different sets of users see, which can help direct their navigation through the planning and reporting process. You can also customize the cards to display certain objects, like a particular form or dashboard, for instance. In addition, you can customize a cluster (a group of cards) and choose which cards exist within them.

What are real life use cases for using navigation flows? The first important thing to know is that navigation flows can be used for any group of users, including administrators. Possible use cases include:

- Hiding specific default Simplified UI cards from all users (all accessible forms, all accessible reports, all accessible business rules, etc.)
- Restricting the Simplified UI cards to just customized ones during a planning process so that certain users can see only what is necessary to complete that planning process
- Customizing user navigation by planning process (one for Budget, one for Forecast, etc.)

You might be wondering...how is this feature different from task lists? It's similar in principle. It's better visually, which makes it more intuitive and very Cloud-like for users. You can add the main card for task lists and reports to your navigation flows but not a specific task list or report. You can, however, link directly to individual forms and dashboards. Navigation flows are definitely the path forward and we'll continue to see more enhancements in this feature.

Key differences between navigation flows and task lists include support for Smart View and Excel. Navigation flows are not yet supported in Smart View, while task lists are supported. And, you can definitely do more with task lists, like order tasks in numerical order, add due dates, alerts, and dependencies, but they are not as visually "pleasing" as navigation flows in the Web user interface.

Create a Navigation Flow

The predefined navigation flow, Default, is read only but it can be duplicated into a new navigation flow and then updated. Navigation flows may be assigned to a user group and then activated or deactivated.

To create a custom navigation flow, you'll have to copy the Default one first and then modify the copy.

1. Select *Navigator >> Tools>> Navigation Flow*.

The main navigation flow management screen displays:

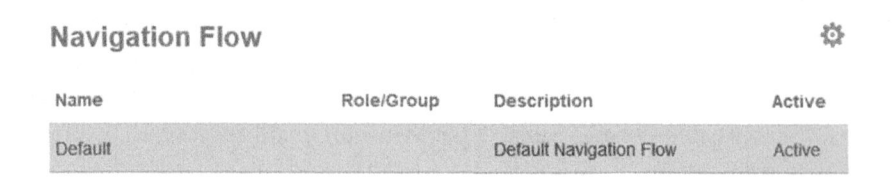

Navigation Flow

Name	Role/Group	Description	Active
Default		Default Navigation Flow	Active

You can click the Default hyperlink to view the details of the Default navigation flow. Again, this one is read only. I'm going to create my own. To create a new navigation flow, the best method is to duplicate the Default navigation flow and then add/hide/rename cards and clusters in the flow. I am going to create two navigation flows, one for administrators and one for users. The administrator navigation flow will have all of the default cards and clusters, plus the custom cards I'll add to support the Vision planning process. The user navigation flow will be a copy of the administrator navigation flow, but with many of the cards hidden that the users will not be using (like Approvals and Rules).

2. Highlight the *Default* navigation flow.
3. From the Actions menu, choose *Create Copy*:

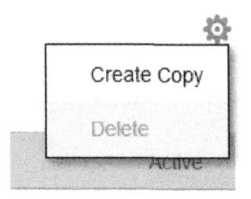

Create Copy
Delete

4. Enter a name for the new navigation flow, "AdminFlow":

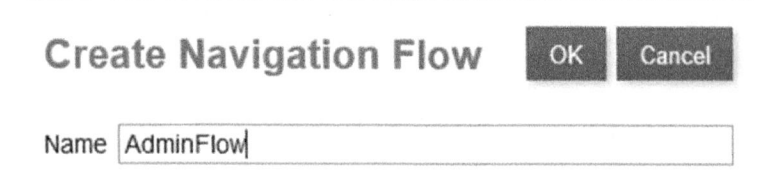

Create Navigation Flow OK Cancel

Name AdminFlow

5. Click *OK*.

You now see it appear in the list with a status of "Inactive." Newly duplicated navigation flows are inactive by default until activated by an administrator. You can create multiple navigation flows for each "visibility category" (explained in a second), but only one navigation flow can be active within each category. This activation process is governed by PBCS. When one navigation flow within a single visibility category becomes active, the others turn off. A PBCS application requires one active navigation flow at all times (and this is the "Default" navigation flow until you create additional navigation flows and make them active).

You can now select the new navigation flow to view and edit the details:

Navigation Flow

Name

AdminFlow

Default

6. Select the hyperlink for *AdminFlow*.

Once you choose to edit this Default navigation flow copy, you'll see all of the wonderful cards and clusters behind it:

396   Chapter 7: Create User Interfaces

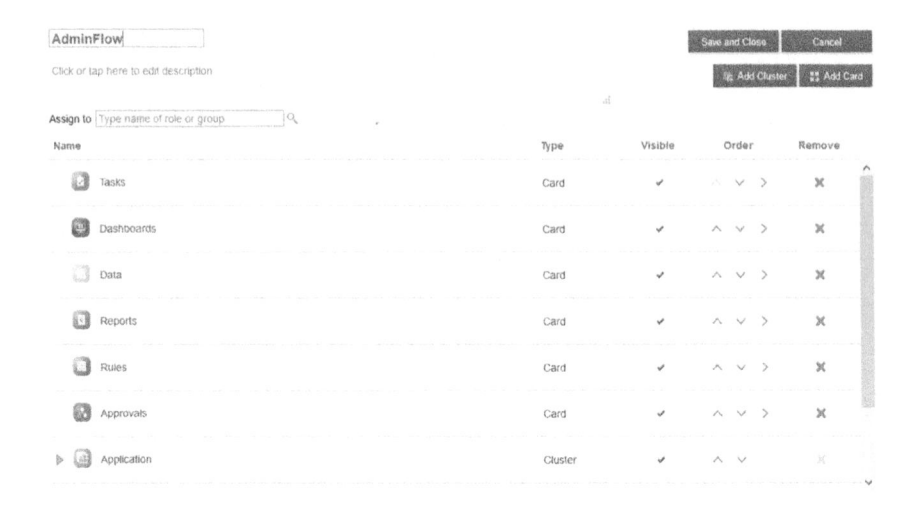

		Type	Visible	Order	Remove
	Tasks	Card	✓	∧ ∨ >	✗
	Dashboards	Card	✓	∧ ∨ >	✗
	Data	Card	✓	∧ ∨ >	✗
	Reports	Card	✓	∧ ∨ >	✗
	Rules	Card	✓	∧ ∨ >	✗
	Approvals	Card	✓	∧ ∨ >	✗
	Application	Cluster	✓	∧ ∨	

Before I start customizing the AdminFlow navigation flow, I'll review a few guidelines for navigation flows.

The following clusters cannot be removed from a navigation flow and are always be visible by administrators:

- Tools
- Application

The following cards cannot be removed or hidden on a navigation flow:

- Settings (in the Application cluster)
- Migration (in the Application cluster)
- User Variables (in the Tools cluster)
- Access Control (in the Tools cluster)
- Navigation Flow (in the Tools cluster)
- Daily Maintenance (in the Tools cluster)

The following rules for the Default navigation flow always apply:

- The "Default" name cannot be modified

- The navigation flow cards and clusters cannot be deleted
- The navigation flow cards and clusters cannot be modified
- The navigation flow can be both activated and deactivated
- The navigation flow can be copied

And here's the list of things you can do with a custom or copied navigation flows:

- Assign access
- Hide and unhide cards
- Create new cards
- Remove existing cards
- Group cards into clusters
- Move cards between clusters
- Rename cards
- Rename tabs
- Switch the icon associated with cards and tabs
- Change the display order of cards and tabs
- Add new and customized horizontal and vertical tabs
- Hide and unhide tabs
- Remove tabs
- Remove navigation flows
- Activate and inactivate navigation flows

Alright, now that those concepts are out of the way, I'll go back to customizing a navigation flow.

7. Click *Add Cluster*.
8. Enter the name "Sales Plan", set Visible to *Yes*, and choose an icon:

398   Chapter 7: Create User Interfaces

Name: Sales Plan
Visible: Yes

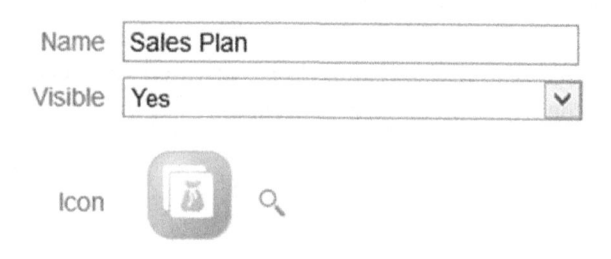

Icon

9. Click *Save and Close*.
10. Use the order arrow icon to move the "Sales Plan" cluster to the top of the list of clusters:

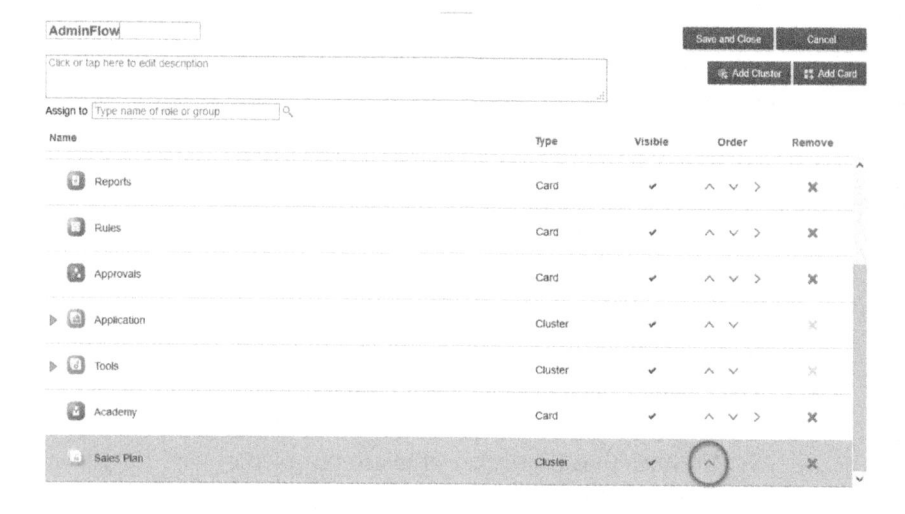

11. Highlight the *Sales Plan* row.
12. Click *Add Card*.
13. Enter the name "Summary", set Visible to *Yes*, and choose an icon.
14. Keep the Page Type to the default of *Single Page* and the Content Type to the default of *Artifact*.

Current artifacts supported for navigation flows include dashboards and simple forms. Composite forms are not supported, which is OK because you can create tabular cards that work like a composite form. I'll do this in a few steps.

15. Click the *Magnifying Glass* icon and search and select the Sales Forecast Home" dashboard:

16. Click *Save and Close*.
17. Click *Add Card*.
18. Enter the name "Enter Plan", set Visible to *Yes*, and choose an icon.
19. Set the Page Type to *Tabular Page*.
20. Set the Orientation to *Horizontal*.
21. Click *Add New Sub Tab*:

22. Enter the Name "Products" set Visible to *Yes*, and leave the icon blank.
23. Set Content Type to *Artifact*.
24. Click the *Magnifying Glass* icon and search and select the Sales Forecast – Products" data form:

25. Click *Save and Close*.
26. Repeat the above steps to add two more sub tabs, selecting the "Sales Forecast – Services & Other" data form with the tab name *Services* and "Sales Forecast – Support" data form with the tab name *Support*:

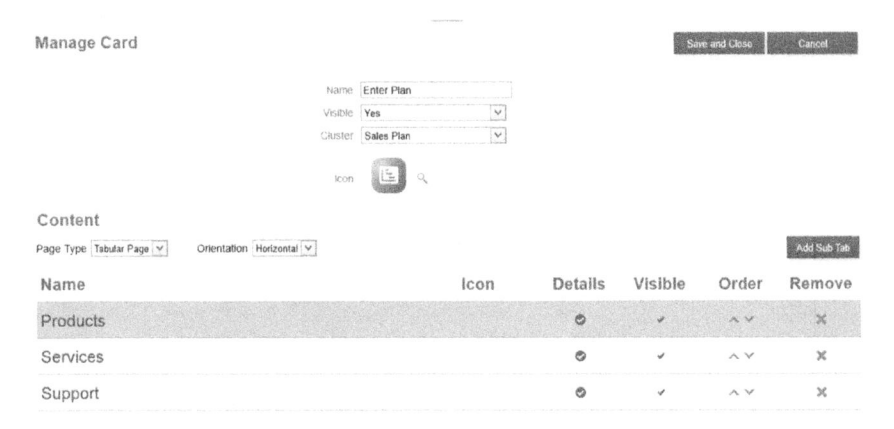

27. Click *Save and Close* to save the Enter Plan card.

Assign Navigation Flow Permission

Navigation flow permissions can occur on three levels: role, artifact, and global. Permissions to navigation flows can be granted to users assigned at the role/group level. In addition, previously assigned artifact security remains intact. For artifacts referenced in the navigation flows, the artifact security still applies (for example, if a user doesn't have access to a data form that is referenced in a navigation flow, they simply won't see it). Global permissions can be granted to all users.

To assign a navigation flow to a role or group,
1. From within the AdminFlow navigation flow, click the magnifying glass icon next to the *Assign to* field to assign the AdminFlow to a group.
2. Select the Groups tab and highlight the *planning-x Service Administrator* group (select either Test or Production, depending on your preference):

AdminFlow

Click or tap here to edit description

Assign to | planning-test Service Administrator

3. Click *Save and Close*.
4. The AdminFlow is now complete!

Name	Type	Visible	Order	Remove
Sales Plan	Cluster	✓	∨	✗
Summary	Card	✓	∨ >	✗
Enter Plan	Card	✓	∧ >	✗
Tasks	Card	✓	∧ ∨ >	✗
Dashboards	Card	✓	∧ ∨ >	✗

5. Click Save and Close.

Hide Cards and Clusters

Now I'm ready to create the end user navigation flow, which is really a copy of the AdminFlow but with some of the cards hidden from users.

1. Highlight *AdminFlow* and select *Create Copy* from the Actions menu.
2. Enter a name "UserFlow" for the new navigation flow.
3. Select *User Flow* to edit the navigation flow details.
4. Select the Rules card and change Visible to *No:*

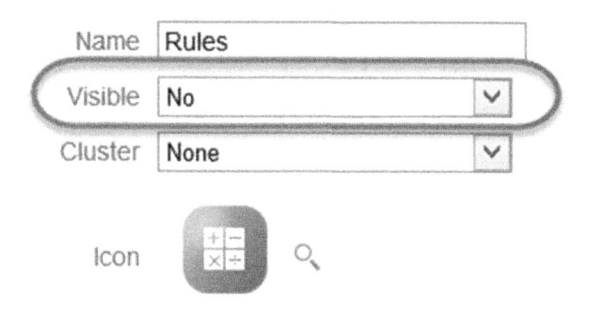

Name	Rules
Visible	No
Cluster	None
Icon	

5. Click *Save and Close.*
6. Repeat the previous step to change Visibility to *No* for the following cards:
    a. Dashboards
    b. Data
    c. Approvals
7. Click the *Magnifying Glass* icon to assign the AdminFlow to a group.
8. Select the Groups tab and select the *User* role:

Look Smarter Than You Are with PBCS 403

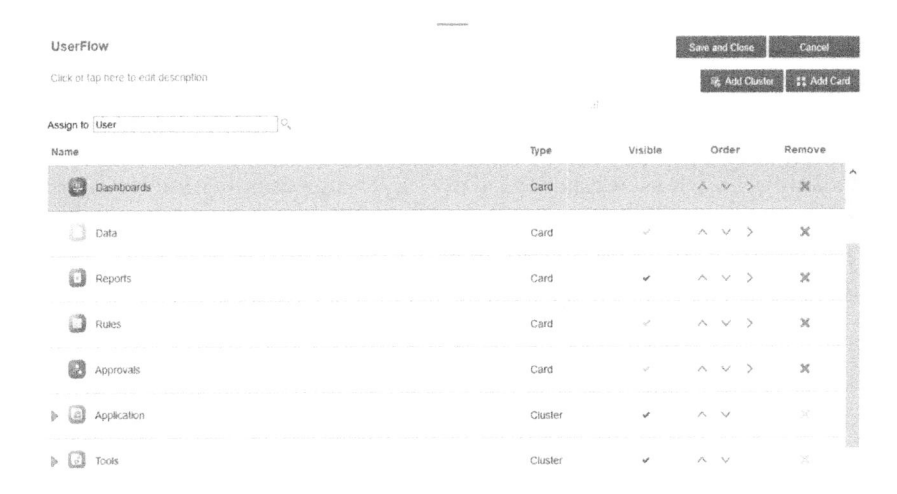

Name	Type	Visible	Order	Remove
Dashboards	Card		∧ ∨ >	✕
Data	Card	✓	∧ ∨ >	✕
Reports	Card	✓	∧ ∨ >	✕
Rules	Card	✓	∧ ∨ >	✕
Approvals	Card	✓	∧ ∨ >	✕
Application	Cluster	✓	∧ ∨	✕
Tools	Cluster	✓	∧ ∨	✕

9. Click *Save and Close*.

Activate a Navigation Flow

Notice that the Default navigation flow is "Active" out of the box. New flows are marked "Inactive" until they are activated by the administrator. I am going to activate the "AdminFlow" and "UserFlow" navigation flows.

To activate a navigation flow,
1. Click the *Inactive* hyperlink next to the navigation flow that you'd like to activate and it changes to "Active":

Navigation Flow

Name	Role/Group	Description	Active
AdminFlow	planning-test Service Administrator		Inactive
Default		Default Navigation Flow	Active
UserFlow	User		Inactive

You do not have to deactivate the other ones first. Since PBCS governs this process, any other active navigation flows assigned to the same visibility category are deactivated automatically.

Now that I've activated them, I might be affected by them (meaning that it's assigned globally or to the administrator's role, a special group that I'm in). If I want to see this navigation flow in action, I'm able to do this by first navigating back to the Home screen and then selecting *Reload Navigation Flow* from within the user menu:

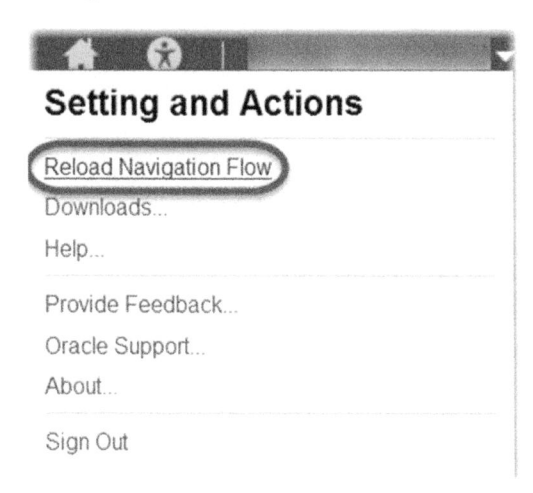

Setting and Actions

Reload Navigation Flow
Downloads...
Help...

Provide Feedback...
Oracle Support...
About...

Sign Out

End User Experience of Navigation Flow

Now when administrators log in (or reload their navigation flow), they see the new *Sales Plan* cluster and cards that we created:

Look Smarter Than You Are with PBCS 405

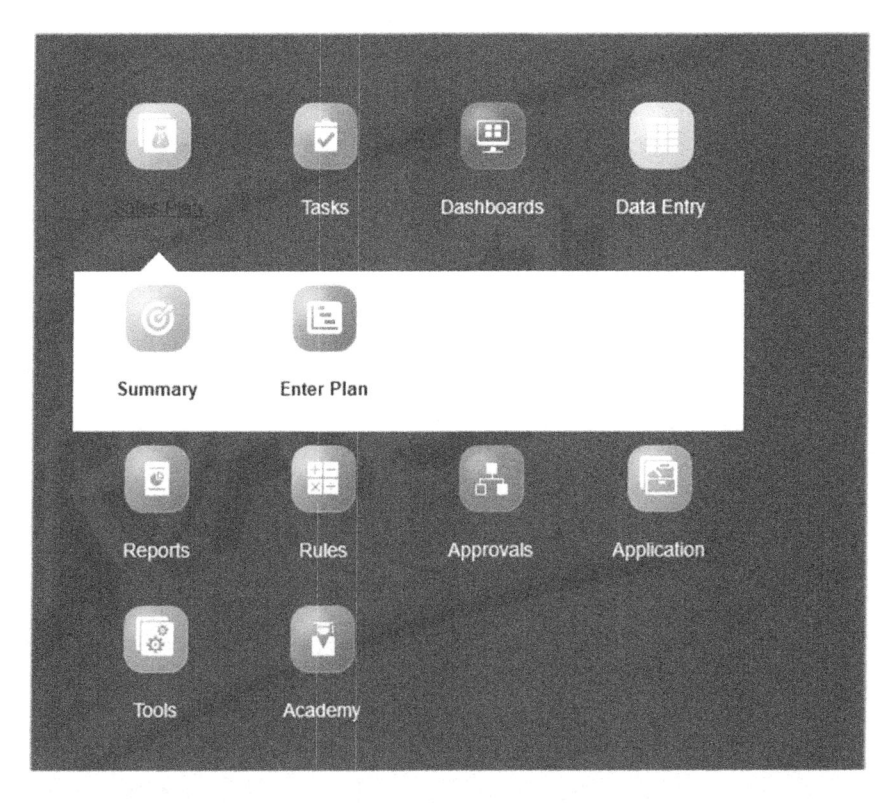

I select the *Summary* card and am taken to the home dashboard:

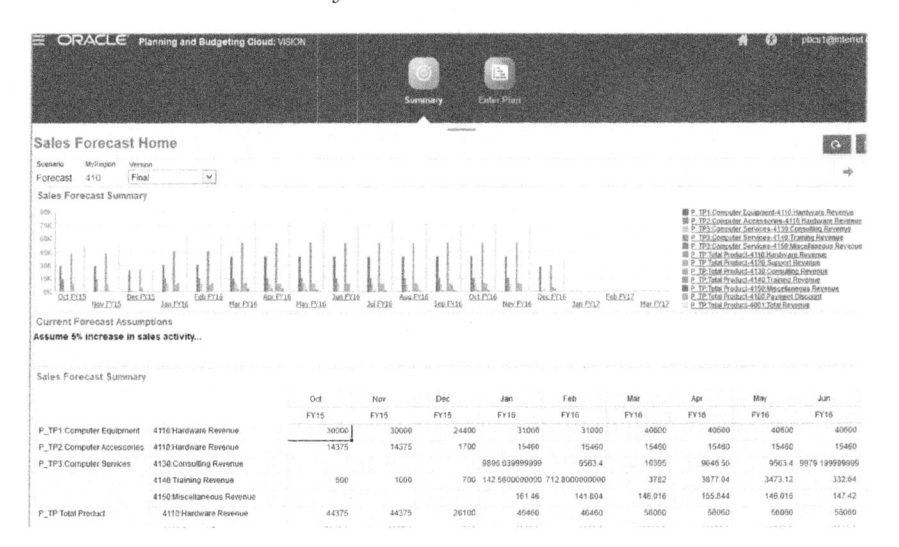

406   Chapter 7: Create User Interfaces

I select the *Enter Plan* card and am taken to the tabular display of the three different forms I previously selected in the navigation flow:

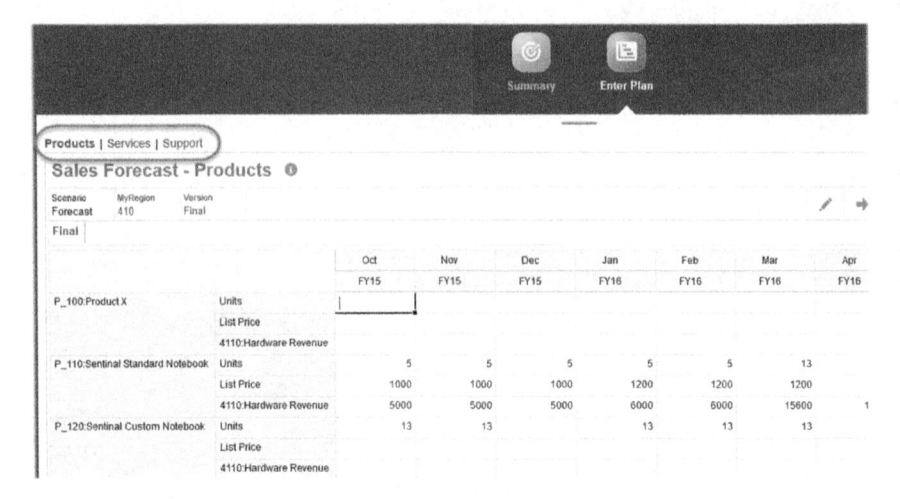

[Screenshot showing Summary and Enter Plan tabs with a Sales Forecast - Products table displaying Scenario, Forecast, MyRegion 410, Version Final columns, and product rows P_100:Product X, P_110:Sentinal Standard Notebook, P_120:Sentinal Custom Notebook with Units, List Price, 4110:Hardware Revenue across months Oct FY15 through Apr FY16.]

When a regular user logs in, notice that they only see the cards that are tagged visible within the UserFlow:

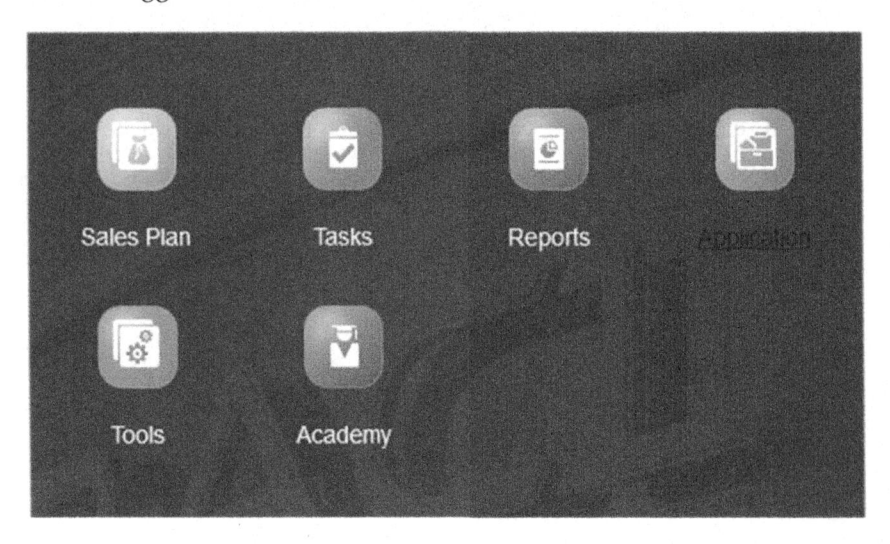

[Screenshot of card icons: Sales Plan, Tasks, Reports, Application, Tools, Academy]

Other Navigation Flow Tips

To edit a navigation flow, you must first inactivate the flow. While it's inactive, users revert back to the Default navigation flow (which can be confusing). After PBCS is in production and live, make sure to update navigation flows during maintenance windows, when users are not in the system.

Navigation flows are pretty cool and you should definitely use them in your PBCS application, but remember they do not work in Smart View. You may want to replicate the form folder structure or task list to replicate the navigation flow steps and organization for users who will use both the web and Excel.

LOG ENTRY: SOL 19, Entry 1

Holy moly! The project might make it! I have an application with dimensions, data, business rules and interfaces. This is awesome. Holy moly!! Okay. Stay calm.

Chapter 8: Assign Security

> LOG ENTRY: SOL 19, Entry 2
>
> The implementation is going to explode!

> LOG ENTRY: SOL 19, Entry 3
>
> Just kidding. Things were going along so well, I thought I would add some drama into this mission.
> Everything is going according to plan and my next step is to set up security.

Users can't get into the system until you assign access. That is a pretty important step. The overall flow of setting up security in the Oracle PBCS is as follows:

1. Create users in *My Services* and provision their role.
2. Create native groups in *Navigator* >> *Tools* >> *Access Control* and assign users and Planning-specific roles to those groups.
3. Assign application access to users or groups within the PBCS application (via dimensions, forms, etc.).

Users can only be created and provisioned by the Identity Domain Administrator through *Oracle Cloud My Services*. I did this step in chapter 2, creating the users and assigning their main PBCS roles. Users cannot be created within the PBCS Simplified UI, nor can their roles be assigned. This is different from on-premises Hyperion Planning where you create users and provision them in Shared Services.

Within Oracle Identity Management there are only five different roles. The table below briefly describes the roles available.

Role	Description
Identity Domain Administrator	Creates users and assigns roles in Oracle Cloud My Services
Service Administrator	Functional administrator for an application
Power User	Grants some functional administrator rights such as creating and maintaining forms, Smart View worksheets, business rules, task lists and FRS reports; controlling approvals process
Planner	Enters data through forms and Smart View, performs ad hoc analysis and drills through to source system
Viewer	Grants view-only access through forms and Smart View

Jump back to Chapter 2 to learn the step to create users in My Services and provision their roles.

However, within Access Control, there are more detailed, Planning-specific roles. More on this in a bit.

NATIVE GROUPS

The next step in the security process is to define native groups. Using group access save you time when creating and maintaining application security.

Access Control in Oracle PBCS is the place where you perform a couple of different administrative tasks for your applications. *Access Control* can be found within the *Tools* cluster or from the *Navigator* menu. Relevant to the current phase of this mission, this is where I can create and manage native security groups for assigning application security. I can also assign some more detailed, Planning-specific roles here.

The *Manage Groups* section allows you to create, import, export and manage native groups for security assignments:

Name	Description	Actions
International_Sales_Grp		⚙
Planner		⚙
Planning Administrator	Planning Administrator	⚙

Manage Groups | Provision Roles | Provisioning Reports | User Login Report

Oracle PBCS supports native user groups for security assignments. You can assign a group of users to native groups and then assign application security to a group level or user level. Native groups can also be imported.

As I mentioned, you want to use group security assignments as much as possible. Groups reduce the overall maintenance for your security application. You define security once and as users come and go, they can be added to and removed from groups. If security requirements change, you update the group security once versus many times for individual users. Native groups that can contain other groups are called nested groups.

You might create different user groups based on what the user can do. For example, you might create a group called "Planner" to house most end users and common security definitions across all users. You might also create a group called "Power" for the budget and financial planning office. You will likely create different security groups for your Entity dimension so that users can only enter plans for their specific department or division.

To create a native security group,
1. Select *Navigator >> Tools >> Access Control*.
2. Select *Manage Groups*.
3. Select *Create* and the *Create Group* window displays.
4. Type in the group name "International_Sales_Grp" and optionally add a description:

Look Smarter Than You Are with PBCS 411

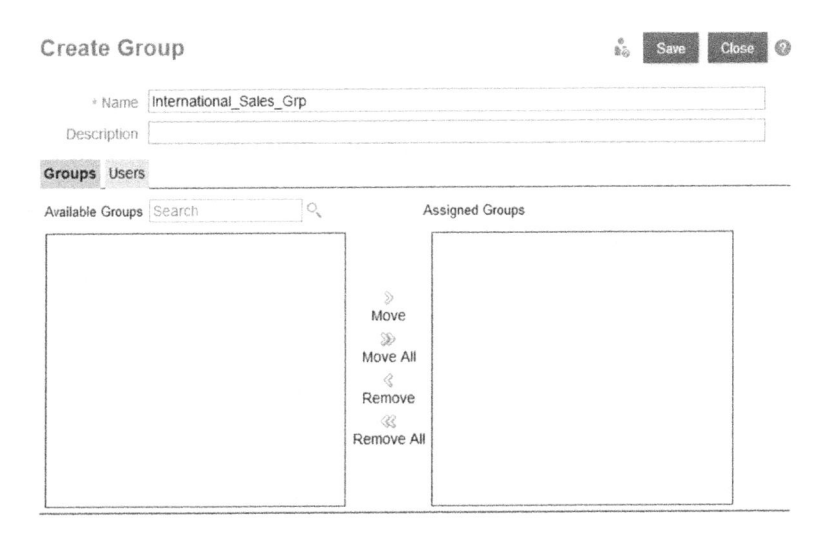

[Create Group form screenshot with Name: International_Sales_Grp, Groups/Users tabs, Available Groups and Assigned Groups panels with Move, Move All, Remove, Remove All buttons]

Next, you can select desired available groups on the Groups tab (either native or external) to assign (also called "nested" group security). You can search for specific groups or search for all groups. Check the group and use the arrow icons to move it into the "assigned" section.

On the Users tab, you select desired available users (either native or external). You have the same search capabilities for specific users as you did for groups. Use the arrow icons to assign the selected users.

5. Click *Save* to create the group and click *OK* to close the Create Group window.
6. Repeat the above steps to create a group called "Vision Planners".

PROVISION APPLICATION-SPECIFIC ROLES

The *Provision Roles* section allows you to assign either groups or users to application-specific roles. These roles provide more granular access to PBCS functionality:

412   Chapter 8: Assign Security

Manage Groups | **Provision Roles** | Provisioning Reports | User Login Report

Name	Description	Actions
International_Sales_Grp		⚙
Planner		⚙
Planning Administrator	Planning Administrator	⚙

The available Planning application roles currently include:

Available Roles
- ☐ Ad Hoc Grid Creator
- ☐ Ad Hoc Read Only User
- ☐ Ad Hoc User
- ☐ Approvals Administrator
- ☐ Approvals Ownership Assigner
- ☐ Approvals Process Designer
- ☐ Approvals Supervisor
- ☐ Calculation Manager Administrator
- ☐ Mass Allocation
- ☐ Task List Access Manager

Ad Hoc Read Only Users can use ad hoc grids, but can't write back to them. Ad Hoc Users can view and modify ad hoc grids, but can't save them. Ad Hoc Grid Creators can create, view, modify, and save ad hoc grids for other users.

The Approvals Administrator is the full administrator of the approvals process and includes all functions of all other Approvals roles. Therefore, this person can take ownership of the process, resolve issues, assign owners and reviewers, etc. The Approvals Ownership Assigner can assign owners and reviewers, as well as tag users who should be notified about the process. The Approvals Process Designer can do all the roles of the Approvals Ownership Assigner, plus: change the scenario and version assignment for a planning unit, change secondary dimensions and members of Entities to which they have write access, and change the web form data validation rules. The Approvals Supervisor can take any action on a planning unit, as well as start and stop it.

The Calculation Manager Administrator has full rights to Calculation Manager and can design, develop, update, and delete calculation objects, as well as assign security to rules and rulesets. The Mass Allocation role allows the users to utilize the Mass Allocation feature on data forms. Carefully assign this feature to users who understand that every time they run a Mass Allocation, they are running a business rule. Security is also "overlooked" by the Mass Allocate feature. Finally, the Task List Access Manager governs the security of tasks to users.

To assign a Planning-specific role to a group,
1. Select *Navigator >> Tools >> Access Control*.
2. Select *Provision Roles*.
3. Change the drop down to *Groups* and press the search magnifying glass to return a list of all groups.
4. Select the Actions menu next to the group that you wish to change and select *Provision*:

Name	Description	Actions
International_Sales_Grp		Provision
Planner		Deprovision
Planning Administrator	Planning Administrator	Provision Report

5. Check the boxes next to the roles that you wish to provision and then use the middle buttons to move them over:

Provision Group: International_Sales_Grp

Available Roles:
- Ad Hoc Grid Creator
- Ad Hoc Read Only User
- Approvals Administrator
- Approvals Ownership Assigner
- Approvals Process Designer
- Approvals Supervisor
- Calculation Manager Administrator
- Mass Allocation

Assigned Roles:
- Ad Hoc User
- Task List Access Manager

6. Press *OK*.

SET PBCS APPLICATION SECURITY

After the users and roles have been created in My Services and the native groups created in Access Control, the final part of PBCS security is to assign access to all of the components. You assign member specific security for the Account, Entity, Version, Scenario, and user-defined dimensions (Product). You also need to assign security to data form folders, data forms, business rules, and task lists. Thankfully, the steps to do so are the same for all objects.

When assigning application security, you select the Users or Groups tab. Select the desired user/group and choose *Read*, *Write*, or *None* and choose *Member*, *Children*, *Children (Inclusive)*, *Descendants*, or *Descendants (Inclusive)*:

Member security is assigned for the selected object. In the case of dimensions, this object is a member. *Children* security is assigned for the children of the member in the dimension, but not the member. *Children (Inclusive)* security is assigned for the member and its children in the dimension. *Descendants* and *Descendants (Inclusive)* are similar to Children / Children (Inclusive) except that all members below the selected member is assigned access.

If you need to edit or delete security, you select the *Action* menu option. Click *Edit Access* or *Remove*:

Assign Access for 4001
Users Groups

Action ▼	View ▼	✚ ✏ ✖	Detach		
Add Access	Ctrl+W			Access Rights	Relation
Edit Access	Ctrl+E			Write	Descendants (inclusive)
Remove Access	Ctrl+Del			Write	Descendants (inclusive)
				Read	Descendants (inclusive)

Security Design Best Practices

Inheritance may determine the user's or group's access permissions. Access permissions assigned to members take precedence over inherited access permissions. You can include or exclude the member from the access permissions setting.

To save time in the security definition process, you may want to create a Planner group for all planners (as I mentioned above). Assign common security like Scenario and Version members in the Planner group. Then create Entity specific or Account specific security groups may be created and assigned for more granular security. The Entity specific or Account specific groups should be assigned to the Planner group to inherit the common security assignments.

ASSIGN MEMBER ACCESS

To assign metadata (or dimension and member) access,
1. Select *Navigator >> Create and Manage >> Dimensions*.
2. While in the Dimension Editor for Account, click the parent member of the descendants that users need access to. I'm first going to grant access to Account member *4001*:

416   Chapter 8: Assign Security

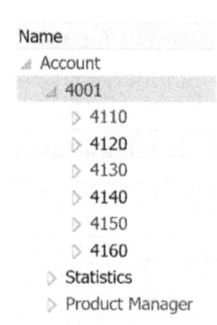

```
Name
⊿ Account
   ⊿ 4001
      ▷ 4110
      ▷ 4120
      ▷ 4130
      ▷ 4140
      ▷ 4150
      ▷ 4160
   ▷ Statistics
   ▷ Product Manager
```

3. Click the *Assign Access* icon:

   Dimension   Account

4. Open the *Groups* tab.
5. Click the *Add icon*.
6. Select the *Vision Planner* group:

```
Add Access for 4001                                              ×
 Users   Groups
 Group
 Finance Management
 International_Sales_Grp
 iProject_Users
 Planning Service Administrator
 Vision Planner


 Type of Access
 ○ Read  ● Write  ○ None   Descendants (inclusive) [v]

 Help                                              Add   Close
```

7. Click the radio button for *Write* and select *Descendants (inclusive)* from the drop-down menu:

Type of Access
○ Read ◉ Write ○ None   Descendants (inclusive) ⌄

8. Click *Add*.

Security for the 4001 member is complete.

9. Using the steps above, complete metadata security according to the following table:

Member	Security Access	Group / User
Account – 4001, Statistics, Product Manager	Write – Descendants (inclusive)	Group: Vision Planner
Account – 4110	Read – Member	Group: Vision Planner
Account – 4120	Read – Member	Group: Vision Planner
Account – Average Price	Read – Member	Group: Vision Planner
Entity – 410	Write – Descendants (inclusive)	Group: International Sales Grp
Entity – 405	Write – Descendants (inclusive)	Users: Elaine, Larry
Scenario – Plan, Forecast	Write – Member	Group: Vision Planner
Scenario – Actual	Read – Member	Group: Vision Planner
Version – Pass1, Pass2, Final	Write – Member	Group: Vision Planner

Access must be granted to the Account, Entity, Scenario, and Version dimensions. Why isn't security assigned by Periods or Years? As mentioned before, all users have access to all periods and years. You control write access for periods by defining the Start Yr., Start Period, End Yr., and End Period in the Scenario dimension.

You'll notice that certain account members such as 4110 and 4120 have Read access for planner rather than Write access. This is because those accounts have member formulas that calculate the value and I don't want any users inputting data where it should be calculated instead.

In a few cases above, I assigned access to a specific user. A better design principle would be to use a security group instead, like I did for the International Sales group.

Note! Security cannot be edited for the Sandboxes Version members (although the children for this member are created by users).

By now you're familiar with refreshing the database to save changes to Essbase. The security information you've just assigned is only stored in the relational database. The refresh to Essbase creates security filters required for the Essbase database. Essbase must be in sync with the security information stored in the underlying PBCS relational repository.

10. Refresh the database.

Note! Service Administrators always have access to everything, therefore, access does not need to be granted for them.

ASSIGN FORM ACCESS

You can assign security at the form folder or individual data form level. All data forms inherit the form folder security definition, so if you can apply security at a folder level, it is definitely more efficient to do so.

To assign form folder or data form access,
1. Select *Navigator >> Create and Manage >> Forms*.
2. Assign access to either the *Forms* or *Vision Users* folder. Assign *Read* access to the "Vision Planner" group:

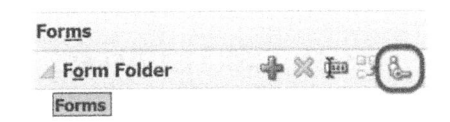

You can also apply security at the form level. If you need to assign unique data form security, select the form and click :

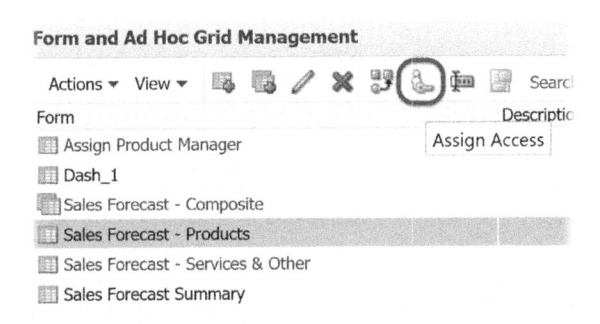

Open the *Groups* tab and assign the correct access. *Read* access allows users to view the form. *Write* access allows the user to change the data form definition and layout if they are provisioned as a Power user role in My Services.

ASSIGN BUSINESS RULE ACCESS

To assign business rule access to the Planner role,
1. Select *Navigator >> Create and Manage >> Rules Security*.
2. Click the Business Rules Folder *CalcMgrRules* and click :

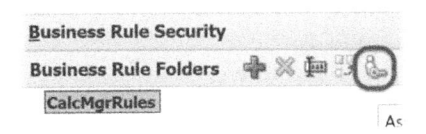

3. Grant *Launch* access to the "Vision Planner" group.

You assign either *Launch* or *No Launch* access. You can apply security at the individual business rule level. If you need to assign unique business rule security, select the desired rule and assign the appropriate access using the steps above.

ASSIGN TASK LIST ACCESS

To assign task list access,
1. Select *Navigator >> Create and Manage >> Task Lists*.
2. Highlight the desired Task List and click:

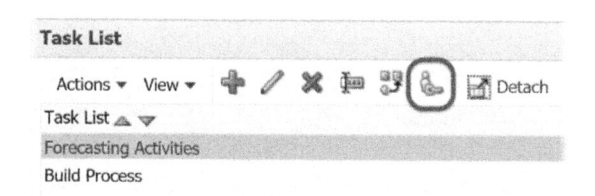

3. Grant the *Assigned* access to the "Vision Planner" group:

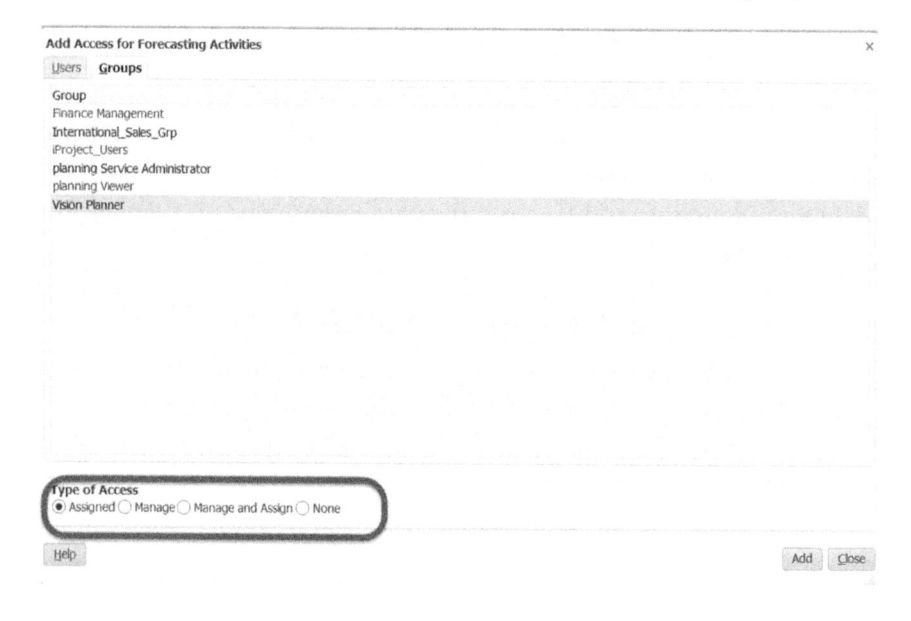

4. Click *Add*.

Assigned access allows users to view and follow the task list. *Manage* access allows the user to update the task list, add new tasks, remove tasks, or set due dates. *Manage and Assign* lets the user both use and manage the task list. You can also remove security (if inherited) by using *None* access.

And those are the steps to give users access to the application!

LOG ENTRY: SOL 20, Entry 1

I think I'm done. Done.
Looking back to when I thought the project would die and what I've accomplished since then… it was actually pretty easy. Much easier than saying being stranded on Mars.
Now, how do I let the folks back on Earth know that the sales forecasting application is ready?

Meanwhile, back on earth…

After the webcast, Rockstar i.n.t.e.r.R.e.l. Consultant Cathy Son stared at the ceiling, monitoring Cloud access. Implementing EPM solutions at i.n.t.e.r.R.e.l had sounded exciting when Director Glen Chang had recruited her out of school. But it turns out the Cloud monitors itself. Her job turned out to be sending emails.
As she scrolled through the logs, she saw something that made her heart stop. A login for roske@interrel.com. But that project was dead! However if he logged into the Cloud, that could only mean one thing. The project was still alive and Edward was trying to implement in the Cloud.
"I need Director Glen Chang's contact information now," she thought to herself. Director Chang was in charge of i.n.t.e.r.R.e.l operations and would know what to do next.

Chapter 9: Automate & Migrate

> **LOG ENTRY: SOL 20, Entry 2**
>
> While I'm trying to figure out how to communicate with Vision and i.n.t.e.r.r.e.l., I guess I'll go ahead and automate some of the PBCS processes.

JOB SCHEDULER

The PBCS Simplified UI has a Job Scheduler to run many of the PBCS jobs (now or at a future time).

Supported jobs include:

- **Rules** – run a business rule
- **Import data** – import data with the Simplified Planning UI
- **Import metadata** – import metadata with the Simplified Planning UI
- **Export data** – export data with the Simplified Planning UI
- **Export metadata** – export metadata with the Simplified Planning UI
- **Refresh the database** – refresh the database, pushing changes from UI to the underlying Essbase databases
- **Cube map** – execute the map to reporting feature, pushing data from one cube to another
- **Invalid Intersections Reports** – run the Invalid Intersections report
- **Clear Cube** – run the Clear Cube action

To schedule a job within PBCS, you must first save tasks as jobs. As an example, I will save an Export Data task as a job. Data files must also be uploaded into the Inbox / Outbox for some tasks (you can automate this step with EPM Automate; more on this in just a moment).

Save Tasks as Jobs

I'm going to create a job that exports the Product Manager assignments from PBCS. A majority of the jobs that can be scheduled are found in the *Actions* menu of the Overview, Cubes, and Dimensions tabs.

To create and save a job,
1. Select *Navigator >> Application >> Overview*.
2. Go to *Actions >> Export Data*:

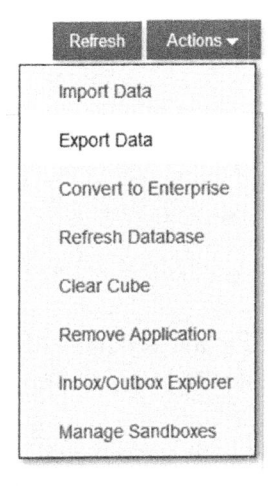

3. Click *Create* and the following window displays:

424   Chapter 9: Automate & Migrate

Export Data

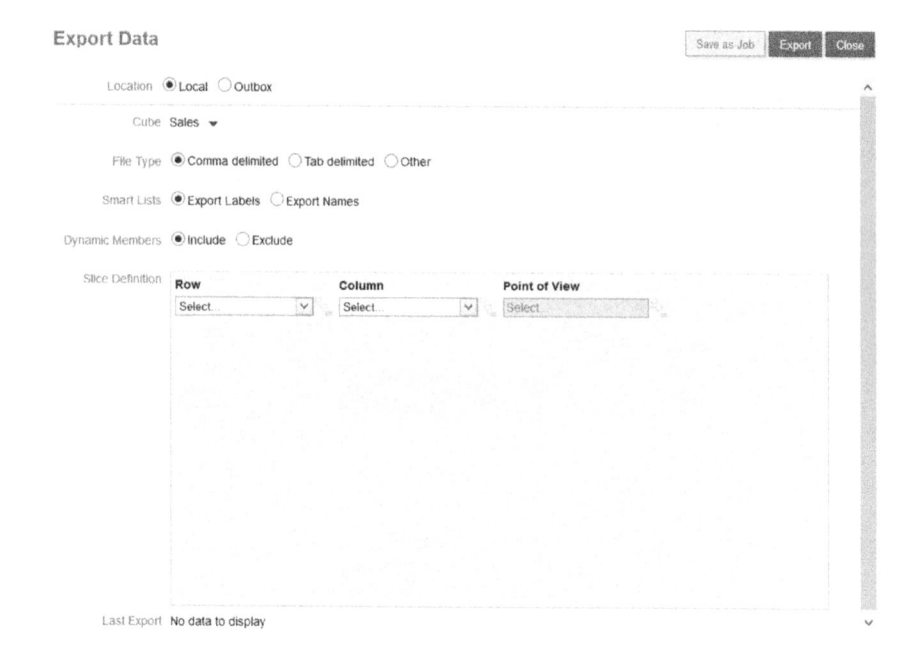

[Screenshot of Export Data dialog showing: Location (Local/Outbox), Cube: Sales, File Type: Comma delimited / Tab delimited / Other, Smart Lists: Export Labels / Export Names, Dynamic Members: Include / Exclude, Slice Definition with Row, Column, Point of View selectors. Last Export: No data to display.]

4. Select *Outbox* for the Location (this is a requirement if you want to schedule this task through Job Scheduler).

Local allows immediate save of the file to your local computer. *Planning Outbox* places the file in the PBCS Inbox / Outbox.

5. Select the desired cube to export data from. Choose the *Sales* cube.
6. Choose the delimiter and for Smart Lists, whether you want export the names or the labels. Select *Comma delimited* and *Export Labels*.
7. Complete the Slice Definition section. Here, select dimensions and members for the Row, Column, and POV:
    a. **Rows**: level-0 Products
    b. **Columns:** Product Manager for Account
    c. **POV**: level-0 members under YearTotal
    d. **POV**: Basedata
    e. **POV**: FY16

Look Smarter Than You Are with PBCS   425

   f. **POV**: Plan
   g. **POV**: Final
   h. **POV**: The Entity "0" which is located in *Total Entity >> TD*):

Export Data

Location	○ Local ● Outbox
Cube	Sales ▼
File Type	● Comma delimited ○ Tab delimited ○ Other
Smart Lists	● Export Labels ○ Export Names
Dynamic Members	○ Include ● Exclude

Slice Definition

Row	Column	Point of View
Product	Account	Select...
ILvl0Descendants(Product)	Product Manager	Period ILvl0Descendants(Period) HSP_View BaseData Years FY16 Scenario Plan Version Final Entity 0

8. Click *Save as Job*.
9. From this screen, you can select the task to edit (e.g., select *Export Product Manager* and you can update the export task parameters and member selections):

Export Data

Type	Name	Modified	Actions
	Export Product Manager	pbcs1@interrel.com 2/18/16 2:40 AM	⚙
	ExportLevel0_Vision	admin 2/15/16 9:27 PM	⚙

Now that the task job has been created, I am ready to schedule it!

Schedule a Job

To schedule a job,

Chapter 9: Automate & Migrate

1. Select *Navigator >> Application >> Jobs*. A list of any upcoming jobs along with recently run jobs display.
2. Click *Schedule Jobs*.
3. Click the radio button for *Export Data*.
4. Click *Next*. Enter the scheduled job parameters:
   a. When do you want to run the job? Run now or schedule to start from a selected day and time.
   b. How often do you want to run the job? Define a name, reoccurrence pattern, and optional end date:

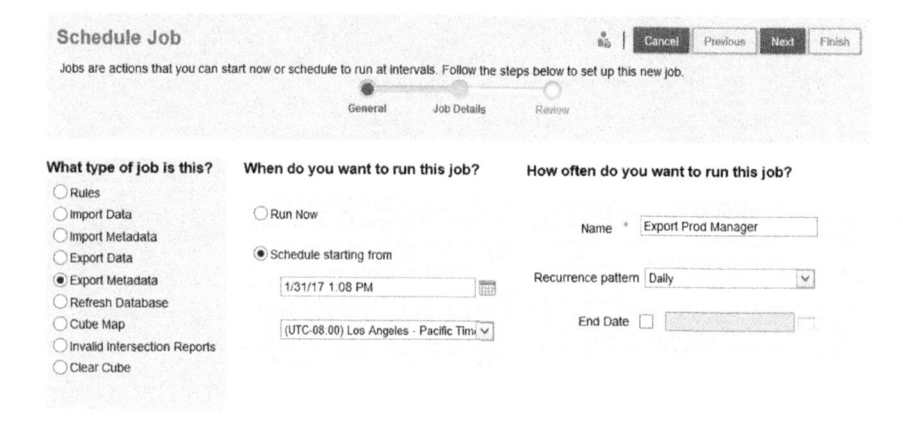

5. Click *Next*.
6. Select *Export Data* job to schedule.
7. Highlight the *Export Product Manager* job that I created in the Simplified UI:

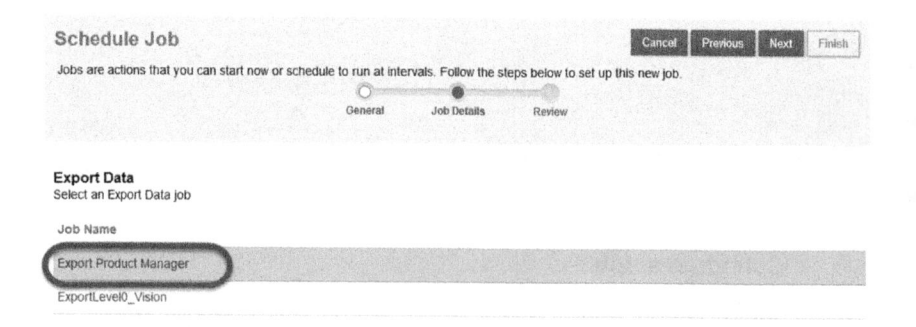

8. Click *Next*.
9. Review and click *Finish*:

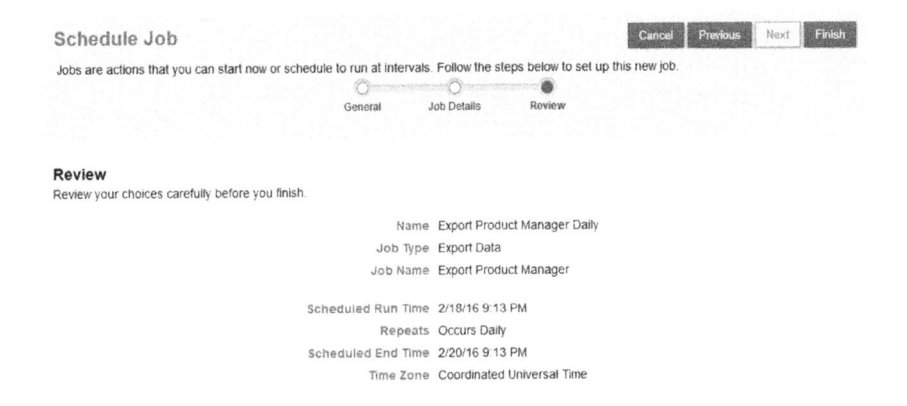

Job Console

As mentioned earlier, from the Job Console you can view pending and recently run jobs. Jobs are retained in the Job Console for 90 days. The jobs from the scheduler and other non-scheduled jobs from PBCS activity display here:

Select any job in the Recent Activity pane to view the details. These details include the job type, who it was run by, status, start and end times, and some other job specific details (e.g., if it was an Export Data job, you would see how many records were read and written and also be able to download the exported data file). You can also change the level of of the messages that you see:

Chapter 9: Automate & Migrate

You can filter jobs by using the *Filter* icon:

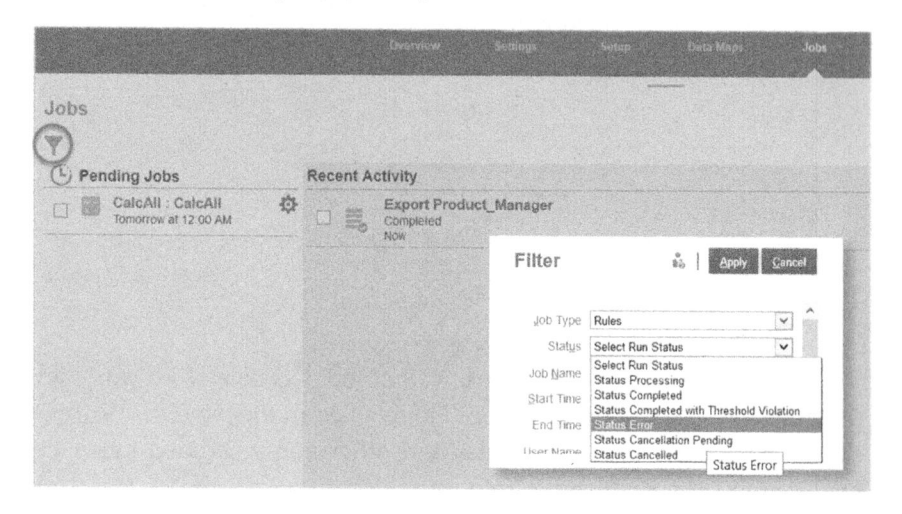

Note! You'll see a lot more job types here in the filter than what you are allowed to schedule.

I'll choose to filter Job Type by Rules and I see all of the recently run Business Rules from PBCS (which were run from the UI and not scheduled). The big thing to remember is that the Job Console shows you both scheduled jobs and jobs run from PBCS Simplified UI:

You can also search the Job Console activity. In my example below, I searched for all jobs containing a reference to "Product Manager":

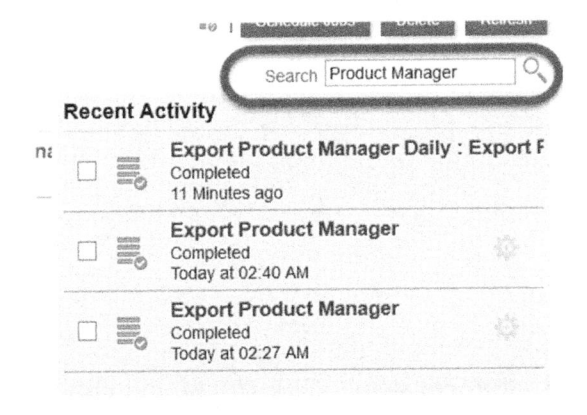

You can manage, edit, and delete jobs from the Job Console.

You also have the option to cancel Rules and RuleSets jobs if they are in a processing state. You cannot cancel import, export, mapping, or refresh jobs.

Inbox / Outbox Explorer

You can export, upload, and download files to the Inbox / Outbox Explorer, a central place where files are stored within the PBCS application. To access the Inbox / Outbox Explorer, go to *Navigator >> Application >> Overview*. Select *Actions >> Inbox / Outbox Explorer*.

> **Note!** The Inbox / Outbox Explorer is only available in the Simplified UI.

The Inbox / Outbox Explorer displays with any currently uploaded files:

Type	Name	Last Modified	Size	Actions
	Export Product Manager.zip	2/18/16 9:17 PM	1.0 KB	⚙
	Actual_Dollars_FY14.csv	1/18/16 5:56 PM	7.1 KB	⚙
	ExportLevel0_Vision.zip	2/16/16 11:50 PM	5.0 KB	⚙
	SalesRpt_Export_Data	2/15/16 11:24 PM	399.5 KB	⚙
	ProductManagerLoad.csv	2/18/16 2:53 AM	13.6 KB	⚙
	epmapplicationsnapshot.xml	2/18/16 8:13 AM	2.2 KB	⚙
	VisionForecastDataExport2.txt	2/15/16 9:30 PM	295.6 KB	⚙
	VISION_EXPORT	1/27/16 3:35 AM	0.1 KB	⚙

To upload a file, simply click *Upload* and browse to the file to upload, and to download a file, go to *Actions >> Download File*.

You can also delete files (it is good to keep the Inbox / Outbox Explorer "clean"). Objects in the Inbox / Outbox Explorer remain even if the application is deleted.

Calculation Manager places files here if you use the Data Export command within a rule to export a slice of data. The syntax for this type of rule looks like the following (see the Business Rule section for more detail):

```
DATAEXPORT "File" ","
"/u03/lcm/VisionForecastDataExport2.txt" "NULL";
```

The complete rule looks as follows:

```
FIX ("BaseData")
SET DataExportOptions
{
            DataExportLevel "ALL";
            DataExportColFormat ON;
            DataExportColHeader "Account";
            DataExportDynamicCalc ON;
            DataExportOverwriteFile ON;
            DataExportDimHeader OFF
};

FIX("Forecast", "Actual",
@Relative("Years",0),
@Relative("Entity",0),
@Relative("Product",0),
"BegBalance":"Dec",
"Units",
@Relative("4001",0),
"4001",
@Relative("Version",0))

DATAEXPORT "File" ","
"/u03/lcm/VisionForecastDataExport2.txt" "NULL";

ENDFIX
ENDFIX
```

Data Management also uses the Inbox / Outbox Explorer to place export files when exporting data from a PBCS cube.

So if I can automate jobs with PBCS using the Job Scheduler, why would I ever need a utility like EPM Automate? Job Scheduler can automate tasks within PBCS, but if you need to create a complete lights out script that requires upload of files or download of files or scripting a series of steps together (e.g., upload data file, load data file, calculate data, export data, download file), you have to use EPM Automate.

EPM AUTOMATE

EPM Automate is the automation utility of PBCS (and other Cloud products) that allows the administrator to remotely perform many administrative tasks. Administrators create scripts using the utility that can then be automated using the Windows Scheduler. You must be a Service Administrator to run the EPM Automate Utility.

Note! EPM Automate is only supported on 64-bit operating systems.

The following tasks can be scripted and executed with EPM Automate:

- Import and export metadata and data
- Refresh the application
- Run business rules
- Copy data from one database to another
- Upload file into the PBCS Inbox / Outbox Explorer
- Upload file into Data Management folders
- Run a Data Management rule or batch and get the output log file
- Download files from the Inbox / Outbox and from Data Management folders
- Export and import application and artifact snapshots
- List the files in the Inbox / Outbox
- Delete files from the Inbox / Outbox
- Take a snapshot of the entire instance
- Run a provisioning report
- Run an audit report to see who has logged in and for how long
- Update substitution variables
- Import and export Data Management mappings
- View the value of a substitution variable using the getsubstvar command
- Use exit codes and detailed error messages
- Download activity reports

- Import of identity domain artifacts from application snapshots (which simplifies the cloning of a service instance by avoiding the step of manually importing users and roles into the identity domain)
- Import identity domain artifacts
- Replay the running of Financial Reporting reports to performance test

Install EPM Automate by going to your logged in ID in the upper right-hand corner and select *Downloads*:

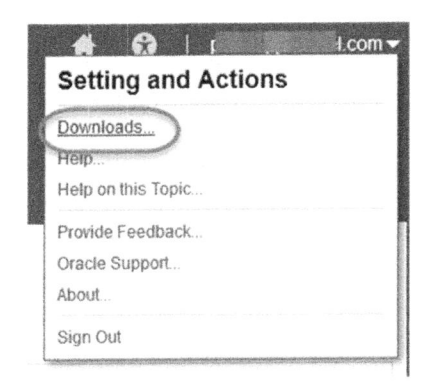

Select the version of EPM Automate for the desired operating system:

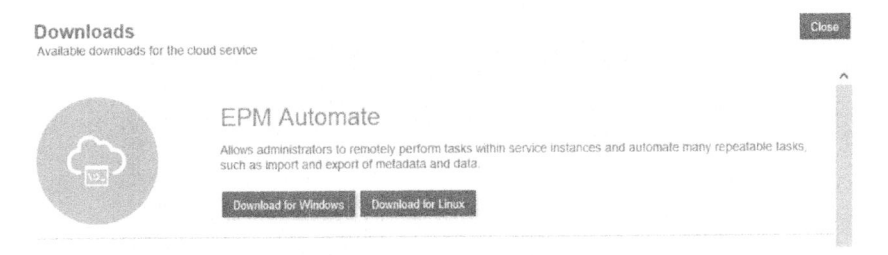

You may install multiple instances of EPM Automate (especially if you need to run tasks in Production and Pre-Production at the same time). If you need to do this, execute the utility from separate directories:

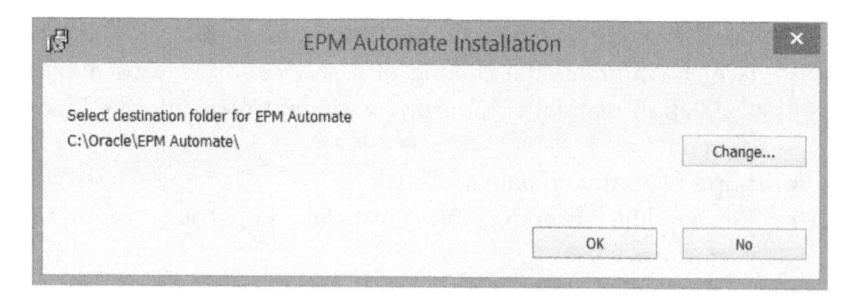

[EPM Automate Installation dialog: Select destination folder for EPM Automate — C:\Oracle\EPM Automate\ — Change... / OK / No]

Launch the EPM Automate client on your computer and log in. Use the following as a guideline for logging in:

```
C:\Oracle\EPM Automate\bin>epmautomate login username password PBCSURL domain
```

Note! To receive guidance directly from the tool, type "epmautomate help" and press *Enter*. You can also use this in conjunction with specific commands. For example, for help logging in you can type "epmautomate login help".

Type "epmautomate listcommands" to see the entire list of tasks possible:

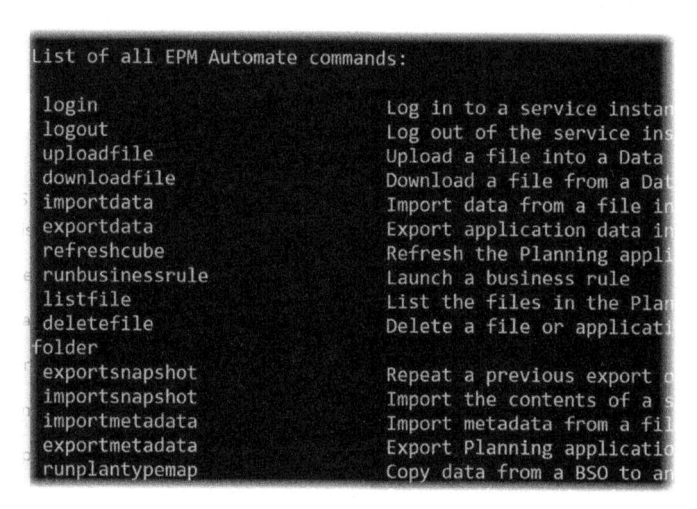

```
List of all EPM Automate commands:

    login              Log in to a service instan
    logout             Log out of the service ins
    uploadfile         Upload a file into a Data
    downloadfile      Download a file from a Dat
    importdata         Import data from a file i
    exportdata         Export application data i
    refreshcube        Refresh the Planning appli
    runbusinessrule    Launch a business rule
    listfile           List the files in the Plan
    deletefile         Delete a file or applicati
    folder
    exportsnapshot     Repeat a previous export
    importsnapshot     Import the contents of a
    importmetadata     Import metadata from a fi
    exportmetadata     Export Planning applicatio
    runplantypemap     Copy data from a BSO to a
```

To automate tasks, create a script to run commands and use the Windows Task Scheduler to schedule them.

Where Do I Put the Data Files?

Files that are used to import / export data and metadata are placed in the Simplified UI Inbox / Outbox Explorer. Files uploaded to the Data Management Inbox and Outbox are accessible in Data Management (not in the Simplified UI Inbox / Outbox). One thing that is a little confusing is that if you create a data load rule in Data Management to export data from an EPM application, that export file is placed in the Simplified UI Inbox / Outbox. Application Snapshots created using EPM Automate are stored in the Snapshots section under *Navigator >> Migration*.

Note! On Windows-based machines, the EPM Automate commands are not case sensitive. In addition, quotes are not necessary unless spaces are used in the directory / file names.

EPM Automate Commands

I've just listed some of the EPM Automate commands for you here. For the full list, check out the Oracle *Working with EPM Automate for Oracle Enterprise Performance Management Cloud* online documentation.

Command	Description	Syntax and Parameters
help	List supported commands or display information on specific command	epmautomate help
encrypt	Uses AES to encrypt password and store it in a file (one time process)	epmautomate encrypt PASSWORD KEY PASSWORD FILE
login	Log into Enterprise Planning Cloud	epmautomate login USERNAME PASSWORD URL IDENTITYDOMAIN
logout	Logout of Enterprise Planning Cloud	epmautomate logout
uploadfile	Upload file from local computer to Planning Simplified UI Inbox / Outbox	epmautomate uploadfile *"DIRECTORY/DATAFILE"* epmautomate uploadfile "C:/pbcsdat/monthlydata.csv"
uploadfile	Upload file from local computer to Data Management folder; you add the [DATA_MANAGEMENT_FOLDER] parameter at the end	epmautomate uploadfile *"DIRECTORY/DATAFILE"* [DATA_MANAGEMENT_FOLDER] epmautomate uploadfile "C:/DataManagementdat/monthlydata.csv" inbox/repository

Command	Description	Syntax and Parameters
downloadfile	Download file from the Planning Simplified UI Inbox / Outbox	epmautomate downloadfile "FILE_NAME" epmautomate downloadfile "ExportProductManager.zip"
downloadfile	Download file from Data Management folder	epmautomate downloadfile "[FILE_PATH]/FILE_NAME" epmautomate downloadfile outbox.csv
importmetadata	Import metadata from Inbox / Outbox into the Enterprise Planning Cloud application using a Planning Job Filenames must match file names in the job OR follow this format "metadata_DIMENSIONNAME.csv"	epmautomate importmetadata JOB_NAME [FILE_NAME] epmautomate importmetadata importAccount importAccount.zip

Command	Description	Syntax and Parameters
exportmetadata	Export metadata to Inbox / Outbox into the Enterprise Planning Cloud application using a Planning Job; Will export in ZIP file only	epmautomate exportmetadata epmautomate exportmetadata dailyAccountexport Accountexport.ZIP
refreshcube	Refresh the database	epmautomate refreshcube
importdata	Import data from Inbox / Outbox into the Enterprise Planning Cloud application using a Planning Job Filenames can be ZIP, CSV For Essbase Cloud format, use TXT	epmautomate importdata JOB_NAME [FILE_NAME] epmautomate importdata dailydataload dailydata.zip
exportdata	Export data to Inbox / Outbox into the Enterprise Planning Cloud application using a Planning Job; Will export in ZIP file only	epmautomate exportdata JOB_NAME [FILE_NAME] epmautomate exportdata dailydataexport dailyData.zip

Command	Description	Syntax and Parameters
rundatarule	Run Data Management load rule; Valid import modes are: APPEND, REPLACE, NON Valid export modes are: STORE_DATA, ADD_DATA, SUBTRACT_DATA, REPLACE_DATA, NONE	epmautomate rundatarule RULE_NAME START_PERIO DEND_PERIOD IMPORT_M ODE EXPORT_MODE [FILE_ NAME] *Multi-period Import*: epmautomate rundatarule VisionActual Mar-15 Jun-15 REPLACE STORE_DATA inbox/Vision/GLActual.dat *Single-period Import*: epmautomate rundatarule "Vision Actual" Mar-15 Mar-15 REPLACE STORE_DATA inbox/Vision/GLActual.dat
runbatch	Run Data Management batch	epmautomate runbatch BATCH_NAME
runbusinessrule	Run business rule; Optionally define values for run time prompts using PARAMETER	epmautomate runbusinessrule RULE_NAME [PARAMETER = VALUE]
runplantypemap	Runs a Planning job to copy data from one plan type to another	epmautomate runplantypemap JOBNAME [clearData=true|false]

Command	Description	Syntax and Parameters
listfiles	List file in Planning simplified UI Inbox / Outbox	epmautomate listfiles
deletefile	Delete a file from Planning simplified UI Inbox / Outbox	epmautomate deletefile FILE_NAME
exportsnapshot	Export a previously run snapshot to create snapshot in Application Management	epmautomate exportsnapshot SNAPSHOT_NAME
importsnapshot	Imports a snapshot into the instance, updating / overwriting artifacts	epmautomate importsnapshot
resetservice	If you see severe performance issues, this command will restart the service instance	epmautomate resetservice
feedback	Send feedback to oracle	epmautomate feedback "comment"
recreate	CAUTION – this will restore service to a clean slate and delete everything!	epmautomate recreate-f

EPM Automate Status Codes

EPM Automate returns a status code of a particular operation. You are looking for the status code "0"! Other error codes for EPM Automate include:

- 0 – Operation completed without errors
- 1 – Functional errors reported by REST APIs
- 6 – Service is not available
- 7 – Errors caused by use of invalid command or parameter
- 9 – Failure due to invalid credentials
- 11 – Indicate internal server errors
- Other error codes (2,3,4,5,8, and 10) are no longer applicable

Now that I've introduced EPM Automate, I'm ready to write some scripts! To follow along, I will be using the Windows version. Check out the Oracle documentation for details on Linux scripting.

Encrypt the Password

First I want to encrypt my password and create a password file.

To encrypt a password for an EPM Automate script,
1. Launch EPM Automate (go to *Start* >> *Programs* >> *EPM Automate* or launch a DOS command prompt).
2. The EPM Automate screen displays:

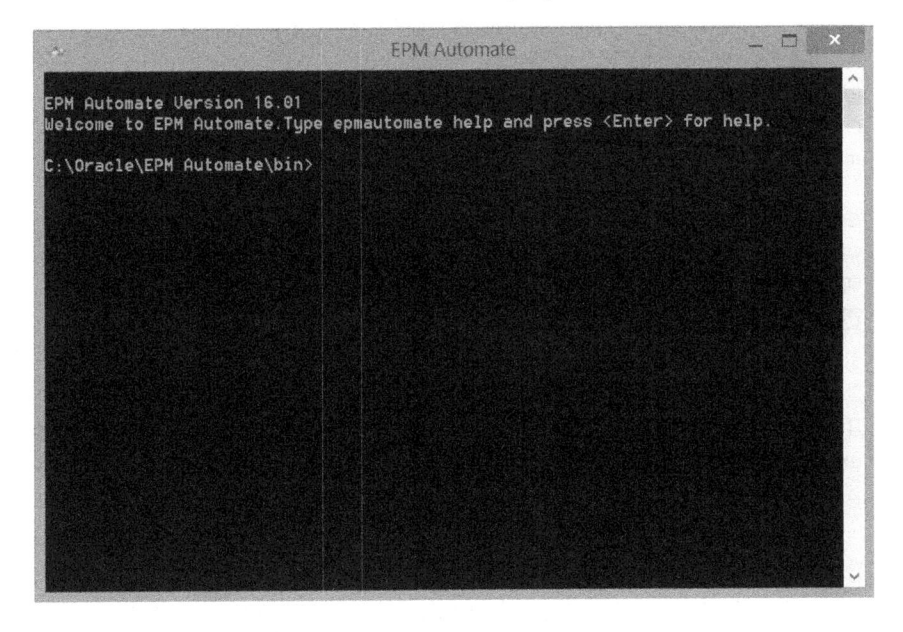

```
EPM Automate Version 16.01
Welcome to EPM Automate. Type epmautomate help and press <Enter> for help.

C:\Oracle\EPM Automate\bin>
```

3. I can optionally navigate to any desired directory where I plan to perform operations. I will stay here in the *Oracle\EPM Automate\bin* directory.
4. Type "epmautomate encrypt *password* myKey C:\EPMAutomateFiles\password.epw":

```
C:\Oracle\EPM Automate\bin>epmautomate encrypt H       3 myKey C:\EPMAutomateFil
es\password.epw
encrypt completed successfully
```

Automate a Planning Job

I just reviewed how to create a Planning job in the previous section. Many EPM Automate Utility commands require jobs to be created within the application such as import data jobs, export of data jobs, and "Cube Map" jobs (aka, copy data from one cube to another).

To automate a PBCS job,
1. In the EPM Automate interface, type the following using your own username, domain, PBCS URL, and file name (step by step is recommended). Remember the first line of the script should be all one line through the identity domain:

```
epmautomate login ServiceAdmin
C:\EPMAutomateFiles\password.epw PBCSURL
myIdentityDomain

epmautomate exportdata ExportProductManager
epmautomate listfiles
epmautomate downloadfile ExportProductManager.zip
epmautomate logout
```

Note in the above example, there are no carriage returns in the first three lines (it will be one long string of text on your screen). This executes the ExportProductManager job and places the file in your EPM Automate / Bin folder.

Now let's compare Job Scheduler and EPM Automate. Note that the Job Scheduler allows me to automate the export of the Product Manager data just as the EPM Automate utility did. The difference is that the EPM Automate utility has additional commands that allow you to download the exported file (to be picked up by another process if dictated by requirements):

2. Save the syntax / commands as a script batch file in the C:\Oracle\EPM Automate\bin directory:

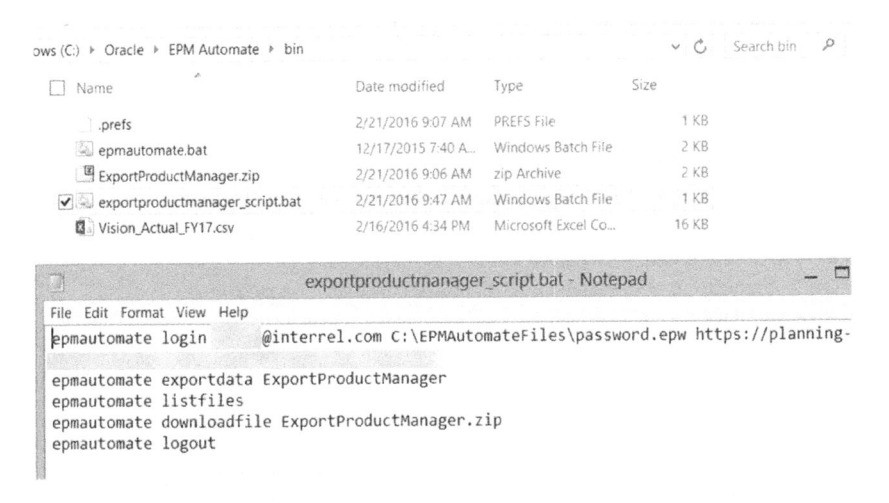

```
epmautomate login          @interrel.com C:\EPMAutomateFiles\password.epw https://planning-
epmautomate exportdata ExportProductManager
epmautomate listfiles
epmautomate downloadfile ExportProductManager.zip
epmautomate logout
```

Automate a Nightly Process

Now let's take things up a notch by creating a more robust script. Here's an example of what an entire nightly process script might look like: logging in, updating a dimension, refreshing the cube, loading data, running a business rule, and then logging out.

```
@ECHO off
REM Nightly script for EPM Automate
REM Created by: interRel Consulting
REM Created on: March 9, 2016

SET url=https://servicename-
domain.pbcs.usx.oraclecloud.com
SET user=admin
SET pwd=C:\EPMAutomateFiles\password.epw
SET domain=MyServicesDomain
SET returnvalue=0

ECHO Logging In
CALL epmautomate login %user% %pwd% %url% %domain%
@ECHO off
IF %ERRORLEVEL% NEQ 0 (
ECHO Login failed with error %ERRORLEVEL%.
GOTO :END
)

ECHO Updating Product dimension
CALL epmautomate importmetadata ImportProduct
@ ECHO off
IF %ERRORLEVEL% NEQ 0 (
ECHO Product dimension failed with error
%ERRORLEVEL%.
GOTO :END
)

ECHO Refresh cube
CALL epmautomate refreshcube RefreshCube
@ECHO off
IF %ERRORLEVEL% NEQ 0 (
ECHO Refresh cube failed with error %ERRORLEVEL%.
GOTO :END
)

ECHO Load sales data
CALL epmautomate importdata LoadSalesFY16
@ECHO off
IF %ERRORLEVEL% NEQ 0 (
ECHO Loading of sales data failed with error
%ERRORLEVEL%.
```

```
GOTO :END
)

ECHO Run CalcAll business rule
CALL epmautomate runbusinessrule CalcAll
planType=Sales
@ECHO off
IF %ERRORLEVEL% NEQ 0 (
ECHO Run business rule failed with error
%ERRORLEVEL%.
GOTO :END
)

ECHO Logging Out
CALL epmautomate logout
@ECHO off
IF %ERRORLEVEL% NEQ 0 (
ECHO Logout failed with error %ERRORLEVEL%.
GOTO :END
)

:END
ECHO Return code: %ERRORLEVEL%
SET returnValue=%ERRORLEVEL%
EXIT /B %returnValue%
```

This script is based on the Oracle documentation and is written for MS-DOS batch. Statements like "REM" are used for commenting the code, "SET" creates and assigns variables, and "ECHO" writes comments out to the command window / log file. Special statements for error trapping (e.g., "IF %ERRORLEVEL% NEQ 0...") have also been included to show a more realistic example. This script uses variables (e.g., %user%) to make maintenance easier. The script is called by another file in order to capture the actions to a log file that can be reviewed after the fact. The following steps cover the basics of each EPM Automate command.

I need to set up the objects referenced from the EPM Automate commands. Most formal processes called by this script such as importing metadata, refreshing the cube, and loading data, require an official job in PBCS.

I'll set up these jobs in order. First, I'll upload all the files that I'll need to run these jobs.

To upload job files,
1. Select *Navigator >> Application >> Overview*.
2. Select *Actions >> Inbox / Outbox Explorer*.
3. I have not previously uploaded the Product dimension source file, so I'm going to upload it now.
4. Click *Upload*.

Note! In order to save metadata and data imports as jobs, the source files must be located in the Planning Inbox. Refreshed files can be uploaded through EPM Automate.

5. Browse to the local file, select it, and then click *Upload File*.
6. Now I need to upload the FY16 Actuals data file. Repeat the previous two steps to upload this data file as well.
7. *Close* out of the Inbox / Outbox Explorer.

Next, I'll set up the "ImportProduct" job, which updates the Product dimension by importing metadata for it.

To set up a job,
1. Select *Navigator >> Application >> Dimensions*.
2. Click *Import*.
3. Click *Create*.
4. Select *Planning Inbox* at the top of the screen since the file is already on the server.

Location ○ Local ● Planning Inbox

5. Next to the Products dimension, select a delimiter type – in my case I'll keep the default of *Comma delimited* since my file is of CSV type.
6. Type in the name of the newly uploaded file on the server.

Product	Product.csv	◉ Comma delimited
27 Members		

7. Ignore the option to the right to *Clear Members*. This option would clear the members first, prior to uploading the new metadata file.

This step is recommended if there are significant changes to the sort order and it's OK to delete the data associated with any deleted members.

8. Click *Save as Job* to save this import as a formal job process.
9. Name the job. I'm going to call this "ImportProduct".
10. Keep the option to *Refresh Database if Import Metadata is Successful* unchecked.

This option refreshes the dimension within the underlying Essbase database only if the metadata import is successful. I'm going to handle this in a separate step in EPM Automate.

11. Click *Save* and then *OK* at the confirmation window.
12. Close out of the screen and you'll see the new job listed in the Import Metadata screen.
13. Close out of this screen as well.

Now I need to create the job to refresh the Essbase cube. To do this,

1. Select *Navigator >> Application >> Overview*.
2. Select *Actions >> Refresh Database*.
3. Click *Create* to create a new process.
4. Now select the options that relate to actions before and after the refresh. This is job-dependent. I have made the following selections:

Refresh Database

Before Refresh Database
Enable Use of the Application for
○ All users ● Administrators
☑ Log off all users
☑ Kill all active requests

After Refresh Database
Enable Use of the Application for
● All users ○ Administrators

5. Click *Save as Job*.
6. Name the job. I'm going to call this "RefreshCube":

> **Save as Job**
> * Name RefreshCube

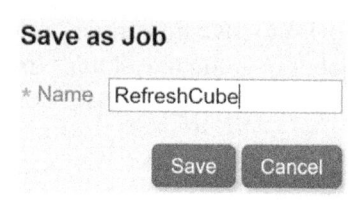

7. Click *Save*.
8. Click *OK* at the confirmation window.
9. Click *Close* and then *Close* again.

Next, I need to create one last job to load data. To do this,
1. Select *Actions >> Import Data*.
2. Click *Create*.
3. Change the location at the top to *Planning Inbox*.

Note! In order to save a data import as a job, the source file must be located in the Planning inbox.

4. Choose the other options that make sense for this data load.
   a. **Location** – Planning Inbox
   b. **Source type** – Planning
   c. **File type** – Comma delimited
   d. **Source file** – Actual_Sales_FY16.csv
   e. Do not check *Include Metadata*

This data file is based on a Planning data file export, so it's in the native Planning format. It's also comma delimited. Since there is no new metadata in the file, for performance reasons I have chosen to uncheck *Include Metadata*:

Import Data

Location	○ Local ● Planning Inbox
Source Type	● Planning ○ Essbase
File Type	● Comma delimited ○ Tab delimited ○ Other
Source File	Actual_Sales_FY16.csv
Include Metadata	☐
Date Format	MM-DD-YYYY
Last Import	Completed

5. Click *Save as Job*.
6. Name the job and click *Save*. Click *OK* at the confirmation window.
7. Click *Close*.

You'll now see the new job in the Import Data list:

Import Data

Type	Name
	LoadSalesFY16

8. Click *Close* again.

Now that the formal jobs have been created and I know that I'm using an existing business rule, I'm ready to write my EPM Automate script and test it.

```
@ECHO off
REM Nightly script for EPM Automate
REM Created by: interRel Consulting
REM Created on: March 9, 2016

SET url=https://servicename-domain.pbcs.usx.oraclecloud.com
SET user=admin
SET pwd=C:\EPMAutomateFiles\password.epw
SET domain=MyServicesDomain
SET returnvalue=0
```

The first part of the script (above), sets up the housekeeping part. Header commentary and variables are set in this section.

The next part of this script logs into the server. Parameters for the "login" command include the username, password, PBCS URL, and PBCS domain. This script uses the basic EPM Automate login command and the parameters are filled in by the variables set at the top of the script.

```
ECHO Logging In
CALL epmautomate login %user% %pwd% %url% %domain%
@ECHO off
IF %ERRORLEVEL% NEQ 0 (
ECHO Login failed with error %ERRORLEVEL%.
GOTO :END
)
```

I've embedded some generic error trapping logic that's used in each command section. The "IF" logic checks for an error after the command runs. If there is an error (it knows this by checking to see if the error code is not equal to zero, which is a successful code), the script skips to the ":END" section (described later in this section).

```
ECHO Refresh cube
CALL epmautomate refreshcube RefreshCube
@ECHO off
IF %ERRORLEVEL% NEQ 0 (
ECHO Refresh cube failed with error %ERRORLEVEL%.
GOTO :END
)
```

Now that the dimension has been updated, I need code to do a database refresh. Otherwise, there could be a disconnect between PBCS and Essbase during the data loading step (since I elected to not check the option to include metadata on the data load). I could have skipped this step, but I chose not to use the inherent option in the import metadata job. This was done for error trapping purposes. Parameters for the "refreshcube" command include the name of the job that does the database refresh.

```
ECHO Load sales data
CALL epmautomate importdata LoadSalesFY16
@ECHO off
IF %ERRORLEVEL% NEQ 0 (
ECHO Loading of sales data failed with error %ERRORLEVEL%.
GOTO :END
```

Now that Planning and Essbase are in sync, I can load data into Essbase. Parameters for the "importdata" command include the job name and then an optional parameter to override the job's data file.

```
ECHO Run CalcAll business rule
CALL epmautomate runbusinessrule CalcAll planType=Sales
@ECHO off
IF %ERRORLEVEL% NEQ 0 (
ECHO Run business rule failed with error %ERRORLEVEL%.
GOTO :END
)
```

If I'm loading data into a BSO cube, I need to aggregate my data after loading it (unless I'm using hybrid aggregation). I have a nifty business rule called CalcAll that takes care of this. The "runbusinessrule" command has several parameters. The first parameter is the business rule name in Calculation Manager. The next parameter is the cube that the rule needs to be run against. Finally, there are optional parameters for any run-time prompts called by the business rule (which don't apply in this example).

```
ECHO Logging Out
CALL epmautomate logout
@ECHO off
IF %ERRORLEVEL% NEQ 0 (
ECHO Logout failed with error %ERRORLEVEL%.
GOTO :END
)
```

The final, formal command involves logging out. The "logout" command is simple and has no parameters.

```
:END
ECHO Return code: %ERRORLEVEL%
SET returnValue=%ERRORLEVEL%
EXIT /B %returnValue%
```

The last section of the code is for housekeeping purposes. It figures out the current error code (if there is one) and then returns it.

Here is the final sequence of commands resulting from this script:

Look Smarter Than You Are with PBCS

```
Logging In
Login successful
Updating Product dimension
Processing...
Retrieving status...
importmetadata completed successfully
Refresh cube
Processing...
Retrieving status...
refreshcube completed successfully
Load sales data
Processing...
Retrieving status...
importdata completed successfully
Run CalcAll business rule
Processing...
runbusinessrule completed successfully
Logging Out
logout completed successfully
Return code: 0
```

Automate a Data Load in Data Management

EPM Automate can run data load rules and batches that are created in Data Management.

To automate a data load in Data Management,
1. First place the *Vision_Actual_FY17.csv* file in your c:\EPMAutomateFiles directory. (email info@interrel.com for a copy of the file)
2. In the EPM Automate interface, type the following (step by step recommended) and hit *Enter*:

```
epmautomate uploadfile
c:\EPMAutomateFiles\Vision_Actual_FY17.csv inbox
```

```
epmautomate rundatarule LoadVisionSalesFY17 Jan-17
Dec-17 REPLACE STORE_DATA
inbox/Vision_Actual_FY17.csv
```

```
C:\Oracle\EPM Automate\bin>epmautomate uploadfile Vision_Actual_FY17.csv inbox
Processing...
100% completed
uploadfile completed successfully

C:\Oracle\EPM Automate\bin>epmautomate rundatarule LoadVisionSalesFY17 Jan-17 De
c-17 REPLACE STORE_DATA inbox/Vision_Actual_FY17.csv
Processing...
Retrieving status...
rundatarule completed successfully

C:\Oracle\EPM Automate\bin>
```

The rule shows a successful execution in Data Management:

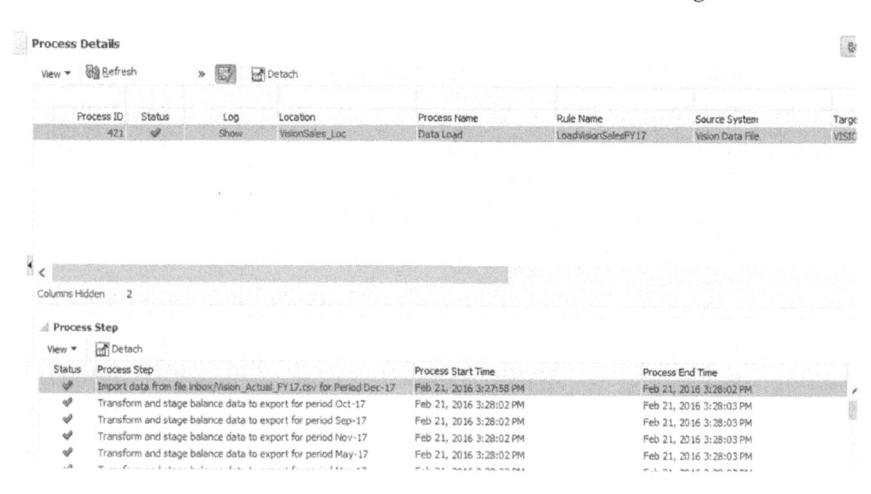

Adding Scripts to the Windows Task Scheduler

It's possible to schedule EPM Automate scripts through Windows Scheduler on a Windows-based computer.

Note! The following screen shots are from Windows 10.

To schedule EPM Automate scripts to run in a Windows Task Scheduler,

1. On the computer where you wish to schedule tasks using Windows Task Scheduler, launch the Control Panel and navigate to *Administrative Tools*.
2. Open *Task Scheduler*.
3. Select *Action >> Create Basic Task*:

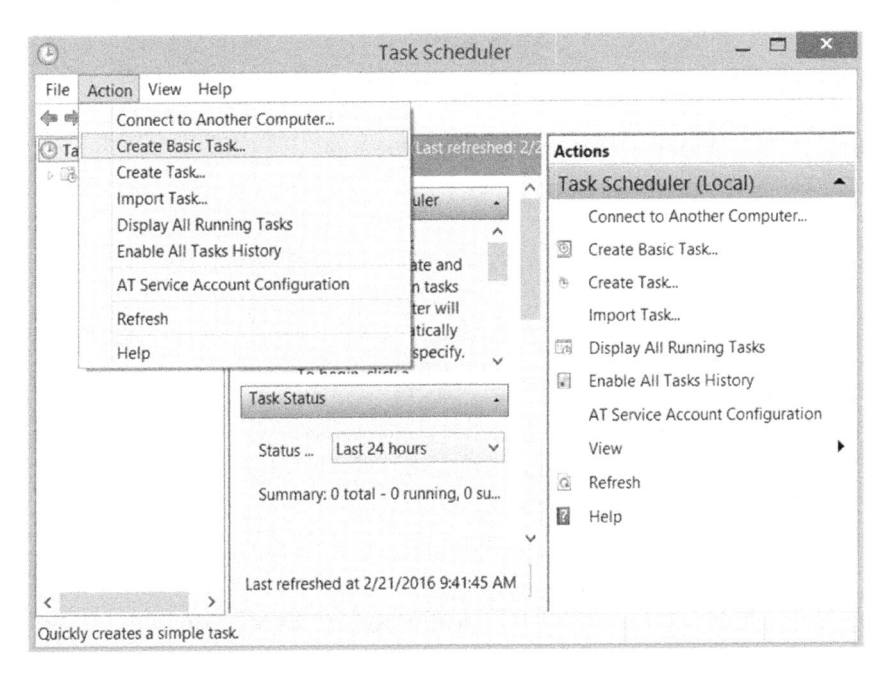

4. Enter the task name.
5. Click *Next*.
6. Under Task Trigger, select the schedule and click *Next*:

Chapter 9: Automate & Migrate

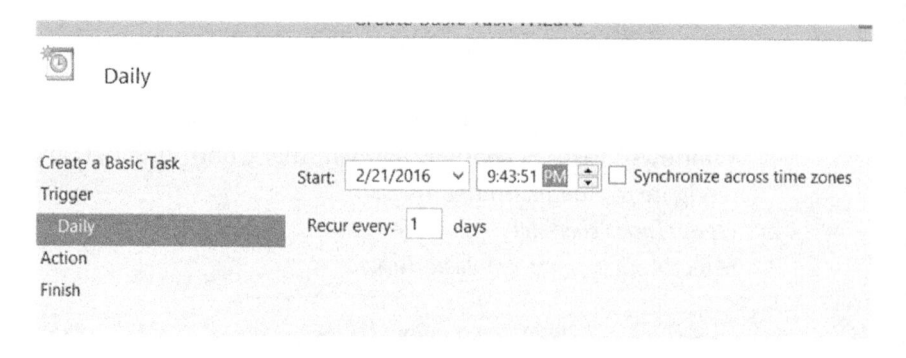

Daily

7. Define any other schedule parameters and click *Next*.
8. Under Action, select *Start a Program*:

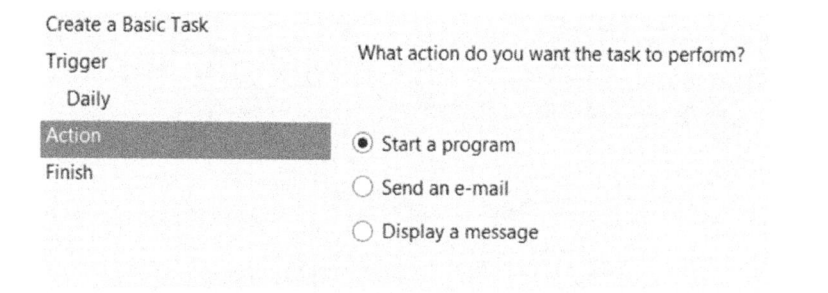

9. Select the script to schedule.
10. Optionally add arguments.
11. In *Start in*, enter the location where EPM Automate utility is installed:

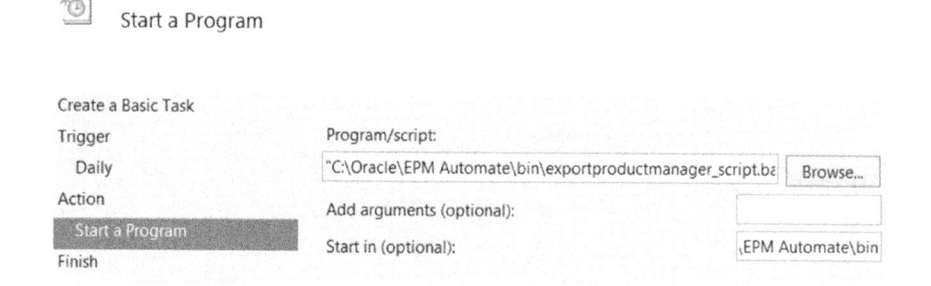

Start a Program

12. Click *Next*.

13. Check the option *Open the Properties dialog for this task when I click Finish*.
14. Click *Finish*.
15. Under the General tab in task properties, define security options for running the script when a user is logged in or not, and whether or not to run with highest privileges:

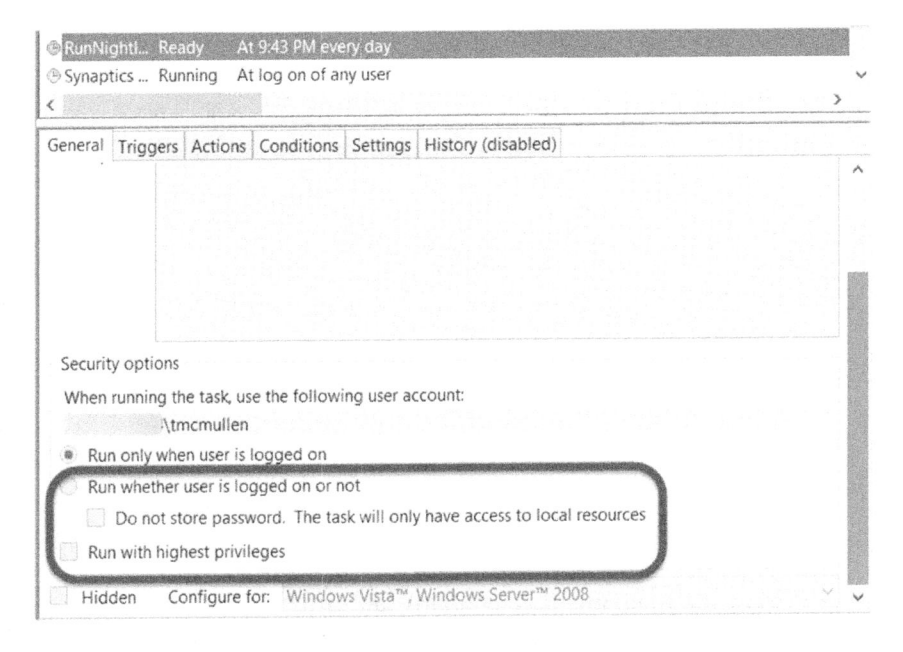

```
RunNightl...   Ready      At 9:43 PM every day
Synaptics ...  Running    At log on of any user
```

| General | Triggers | Actions | Conditions | Settings | History (disabled) |

Security options
When running the task, use the following user account:
    \tmcmullen
● Run only when user is logged on
○ Run whether user is logged on or not
    ☐ Do not store password. The task will only have access to local resources
☐ Run with highest privileges
☐ Hidden   Configure for: Windows Vista™, Windows Server™ 2008

Voila! I now have a fully automated nightly process that runs each night to my PBCS application.

MIGRATION

Migration is the place where you can export or import application artifacts (basically any object or component in your application…but it sounds cooler when you use the term "artifact") or the entire application. Application snapshots are uploaded and downloaded from the Migration area. You can also run artifact update reports and migration reports. For any on-premises Hyperion Planning administrators, the migration features and functions are essentially a Cloud version of the familiar on-premises tool Life Cycle Management.

You access Migration by selecting *Navigator >> Application >> Migration*. Three tabs display for Migration: Categories, Snapshots, and Reports.

The *Categories* tab lists artifacts for the current PBCS application, grouped by Planning, Data Management, Calculation Manager, Groups and Membership, and Reporting:

Categories | Snapshots | Reports

Name
☐ Planning
☐ Data Management
☐ Calculation Manager
☐ Groups and Membership
☐ Reporting

- **Planning** – contains the core PBCS application artifacts for the current application including data forms, data, dimensions, and more
- **Data Management** – contains all of the Data Management (FDMEE Cloud) artifacts
- **Calculation Manager** – contains all of the Calculation Manager objects like rules, rule sets, and variables
- **Groups and Membership** – contains the native group definition and assigned users to those groups
- **Reporting** – contains all of the Financial Reporting objects like reports, books, and batches along with any other artifacts imported into the reporting and analysis repository

The *Snapshots* tab contains all of the imported and exported snapshots. It's up to your administrator to keep this area clean – snapshots will stay there until they are removed. You can rerun an export snapshot from this section or it can be scheduled to run with EPM Automate. You can also delete and rename snapshots:

Categories | **Snapshots** | Reports	
Name	Actions
▷ Artifact Snapshot	⚙
▷ Artifact Snapshot_2016 11 07	⚙
▷ Book Snapshot 16-12-15(1)	⚙

Also notice that the *Artifact Snapshot* is taken each night; this is completed automatically for you each day (and is overwritten each day). You can set up a scheduled process to download it each day and keep it for a period of time as a backup. You'll see in just a bit how easy it is to import a snapshot in the event that you to need to restore from backup.

The *Reports* tab contains the Artifact Updates and Migration Status reports:

Categories | Snapshots | **Reports**
Name
Artifact Updates
Migration Status

An *Artifact Updates* report provides a list of artifacts that have been updated based on a specified date range and artifact category. You can also specify an artifact type and user. The report includes the application name, artifact name, artifact type, name of the user who modified the artifact, date of the artifact update, and the location of the artifact.

A *Migration Status* report provides status information about a migration into the PBCS instance or a backup of the PBCS instance. You can view the user who performed the migration/backup, the start time, the end time, and the list of artifacts migrated. In addition, the overall status of the migration/backup is displayed. For failures, you can view the artifacts that failed along with error messages on why the artifact failed to migrate/backup.

> **Note!** Migrations by the user epm_default_cloud_admin include the daily maintenance backup process. There should be one entry in the report by day for this user. You can check these out to see how long the daily backup is taking and whether or not it was successful.

```
Meanwhile, back on Earth...
    When Project Commander McMullen had first heard
that Roske and the implementation were still alive
from Director Chang, she was flooded with relief. Of
course, Roske would find a way!
    So now she had to see what she could do to help
Roske. His application was in good shape. Still, she
could improve a few things. Let's import this baby to
see if any "tweaking" is needed.
```

Why would I want to import from or export to Oracle PBCS? Oh, let me count the reasons. You want to move an on-premises Hyperion Planning application to the Cloud or vice versa. You want to move a PBCS application from the Test instance to the Production instance. You have an issue and Oracle Support requests a copy of your application. You want to make a backup or snapshot of the application before major change. In short, you will definitely need to do this at some point in your Oracle PBCS administrator life.

Export PBCS Application

To export the entire PBCS application from a Cloud instance,
1. In the Simplified UI, select *Navigator* >> *Application* >> *Migration*.
2. Select the *Categories* tab.

3. Check the boxes next to *Planning, Data Management, Calculation Rules, Groups and Membership,* and *Reporting*:

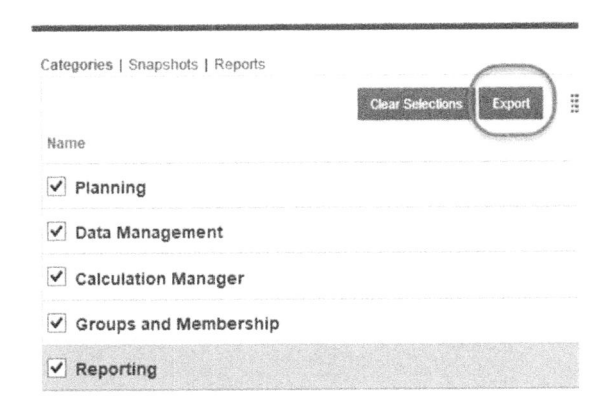

4. Click *Export*.
5. Give the application export a name (if you don't like the default) and click *OK*. It's best to include the date somewhere in the name:

6. The Migration Status report should display:

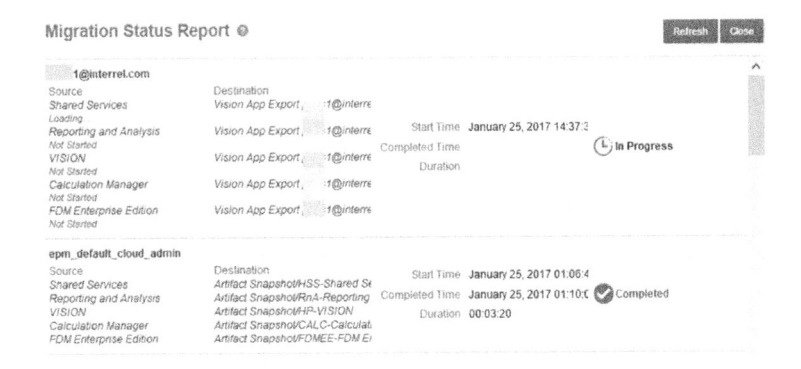

7. Click *Refresh* to see the report status update.

You can also close the migration status report. The migration continues to run in the background.

8. When the application export is complete, select the *Snapshots* tab. The export is now listed:

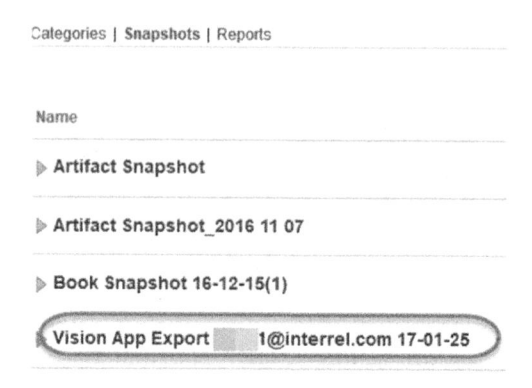

```
Categories | Snapshots | Reports

Name

▷ Artifact Snapshot

▷ Artifact Snapshot_2016 11 07

▷ Book Snapshot 16-12-15(1)

▷ Vision App Export    1@interrel.com 17-01-25
```

9. Select the snapshot and click the *Actions* icon. Notice that you can *Delete, Download, Repeat Export, Rename, Import,* and view a list of artifacts (and even export them) that have been *Modified Since* that backup was taken:

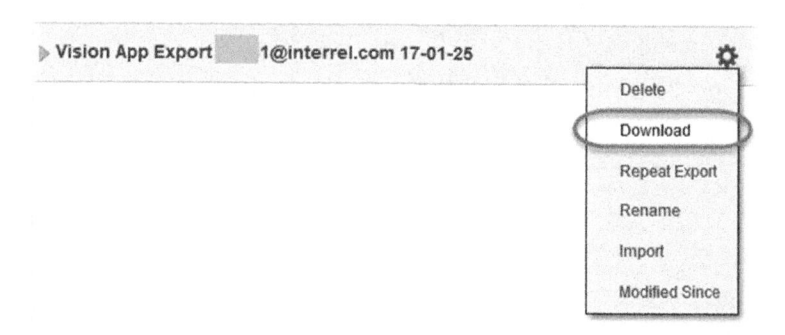

```
▷ Vision App Export    1@interrel.com 17-01-25          ⚙

                                              Delete
                                              Download
                                              Repeat Export
                                              Rename
                                              Import
                                              Modified Since
```

To manually download an application snapshot from PBCS,

10. Select the desired snapshot and click *Download*.

When performing a migration, you can choose to export the entire application (as I just did) or export individual artifacts (e.g., a

Look Smarter Than You Are with PBCS   463

business rule, data, or data form). You can drill into the main categories to select desired artifacts. For example, I can select the hyperlink for Planning and drill into the artifacts to select two new forms that I would like to migrate from test to production. The snapshot that is created only contains the two checked data forms:

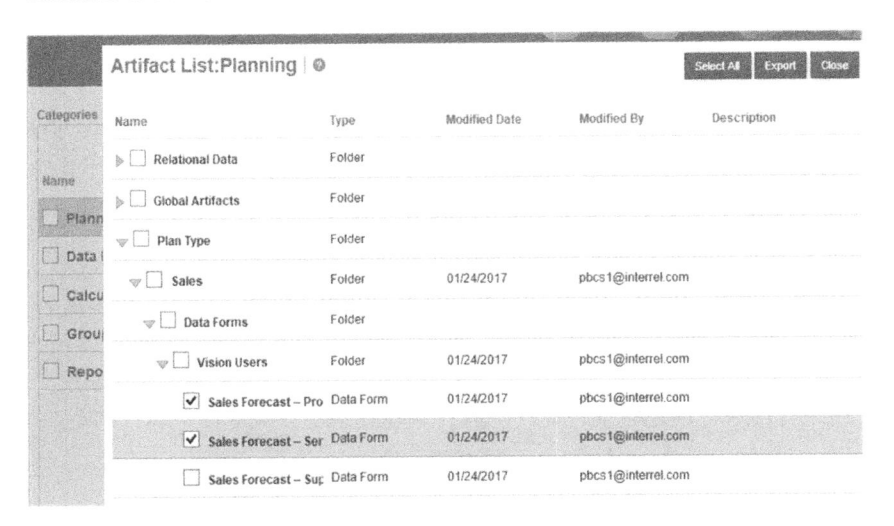

Artifact List:Planning					Select All Export Close
Name	Type	Modified Date	Modified By	Description	
▷ ☐ Relational Data	Folder				
▷ ☐ Global Artifacts	Folder				
▽ ☐ Plan Type	Folder				
▽ ☐ Sales	Folder	01/24/2017	pbcs1@interrel.com		
▽ ☐ Data Forms	Folder				
▽ ☐ Vision Users	Folder	01/24/2017	pbcs1@interrel.com		
☑ Sales Forecast – Pro	Data Form	01/24/2017	pbcs1@interrel.com		
☑ Sales Forecast – Ser	Data Form	01/24/2017	pbcs1@interrel.com		
☐ Sales Forecast – Sup	Data Form	01/24/2017	pbcs1@interrel.com		

Import PBCS Application

The administrator can import an application and its artifacts once it's located in Application Snapshots. When you import a snapshot, it is an "additive" and overwrite process. It imports artifacts and overwrites any artifact with a common name. Depending on your requirements, you might have to delete the application before importing a new snapshot (*Navigator* >> *Application* >> *Overview* and choose *Remove Application*).

You might run into errors if users have been provisioned to one Cloud instance but not the target Cloud instance. If the users do not exist, the application still imports successfully but you see an error related to that user for security and possibly even user variables. If the errored user does not need access to the target Cloud instance, you can ignore these error messages. If the user does need access, make sure to provision them in My Services.

Note! Only follow along with these steps if you want to actually import the artifact into the target Cloud instance.

To upload an application snapshot into PBCS,
1. Select *Navigator >> Application >> Migration*.
2. Select the *Snapshots* tab.
3. Click *Upload*.
4. Browse to the snapshot zip file containing the necessary artifacts (for example the zip file created when I exported the PBCS application in the earlier section):

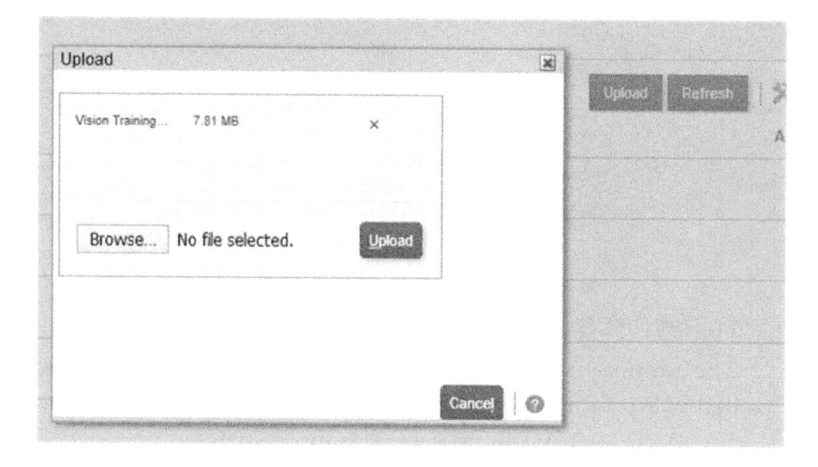

5. Click *Upload*.
6. Click *OK* after the file is successfully uploaded.

Sometimes you might want to override the default migration options. To set migration options (if your requirements dictate settings other than the default),
1. From within Snapshots, click on the *Tools* icon next to the Refresh button.
2. Set the desired import options:

Import Options	
Reporting - Replace Newer Artifacts Only	No
Reporting - Exclude Job Output On Import	No
Data Management - Skip Validation	No
Groups and Membership - Import Mode	Create or Update
Groups and Membership - Max Errors Threshold	100

You can set replacement options, skip the validation on Data Management, and set options for groups and memberships.

3. Click *Save and Close* to save the chosen options.

To import an application snapshot into PBCS,
1. If not already there, select *Navigator >> Application >> Migration*.
2. Select the Snapshots tab.
3. Select the desired snapshot and from the Action ⚙ icon, choose *Import*:

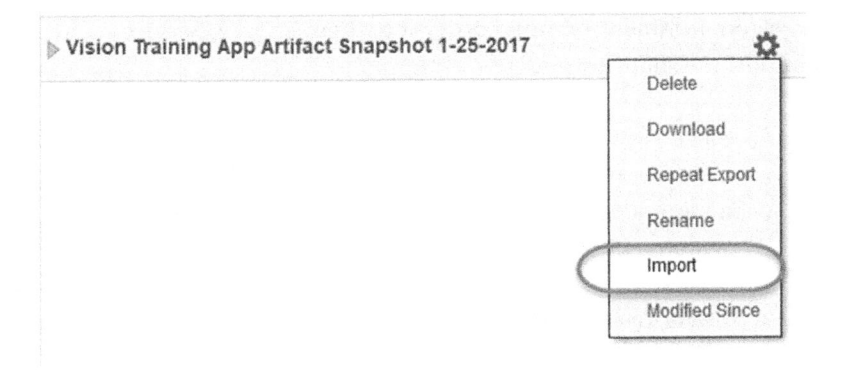

▷ **Vision Training App Artifact Snapshot 1-25-2017**

- Delete
- Download
- Repeat Export
- Rename
- Import
- Modified Since

4. Click *OK* to proceed forward.

The Migration Status report displays automatically. Click *Refresh* to see the updated status. If you see a message of "Failed", click on the *Failed* hyperlink to view any error messages:

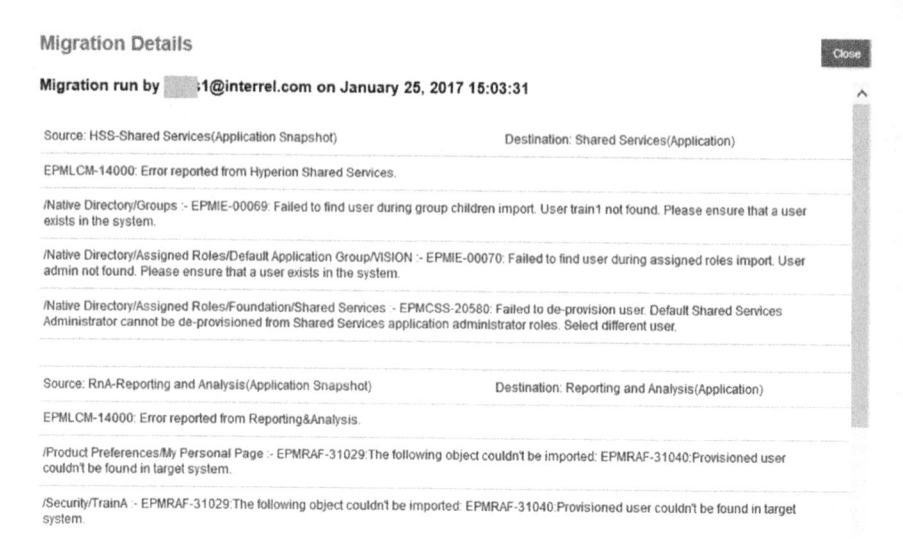

Migration Details

Migration run by ___1@interrel.com **on January 25, 2017 15:03:31**

Source: HSS-Shared Services(Application Snapshot)	Destination: Shared Services(Application)

EPMLCM-14000: Error reported from Hyperion Shared Services.

/Native Directory/Groups :- EPMIE-00069: Failed to find user during group children import. User train1 not found. Please ensure that a user exists in the system.

/Native Directory/Assigned Roles/Default Application Group/VISION :- EPMIE-00070: Failed to find user during assigned roles import. User admin not found. Please ensure that a user exists in the system.

/Native Directory/Assigned Roles/Foundation/Shared Services - EPMCSS-20580: Failed to de-provision user. Default Shared Services Administrator cannot be de-provisioned from Shared Services application administrator roles. Select different user.

Source: RnA-Reporting and Analysis(Application Snapshot)	Destination: Reporting and Analysis(Application)

EPMLCM-14000: Error reported from Reporting&Analysis.

/Product Preferences/My Personal Page :- EPMRAF-31029:The following object couldn't be imported: EPMRAF-31040:Provisioned user couldn't be found in target system.

/Security/TrainA :- EPMRAF-31029:The following object couldn't be imported: EPMRAF-31040:Provisioned user couldn't be found in target system.

As mentioned earlier, common failures are usually related to differences in provisioned users between Cloud instances. This particular application migration / import was still successful with the exception of these few errors. If the users should be provisioned in the target environment, simply provision them in My Services and then reimport the snapshot.

Note! Since PBCS allows only one application per instance, the existing application is overwritten. If an application does not exist, a new one is created with the imported artifacts.

5. Verify the migration and make sure everything you need has been imported.

If you imported a brand new application, you might have to log out and log back in to see the imported artifacts.

In the example above, I imported in the entire snapshot file. You can also pick and choose the artifacts to import from a larger snapshot. You can expand the snapshot to see the main PBCS categories:

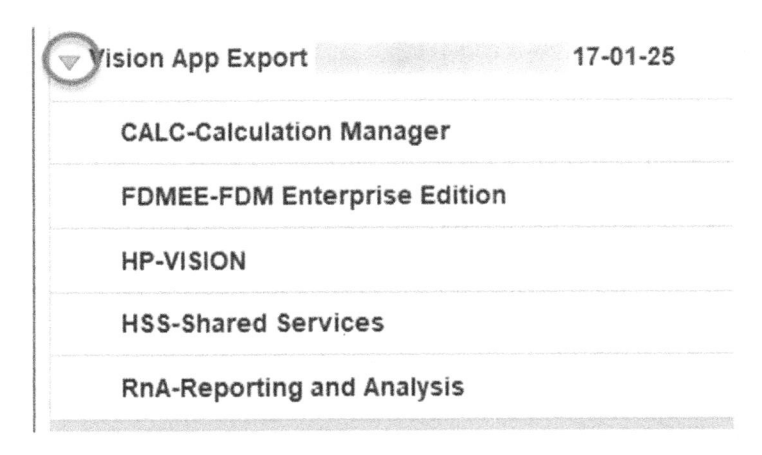

Vision App Export	17-01-25
CALC-Calculation Manager	
FDMEE-FDM Enterprise Edition	
HP-VISION	
HSS-Shared Services	
RnA-Reporting and Analysis	

Next you can select the desired category hyperlink to select specific artifacts to import:

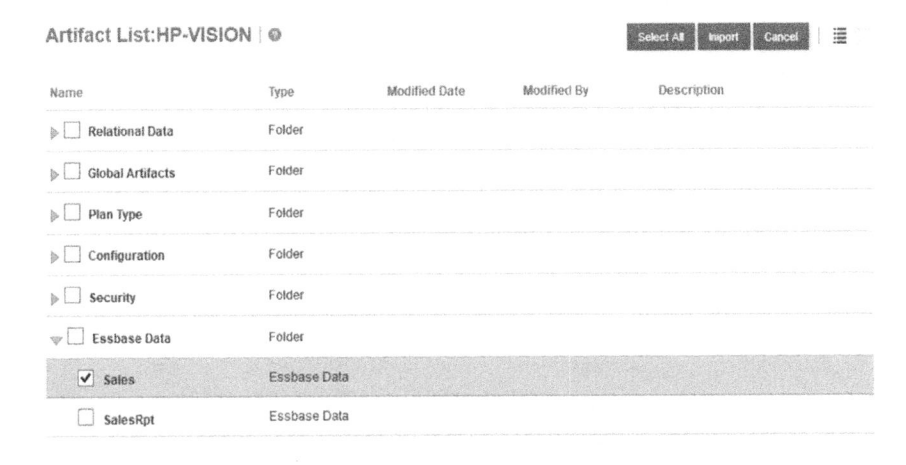

Artifact List:HP-VISION

Name	Type	Modified Date	Modified By	Description
▷ ☐ Relational Data	Folder			
▷ ☐ Global Artifacts	Folder			
▷ ☐ Plan Type	Folder			
▷ ☐ Configuration	Folder			
▷ ☐ Security	Folder			
▽ ☐ Essbase Data	Folder			
☑ Sales	Essbase Data			
☐ SalesRpt	Essbase Data			

Once the artifacts are selected and ready, click *Import*.

Export On-Premises Hyperion Planning Application

If you have an on-premises Hyperion Planning environment and would like to migrate to Cloud, you likely need to move your Hyperion Planning application to PBCS. The steps to export an application from on-premises Hyperion Planning is similar to the export steps in PBCS but there are a few slight differences. One main difference is that you work in "Life Cycle Management (LCM)" or the Shared Services Console.

Note that there are some on-premises artifacts that are not supported in Oracle PBCS, like Essbase calc scripts and Essbase data load rules. You receive errors for any non-supported artifacts when you try to import them into the Cloud. Also, there may be errors depending on your on-premises version. For example, in Hyperion Planning version 11.1.2.3.500, you might have issues exporting data via Life Cycle Management. Uncheck the data option if you run into issues and use an Essbase data export to load data manually via the PBCS Simplified UI.

To export an on-premises Planning application,
1. Go to *Navigate >> Administer >> Shared Services Console*:

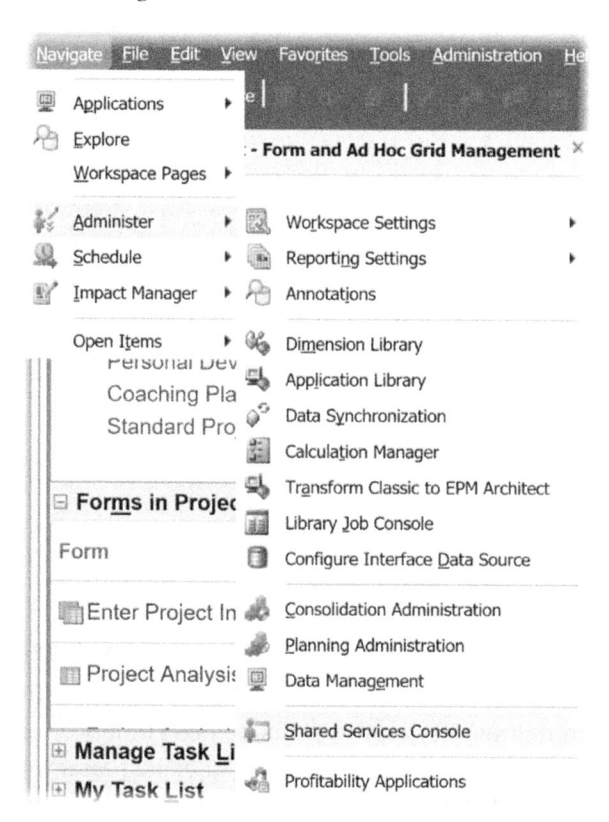

Look Smarter Than You Are with PBCS   469

2. Go into the *Application Groups* folder then find the application to export in the Planning folder.
3. Select the artifacts to export:

Name	Type
☑ Configuration	Folder
☑ Global Artifacts	Folder
☑ Plan Type	Folder
☑ Relational Data	Folder
☑ Security	Folder

4. Click *Export* and name the File System Folder.
5. Click *Export* again. Wait for a "Completed" status in the Migration Status Report:

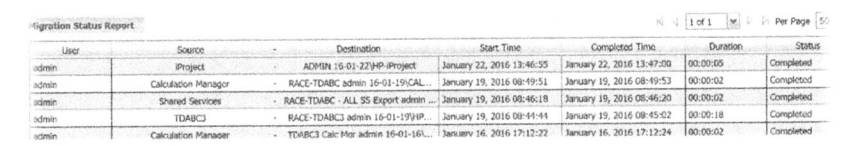

Once completed, the application export is located in the File System folder of Shared Services. Right-click the exported folder for the following options:

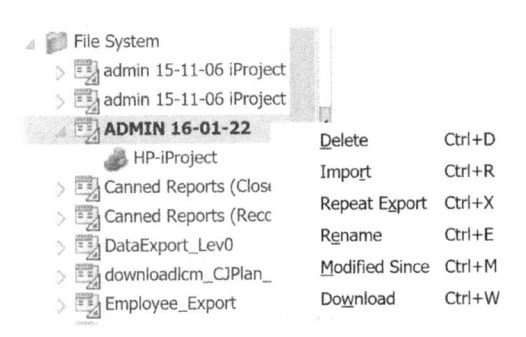

Delete	Ctrl+D
Import	Ctrl+R
Repeat Export	Ctrl+X
Rename	Ctrl+E
Modified Since	Ctrl+M
Download	Ctrl+W

Download the export file locally.

Note! To import an on-premises Planning application to PBCS, download the file to your computer so that it can be uploaded to PBCS.

You now have a snapshot that you can import using the PBCS import steps noted in the previous sections. As I mentioned before, there are some on-premises artifacts that are not supported in Oracle PBCS like Essbase calc scripts and Essbase data load rules. You should expect to receive errors for any non-supported artifacts when you try to import them into the Cloud.

Easy as pie to migrate applications to the Cloud!

LOG ENTRY: SOL 20, Entry 3

My email works. Huh?! So I can communicate with i.n.t.e.r.R.e.l. Guess I should have checked that first thing.

After pondering how I was going to communicate my success at getting the PBCS application up and going, I received an email from Project Commander McMullen. They could access the application!

Now that I can communicate with i.n.t.e.r.R.e.l, Project Commander McMullen thinks she can build a better sales forecasting application than me. I figure out how to do this all by myself in the Cloud and now she's taken my application and changed it! She exported my application using LCM to her instance and now has some "tweaks."

I think I'm having some interference and her email just isn't coming across. (Really I'm going to just ignore her comments for this phase and turn this application over to the end users.)

Time to go live!

Chapter 10: End User Activities

> LOG ENTRY: SOL 21, Entry 1
>
> Now that I've successfully completed the sales forecasting application, the users are ready to enter their sales forecast data. I'll turn it over to End User Specialist, Opal Alapat, to help users enter their plans in the PBCS.
>
> What's next for me? It's time for some well-earned R&R. Surprisingly, Glee is growing on me. Maybe it is because I don't have any other option. I wonder if the New Directions glee club will finally make it to Nationals?

NAVIGATE SIMPLIFIED UI

The Simplified UI is a streamlined UI for users of PBCS. In order to provide ease of use for tablets, this interface does not have any right-click options and everything is large enough to click with a finger. Depending on the Cloud version and updates made to these cards and clusters, the user experience and navigation may look a little different:

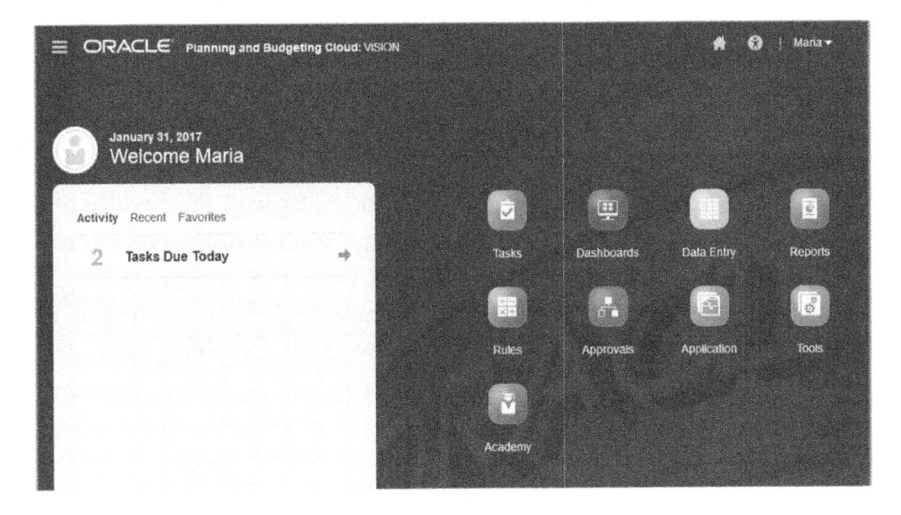

Alright, let's get started!

REVIEW DASHBOARDS

Dashboards are great to see the big picture of things. They are created by the administrator and can be viewed by users (if they have security access to the specific intersection of data represented in the dashboard). Four quadrants are available and each quadrant contains one dashboard object. Dashboard objects include a variety of charts, URLs, and commentary text:

FOLLOW TASKS

As it is with most things in life, a little bit of guidance and support can go a long way. You've already seen that data form instructions help you in your planning process. Think of task lists as having your own personal tour guide through the budgeting and forecasting process.

The wizard-like task list itemizes the steps users need to complete as they work through the budget. It even has helpful instructions and due dates for those who do not spend their entire lives strapped to a computer doing budgeting. Administrators and power users can create and manage tasks and task lists.

This brings you to the Task List summary view where you see the task list steps, their status (complete or incomplete), due date, completed date, and any defined instructions:

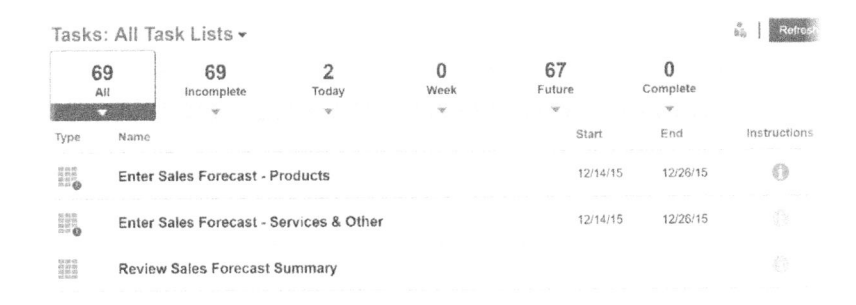

Tasks: All Task Lists ▼							Refresh
69 All	69 Incomplete	2 Today	0 Week	67 Future	0 Complete		
Type	Name			Start	End	Instructions	
	Enter Sales Forecast - Products			12/14/15	12/26/15		
	Enter Sales Forecast - Services & Other			12/14/15	12/26/15		
	Review Sales Forecast Summary						

According to the task list dashboard pictured above, no one at the company is very productive because not a single item has been completed.

You can also switch to a hierarchical view of task lists by toggling the hierarchy icon:

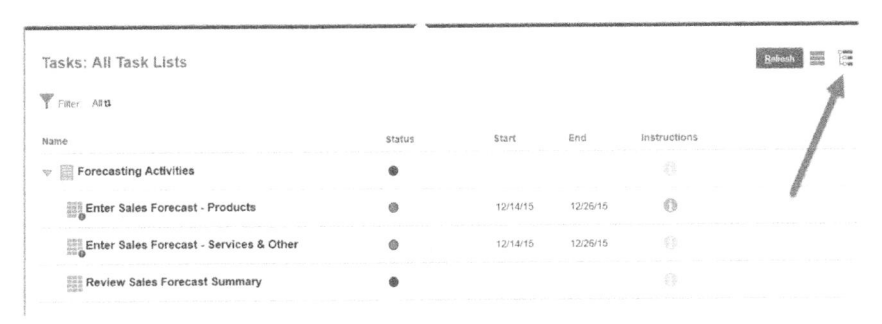

Tasks: All Task Lists					
▼ Filter: All ≡					
Name	Status	Start	End	Instructions	
▽ Forecasting Activities	●				
Enter Sales Forecast - Products	●	12/14/15	12/26/15		
Enter Sales Forecast - Services & Other	●	12/14/15	12/26/15		
Review Sales Forecast Summary	●				

To complete a task,
1. Click on an incomplete task and perform the task (if the task opens a form, input data and save the form – more on inputting data to a form very shortly).
2. When the task is complete, check the box for *Complete*:

    | Save | Refresh | Actions ▼ | ☑ Complete | Previous | Next | Close |

3. *Close* the task. You'll notice that there is a pleasant green check mark next to the completed task:

Type	Name
	Enter Sales Forecast - Products
	Enter Sales Forecast - Services & Other
	Review Sales Forecast Summary

Move onto other tasks created by the administrator to complete the entire task list.

To view instructions for a task, simply click the *Instructions* icon:

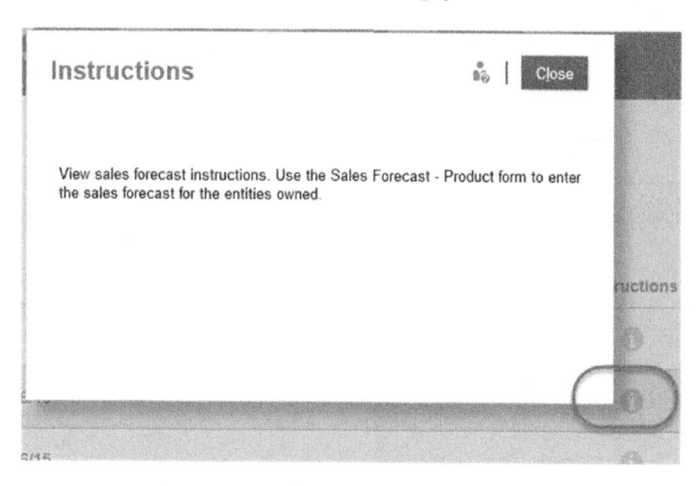

DATA ENTRY

From the Simplified UI, click *Data Entry* (known as "Plans" and "Data" in previous Cloud versions) to access to data forms and ad hoc grids organized in form folders directly:

Data Entry

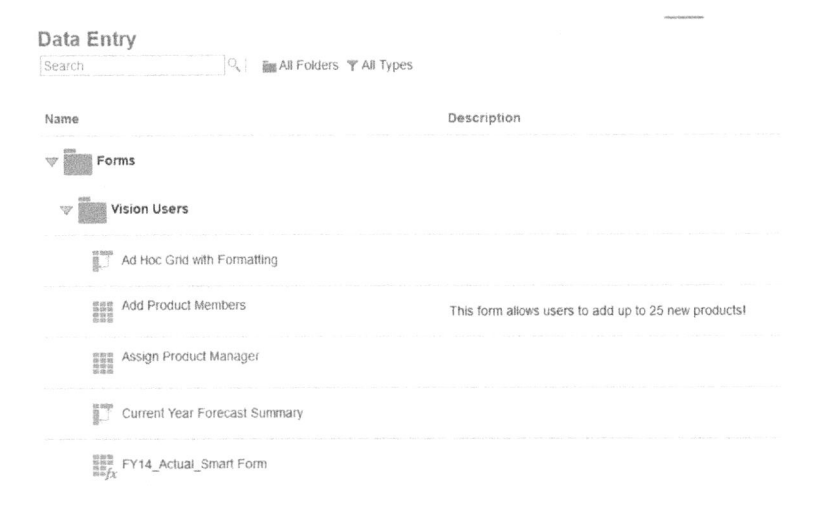

Name	Description
▽ Forms	
▽ Vision Users	
Ad Hoc Grid with Formatting	
Add Product Members	This form allows users to add up to 25 new products!
Assign Product Manager	
Current Year Forecast Summary	
FY14_Actual_Smart Form	

Before you enter data, let's review some of the data form components:

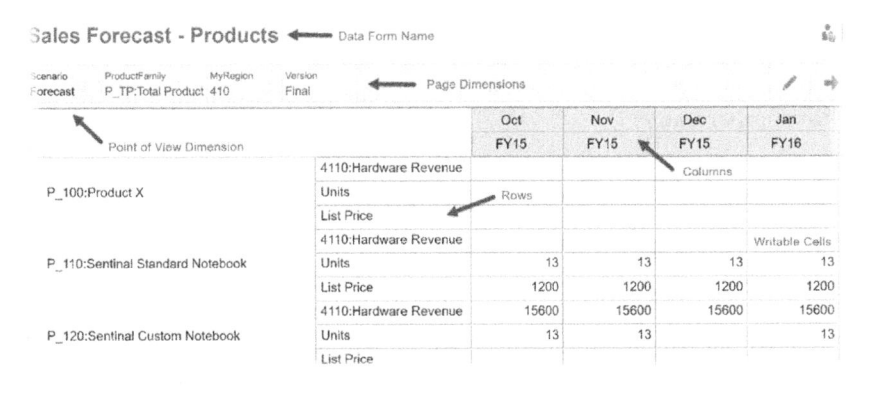

Sales Forecast - Products ← Data Form Name

Scenario: Forecast | ProductFamily: P_TP:Total Product | MyRegion: 410 | Version: Final ← Page Dimensions

Point of View Dimension

		Oct FY15	Nov FY15	Dec FY15	Jan FY16
	4110:Hardware Revenue			Columns	
P_100:Product X	Units	Rows			
	List Price				
	4110:Hardware Revenue				Writable Cells
P_110:Sentinal Standard Notebook	Units	13	13	13	13
	List Price	1200	1200	1200	1200
	4110:Hardware Revenue	15600	15600	15600	15600
P_120:Sentinal Custom Notebook	Units	13	13		13
	List Price				

A data form contains one or more dimensions in the rows and columns of the form. You may see a list of members or a hierarchy of members that you can collapse or expand, allowing you to view and plan data at a summary or detailed level:

	4110:Hardware Revenue	1000	1000
⊟ P_TP2:Computer Accessories	Units	81	81
	List Price	835	835
	4110:Hardware Revenue	14375	14375
⊞ P_TP3:Computer Services	Units		
	List Price		
	4110:Hardware Revenue		
⊟ P_TP:Total Product	Units	149	149

A data form has a Point of View, which as I've mentioned is a fixed set of members for dimensions that are not in the Page, Rows, or Columns. For example, if the data form should always use the Forecast scenario, you will probably add it to the Point of View. In general, users can't change the Point of View (often called POV, for short) selections. One exception is when dynamic user variables have been configured for the form.

A data form may also contain one or more Page drop-down boxes. A Page component is a drop-down list of members from a dimension. In the Forecast Sales – Products data form, the Page dimensions include: Product, Entity, and Version. You can choose the desired member from the Page drop-down by checking the box next to the member name:

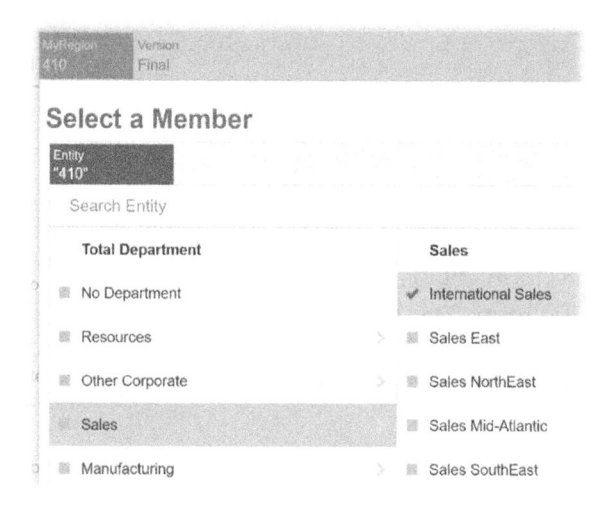

MyRegion	Version
410	Final

Select a Member

Entity
"410"

Search Entity

Total Department		Sales	
▪ No Department		✓ International Sales	
▪ Resources	>	▪ Sales East	
▪ Other Corporate	>	▪ Sales NorthEast	
▪ Sales		▪ Sales Mid-Atlantic	
▪ Manufacturing	>	▪ Sales SouthEast	

You'll notice the data hasn't changed. You have to click the arrow button (a.k.a. the *Go* button) to refresh the form:

Once you've selected the page options, you are ready to enter data into valid data cells by typing some numbers (or in some cases, text) into the data form.

There are four primary types of cells in a data form, each indicated by a different color (although hard to distinguish in the screen shot – darned black and white printing!):

White Cells	Valid data cells available for input
Yellow Cells	"Dirty" cells; A cell that is "dirty" indicates that data has been changed but not saved
Gray Cells	Read-only cells. You cannot edit or input data into these cells
Green Cells	Cells that have been recently changed and auto-saved

		FY15	FY15	FY15
	List Price	700	700	700
	4110:Hardware Revenue	5600	5600	
P_150:Other Computer	Units	13	13	13
	List Price	500	500	500
	4110:Hardware Revenue	6500		6500
P_160:Tablet Computer	Units	9	8	8
	List Price		800	800
	4110:Hardware Revenue	64	640	0
⊟ P_TP1:Computer Equipment	Units	80	68	47
	List Price	3700	3700	3700

A quick note on navigating the data forms: if you want to move horizontally, say from "Jan" to "Feb" to "Mar" while in the same row, then click *Tab*. If you want to move vertically, down the month of Jan for each row, then press *Enter*. Tab moves you from left to right, and Enter moves you from top to bottom when in data entry mode.

Before you get in too much of a hurry to input data in the forms, it might be helpful to view some instructions created by the administrator. To view instructions for a form, simply click *Data Entry* and click the *Instructions* icon:

EVERYTHING'S UNDER A MENU

Context sensitive *Actions* menus and right-click menus are used throughout the Simplified UI; the items under the Actions menus depend on what screen the user is in. In a data form, users can analyze with ad hoc analysis, create new ad hoc grids, run business rules, execute Smart Push, view validation messages, or clear the form's formatting:

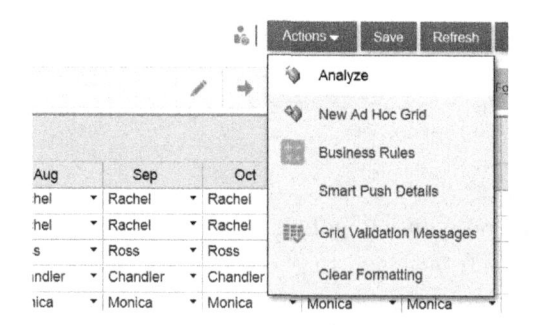

Many context sensitive actions are also available in right-click menus:

Look Smarter Than You Are with PBCS 479

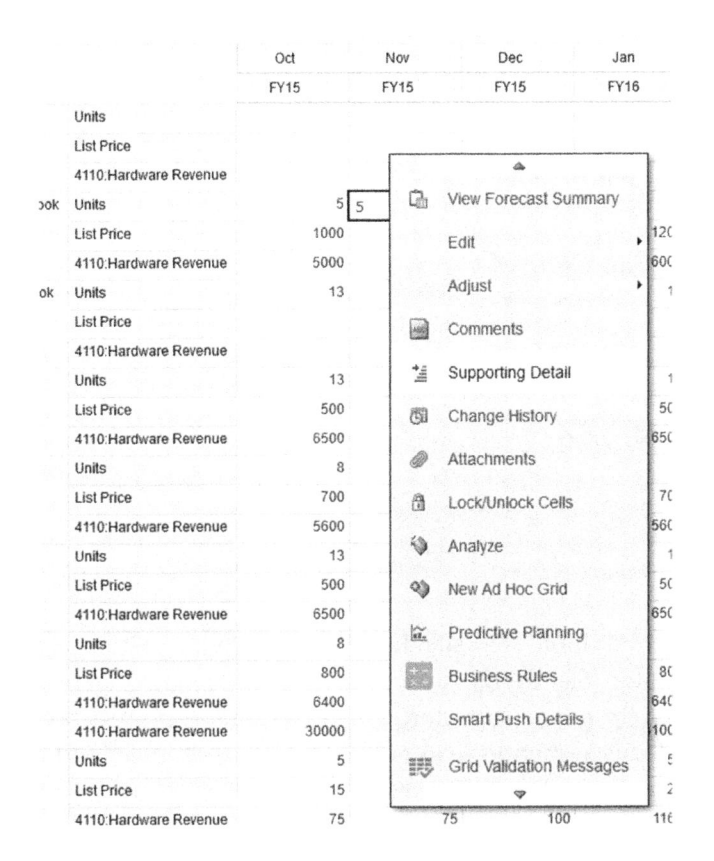

		Oct	Nov	Dec	Jan
		FY15	FY15	FY15	FY16
	Units				
	List Price				
	4110:Hardware Revenue				
ook	Units	5	5		12(
	List Price	1000			60(
	4110:Hardware Revenue	5000			1
ok	Units	13			
	List Price				
	4110:Hardware Revenue				
	Units	13			1
	List Price	500			5(
	4110:Hardware Revenue	6500			65(
	Units	8			
	List Price	700			7(
	4110:Hardware Revenue	5600			56(
	Units	13			1
	List Price	500			5(
	4110:Hardware Revenue	6500			65(
	Units	8			
	List Price	800			8(
	4110:Hardware Revenue	6400			64(
	4110:Hardware Revenue	30000			10(
	Units	5			
	List Price	15			2
	4110:Hardware Revenue	75	75	100	11(

Menu options shown: View Forecast Summary, Edit, Adjust, Comments, Supporting Detail, Change History, Attachments, Lock/Unlock Cells, Analyze, New Ad Hoc Grid, Predictive Planning, Business Rules, Smart Push Details, Grid Validation Messages.

PBCS provides options for users to interact with the data in data forms. There are menus for editing data, performing ad hoc analysis, and formatting:

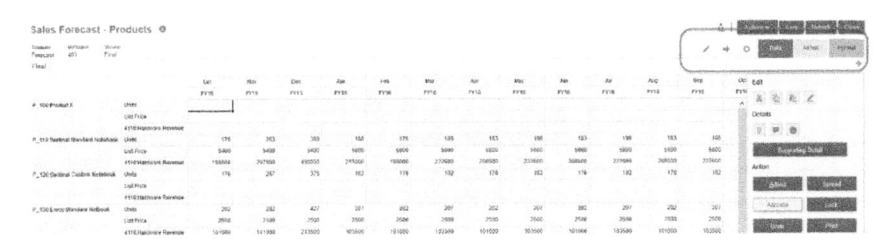

Below are the options available under the *Data, Ad Hoc,* and *Format* menus respectively:

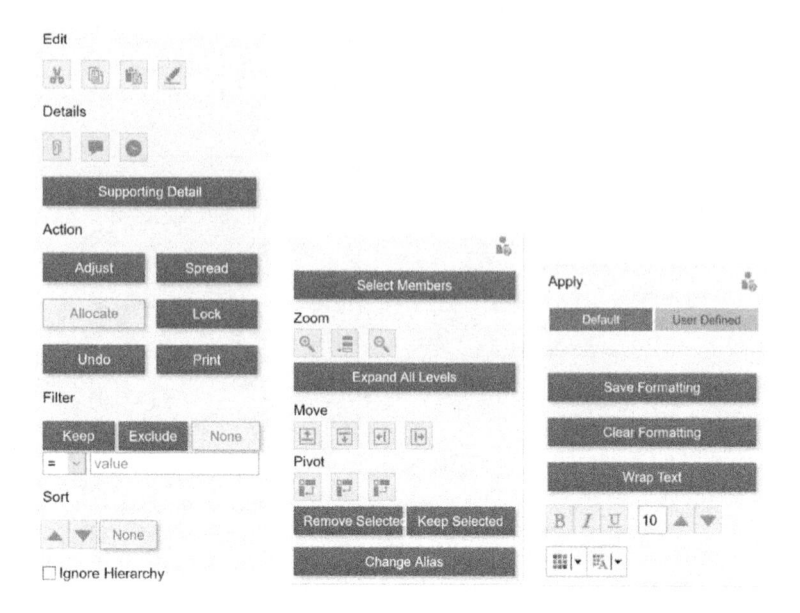

In addition to standard menu items within PBCS, the administrator may design some custom menu items under the Actions menu to help guide users through the planning process. Refer to the Action Menus section to read how an administrator can add additional action menu items for data forms.

Apply Filtering in a Data Form

Through the Data menu, you can apply filtering on data and metadata. Simply click the *Data* menu and go to the Filter section (or optionally you can right-click on the column and select *Filter*) to keep or exclude certain values or records:

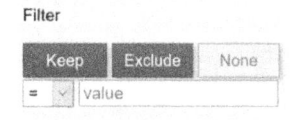

Filters are session specific. If you navigate away from the data form, you lose the filter.

Apply Sorting in a Data Form

You can also apply sorting in the hierarchy for data or metadata. Go to *Data >> Sort* (or optionally you can right-click on the column and select *Sort*) and click the arrow for *Sort Ascending* or *Sort Descending*:

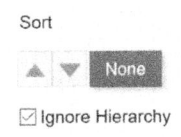

Sorting is session specific. If you navigate away from the data form, you lose the sort.

SELECT SMART LIST VALUES

Users can choose text values from pre-defined drop-down lists within a data form. These pre-defined lists are called Smart Lists and are created by the administrator. See the example below in which a user can select a Product Manager for each Product and Period:

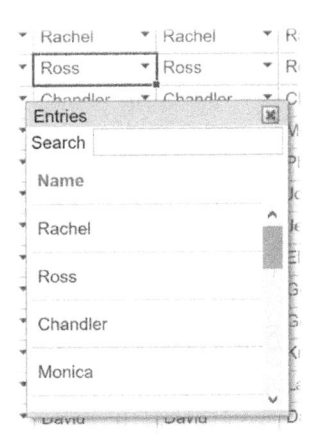

You can use Smart List values in business rules and reports.

ENTER TEXT & DATES

You can also enter free form text values or dates in data forms if enabled by the administrator (done by creating members with the "text" data type). Simply type in the empty cell. Be aware, keep it brief because display options are not optimized for text cells.

Refresh a Data Form

Let's face it, we've all made mistakes. What if you enter data but you don't want to save what you've done? Should you delete all of the values that you typed in? Try this and notice how the cells are still marked as "dirty" even though I deleted all of the data. If you want to make these cells "clean" again or go back to the original data values in the form without saving, one option is to refresh the data form.

Note! If the Autosave feature is turned on for the form, the best way to clean your cells is to undo your changes by pressing *Ctrl-Z*.

To refresh a data form (and not save data changes),
1. With the data form open, click *Refresh*.
2. The window below appears. Click *OK*:

Warning
There is unsaved data. If you proceed, this data will be lost. Do you wish to continue?
OK   Cancel

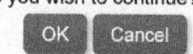

3. If you click *OK*, the form's data reverts back to the original values.

Save a Data Form

To save data, all you need to do is click *Save* (next to the actions menu). In general, Save recalculates the form's subtotals and possibly runs business rules associated with the form (this depends on how the administrator designed the form). If you change data and you try to leave the form without saving, you receive a prompt to save. Click *OK* to save and *Cancel* to discard.

If the Autosave feature is turned on (explained in more detail shortly), users don't need to manually save their form multiple times (unless business rules set to run on save need to be launched). The Autosave feature saves data once the user clicks out of their current cell.

Shortcut Keys

Users are granted further ease of use when inputting data into forms with the availability of shortcut keys in the Simplified UI. Shortcut keys can be used in simple forms and on the desktop only (not on a tablet).

The shortcut keys provided below are a combination of shortcuts that were available prior to PBCS and those new with the PBCS Simplified UI:

Shortcut Keys	Description
Ctrl+Home	Move to the first cell of the form
Ctrl+Z	Undo previous action(s) – can undo multiple actions at a time
Tab	Move to the next cell to the right
Enter	Move down one cell
K	Indication of a number in the thousands. For example, entering "5K" will result in 5,000
Up / Down arrow	Move up one cell / down one cell
Ctrl+Alt+B	Bold a value

Autosave & Undo

Administrators have the option to enable Autosave when creating data forms. Autosave is a neat, new feature in the Simplified UI that saves data input into a cell when a user tabs out of the cell. If a user mistakenly saves data by tabbing out of a cell, a Ctrl+Z shortcut undoes the mistake.

If Autosave is enabled, the cells turn green to indicate a saved cell (this would look really cool if the book was printed in color):

		Oct FY15	Nov FY15	Dec FY15
Training_P_291	4140:Training Revenue	500	700	750
Miscellaneous_P_292	4150:Miscellaneous Revenue			
Consulting_P_294	4130:Consulting Revenue			
Total Product	4120:Support Revenue	9895.5	9895.5	6606

Additionally, an option to *Run Form Rules* on Autosave can be enabled by the administrator to update dynamically calculated cells that depend on the autosaved cell values that were input by the user. If rules were run and Ctrl+Z is used, the rules that were run as a part of the Autosave is undone as well.

ADJUSTMENTS & DATA SPREADING

Adjust

Have you ever finished your budget only to be told by someone above you in the org chart that you need to increase revenue or decrease expenses? Rather than go back to the beginning every time you need to revise, Planning provides the ability to adjust data in cells by either a specific amount or a percentage. In the Simplified UI, only one cell can be adjusted at a time. Let's go through an example in the Simplified UI.

To adjust a cell,
1. Select the cell to adjust.
2. Open the *Data* menu and click *Adjust* (under Action section (or optionally you can right-click on the cell).
3. Type in the number or percentage to adjust by:

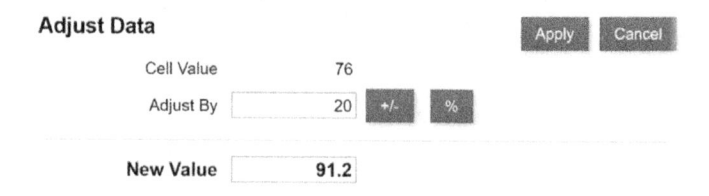

Adjust Data

Cell Value	76
Adjust By	20
New Value	91.2

4. Review the new value.
5. Click *Apply* to adjust the data.

Time Spreading

Time Spreading allows you to enter data at a summary level (like at the quarter or year level) and then have PBCS automatically push the data down to the time periods underneath. Let's explore time spreading in more detail.

While working in a data form, you can:

- Spread the value in a summary time period back to its base time periods
- Spread values among members based on the proportional values of existing data
- Spread values based on a calendar's weekly distribution in a quarter: 4-4-5, 5-4-4, 4-5-4, or None (this depends on how the administrator set up the application)

To spread, or distribute, data based on the Periods dimension,
1. On the data entry form, select the cell for the summary time period whose new value you want to spread.
2. Enter the new value.
3. When you leave the cell, the new values should spread to the time periods beneath the summary time period.

So how are the data values spread? It depends on the type of account or measure for which you are planning. For Revenue, Expense, and Saved Assumption Account (Flow) values entered at upper levels are spread to the children based on a percentage of the values already there. It sort of goal-seeks in a way. If there are no existing values, values are spread evenly or based on weekly seasonal distributions (4-4-5, 5-4-4, or 4-5-4).

For Asset, Liability, Equity Accounts, and Saved Assumption with Time Balance First, values entered at upper levels are placed in the first child. Other children remain unchanged. For example, if you change

Qtr 1 from "30" to "50", January changes to "50". February and March remain unchanged. If there are no existing values in any of a member's children, values entered at upper levels are placed in all children.

For Asset, Liability, Equity, and Saved Assumption Accounts with Time Balance Last, values entered at upper levels are placed in the last child. Other children remain unchanged. For example, if you change Qtr 1 from "30" to "50", March changes to "50". January and February remain unchanged. If there are no existing values in any of a member's children, values entered at upper levels are placed in all children.

Let's see an example of Time Spreading in action. Notice below I have January through March, rolling up to Q1:

	Jan	Feb	Mar	Q1
Units	500	400	400	1300
List Price				

Enter a new value into Q1. Once applied, the values are spread proportionally based on the existing data distribution:

	Jan	Feb	Mar	Q1
Units	600	480	480	1560
List Price				

You can temporarily lock a cell so that it is not impacted by spreading (PBCS ignores the locked cell) by selecting *Data >> Action >> Lock*.

Note! Months that have already been locked by administrators, cells with supporting detail, and other read-only cells are also skipped.

Grid Spread

Grid Spread allows you to increase or decrease cell values in your form by number or percentage. When using Grid Spread, the calculations are performed right then and there on your computer (the client), and you're able to see the calculation results so you can decide whether to save or not to save (to paraphrase Hamlet). Grid Spread in PBCS is available for users if enabled by the administrator.

There are three types of spreads: Regular, Chunky, and Extra Creamy. Wait, those are for peanut butter. There are three types of *Grid Spreads* – Proportional Spread, Evenly Split, and Fill:

- **Proportional** – divides a value across members and dimensions in proportion to the values that are already there
- **Evenly split** – divides a value evenly across the base level members
- **Fill** – fills the base members with a specified value

To perform a grid spread in a data form,
1. Select the upper level cell to adjust.
2. Click the *Data* button near the top right of the data form (or optionally you can right-click on the cell).
3. Under Actions, click *Spread*.
4. Adjust the cell by a number or percentage and select a spread method:

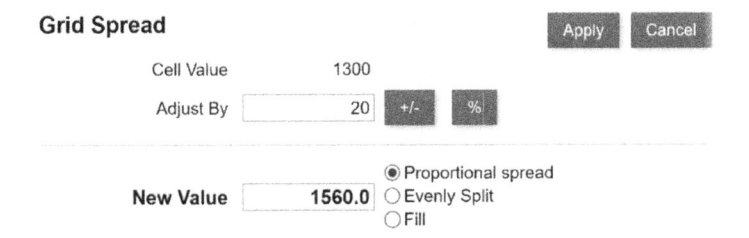

Grid Spread

Cell Value	1300
Adjust By	20 +/- %
New Value	1560.0 ◉ Proportional spread ○ Evenly Split ○ Fill

5. Click *Apply* and review.
6. Click *Save* to save changes.

Note! The Simplified UI only allows one cell to be selected at a time. As a result, Grid Spread in the Simplified UI can be done one cell at a time.

ATTACHMENTS, COMMENTARY, & DETAIL

Add Attachments to Data Forms

Sometimes you have some supporting information in the form of reports and you'd like to attach them to your planning data. In PBCS users can attach reference documents to a cell on a form by inputting a reference URL.

I'll walk through a basic example to show you how to do this.

To add an attachment to a data form,
1. Select a cell in a data form to add an attachment to.
2. Go to *Data* >> *Details* >> *Attachment* (paper clip icon) (or optionally you can right-click on the cell):

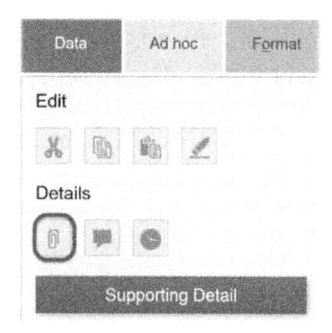

3. Enter a Reference URL and click *Post*:

Note! The report URL can be copied by going to *Explore* (in the PBCS repository), right-clicking the report, going to *Properties*, then copying the *SmartCut* URL segment:

Attachments

admin
1/13/16 11:54 PM
/workspace/browse/get/VISION%20Reports/Total%20Revenue%20by%20Product
Edit Delete

Enter Reference URL

Post Close

General Properties

* Name: Total Revenue by Product
Description:

UUID: 00000151b11bb964-0000-53ce-0ac80c29
Owner: admin admin(admin) Change Owner
SmartCut: /workspace/browse/get/VISION%20Reports/Total%20Revenue%20by%20Product

To open the attachment, click the cell containing the attachment, click the *Attachments* icon, and click the URL. Since the URL links to a Financial Reporting Studio report in HTML view, you may need to enter some additional information, such as run-time prompt entries, to view the report.

Add Supporting Details

What you shouldn't do is come up with your budget outside of PBCS and then copy the summary values in. If you want to show where a summary number comes from, Supporting Detail allows you list out the assumptions and drivers you used to calculate the required number on the form.

Some people refer to Supporting Detail as "line item detail" because it allows end users to provide detail below the bottom-level in the PBCS model. For example, there may be an account called "Travel" and you want to include details for each trip that makes up the travel account. You can build a hierarchy of supporting detail under a cell or cells using different methods for aggregation (+ - * / ~).

To enter or view Supporting Detail,
1. Select the desired cell and go to *Data >> Supporting Detail* (or optionally you can right-click on the cell):

The Supporting Detail window displays.

2. Click *Actions* and use the following actions to enter supporting detail lines: *Add Child* adds a line below the selected line and *Add Sibling* adds a line next to the selected line, etc.):

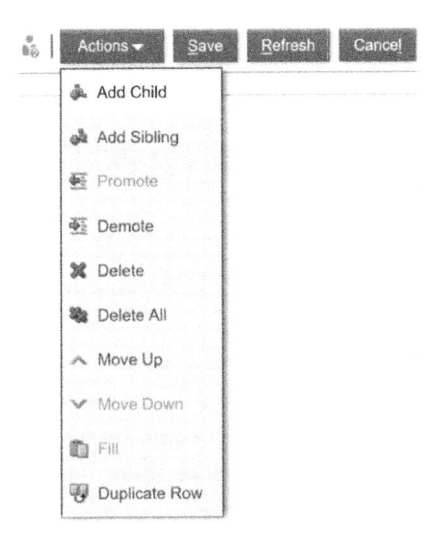

[Actions menu screenshot showing: Add Child, Add Sibling, Promote, Demote, Delete, Delete All, Move Up, Move Down, Fill, Duplicate Row]

3. Once the lines are added in the supporting detail window, you can add text to label the details, select an operator and enter the amount:

Supporting Detail

	Operator	Oct
Base	+	70.0
Additional	+	16.0
Total		86.0

4. Click *Save*.

The form saves and the cell with the supporting details is shaded a deep blue color:

	Oct	Nov
Units		
List Price		
4110:Hardware Revenue		
Units	86	106
List Price	30	30
4110:Hardware Revenue	2580	3180
Units	151	151
List Price	250	250

Print Supporting Details

You might want to print the supporting details included on a data form. The option to print supporting details is set by default by the administrator during form creation, or it can be selected at the time of printing.

Administrators can include supporting details in printed forms by default by simply checking the *Include supporting detail* option under Printing Options in the form Layout tab.

To enable supporting details at the time of printing,
1. Go to *Data Entry* and select the form to print.
2. Go to *Data >> Print*:

3. Check *Include supporting detail* under Printing Options:

```
Printing Options

Paper Size    Letter

        Print Form  ☑    Include      ☑   Normal Order
              Name         supporting
    Repeat Column  ☑       detail
           Headers
       Repeat Row  ☑
          Headers
   Print Grid Lines  ☑
    Print POV/Page  ☑
       Print Footer  ☑
     Print in Black  ☐
        and White
```

4. Click *Print Preview*, then *Open* or *Save* the file to do what you wish with it.

Add Comments

Once in a while, you'll want to comment on an individual value in your form. Maybe a variance is off and you want to explain why or maybe you need to explain why "Going to Cabo" is a legitimate business expense.

Comments let you add commentary to your plan. Cell-level text comments can be added to any intersection at any level in a data form using the Actions menu or right-clicking in the desired cell:

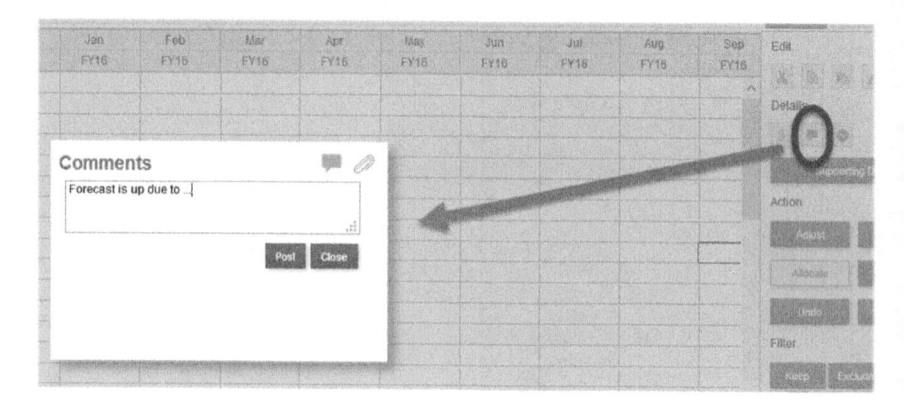

All users who have read access to the cell can read the cell text comment. The comment can be printed within the data form.

To enter comments in a data form, simply click on a cell and go to *Data*. Under Details, click the *Comments* icon.

FORMATTING

PBCS allows user-defined formatting for all forms and grids in the Simplified UI. Default formatting or user-defined formatting can be applied to the data forms. Formatting can be saved or cleared, if desired. The option to wrap text in data cells is also available. Form numbers or text can be bolded, italicized, or underlined, and the font sizes can be adjusted as well.

To format a form, simply click the *Format* menu and add your desired formatting options:

Look Smarter Than You Are with PBCS 495

A sample of a form with some formatting is shown below (cell color, cell text color, and bolded values):

		Jan	Feb	Mar	Q1
P_000:No Product	Units	500	400	400	1300
	List Price				
	4110:Hardware Revenue				
P_100:Product X	Units				
	List Price				
	4110:Hardware Revenue				
P_110:Sentinal Standard Notebook	Units	13	13	13	39
	List Price	1350	1200	1200	3750
	4110:Hardware Revenue	17550	15600	15600	48750
P_120:Sentinal Custom Notebook	Units	13	13	13	39
	List Price				
	4110:Hardware Revenue				
P_130:Envoy Standard Netbook	Units	13	13	13	39

As an added bonus, users can adjust the height and width of a column or row with a click and a drag, or by right-clicking a row or column and entering in a pixel value:

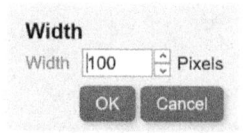

VIEW MEMBER FORMULAS

Have you ever wondered, "Where in the heck did this number come from?" The PBCS administrator usually creates a number of calculations for the Planning application that automatically derive numbers based on your plan inputs. In many cases, this is done using member formulas. You can view the logic behind the member formula calculations. In the example below, the administrator has enabled *Member Formula* on the Sales Forecast – Products data form.

Once the administrator has enabled the Member Formula option for a specific row or column, users can view the formulas in the data forms.

Click the *Formula* icon to view:

P_120:Sentinal Custom Notebook	Units	106	106
	List Price	350	350
	4110:Hardware Revenue *f*	37100	37100
P_130:Envoy Standard Netbook	Units		
	List Price		
	4110:Hardware Revenue *f*		

The member formula appears in a box:

Member Formula
If (@ISMBR("Forecast"))
"Units"*"List Price";
ENDIF

ANALYZE

Users can perform ad hoc analysis within a data form with the Analyze feature. Security is honored through ad hoc grids so users can still read and update data where they have been assigned access.

Users can perform the following ad hoc actions:

Ad Hoc Option	Description
Pivot	Move a dimension from and to Page, Row or Column
Move	Move a dimension Up, Down, Left or Right when more than one dimension is listed in a Row, Column or Page
Zoom In Next Level	Drill down into the next level of a hierarchy of a dimension
Zoom In Bottom Level	Zoom into all Level 0 members of a specified parent member
Zoom Out	Drill up a hierarchy to the parent of the selected member
Expand All Levels	Expand the entire hierarchy of the selected member
Keep Selected	Keep the selected member(s) and remove all other members in that dimension
Remove Selected	Remove the selected member(s) and keep all other members in that dimension
Select Members	Launch a member selection window for the member selected
Change Alias	Toggle between alternate alias tables for an application

To use the Analyze feature in a data form, go to *Actions >> Analyze* (or optionally you can right-click in the grid):

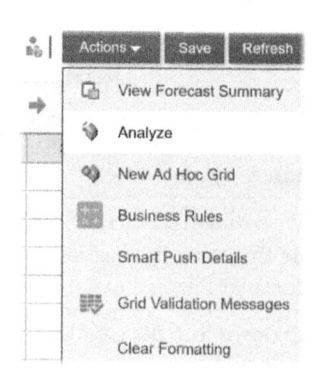

498   Chapter 10: End User Activities

[Actions menu showing: View Forecast Summary, Analyze, New Ad Hoc Grid, Business Rules, Smart Push Details, Grid Validation Messages, Clear Formatting]

Once in Analyze mode, users can use typical analytic functions like zooming, pivoting, and selecting members by going to the *Ad hoc* menu:

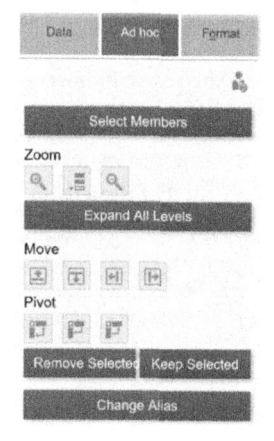

[Ad hoc menu showing: Select Members, Zoom, Expand All Levels, Move, Pivot, Remove Selected, Keep Selected, Change Alias]

Users can save the form definition for future use by selecting *Actions >> Save Ad Hoc Grid*:

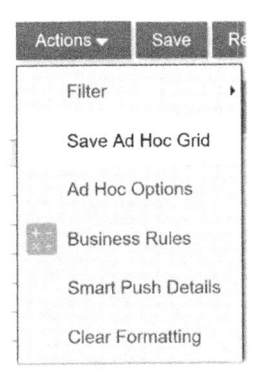

You enter a name for the definition:

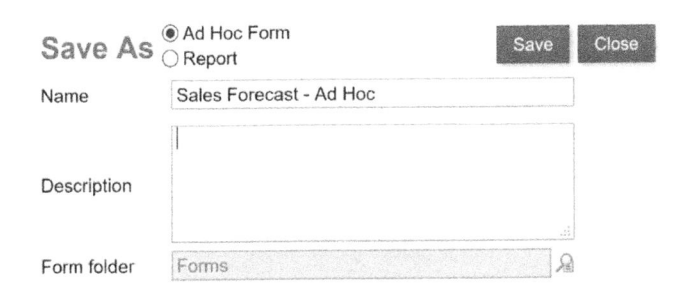

By default, the ad hoc grid is saved under *Data Entry* in the *Forms* folder.

Note! *Save* does not save the ad hoc definition such as the POV. *Save* only saves any data changes that you made in ad hoc mode.

You can change the default ad hoc options to support your analyzing experience. Click *Ad Hoc Options* within an ad hoc form:

The Ad Hoc Options window opens with various property options (not all options are shown below):

Ad Hoc Options

Member inclusion	☑ Include selection ☐ Within selected group
Zoom in levels	⦿ Next level ○ All levels ○ Bottom level
Ancestor Position	○ Top ⦿ Bottom
Navigate without refreshing data	○ Yes ⦿ No

Suppress

Zeros	☐ Row ☐ Column
	☐ Repeat Members ☐ Missing Blocks on Rows

Precision

	Minimum	Maximum
Currency values	0	None
Non-currency values	0	None
Percentage values	0	None

Under Ad Hoc Options, you can choose the drill behavior – do you want to keep the member that you zoom on or not? Do you want to show the member name, the alias, or both? Do you want to suppress missing data? You can set options for these under Ad Hoc Options.

Available Ad Hoc Options include member inclusion, display of member names and aliases, ancestor position, indentation, suppression (including suppression of data for columns), precision, and replacement options for missing or no-access data cells.

The Analyze feature is great for taking an existing data form's structure and then going to "ad hoc" mode. To create a grid completely from scratch, users can create ad hoc grids.

USE SMART FORMS

Simply put, Smart Forms are saved ad hoc grids that allow Excel formulas and grid labels to be added that are not defined in the

Look Smarter Than You Are with PBCS   501

application. Smart Forms are available in the Simplified UI and in Smart View.

In the Simplified UI, Smart Forms can be found when filtering on *Smart Form* in the Data Entry area:

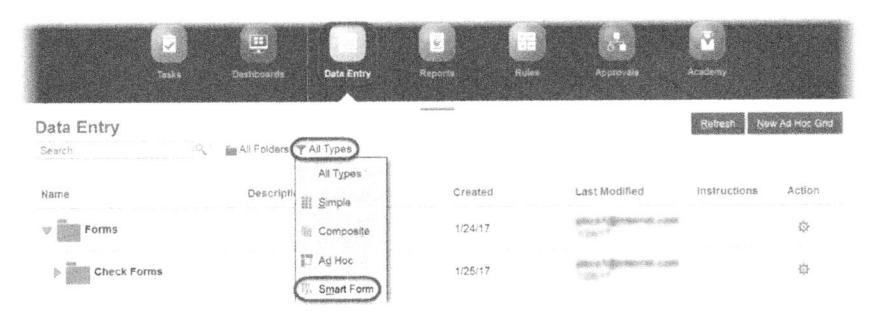

Hover over the calculated cells to view the formulas:

To view Smart Forms in Smart View, connect to the application and open the form. Then double-click the form to open. Grid labels show as orange and the calculated cells show as light green:

RUNNING BUSINESS RULES

If you need to run either simple or complex calculations on your Planning data, then business rules are going to be your weapon of choice. Business rules perform calculations on data, like aggregating data from detail levels to summary levels, allocating data from summary levels to detailed levels, copying data, clearing data, and more. Business rules, in most cases, are created by the PBCS administrator.

Some business rules are attached to data forms and automatically run when you save the form. You can also launch a business rule associated with a data form by going to *Actions >> Business Rules* or right-clicking in the grid.

Some business rules may not be associated with a specific data form. Go to *Rules* to select and run any business rule in the PBCS application by clicking the *Launch* arrow. The list of business rules for which the current user has access is shown. Users have the option to filter business rules by Cube or Rule Type:

Type	Name	Description	Launch
	CalcAll		→
	Calculate MyForecast		→
	Seed Forecast based on Actuals		→
	Export Forecast and Actuals Data		→
	CalcAccts_Script		→

Business Rules
All Cubes All Rule Types

Depending on the rule, it may run a few seconds or a few minutes. A message displays letting you know the business rule has run successfully (or if it failed in misery with errors).

Run-time Prompts

Sometimes you may be prompted to enter some information for the business rule. What market should be calculated? What period should be calculated? What percent should be used in the bonus calculation?

Business rules have the ability to prompt users for values when they are launched. This is conveniently called a "run-time prompt." Say you need to recalculate your department budget after submitting data. A single business rule is created for all the departments, and all you have to do is select your specific department when prompted by the business rule. The rule runs for your department.

For example, you may create a business rule that prompts users to select a Scenario, Version, and Segment. A *Member Search* icon is available to search the dimensions for a specific member or members. If you know the desired member name exactly, simply type it in. Click the *Launch* icon to run the business rule.

The administrator dictates the rules for run-time prompts. They can be single or multiple members, numeric value, Smart List value, or text value. Members available for run-time prompts are limited by your security and any other limitations defined by the administrator.

APPROVALS

Approvals can be used as a mechanism for reviewing, tracking, and approving plans via the Simplified UI or Smart View. The administrator may define approval paths for plans, set validations to highlight exceptions, view audit information for plans and comments, and annotate the plans.

Approvals are managed by Planning Units. The Planning Unit consists of the Entity, Scenario, and Version dimensions. Once Planning Units are initiated, users enter their plans in the data forms and run business rules, then submit their plans for review and approval.

Under Approvals, users can view the status of approvals and sort through them by Approvals Status, Current Owner, or Planning Unit Name.

The administrator must complete several steps before you are ready to use Approvals. Check out the Oracle documentation for more information. This is a way-cool journey that I will take in a future version of this book.

RUN REPORTS

Reports that were created via Financial Reporting Studio or Ad Hoc Grids that are saved as reports are saved in the Reports section of the Simplified UI. Simply click the *Reports* icon from the Simplified UI main menu:

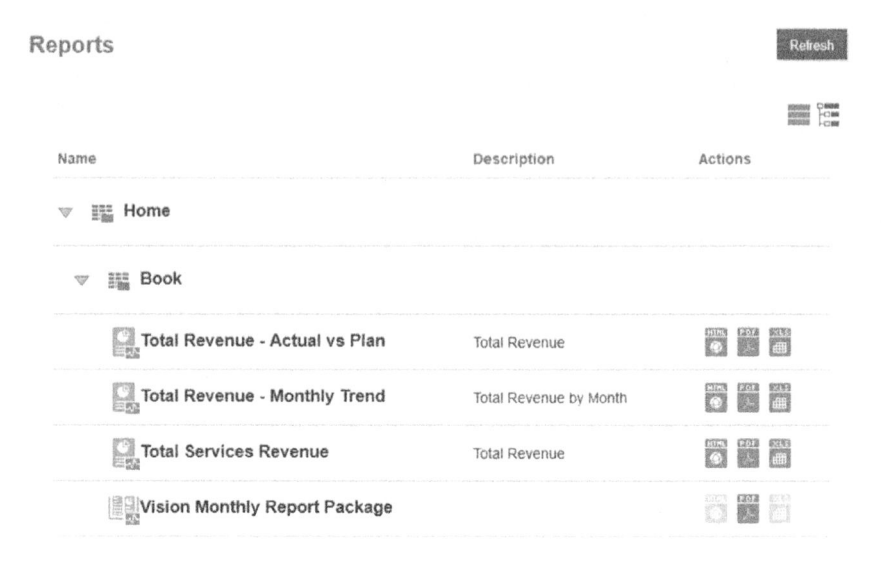

Reports

Name	Description	Actions
▽ Home		
▽ Book		
Total Revenue - Actual vs Plan	Total Revenue	HTML PDF XLS
Total Revenue - Monthly Trend	Total Revenue by Month	HTML PDF XLS
Total Services Revenue	Total Revenue	HTML PDF XLS
Vision Monthly Report Package		HTML PDF XLS

The reports can be viewed in HTML, Excel, or as a PDF:

Some reports require users to specify the members for each dimension for the user point of view:

Total Revenue by Product

Account	4001	Version	Final
HSP_View	BaseData	Entity	410

Other reports may be designed to use report prompts. End users answer prompts and the report is displayed:

The following prompt has been defined in the report. You may use the default values shown, or select other members.

Respond to Prompts at Report Level

Prompt	Selection	Type	Source
Enter Years:	FY15	Report	Report: Total Revenue by Product Grid: All

Finally, the report opens in another window:

Account: 4001 | HSP_View: BaseData | Version: Final | Entity: 410

Total Revenue by Products - FY15

(Report in Thousands)

	Jan	Feb	Mar	Apr	May
	Actual	Actual	Actual	Actual	Actual
Total Product					
Computer Equipment					
Product X					
Sentinal Standard Notebook					
Sentinal Custom Notebook					
Envoy Standard Netbook					
Envoy Custom Netbook					
Other Computer					

Note! In HTML view, POV members can be changed; simply click the blue dimension buttons at the top of the report.

SETTINGS

Define Application Settings

Users can also select a number of settings to make PBCS behave like it's your own personal budgeting product. The Application Settings tab is where you can access and make changes to several preference options. You can enable e-mail notifications so that you automatically receive e-mail notifications when you become the new owner of a planning unit. You can also control the display of member names or their aliases, set number formatting options, or change the time zone.

To access application settings, select *Navigator >> Application >> Settings*:

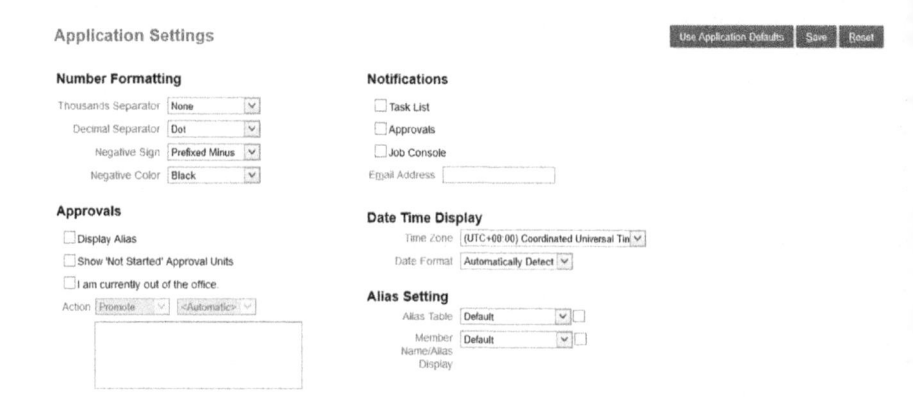

Depending on the user's provisioning, they may also be to access the application settings by selecting *Navigator >> Create and Manage >> Preferences*.

Users have the option to stick with the application defaults (defined by the PBCS administrator) or define their own application settings. Be sure to click *Save* once settings have been defined:

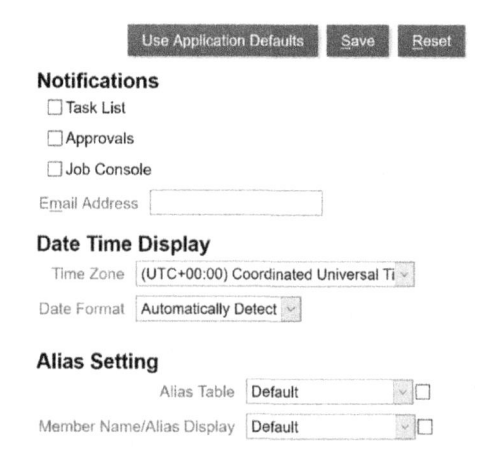

Review My Jobs

Users can view the jobs they have run by selecting *Navigator >> Application >> Jobs*. The list shown is filtered for the user's jobs:

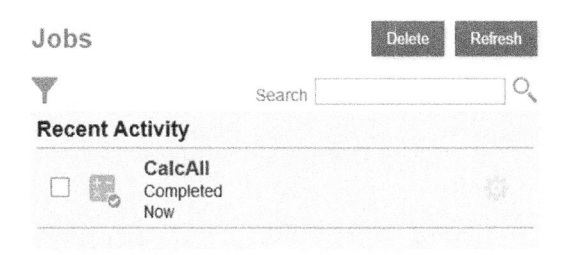

```
Jobs                          Delete   Refresh
▼              Search                    🔍
Recent Activity
    ☐  📋  CalcAll
           Completed
           Now
```

Set User Variables

User Variables allow data forms to be filtered for just the members end users want to see. For example, an end user may have read access to all entities but write access for the International Sales entity. When he inputs the sales forecast, he really only cares about International Sales. So the administrator sets up a User Variable called "MyRegion" and designs the Sales Forecast – Products form to select this variable. The end user sets his MyRegion variable to "International Sales" and the form only shows International Sales and not the other entities.

The Sales Forecast – Products data form was created to contain one User Variable: MyRegion. If you open the data form without defining a User Variable for MyRegion, you get an error message that states that "members must be selected before the form can be opened." You cannot open a data form that contains a User Variable if you haven't selected a member for that variable.

Depending on provisioning, users can define their User Variable settings by selecting *Navigator >> Tools >> Variables* or selecting *Navigator >> Create and Manage >> Preferences*.

To set the User Variables,
1. Navigate to the user variable settings by selecting *Navigator >> Tools >> Variables* (or selecting *Navigator >> Create and Manage >> Preferences* and click the *User Variables* tab):

User Variables

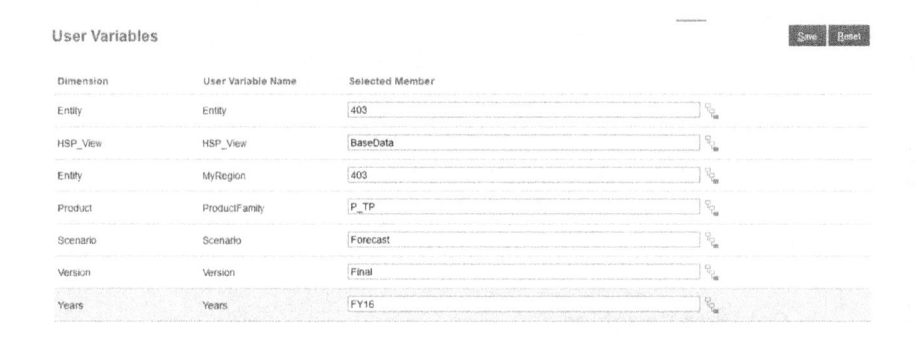

Dimension	User Variable Name	Selected Member
Entity	Entity	403
HSP_View	HSP_View	BaseData
Entity	MyRegion	403
Product	ProductFamily	P_TP
Scenario	Scenario	Forecast
Version	Version	Final
Years	Years	FY16

2. Use the Member Selector to designate a member for both user variables:

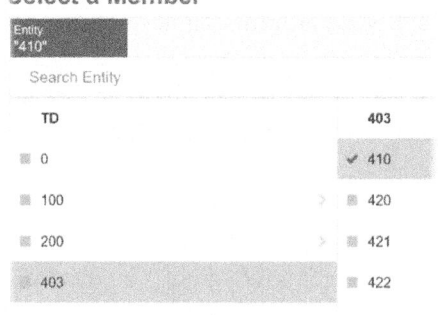

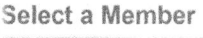

Select a Member

Entity: "410"

Search Entity

TD		403
☐ 0		✓ 410
☐ 100	>	☐ 420
☐ 200	>	☐ 421
403		☐ 422

Note! You can type "P_TP1" or any other member name into the text box if you know the exact spelling of the member name.

3. Click *Save*.
4. Open the Sales Forecast – Products form and notice the form defaults to the member that was selected for MyRegion:

Sales Forecast - Products

Scenario: Forecast MyRegion: 410 Version: Pass1

		Oct FY15	Nov FY15
P_100:Product X	Units	86	106
	List Price	30	30
	4110:Hardware Revenue	2580	3180

As you can see, user variables provide huge time savings when it comes to data form development for power users and administrators.

ADD MEMBERS ON THE FLY

The administrator might enable a feature called "add new members on the fly" which allows users to add members dynamically from within forms.

To add members on the fly (if enabled and configured by your administrator like I did for new products),
1. From the Simplified UI, navigate to *Data Entry >> Add Product Members* data form and open it.
2. Right-click on one of the dimension members in the POV bar. You see a custom action menu, *Enter new product members*. Click on it.

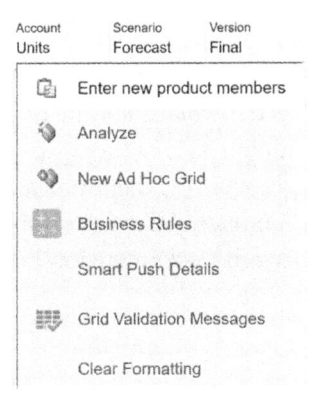

Account: Units Scenario: Forecast Version: Final

- Enter new product members
- Analyze
- New Ad Hoc Grid
- Business Rules
- Smart Push Details
- Grid Validation Messages
- Clear Formatting

3. Enter a new product "External Hard Drive":

AddDynamicProducts

* Product Name | External Hard Drive |

4. Click *Launch* to launch the rule. If the rule launches successfully, a confirmation message shows:

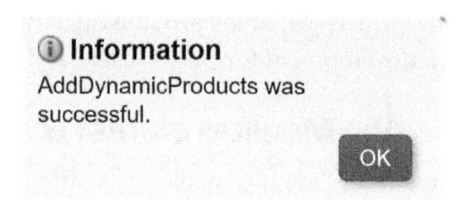

> ⓘ **Information**
> AddDynamicProducts was successful.
>
> OK

Up to 25 new products can be added under the New Products member, based on the criteria originally set in the member properties. The new products are listed in the data:

Add Product Members

Account Units	Scenario Forecast	Version Final	Entity No Entity	Period Apr
		FY16		
External Hard Drive				
⊟ New Products				

The next time the PBCS administrator refreshes the database, the new product names replace the placeholders originally created.

Once the new member is added, users may not change the member name. If the business rule is set up properly, there are options to let users delete the new member. Administrators can update the member name or delete the member in the Dimension Editor.

PREDICTIVE ANALYTICS

PBCS supports Predictive Analytics, a statistical forecasting feature that is accessible to all PBCS users over the web and in Smart View. Predictive Analytics provides the following features and benefits:

- Utilize statistical prediction scenarios
- Enables sanity check during forecast cycles
- Ability to compare accuracy of forecasts versus statistical predictions
- Uses Crystal Ball's Predictor to analyze historical data and projects trends and patterns into the future. Crystal Ball Predictor is a powerful time-series forecasting tool that leverages Microsoft Excel. It can create professional forecasting charts and reports
- Users review forecasted values, override if needed, then submit back to Planning
- Automatically forecast best and worst case scenarios in addition to base case

To predict future values, you first create a valid form to be used. Predictive Planning accesses historical data for the members on the form, analyzes the data for trends and seasonal variations, and then predicts future values based on this information. Once the form is created, open the form and select *Predictive Planning* from the Actions menu. The results displays with the historical data, forecast, and the predictions. You can use the information to help update your forecasts.

PLAN IN EXCEL USING SMART VIEW

Good news! Smart View and all the neat things you can do with it are also available with PBCS. If you are not familiar with Smart View, it is NOT just another Excel add-in for Oracle EPM. Its capabilities are far greater than any other Hyperion Excel add-in you've seen to date. Smart View provides a common Microsoft Office interface to multiple tools including Essbase, Financial Management, on-premises Planning, Financial Reporting, and more. This means you can use Microsoft Excel to input data and Microsoft Excel, Word, or PowerPoint to view, manipulate, report, and share data.

Combining the powers of PBCS and Smart View allows planners to update data in forms, calculate data using business rules, and utilize most of the other features available through the PBCS web client, all through Microsoft Excel (if you are a financially minded individual, you know that Excel is as valuable as your left hand). The chart below shows the similarities between the PBCS web client and Smart View (everything you can do in the web from an end user perspective you can do in Smart View):

Feature	Enterprise Planning Cloud Web Client	Smart View
Web	Yes	No
Enter Data	Yes	Yes
Launch Business Rules	Yes	Yes
Supporting Detail	Yes	Yes
Cell Text	Yes	Yes
Adjust	Yes	Yes
Mass Allocate, Grid Spread	Yes	Yes
Linked Excel Formulas	No	Yes
View Instructions	Yes	Yes
Workflow	Yes	Yes
Copy / Paste	Yes	Yes
Client Install Required	No	Yes
Composite Forms	Yes	Yes
Update User Variables	Yes	Yes
Smart Form	Yes (but not editing)	Yes
Task List	Yes	Yes
Cascade Data	No	Yes

As you can see, almost everything that you can do in the PBCS web client can be done in Smart View. You may have noticed that Smart View requires a client install. To do this, select the drop-down under your logged in ID in the upper right corner and choose *Downloads*.

Choose *Smart View for Office*. Follow the installation process and you will notice a Smart View ribbon in Excel.

Note! Always download the latest version of Smart View. If there is an older version installed on your computer, uninstall it first then install the current version through PBCS.

Let's go over how do use some of these awesome Smart View features, starting with connecting to the VISION application with Smart View.

To connect to an application in Smart View,
1. Open Microsoft Excel.
2. Click the *Smart View* ribbon:

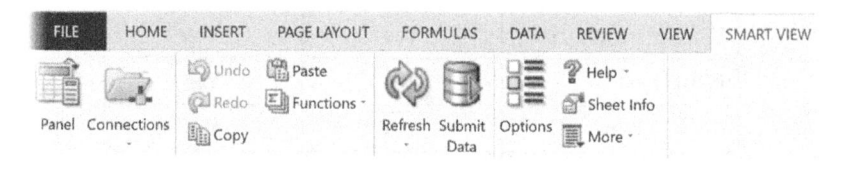

3. Click *Options* and click the *Advanced* tab.
4. In Shared Connection URL, enter the connection URL. A sample URL is below:

https://servicename-test-domainname.PBCS.Cloud.us1.oraclecloud.com/workspace/SmartViewProviders

5. Click *OK*.

Note! The Shared Connections URL only needs to be input once for each instance. If you want to connect to another instance (say you want to change from Test to Production), a new Shared Connections URL must be entered.

6. Click the *Panel* icon (to the very left).

7. When the Panel appears, click *Shared Connections*:

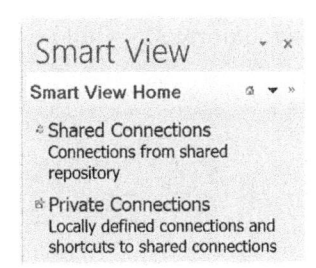

8. Enter the domain. Click *OK*.
9. Enter your username and password. Click *OK*.
10. In the Panel, select *Oracle Hyperion Planning, Fusion Edition* from the server drop-down menu.
11. Expand the server and VISION application folder:

Connection to the application is complete.

To open a data form, input data, and save data in Smart View,

1. In the Panel, expand the *Forms* folder and double-click on the desired form (or click *Open form*).
2. Enter data as you normally would into Excel:

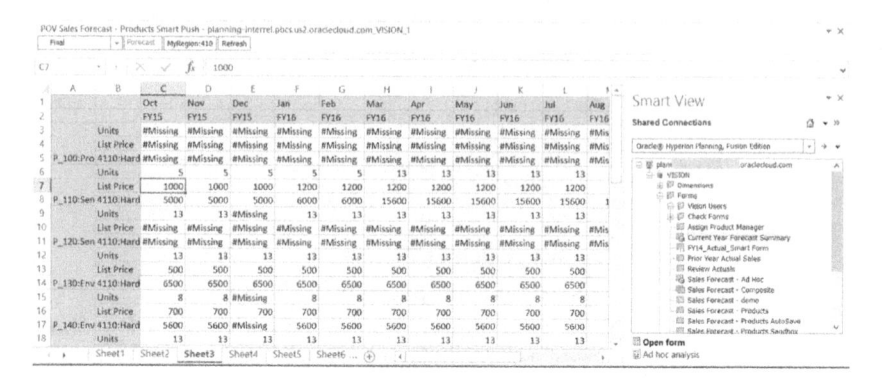

3. To save the data back to PBCS, click *Submit Data* in the Planning ribbon (this ribbon appears when you open a data form):

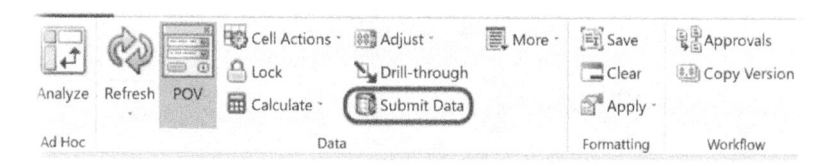

Using the Planning panel, users can also add comments, supporting detail, and attachments, calculate data by running business runs, and adjust data. In addition, users can access and perform Task List activities by opening the Task List folder and double-clicking on a task:

Look Smarter Than You Are with PBCS   517

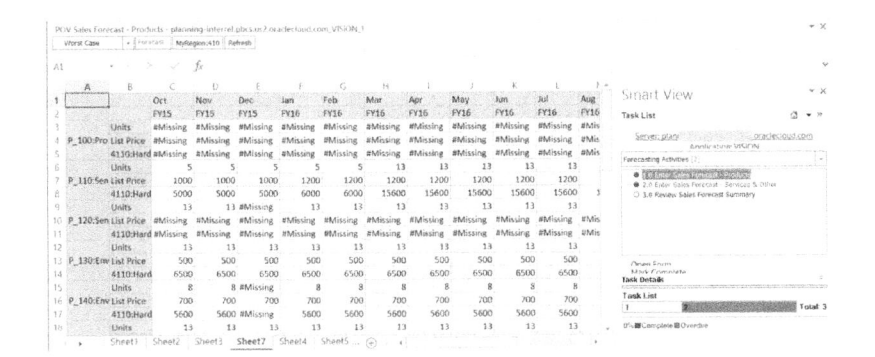

[Screenshot of Smart View ad hoc grid with POV Sales Forecast - Products data showing months Oct FY15 through Aug FY16 across columns, with rows for P_100, P_110, P_120, P_130, P_140 products including List Price, Hard, Units data. Task List panel visible on right side.]

To perform ad hoc analysis in Smart View,
1. Click on a database (a.k.a. cube):

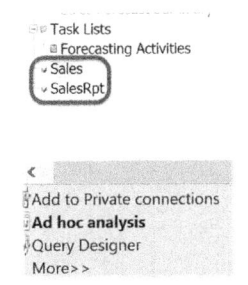

[Screenshot showing Task Lists > Forecasting Activities with Sales and SalesRpt options circled]

[Screenshot showing menu options: Add to Private connections, Ad hoc analysis, Query Designer, More>>]

2. Click *Ad hoc analysis* to open a blank ad hoc grid:

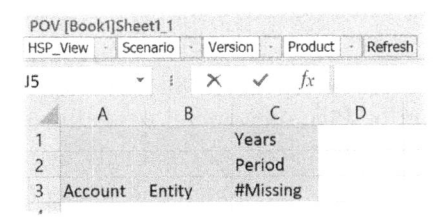

[Screenshot of blank ad hoc grid with POV [Book1]Sheet1_1, showing HSP_View, Scenario, Version, Product, Refresh buttons, and grid with Years, Period, Account, Entity, #Missing]

The Planning Ad Hoc ribbon displays:

[Screenshot of Planning Ad Hoc ribbon showing: Zoom In, Zoom Out, Pivot, Keep Only, Remove Only, Member Selection, Query, Preserve Format, Change Alias, Smart Slice, Save Ad Hoc Grid, Save As Smart Form, Cascade — under Analysis group]

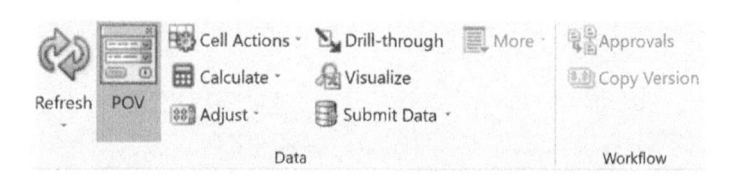

3. Select dimension members (or type them in if you are sure of the exact spelling) and zoom in, zoom out, pivot, and cascade to analyze away!

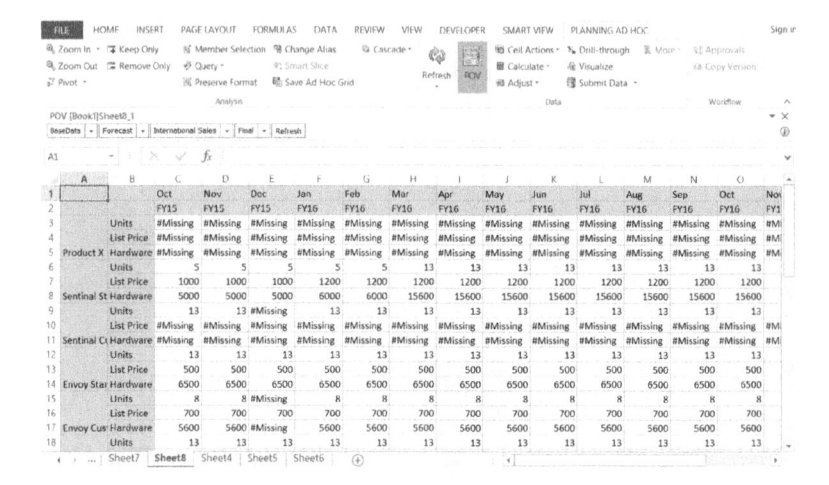

Ad hoc grids can be saved by users for later use.

Note! To perform ad hoc analysis on a data form, click *Analyze* in the Planning ribbon while the form is open in Smart View. Alternatively, you can select a form in the Panel and click *Ad hoc analysis*.

I've really just skimmed the surface with Smart View and all of its functionality. Check out the *Look Smarter Than You Are with Smart View* book as that book contains more details on Smart View features.

RETAIN EXCEL FORMATTING / CUSTOM STYLES

You can apply formatting to data forms and ad hoc grids in Smart View by choosing the Save icon under formatting (note this is not available in Analyze mode):

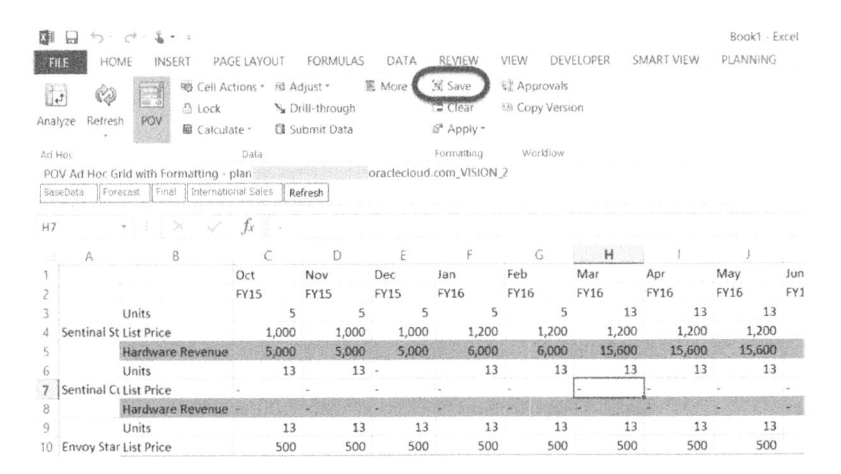

If saving an ad hoc grid, you can choose to *Submit Formatting*:

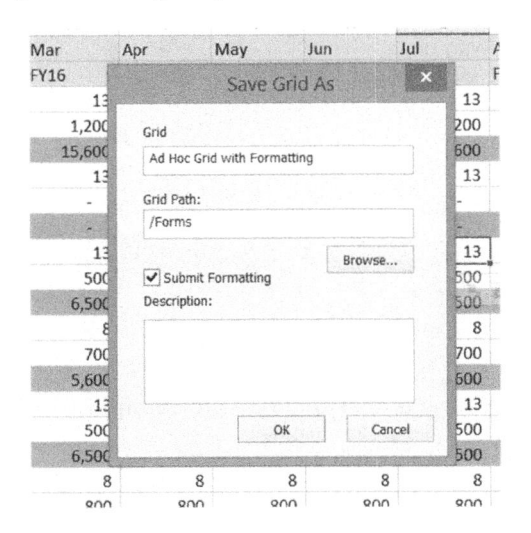

Now when you reopen the data form or ad hoc grid in Smart View, you can reapply the custom formatting. By default, cell styles are applied. Select *Apply >> Custom Styles*:

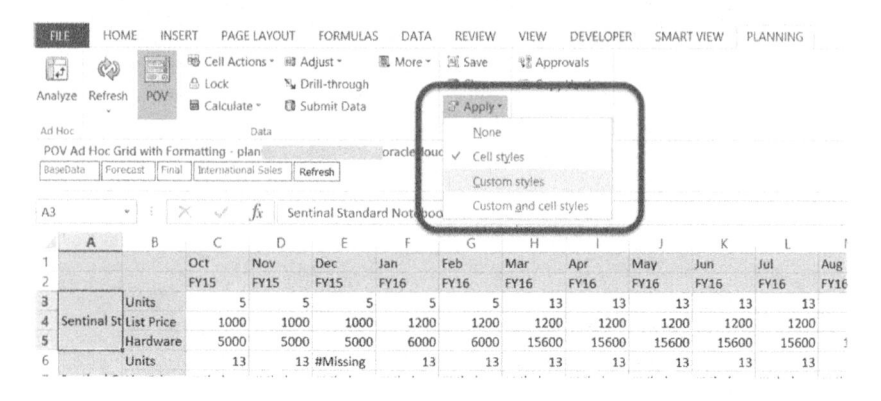

And the formatting is reapplied:

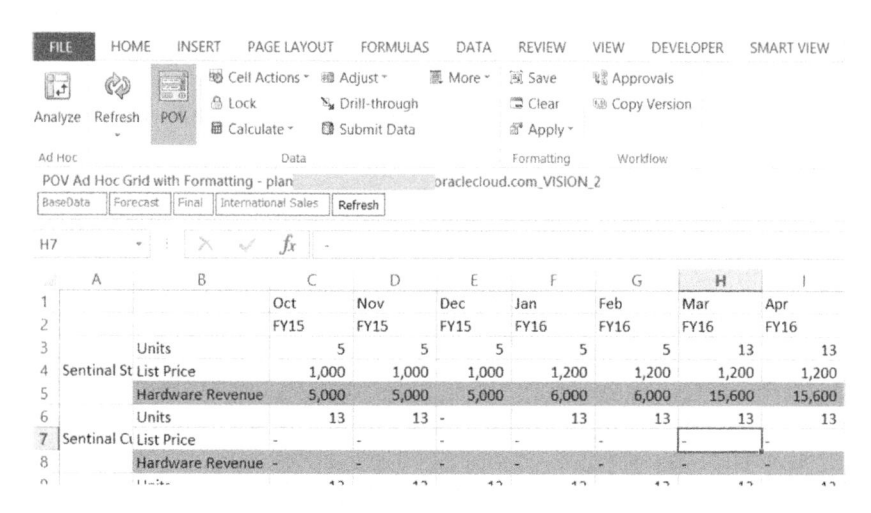

The formatting is also applied in the Simplified UI:

Look Smarter Than You Are with PBCS 521

You can toggle back and forth between custom styles and default cell styles.

A few considerations for this formatting feature:

- Formatting can affect performance and is not recommended for large forms
- Not all Excel formatting options are supported
- Administrators can define formatting for a form, then users with access can overwrite the formatting and save the changes on the form
- Composite forms are not supported

For more information regarding all the features and functionalities of Smart View, check out the *Look Smarter Than You Are with Smart View* book or view the Oracle *Working with Smart View for Office* online documentation.

MOBILE SUPPORT

PBCS supports many, many tasks on mobile devices. Users can review and enter plans, follow tasks, launch business rules, and run reports.

Additionally, there is an EPM mobile app (called "Oracle EPM Mobile App") that is available at the Apple and Android stores to support the approvals process:

> LOG ENTRY: SOL 23, Entry 1
>
> The Vision users love the Oracle Enterprise Cloud. Their planning cycle was shorter. The forecasts were more accurate and enabled better, faster decision making.
> Yeah! Feel my EPM Cloud power!

> LOG ENTRY: SOL 23, Entry 2
>
> So I just received an email from Cloud Specialist Alapat. I'm not quite finished! Users are requesting more functionality around sandboxes.
> Whaaaaaat?

Chapter 11: Sandboxing

> LOG ENTRY: SOL 23, Entry 3
>
> In high school I used to be a board game fanatic. (And maybe I still am.) You may not have guessed this, but I used to be a bit of a nerd. My favorite card and board games were Risk (Lord of the Rings version, of course), Settlers of Catan, and Werewolf. I also liked the Who Wants to be a Millionaire board game version. What I wouldn't give to have a lifeline right now for Vision's last requirement.
>
> Users want more flexibility in creating sandboxes. Thankfully Oracle PBCS has a lifeline built in with a feature called sandboxing. I enabled this feature when I initially set up the application. Just a few more configuration steps away from completing this mission.

Sandboxes allow users to analyze and perform impact analysis on data without affecting the plans of other users. Sandboxes are private to the users and the changes made in the sandbox are not saved to the application and cannot be viewed by other users.

ENABLE SANDBOXES

Sandboxing must be enabled when the application is created and can be enabled by cube for BSO cubes. I did this what seems like forever ago:

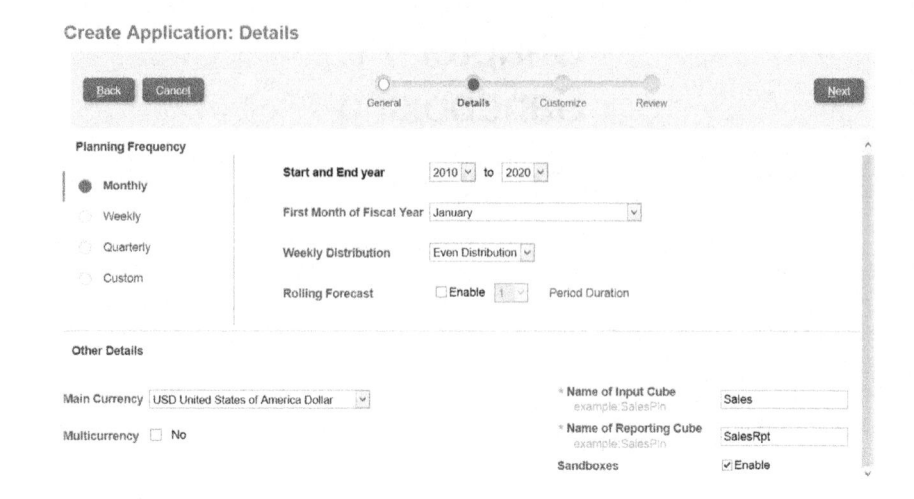

If you add a new cube later in the application and sandboxing has already been enabled on the application, you choose whether to enable sandboxing on that cube:

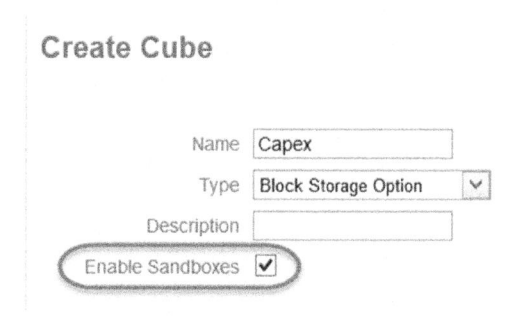

ENABLE VERSION FOR SANDBOXING

Once the application is enabled for sandboxing, you must also enable the desired Version members. Remember back in the dimension build section, I enabled sandboxing for the members Final and Pass1:

Sandboxing Members

Understand the Version Dimension & the Sandbox Members

Now that the appropriate Version dimension members are enabled, a corresponding sandbox member is created for that version:

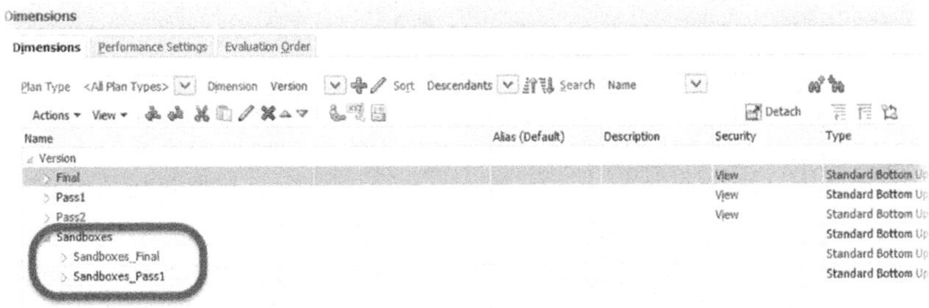

Understanding the HSP_View Dimension

The HSP_View dimension is created when sandboxes are enabled during application creation. This dimension and its members cannot be altered and should not be reordered. The members below are created along with it:

- **BaseData** – where data is stored when users are working in a non-sandbox view in a form
- **SandboxData** – where data is stored when users work in a sandbox
- **ConsolidatedData** – retrieves data from the SandboxData member when it is available; otherwise, it retrieves the data from the BaseData member; this member is dynamically calculated

By default, forms and ad hoc grids are used by the *BaseData* member. When users enter data in a sandbox, the data is housed in the *SandboxData* of the HSP_View dimension rather than *BaseData*. Users can publish the data in a sandbox to *BaseData* so that it can be seen by others and be saved to the application.

Per the Oracle PBCS documentation, Administrators need to update the member formula for the ConsolidatedData member to make sure that the proper sandbox member is referenced. I tried to update the member formula for this member and was not able to actually save the formula.

The documentation recommends adding the following member formula to ConsolidatedData in the HSP_View dimension:

```
IF (@ISLEV("Product",0))
   IF (@ISLEV("Entity",0))
      IF (@ISLEV("Period", 0))
         IF (NOT (@ISMBR(@Relative("Sandboxes",0))))
            BaseData;
         ELSE
            IF (SandboxData == #MISSING )
               IF (@ISCHILD("Sandboxes_Final"))
                  "Final"->BaseData;
               ELSEIF (@ISCHILD("Sandboxes_Pass1"))
                  "Pass1"->BaseData;
               ENDIF
            ELSE
               SandboxData;
            ENDIF
         ENDIF
      ENDIF
   ENDIF
ENDIF
```

The formula validates, which is good:

But I'm unable to save:

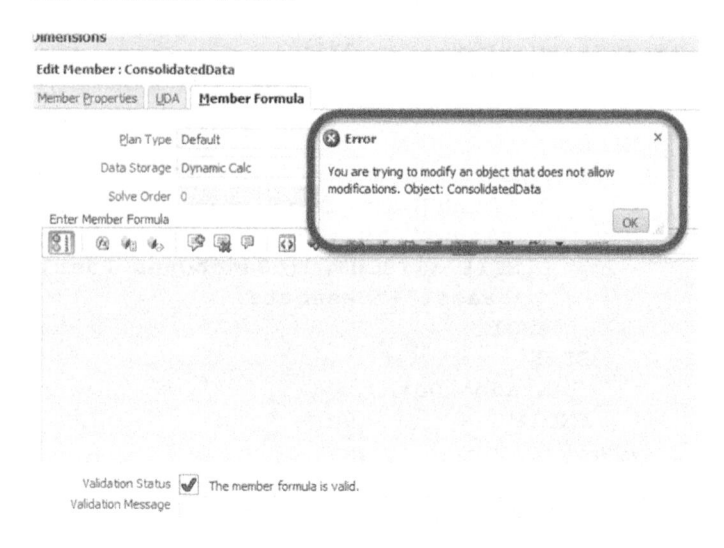

> **Edit Member: ConsolidatedData**
>
> Plan Type: Default
> Data Storage: Dynamic Calc
> Solve Order: 0
>
> **Error**
> You are trying to modify an object that does not allow modifications. Object: ConsolidatedData
>
> Validation Status: The member formula is valid.

Huh? So this is either a bug or the documentation is wrong. I'll just keep going and see if I can MacGyver this to work. What I'll find out shortly is that this step is no longer necessary. ConsolidatedData automatically shows BaseData + Sandbox data appropriately.

Update Member Formulas to Support Sandboxing

Don't miss this step! When you use sandboxing, you need to create or modify member formulas to support sandbox views by referencing the ConsolidatedData member. Otherwise, data does not calculate properly for sandbox views.

To update the member formulas to support sandboxing,
1. Update the member formula for 4110 to point to the ConsolidatedData member in the HSP_View dimension:

```
IF (@ISMBR("Forecast"))
   IF ((@ISMBR(@relative("Sandboxes",0))))
      "Units"->"ConsolidatedData" * "List Price" -
>"ConsolidatedData";
   ELSE
      "Units"*"List Price";
   ENDIF
ENDIF
```

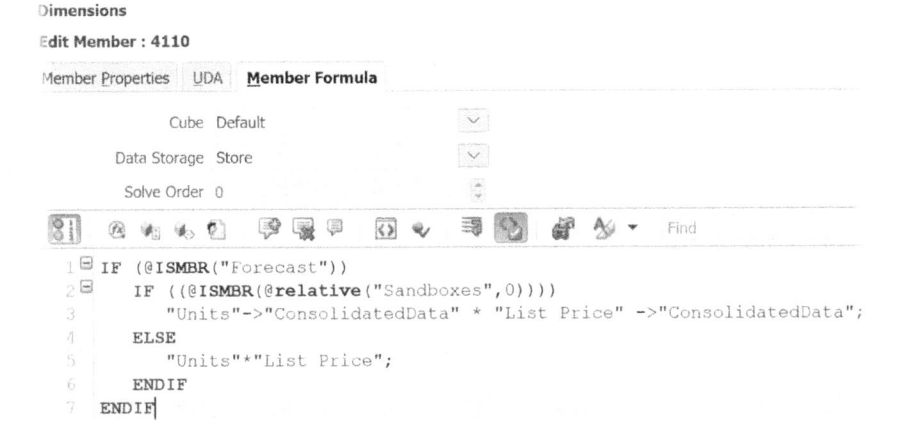

Dimensions
Edit Member : 4110

Member Properties | UDA | **Member Formula**

Cube   Default
Data Storage   Store
Solve Order   0

```
1  IF (@ISMBR("Forecast"))
2     IF ((@ISMBR(@relative("Sandboxes",0))))
3        "Units"->"ConsolidatedData" * "List Price" ->"ConsolidatedData";
4     ELSE
5        "Units"*"List Price";
6     ENDIF
7  ENDIF
```

2. Save the member.
3. Refresh the database.

Only the Calculate Data Form Business Rule Works

The only business rule that works with sandbox views is the "Calculate Data Form" business rule (and "Calculate Currencies," but I'm not using multiple currencies in this application). Thankfully for me, I designed the calculations as member formulas (a recommended practice in PBCS when possible for this very reason).

To verify this,
1. Edit *Sales Forecast – Products* and then *Save As* to a new form called "Sales Forecast - Products Sandbox".
2. Remove the Rule – *Calculate MyForecast*.
3. Add <Calculate Form> to the Selected Business Rule pane (if not already there) and check the option to *Run on Save:*

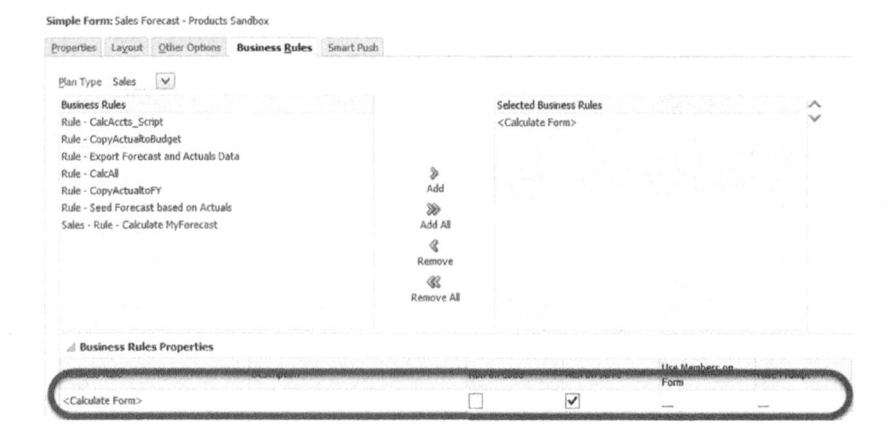

4. Click *Finish* to save and close the form.

Set Sparse Upper Level Members Dynamic

In order for aggregations to work for sandbox versions, upper level members of sparse dimensions must be dynamic, if shown on the data form.

Finally, users are ready to create a sandbox.

CREATE A SANDBOX

To create a sandbox through a form or an ad hoc grid,

1. While in a data form, click ✚ to create a new sandbox:

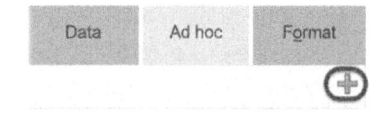

Note! The administrator must check the *Enable Sandboxes* box in Version member properties for ✚ to appear for users.

2. Name the sandbox "Worst Case":

Look Smarter Than You Are with PBCS 531

Create Sandbox [Create] [Close]

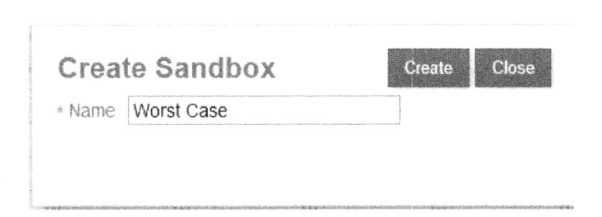

* Name: Worst Case

3. Click *Create*. The sandbox appears as a new tab next to the original form:

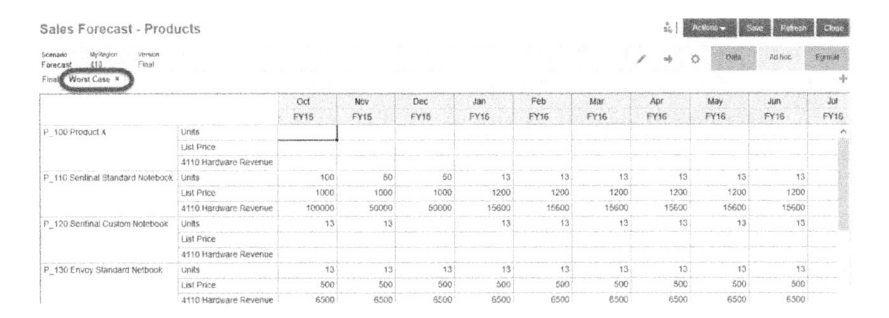

Sales Forecast - Products

		Oct FY15	Nov FY15	Dec FY15	Jan FY16	Feb FY16	Mar FY16	Apr FY16	May FY16	Jun FY16	Jul FY16
P_100:Product X	Units										
	List Price										
	4110:Hardware Revenue										
P_110:Sentinal Standard Notebook	Units	100	50	50	13	13	13	13	13	13	
	List Price	1000	1000	1000	1200	1200	1200	1200	1200	1200	
	4110:Hardware Revenue	100000	50000	50000	15600	15600	15600	15600	15600	15600	
P_120:Sentinal Custom Notebook	Units	13	13		13	13	13	13	13	13	
	List Price										
	4110:Hardware Revenue										
P_130:Envoy Standard Netbook	Units	13	13	13	13	13	13	13	13	13	
	List Price	500	500	500	500	500	500	500	500	500	
	4110:Hardware Revenue	6500	6500	6500	6500	6500	6500	6500	6500	6500	

4. Enter data in the sandbox and view the impact on other accounts or forms. Woo hoo! It worked. The golden yellow cells (although hard to see below in the monochrome print) indicate data in my sandbox that have been calculated:

Sales Forecast - Products San...

		Oct FY15	Nov FY15	Dec FY15	Jan FY16	Feb FY16
P_100:Product X	Units					
	List Price					
	4110:Hardware Revenue					
P_110:Sentinal Standard Notebook	Units	5	5	5	5	5
	List Price	1000	1000	1000	1200	1200
	4110:Hardware Revenue	5000	5000	5000	6000	6000
P_120 Sentinal Custom Notebook	Units	13	13		13	13

All other forms have the sandbox tab until the data is published.

Note! Any Supporting Detail cells previously created in the non-sandbox version cannot be removed in a sandbox version. It allows you to go through the steps, but the supporting detail will come back.

Publish a Sandbox

To publish data from a sandbox to other users, the *Publish* action moves the sandbox data back to the BaseData member. All modified data from the sandbox is published (across different POVS or pages, and across different forms). If multiple planners publish sandbox data to the same member in the base view, the most recently published data overwrites the previously published data.

To publish a sandbox,
1. When ready to publish the data in the sandbox, go to *Actions >> Sandbox >> Publish*:

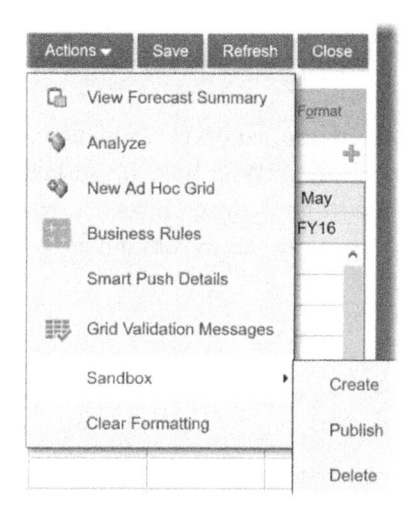

Once the sandbox is published, it disappears and its data is saved to Essbase under the BaseData member.

Other Rules about Sandboxing

A few rules about sandboxing:

- All security is still in effect when users sandboxes

- Planners may have multiple sandboxes and switch between them
- Planners won't impact other planners when sandboxing
- You might need to update member formulas so they calculate properly when viewing base data and sandboxes; to do this you reference the "ConsolidatedData" member
- For a form to support sandboxing, the Version dimension must be on the page or in the POV as a user variable
- The only supported business rules for sandboxes are the default "Calculate Form" and "Calculate Currencies" rules
- Some sandboxing functionality is supported in Smart View (update data in a sandbox):

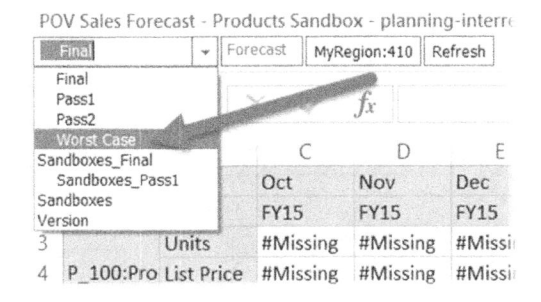

- You can't create, delete, or publish data from Smart View

If you don't see the sandbox options in a data form, it is likely because one of the above rules has been broken.

MANAGE SANDBOXES

Administrators can manage all sandboxes that were created by users and can also see the following information:

- Data in all sandboxes
- Which version member the sandbox is based on
- Who created each sandbox
- When the sandboxes were last modified

Administrators can also delete anyone's sandbox. To manage sandboxes, go to *Navigator >> Application >> Overview*. Choose *Manage Sandboxes*:

Manage Sandboxes				Refresh Delete Close
Sandbox Name		Base Version	Created By	Last Modified
Worst Case		Final	pbcs1@interret.c	2/2/2016

> **LOG ENTRY: SOL 23, Entry 4**
>
> The Vision users love the Oracle Enterprise Cloud with sandboxing. Their planning cycle was shorter. The forecasts were more accurate and enabled better, faster decision making. And now they can what-if and sandbox to their hearts content.
>
> Yeah! Feel my EPM Cloud power! Again.

Chapter 12: Maintain & Support

> LOG ENTRY: SOL 24, Entry 1
>
> Before I can move onto my next Cloud mission, I need to document some of the PBCS maintenance steps for the Vision Administrator. What if something stops working? What if users are in the middle of a process and everything freezes?
> I'm using this log entry to document some of these helpful administrative tips.

APPLICATION MAINTENANCE

You can manage your PBCS application from the Application section (available to PBCS administrators). From the Overview tab, you can view the count of objects, import and export data using the simplified Planning format, convert the application to an Enterprise (EPBCS) application type if you have changed your licensing, refresh the database, clear a specific cube, remove the application (which means "delete"), access the Inbox/Outbox explorer, and manage sandboxes:

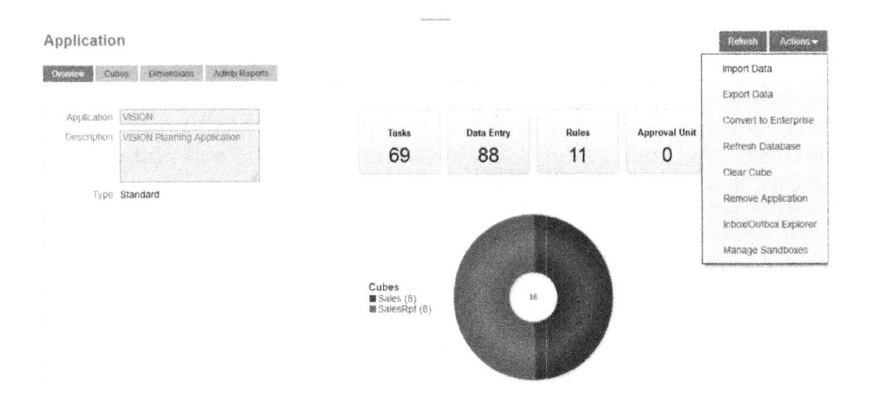

CREATE AND EDIT CUBES

You can create new cubes after the application creation in the Cubes section (simply go to *Navigator* >> *Application* >> *Cubes* tab). In the

Cubes tab, click *Create*. You may create a BSO or ASO plan type and optionally enable sandboxes:

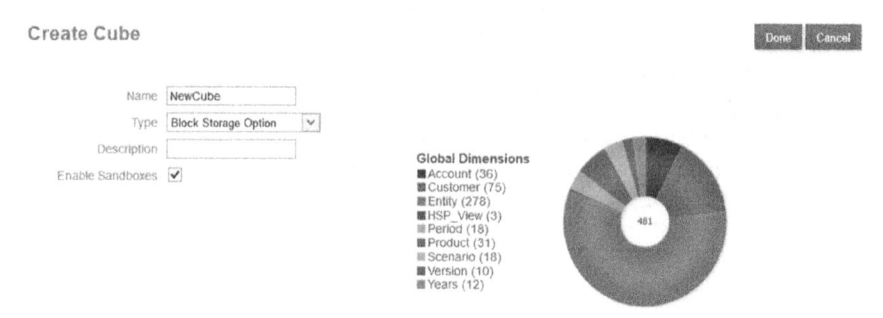

There are a couple of rules governing cube creation:

- You may add up to three BSO cubes and the number of BSO cubes +1 ASO cubes (four total ASO cubes) in PBCS
- You may not delete cubes in PBCS

The global dimensions are automatically created in the new cube and you can add any new custom dimensions for the new cube in the Dimension Editor or Dimensions tab, enabling them for the new cube only.

CLEAR CUBES

If you need to clear a cube, you could do this with a business rule but there is a much easier way! Clear cubes may be run and scheduled from the Job Console.

To partially clear or fully clear a cube,
1. Select *Navigator >> Application >> Overview*.
2. Select *Actions >> Clear Cube*.
3. Select *Create* to create a new clear cube action
4. Enter a name.
5. Select the cube *Sales* (which is BSO and the following options display).
6. Define what should be cleared:

a. Clear all
b. Upper level blocks (common clear requirement for nightly calculations and aggregations)
c. Non-input blocks
d. Dynamic blocks
e. Empty blocks (great tuning opportunity):

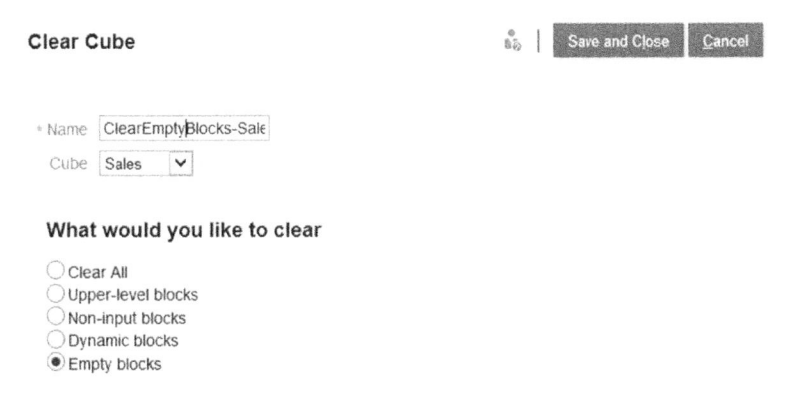

Clear Cube

* Name: ClearEmptyBlocks-Sale
Cube: Sales

What would you like to clear

○ Clear All
○ Upper-level blocks
○ Non-input blocks
○ Dynamic blocks
● Empty blocks

7. Click *Save and Close*
8. Repeat the following steps but select the SalesRpt cube.

Notice that the clear options are different for ASO cubes. You can clear all data, all aggregations (if you've materialized in data), or partial data. For partial data clears, you would write an MDX statement identifying the intersection to clear and then choose either Logical or Physical clear:

SalesRpt Clear

Cube: SalesRpt

What would you like to clear

○ Clear All
○ All Aggregations
● Partial Data

How would you like to clear

● Logical ○ Physical

538   Chapter 12: Maintain & Support

You can also run partial clears from Calculation Manager. Calculation Manager has a Member selector to help you define the MDX syntax.

To execute the saved Clear action,
9. Highlight the saved Clear action.
10. Choose the *Actions* icon >> *Submit*:

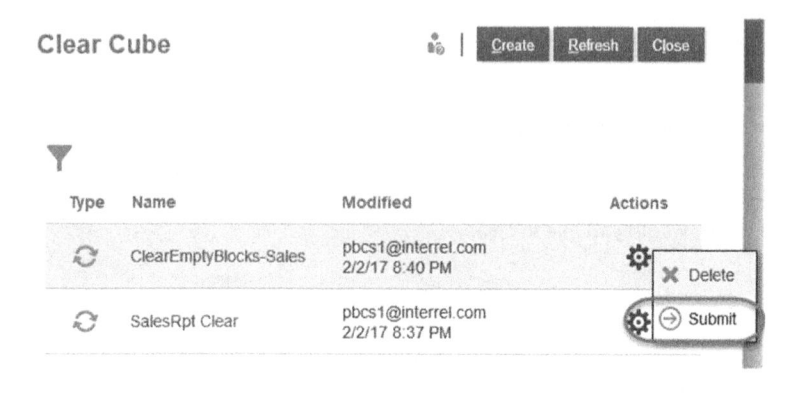

DIMENSION MAINTENANCE

While you will do most of the manual dimension maintenance in the Dimension Editor (*Create and Manage* >> *Dimensions*), you can import and export dimensions in *Navigator* >> *Application* >> *Dimensions* tab. You can also set the dimension sort order and evaluation order for each cube:

VIEW AND SET UNDERLYING CUBE PROPERTIES

It's possible to edit some of the traditional Essbase properties. This has to be done in Calculation Manager.

To view Cube Database Properties (traditional Essbase database properties),
1. Select *Navigator >> Create and Manage >> Rules*. This launches Calculation Manager.
2. In the System View, navigate to *Actions >> Database Properties*:

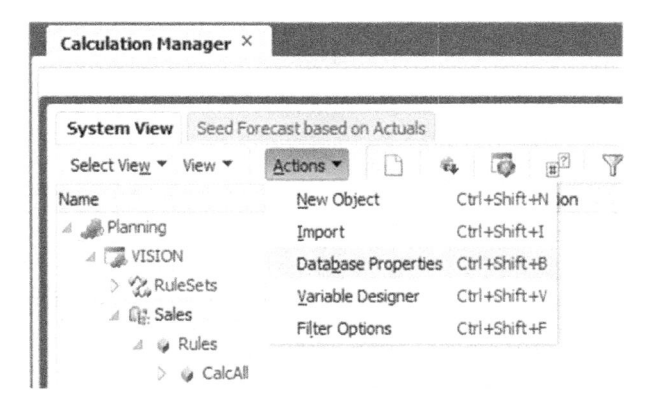

3. In the Database Properties tab, highlight a cube. The properties appears:

Chapter 12: Maintain & Support

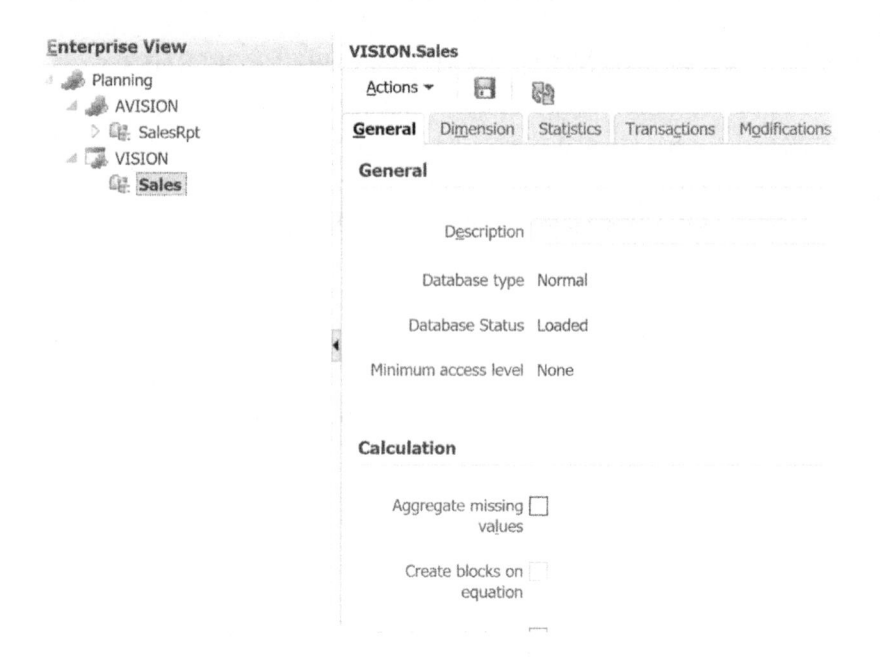

You can modify some of properties in Calculation Manager.

In the General tab:

- **Description** – adds a description to the cube
- **Aggregate missing values** – a global setting to aggregate missing values during database calculation
- **Two-pass Calculation** – a global setting of two-pass calculation; members tagged with two-pass calculation are recalculated after a database default calculation:

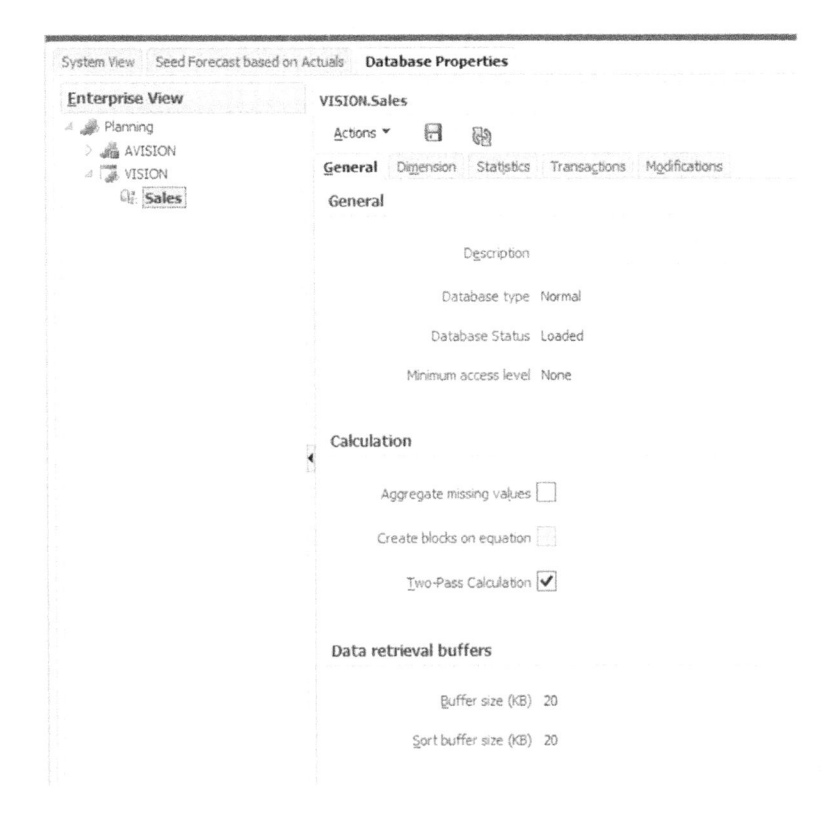

[Screenshot: Database Properties — VISION.Sales, General tab showing Description, Database type: Normal, Database Status: Loaded, Minimum access level: None; Calculation section with Aggregate missing values, Create blocks on equation, Two-Pass Calculation (checked); Data retrieval buffers: Buffer size (KB) 20, Sort buffer size (KB) 20.]

Properties in the Dimension, Statistics, Transactions, and Modifications tabs cannot be modified here. They are for display purposes only. You can view dimension statistics:

VISION.Sales

Number of dimensions: 8

Dimension	Type	Members in Dimension	Members Stored
Period	Dense	21	14
Account	Dense	13	10
Entity	Sparse	127	55
Product	Sparse	28	21
Years	Sparse	12	12
Scenario	Sparse	7	6
Version	Sparse	1544	1543
HSP_View	Sparse	4	3

You can view database statistics like block size and number of blocks:

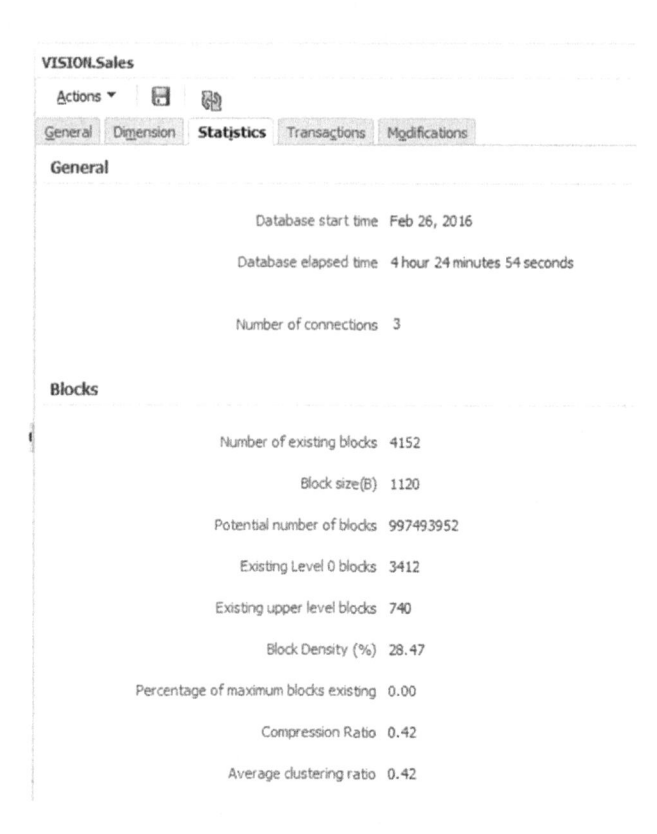

VISION.Sales

General | Dimension | **Statistics** | Transactions | Modifications

General

Database start time	Feb 26, 2016
Database elapsed time	4 hour 24 minutes 54 seconds
Number of connections	3

Blocks

Number of existing blocks	4152
Block size (B)	1120
Potential number of blocks	997493952
Existing Level 0 blocks	3412
Existing upper level blocks	740
Block Density (%)	28.47
Percentage of maximum blocks existing	0.00
Compression Ratio	0.42
Average clustering ratio	0.42

You can view transaction settings:

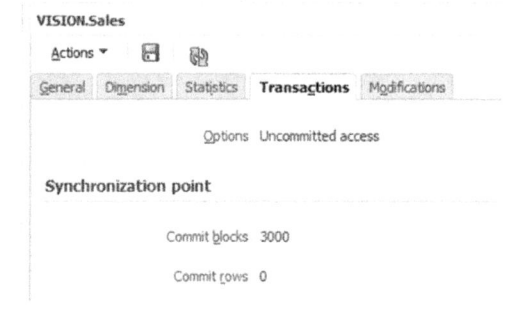

VISION.Sales

General | Dimension | Statistics | **Transactions** | Modifications

Options	Uncommitted access

Synchronization point

Commit blocks	3000
Commit rows	0

You can view information on when the cube was last loaded and calculated:

VISION.Sales			
Operation	User	Start Time	End Time
Data Load	epm_default_cloud_admin@Native Direct Feb 24, 2016		Feb 24, 2016
Calculation	epm_default_cloud_admin@Native Direct Feb 26, 2016		Feb 26, 2016
Outline Update	epm_default_cloud_admin@Native Direct Feb 16, 2016		Feb 16, 2016

The ASO database properties vary some. You can view the data retrieval buffers:

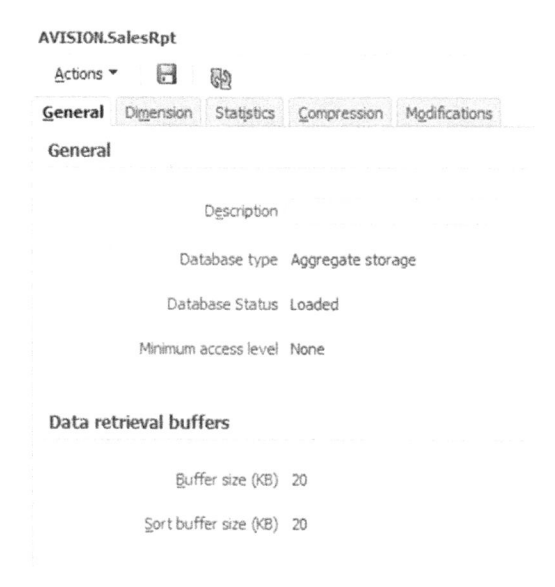

AVISION.SalesRpt

General | Dimension | Statistics | Compression | Modifications

General

Description
Database type: Aggregate storage
Database Status: Loaded
Minimum access level: None

Data retrieval buffers

Buffer size (KB): 20
Sort buffer size (KB): 20

You can view compression information which may be helpful in performance tuning:

Dimension Name	Is Compression	Stored Level0 Members	Average Bundle Fill	Average Value Length	Level0 Mb
<No Compression Dimension>	FALSE	0.0	1.0	8.0	0.25640869140625
Account	TRUE	10.0	3.4297473419458093	3.526	0.11257623596191407
Period	FALSE	13.0	11.6331096196868	3.112	0.06640245466965897
Years	FALSE	11.0	1.920614596670935	3.034	0.14874909210205078
Scenario	FALSE	6.0	1.0	3.028	0.24083186340332033
Version	FALSE	1518.0	1.002004008016032	3.028	0.24044725036621095
Entity	FALSE	105.0	1.453840562151684	3.08	0.18163350677490236
Product	FALSE	21.0	4.373825776886602	3.564	0.10108261230766001
Customer	FALSE	69.0	1.3386880856760375	3.134	0.1938770217895508

For more detailed information on all of these properties, I recommend you check out our *Look Smarter Than You Are with Essbase* book.

FORCE RESTRUCTURE

Fragmentation is a common "side effect" of planning applications. To remove fragmentation from a BSO cube, you can force a restructure. Do this in off times when users are not in the system. Depending on the BSO cube size, this could take a while to complete.

To force a database restructure,
1. Select *Navigator >> Create and Manage >> Rules*. This launches Calculation Manager.
2. In the System View, navigate to *Actions >> Database Properties*.
3. Select *Restructure Database*:

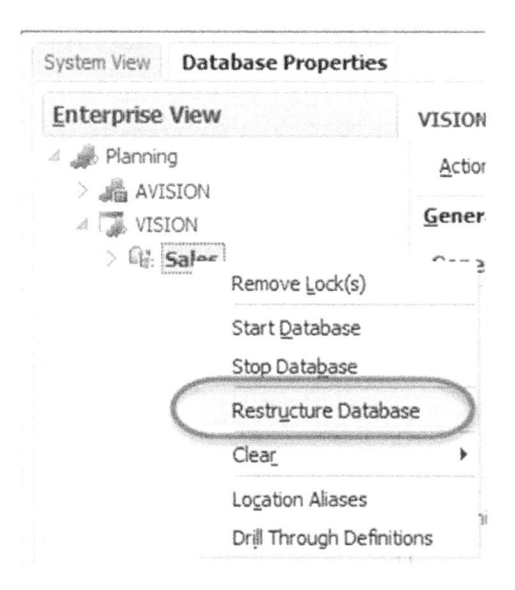

Note that you can also start and stop the cube, run clears (this is the same functionality as *Clear Cube*), and review and define location aliases and drill through definitions.

DELETE APPLICATION

Oracle PBCS supports a single application. To create a new application, you need to delete the existing application if one exists in the instance.

To delete an application,
1. Select *Navigator >> Application >> Overview*.
2. In the Application Overview tab, go to *Actions >> Remove Application*:

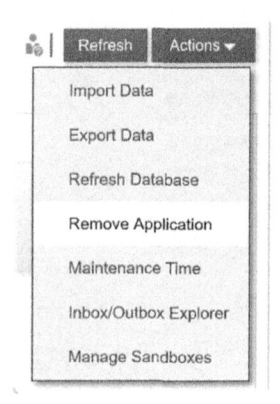

3. Click *Yes*. It takes a few seconds for the application to delete.

You need to log out and log back into the PBCS instance. Once the application is deleted, you can create a new application or import an application in the *Migration* section.

VIEW CLOUD VERSION

To view your current Cloud version,
1. Select the drop-down in the upper right-hand corner next to your ID.
2. Select *About:*

Daily Backups

A snapshot of all of the application artifacts and data is taken each day. It is replaced each day with the previous artifact snapshot:

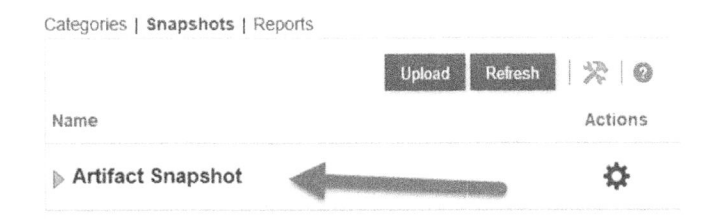

If you want to keep a week's worth of snapshots, you can easily create an EPMAutomate batch process to download the snapshot to a central location each night.

Set Appearance

In *Navigator >> Tools >> Appearance*, you can set the logo image and background image URL. You can change the theme color and the shapes for all users:

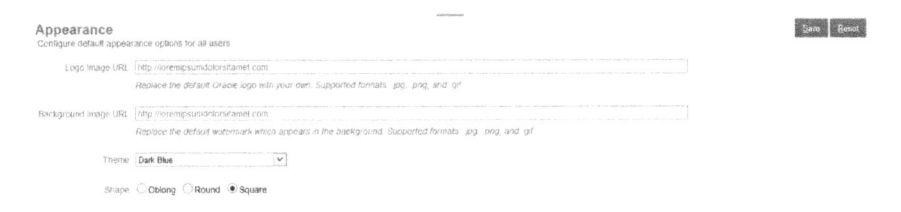

Logos with a size of 125px wide by 25px high can be referenced without having to scale. For larger image logos, Oracle recommends you maintain a 5:1 ratio so the image scales without distortion. The default size for the background image is 1024x768 but you can use a larger image. Oracle recommends that you size the image that fits your biggest screen.

ANNOUNCEMENTS

In *Navigator* >> *Tools* >> *Announcements*, you can create and manage announcements for users that display on the Home screen. Within each announcement, you define the Subject, Start Date, End Date, and Message with formatting:

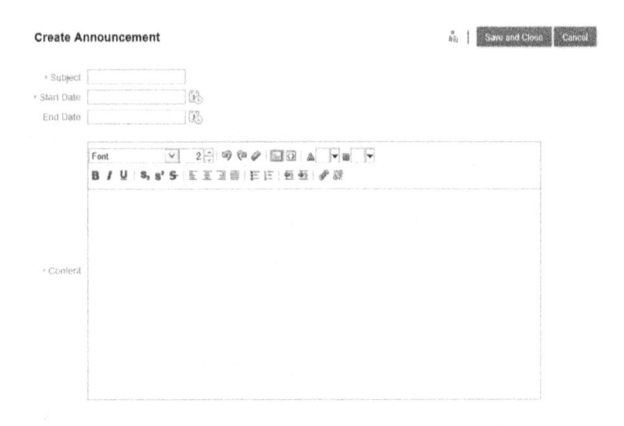

ARTIFACT LABELS

Artifact labels under *Tools* >> *Artifact Labels* enable Administrators to customize artifact labels (think of an artifact label like an alias for an artifact). You might want to change the artifact label based on the user's browser locale for a different language or present a more user friendly artifact name to the user. Artifact Labels are supported for cards, clusters, dashboards, data maps, data validation rules, dimensions, folders, forms, members, Action Menus, menu items, Navigation Flows, cubes, approval unit hierarchies, reports, rules, rulesets, Smart Lists, Smart List entries, tabs, tasks, Task Lists, templates, User Variables, and Valid Intersections. You can export and import Artifact Labels.

You can filter for specific artifact types and then add additional languages ("aliases") for the application along with custom help for artifacts:

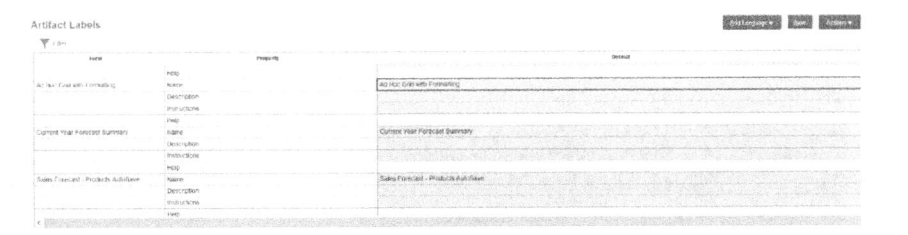

DAILY MAINTENANCE

The administrator can schedule the maintenance time zone and time by going to *Navigator >> Tools >> Daily Maintenance*:

During the maintenance window, the system is backed up and it normally takes about one hour. To ensure that no changes are lost, refresh the database before the scheduled backup time.

RESTARTING THE PBCS APPLICATION

There may be instances where the Planning application needs to be restarted. Since the backend components are not as easily available in the Cloud, a different process is required for restarts. Oracle has created steps to "reboot" (reset) the PBCS environment.

Why would one ever need to do this? There are a couple of important reasons: runaway processes and performance issues to start with. Oracle recommends that this command be used only when severe performance degradation is witnessed or if error messages pop up, indicating that the instance is unusable. Service resets do not affect application customization (for example, locale change, settings related to theme and currency, etc.) and it can take up to 15 minutes to fully reset.

To perform a reset with EPM Automate,
1. Open a command prompt. You'll use the `resetservice` command within EPM Automate.
2. Navigate to the EPM Automate install location. Example:

```
CD C:\Oracle\EPM Automate
```

```
C:\Windows\system32\cmd.exe
Microsoft Windows [Version 6.1.7601]
Copyright (c) 2009 Microsoft Corporation. All rights reserved.

C:\Users\       >CD C:\Oracle\EPM Automate

C:\Oracle\EPM Automate>
```

3. Log in to the Cloud instance. Example of the generic syntax:

```
epmautomate login username password/<password file>
url identitydomain
```

Comments can also be used to track the reasons for restart. Comments must be enclosed within double quotation marks.

4. Type:

```
epmautomate resetservice "Import Metadata processing
is stuck"
```

```
:\Oracle\EPM Automate\bin>epmautomate resetservice "Import metadata processing is stuck"
Are you sure you want to restart the service instance (yes/no): no ?[Press Enter]
yes
Processing...
Retrieving status...
resetservice completed successfully
```

A batch file can also be generated from the above commands to make processing easier in the future.

APPLICATION AND SYSTEM SETTINGS

Advanced Settings

A number of advanced application settings are defined by the administrator, including enabling or disabling the application for use by users (this is helpful if you want to keep users out while performing maintenance) and display defaults for the application.

To define advanced settings,
1. Select *Navigator >> Setup >> System Settings*.
2. Click the *Advanced Settings* tab.

3. Update the settings accordingly and click *Save*:

Oracle Hyperion Planning		
Application Settings		
Advanced Settings Current Application Defaults		
System Settings Custom Tools		
Email Options		
Email Character Set	UTF-8	
Business Rules Notification	No	
Notify These Users		
Application Maintenance Mode		
Enable Use of the Application for	All users	
Substitution Variable Display		
Enable the Display of Substitution Variables	Display All	
Assign Application Owner		
Select User	admin	
Other Options		
Display Users' Full Names	No	
Calculation Module	Calculation Manager	

For more information on each of these settings, check out the Oracle documentation.

Current Application Defaults

The administrator defines the application defaults for users, including defaults for alias table and member and alias display. On the Display Options tab, you can define the number formatting settings like thousands separator and how to show negative numbers. You can also set the Partial Grid Fetch Size to aid in performance for large forms (only retrieves a portion of the data upon initial form load). Users can override these defaults in their preferences.

To define current application defaults,
1. Select *Navigator >> Setup >> System Settings*.
2. Click the *Advanced Settings* tab.
3. Update the settings accordingly and click *Save*:

System Settings and Defaults	
Advanced Settings **Current Application Defaults**	

Application Settings Display Options

Email Options
Task List Notification	No
Approvals Notification	No
Job Console Notification	No

Alias Setting
| Alias Table | Default |
| Member Name/Alias Display | Default |

Approvals Options
| Show Approval Units as Aliases | No |
| Show Approval Units That are Not Started | No |

Attribute Dimension Options
| Attribute Dimension Date Format | MM/DD/YYYY |

Predictive Planning Options
Historical Data
| Scenario (Version) | Actual (Working) |
Predictions
| Prediction Interval (Worst and Best Cases) | 2.5% and 97.5% |

4. Click the *Display Options* tab.
5. Update the settings accordingly and click *Save*:

System Settings and Defaults

Advanced Settings | **Current Application Defaults**

Application Settings | **Display Options**

Number Formatting
Thousands Separator	None
Decimal Separator	Dot
Negative Sign	Prefixed Minus
Negative Color	Black

Page Options
Remember selected page members	Yes
Allow Search When Number of Pages Exceeds	100
Indentation of Members on Page	Indent level 0 members only

Other Options
Partial Grid Fetch Size(Rows,Columns)	25, 17
Date Format	Automatically Detect

CLEAR CELL DETAILS

Clear Cell Details allows the administrator to clear supporting details, comments, and document attachments for a defined intersection of the cube:

Clear Cell Details
Cube: Sales
Clear Options: Account Annotations, Supporting Details, Comments, Document Attachments

Static Dimensions
Dimension	Members
Years	FY16
Scenario	Plan
Version	Final
Select Dimension	

COPY DATA

Copy Data allows the administrator to copy data and supporting details, comments, and document attachments for a defined intersection of the cube. While you can copy data in business rules, you cannot copy the supporting data sets like supporting details, comments, and documents. If you need to copy those details, this is the feature to use! You can define the intersection to a very granular level by members from each dimension:

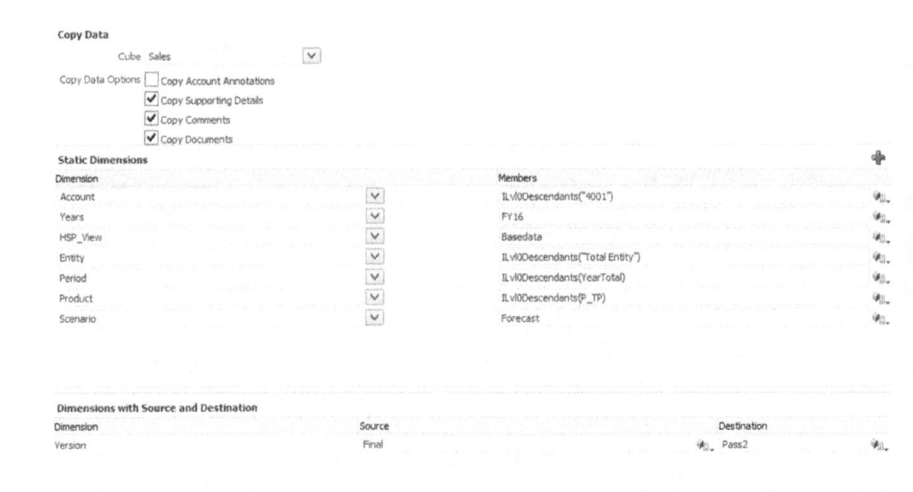

Copy Versions

Copy Version is similar to copy data but there are two main differences: 1) all users can run a Copy Version and 2) Copy Version copies all years, all accounts, all periods, all *other custom dimensions* for a selected set of entities, version, and scenario:

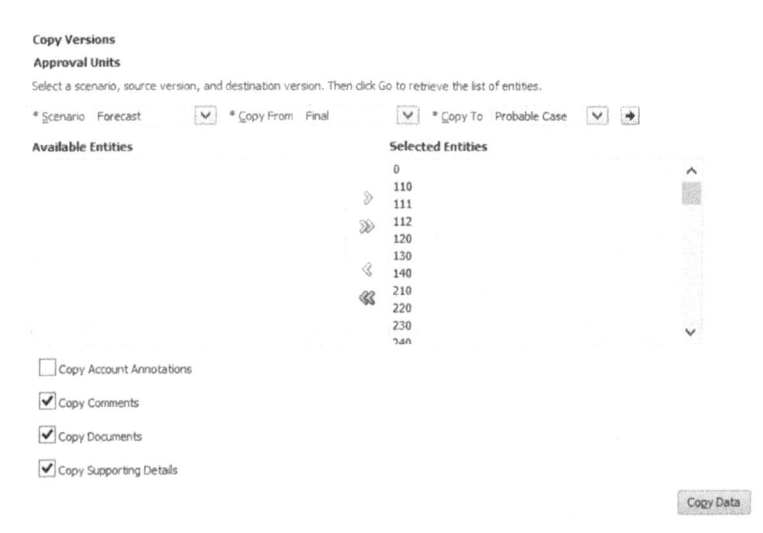

VIEW ACCESS LOGS

PBCS provides out of the box access logs to help you monitor your PBCS usage. This access log is a "data dump" of most of the activity that takes place within PBCS, including date, time, duration, and user ID of the activity.

To download an access log,
1. Select *Navigator >> Application >> Overview*.
2. Choose the *Activity Reports* tab.
3. Select *Download* for the desired day to download the access log:

Date and Time	Activity Reports	Access Logs
2017-02-01 07:12:47	View	Download
2017-01-31 07:08:53	View	Download
2017-01-30 07:08:54	View	Download
2017-01-29 07:08:44	View	Download
2017-01-28 07:12:41	View	Download
2017-01-27 07:08:55	View	Download
2017-01-26 07:12:41	View	Download
2017-01-25 07:12:31	View	Download

4. Open the access log in Excel or another text editor:

VIEW ACTIVITY REPORTS

PBCS provides out of the box activity reports to help you monitor your PBCS usage. This report presents a graphical view of many of the metrics from the access logs, including Number of Users, Percentage of UI Requests over 10 Seconds (0.2%), Top 7 User Interface Requests by Duration, Top 30 Worst Performing User Interface Actions over 10 Seconds, Number of Users by Hour, Number of Users by Usage Duration, Top 10 Most Active Users by Usage Duration, 10 Least Active Users by Usage Duration, Top 10 Calc Scripts by Duration, and Browser Version Usage. You may also view application design changes made over a period of time.

To view an activity report,
1. Select *Navigator >> Application >> Overview*.
2. Choose the Activity Reports tab.
3. Select *View* for the desired day to view the activity report:

Activity Report

2017-02-01 07:12:47

Top 30 Worst Performing User Interface Actions over 10 Seconds

Duration (Min:Sec)	User	Time	Screen	Action	Object
00:19	pbcs1@interrel.com	08:06:32	Planning	LogOn	
00:16	pbcs1@interrel.com	13:07:54	Planning	EfsStructurePSB	

Number of Users by Hour

Task List Report

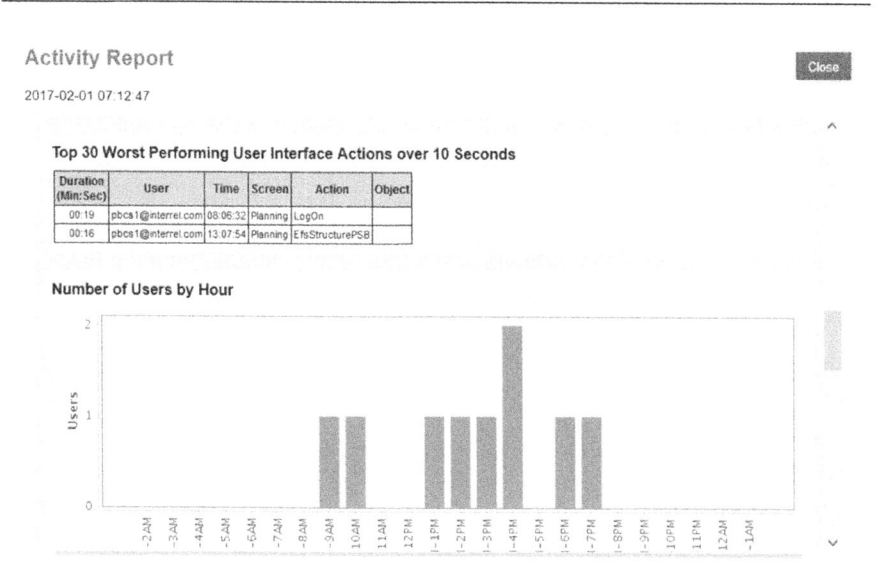

The Task List report shows the status of each task within the selected task list for selected users or groups:

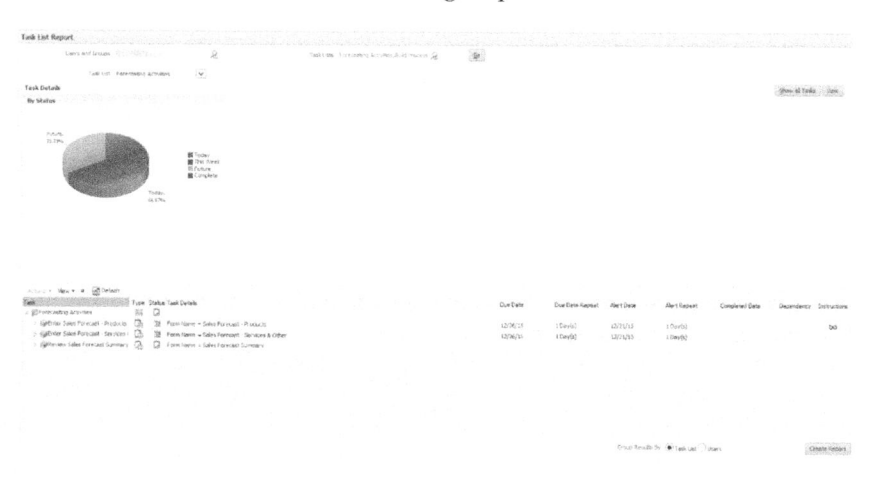

APPLICATION DIAGNOSTICS / APPLICATION MONITOR

The Application Monitor provides administrators an opportunity to review design flaws in artifacts before releasing them to production.

Administrators can evaluate the whole application, specific artifacts, and artifact types:

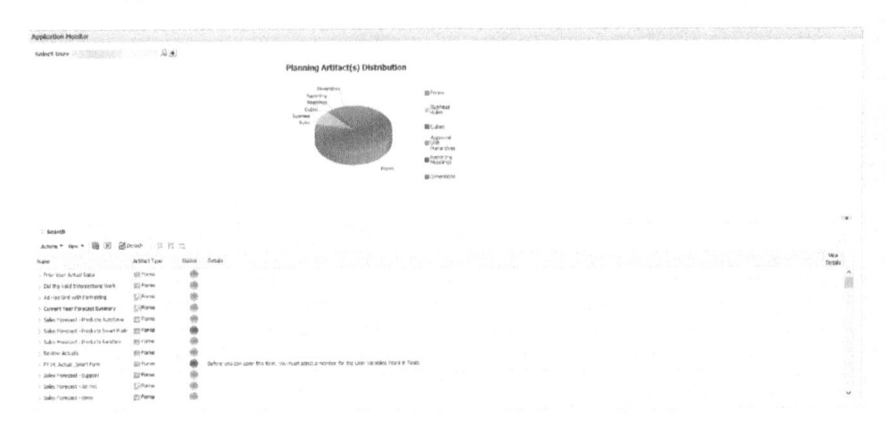

SYSTEM REPORTS

You may run artifact definition reports for forms, approval unit annotations, and access control definitions in *Navigator >> Monitor and Explore >> System Reports*. These are out of the box reports to provide details on artifact definitions often times needed for documentation or audit purposes:

CHANGE HISTORY / AUDITING

Auditing for data, business rule launches, approvals, dimension administration, task lists, etc., can be enabled in PBCS. Open the application and go to *Tools >> Reports*. Click the *Auditing* tab and check the actions to audit. Check *Data* to see the change history in the data forms:

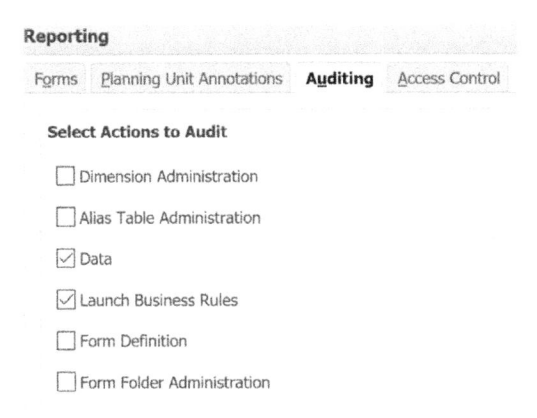

All data changes are tracked, including who made the data change, when the change was made, the previous value, and the new value.

To view the change history for a data cell, open a form and click the *Show Change History* icon under the Data menu:

The User, Date, Old Value, and New Value appears in a window. Cell history is also available through the History option in Smart View. Simply click a cell to view, then go to *Cell Actions >> History*:

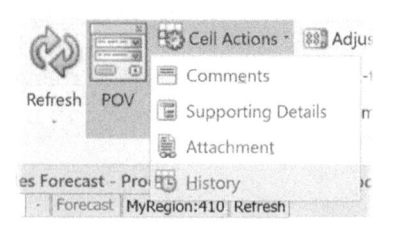

The Change History window appears with a record of the changes.

SET ENVIRONMENT NOTIFICATIONS

There are different types of notifications that Oracle allows administrators to receive. In PBCS, administrators can set up their personal notifications for specific types of events, such as outages.

To set up notifications,
1. Log into the Cloud home page at https://cloud.oracle.com/home.
2. Select *Sign In* in the top right-hand corner.
3. Select the Data Center/Region for your instance and click *My Services*.
4. Sign in with the appropriate credentials.
5. Navigate to the *Notifications* option box in the upper right-hand corner of the screen:

6. Under the *Notification Preferences* tab, take a look at the Categories for notification.
7. Click the checkbox next to the notifications you'd like to receive:

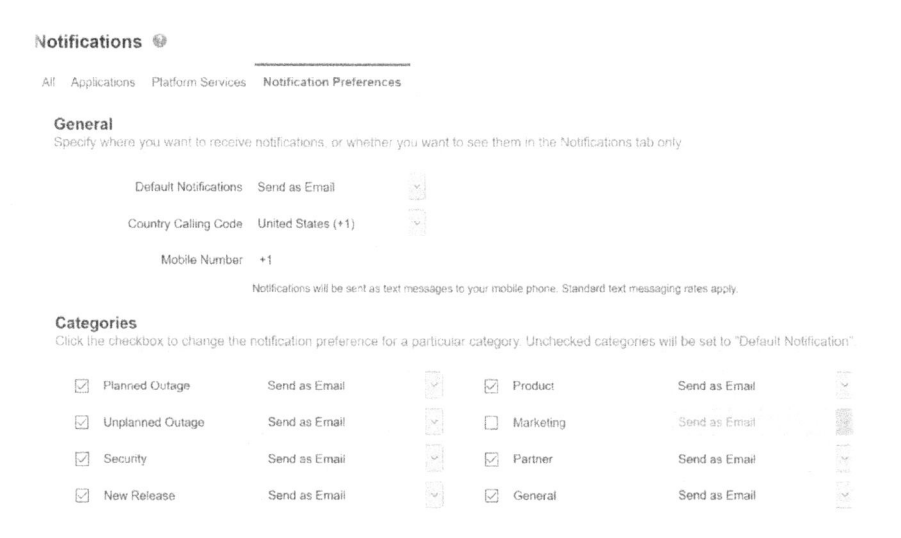

Look Smarter Than You Are with PBCS 561

Notifications

All · Applications · Platform Services · **Notification Preferences**

General
Specify where you want to receive notifications, or whether you want to see them in the Notifications tab only.

Default Notifications	Send as Email
Country Calling Code	United States (+1)
Mobile Number	+1

Notifications will be sent as text messages to your mobile phone. Standard text messaging rates apply.

Categories
Click the checkbox to change the notification preference for a particular category. Unchecked categories will be set to "Default Notification".

☑	Planned Outage	Send as Email	☑	Product	Send as Email
☑	Unplanned Outage	Send as Email	☐	Marketing	Send as Email
☑	Security	Send as Email	☑	Partner	Send as Email
☑	New Release	Send as Email	☑	General	Send as Email

8. Click *Save*.

ACADEMY & LEARNING MORE

The Academy is an educational starting page that provides training opportunities for PBCS:

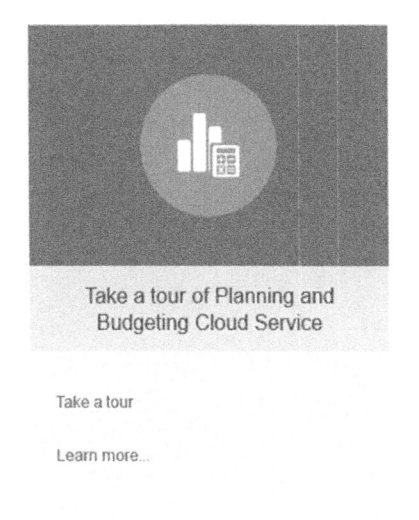

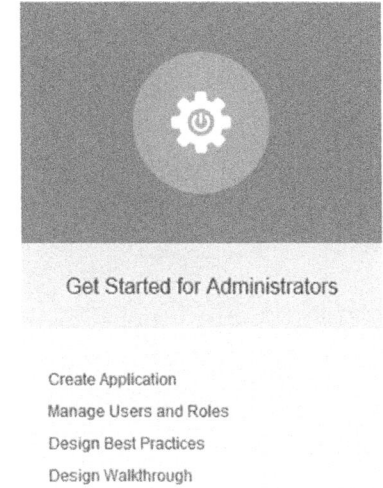

Take a tour of Planning and Budgeting Cloud Service

Take a tour

Learn more...

Get Started for Administrators

Create Application
Manage Users and Roles
Design Best Practices
Design Walkthrough

Other helpful links are:
- Learn about new features at the PBCS Release Readiness home page: https://cloud.oracle.com/en_US/planning-and-budgeting-cloud/releasereadiness
- Main documentation site for PBCS: http://docs.oracle.com/cloud/latest/pbcs_common/index.html

```
LOG ENTRY: SOL 24, Entry 2

    Well, the project didn't die. This Oracle PBCS
thing really works! I wonder what my next mission
will be. Enterprise Performance Reporting Cloud?
Business Intelligence Cloud?
    For now it's time to celebrate with a little
Naughty by Nature and Hip Hop Hooray, "Ho, Hey, Ho …"
```

Epilogue: The EPM Martian

> Meanwhile, back on earth...
>
> "Crap," Danielle said. "Edward Roske and the project are still alive and we haven't communicated it out to anyone besides i.n.t.e.r.R.e.l and Vision? You've got to be kidding me."
>
> Director Chang glared across the room and said, "Not helping, Danielle."
>
> "You don't have to face those darn i.n.t.e.r.R.e.l supporters like Mike Reed and Scot Martin. We should have told them when we first knew the project was alive."
>
> This was going to be rough and Danielle knew it. Not only did she have to deliver the biggest mea culpa in i.n.t.e.r.R.e.l.'s history, every second would be remembered for forever (well maybe thirty minutes). She was confident that none of the concern showed in her voice as she leaned into the computer microphone on i.n.t.e.r.R.e.l.'s regularly-scheduled, free webcast.
>
> "Thank you all for attending today. We have an important announcement to make. We have viewed recent Oracle EPM Cloud logs and have confirmed that Consultant Edward Roske and the Vision implementation are, currently, alive. In fact, he has successfully implemented Oracle PBCS in just a few sols."
>
> After one full second of utter silence, the webcast chat session exploded with questions.

Appendix: *Look Smarter Than You Are with Essbase* Highlights

> LOG ENTRY: Note to Self
>
> Because many of the Cloud applications sit on top of Essbase, I'll review my *Look Smarter Than You Are with Essbase* refresher manual to help define some of the basic Essbase definitions and concepts that will be helpful to implementing the Cloud solutions.

INTRO TO ESSBASE

Essbase is currently produced by a company named Oracle. Prior to the earthshaking acquisition by Oracle, Essbase was produced by a company named Hyperion Solutions Corporation. Although Hyperion was founded in 1981, the Essbase product came along in the early 1990's – compliments of a company whose only product was Essbase: Arbor Software. Up until 1998 when Hyperion and Arbor "merged," the two companies were fierce competitors who were just as likely to spit on each other in waiting rooms as work together (I am kidding, but only slightly).

Good terms to describe these databases: OLAP (On-Line Analytical Processing) or multi-dimensional databases. There were several features that Essbase offered that no previous database could handle.

Multi-Dimensional Databases

First of all, Essbase was a multi-dimensional database (MDDB or MDB, for short). What did the good doctor mean when he said Essbase was multi-dimensional? Simply that any of the dimensions set up in a database could be put in the rows or the columns (or applied to the whole page / report).

Relational databases are two-dimensional: records and fields. Essbase had no theoretical dimension limit (though there was certainly a practical limit).

While any relational database can be set up to give the appearance of having multiple dimensions, it takes a lot of upfront work by developers. Essbase and other OLAP databases have dimensionality built in.

Essbase databases were also optimized for retrieval at any level of the hierarchy – even the very topmost number that might represent every dollar the company has ever made in its history. Relational databases are nicely optimized for retrieval of detailed records but definitely not hierarchical information. By pre-saving summarized information, Essbase allows analysis to happen from the top-down with no decrease in performance.

For OLAP databases, the hierarchy is native to the database itself. This is far different from relational databases that store the data in one table and then have one or more other tables that can be joined in to view data in a rolled-up fashion. For Essbase, the hierarchy is the database. When you change the hierarchy logic in Essbase on how a product is grouped or how a market rolls-up, you actually change where the data is stored.

Because hierarchy is inherent to OLAP databases, drill-down (sometimes known as "slicing and dicing" but never known as "making julienne data") is inherent as well. Essbase is great at doing ad hoc analysis because it knows that when a user double-clicks on Qtr1, she wants to see Jan, Feb, and Mar. This is because the roll up of months to quarters is pre-defined back on the server.

Dimensions

Data is organized within an Essbase database (or cube if you are using PBCS) into dimensions or groupings of related data elements grouped into a hierarchical format. To oversimplify, a *dimension* is something that can be put into the rows or columns of your report or data form (or it applies to the whole page). Different databases have different dimensions.

Have a look at this really simple Profit & Loss Statement:

	Actual	Budget
Sales	400,855	373,080
COGS	179,336	158,940
Margin	221,519	214,140
Total Expenses	115,997	84,760
Profit	**105,522**	**129,380**

It only has two dimensions. Down the rows, I have our "Measures" dimension (often called "Accounts"). Across the columns, I have our "Scenario" dimension – the dimension that contains Actual, Budget, Forecast, and the like.

The only two dimensions so far are Scenario and Measures. The more detailed breakdowns of Measures (Sales, COGS, Margin, etc.) are the members of the Measures dimension. Actual and Budget are members in the Scenario dimension. A *member* identifies a particular element within a dimension.

If I pivot the Measures up to the columns and the Scenario dimension over to the rows, our report will now look like this:

	Sales	COGS	**Margin**	Total Expenses	**Profit**
Actual	400,855	179,336	221,519	115,997	105,522
Budget	373,080	158,940	214,140	84,760	129,380

While it doesn't look very good, it does illustrate a couple of important points. First, a dimension can be placed into the rows, the columns, or the page (as I'll see in a second). If it's really a dimension (as Scenario and Measures both are), there are no restrictions on which dimensions can be down the side or across the top. Second, notice that the values in the second report are the same as the values in the first report. Actual Sales are 400,855 in both reports. Likewise, Budgeted Profit is 129,380 in both reports. This is not magic.

A spreadsheet is inherently two dimensional (as are most data forms and reports for Planning). It has rows and columns. This is great if your company only produces a Profit & Loss Statement one time and then files for bankruptcy, but most companies will tend to have profit (be it positive or negative) in every month. To represent this in Excel, I use the spreadsheet tabs (one for each month):

	Actual	Budget
Sales	31,538	29,480
COGS	14,160	12,630
Margin	17,378	16,850
Total Expenses	9,354	6,910
Profit	8,024	9,940

All Products and Markets.xls — tabs: Jan, Feb, Mar, Apr, May, Jun, Jul, Aug, Sep, Oct, Nov, Dec

I've now introduced a third dimension, Time. It could be across the columns (if you wanted to see a nice trend of twelve months of data) or down the rows, but I've put it in the pages. That is, if you click on the "Jan" tab, the whole report will be for January.

If you're looking for Actual Sales of 400,855, you won't find it now because that was the value for the whole year. I could get it by totaling the values of all twelve tabs onto a summary tab.

Right now, this spreadsheet is not broken down by product or market. Within Excel, it's problematic to represent more than three dimensions (since I've used the rows, columns, and tabs). One way is to have a separate file for each combination of product and market:

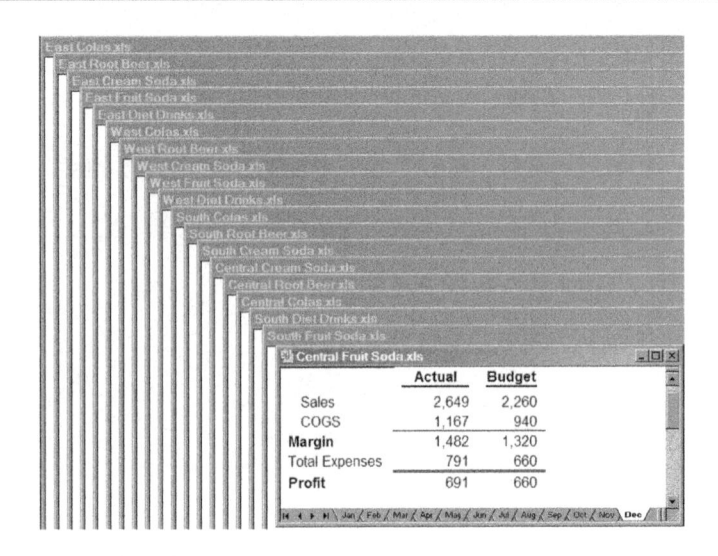

As you can see, this is getting ridiculous. What if I want to pivot our market dimension down to our columns to compare profitability across different regions? To do this, I'd either have to have a series of linked spreadsheet formulas (which would break as soon as I added or deleted a new product or market) or I could hire a temporary employee to print out all the spreadsheets and type them in again with the markets now in the columns.

Now that you understand what a dimension is, let's discuss some terms related to the elements within a dimension. A member or member name is the short, computery name for the member of an Essbase dimension (like "100-10"). An alias is the longer, more descriptive name for a member (like "Cola"). Members are grouped into hierarchies within a dimension.

Dimension Member References

Since I'm discussing dimensions, I'll also cover some "family" topics. The most common way to refer to members in a dimension relative to each other is by using "family tree" relationships:

```
⊟ Product
   ⊟ 100 (+) (Alias: Colas)
        100-10 (+) (Alias: Cola)
        100-20 (+) (Alias: Diet Cola)
        100-30 (+) (Alias: Caffeine Free Cola)
   ⊟ 200 (+) (Alias: Root Beer)
        200-10 (+) (Alias: Old Fashioned)
        200-20 (+) (Alias: Diet Root Beer)
        200-30 (+) (Alias: Sasparilla)
        200-40 (+) (Alias: Birch Beer)
   ⊟ 300 (+) (Alias: Cream Soda)
        300-10 (+) (Alias: Dark Cream)
        300-20 (+) (Alias: Vanilla Cream)
        300-30 (+) (Alias: Diet Cream)
   ⊟ 400 (+) (Alias: Fruit Soda)
        400-10 (+) (Alias: Grape)
        400-20 (+) (Alias: Orange)
        400-30 (+) (Alias: Strawberry)
   ⊟ Diet (~) (Alias: Diet Drinks)
        100-20 (+) (Alias: Diet Cola)
        200-20 (+) (Alias: Diet Root Beer)
        300-30 (+) (Alias: Diet Cream)
```

The members directly below a member are called its children. For example, a Product dimension has five children: Colas, Root Beer, Cream Soda, Fruit Soda, and Diet Drinks. If I ever wanted to refer to those members on a report or data form without hard coding them, I could say "give us all the children of Product."

The advantage to this (aside from the saving in typing) is that if a new product line needs to be added (say, "Water"), I don't have to modify our reports and data forms. Any report or data form designed to display the children of Product will pick up the new "Water" product and add it to the list automatically.

If Colas, Root Beer, and the other rugrats are all the children of Product, what relation is Product to its children? Assuming you didn't fail "Birds and the Bees 101," you'll know that Product must be the *parent* of Colas, Root Beer, and the rest. In other words, the parent of any member is the one that the member rolls up into. Qtr2 is the parent of May. Year is the parent of Qtr2.

Since Colas and Root Beer are both the children of Product, Colas and Root Beer are siblings. This is simple, but what relationship do January and May have? Well, their parents are siblings so that makes them... cousins. Correct, but "cousins" while technically correct isn't used that often. In general, people say that January and May are at the "same level."

What if you want to refer to all the members into which May rolls (not just the one right above)? Well, those are its ancestors, which in this case would be Qtr2 and Year. Correspondingly, the descendants of Year would include all four quarters and all twelve months.

Note that there are members that don't have any children. If our database doesn't go below the month level, May is barren. I refer to childless members as being "level-0." If you want all bottom, child-less members of a dimension, just ask for the level-0 members. For example, the level-0 members of the Year dimension are the months.

Level-0 (bottom level) members also are sometimes referred to as "leaves," because they're at the edges of the family tree. I sometimes refers to level-0 members as "the ones who have to sit at the little table in the living room on Thanksgiving," but I think I'm the only one, because that's rather a lot to say.

All of the parents of the level-0 members are referred to as level-1. Since the level-0 members of the Year dimension are the months, then the level-1 members are the quarters. For the Market dimension, the level-1 members are the regions: East, West, South, and Central.

Just as the parents of the level-0 members are level-1 members, the parents of level-1 members are level-2 members, their parents are level-3 members, and so on up the hierarchy. There are many places in Essbase that you can specify, for example, "All the level-2 members of the Product dimension," so remember that levels count up from the bottom of a dimension starting at 0.

If you want to count down the hierarchy, use generations instead of levels. The dimension itself is considered generation-1 (or "Gen1," for short). Its children are Gen2. For the Year dimension, the Gen2 members are the quarters.

Yes, the quarters are both level-2 and generation-2. Why do I need both levels and generations? Well, in some dimensions with many, many levels in the hierarchy, you'll want to count up from the bottom or down from the top depending on which is closer. I've seen a dimension with 17 levels in the hierarchy, and it was nice definitely to have both options available. The children of gen2 members are gen3 and so on down the hierarchy.

> **Note!** Why do generations start counting from 1 and levels from 0? It's because Generation 0 is considered to be the outline itself making its children, the dimensions, generation-1.

While counting with generations is pretty straight-forward, levels can sometimes be a bit tricky. Look at this portion of the Measures dimension:

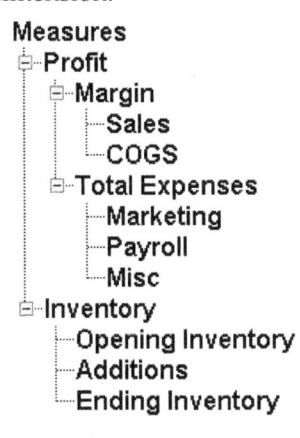

Measures
- **Profit**
  - **Margin**
    - Sales
    - COGS
  - **Total Expenses**
    - Marketing
    - Payroll
    - Misc
- **Inventory**
  - Opening Inventory
  - Additions
  - Ending Inventory

For this dimension, Gen1 is Measures. Gen2 is Profit and Inventory. Gen3 is Margin, Total Expenses, Opening Inventory, Additions, and Ending Inventory.

So far this is looking pretty easy, but let's switch our focus to the levels. The level-0 members are Sales, COGS, Marketing, Payroll, Misc, Opening Inventory, Additions, and Ending Inventory. The level-1 members are Margin, Total Expenses, and Inventory. What are the level-2 members? Profit (because it's the parent of level-1 members Margin and Total Expenses) and Measures (because it's the parent of level-1 member Inventory).

The trickiness is that Measures is *also* a level-3 member because it's the parent of Profit, a level-2 member. This means that if you ask Essbase for level-2 members, you'll get Measures, but you'll also get Measures if you ask for level-3 members. Notice that this counting oddity does not occur with generations.

BLOCK STORAGE DATABASE

Dense & Sparse

Before defining dense and sparse, I'll start with defining a member combination. A member combination is the intersection of members from each dimension. See the following examples of member combinations for the following sample outline:

```
Year Time (Active Dynamic Time Series Members: H-T-D, Q-T-D) (Dynamic Calc)
    Qtr1 (+) (Dynamic Calc)
    Qtr2 (+) (Dynamic Calc)
    Qtr3 (+) (Dynamic Calc)
    Qtr4 (+) (Dynamic Calc)
Measures Accounts (Label Only)
    Profit (+) (Dynamic Calc)
    Inventory (~) (Label Only)
    Ratios (~) (Label Only)
Product {Caffeinated, Intro Date, Ounces, Pkg Type}
    100 (+) (Alias: Colas)
    200 (+) (Alias: Root Beer)
    300 (+) (Alias: Cream Soda)
    400 (+) (Alias: Fruit Soda)
    Diet (~) (Alias: Diet Drinks)
Market {Population}
    East (+) (UDAS: Major Market)
    West (+)
```

Example member combinations:

- Qtr1 -> Profit -> 100 -> East -> Actual
- Year -> Profit -> 100 -> East -> Actual
- Jan -> Sales -> 100-10 -> New York -> Budget
- Jan -> Sales -> 100 -> New York -> Budget

Note! The symbol "->" is known as a cross dimensional operator in Essbase (more on this later). For now, when you see the "->", think of the word "at." I am referencing the data value at Qtr1 at Profit at 100 at East at Actual.

Dense data is data that occurs often or repeatedly across the intersection of all member combinations. For example, you will most likely have data for all periods for most member combinations. You will most likely have data for most of your accounts for member combinations. Time and accounts are naturally dense.

Sparse data is data that occurs only periodically or sparsely across member combinations. Product, Market, and Employee dimensions are usually sparse:

	Products			
	X			
			X	
	X			
		X		
				X

Markets (row label)

Sparse

	Time				
	X	X		X	
	X	X	X	X	X
	X	X	X		X
		X	X	X	X
	X		X	X	X

Measures (row label)

Dense

You, as the administrator, will assign a dense / sparse setting to each dimension. This will dictate how the Essbase database is structured.

Why can't you see the dense / sparse setting for the Product Manager dimension or any other attribute dimensions? If you answered "attribute dimensions are always sparse", pat yourself on the back.

Block Structure

The Essbase database is composed of a number of blocks. A block is created for each intersection of the sparse dimensions. In the example below, Market and Product are sparse. See a block for each sparse member combination in the example below:

Cola->East

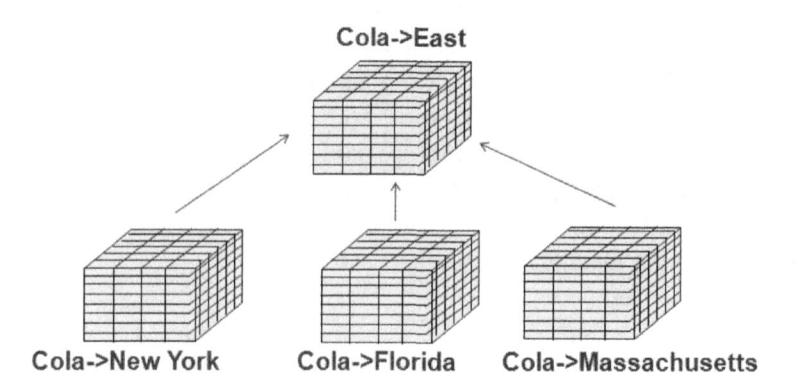

Cola->New York   **Cola->Florida**   **Cola->Massachusetts**

There are four types of blocks:

- Input blocks are blocks where data is loaded or input.
- Calculated blocks are blocks that are created through consolidation or calculation.
- Level zero blocks are blocks that are created from the level zero members of all dimensions.
- Upper-level blocks are all blocks that contain at least one upper level member (non-level zero).

Each block is made up of cells. These cells are created for each intersection of the dense dimensions. In the example below, Time, Measures, and Scenario are dense dimensions. See the cells for each dense member combination in the example below (I've highlighted one specific cell "Profit" at "Jan" at "Actual"):

Look Smarter Than You Are with PBCS 575

[Figure: 3D cube diagram showing dimensions — Time (Jan, Feb, Mar, Qtr1, Apr, May) across the top, Measures (Profit, COGS, Margin, Mkt exp., Payroll, Misc., Tot. Exp., Sales) on the left, and Scenario (Actual, Budget, Var, Var%) along the bottom.]

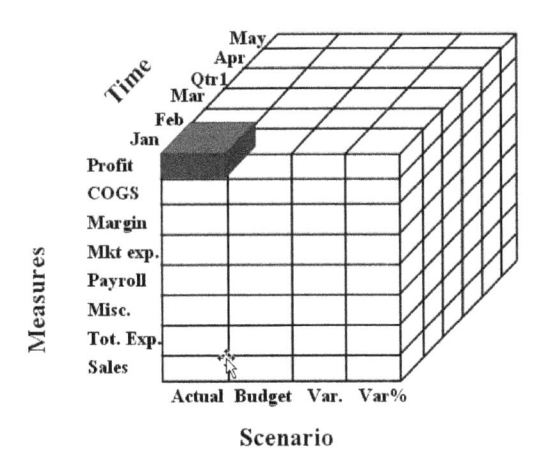

Outline Consolidation

Essbase is built to perform outline consolidations. You assigned a consolidation attribute to each member that tells Essbase how to perform the consolidation, whether it should add to the total, subtract from the total, and so forth. Unary operators include +, -, *, /, %, and ~. The consolidation will use these operators and follow the path of the hierarchies for each dimension.

So what do outline consolidation and dense / sparse have to do with each other? Essbase will perform dense calculations first and then sparse calculations.

The default calculation order for Essbase is the following:

- First, Accounts
- Second, Time
- Third, remaining dense dimensions
- Fourth, remaining sparse dimensions
- Finally, Two Pass Calculation (as applicable)

Let's follow the path of an Essbase consolidation to help you better understand. In the example below, the highlighted cells indicate cells loaded with data:

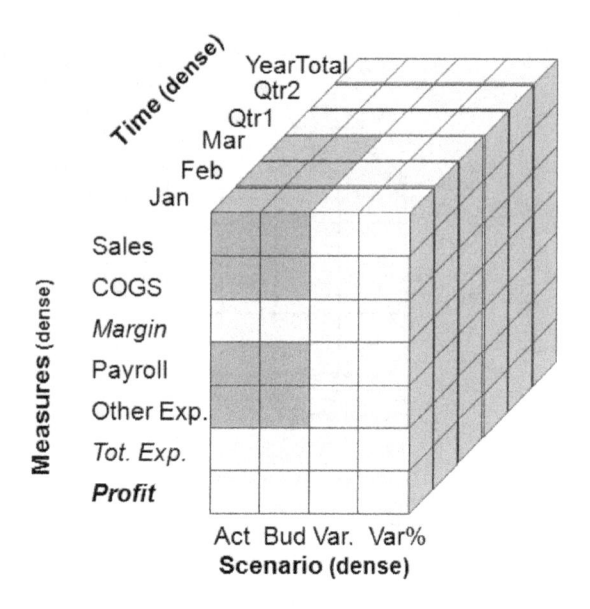

Next, you see those cells populated with the Accounts dimension calculation (see Profit, Margin, Tot. Exp):

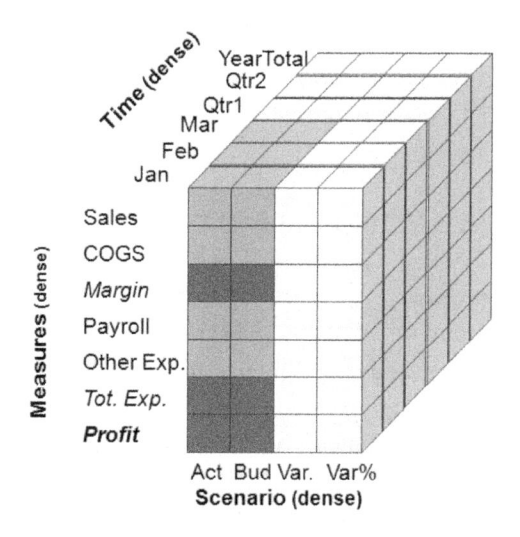

Finally, the cells in the upper portion of the block represent those cells populated with the Time dimension calculation (Qtr1, Qtr2, YearTotal):

Look Smarter Than You Are with PBCS 577

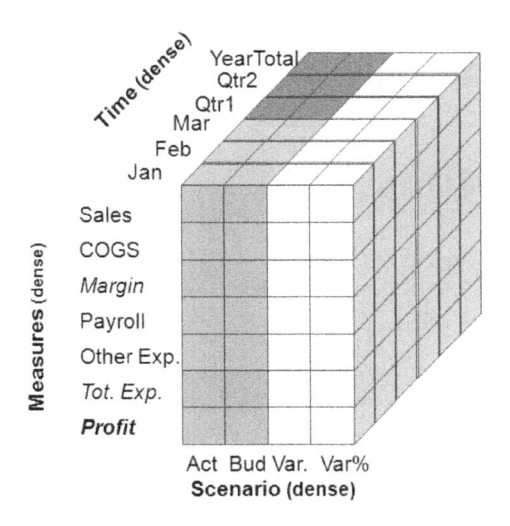

Why don't the variance and variance % members show calculated data values? 99% of the time you will tag these two members with the dynamic calc property so data will never be stored and in most cases, you won't need to calculate the Scenario dimension (and in most cases, this is a sparse dimension instead of a dense dimension; but I'm getting a bit ahead of ourselves).

Here is another view of this dense calculation. Data is loaded to Sales and COGS members for each month. I am looking at the block for Vermont, Cola, and Actual (there's that cross dimensional symbol that means "at"):

Vermont -> Cola -> Actual

Accounts	Jan	Feb	Mar	Qtr1
Sales	124.71	119.43	161.93	
COGS	42.37	38.77	47.28	
Margin				

First I consolidate the Accounts dimension, calculating the Margin member:

Vermont -> Cola -> Actual

Accounts	Jan	Feb	Mar	Qtr1
Sales	124.71	119.43	161.93	
COGS	42.37	38.77	47.28	
Margin	82.34	80.66	114.65	

Next I consolidate the Time dimension, calculating the Qtr1 member:

Vermont -> Cola -> Actual

Accounts	Jan	Feb	Mar	Qtr1
Sales	124.71	119.43	161.93	406.07
COGS	42.37	38.77	47.28	128.42
Margin	82.34	80.66	114.65	277.65

Once the Dense calculation is complete, the sparse calculation is next. The Vermont -> Cola -> Actual block and the New York -> Cola -> Actual block are added together to create the East -> Cola -> Actual block:

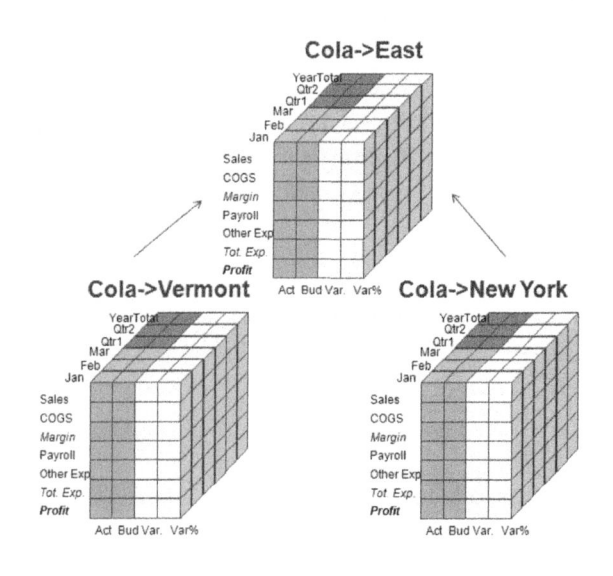

Note! This unevenness of some dimensions is also known as a ragged hierarchy.

AGGREGATE STORAGE DATABASE

Essbase allows two database types: aggregate storage databases (ASO) and block storage databases (BSO). ASO databases are designed to handle more dimensions and members, smaller batch windows for loads and aggregations of sparse data, and smaller database footprints.

Benefits of an ASO cube in PBCS applications include unified dimension maintenance and security for BSO and ASO planning and reporting. No aggregation is required for ASO databases so results at upper levels are available immediately.

Users can use ASO cubes to provide write back to databases with larger number of dimensions and members. ASO cubes provide a higher level of granularity for requirements that dictate detailed planning.

In ASO databases, there are three types of hierarchies: stored, dynamic, or multiple hierarchies ("Hierarchies Enabled"). Stored hierarchies will aggregate according to the structure of the outline. For example, months will roll up to quarters up to a year total in the Period member. This aggregation is really fast (the nature of ASO databases); however, stored hierarchies may only have the + for any member and ~ consolidation tags for members under a label only parent (other assigned consolidation tags are ignored). Also, stored hierarchies cannot have member formulas; there are a few other restrictions on label only assignments.

Dynamic hierarchies are calculated by Essbase (versus aggregated like in stored hierarchies) so all consolidation tags and member formulas are processed. The evaluation order for the calculation of members is dictated by the solve order. Dynamic hierarchies, as expected, do not calculate as quickly as stored hierarchies.

The Solve Order member property tells the ASO database the order to complete calculations. Why is this important? You want to calculate the correct numbers in the correct order. Think about the order of operations for basic math. 4 + 5 * 2 does not equal (4 + 5) * 2. Solve order is the way you control the order of calculations in ASO databases. This is a property specific to ASO cubes and does not apply to BSO.

You can also have multiple hierarchies within a single dimension. The hierarchies within a dimension can be stored, all dynamic, or have one hierarchy stored and the other hierarchies dynamic. Multiple hierarchies can contain alternate hierarchies with Shared Members or completely different hierarchies.

Hybrid Aggregation

Hybrid aggregation databases were introduced in Essbase 11.1.2.3.500 as a new alternative to BSO databases and are supported in on-premises versions of Hyperion Planning and Essbase. Hybrid aggregation databases are not supported for PBCS yet but I anticipate this feature coming soon!

With the latest on-premises version, 11.1.2.4, hybrid aggregation supports many common functions, and it's a good candidate for your cubes unless you have a valid reason for using either straight BSO or ASO.

Design considerations for hybrid aggregation cubes are very much the same as the design considerations for a Block Storage application. Users can write back to stored dimensions at any level, and the same calculation engine in BSO is still available to hybrid aggregation applications; however, dynamic dimensions in a hybrid aggregation application benefit from lightning-fast aggregations like an ASO application. On the downside, the dimensions are somewhat constrained still, like a BSO application, although larger BSO applications are possible if they use dynamic dimensions.

Hybrid aggregation applications are truly a blend of both ASO and BSO, which makes them perfect for reporting applications or Planning applications where there is a desire to see the latest aggregated numbers as fast as possible.

Hybrid will be the default setting for many Cloud Essbase based products in the future (I think).

COMPARING ESSBASE DATABASE OPTIONS

First, a quick disclaimer: this chapter was written mainly for Essbase 11.1.2.4. The hard working developers have enhanced the ASO engine dramatically in versions 9, 11.1.1.x, and 11.1.2.x, so comparing the two database types has been a rapidly moving target. If you are on Essbase 7x or an early version of System 9, you will see more differences than noted in the discussion below.

Let's start with the most important point – what does the user see? The beauty of ASO, BSO and hybrid aggregation databases is that front-end tools like the Excel Add-In, Smart View, and OBIEE really don't care if the database is BSO or ASO or a combination of both (even MaxL sees only minor differences between the two). The three types seem like multidimensional databases that have Zoom In and Zoom Out and Keep Only and Remove Only and Pivot and all that nice stuff. There are some minor differences, but for the most part the database type is pretty much transparent to the end-user.

What else is the same? The three types of databases are defined by their outline. Most dimension and member properties like dimension type, data storage (store, never share, label only), consolidation tags, and aliases are consistent for all three application types. How you build dimensions and load data is essentially the same. Certain rule files properties are database type specific, but the overall interface and steps are the same.

Calculating the databases is where I really begin to see the differences between them. In ASO databases, after data values are loaded into the level 0 cells of an outline, *the database requires no separate calculation step*. From any point in the database, users can retrieve and view values that are aggregated for only the current retrieval. ASO databases are smaller than block storage databases, enabling quick retrieval of data. For even faster retrieval, administrators can pre-calculate data values and store the pre-calculated results in aggregations. You can add in calculated members with member formulas in ASO. The syntax for the formulas is MDX.

On the other side of the house, BSO databases also have member formulas, but they use a different syntax: Essbase calc script syntax. In most cases, you will need to aggregate the BSO database after performing a data load. You will use the default calc script or one that you manually create to roll up all of the values for the dimensions in the database. These BSO calc scripts can perform complex business logic and allocations.

For hybrid aggregation applications, once data is loaded there may or may not be a need to aggregate the database depending on the dimensions and member properties of the Sparse dimensions. If not all Sparse dimensions are dynamic, a more limited aggregation script may need to be run. In hybrid applications, member formulas and calculation scripts are available just like BSO apps, and hybrid aggregation uses the same syntax as the BSO Essbase calculator engine.

Write back is another differentiator. For block storage databases, users can write back to any level in the database if they have permissions, while aggregate storage databases only allow write back to level zero members. Hybrid applications allow write back to any level as long as the dimension is stored and not dynamically calculated. If most dimensions are marked as dynamic in a hybrid app, then write back at level zero would be permitted like an ASO application.

Under the covers, the types of databases are radically different. ASO outlines have two types of hierarchies: stored and dynamic. BSO outlines define dense and sparse dimensions. Hybrid applications also have dense and sparse dimensions, but some sparse dimensions can be dynamically aggregated. ASO databases are stored in a series of tablespaces while BSO databases are stored in a series of index and page files and hybrid applications are a combination of both. How you tune each database is very different.

All of these concepts are covered in much greater detail in the *Look Smarter Than You Are with Essbase* book, but I wanted to have one place to summarize the great ASO versus BSO versus hybrid aggregation debate.

General guideline – use ASO when requirements dictate large numbers of dimensions and members that simply "roll up" (i.e. minimal complex calculations are required).

Note! General guideline – Use BSO for applications that require complex calculations and write back capabilities to any level.

General guideline – Use hybrid aggregation to achieve the best of both worlds. This will likely become the default option.

DIMENSION ORDER FOR BSO CUBE

Dimension order is critical for Essbase performance. The administrator may want to test different iterations of dimension order to determine the optimal structure. The hourglass methodology involves the largest dense dimensions to the smallest dense dimension to be ordered first, then the smallest sparse dimension to the largest sparse dimension to be ordered last. The hourglass format works well when parallel calculations is not utilized. If parallel calculations are being used, a different dimension order would be more optimal.

First, a few definitions:

- **Dense dimensions** – dimensions that define the internal structure of the data block; they should reside at the top of the order
- **Aggregating Sparse dimensions** – dimensions that will be calculated to create new parent values; these dimensions should reside directly after the last dense dimension. Placing these dimensions as the first sparse dimensions positions them to be the first dimensions included in the calculator cache, which gives them an ideal location for optimized calculation performance.
- **Non-Aggregating Sparse dimensions** – dimensions that organize the data into logical slices (e.g., Scenario, Version and

Years); it is not crucial for these dimensions to be included in the calculator cache because their members are typically isolated in FIX statements

With these types of dimensions in mind, you can create the optimal dimension order. This method is sometimes called an "hourglass on a stick." The general starting point would be to have Period first, then Account. If there is a sparse dimension that is frequently in rows, consider moving that dimension to be the first sparse dim after the dense dimensions.

What was just presented is a basic guideline for dimension ordering; for best results, test iterations of dense and sparse dimensions to figure out the optimal settings for your application.

Appendix: Glimpse into EPBCS

Enterprise Planning Cloud (referred to as EPBCS) is a Cloud solution that delivers prebuilt frameworks for planning processes using the Planning and Budgeting Cloud (PBCS) underlying solution. The current EPBCS frameworks include Financials, Workforce, Capital, and Projects. The frameworks are configurable and you choose what you want to enable and use. The EPBCS frameworks are automatically upgraded by Oracle. Some of the out of the box content delivered with EPBCS are drivers & KPIs, calculation rules, forms, reports, and dashboards. In summary, EPBCS is PBCS with prebuilt configurable artifacts to support common business planning processes.

FINANCIALS FRAMEWORK

The Financials framework contains prebuilt content to support plans and forecasts for detailed revenue, detailed expense, income statement, balance sheet, and cash flow. You may incrementally enable Revenue/Gross Margin, Expense, Balance Sheet, Cash Flow, Income Statement, and Analysis. The Financials framework integrates with the Capital, Workforce, and Projects frameworks if you need more granular planning for those business processes.

The Home dashboard delivered out of the box (but configurable) shows a snapshot of the Financial plan:

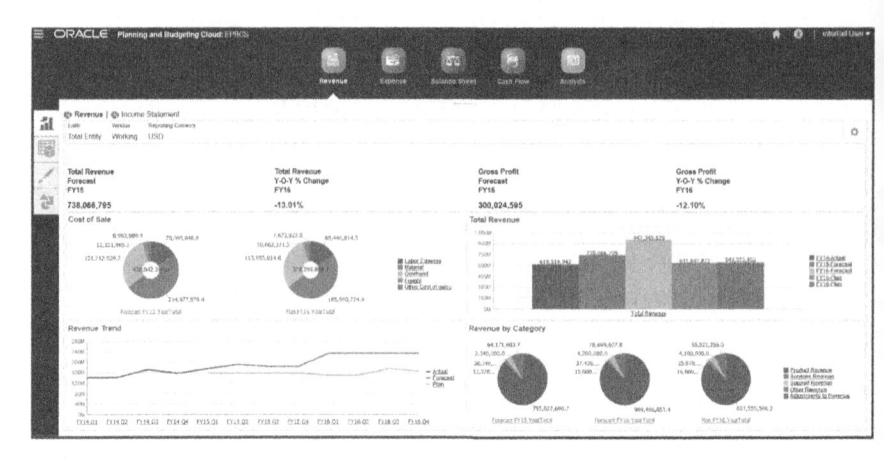

EPBCS supports driver-based, trend-based, or direct input for revenue and expense plans (depending on what you have enabled and configured). For driver-based plans, users enter and update drivers by defining trends for drivers and/or adding percent increases and decreases. The resulting revenue or expense is calculated based on the driver and users can layer in adjustments on top of the calculated result:

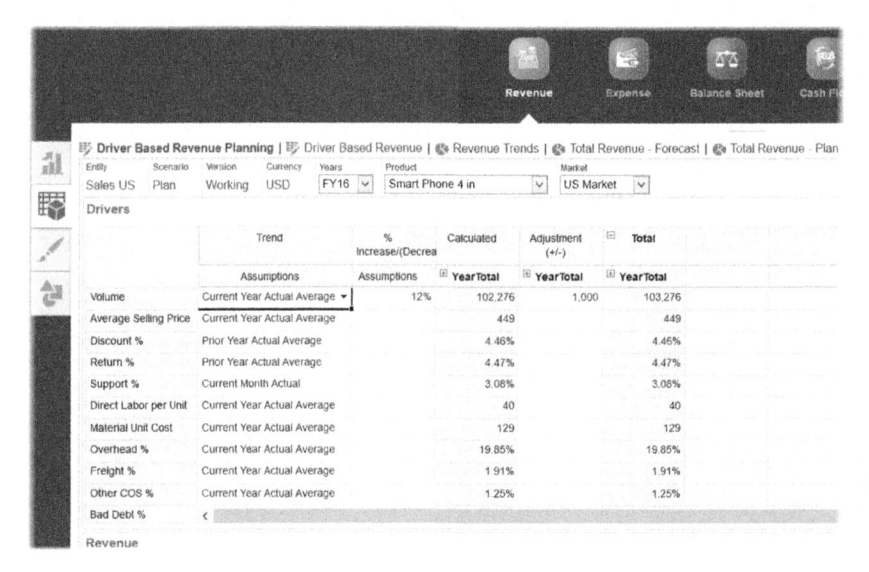

Users can also plan expenses at an account level using trend-based planning. Users select the trend assumption (e.g., CY Actual) and can add an increase/decrease %. The resulting trend-based forecast amount is calculated and users can layer in another increase/decrease adjustment dollar amount:

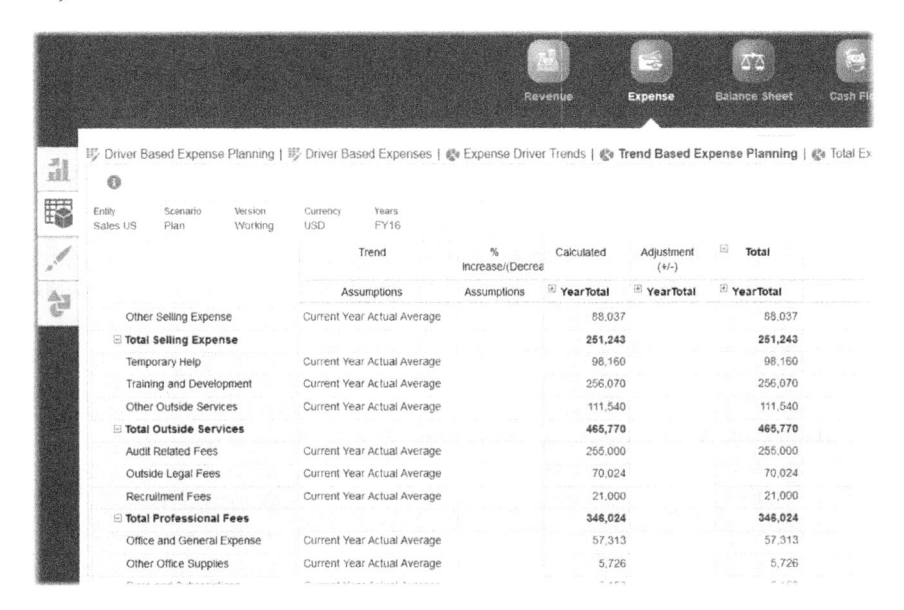

	Trend	% Increase/(Decrea	Calculated	Adjustment (+/-)	Total
	Assumptions	Assumptions	YearTotal	YearTotal	YearTotal
Other Selling Expense	Current Year Actual Average		88,037		88,037
Total Selling Expense			**251,243**		**251,243**
Temporary Help	Current Year Actual Average		98,160		98,160
Training and Development	Current Year Actual Average		256,070		256,070
Other Outside Services	Current Year Actual Average		111,540		111,540
Total Outside Services			**465,770**		**465,770**
Audit Related Fees	Current Year Actual Average		255,000		255,000
Outside Legal Fees	Current Year Actual Average		70,024		70,024
Recruitment Fees	Current Year Actual Average		21,000		21,000
Total Professional Fees			**346,024**		**346,024**
Office and General Expense	Current Year Actual Average		57,313		57,313
Other Office Supplies	Current Year Actual Average		5,726		5,726

Finally, users have the option to directly input forecasts and plans:

	Jan	Feb	Mar	Q1	Apr	May
Product Revenue						
Services Revenue	1,333,333	1,333,333	1,333,333	4,000,000	1,333,333	1,333,333
Support Revenue						
Other Revenue	341,667	341,667	341,667	1,025,000	341,667	341,667
Discounts						
Returns						
Adjustments to Revenue						
Total Revenue	**1,675,000**	**1,675,000**	**1,675,000**	**5,025,000**	**1,675,000**	**1,675,000**
Labor Expense						

WORKFORCE FRAMEWORK

The Workforce framework supports compensation planning, other employee-related expense planning for items like travel and training, strategic workforce planning, and demographics analysis. Compensation planning supports the traditional planning of compensation expenses driven by Finance, typically in a 1-2 year planning horizon. Strategic Workforce Planning is a different process, usually driven by HR, to help organizations plan the resources needed to execute strategic plans.

The configurable compensation expense planning portion of the Workforce framework allows users to plan workforce expenses by employee, by job code, or both employee and job code. Out of the box functionality for managing new hire requisitions, transfers, job changes, and planned departures. Like Financials, a home dashboard presents a snapshot of the compensation expense plan:

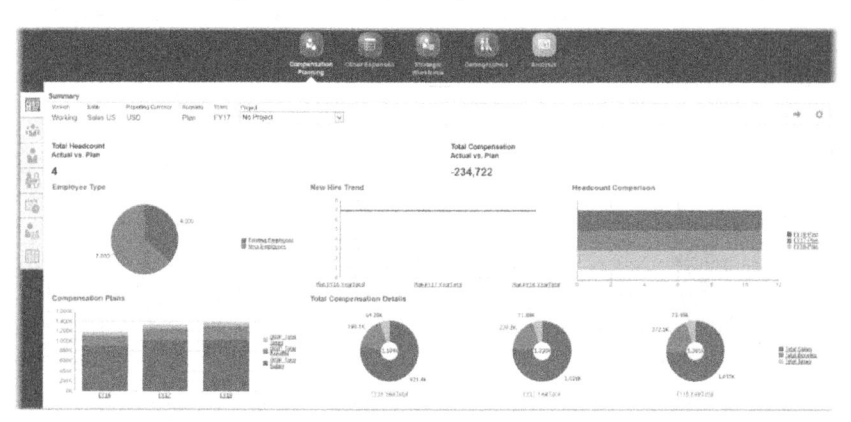

Users can add and manage new hire requisitions and calculate the updated compensation expense:

Users can manage existing employees, updating their job details, perform transfers, plan departures, and calculate the updated compensation expense:

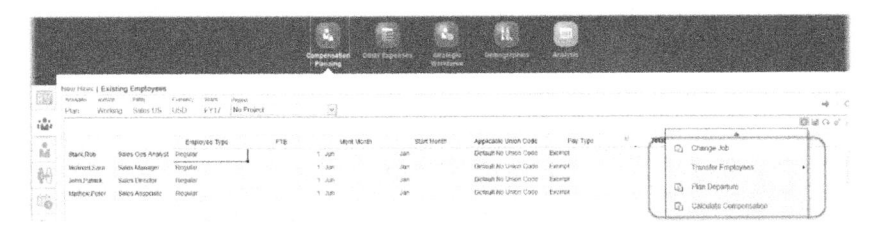

Other related employee expenses may be planned at the employee or entity level:

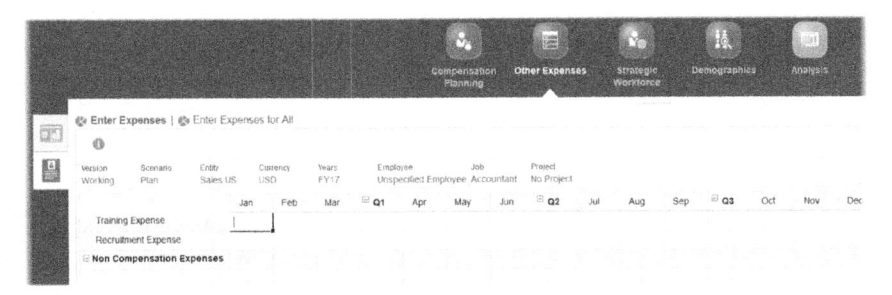

A wizard-driven configuration tool facilitates the setup and planning for benefit and tax expense.

Strategic Workforce Planning allows for long range planning by skill set, allowing the alignment of strategy with execution and costs. Strategic Workforce Planning uses drivers like attrition rates, retirement rates, and transfer rates to determine headcount and related costs of employees by skill set. This information helps organizations understand whether they have the right skill mix to execute on strategic initiatives.

590   Appendix

The Demographics portion of the Workforce framework supports reporting and analysis by employee level demographics:

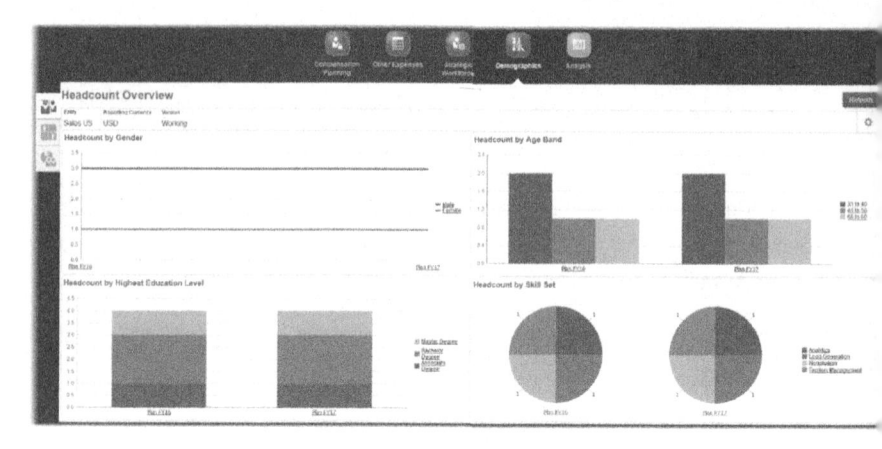

CAPITAL FRAMEWORK

The Capital framework supports the planning of new capital investments, management of existing assets and leases, and planning for intangibles. Functionality is delivered for new capital requests and planning, impacted P&L, cash flows, and funding requests:

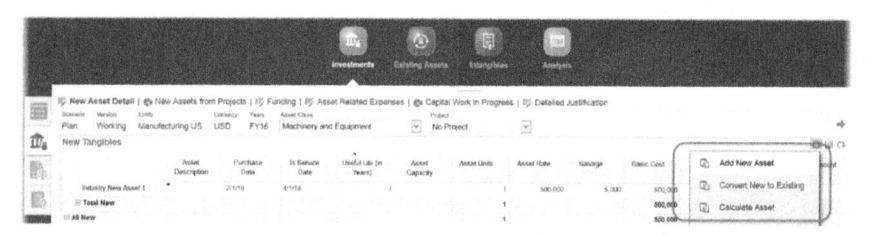

Users can manage existing assets, plan asset-related expenses, insurance, repairs, and maintenance. Existing assets may be transferred, retired, or replaced:

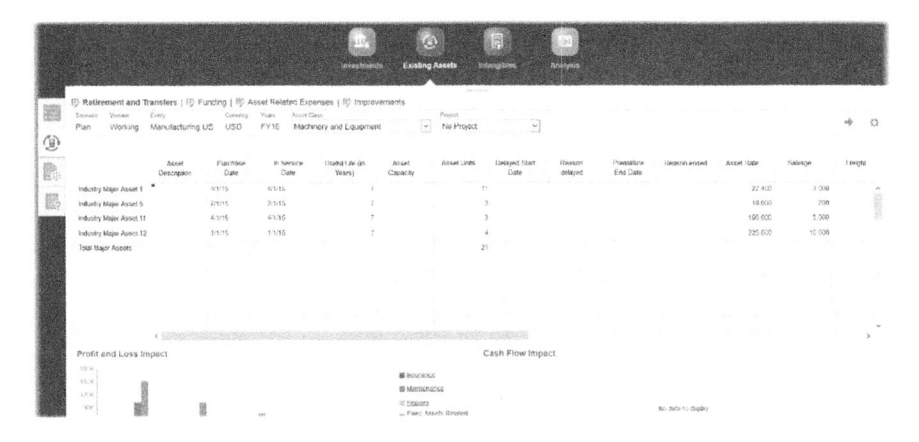

Reporting and analysis dashboards and reports support the overall review and management of the capital planning process, including reviews for overall capital expense spend, asset summary reports, capital plan versus actuals, and financials impacts across asset class and business unit.

PROJECTS FRAMEWORK

The Projects framework supports projects-based planning for internal and external projects, contract projects, and capital projects. Out of the box functionality is delivered to support new project requests, management of existing projects, forecast updates, and project variance reporting and analysis. Both expense and revenue planning are supported for projects planning and along with project prioritization and approvals. The home dashboards show snapshots of project status and expense:

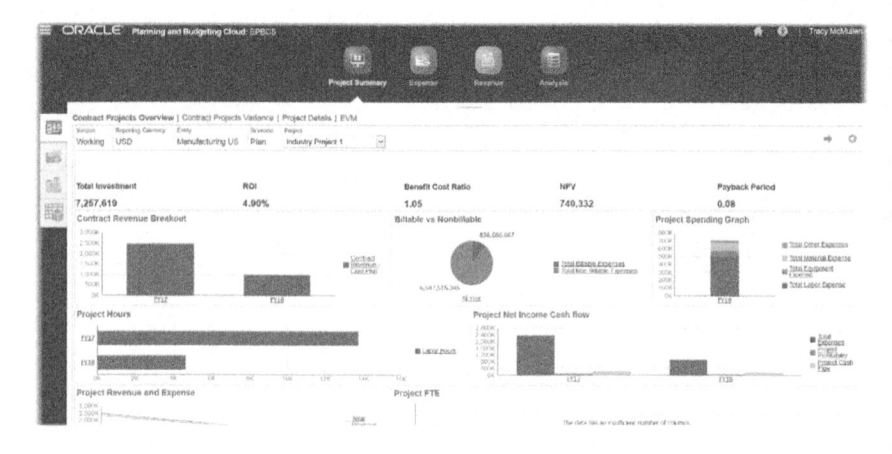

New projects can be added, approved, or deleted by users:.

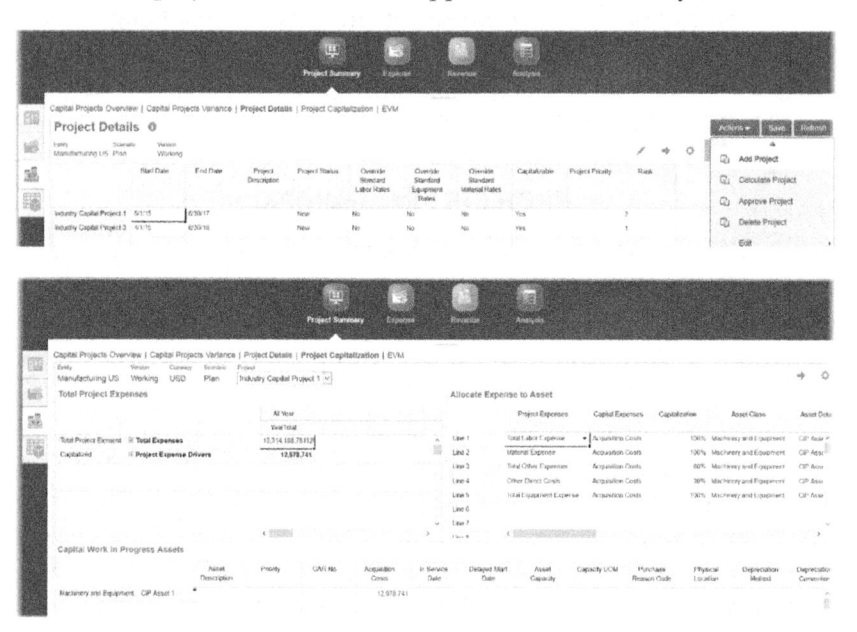

The Projects framework supports direct summary level expense planning. It can also integrate with the Workforce framework to pull in employee details for projects planning, as well as the Capital framework to pull in asset details:

Look Smarter Than You Are with PBCS 593

[screenshot of Expense Assumptions form with Labor | Material | Equipment | Other tabs, showing columns for Phase, Job, Employee Resource, Assignment Start Date, Assignment End Date, FTE, Assignment Location, Skill Set, Total Labor Expense, with rows Line 1 (No Stages, CNC Operator, Unspecified Employee, 6/1/15, 6/30/17, 12, Location 1, 4,915,891), Line 2 (No Stages, Engineer, Unspecified Employee, 5/1/15, 12/31/15, 10, Location 1, 6,072,000), Line 3 (No Stages, Project In Charge, Unspecified Employee, 5/1/15, 6/30/17, 1, Location 1, 425,850), Line 4]

ENABLE AND CONFIGURE EPBCS

EPBCS allows you to customize and enable the frameworks and functionality within the frameworks to meet your current requirements. The *Configure* card is the primary place where you set up the EPBCS application. Oracle has defined most of the configuration steps for each business process framework and those are found in *Configure*:

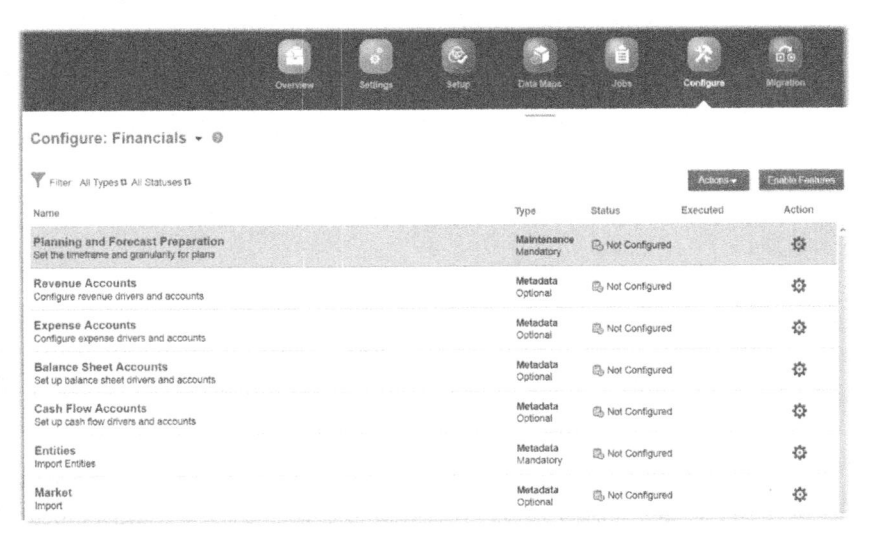

[screenshot of Configure: Financials screen showing navigation tabs (Overview, Settings, Setup, Data Maps, Jobs, Configure, Migration) and configuration table]

Name	Type	Status	Executed	Action
Planning and Forecast Preparation — Set the timeframe and granularity for plans	Maintenance Mandatory	Not Configured		⚙
Revenue Accounts — Configure revenue drivers and accounts	Metadata Optional	Not Configured		⚙
Expense Accounts — Configure expense drivers and accounts	Metadata Optional	Not Configured		⚙
Balance Sheet Accounts — Set up balance sheet drivers and accounts	Metadata Optional	Not Configured		⚙
Cash Flow Accounts — Set up cash flow drivers and accounts	Metadata Optional	Not Configured		⚙
Entities — Import Entities	Metadata Mandatory	Not Configured		⚙
Market — Import	Metadata Optional	Not Configured		⚙

Click *Enable Features* to enable the desired EPBCS frameworks. (Tip: Options with check boxes can be added. Options with radio buttons, once set, cannot be changed):

Financials - Enable Features

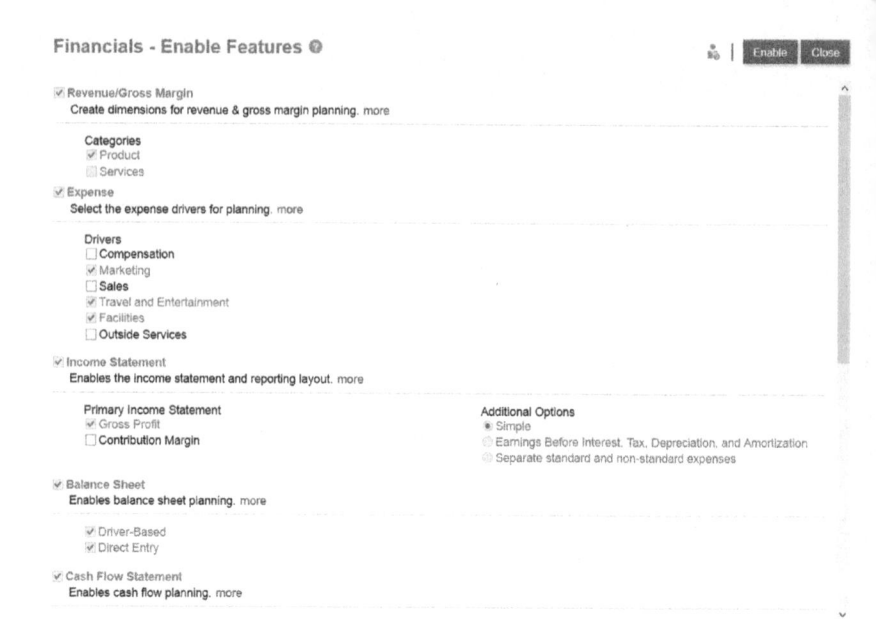

- ☑ Revenue/Gross Margin
  Create dimensions for revenue & gross margin planning. more
  - Categories
    - ☑ Product
    - ☐ Services
- ☑ Expense
  Select the expense drivers for planning. more
  - Drivers
    - ☐ Compensation
    - ☑ Marketing
    - ☐ Sales
    - ☑ Travel and Entertainment
    - ☑ Facilities
    - ☐ Outside Services
- ☑ Income Statement
  Enables the income statement and reporting layout. more
  - Primary Income Statement
    - ☑ Gross Profit
    - ☐ Contribution Margin
  - Additional Options
    - ◉ Simple
    - ○ Earnings Before Interest, Tax, Depreciation, and Amortization
    - ○ Separate standard and non-standard expenses
- ☑ Balance Sheet
  Enables balance sheet planning. more
    - ☑ Driver-Based
    - ☑ Direct Entry
- ☑ Cash Flow Statement
  Enables cash flow planning. more

In summary, the basic steps to implement EPBCS are:
1. Enable and configure the desired options upon application creation
2. Then enable and configure each framework that you'd like to implement
3. Load in your metadata (dimensions and hierarchies)
4. Load data
5. Define and assign security

Likely, there are some customization steps in there too.

EPBCS vs. Custom PBCS

So should you purchase and implement EPBCS or PBCS? With EPBCS, you get PBCS plus prebuilt content that should shorten implementation and support time. I definitely recommend taking a strong look at EPBCS. You can leverage out of the box, best practice designed features created and maintained by Oracle. You can configure and enable just the portions of EPBCS that you want. Oracle will continue to enhance and add functionality to EPBCS.

However, if you have very custom requirements and/or very simple requirements, it's possible that PBCS would support your needs.

INDEX

Academy, 561
Account, 68, 87, 95
Account Annotations, 323
Account Reconciliation Cloud, 13
Account Reconciliation Manager, 13
Account Type, 90
Action Menu, 335, 337, 478
Ad Hoc Analysis, 496, 517
Ad Hoc Grid, 381
Ad Hoc Grid Creator, 412
Ad Hoc Options, 500
Ad Hoc Read Only Users, 412
Ad Hoc User, 412
Adjust, 484
Aggregate Storage Database, 57, 579
Aggregating Sparse Dimension, 126, 583
Aggregations, 581
Alias, 68
Alias Display, 324
All Years, 100, 101
Alternate Hierarchy, 73
Analyze, 381, 496, 500
Application, 56
Application Creation Wizard, 61
Application Settings, 505
Application-Specific Roles, 411
Approvals, 503
Approvals Administrator, 412
Approvals Process Designer, 412
Approvals Supervisor, 412
Artifact Snapshot, 459
ASO, 57, 65, 129, 579
Assign security, 414
Attach documents, 324
Attachment, 488
Attributes, 73
Audit Trail, 558
Autosave, 314, 323, 483

BaseData, 103, 266, 526
BI, 3
BICS, 10, 15
Block Storage Database, 57
Blocks, 573, 574
Bottom Up Version, 84
BSO, 57, 65
BSO Calc Functions, 74
BSO Dimension Order, 126, 583
Business Rule, 58, 245, 266, 267, 270, 419, 501, 502

Calculate Data Form, 270
Calculate Data Form business rule, 290
Calculation Manager Administrator, 413
Cell Color, 477
Cell Text, 493
Cells, 574
Change History, 534, 558

Chart Type, 357
Cloud, 5
Cloud Support Case, 39
Cloud.oracle.com, 19
Comments, 493
Composite Form, 278, 312
ConsolidatedData, 103, 526
Consolidation Operators, 71
Context Sensitive Menu, 478
Continuous Forecast. *See* Rolling Forecast
Copy Scenario, 78
Country, 68
Create custom dimension, 104
Create Users, 29
Cross-Dimensional Operator, 572
Ctrl+Z, 314, 483
Cube, 56
Custom ASO Dimension, 131
Custom Dimension, 68, 104
Customer Support ID, 28

Dashboard, 352, 353, 472
Data Center, 3
Data Entry, 474
Data Form, 58, 277, 418, 475
Data Management, 150
Data Management Application Settings, 156
Data Management file requirements, 154
Data Management Steps to Build an Integration, 151
Data Map, 52, 237, 249, 268, 318
Data Storage, 69

Data Type, 69, 91
DATAEXPORT, 271
Date Cell, 481
Default BSO Calculation Order, 575
Default Value, 264
Delete application, 545
Dense, 573, 582
Dense Data, 126
Dense Dimension, 126, 583
Dimension, 58, 67, 113, 565, 566
Dimension Editor, 67
Dimension Management Cloud, 17
Dimension Properties, 286, 292, 324
Dimension Template for Import, 106
Dimensions, 340
Display properties, 288
DMCS, 17
Download a file, 429
DTS. *See* Dynamic Time Series
Dynamic Calc, 70, 577
Dynamic Hierarchies, 130, 579, 582
Dynamic Report, 389
Dynamic Time Series, 102
Dynamic User Variable, 300

E-mail Notifications, 505
Enter data, 475
Enterprise Performance Reporting Cloud, 12
Enterprise Planning pricing option, 57

Entity, 109
EPBCS, 10
EPM, 3
EPM Automate, 225, 432
EPM Automate Utility, 242
EPM Cloud, 17
EPRCS, 12
Error Trapping, 450
Essbase, 3, 69
Essbase Administration Services, 245
Evaluation Order, 128
Excel
  New Features in 2016, 504
Excel View - Financial Reports, 504
Exchange Rate Type, 91
Expense Reporting, 87
Export data, 148, 222, 271
Export metadata, 111
Export PBCS Application, 460, 561

Family tree relationships, 568
FCCS, 14
FDMEE, 18, *See* Financial Data Quality Management, *See* Financial Data Quality Management, *See* Financial Data Quality Management
Filter Data Form, 480
Financial Consolidation and Close Cloud, 14
Financial Data Quality Management, 150
Financial Planning, 87

Financial Reporting, 503
Financial Reporting Studio, 361, 503
Financial Reports, 361
Flat File, 106, 139
Flying Cars, 4
Focused aggregation, 261
Form Folder, 277
Form Layout, 292
Format Forms, 494
Formatting, 505, 519
FR Desktop Studio, 376
FR Web Studio, 361, 362, 376
Free Form Text, 481
Frozen, 4
FRS, 361

Generations, 570, 571
Graphical business rule, 249, 255
Graphical Mode, 248
Grid, 363
Grid Properties, 285
Grid Spread, 324, 486

HSP_View, 68, 84, 103, 525
HTML View, 489
Human Capital Planning, 87
Hybrid, 17
Hybrid aggregation, 57, 65
Hybrid Aggregation, 580, 581, 582, 583
Hybrid Aggregation Mode, 104
Hyperion, 564

Identity Domain, 24
Identity Domain Administrator, 24, 408

Ignore, 72
Implicit Sharing, 70
Import data, 141, 154
Import PBCS Application, 463
Import users, 33
Inbox / Outbox Explorer, 273, 429
interRel, 6
Inventory Planning, 87

Job Console, 268
Job Scheduler, 422, 425

Label Only, 70
Launch Business Rules, 503
LCM, 468
Level-0 member, 570
Levels, 570, 571
Life Cycle Management, 468
Lock Cell, 486

Maintenance time, 549
Mark Watney, 3
Mass Allocation, 413
Master Composite Form, 322
MaxL, 581
MDX, 581
Measures, 566, 571
Member, 566
Member Formula, 74, 82
Member Name Display, 324
Member Properties, 68
Member search, 54
Member Search, 54
Member selection filters, 55
Member Selector, 53, 293
Members on the fly, 338, 509

Members On the Fly, 338
Metadata Access, 415
Microsoft Office, 40, 511
Microsoft Office Integration, 361
Migration, 460, 463, 561
Monitor Service status, 35
Monitor usage metrics, 36
Multi-Dimensional Databases, 564
My Account, 23
My Services, 23, 408

Native Essbase format, 141
Native Planning format, 142
Navigation Flow, 392
Navigator, 92
Never Consolidate, 72
Never Share, 70
New 2016 Feature, 93
New Features in 2016, 135, 280, 283, 286, 361
New Features in 2017, 119, 433
Non-Aggregating Sparse Dimension, 127, 583
Notifications, 37, 560

OLAP, 564
Oracle, 564
Oracle Enterprise Planning Cloud Version for this book, 61
Outline, 571
Outline Consolidations, 575

Page, 476
Partial Data Clear, 274
Partial Grid Fetch Size, 551

PBCS, 40
PDF View, 504
Performance, 126
Period, 101
Plan type, 56, 126, 129, 535
Plan Type, 539
Point of View, 476
Predictive Analytics, 511
Provision Roles, 411

Read Only, 307, 309
Refresh, 482
Refresh the Database, 79
Report Book, 361
Reports, 360, 503
Restarting Instance, 549
Rolling Forecast, 64, 301, 303
RTP. *See* Run-time prompt
Run-time prompt, 502

Sales Planning, 87
Sandbox, 64, 84, 103, 525
SandboxData, 103, 526
Sandboxes, 523
Save Tasks, 423
Scenario, 75, 566
Schedule Jobs, 268
Script business rule, 260
Script Mode, 248, 260, 264
Security, 414
Segment Properties, 287
Select Level 0 Members, 310
Servers, 3
Service Administrator, 25
Set time zone, 505, 549
Shared Connection URL, 514

Shared Services Console, 468
Shortcut Keys, 483
Simple Form, 278, 290
Simplified Interface, 40
Simplified UI, 471
Skip Missing, 89
Slice Definition, 149
Smart Form, 325
Smart List, 91, 92, 130, 309, 481
Smart Push, 52, 237, 249, 268, 320
Smart View, 113, 361, 511, 514
Smart View Panel, 515
SmartCut, 488
Snapshot, 361
Solve Order, 130, 579, 580
Sort Data Form, 481
Source Plan Type, 87
Sparse, 65, 573, 582
Sparse Data, 126
Sparse Dimension, 70
Store, 70
Stored Hierarchies, 130, 579, 582
Subscription ID, 28
Substitution Variables, 137, 302
Supported Data Sources for PBCS, 139
Supporting Detail, 323, 489, 492
Sync data, 216
System 9, 3

Tablespaces, 582
Target Version, 84
Task, 348, 472
Task List, 58, 348, 420, 472, 516
Task List Access Manager, 413

Task List Alerts, 350
The Approvals Ownership Assigner, 412
Time, 68
Time Balance, 89
Time Spreading, 485
Two Pass, 72

UDA, 73
Undo, 314, 483
UPDATECALC, 251
Upload a file, 429
User Defined Attribute, 73
User Interfaces, 40
User Preferences, 505
User Variable, 133, 507

Valid for Plan Type, 71

Valid Intersection, 328
Validation Rule, 323
Validation Rules, 289
Variable Designer, 262
Variance, 74, 81
Variance Reporting, 87, 88
Version, 84
View Member Formulas, 324, 496

Web Client vs. Smart View, 512
Wildcard search, 54
Workforce Planning, 57
Workspace, 40

XREF, 87, 131

Years, 100

Made in the USA
Las Vegas, NV
19 April 2022